Shanghai Love

Shanghai Love

Courtesans, Intellectuals, and Entertainment Culture, 1850–1910

CATHERINE VANCE YEH

UNIVERSITY OF WASHINGTON PRESS • *Seattle & London*

This book was published with the assistance of the Getty Foundation.

Designed by Veronica Seyd
Printed in United States of America
12 11 10 09 08 07 06 5 4 3 2 1

University of Washington Press
PO Box 50096, Seattle, WA 98145
www.washington.edu/uwpress

Library of Congress Cataloging-in-Publication Data

Yeh, Catherine Vance.
Shanghai love : courtesans, intellectuals, and entertainment culture, 1850–1910 / Catherine Vance Yeh.
p. cm.
Includes bibliographical references and index.
ISBN 0-295-98567-4 (hardback : alk. paper)
1. Shanghai (China)—Social conditions. 2. China—History—1861–1912. I. Title.
HN740.S484Y44 2006
306'.0951'13209034—dc22 2005020856

The paper used in this publication meets the minimum requirements of American National Standard for Information Sciences—Permanence of Paper for Printed Library Materials, ANSI Z39.48–1984.

Jacket front: Hand-colored postcard of courtesans in theatrical costumes, Yaohua Studio Shanghai, 1890s (courtesy Regine Thiriez, Paris)
Jacket back: "Zhu Ruchun in male costume," *Haishang jing hong ying*, 1913

For R

Contents

Acknowledgments

Many have helped to bring this book to completion. It all began in 1988, while I was in China on a Fulbright scholarship. During that time, I regularly met with Professor Wu Xiaoling. In one of our conversations, I told him of my interest in the late Qing courtesan culture, whereupon he brought out a collection of books. He laughingly told me that he had preempted Professor Zheng Zhenduo, for whom these books had been waiting in a secondhand bookstore in the Dong'an market in Beijing in the early 1960s. It is an exceedingly precious and unique collection. Many of the items are not available in any major library, as I found out years later when I started research on this topic and began a systematic search for such works. My deepest gratitude thus goes to the late Professor Wu Xiaoling. Other scholars were extremely generous in sharing their materials with me. In this regard, I wish to thank Nancy Norton Tomasko, Princeton University, and Lothar Wagner, Institute of Chinese Studies, University of Heidelberg, for letting me use their collections of Shanghai city guides. Régine Thiriez, Paris, gave me copies of photographs of Shanghai courtesans from her collection and also taught me much about photographic analysis. Ingeborg Klinger, University of Heidelberg, helped with making photographic reproductions. The staffs of the Shanghai City Library, the Shanghai City Archive, the Harvard-Yenching Library, the C. V. Starr East Asian Library at Columbia University, the School of Oriental and African Studies at the University of London, and, of course, the Institute of Chinese Studies at the University of Heidelberg have been exceedingly kind and supportive of my research.

I would like to thank the members of the University of Heidelberg research group Structure and Development of the Chinese Public Sphere, who heard and discussed draft versions of most of the book's chapters. Their critical comments helped me to clarify my own thinking. I would also like to thank Barbara Mittler, who read through the manuscript and gave me her notes; Nanny Kim and Holger Kühnle, who helped me in the final stage of preparing the manuscript; and Michael Schön, for reading the chapter on city guides and offering critical comments and corrections.

I am indebted to Leo Ou-fan Lee and Christian Henriot, who were kind enough to read the entire manuscript and provide me with detailed and insightful criticisms, comments, and corrections. They gave the work a final harsh but extremely important push. I would also like to thank the four anonymous scholars who read the manuscript for the University of Washington Press, for their rich and stimulating comments and suggestions, and to acknowledge their contribution to the revision of this work.

Many chapters in this book grew out of papers presented at conferences. Here, I would like to thank Marianne Bastid-Bruguière, Paris, for her invitation to the Conference on European Thought in Chinese Literati Culture in the Early Twentieth Century, in Garchy, in 1995; Professor Charles LeBlanc, who invited me to attend the European and American scholars' exchange in Montreal; Michael Hockx, for inviting me to join the Literary Field of Twentieth-Century China conference in Leiden; and the Shanghai Academy of Social Sciences, for the invitation to the conference on urban studies, where I also had many thought-provoking discussions with Professor Xiong Yuezhi, Professor Luo Suwen, and other scholars. Invitations to speak on my project came from colleagues at the University of California, Berkeley; the University of California, Santa Barbara; Oxford University; the School of Oriental and African Studies at the University of London; and Harvard University. My gratitude to them all.

The generous support of various foundations was instrumental in allowing me to complete this work. I would like to thank the Chiang Ching-Kuo Foundation for International Scholarly Exchange, which supported my research for two years, and the German Research Foundation (Deutsche Forschungsgemeinschaft), which supported me for three more years as part of the "Theatricality" project. My thanks also go to Professor Monica Übelhör, Marburg University, and Professor Erika Fischer-Lichte, Free University, Berlin, for the many intense and stimulating discussions in the "Theatricality" research framework.

It is with deeply felt gratitude that I would like to thank Rudolf Wagner, who throughout the years was the first to hear all the ideas, read all the chapters, and offer his love and critical comments.

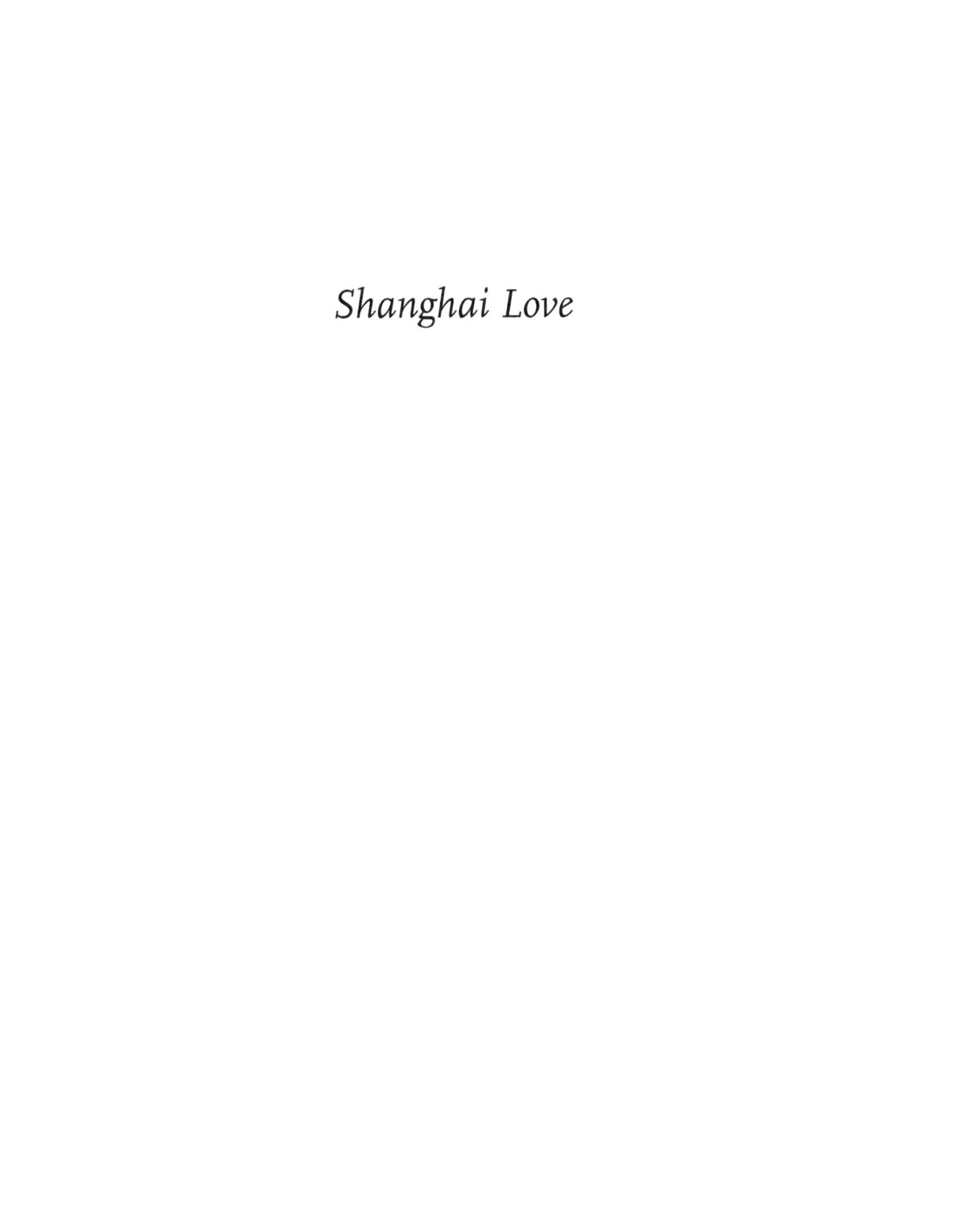

Shanghai Love

Introduction

During the biannual Shanghai horse race of 1899, the newspaper *Entertainment* (Youxi bao) reported:

> Yesterday was the second day of the races and more people participated than on the first day. Especially noteworthy were the top courtesans; dressed without exception in the height of fashion, they were dashing up and down through the Foreign Settlements [in their carriages], [creating such a] thrilling view as to provide more than enough excitement to one's spirit.
>
> For the record: Yesterday, Lin Daiyu wore a blue satin gown trimmed with pearls; she was riding in a four-wheeled carriage drawn by black horses, with her coachman dressed in a gray crêpe-de-Chine jacket and a black-rimmed straw hat. Lu Lanfen [was dressed in] in a pearl-trimmed gown of lake-green color; she rode in a black carriage with her coachman [dressed] in a starched light-blue cotton uniform with a black vest and a straw hat. Jin Xiaobao [wore] a flowered gown with black butterflies on a white background; she rode in a yellow carriage with red wheels, her coachman [dressed] in a lake-green silk uniform with a black-trimmed straw hat. Zhang Shuyu [was dressed in] a pearl-hemmed blue gown; she rode in a black carriage accompanied by Gu Yu, who wore a moon-white pearl-hemmed gown; their coachmen each had on black summer hats and wore light white-gray uniforms.[1]

The report describes the top-ranking courtesans out riding in public, exhibiting their latest fashions, competing with one another in displays of conspicuous consumption, and vying for attention. Their coachmen were dressed up as part of the show. The first four—Lin Daiyu, Lu Lanfen, Zhang Shuyu, and Jin Xiaobao—were the top-ranking Shanghai courtesans during the 1890s, and their names signaled style, fashion, and notoriety. It was their business to create a sensation as trendsetters and public figures.

The scene is extraordinary in many ways. It highlights the ability of Shanghai courtesans to parade around the Foreign Settlements in such an ostentatious manner. Their behavior, moreover, has become the subject of reporting by an emerging entertainment press and is portrayed in a manner that suggests they were Shanghai's leading figures and the city's prime spectacle. Seen in the larger historical context of the time, their public presence was sensational indeed. In the rest of the Qing empire, and even in the capital Beijing, women—including courtesans—largely were not allowed to attend public entertainments. They were excluded from the public arena altogether, which makes it all the more remarkable that these courtesans were riding carriages in broad daylight to attend a fashionable and gaudy event such as a horse race.

What, then, were the conditions that allowed the Shanghai courtesan to be so brazen in parading her new persona? How did she manage to displace the beauties of the emperor's court in setting fashion and, far from incurring disdain as a "public woman," become lionized as the socialite with whom one had to be seen? Courtesans and prostitutes have had a strong impact on women's fashion and social manners in other cities and in earlier times—for example, Tang dynasty Chang'an (618–907), Ming dynasty Nanjing (1368–1644), Renaissance Venice (1420–1600), Tokugawa period Edo (1603–1867), and Second Empire Paris (1852–70). The influence they enjoyed elsewhere, however, does not explain the courtesan's degree of visibility in Shanghai at this time and her power to affect popular taste to a degree that some of the city's leading lights as well as Chinese officials found alarming.

Aided in no small way by the press, the new medium of Chinese-language mass communication that had been spreading outward from Shanghai's Foreign Settlements since the 1870s, the Shanghai courtesan of the late Qing established herself as the city's first modern professional woman. She was the first to articulate the manner in which urban women would behave, and in many aspects, her lifestyle and habits prefigure those of the Shanghai urbanite of the Republican period.

This study aims to shed light on the rise of a new kind of commercially driven entertainment culture in the Shanghai Foreign Settlements during the late nineteenth century, as reflected in the scene described above, and probes its implications for the larger transformations of the time. The three key players are the city, the courtesan, and the new class of urban intellectuals, many of whom belonged to China's first generation of journalists. The Foreign Settlements provided the civic culture, the institutional and legal environment, and the economic base for the development of a new brand of urban entertainment. The Shanghai courtesan was the force that pushed most unabashedly for the transformation of traditional cultural and social values. Her incorporation of Western material goods into a world of luxury, ease, and enjoyment, her re-casting of the new as a desirable part of her lifestyle in contrast to its traditional low status, and her exploration of the public arena were instrumental in defining the contours of Shanghai urban culture. Close behind were the men of letters, mostly from the adjacent, rich Lower Yangtze Valley region (Jiangnan), who redefined their social status and became the first urban intellectuals. By entering Shanghai's booming book, print, and education markets, they became the image makers of modern times. Much of Shanghai urban culture was about image and image making. The shock of Shanghai's new was both attractive and intriguing to contemporaries. In order to reconcile this contradiction, the narration of the city found a symbol in that unique creation of the Foreign Settlements, the Shanghai courtesan.

One way in which to understand the new entertainment culture is to study the symbiotic and symbolic relationship between this new city and its courtesans. But are we not focusing on a supposedly marginal phenomenon and group, which must therefore have had an equally marginal influence on the grand transformations of modern China? The process of a political, social, and values transformation of this magnitude in China has heretofore been studied mostly on the basis of the normative pronouncements and acts of political, financial, and intellectual leaders. The viability of this approach is a matter of opinion and has not, I believe, been sufficiently evaluated against the particular realities of China at the time.

The first factor we must acknowledge is the structural imbalance that makes a single marginal place "in a corner by the sea," as one of the most important early writers on the city, Wang Tao (1828–1897) called Shanghai, into the modernizing engine of a huge empire. The second is the multiethnic community of marginal sojourners from throughout the world and across China that collectively developed a hybrid way of life under the benign eyes of the Committee on Roads and Jetties (later the Municipal Council), which consisted of unpaid, short-term, part-time members of the foreign business community who had little interest in administering morals or handing out monopolies. Third, the explosive development of a modern publishing industry with new media such as newspapers and journals quickly opened distribution channels throughout the empire and provided the ground in which new lifestyles, values, and forms of thinking could be played out. And finally, there is the large, glittering, immensely attractive and thoroughly marginal world of entertainment arising in this new type of civic environment, with the courtesan at center stage, offering the options of make-believe, role-play, and exploration of the new. These combined lures attracted a rapidly growing number of tourists and sojourners, and, along with the breathless reports and images communicated in Shanghai's books and papers, helped to spread—mostly without grand words and programs—the impact of the "modern" throughout the country. Under these conditions, the "marginal" does not seem to be a bad address. Shanghai's entertainment culture was the available, open, and public space where a modern and distinctly urban sensibility developed below and beyond the lofty, normative words of political leaders and ideological reformers.

In fact, it might be here that many of the unplanned, messy, and real modernization processes actually took place. This study thus focuses on the development of an urban entertainment culture in the Shanghai Foreign Settlements and its impact on social and cultural change. Implied is the claim that the concept as well as the content of Shanghai entertainment were utterly new, distinctly urban, modern, and cosmopolitan in character and linked globally to similar developments in other urban centers such as Paris, in which Alain Corbin has dated the "coming of leisure entertainment" to about 1850.[2]

During the fifty years between the 1860s and the 1910s, the Shanghai Foreign Settlements came to occupy a pivotal geographical place and social role in China's transition to modernity, as its commercial practices, urban development, and lifestyle were providing the model. Although not necessarily followed in all its ramifications, this model was a constant stimulus and provocation that marked even those who rejected it.

Urban Studies and the Shanghai Entertainment Culture

A study of entertainment culture faces manifold challenges. Primary among these is the subject matter itself. In examinations of cities and urban culture, entertainment has traditionally received little attention, either in terms of economy or cultural makeup. Urban entertainment owes its low status to the suspicion that it might be a lightweight scholarly topic compared, for example, to the study of the words and deeds of politicians, reformers, and military men. This suspicion reflects apprehension about the moral stature of entertainment personnel and their activities. Furthermore, entertainment does not easily accommodate itself to any one of the academic discursive formations that carve up our perception of reality; instead, it languidly straddles their borders.

In nineteenth-century official reports, entertainment certainly is not an economic concern, because it involves neither trade in goods, nor industrial production, nor capital flows. Foreign consuls in the Shanghai Foreign Settlements had no category for it, and while their quarterly reports listed every Nankeen that had gone through the port, this important branch of the Shanghai economy was never mentioned. Today, however, even old financial and industrial centers such as London, New York, and Paris depend on the tourism-related appeal of entertainment as their single most important revenue generator. Entire countries rely on tourist entertainment as their main source of income. This fact has become painfully clear to urban planners and city administrators and has led to a complete reorientation of priorities; however, this acknowledgment has not yet, to the best of my knowledge, translated into a reorientation of urban historical studies, especially with regard to China. A fine example is the monumental work on the city in late imperial China, edited by William Skinner, which pioneered Chinese urban studies; the word "entertainment" did not even make it into the index of the book.[3]

In studies of Shanghai, the city is approached from a variety of angles and scrutinized under various hypotheses: as the engine of change and the key to modern China, the isolated bridgehead of imperialism, the city of the workers' movement, or the birthplace of Chinese nationalism.[4] Others have viewed Shanghai from the perspective of administration, trade, and commerce; as an immigrant society; and as a marketing center that was already thriving centuries before the foreigners arrived.[5] More recently, some scholarly work has been done on the everyday life of Shanghai's common people.[6] Although these studies have contributed greatly to our understanding of many facets of the city's history and structure, it is amazing that Shanghai's significance as China's most important entertainment center in the late nineteenth century has been consistently overlooked, although this was crucial for its image and consequent attractiveness to financiers, traders, and short-term visitors.

Happily, the situation has begun to change in recent years. A number of very substantial studies on Shanghai prostitution have been published, which evidently also deal with entertainment. Those in Western languages include Christian Henriot's book *Belles de Shanghai* (1997); the topic and his scholarship evoked such interest that an English-language translation, *Prostitution and Sexuality in Shanghai,* followed in 2001.[7] Gail Hershatter published her *Dangerous Pleasures* (1997), and David Der-wei Wang devotes a chapter in his *Fin-de-Siècle Splendor* (1997) to depictions of Shanghai courtesan entertainment in late Qing novels.

Henriot approaches the topic of Shanghai prostitution as a historian, in the great tradition of one of his teachers, Alain Corbin, author of *Women for Hire*, and provides a closely documented and well-grounded analysis of the institutions, authorities, and organizations involved in administering prostitution in Shanghai between the late nineteenth and the mid-twentieth century. He discusses in detail the historical background of the courtesans' move, which began in 1853, during the Small Sword Uprising (1853–55), from the walled city of Shanghai into the Foreign Settlements. There, they were later joined by courtesans from other Jiangnan towns who were fleeing the Taiping Rebellion (1850–64). He maps the entertainment district and investigates the ages and regional backgrounds of these women as well as their reasons for entering and leaving the trade, drawing on both printed sources and the archive of the French Settlement's Sanitary Police, which is rich in raw data, especially for "wild chicken" (*yeji*), or street prostitutes.

Henriot's main argument is that the development of Shanghai prostitution reflects a major shift in sexual practice, from an exclusive privilege of elite men who patronized high-class courtesans to a mass market phenomenon. This sexualization and commercialization began with the opening of the Shanghai Treaty Port and was completed sometime after World War I. In his desire to offer an objective version of the history of Shanghai prostitution, Henriot focused on the archival records of the Sanitary Police in the French Settlement. (This approach to dealing with such morally awkward subject matter proved its worth in Corbin's study on Paris prostitution.)[8] In the process, Henriot's own efforts to reach a cultural understanding of courtesan entertainment are somewhat sidelined in his book.[9]

While I agree with this broad outline and have been much inspired by this argument, my own research has convinced me that in the midst of this seemingly linear process, in which old-style courtesan entertainment was replaced by new urban prostitution, the Shanghai Foreign Settlements experienced a development that was uniquely theirs. For more than two decades, the premier Shanghai courtesans escaped the traditional spatial, ritual, functional, and social enclosures reserved for courtesans, reset the relationship with their clients so as to aggrandize their own power, and presented themselves as "public women" in the very literal sense of being strong, self-assured, public female entertainers with such a knack for creating and capturing the spirit of this booming metropolis that they eventually became its most highly prized emblem.

Only by the late 1890s, when the new urban intellectuals had attained a degree of sophistication and irony, did their depictions take on the fake glories of the city and its courtesans. This reflects a shift in their attitudes, not in the social realities of courtesan entertainment. From Chinese sources of the 1920s, such as the entertainment paper *The Crystal* (Jingbao), it would seem instead that courtesan entertainment was still very much alive after World War I. The notion that it disappeared might be related to its loss of place as bona fide entertainment after 1917 in the context of the New Culture Movement, which disdained such backward traditions. My study focuses on this group of leading courtesans in the crucial decades between 1870 and 1900 in the place where everything that was new and modern in China seemed to happen.

Hershatter's study, *Dangerous Pleasures,* examines the same decades as Henriot's does. It is the result of much meticulous research and offers a rich and lively discussion of prostitution from a feminist perspective. By piecing together the lives and biographies of several top Shanghai courtesans and allowing their voices to be heard, this work makes an important contribution to our understanding of the complex interaction between the private and professional lives of these women and of their relationship to the Shanghai environment. It offers a new angle on the historical picture of courtesan entertainment. Inspired by Hershatter's work, I have pursued the question of how these women might have thought about themselves and their contribution to Chinese modernity.

In other aspects, my approach differs substantially from Hershatter's. Her main concern is to narrate the lives and labors of Shanghai prostitutes within the broader context of their social and economic exploitation as sex workers. She approaches her subject largely from the perspective of power and control, as part of the wider picture of China's evolving modern statehood, and studies the attempts of the Republican state to regulate and control prostitution. In "volatile and virtually colonized Shanghai," she argues, the social elite felt even more keenly the "instability of China's semicolonial situation."[10] Thus, the debates over prostitution should be seen in the context of the Chinese (male) elite's anxiety about the fragility of China's sovereignty and the feeble attempts to define a Chinese modernity.[11]

My study approaches the question of power and control in a much more open-ended manner. The focus on entertainment and entertainment culture brings greater visibility to the ways in which segments of Shanghai entertainment culture and the individuals behind them affected social change. In such a scenario, power and control are not predetermined. For example, the Chinese state was not an important actor in Shanghai entertainment culture and its power to transform society, although later in the Republican period, this changed to some extent. Analytical points therefore must be anchored in a particular historical time frame. Specifically, I would suggest that the "male anxiety" in Hershatter's argument has a specific historical date. It did not predate the rise of Chinese nationalism in the twentieth century. It does, however, have a historical antecedent, the anxiety about their own identity besetting the men of letters who had been arriving in the Foreign Settlements since the 1870s. This anxiety had to do with the unabashed commercial spirit of the Settlements rather than with sovereignty or nationhood. My analysis demonstrates that the shift in the way these men described courtesan entertainment and the city itself reflects a change in their self-perception and mentality.

In his *Fin-de-Siècle Splendor,* Wang discusses some of the same novels that I examine in this book. They were published in Shanghai at the turn of the twentieth century and feature Shanghai courtesans as their main characters. Wang's point of departure is the claim made by May Fourth writers and literary historians that modernity in Chinese literature began only in the 1920s and with a particular group of fictional works written in the new vernacular. This largely successful claim transformed the modern sensibilities in late Qing novels into the "repressed modernities" of Wang's book title. The modernity of the late Qing courtesan novels is their redefinition of the realm of love and desire by means of a transgression or an ironic exaggeration of erotic and sentimental conventions. What might at first seem decadent, the novels' excessive focus on sex and desire, is precisely the point at which a new code of behavior was brought into being in the guise of "waywardness." Wang takes this term from Lu Xun (1881–1936), author of the most influential early history of Chinese fiction. As opposed to the May Fourth fiction, with its clearly foreign models, Wang sees the late Qing novels and the particular patterns of their modernity emerge out of a mostly internal cultural process. He asserts that modernity should not be understood as a linear developmental model; it did not appear first in one place and was then followed by "belated moderns." He sees instead "the advent of the modern at any given historical juncture as the effect of a fierce competition of new possibilities."[12] While the point is certainly well taken that late-nineteenth-century modernity took on particular shapes in different places, I find that there is strong and even overwhelming evidence to support the view that the writers of these novels were in many ways globalized. Their novels were serialized in Western-style media, the periodical and the newspaper, and the majority of the writers worked as journalists in these media. They had moved to Shanghai because it was "the West" in China, and they introduced the truly modern fictional protagonist into their novels: the city, the metropolis, Shanghai. They were part of a world fashion of the time, which, despite its variety, had definable core features that were absorbed, adapted, and transformed by the different metropolitan centers, and often with a time delay. The same is true for the main protagonist of these novels, the Shanghai courtesan. While her new Shanghai personification certainly talks back to traditional perceptions of courtesans, it also eagerly absorbs the world's fashions and fancies. Through association with her, the modern and the Western unwittingly become part of the interior decoration of paradise. She might be an unlikely modernizer, but she is undeniably an effective one, not least of all because she does not proselytize. Wang touches on the importance of this new urban center in these novels, especially *The Biographies of Shanghai Flowers*, but takes it no further.

Of direct importance to my study is Wang's observation that the figure of the courtesan in late Qing fiction "may well have prefigured the emotionally and behaviorally defiant postures of the 'new woman'" portrayed in 1920s women's writing.[13] Although he did not pursue this idea in his discussion of the novels, it is nonetheless daring and insightful. Again, the crucial link between the city of Shanghai and the production of this "new woman," both figuratively and literally, is not made. When Wang stresses the relationship between Shanghai and its courtesans, he sees them mainly as representing desire.[14] If one examines the courtesan novels as a whole, it becomes apparent that desire is merely the familiar outer garment in which the authors dress up Shanghai's outrages and excesses. The fundamental structure shared by all the courtesan novels is the city. From this perspective, development of critical perception in this group of novels, discussed first from a moral standpoint by Lu Xun and in terms of narrative innovation by Wang, is rooted in the changing perception of what Shanghai stands for.[15] My study concentrates on this aspect of the relationship between the city and the Shanghai courtesan as literary figure. The rise of locale as a dominant element in fiction and the symbolism attributed to the urban center connote the advent of the modern.

Works on Shanghai prostitution by modern Chinese historians include Sun Guoqun's *A Secret History of Prostitution in Old Shanghai* (Jiu Shanghai changji mishi) and Xue Liyong's *History of Shanghai Prostitution* (Shanghai changjishi). Although both are rich in materials, they share the same neglect of documentation, an indication that studies in this field are still somewhat more anecdotal than scholarly in form. Sun Guoqun, whose work is one of the first such studies by a Chinese scholar, was not able to distance herself from the master discourse within her country, which springs from the premise that prostitution is evil. Her historical discussions are thus framed as exposés of the exploitation of women by the capitalist system. Xue Liyong, who previously had published an article on Shanghai prostitution, argues that the Shanghai courtesan was part of the evolving commercial culture of the city and played an important role in the formation of Shanghai urban culture. Unfortunately, this potentially important study contains many factual errors, and the author's arguments are not supported by historical documentation.

These studies nonetheless have contributed substantially to our understanding of the Shanghai courtesan from the perspectives of urban social history, gender studies, and literary representation. In a dialogue with these works, and through exploration of hitherto unused sources and trajectories of inquiry, my study attempts to explain why the Shanghai courtesan was such a pervasive figure in late-nineteenth-century representation, and in particular in relation to the city. How did this relationship both render and reflect the particular kind of impact she was able to generate? This impact was crucial in the formation of a new type of urban entertainment culture and modern lifestyle that easily blended things East and West and in the cultural construction of a new identity by people moving into this hybrid place.

This book follows a hermeneutical cultural history approach. It does not start out with privileging one type of source over another but tries to read them into one another within the confines of their own genre and media codings. It tries to develop an understanding of them in their own terms and as part of a living, historical universe of meaning. At the same time, it offers these sources the concepts and perspectives of our own time in order to unfold layers of meaning of which even their authors were not aware.

The approach differs from a focus on verifiable historical facts by accepting that the image of Shanghai and the courtesans might have been as real and powerful at the time as were the actual city and people themselves, and even more so. It does not view descriptions and depictions as simple constructions of reality, grounded only in the imaginations and agendas of their authors. Instead, it assumes that some fictional works are possibly based on broad quasi-sociological observation, while supposedly realistic biographies of courtesans might be interwoven with subterranean reflections on the male authors' selves. Rather than setting out to document the history of female oppression, this study accepts the possibility that Shanghai courtesans might have been creative and proactive in making the best of their new environment to the point that they unintentionally paved the way for an urban modern culture in China and were much more effective than the bold words of the great reformers.

The Historical Setting and the Rise of Entertainment Business

The Shanghai Foreign Settlements were established on the mudflats along the Huangpu River in 1841, as a consequence of the Treaty of Nanjing, which ended the first Opium War. The name "Shanghai" was still attached to the old walled city a bit to the south, and the Foreign Settlements—the International Settlement, which was administered by the British and the Americans, and the French Settlement—were at a safe distance, separated by a creek. As people of different backgrounds came or fled to the Settlements with their hopes and expectations, their vision of their future city was little impeded by old structures of any kind, on the ground, in their minds, or in traditional power relations. Thus, they were able to influence the development of the city in a very decisive way.

Since the early 1860s, Westerners were already using the term "model settlement" to describe the place. Although it never was neatly defined, the contexts in which it was used implied harmonious relationships among the different races, civic order, and a proper balance between public and private interest.[16] The residents also took pride in the Settlements for the lively social life and cultural activities. As one of the old residents of Shanghai wrote at the turn of the twentieth century, Shanghai could congratulate itself on being better at entertainment than any other treaty port.[17]

In the late 1850s, Chinese refugees fleeing the Taiping Rebellion, many from the moneyed classes, began pouring into the Settlements, which became the favorite abode of wealthy merchants and high officials alike. In the ensuing years of chaotic development, the city could not maintain separate sectors for Chinese and Westerners, as specified in the original treaty, even though such sectors existed and continued to exist in other treaty ports, such as Tianjin. This situation produced a unique intermingling of settlers from many different Chinese and foreign domains within a singularly well-managed urban environment.

As the Settlements grew rapidly into the most important commercial center on Chinese soil, entertainment, which was an important part of Shanghai's economic life, developed to such an extravagant extent that the city became the leading tourist attraction for mainland as well as overseas Chinese; by the 1910s, it was even a choice spot for international visitors. The quality of life associated with the city and its entertainment did much to attract commercial and financial capital.

By the 1880s, Chinese sojourners and visitors to the city routinely talked about it in terms of the paradise of Penglai, Island of the Immortals. While there were antagonistic voices, writers generally were most impressed with the care lavished on the public spaces and the comfort provided by an infrastructure that ranged from paved roads to a system for separating fresh water and sewage. As one writer exclaimed in his 1887 *One Hundred Ballads on Shanghai* (Shenjiang baiyong): "Upon entering Wusong port[,] one's horizon opens, one wonders whether one has not entered Penglai in this life; if Liu [Chen] and Ruan [Zhao] [from the Eastern Han dynasty] were brought back once again, they would have mistaken [what they see here] as the peach [the fruit that soothed all their earthly sufferings] and refused to ever leave again."[18]

In Shanghai, visitors were impressed by the wide, clean avenues and well-regulated traffic, which featured the strange convention of people who were traveling in one direction all driving on the same side of the street. They admired the grand buildings with their diverse architectural styles, the public parks, tap water (1880), water closets, and the trees planted along the bank of the Bund and the streets in residential districts. They were overwhelmed by the glitter of the street lamps—lit by gas (1864) and, later, electricity (1882)—which transformed night into day. All these material wonders were further glorified by the allure of the Shanghai courtesans moving among them.

For the Chinese, the notions of "paradise" and "island" seemed to have a causal relationship; paradise is possible only in a small, isolated place. The Settlements were run by foreigners and therefore made up an island, a de facto independent political entity, on Chinese soil. They were shielded from the conflagrations that were tearing China proper apart and consequently offered a haven where people could be safe and make money without the traditional social constraints or interference from Qing officialdom. At the same time, the foreign consulates were frequently frustrated by their lack of control over the city and its foreign inhabitants, including the Municipal Council.

The Shanghai entertainment industry developed under two vitally important conditions provided within the Foreign Settlements. The first was effective control over organized crime, which became a serious social concern only after 1900.[19] Organized crime tends to prey on entertainment; this association undercuts the cultural status of entertainment and reduces its innovative potential. The second was the efficient management of the city's civic sector. Its clean and orderly appearance along with its modern infrastructure provided an optimal physical and cultural ambience. In both respects, Shanghai entertainment differed radically from that offered in earlier Chinese centers.

Shanghai's reputation as the Paris of the East or the Penglai of this life was the result of the city's particular multicultural mix. Although Shanghai was a semicolonial political entity, the imperialism paradigm would not help in understanding the particular situation or the source of the city's vitality. Shanghai's governing council was run by foreigners, but beyond securing the general existence of the place, foreign governments had little say, especially in the International Settlement. In fact, there was often fundamental disagreement and conflict between European governments and foreign settlers.[20] Meanwhile, a multiethnic culture was forming in the city, with Western and Chinese elements blending and connecting at many levels. Doing business and understanding the other's business culture was one important example. Chinese merchants operating within a Western legal framework and system of taxation was yet another. Communication among the city's short- and long-term sojourners was carried out in a mixture of different regional as well as international languages, with Pidgin English the most common language of business. The city had at least seven kinds of post offices and many systems of accounting for time and holidays. The members of the different communities compromised and adjusted. The Shanghai Municipal Council made a tremendous effort to create an urban infrastructure on a par with those of Paris and London, and the city quickly gained the admiration of visitors and evoked pride in its residents.

What about power and foreign domination? Tax-paying Chinese merchants were not allowed to join the Foreign Ratepayers' Association or participate in city management. However, the Chinese during this early period do not appear to have exerted much pressure to be included; they seemed content with being able to address the City Council directly with their grievances and take independent action when they deemed it necessary.[21] A morally charged discourse about imperialism and colonialism would sound like an anachronistic and retroactive imposition and would have made little sense to Shanghai's sojourners of the late nineteenth century. The notion of hybridity might be better suited to capturing the situation.[22] The members of this temporary community crossed all kinds of national and cultural boundaries and accepted the rules of the place because the benefits were clearly known. Even the so-called Chinese in Shanghai were far from being homogeneous. They identified less with their "country" than with their native places, to which they often returned. Many had come to Shanghai as British subjects from what is today Malaysia or Singapore and insisted on being treated as such. There was a sizable number of children of ethnically mixed background (the first Shanghai school was built for them), and they embodied the city's hybridity. This cultural interplay and transference made Shanghai the most open city on Chinese soil.

The cultural importance of entertainment was apparent from the early stages of the founding of the Settlements. It was one of the most visible and effective mediating forces between Chinese traditional culture and the foreign and modern challenge. This study reads entertainment in the context of a newly emerging, modern, urban community engaged in a polyphonous search for its identity.

The Makers of Shanghai Entertainment Culture

Leisure pursuits were transformed into a key ingredient of the Shanghai economy through the interaction of a willing market and enterprising individual players who saw the opportunity and pursued it. The money and institutions were in place for the development and commercial exploration of entertainment for affluent sojourners, most of whom were in town without their wives and families. The courtesans were among the first to spot the favorable conditions of this environment. Finding little opposition, they set out to reinvent themselves as public figures for life and business in the Settlements.

Courtesan entertainment has a long history in China, with the capital city and powerful regional administrative and commercial centers setting the tone. By contrast, during the Manchu Qing dynasty (1644–1911), official courtesan entertainment, known as *guanji,* was abolished in the capital shortly after the founding of the dynasty, and the ban was later implemented throughout the country. Prostitution and private courtesan entertainment did not disappear but were continuously subjected to arbitrary bans and closures by local officials. The survival and, in some towns, success of courtesan entertainment depended on the discretion of the local official, as it did not have legal protection.[23] Qing officials were banned by law from visiting such establishments, and offenders faced severe punishments. The age-old patronage culture linking officials and courtesans was suppressed.

The scene described in *Entertainment*, quoted at the beginning of this chapter, was so uniquely Shanghai that it could not have taken place anywhere else in the empire. The Foreign Settlements were a radical contrast to the Shanghai district town next door, walled up and resistant to the new lifestyle, modern city management, and improvements such as roads and sewage systems springing up just over Yangjingbang Creek.[24] Perhaps the pressure from this noisy competitor right beyond the walls made the town gentry even more conservative. As it was, the Settlements and the walled city coexisted rather peacefully. In time, however, the Settlements came to dominate economically as well as spatially, and increasingly, to the new reader of newspapers and potential tourist, the name "Shanghai" evoked only the lure of the Settlements.

Within the particular social, financial, and legal environment of the Settlements, the courtesans' entertainment business grew rapidly from the 1850s onward. During the early period, they, like others, were refugees. They escaped from war in the walled city and moved to the safe haven of the Foreign Settlements. Joining them were other courtesans from the greater Jiangnan area, including cities such as Suzhou, which up to that time had completely eclipsed Shanghai Prefecture in urban entertainment. In fact, the soft Suzhou vernacular remained the professional language of Shanghai courtesans, and even those who had grown up in the new metropolis were eager to learn it. The Settlements comprised an immigrant community. Everyone was as much Shanghainese as anyone else.[25] Absent was the traditional gentry class, whose social stature would have permitted it to regulate and, to an extent, enforce standards of proper public behavior. Absent—less in a strictly legal sense than in an actual one—was the Qing court, with its standards and sumptuary laws.[26] And there was the chance, which the courtesans eagerly seized, to develop rules and rituals that reflected the new social dynamics.

Contemporaries noted the synergy between the courtesans and the Settlements. A biography of a famed courtesan had this to say in 1907:

> Since the opening of the Foreign Settlements [here called "foreign trading post" (*yangchang*)], the outsiders have asserted their extraterritorial rights in our land. The governing principles were based on foreign laws, and the courtesans as well as others were protected by it, quite unlike the strict control exerted over them in the rest of the country. Therefore, in the Foreign Settlements they are much more active and visible in openly advertising their business; their clients find no obstacle to patronizing them and to enjoying themselves without scruples. This is unlike the inland situation, in which one is more cautious and would hesitate to go about it so boldly.[27]

In strictly legal terms, the International Settlement had no special provisions protecting courtesans and prostitutes; in the French Settlement, their registration and taxation made their legal position only slightly better. The Municipal Council's general policy of reducing the Chinese government's legal presence in the Settlements, even in matters concerning Chinese residents, provided the courtesans with sufficient coverage and protection against the Chinese authorities. In court cases in the Settlements, the legality of the courtesans' business never was an issue.

In this book, I often use the term "courtesan" in the singular to represent a collective. The composition of this collective changed all the time. From the perspective of the rise of Shanghai entertainment and its culture, however, the members of this collective were held together by a constant movement of information, fashion, and competition. The difference between prostitutes and courtesans is in their training and line of business; the prostitute openly sold sex, and the courtesan purveyed cultural entertainment. Although both catered to the whims of men in one fashion or another, the top courtesans paraded in the limelight and created far greater public interest. As a consequence, they had greater public influence.

The Shanghai courtesan's status as one of Shanghai's wonders was the result not only of her own self-promotion but of an image furthered by the Shanghai print industry, especially the entertainment press. This industry noted the market value of the courtesan as an emblem of Shanghai's appeal and decadence and developed a rich array of print products about her, from illustrations to biographies to daily reports. Thus, the courtesan's self-staging as the trendsetting public Shanghai figure was reflected, multiplied, and enhanced through print narrations and illustrations of her and this unique city.

The press, particularly the entertainment press, was an equally singular feature of the Settlements and would have been unthinkable in the rest of the Empire. With the founding of the Chinese-language newspaper *Shenbao* and the opening of the Shenbaoguan publishing house in 1872, the Settlements rapidly developed into China's print capital and became, as Rudolf Wagner has argued, coterminous with the "modern" Chinese public sphere.[28] Again, Shanghai defies the assumption that in these times of turbulent change, which saw China's transformation into a nation along with a dramatic realignment of the country's social structure and its elite, the press would inevitably be constantly absorbed in deep thoughts about this critical historical juncture. Until recently largely unstudied, but still there for all eyes to see, the Shanghai Chinese-language papers devoted as substantial a part of their attention to pleasure and entertainment as other foreign-language papers did. Eventually, the growth of this market made entertainment newspapers, with their characteristic blend of courtesan and stage news and political satire, commercially viable. In their daily reporting, these papers fleshed out the courtesan's image as the emblem both of Shanghai's "prosperity and glamour" (*fanhua*) and of its folly and outrageousness.

The men working in the press and the print industry were called—not without a tinge of irony—"Foreign Settlements' men of letters" (*Yangchang caizi*).[29] They expressed their contradictory sentiments about the city through the image of the courtesan. The Shanghai courtesan's rise to prominence was a challenge to these literati, who had moved from the status of gentry elite to that of salaried urban employees. Their traditionally close relationship with courtesans, epitomized by the legendary late Ming enchantments between the grand courtesans and the famous literati of the time, became a burden, as it was a constant reminder to the literati of the change in their relative social status.[30]

These men, whom I refer to variously as literati, men of letters, or *wenren*, are not a clear-cut, stable category. Contemporaneous texts identify them as men who "seek the company of courtesans" (*yeyou*). Any one of them might be a merchant, an official, or a teacher, serve in the military, or work for a foreign firm as a journalist, editor, or "comprador" (*maiban*). The group essentially is defined by an elevated level of education that enabled its members to display a certain cultural connoisseurship while they also had to work for a living. (Nor were the courtesans a clear-cut group. As mentioned earlier, courtesans were constantly moving in and out of various roles such as wife, concubine, madam, performer, entertainer, and lover, playing some of them simultaneously and others sequentially.)

In part to cope with their new situation in life, the men of letters fell back on an age-old tradition: they adopted the attitude of someone who is just "playing" (*youxi*). Literati who felt unappreciated by or dissatisfied with the world, yet were powerless to influence it, had assumed this guise in the past. Thus, the *youxi* attitude was a sign easily recognized by others. In this pose, the Shanghai *wenren* announced their dissatisfaction with the world and also made excuses for the compromise they made by joining the market. Their portrayal of the Shanghai courtesan is therefore an indirect comment on their own self-assessment and relationship to their Shanghai environment.

Organization

This study is organized along different trajectories rather than in chronological order.

Chapter 1 focuses on the impact of the Shanghai courtesan on the city's public culture. By analyzing the fashions, furniture, and public behavior of the leading courtesans and the fixation on courtesans that resulted among their contemporaries, the chapter traces their transformation into the ultimate emblem of Shanghai's prosperity. In moving their place of business from the traditional secluded, indoor locations into Shanghai's public space, the courtesans were able to strongly influence fashion, taste, and public behavior. Thus, they unintentionally became the model for modernity.

Chapter 2 investigates the new ritual practices governing courtesan houses in the Foreign Settlements. A comparison with earlier courtesan rituals practiced in the walled city and the Jiangnan region supports the argument that a unique set of such rituals developed within the Foreign Settlements, reflecting the new standing and dramatically increased freedom the top-ranking Shanghai courtesans carved out for themselves in relation to their clients, the madams, and the public.

Chapter 3 takes up this new pattern of ritualized play and addresses the specific role models Shanghai courtesans used to fill out this abstract framework. The role-play arose from the courtesans' obsession with the novel *Dream of the Red Chamber* (Honglou meng), by Cao Xueqin (1715–1763), and the assumed familiarity of their clients with this novel. Theatricality has traditionally been part of the courtesan persona. This game focused on *qing*, which means sublime love or passion, and the role-play was based on the love between the two most celebrated protagonists of the novel, the frail beauty Lin Daiyu and Jia Baoyu. The implications of this game are significant. It cast Shanghai as a dreamscape in place of the novel's Daguan Yuan, a garden in which the young people pursue their passions shielded from the outside world. And it equated the courtesan and her client with the lovelorn heroine and hero. Through this scenario, the courtesan established a new identity that signaled the nature of the game, its rules, and her expectations. In it, the client had a romantic but decidedly meek role to play, while the courtesan assumed a new and playfully dominant status.

Chapter 4 explores the process by which Shanghai men of letters created the image of the Shanghai courtesan. This cultural production coincided with the transitional period in the lives of these men, when many of them had started to "plow with the pen" (*pa gezi*) in the rapidly growing Shanghai print industry. Studies of the different types of works produced between the 1860s and the 1890s show that although the historically close link between the literati and the courtesans was at the root of this production, the men of letters used the print media to articulate their own contradictory sentiments toward themselves, the city, and its courtesans. The print entertainment that developed during this period thus had the courtesan as its dominant character.

Chapter 5 studies the role of the entertainment press and the rise of Shanghai courtesans from their traditional low social status to the position of the first modern national stars around whom an emerging star culture formed. This predates the celebrity-making process that developed around the film stars of China's burgeoning motion picture industry in the 1920s and 1930s. One of the most important means of promoting this development was the kind of entertainment newspaper later known as the "little paper" (*xiaobao*), which arrived on the scene around 1897. Mainly devoted to the Shanghai courtesan, these papers singled out top courtesans in their reporting and spread their names and stories daily throughout the country's major cities. Courtesans were quick to recognize the potential of these media and used them to promote their own agenda. The star and the star culture thus became part of the new landscape of Shanghai's commercial print industry and entertainment culture.

Chapter 6 studies the changing image of the Shanghai courtesan as she became one of the major fictional figures in late Qing novels. Through an analysis of the literary and illustrative representations of courtesans in the new wave of courtesan novels, the chapter argues that this body of literature comprises what may be considered the first modern Chinese urban novels. The illustrations, furthermore, were a breakthrough in their own right as they introduced the image of the female into the urban landscape.

Chapter 7 deals with the creation of a collective identity for the city. By analyzing conflicting representations of the city shown in city guides since the 1870s, this chapter documents the different narrative strategies pursued by early Chinese and Western sojourners in articulating the city's image. The narration in these city guides tells us more about what people wanted the city to be than what it was. The development of a coherent city identity is found less in the historical data than in the dreams and aspirations of the city's sojourners as expressed in the language, imagery, and symbols they used to describe it.

The conclusion takes up three broader issues arising out of the study of Shanghai entertainment culture during the late nineteenth and the early twentieth century. The first is the unwitting role of entertainment in social change and what is considered modernization. The second is the relationship among entertainment culture, business interests, and the emerging Chinese public sphere. And the third is the potential of approaches such as gender and colonialism studies for examining the Shanghai courtesan and the rise of Shanghai's entertainment culture.

Source Materials

The study of entertainment as a cultural phenomenon is complicated by the undefined borders of the source material, the difficulty of access in view of the paucity of reprints of such "marginal" material, and the need to develop methods suited to handle and integrate these sources. Source materials are of an unsettling variety and include postcards and city maps; guidebooks introducing individual courtesans; novels and poetry; photographs; demographic statistics; advertisements; descriptions and illustrations of architecture, furniture, and fashionable clothing; tabloid newspapers; and memoirs. Rarely are these materials bona fide sources of well-defined academic disciplines. It is often a daunting task to see beyond the intended function of these materials and discern their unintentional role in the construction of a cultural milieu.

Take, for example, a photograph of a courtesan. It is first of all a collective product, with the photographic studio providing some choice in setting, lighting, and backdrop; the courtesan's dress designed by her or someone else so as to evoke certain associations; and her facial expression selected to communicate the drama being staged. The photograph itself may have many different functions: a courtesan's gift to clients, a memento for certain events in the ritual of courtesan life, evidence that the Shanghai postcard was becoming an instrument of self-representation for the city, or a curiosity printed and sold by the studio to locals and tourists. The postcard is proof of a technology that was accepted and spreading among urbanites, of a commercial market for imagery, and might have been the basis for the illustrated entertainment offered by journals and newspapers. As I am not a specialist on photography or any of the related subjects, I had to learn and discover as I went along, constantly facing the pitfalls of the amateur and sometimes being saved by the gracious intervention of a specialist in this particular field. I found that this openness toward different materials and the information they might provide contributed much to my endeavor, and I was greatly encouraged by a similar boldness on the part of other scholars in the field of cultural studies.

Sources used in my study of Shanghai entertainment culture are vulnerable to one serious challenge. They might be regarded as belonging to a type of discourse that shares the same basic values and perspective, with hardly any dissent expressed. The information found in, for example, "brush notes" (*biji*), or "bamboo twig ballads" (*zhuzhi ci*), and the entertainment newspapers might appear to be of one voice, but they could in fact represent widely different positions and viewpoints. Discourse has its bias or blind spots, and this is true as well for those types of discourse, such as statistics, that would deny it most strenuously. Statistics might seem extremely unbiased and give the impression of standing on quantifiable facts, yet we are quite aware that this is a myth. Statistics are one method of recording data and lend themselves to treating certain questions and not others. The statistics relevant to this study have been compiled not from questionnaires sent to representative samples but from courtesan connoisseurs with very particular tastes, circles of friends, and access to information, from which they selected those facts they wished to record. I have tried to aggregate these intrinsically unstable data whenever I felt it might help to harden information. Otherwise, however, a statistical sampling would obviate my actual focus, namely, how people felt about or saw things.

Sources dealing with courtesans are a case in point. It has been argued that our knowledge of this group comes from a rather unified group of texts—the writings of men from the cultured elite who tended to present the courtesan in an idealized manner—which doesn't offer information on other groups such as street prostitutes and might even hide the truth about courtesans.[31] In the context of my own research into the Shanghai entertainment culture, I do not regard the information contained here as sociographic fact but as part of the mythmaking process that unfolded around Shanghai entertainment. Myth and fantasy are as true and powerful as demographic or economic data. They can and do translate into jobs, markets, investment, migration, and energy that makes things happen. In examining the process of urban mythmaking, I have tried to discover its origin and how Shanghai courtesans used it to their advantage.

Fictional sources such as late Qing novels are an important and valuable body of materials for this period. While fictional sources do not provide raw sociological data, it is too easy to dismiss them as pure "fiction." We must look at their particular agenda. During the late Qing period, the dominant fashion in fiction writing was social and political exposé. Much of the credibility of writers and their work depended on insider knowledge, which included sharp "sociological" observations of the exclusive world of courtesans and their clients. The writers claimed that they would show the true inner workings of a world that was not accessible to all, but their success hinged on the judgment of other insiders and connoisseurs. Naturally, the genre lends itself to exaggerations and constructions. For these writers, however, the incentive was to get it right. They did this by crafting general observation of social phenomena and processes by means of fictional individuation, which in itself was often based on thinly disguised real-life figures. To be on the safe side, I have used novels to substantiate suggestions from a broad range of nonfictional as well as narrative sources but did not use these novels as the sole or primary evidence with which to establish basic features.

Entertainment newspapers themselves may be considered questionable sources. These early papers are sometimes, and quite wrongly, associated with what is generally subsumed under the term "tabloid press." While it is true that the focus of the reporting by the early *xiaobao* was very different from that of major dailies such as *Shenbao*, the editors and journalists of these *xiaobao* took their model and measure from the professional big dailies. Journalists such as Li Boyuan were serious about the factual accuracy of their reports. The early *xiaobao* thus are an extremely important source in terms of both the factual record and the culture of Shanghai entertainment. In them, we find a dimension of entertainment life with traces of events, lives, and personalities that were instrumental in shaping Shanghai entertainment and which were largely written out of the major dailies and other sources. They are part of this culture, and they are its critics.

1 *Modeling the Modern*

Courtesan Fashion, Furniture, and Manners in Late-Nineteenth-Century Shanghai

The Shanghai courtesan, her public manners, her attire, and the decoration of her boudoir have been objects of continuous public fascination from the 1860s to the turn of the century. Her public and private persona as well as her lifestyle seem to have captivated the imagination. While the reaction was not always positive, this strong attention shows that the Shanghai courtesan—like women of the same profession in sixteenth-century Venice, eighteenth-century Edo, and nineteenth-century Paris—had become a force to be reckoned with. The constant, calculated provocations and the titillation of her social behavior and lifestyle gave her considerable power in the public arena and influence on fashion and taste. Chinese courtesans of the late Ming already had the reputation of being leaders in fashion and champions of the new, yet in Shanghai their stature took on added dimension.[1] In Shanghai, they were operating as public figures, and their impact was pervasive. They were the emblem and the most uninhibited advocates of Shanghai Settlements culture, with its particular mix of East and West, tradition and modernity.

As the entertainment business in Shanghai boomed, developing into a major moneymaking enterprise that attracted visitor and sojourner alike, the Shanghai courtesan, with her exceptional social position, her pursuit of glamour and fashion, and her desire to shock society with ever more "outrageous" public manners, became the trendsetter in the latter half of the nineteenth century. Given her intense public presence and impact, the Shanghai courtesan's sphere of influence was unique within the Empire. Before the official courtesan establishments were closed in the seventeenth century, shortly after the founding of the Qing empire, the courtesans participated in official and public ritual functions, leading spring processions and entertaining at official functions. Afterward, prostitution and courtesan entertainment lived on in private establishments that were not officially licensed or taxed, flourishing in and around commercial or administrative centers such as Suzhou, Yangzhou, Nanjing, and Canton. Beijing was hardest hit by the closure, as the establishments were disbanded and never recovered. New ones sprang up in the theater district outside Qianmen, but since Qing law prohibited officials and officials-in-waiting from patronizing courtesan or prostitution houses, business languished.[2] Certain regional differences notwithstanding, courtesan entertainment and prostitution went underground. They were no longer part of court or public culture. As a consequence, they became strictly "indoor" businesses, hidden from the larger public in a confined and separate social space. The legal limbo in which these businesses found themselves also meant that they were subject to the whims of local officials. Many Qing sources elaborate on the often devastating results of the delegitimization of courtesan establishments.[3]

The effects were felt even in the little district town of Shanghai, a mere backwater compared to the major centers of Nanjing and Suzhou. Constant threats of closure from local officials as well as the extortion made possible by lack of legal protection had prompted the courtesans to move to the new Shanghai Foreign Settlements during the Small Sword Uprising, never to return.[4] Eventually, the walled town also banned them from entering its parks, such as the Yu Yuan or the Yeshi Yuan.[5] Their Western-style carriages, which had become essential for their public self-staging, were too wide for the narrow streets of the walled city; as a consequence, the Foreign Settlements became their exclusive operating arena.[6] Making the best of the opportunities offered there, they successfully expanded their business activities into the public realm, establishing all-female storytelling halls, giving theater performances, and driving out to the public parks for afternoon tea with clients. In this way, they effectively used the public realm as a stage on which to promote their image and, in so doing, changed the face of their profession.

The recent work of Christian Henriot and Gail Hershatter has brought to light many of the institutional parameters and social facets of late Qing Shanghai courtesan life. What I propose to examine here is the cultural impact of these courtesans. From this angle, the courtesans appear as movers in their own right rather than merely objects of male projections and descriptions. The study is informed by the self-staging of the courtesans and the reactions of the public, including the media.

Western Material Culture and the Image of the Courtesan

Shanghai's fast-growing print industry reflected the city's increasing prosperity and self-confidence by producing a fair number of city and entertainment guides as well as high-quality illustrated Shanghai albums. They are in no way unified in form and content except that they reserved, in their characteristic aggrandizement of the city, a privileged position for the Shanghai courtesan, who became their most frequently illustrated subject.

Characteristically, the illustrations of courtesans and the courtesan house reflect a general mood of extravagance, fun, and novelty. The courtesans appear in a variety of ways: as the individual "famous courtesan," or *mingji*, as an entertainer, as a professional woman mentioned by name, and as entertainment itself in the guise of the many different services she offers.

Traditionally, the notion of *fanhua* (glamour and prosperity) has been associ-

1.1. "Drinking at the chrysanthemum mountain accompanied by courtesans" (Juhua shanxia xiaji yinjiu). Lithograph. The prominent position of the staircase, which is very unusual in Chinese architecture and in illustrations, represents a mixture of Chinese and Western styles that is typical of Shanghai. Note the Western-style kerosene lamps suspended from the ceiling and at the head of the stairs and, on the far side of the right wall, also another sure sign of Shanghai, a glass-pane window. (Dianshizhai, Shenjiang shengjing tu, *1884, 2:4)*

ated with the courtesan figure, *fanhua* being a core quality of a powerful and attractive city. In this sense, the courtesan appears in descriptions of former capitals such as Nanjing or trading centers such as Yangzhou. While the Shanghai depictions link up with these predecessors in language and style of illustration, they introduce distinctive, new features. This is true even when the courtesan is depicted in a most traditional manner. The lights suspended from the ceiling in figure 1.1 are Western-style kerosene lamps, and, as a contemporary description puts it, they "turn night into day" in a manner no amount of candles can match.[7] The candles shown in the illustration are there only as traditional elements in the Shanghai courtesan ritual *Juhua shan* (Drinking at the chrysanthemum mountain), which took place once a year. The window to the right has glass panes instead of the traditional paper. Two other illustrations of traditional courtesan entertainment show that Western-style kerosene lamps and Western-style large mirrors had become fixtures in the internal decoration of courtesan quarters (figs. 1.2, 1.3).

1.2. "Illustrations of Shanghai fun: Listening to the singing of Jin Xiaobao from Daxingli Lane" (Haishang kuaile tu: Daxingli Jin Xiaobao ting tangchang). Lithograph. Jin Xiaobao was one of the four famous courtesans of Shanghai during the 1890s. Visiting her house to listen to her singing was one of the more traditional parts of courtesan entertainment. A Western-style kerosene lamp hangs from the ceiling. (Hushang Youxizhu, Haishang youxi tushuo, *1898, 4)*

1.3. "Illustrations of Shanghai fun: To tea at the changsan courtesan establishment" (Haishang kuaile tu: Changsan shuyu da chayuan). Lithograph. Patrons typically had tea at the houses of courtesans with whom they were familiar. The illustration features a large Western-style mirror. (Hushang Youxizhu, Haishang youxi tushuo, *3)*

While the illustrations and descriptions resemble an advertisement for the individual courtesan—showing her portrait, her services, and the exact location of her premises—they also made her a part of the city's self-representation. They display the courtesan prominently alongside the glamorous comforts of this Western-style city with its renowned fire brigade, police force, street lamps, wide and unencumbered avenues, public parks, running water, water closets, and Western-style city management with its unique, for China, financial and legal institutions. Although the other features of the city—such as history, economic power, or culture—are introduced in their own right, the image of the courtesan is often shown surrounded by novelties that might have belonged originally to the West or the city's Western installations but have become part of her world.

What then is conveyed by portraying the city through the image of the courtesan? And what is the courtesan's function in this agenda? Since these guides present Shanghai as something unique, what is specifically new in the image of the Shanghai courtesan that differs from her traditional representation? A closer look at some of these illustrations reveals a new set of information, and with it appears a new layer of meaning.

Courtesans are shown offering clients a round of the Western game of billiards in the Zhang family's Weichun Garden, which is generally known as Zhang Garden, the first "modern" amusement park in Shanghai, which opened to the public in 1885 (fig. 1.4). They are also depicted dining with clients in the famous Western-style Chinese restaurant Yipinxiang on Si Malu, called "Fuzhou Road" in Western maps (fig. 1.5). This restaurant had all the accoutrements of high-style foreignness—Western-style tables, tablecloths, chairs, a fireplace, a clock on the mantelpiece, and gas lamps suspended from the ceiling—and the courtesan and her client could amuse themselves by eating with knives and forks.

Courtesans are also shown parading through the city and its various scenic drives with their clients in Western-style open carriages (fig. 1.6). In these illustrations, they move through a characteristic Shanghai urban setting, which includes Western-style buildings and installations such as electric street lamps, fire hydrants, and different kinds of horse-drawn coaches (figs. 1.7a, 1.8). The central position of Western-style furniture and surroundings as markers of high style is unmistakable. Within this new setting, the courtesan image acquires a new meaning.

Unlike traditional portrayals, which place the courtesan in a courtyard, in the private house of a wealthy patron, or next to a window in her room and looking out onto a garden, the new Shanghai illustrations make her an essential and illustrative part of the urban landscape itself. The precise relationship between the courtesan and the city is shown metaphorically in figure 1.9. The picture can be seen as consisting of two parts. On the left is the city with its Western-style buildings and electric lights (including wires), and on the right, the courtesan and her client ride through this cityscape. The courtesan's role in the picture is to lend a particular reading to the city. She is the Chinese commentary on these Western innovations. As the embodiment of the *fanhua* of entertainment and the easy life, she ensured that the Westernized cityscape and installations were non-threatening as well as fashionable, fascinating, and valued. Thus, her newly assigned role was to redefine the meaning of *fanhua* for particular features of Shanghai.

1.4. "Illustrations of Shanghai fun: Playing billiards at Weichun Garden" (Haishang kuaile tu: Zhangshi Weichun Yuan da danzi). Lithograph. Courtesans and their patrons play Western-style games in public at this garden, also known as Zhang Garden, which was free for all to enter. (Hushang Youxizhu, Haishang youxi tushuo, *1898, 2)*

1.5. "Illustration of Shanghai fun: Having a Western-style meal at Yipinxiang on Si Malu" (Haishang kuaile tu: Si Malu Yipinxiang chi dacai). Lithograph. The courtesan and her maid are seen dining with the patron and his friend at one of Shanghai's most famous restaurants, which offered a Western-style environment. (Hushang Youxizhu, Haishang youxi tushuo, *1898, 5)*

1.6. "Illustrations of Shanghai fun: A visit to the gardens in a four-wheeled open carriage" (Haishang kuaile tu: Caipiye shuanglun you huayuan). Lithograph. Accompanying a patron on an outing in the carriage was a new type of courtesan entertainment. (Hushang Youxizhu, Haishang youxi tushuo, *1898, 2)*

a

1.7a, b. "Illustrations of Shanghai fun: The chivalrous top-ranking courtesan Zhang Shuyu goes for a ride" (Haishang kuaile tu: Xia mingji Zhang Shuyu zuo mache). Lithograph. Zhang Shuyu was one of the four courtesan stars of Shanghai in the 1890s. The illustration (a) portrays many Shanghai icons: the open carriage, the street lamp, the wooden plank floors in the lanes of the linong, and glass-pane windows. The short biography (b) that precedes the illustration was written in praise of the courtesan by a patron. (Hushang Youxizhu, Haishang youxi tushuo, *1898, 1)*

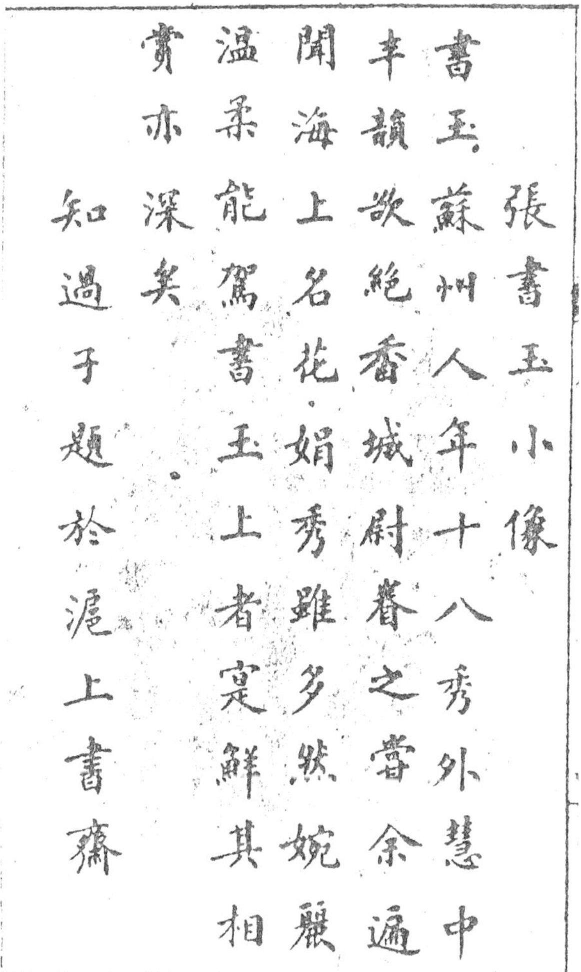
張書玉小像
書玉蘇州人年十八秀外慧中丰韻欲絕香城尉眷之嘗余遍閱海上名花娟秀雖多然婉麗溫柔能駕書玉上者寔鮮其相賞亦深矣。
知過子題於滬上書齋

b

By the 1880s, the Shanghai courtesan, like the Paris courtesans of the Second Empire, who, while "formerly confined to the edges of society had more and more usurped the center of things and seemed to be making the city over in their image,"[8] had become the emblem of the city's claim to be a paradise of entertainment, comfort, wealth, and security, guaranteed by the invisible hand of the foreigner. In her role as an entertainer, she marked the availability of these features as commodities irrespective of the customer's standing in the traditional social hierarchy. The illustrations operate on a double perspective: the city shows what it can offer, and the visitor sees what he can get.

The courtesan was best qualified to represent the combination of tradition and Western innovation under the banner of *fanhua*. Unlike any other figure, she was able to subvert without offending. In traditional culture, she already had the license to be innovative, even outrageous. The literary and artistic motif of the courtesan had great potential for representing the unusual, and the courtesan's success in being

1.8. "Wang Xiaobao" (Wang Xiaobao). Lithograph. The courtesan stands behind a Western-style fire hydrant. (Huayu Xiaozhu Zhuren, Haishang qinglou tuji, *1892, 2:19)*

attractive might have rendered the unusual acceptable. The Shanghai courtesan glorified the prosperity of the city and mediated between traditional culture and provocative Western-style innovations. In this process, the Western innovations did not appear as the advent of a new agenda of technology and commerce but were socially accommodated in the category of the curious, fascinating, and exotic.

The courtesan's image thus changed from being a supplement to traditional

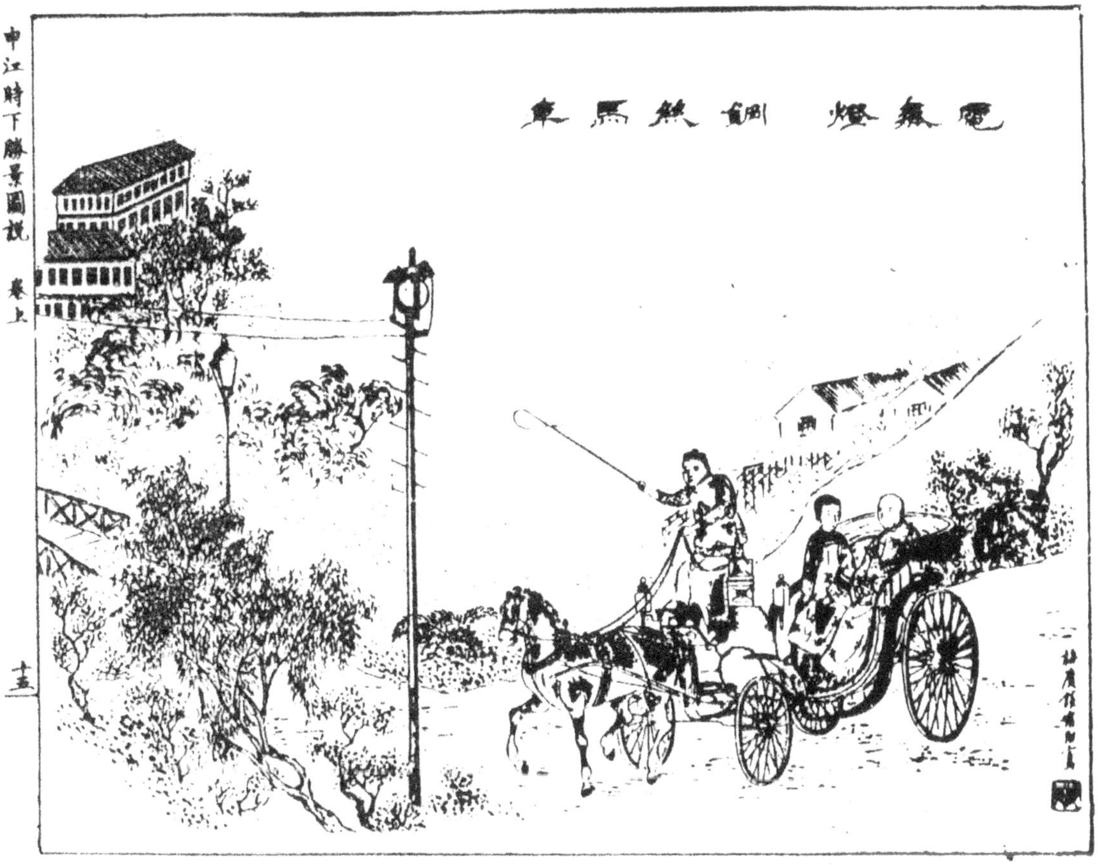

1.9. "The electric light and the steel-frame horse-drawn carriage" (Dianqideng, gangsi mache). Lithograph. Riding with a courtesan is one among many extraordinary sights in this depiction of two other Shanghai wonders, the electric light and the Western-style open carriage. (Meihua'an Zhu, Shenjiang shixia shengjing tushuo, *1894, 1:15)*

culture, as well as a relief from some of its constraints, to that of being a trendsetter and transmitter of the new. In this spirit, the guides to the city and its entertainment life made her the city's new icon. The regular linkage of her image with objects of Western material culture helped to insert this connection into the consciousness of readers. Shanghai courtesans appear to have encouraged and supported this linkage in every possible way. In the Foreign Settlements, their marginal social position kept the forces of tradition from focusing too much attention on their behavior; the weak Chinese administrative presence in the Settlements enhanced their leeway and proved crucial for the development of their business; and their profession prompted them to seek out the novel and amusing. The courtesan was seen as the most vivid, publicly acceptable persona for interpreting and representing the city's newness and foreignness as high-register, desirable extravagance. These illustrations, in their arrangement and, more important, their iconography visually established this link.

The Courtesan House

Illustrations of the objects surrounding Shanghai courtesans were inspired by the lifestyle of these women, who, by the 1880s, had attained a prominence that allowed them to set the tone of fashion in the city. In their efforts to demonstrate their position as trendsetters, they helped to translate Western accessories into emblems of novelty, extravagance, and high fashion. Their status was reinforced and visualized by the illustrations in the city guides. The link between the Shanghai courtesan and Western accessories is notably absent in depictions of courtesans from other cities such as Beijing, Suzhou, and Nanjing and is also not shown in illustrations of residences of officials and wealthy Shanghai families.[9]

There were roughly three phases in the development of fashion by the Shanghai courtesan. In the first phase, before the courtesans moved into the Foreign Settlements, Suzhou set the fashion.[10] The second phase came in the Settlements, during the 1860s, when Shanghai courtesans developed a mixture of Beijing, Canton, and Western elements into high fashion.[11] By the 1880s and 1890s, the third phase, Shanghai courtesans were defining trends for the Jiangnan region, and their reputation gradually spread throughout the country, as explained below.

In terms of furniture and accessories, Shanghai shops offered much to choose from, and some seemingly Western items might very well have been reimports from Canton. According to the first Chinese-language Shanghai city guide, published in 1876, shops in the city specialized in fashionable goods from the West, Beijing, and Canton. "Shops with Beijing goods" (*Jinghuo pu*) featured items such as feather fans, court shoes, and embroidered wares; they were concentrated in the popular Chinese retail district of East Qipan Road and West Qipan Road (Se Ge Bae Ka and Tong De Bae Ka on the English map of 1902) and Baoshan Road (the middle section of Canton Road, today's Guangdong Road). Four or five such establishments were already doing business during the 1870s and 1880s. Shops offering Western goods were located mainly on and around Nanjing Road.[12] The most famous among them, Vrard & Company (also known as Hengdali), at 2 Keangse Road (Xin Kai He Road)—a "must," according to all Shanghai city guides—was immortalized in late Qing novels.[13] Founded in 1864, this German shop specialized in clocks and watches, Western scientific instruments such as microscopes, and musical instruments as well as all kinds of playful accessories including music boxes with singing birds and wind-up dancing lions. A 1909 guide lists fourteen such stores.[14] Among the variety of stores, some carrying only Western-style furniture and lamps, "shops for both Western and Cantonese goods" (*Yang Guang huo pu*) were by far the most popular.[15] For the 1870s and 1880s, the guides list one hundred mixed shops in the walled city and the Foreign Settlements, with Yuesheng Quanheng and Huazhang being the most famous.[16] Also of interest to this study are shops for Cantonese-style rattan furniture; they offered goods made for export to the West that were based on Western models. This type of furniture frequently showed up in courtesan households alongside furniture that actually was imported from the West and was regarded as Western.[17]

From the 1870s onward, comments on Shanghai urban life in bamboo twig ballads, courtesan guides, and brush notes by Shanghai residents and in the diaries of visitors raised the claim that the Shanghai courtesan, in her quest for style and notoriety, was largely responsible for many new Shanghai trends. Prior to the 1870s, descriptions of courtesan entertainment were confined for the most part to the rituals involved, and courtesan life was much in a world of its own. Wang Tao (1828–1897), one of the earliest Shanghai sojourners who has provided much of our knowledge of this period, paid no attention to either furniture or clothing fashions in his elaborate account of courtesan entertainment in the walled city. Obviously, there was nothing extraordinary to note. Only later do he and others comment on courtesans, now in the Settlements, setting new fashions in clothing, furniture, and public manners.[18]

Personal accessories also underwent changes in fashion during the 1870s–80s. Courtesans preferred the imported perfume called "fragrant water" (*xiangshui*) to the burnt incense they had used for centuries to perfume their clothes, beds, and bodies.[19] The feather fan with a carved bone handle, a new import from Beijing, replaced the traditional round fan popularized earlier by Nanjing courtesans,[20] and the newest rage, pearl-embroidered headgear, replaced the emblem of Suzhou courtesanship, the flower arrangement for the hair, with an accessory that exemplified Shanghai's bent for conspicuous consumption (fig. 1.10). As the pearls came from Canton, this ornament nicely epitomized the spirit of the city as a hub of world trade.[21]

The illustrations of the interiors of courtesan houses, the descriptions of all that was new and thrilling in the courtesan world, and the different versions of Shanghai courtesan guidebooks enable us to identify those accessories first introduced to the public by Shanghai courtesans. These guidebooks differ from the city guides in their exclusive focus on the courtesan world. In general terms, they refer to the interior of the houses of the two highest courtesan categories, the *shuyu* and the *changsan*,[22] as "rich and splendid, comparable only to that of the highest lords of the land."[23] A visitor to the city in the late 1870s notes that every object displayed in these houses was of the richest and finest quality, so that "one is dazzled and overwhelmed; [the setup] conveys the mesmerizing atmosphere of a world of dissipation."[24]

Already during the 1870s and 1880s, the leading courtesans took pains to ensure that their addresses were in the most fashionable neighborhoods, especially those close to the entertainment district around Fuzhou Lu.[25] In the 1890s, top-ranking courtesans lived in a Western-style building in this area. Lu Lanfen resided at Zhaogui Lane on the corner of Fuzhou Road, Jin Xiaobao lived nearby in Daxing Lane, and Zhang Shuyu was on Shangren Xi Lane.[26] Lin Daiyu, who had just returned from a trip to Tianjin, also had her establishment on Daxing Lane, but she was considering a move to a spacious five-room house on Nanjing Road, one of the most expensive places to live.[27] Zhu Ruchun, who achieved fame in the 1890s, had moved into the first spacious five-room two-story house to be erected in Yangqing Lane, and the papers added that she had furnished it in fine taste.[28]

Typical furnishings for one of these courtesans included a large Western-style mirror hung at a tilt on the wall; bright kerosene or gas lamps; clocks of all kinds and dimensions; a Western-style cast-iron stove instead of the traditional charcoal-filled pan (fig. 1.11); pairs of calligraphy-painted glass or silk lamp shades suspended

1.10. High-ranking Shanghai courtesan with a man's feather fan in a Chinese studio. Photograph, Shanghai, 1870s–80s. The decorative sash hanging down the front of the courtesan's skirt was in fashion between the mid-1860s and late 1880s. She wears pearl hair ornaments and pearl earrings, but the bun at the back of her head is adorned with flowers. The hair dress suggests a date between the mid-1870s and mid-1880s. As in most courtesan photographs of this period, books are an important prop that signals elevated cultural levels. For a comparable hairstyle, see figure 1.1. (Courtesy School of Oriental and African Studies, London)

from the ceiling; and a three-legged, round, European-style tea table known in courtesan houses as *bailingtai*, for its likeness to the small feeding platform in a birdcage (fig. 1.12). Western-style curtains provided graceful cover for windows (fig. 1.13).[29] From pictures of Western-style restaurants of the time, one can easily see where the courtesans got their ideas (fig. 1.14).

Other common furnishings include a Western-style reclining rattan sofa in a

1.11. "Xie Yuexiang" (Xie Yuexiang). Lithograph. Courtesan performers in a storytelling hall with a Western-style cast-iron stove in front of the table. Note the short bangs, an 1890s fashion. (Huayu Xiaozhu Zhuren, Haishang qinglou tuji, *1892, 4:9)*

spot by the window and a leather armchair near the bed.[30] Illustrations also show upholstered chairs with rounded backs, framed landscape-and-figure paintings hung at a tilt, washstands with mirrors, and the sofa, which combined Chinese woodwork and Western-style cushions (figs. 1.15, 1.16). Western wallpaper was equally favored.[31] According to a contemporary novel, Western-style pillows and candleholders were likewise popular in courtesan households.[32] One of the courtesans' favorite musical instruments was the portable Western organ, which Vrard & Company advertised as the *bayin he.*[33]

1.12. "Images of the Four Great Golden Diamond Cutters: Image of Lin Daiyu, the leader among the courtesans in the Shanghai Settlements" (Si Da Jin'gang xiang: Hubei huaying tongling Lin Daiyu xiaoxiang). Lithograph, based on a studio photograph. The pose, with one hand resting on a small, high table, is similar to that of the courtesan in figure 1.10, but the table is now Western. (Hushang Youxizhu, Haishang youxi tushuo, *1898, 1)*

1.13. "Illustrations of Shanghai fun: Slippery fellows making out with the prostitutes at the racecourse" (Haishang kuaile tu: Paomating huatou "diao bangzi"). Lithograph. There were many brothels along the Shanghai racecourse. Note the Western-style curtains in the second-floor window. (Hushang Youxizhu, Haishang youxi tushuo, *1898, 7)*

*1.14. "Having a Western-style meal" (Chi dacai). Lithograph. Note the foreign style of the furniture and curtains. (*Haishang qinglou lejing tu*, 1892, 4)*

1.15. "Ma Qiaozhu" (Ma Qiaozhu). Lithograph. Note the Western-style upholstered chair and the sweeping curtain. (Huayu Xiaozhu Zhuren, Haishang qinglou tuji, *1892 3:1)*

1.16. "Xie Xiangyun" (Xie Xiangyun). Lithograph. The Western-style, framed landscape-and-figure painting on the wall is hung at a tilt in the Western manner of the time. At the center of the illustration is a Western-style washstand with an attached mirror. (Huayu Xiaozhu Zhuren, Haishang qinglou tuji, *1892, 3:3)*

外科新藥黑鬼血白鶴涎之能力

上海中法藥房新發明外科二藥。一名黑鬼血。外治極效。無論癰疽發背對口搭手。以及癩疥惡瘡無名腫毒一切。凡未潰者。以毛筆醮敷患處。無不立愈。每瓶售洋五角。一名白鶴涎。乃內消聖藥。善解血毒熱毒風毒火毒濕毒痰毒並山嵐瘴癘等毒。服之毒退病消。永無後患。每瓶亦祇售洋五角。有疾者外以黑鬼血塗治。內服白鶴涎退消。竊謂外科當無不治之症。況厥價極廉。病家當樂於購試也。

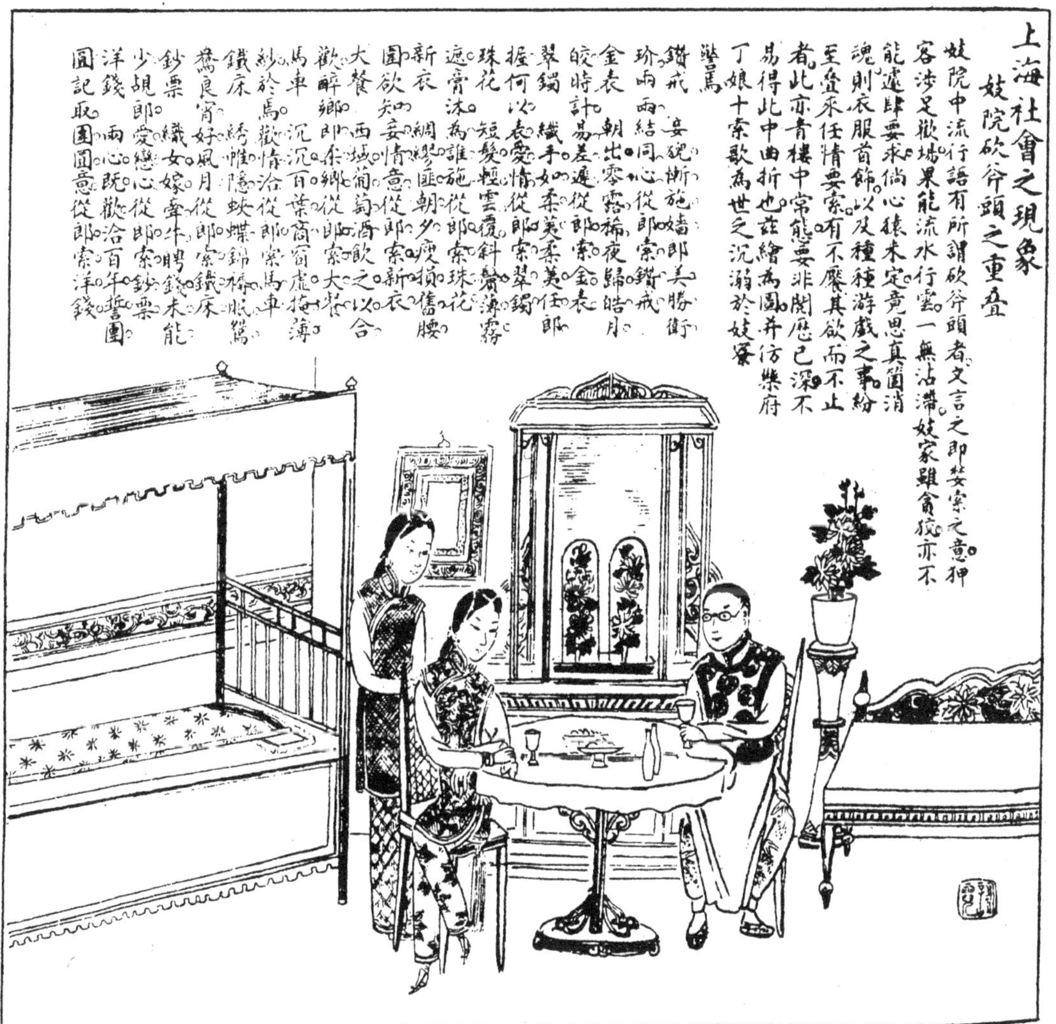

1.17. *"Events in Shanghai society: The manifold 'axing' [courtesan soliciting gifts from a patron] in the courtesan house" (Shanghai shehui zhi xianxiang: Jiyuan kan futou zhi chongdie). Lithograph. The Western-style bed without curtains is shown together with other Western-style furniture and accessories such as a tablecloth, sofa, chairs, and framed mirrors. (*Tuhua ribao*, no. 54 [1909], 7)*

Perhaps the most important change in style was the bed. First references to the new "bed without curtains" or "iron bed" date to the mid-1880s.[34] In later illustrations, such as figure 1.17, it was shown together with other types of Western-style furniture and accessories.[35] All of these new items are shown alongside traditional Chinese furniture and decorations. There seems to be neither conflict nor stress between the different elements. In the setting of the courtesan house, these foreign goods are transformed into and presented as symbols of glamour and desirability.

An inventory of the fashionable furniture ordered from specialized shops by a Shanghai courtesan is described in the novel *Dreams of Extravagance in Shanghai* (Haishang fanhua meng), published in 1898. In it, the courtesan gives a list to a client who has just committed himself to her; she wants a whole new set of furniture for her establishment. When he joins her later for a dinner party with the receipt in his hand, the only entry he understands is the total of $526.45. As he has arrived recently from Suzhou, he has no idea what the words on the list mean. The receipt is from the department store Zhang Fuli Gongsi, also known as Fuli Gongsi (Hall and Holtz). Founded in 1893 and located on Nanjing Road, it was Shanghai's first such department store and took pride in offering the latest in fashion and taste. The items listed on the receipt were eventually interpreted to the client by a friend who was a comprador for a foreign firm and thus was more knowledgeable. The following articles were included: one "si-po-ling pao-tuo-mo-sha-fa" [spring-bottom sofa (bed)], one "shafa" [sofa–reclining chair], one "die-lai-xin tui-bo-er" [dressing table], one "di-ling tui-bo-er" [dining table], one "hua-tou-lu-bo" [wardrobe], two "kai-hen xi-tie-qian-ai" [cane chairs], one "liu-gen ge-la-si" [looking glass], one "hua-shu si-tui-hen-te" [washstand], one "ban-xin tuo-bo" [bathing tub], six "qian-ai" [armchairs], one pair of "ti-pa-ai" [tea tables], one [set] of Western dinnerware, including a "te-lai-suan"[?].[36]

This list ironically exaggerates a historical fact, namely, the degree to which these foreign items, including their transliterated names, were seen as the height of chic by the courtesans. The client's willingness to buy these goods for the courtesan is the token of his devotion, and proof of his financial standing. This was not portrayed as an isolated incident. The owner of the department store seems quite familiar with the procedure, and the comprador's ability to explain the items indicates that they had already become part of Shanghai chic.[37]

The new glamour accorded fashion is visible in the revived popularity of the old term *shimao*, with the meaning "fashionable," as it was first used in the courtesan world. The renewed use of this term might be due to the phonetic resemblance to the term "smart," common in the sense of "fashionable in dress" in the British Isles since the eighteenth century. An "outstanding and fashionable courtesan" was described as *shimao guanren*,[38] while someone who rushed after the latest fashion was ridiculed as "besotted with fashion" (*gan shimao*).[39] Prior to the late nineteenth century, the term that described fashionable clothing, makeup, and accessories was *shishi zhuang*.[40] In the late 1850s, Wang Tao used the term *shixia ji* for "fashionable courtesan," but *shixia* also occurred in terms for clothing.[41] At this time, the term *shimao* stood for urban chic.

The courtesan Hu Baoyu was a powerful figure in the fashion world of the city during the 1870s and early 1880s.[42] Her position as one of the most sought-after courtesans of the time was based on her extravagant clothes, her sexual skills, the interior decoration of her house, her good cooks, and her love of novelty. She became a legend during her lifetime. The novel *The Nine-Tailed Fox* (Jiuwei hu) is entirely devoted to her life and adventures.[43]

She is also the subject of the first full-length biography of a Shanghai courtesan, a work attributed to Wu Jianren, the leading political novelist of the late Qing.[44] This biography bluntly ascribes her success to her capacity to "create fashions" (*zhizao fengqi*) and describes her as one of Shanghai's most cunning and successful professionals. In an instant, she could judge a client's character and his potential for spending. She would pick out, "with the speed of lightning," a potential patron from among the wealthiest. For herself, she "always chose the most beautiful youth to satisfy her lust" and supported her lover of the moment financially as a "kept" man. The author justifies this biography by pointing out Hu Baoyu's impact during the formative years of the Shanghai Settlements culture. She became celebrated and powerful by continuously pursuing the new while maintaining high professional standards, which gave her business the necessary vitality and freshness.[45]

Hu Baoyu's fame as an innovative entrepreneur was noted by many contemporaries and is substantiated by a flurry of anecdotes. Frustrated with the narrow constraints of Suzhou-dominated Shanghai courtesan practices, she ventured on a journey that took her as far as Canton; when she returned, she brought Cantonese furniture with her. This established the fashion of Cantonese redwood furniture in Shanghai courtesan houses.[46] Legend also had it that she learned English from the *xianshui mei* (sisters from the ocean waters), that is, Cantonese prostitutes, who also received Westerners as clients. She was even seen riding proudly with them in an open carriage through the main Shanghai thoroughfares, an extremely unusual act at a time when the hierarchy among courtesans would have prevented her from associating with the lowly *xianshui mei*. She set off another fashion rage when she appeared with bangs in the manner of the Cantonese courtesans. It was said that her adoption of the style was prompted by her curiosity about foreign men, with whom Cantonese courtesans were so successful.[47] This certainly does not exclude the possibility that business considerations played a role. As other sources point out, Hu Baoyu's wealth originated with a Western client.[48] Ma Xiangbo (1840–1939), one of Shanghai's most renowned scholars, noted that the Cantonese courtesans and prostitutes whose main clients were foreigners were among the largest depositors when the Hong Kong Shanghai Bank (Huifeng Yinhang) was first founded in 1865.[49] It seems that after her "lessons" with the Cantonese *xianshui mei*, Hu Baoyu soon succeeded in having a foreigner among her clients, thus breaking with the tradition of Shanghai *changsan* courtesans of Suzhou origin to keep aloof from such clientele (fig. 1.18).

Hu Baoyu's establishment also had a famous "Western room," which was decorated entirely with imported furniture for the entertainment of both Chinese and Western clients. It is mentioned and described in various courtesan biographies and guides. According to one fictional account, her establishment occupied a five-room house, with a large main hall, a guest room, a dining room, and a study. The

1.18. *"To taste the '[Western] exotic,' [Hu Baoyu] entertains a foreigner" (Chang yi wei, shenpei waiguoren). Lithograph. Hu Baoyu's liaison with a Western client was fictionalized and illustrated in* The Nine-Tailed Fox *(Jiuwei hu), 1918. This illustration for chapter 10 of volume 2 shows her newly adopted Cantonese hairstyle. The photograph on the wall must show Hu Baoyu herself. (Menghuaguanzhu Jiang Yinxiang,* Jiuwei hu, *in* Zhongguo jindai xiaoshuo daxi, *n.p.)*

rooms were so lavishly decorated that the house was compared to a "crystal palace."[50] One of her clients left the following description:

> The rooms are filled with [precious and refined objects such as] playing cards of ivory, scroll-paintings with jade handles, precious *ding* [bronze sacrificial vessels], hand-warming pots of gold, a chess game made of jade. With books lining the four walls, [the study] appears magnificent and tasteful. It may be that someone helped her to make these arrangements. Set apart is a room, lavishly decorated with Western-style furniture and clean without a flicker of dust. On its walls there is shiny silver wall-paper, and the floors are covered with multicolored rugs; from the ceiling hangs a Western-style turning fan, which cools the entire room during summer; and for winter an exotic Western stove is provided. The bed in this apartment is also Western in style, and without curtains. This room is the ultimate in extravagance and beauty.[51]

In the process of adopting new furniture from the West, the courtesan and her house were also transformed. With her new image, she communicated a new set of values. She not only introduced the symbol of change, Western furniture, into her house as part of her setting but, more important, indicated that change meant mostly if not exclusively the inclusion of Western goods. With her house, the courtesan gave a fresh interpretation to the traditional notions of wealth and fashion. Although the inclusion of exotic foreign objects and materials had been part of that lore at least since Tang times, the setting of the Foreign Settlements made the message all the more provocative and potent. For the Shanghai courtesan, competing in the display of glamour and ever newer innovations was part of doing business in that city.

The house of the premier courtesan, where men from a wide variety of social and geographic backgrounds attended entertainments and banquets, marked off an exclusive space, which, despite its essential privateness, was also very public. Unlike the manifestly public spaces such as the teahouse or the public garden, however, the exclusivity of the courtesan house made it subversive. Through curiosity and competition among courtesans, Western civilization entered in the form of accessories of pleasure and inscribed itself in this form on what became the refined urban taste in decorating the private and public spaces of Chinese life.

The guidebook descriptions and illustrations played an important role in the transfer of the new fashions and taste, with their blend of Chinese and Western material culture, from the courtesan quarters to the public consciousness (see, for example, figs. 1.19, 1.20). Clients also spread the word. Courtesan novels of the period describe women asking the wives of men who frequent courtesan houses to share their knowledge of courtesan fashion and behavior.[52] Some wives, concubines, or even daughters were driven by such curiosity that they disguised themselves in men's clothes and accompanied their husbands or fathers to the courtesan establishments.[53] There were also wives who, because of their own sexual preferences, became clients in courtesan houses.[54] In one story, an official holds a dinner party in a Shanghai

*1.19. "Zheng Jinhua" (Zheng Jinhua). Copperplate engraving. The setting, which includes a hanging clock, conveys the complex interaction between Chinese and Western material culture. (*Jingying xiaosheng chuji*, 1887, 27, courtesy Columbia University Libraries, New York)*

*1.20. "Hu Xiulin" (Hu Xiulin). Copperplate engraving. The clock, artificial flowers covered by Victorian-style glass domes, and kerosene lamp prominently displayed on the table convey a sense of glamour and high fashion. A feather fan (also in figure 1.15) is inserted at the corner of the neatly folded bedding. The fan and the hairstyle signal a date between the mid-1870s and mid-1880s for the photograph on which this copper engraving is based. (*Jingying xiaosheng chuji*, 1887, 7, courtesy Columbia University Libraries, New York)*

courtesan house in order to satisfy his elderly mother's desire to gain firsthand knowledge of these famous establishments. He orders his wife and concubine to accompany her. The old lady is so enchanted with the courtesan that she offers a gold ornament from her hair as a token of appreciation.[55]

Other entertainment establishments made the new furniture fashions publicly accessible and visible. A good example is the Female Storytelling Hall, with its top courtesan performers. The novel *Dreams of Shanghai's Glamour* tells how, in the 1890s, the hall's managers refitted the interior for the New Year festival, duplicating the typical furniture arrangement and decoration found in courtesan houses. The particular arrangement was first recorded in the 1870s and developed into ever more elaborate forms during the 1880s. It entailed covering the best tables in the hall with thickly woven "Persian rugs" (*taitan*) and placing on each table glass bowls full of fruit and sweets, a clock, and flowers arranged in baskets and vases.[56] This novel type of public place for performances by courtesan singers became the courtesans' stage for displaying their latest clothing fashions in the midst of their new-style interior decoration.

Furniture has its own way of shaping bodies and human relations. This new furniture suggested different ways of sitting, reclining, and relating to others. While traditional furniture seemed to convey distance, order, and hierarchy within a broader clan structure, the new forms created a sense of intimacy within modern comfort. The cultural structure of this furniture suggested and supported the urban bourgeois lifestyle of a nuclear family, which was later known under the new term "small family" (*xiaojiating*). The Shanghai courtesans were among the first to openly rebel against the old family structure, and they made it a condition for marriage or living together outside courtesan establishments that they would remain in Shanghai instead of returning to a husband's native place, where they would be under the first wife's control. For example, Lu Lanfeng and a Mr. Xi, the owner of a specialty shop for cloth dyes, set up what was called at the time a *sidi* (private home) in a "small lane," or *linong* (normally read *lilong* but pronounced *linong* in this combination), off Liu Malu (Sixth Avenue). Their nuclear cohabitation, during which Lu had a baby, ended tragically when Mr. Xi died after being kicked in the chest by an opera singer, Lu's jealous former lover, who had come to their door.[57] By the 1890s, this apartment arrangement had become a rather common demand among Shanghai courtesans.[58] The Western-style architecture of Shanghai's buildings and *linong* housing blocks also promoted this furniture and its attendant social implications because it was designed for smaller families.

The various guides with their detailed descriptions reflect the courtesans' success in presenting Western civilization as *qi*, or the extraordinary (here with the added meaning of exotic), which transformed courtesan houses into veritable showcases of the Western as fashionable. With the transformation of her house, the courtesan and her image changed. Many illustrations and later photographs of Shanghai courtesans use the mirror motif, with the courtesan presented through her reflection in a mirror. An illustration from *Mirror Reflections and Flute Sounds* (Jingying xiaosheng chuji) (1887) frames the courtesan's image in a mirror in the manner of a Western-style portrait (fig. 1.19).[59] Another illustration from the same album depicts

1.21. "Courtesan of the late Qing period" (Qingmo de mingji). Photograph. Hairstyle and clothing indicate a date around 1900. (Tang Zhenchang, Jindai Shanghai fanhua lu, *71)*

two courtesans gazing at each other through mirrorlike structures (fig. 1.20). In these illustrations, the courtesan no longer faces the viewer but is seen as an image or a reflection. The mirror doubles the image of the courtesan, displaying her back and her reflected front in fresh erotic and aesthetic dimensions. The scenes are a play on the transitory and illusory nature of courtesan life; the mirror metaphor ultimately comes from Buddhist sources.

The notion of *fanhua* represented by the Shanghai courtesan incorporates Western accessories with ease. This unprecedented and perfectly nonideological alliance is exemplified in the image of the courtesan reclining on a grand leather sofa (fig. 1.21). There is no sense of awkward accommodation here, only a heightened unity of glamour and seduction in the presence of this rarefied, exciting commodity.

The Hunter's Hat and Iconoclastic Lingerie

Creative adaptation and imitation of Western clothing was another way in which Shanghai courtesans brought the West into Chinese fashion. If the transfer of the latest fashions in furniture took the indirect route via Canton, in clothing the courtesan herself was the pioneer. As she moved into the public arena, her heightened visibility enhanced her role, to the chagrin of many in the city who saw this as a brazen challenge to their preferred order of things, even in Shanghai. Exposed to the stimulus of a great diversity of Chinese, Manchu, Japanese, and Western, male and female, stage and real-life costume and free from the pressures of other places in China where styles and colors still carried definite social meaning and could not be chosen at random, the Shanghai courtesan enjoyed considerable leeway in her clothing. And she made the most of it.

Courtesans and prostitutes have the reputation of being the most outrageously dressed women. This is as true for the sixteenth-century Venetian *cortegiane* as for the eighteenth-century geisha in Genroku Japan and the nineteenth-century *grandes courtisanes* of France's Second Empire.[60] But much as in Edo (1600–1867) and Meiji (1868–1912) Japan, where courtesans could operate only within entertainment quarters located on city outskirts, such as Yoshiwara in Edo and Shimabara in Kyoto, courtesans had a limited influence on broader segments of society in earlier centers such as Suzhou and Yangzhou.[61] The Shanghai courtesans' disproportionate impact on fashion was directly connected to their singular freedom of movement in the public realm. Their quest for fashion and iconoclastic novelty created an infectious atmosphere among women and even had an effect on men's dress. With their outrageous costumes, the sumptuous interior decoration of their quarters, and their free public manners, they in effect challenged the supremacy of Beijing, where the court once had enjoyed a powerful and not altogether pleasant hold on the nation's taste and apparel. Perhaps more profoundly, through their pursuits and public manners, the courtesans helped shape a new type of urbanite performance, in which looking and being looked at became absorbing activities in their own right.[62] The Suzhou courtesans shown in figure 1.22 were seen as imitating their Shanghai colleagues.

[The Qing code contained many prescriptions for dress as well as sumptuary laws that, for example, barred merchants from wearing clothes and colors signaling official rank and status. Textile museums in China and elsewhere have kept a sizable variety of the dress worn during the period, and they confirm that social practice largely corresponded to these laws. Although the regulations pertained chiefly to men, they implied a pervasive ban on wearing certain fabrics and colors, mainly those reserved for the court and the emperor himself. Shielded from these laws and regulations in the International Settlement and by certain customary rights of their profession, Shanghai courtesans developed their own, often provocative ideas about the suitability of colors, as did many of the young men in Shanghai. This caused much shock and excitement among their contemporaries, who were sure to mark such sensational events in their records with appropriate disapproval.

For their underwear, some courtesans selected gardenia yellow, which happened to be the cardinal color for men's outer dress when paying respects to their elders or teachers.[63] Courtesans wore crimson crepe skirts during the New Year festival, a costume traditionally worn by maidens for their marriage ritual and a color otherwise reserved for honored officials attending court ceremonies.[64] One commentator exclaimed: "Only in Shanghai can such a thing happen; no other place dares to be so bold as to exceed the boundaries of propriety to such an extent!"[65]

The relationship between sumptuary regulations and their application is always messy. *Things Seen in the World* (Yueshi bian), a seventeenth-century work on life and customs in the Shanghai walled city, describes the development of fashion during the late Ming and early Qing periods. It notes cases in which the locals trans-

1.22. "Events in Suzhou courtesan establishments: One hundred times passing without being worn out" (Suzhou quyuan zhi xianxian: Baibian xiangguo yi wei lan). At this time, Suzhou courtesans, influenced by Shanghai courtesans, had recently taken up riding in open carriages with their patrons. Suzhou had only one paved road, however, and the courtesans could ride up and down only on this street. (Tuhua ribao, *no. 330 [1910], 7)*

gressed existing dress codes; in some cases, courtesans and prostitutes, opera singers, or "lowly servant girls" were the culprits.[66] But the record does not note any reaction in the community; it simply states that it was a worry for the "leaders of public morals" (*zhuchi shidao zhe*).[67] The demeanor and fashions of Shanghai courtesans were recorded in photographs and illustrations beginning in the 1860s (figs. 1.23a-f). These fresh styles and attitudes eventually caught the attention of the new urban media.

Popular papers such as *Entertainment* (Youxi bao), founded by the political novelist Li Boyuan in 1897, contained almost daily reports on fashion in the Shanghai courtesan world, including the minutest details about the color and cut of their newest outfits. An article titled "Lin Daiyu in stunning dress" raves about the courtesans' display of beauty and about their competition in fashion on the occasion of the Shanghai Derby's autumn race.[68] A detailed report about Lin Daiyu's pearl-embroidered coat helped to make this garment a rage among upper-class wives.[69] Another article reports on the four most famous courtesans—Lin Daiyu, Jin Xiaobao, Zhang Shuyu, and Lu Lanfen—discussing the date on which they should first appear with their winter hats for afternoon tea at the fashionable Zhang Garden. The article comments with some irony: "Evidently, as these Four Great Golden Diamond Cutters are such important personalities, the decision of when to start wearing their winter hats must be made ten days in advance, and the day must be auspicious; an ordinary day just would not do for them!"[70] The courtesans were willing to go to great lengths in their attempts to gain notoriety. "Coachman uniform makes for a sensation" ran the headline of another article, which bemoaned through its fascination the total lack of propriety in the way the courtesans outfitted their coachmen, "going even so far as to dress [them] in flower-patterned foreign brocade, gold-trimmed felt hats, and small boots as if they were opera singers on stage" (see, for example, the coachman in figure 1.7). The last comment is a swipe at the new craze among courtesans of taking opera singers as lovers.[71]

The *Qing Historical Anecdotes Arranged by Categories* (Qingbai leichao) summarized the trends in Shanghai courtesan fashion of the 1890s and early 1900s in the following words:

> During the transition from the Guangxu to the Xuantong reigns [early 1900s], their [the courtesans'] clothes became ever more strange and exotic, with a countless variety of styles. The jacket is now so short as to reach only to the waist, and their bodies are tightly wrapped like firewood, with sleeves reaching only to the elbows. With their fanciful and original clothing, the courtesans set out to lead in fashion in order to entice and please their potential customers. Driven by these fashions, women from respectable families without exception all imitate the courtesans as they earlier imitated the women living in the [emperor's] inner quarters. The Shanghai courtesans also began the fashion of wearing the Western hunter's hat and the Western overcoat, all of which belong to the clothes worn by Western men. [Wearing these men's outfits, the courtesans] would move about on foot. Among the throngs of people on the street, one can hardly tell that they are women.[72]

1.23a–f.

(a) Shanghai courtesan with hat. Photograph, 1860s. Note the very wide sleeves, the lack of collar on the jacket, and the handkerchief in the courtesan's hand. She is seated in a typical Western-style photography studio. The setting includes a spittoon, a rug-type tablecloth, and books, a frequent accessory of the courtesan in photographs. (Private collection, Los Angeles)

(b) Shanghai courtesan. Photograph, around 1870. The courtesan is seated with a typical Western-type studio curtain on the left and is surrounded by Chinese furniture. Note the small mirror on the table, the open book below, the folding fan in her hand, and the wide outer and retreating inner sleeves of her garment. (Private collection, Los Angeles)

(c) Shanghai courtesan. Photograph, around 1880s. Note the headband in the form of a half moon shaping the woman's face. This fashion allows us to date the photograph. The flowers on the table are a regular feature in courtesan photographs, suggesting their vocation through the pun on hua *(flower).*

(d) Shanghai courtesan. Photograph, 1890s. The courtesan is wearing pants and sits cross-legged, showing her small feet. She holds a book in one hand and a folding fan and a handkerchief in the other. The sleeves of her garment are not as wide, and the inner garment is not visible. Her upper garment has the beginnings of a small collar. She sits on a Western-style rattan chair, typical of European studios at the time. The water pipe on the table is a frequent courtesan accessory. (Courtesy Régine Thiriez, Paris)

(e) Shanghai courtesan. Photograph, around 1900. Note the short bangs, the collar, and the short, narrower sleeves. (Courtesy Régine Thiriez, Paris)

(f) Shanghai courtesan. Photograph, around 1910. The outer sleeves are shorter and even slimmer, with the inner sleeve prominently displayed, and the collar has risen to the earlobe. The courtesan's hair is tightly bound in an inverted V shape, and she wears a pearl-embroidered headband, probably influenced by European fashions of the time. (Bian Yuqing, Shanghai lishi mingxinpian, *114)*

Courtesans wearing Western men's or women's clothing was also a widely reported fashion. An 1888 lithograph in *Dianshizhai Illustrated Magazine* (Dianshizhai huabao) is a fine example (fig. 1.24).[73] The text reports that some men of fashion threw a dinner at which all the courtesans summoned to attend were to appear in different fashion styles; the illustration shows them arriving in Western, Japanese, and Manchu women's styles as well as in late Qing Manchu and Chinese men's outfits. By including Beijing Manchu male and female fashions in their own outfits, Shanghai courtesans subsumed the Manchus and the capital under the same "exotic" agenda that encompassed Western and Japanese elements.

An 1897 *Entertainment* report describes the appearance and public behavior of a courtesan dressed in men's clothes: "Last night around nine o'clock, a top courtesan [*jiaoshu*] who had changed into men's clothing paraded on Foochow Road. She was wearing a long gown of silk gauze, silk-topped boots, and long pants underneath. She carried a folding fan made entirely out of bone, and she sported a cigar! Lingering about on Foochow Road, she looked around, radiant with smiles."[74]

Walking without the help of a maid was difficult for courtesans, since most had bound feet. Thus, a new type of shoe was fashioned for them, with an instep that fit between a normal shoe and the bound foot. Later, leather boots were made with this instep, so that women with bound feet could fasten the boots to their feet.[75]

The newspapers reacted to these new trends with exasperation. This occasionally translated into efforts to justify current fashion as in fact a revival of traditional costume together with denials that European fashions had any influence at all on Shanghai courtesans.[76] Yet, many of the new styles exhibited by the courtesans, especially the tight top, strongly suggest such an influence.[77] In Shanghai's international environment, courtesans had many opportunities to study Western men's and women's fashions at close range. In an 1894 city guide, courtesans are said to sport such Western-style clothing on outings in their carriages.[78] They mixed foreign and Chinese native fabrics bought from specialty shops[79] and had the outfits made to order by their tailors.[80]

Absorbing Western and other influences, the courtesans created a rapid succession of new looks that were unmistakably Shanghai.[81] Contemporary observers had already noted their impact on fashion not only in the city but outside it as well. Fritz Secker, editor of Shanghai's German-language paper *Der Ostasiatische Lloyd*, wrote in 1913: "And what happens in Shanghai influences the entire nation. The luxury among both men and women is becoming excessive. In dress, there hardly is a difference left between honest and dishonest women. . . . What started as the gregarious dress of public women has now been accepted by all others. The old customs have been swept away."[82] Regular papers such as *Shenbao* often lamented the courtesans' corruption of "honest" women's fashions, and even the entertainment papers expressed concern about the dangerous influence of courtesan (and opera singer) fashions on the city's female population.[83] Editorials pointed out the rapid disappearance of proper taste and class distinctions among the different segments of society, especially female society. An editorial in *Entertainment* excuses the courtesans' "outrages" as being in the nature of their profession but is incensed that "women from rich and mighty families are eager to keep up with fashion in every

*1.24. "Each flower is unique" (Huayang yi xin). Lithograph. The illustration shows courtesans arriving at a dinner party wearing different styles of clothing. (*Dianshizhai huabao, *no.* yin, *3 [1888]: 18)*

way and are concerned only with not being a match for the courtesans in the color and cut of their dresses; even in their makeup and style of walking, they imitate the courtesans to the minutest detail." This, the paper exclaims, makes these wives appear exactly as if they are courtesans. But "Alas! The beautiful dresses of the courtesan are there to woo their clients; now as to the [married] women in ordinary, scholar, and gentry families, they should be parsimonious and simple, but they are imitating the courtesans in all they do—I fail to understand, whom are they trying to woo?"[84] An editorial in *The Guide* (Zhinan bao), cries out in the same vein: "The concubines of the rich and mighty and of the high officials also imitate the courtesans. Without any self-respect they are mixing with others in the theaters and sit high up in their carriages to offer themselves to the general gaze and to be gossiped about, and they feel very pleased about it. But what, please, is the purpose of all their looking around and competing [since, as concubines, they are already married]?"[85]

The newspaper also chides the courtesans for undermining social order by arraying themselves in a kind of jewelry formerly given to officials in recognition of their services, having themselves photographed with clients in exotic outfits, and racing their open carriages through the streets with their clients holding the reins (fig. 1.25).[86] It protested that these behaviors were encouraging a fad of conspicuous consumption and sumptuary competition that had proved infectious among the city's men and women.[87]

Grooming was an integral part of the professional life of a courtesan. This task was usually done at midday. (Entertainment guidebooks as well as novels from the period show that Shanghai courtesans kept very late hours; this was made possible by the introduction first of kerosene and gas lamps and later, beginning in the 1880s, of electricity.) The courtesan rose sometime during midday and spent much of her time having her hair arranged by a professional hairdresser, who came every day to her house. Makeup would follow. Although not much has been written on this topic, courtesan biographies reveal that some courtesans preferred brilliant makeup regarded as *yan* (rich in color) over the refined light touch known by the term *dan* (delicate). The latter has no real equivalent in Western languages, as translations such as "insipid" or "without flavor" have negative connotations. It was Lin Daiyu who started the fashion of thick makeup and extremely dark shading of the eyebrows (fig. 1.26).[88] This is quite the opposite from the advice given in the normative discourse on beauty. Handbooks on how to be a *meiren* (beauty) offer a point of reference here. According to *The Arts of a Beauty* (Yuerong bian), the principle in makeup is subtlety, with a blend of *nong* (strong) and *dan* (delicate) and only one hair ornament. The handbooks emphasize creating the flair for simplicity that suited a *meiren* secluded in the private realm.[89] Lin Daiyu's sense of fashion certainly did not share this goal. She had no interest in conveying the style of traditional beauty that seemed so out of tune with the bolder and even provocative beauty flourishing in this public, urban environment. Self-staging was very much part of the public persona of the courtesan, and Lin Daiyu was also an active and well-known opera singer who regularly performed at the theater in the Zhang Garden with the all-female Maoer opera troupe (*maoer xi*). Her inspiration for this makeup might have come from the stage.

The new clothing sculpted the body and gave it a new language. The latest fashions worn by the Shanghai courtesan became the city's insignia of change. Photographs from the 1890s to the 1910s show clothes with an ever tighter fit being worn by courtesans (fig. 1.27). The shorter sleeves of the upper garment exposed the wrist and part of the arm; the pants, too, were closer fitting and revealed more of the figure.

These clothes not only emphasized a woman's body contours but made possible and demanded changes in movement and gesture. The bodies wrapped in these clothes became the city's continuously evolving public sculptures. As they began moving in new ways, new manners developed. This was most clearly seen when courtesans wore men's clothing (figs. 1.28, 1.29). Their body posture changed, and adopting a familiar male pose, they conveyed a sense of power and freedom. The

外科新藥黑鬼血白鶴涎之能力

上海中法藥房新發明外科二藥一名黑鬼血外治極效。無論癰疽發背對口搭手以及癩痔惡瘡無名腫毒一切凡未潰者。以毛筆醮敷患處無不立愈。每瓶售洋五角一名白鶴涎乃內消聖藥善解血毒熱毒風毒火毒濕毒疫毒並山嵐瘴癘等毒服之毒退病消永無後患。每瓶亦祇售洋五角有疾者外以黑鬼血塗治內服白鶴涎退消。竊謂外科當無不治之症況廉價極廉病家當樂於購試也。

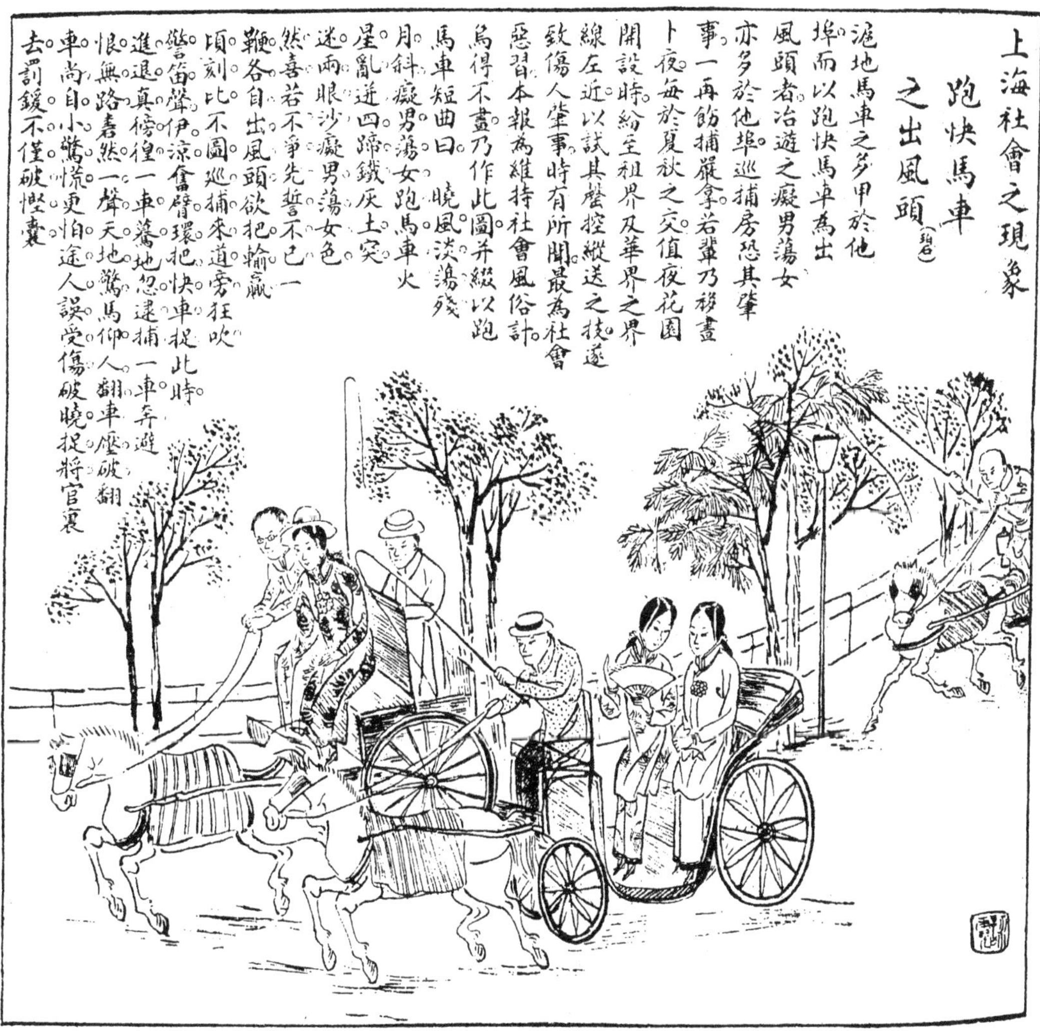

*1.25. "Events in Shanghai society: Showing off by racing in a carriage" (Shanghai shehui zhi xianxiang: Paokuai mache zhi chufengtou). Lithograph. The fashion of courtesans riding in open carriages with their clients, an imitation of Western men and women sitting together in carriages, could turn into a hazardous venture. When several parties met, the result was often a dangerous race. Worse, clients often took the reins from the grooms, as seen in the first carriage. Note the street lamp to the right, which had been an insignia of Shanghai since the 1880s. (*Tuhua ribao*, no. 25 [1909], 7)*

1.26. Shanghai courtesan. Photograph, around 1910. Note the strong makeup for the eyebrows, made popular by Lin Daiyu. (Private collection, Los Angeles)

new body movements also suggested novel roles for women, and not just these women. They were public personae, and the city became their showcase.

The Horse-Drawn Carriage and the Courtesan Star

Riding in a carriage with a patron became a fashion in the 1870s, although it did not immediately become a regular feature of courtesan entertainment. Several decades later, however, in 1894, a foreign reporter in Shanghai wrote of Foochow Road: "When the shades of evening are beginning to fall fast, and during the hours of night when the roll of the carriages dies away, you will see innumerable palanquins making their way hither and thither; their occupants are mostly almond-eyed beauties in the gayest and richest attire. Where they are bound to, is one of the mysteries of Foochow Road."[90] And later, Fritz Secker, editor of *Der Ostasiatische Lloyd,* observed that during the day, Foochow Road (called Si Malu) is "hardly different from any other road. It has a sober and business-like appearance. . . . Once dark-

1.27. "The fifth photograph session of the Ten Beauties in Shanghai" (Shanghai di wu ci Shi Mei tu sheying). Photograph. Tighter and more revealing clothes had become fashionable among courtesans by the time this photograph was taken. (Xiaoshuo shibao, *no. 9 [1911])*

ness descends onto Shanghai, Foochow Road is as if touched by a magic wand. The magician is an evil female called craving for pleasure and dissipation."[91] Evenings were of course the busiest time for courtesans on their way to serve as entertainers at dinner parties, companions at the theater, or performers at the Female Storytelling Hall. The flurry of their comings and goings altered the atmosphere on the street.

Courtesans were, however, also highly visible during the day, riding through the city in their open horse-drawn carriages.[92] The victoria was the most popular carriage among the courtesans (see fig. 1.25). It was introduced to Shanghai in the 1880s and was beloved for its comfortable spring-box and noiseless rubber tires. Other popular carriages were the double victoria, the landau, and the brougham, which offered protection against inclement weather. The double victoria, designed so that passengers faced each other, provided more space and encouraged sociability.[93] Visitors judged the glimpse of a courtesan passing by in a carriage to be among the most stunning of Shanghai sights and consequently commented upon it often.[94] Basing himself partly on the bamboo twig ballads published in Shanghai, Wang Tao wrote in the 1870s from distant Hong Kong: "Recently the price for hiring a Western-style horse-drawn carriage has come down, and the courtesans love

翁梅倩 林黛玉 藍橋別墅 梁溪李庽

*1.28. "Weng Meiqian, Lin Daiyu, Lanqiao Bieshu, Liangxi Li Yu" (Weng Meiqian, Lin Daiyu, Lanqiao Bieshu, Liangxi Li Yu). Photograph. These courtesan stars of the late nineteenth and the early twentieth century are wearing men's clothing. (*Haishang jing hong ying*, 1913, n.p.)*

祝如椿男裝

1.29. *"Zhu Ruchun in male costume" (Zhu Ruchun nanzhuang). Photograph. (*Haishang jing hong ying, *1913, n.p.)*

to take a ride after they have finished their makeup and dress for the evening. As the sun is setting, vigorous horses would gallop eastward (toward Jing'an Temple) like lightning or a gush of wind; the bystanders get only a glimpse, but this [is enough to] dazzle their senses and confuse their hearts."[95]

These scenes eventually made it into the newspapers. An illustrated report in the 1884 *Dianshizhai Illustrated Magazine* states: "No place has more horse-drawn carriages than our city [Shanghai], and none has more courtesan establishments. Every day around five or six o'clock in the afternoon, people are in the habit of taking friends or going with courtesans for a ride to Jing'an Temple for one or two dollars. Both sides of the roads are shaded by trees. The roads are full of such carriages. This is one of the famous sights of Shanghai." The illustration for another news item shows a mother in shabby clothing trying to pull her son out of a carriage in which he sits with a courtesan. She tells the onlookers that her son has squandered the family fortune (fig. 1.30).[96] A later description, published in the 1890s, characterizes these outings in an equally unromantic way under the heading "Riding in a carriage" (Zuo mache):

> Each afternoon after four o'clock, it is the popular thing to take a ride in a horse-drawn carriage toward Jing'an Temple or along the river. . . . There are [patrons] taking rides with their courtesans. They would surely go once or twice along Fuzhou Road just to show off. The men are dressed in Beijing fashion, and the women wear all kinds of gorgeous outfits. They go so far as to imitate the fashions of Manchu, Western, or Japanese women, swaggering about town and sure that this is something to be proud of. Such vulgar customs are ridiculous indeed![97]

These public parades became regular news items.[98] An 1898 newspaper reports on how Zhu Ruchun spent the day after her recent divorce and return to the courtesan profession:

> Jiaoshu[99] Zhu Ruchun has once again returned to her old profession, as we have reported previously. . . . On the 21st, accompanied by her maid, she took a ride in a horse-drawn carriage and [was seen] swaggering around Si Malu. In the evening, they went to the Yipinxiang restaurant to have a Western-style dinner in room number 30 with two other women. Ruchun was wearing a flower-patterned embroidered jacket, but she did look a little thin and pallid, unlike her glamorous old self.[100]

Riding in a carriage, dining at a fashionable restaurant, and going to the theater were common pastimes and business activities for Shanghai courtesans at this time.

The Shanghai courtesan emerges from behind and through her affected exhibitionism and pursuit of the exotic as a new type of urban personality. The world in which she moved was larger even than that of most men in Shanghai, and also freer on some levels. Her relationship to the city was of a particular kind. She operated among the upper echelons, as her guests were oftentimes the nation's highest-ranking officials, most famous scholars, and wealthiest merchants. Following calls from clients, as was the rule—and drawn by a sense of adventure—she explored

*1.30. "Taking out a courtesan and disregarding one's family" (Xia ji wang qin). Lithograph, illustration by Wu Youru. The young man in this illustration has pawned the family property to finance his visits to courtesan establishments. His mother intercepts him as he returns from a ride to Jing'an Temple with a courtesan. The mother, who has been reduced to poverty, takes hold of the young man's queue and prepares to drag him away. (*Dianshizhai huabao, *no.* yi, *2 [1884]: 9)*

the wide range of the city's public facilities: its quiet streets and lively avenues, parks, and racetrack.[101] She was immersed in the city and responded actively to its leeway and speed. True, her brazen public behavior earned her much scorn, but she managed to stage herself as one of the city's more colorful public sights.

By the 1890s, the entertainment papers would publish articles critical of the lifestyle of the young gents in the Settlements. In ironical exasperation, one article bemoaned the ease with which major changes in lifestyle were adopted while political change remained so difficult to achieve. "Who are they who easily adopt the new? The Shanghai Settlements youth. They are the ones who take on the Westerners' lifestyle, food, and clothing fashions. When they travel, it must be by carriage; when they eat, it must be Western-style food; when they speak, it must be Western language." The article goes on to criticize these youths by pointing out that the Westerners' carriages are extremely modest compared to the extravagant vehicles used by these young men; Westerners eat their food with decorum whereas these youths use the occasion to show off by appearing in the company of courtesans.[102] To be seen with a gorgeous Shanghai courtesan was the unmistakable sign of sophistication and high living.

In a more romantic vein, Xiaolantian Chanqing Shizhe described the experience of riding with a top-ranking courtesan:

> I still remember the evening of the Autumn Festival. She [Zhou Wenqing] accompanied me to view the moon during a ride in a Western-style boat-shaped open carriage. At lightning speed, we drove out toward Jing'an Temple with the cool breeze in our faces. By the time we got there, the place was already crowded with vehicles. We got off and walked into the Shen Gardens. Wherever we turned, we saw the most sumptuously dressed courtesans coming toward us. The flowers in their hair filled the air with intoxicating fragrances. . . .
>
> Unwilling to leave, we lingered a little longer after some tea. Finally, we got back into the carriage and drove to the racecourse to view the electric lights, their brilliant rays competing with the moon. What a sight of man-made wonder! From there, we drove to the Bund and went toward the Hongkew iron bridge, all the while gazing at the Huangpu River, which was like a painting with its thousands of sails and the iron steamships towering above them.[103]

For this author, the experience had been to live the height of fashion and at the same time to replay the myth of the dashing scholar of old accompanied by the grand courtesan. The courtesan might have realized that the occasion was loaded with cultural meaning for her patron and played along. This was part of the entertainment she offered and was thus part of her business.

By the 1890s, public appearances were an established part of a courtesan's services. These included accompanying clients to all kinds of amusements and being "on call" (*jiaoju*) in the public realm. As she accompanied her client, the courtesan mapped the city. One source neatly sketched the route she took (fig. 1.31).[104]

The tour started off at Foochow Road, the central courtesan district and the most extensively described street in Chinese- and Western-language city guides. It was

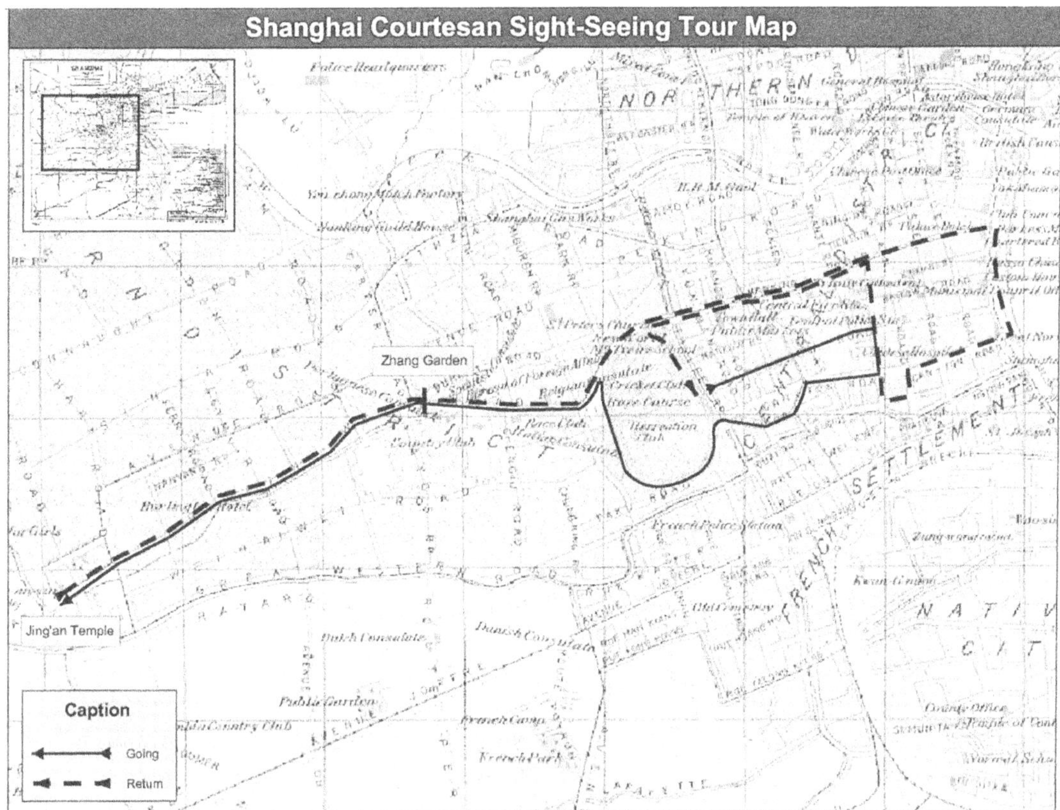

1.31. Reconstruction of the pleasure ride on which Shanghai courtesans took their clients during the late nineteenth century. (Constructed with the help of Institut d'Asie Orientale, ENS-LSH, Lyon, France)

the heart of Shanghai's entertainment business, with many of the most famous teahouses, restaurants, theaters, and storytelling halls located either on the street itself or in its vicinity.[105] After passing such teahouses as Prosperous Peace of the Four Seas (Sihai Shengping Lou) and One above the Others (Gengshang Yiceng Lou), Western-style restaurants such as First-Class Taste (Yipinxiang), billiard halls such as the Variety Club (Hua Zhong Hui) and Lang Gardens (Langyuan), and publishing houses,[106] the carriage traveled toward Medhurst Circle (Maijia Quan), named for the missionary Walter Henry Medhurst. The lawn at Medhurst Circle was famous for being fenced instead of walled in. Medhurst Circle was the location of the London Missionary Society Press (Mohai Shuguan), one of the earliest missionary publishing houses, and alongside it were the Grand English Church and Shanghai's first missionary charity hospital. From Shandong Road, the carriage entered Baoshan Street at the juncture of Guangdong Road, the wealthiest business and entertainment area in the vicinity of Foochow Road.[107] It then turned down Beihai Road and passed Shanghai's first science college, Gezhi Gongxue, with its attached public reading room, crossed Zhongnicheng Bridge, and circled the racecourse.

Finally, after a scenic ride of about twenty minutes along Bubbling Well Road (Jing'ansilu), with its fancy Western mansions, including the one *Shenbao* editor Ernest Major had built for himself, the carriage entered Zhang Garden.[108] A 1909 illustration shows client and courtesan being photographed at the gate to this park (fig. 1.32). Zhang Garden housed the legendary Ankaidi building, the name a transliteration of "Arcadia," the idyllic Greek landscape that provides the setting for many Hellenistic romantic love novels. The Ankaidi, which had been set up by a Chinese businessman, contained a five-hundred-seat theater for performances of Beijing and Suzhou opera, a smaller theater where the all-female Maoerxi opera troupe performed daily, a teahouse, Western-style ball courts, a billiard hall, and a room for electric games featuring what were then considered "fantastic"—an electric light, fan, and doorbell and an electric lion that roared when a button was pressed.[109] The theater eventually became the first hall in China that could be rented for public meetings.[110]

On the drive back to town, the carriage crossed Nanjing Road, entered Wangping Street, and then turned south and drove onto Qipan Street. These two streets, with their publishing houses, newspaper establishments, and bookstores, where most new-style men of letters worked and lived, were the hub of the city's intellectual life and publishing industry.

From there, the carriage turned east onto the Bund. Along the Bund, Western and Chinese commercial institutions displayed themselves in all their grandeur; this short segment of the route embodied much of the city's commercial might. As the courtesan took her client through the English section of the Bund, he, in the words of a late Qing novel, "could see the waters of the Huangpu, calm and smooth, with sails and masts like trees in a forest. Startled he looks up and sees on the further bank of the river the bronze statue of Gordon, a British adventurer who had hired himself out to the Qing court to help put down the Taiping Rebellion. Then coming toward him is a stone column, which he realizes must be the Obelisk."[111]

Finally, the carriage entered Nanjing Road, with all its fancy retail stores, the main commercial street of the city. This was the Times Square of Shanghai, where people of all races and backgrounds converged.[112] The architecture on the street offered a mixture of different foreign and Chinese styles, although foreign buildings occupied both sides of the road for only two blocks, up to Jiangxi Road. That is to say, from the 1870s to the early 1900s, large parts of Nanjing Road were dominated by Chinese-style buildings. Along with the display of worldly goods, the carriage would pass Hong, or Situ, Temple, one of the most active temples in the Settlements, which counted courtesans and opera singers among its frequent worshipers. Next came the Mixed Court, which was created in 1869 to handle disputes between Chinese and foreigners, where a Chinese and a Western legal assessor shared the bench; the imposing Town Hall with its impressive Public Library; and the covered market, among the earliest Western-style public institutions, developed after the 1860s, where Chinese vegetable sellers could offer their wares in a place set aside for the purpose instead of setting up stands by the roadside, where they interfered with traffic. From the market, the carriage returned to Fuzhou Road via Hubei Road, and the ride came to an end.[113]

The courtesan's ride highlighted certain sights as points of interest and gave

1.32. "Zhang Garden" (Zhang Yuan). Lithograph. As the visitor approached the garden, photographers offered their services. Being photographed with a Shanghai courtesan was one aspect of "Shanghai fun." ("Minhu ribao tuhua," Minhu ribao, *April 30, 1909)*

her a say in determining and defining the city's attractions. She was the one who showed Shanghai to her client, and she selected as most attractive those areas of the city that interacted best with her own lifestyle and interests. In planning her route, she also targeted those to whom she would show herself. This audience in turn was elevated to the status of potential client. The courtesan thus moved through the city as a part and a representation of its complex makeup, traditional in her entertainer's role and modern in her freedom. She exhibited herself on these streets, imposing her image on that of the city, so that even the reluctant were forced to acknowledge her. For her client, she embodied the allure and glamour of the city, which he entered with her. The visitor evaluated the courtesan in the context of the city's manifest commercial success and the relative security and stability secured by its Western-style environment. Being seen in such a setting allowed the client to display his wealth and style, while being seen with a fashionable client elevated the courtesan's status and augmented her prestige. Their tour inserted them both into the imaginary narrative of this Arcadia on Chinese soil.

Going to the races was one of the most important events in the self-staging of Shanghai courtesans. People from all regions and nations mingled freely and placed their bets at the Shanghai Derby.[114] It is said that Hu Baoyu started the fashion among courtesans of driving to the races in a carriage. Always eager for novelty, she also began the fad of embellishing the horses and carriage with red ribbons.[115] Aiming to compete and impress, the courtesan dressed in her most lavish costume and surrounded herself with devoted lovers, patrons, and friends. High above the crowd, she held court and, like today's film stars, would offer her latest innovations and fashions to view.[116]

Competition for attention often became a public nuisance. There were many reports of traffic accidents caused by chauffeurs or clients of courtesans racing each other on crowded streets.[117] And the courtesan fashion of taking a night ride with a lover or a patron during the hot summer months led to scandalized reports of pairs being caught making love in their carriages, which was illegal.[118] *Dianshizhai Illustrated Magazine* ran many stories on the topic, including one about an accidental injury to a client (fig. 1.33). While such scandals might have earned courtesans some scorn, mostly of the amused sort, the reports heightened their public profile and were thus beneficial to their business.

Public Manners, Lifestyle, and New Business Ventures

The Shanghai Settlements helped foster the idea of the public realm as a legitimate business arena. The courtesans used this space for self-advertisement by staging their appearances. Each afternoon, they congregated for another public performance in the teahouses situated on the most fashionable streets of the commercial districts. At the Ankaidi teahouse, the Four Great Golden Diamond Cutters (Si Da Jin'gang) dominated the scene. As they arrived, all eyes were drawn to them. They set themselves up in the most conspicuous spots on each side of the door. Every day, they were scrutinized from top to toe, their manners studied in detail and their conversation recorded. "Honest" women who came to the teahouse with their families were sure to learn about the latest in fashion, manners, and scandal.

The theater was another important public space for courtesan business as well as pleasure. In places such as Beijing and Tianjin, the rule forbidding women to enter the theater remained in force until the end of the nineteenth century.[119] They could enjoy opera only in private settings such as family parties (referred to as "singing in [private] halls" [*tangchang*]). Even when women were finally allowed to attend the theater in Beijing, visitors from Shanghai were amazed to observe that men and women sat in different sections. From the moment theaters opened in the Shanghai Foreign Settlements, courtesans were devoted customers, and other women soon followed.[120] This was such a unique sight that many authors of bamboo twig ballads felt compelled to note it at the time.[121] The presence of women in such places of public entertainment continued to irritate some Chinese officials and literati. They probably were aware that it would be impossible to ban women from attending the

1.33. "The craving for sex makes them forget about their lives" (Tanse wangming). Lithograph. The illustration depicts a client making love to a courtesan in a carriage. According to the story, he was extremely excited and could not stop, even when they attracted public attention. The courtesan followed her maid's advice and tried to bite him at an acupuncture point on his upper lip, to calm him, but instead bit off part of his nose. (Dianshizhai huabao, *no.* yi, *3 [1885]: 22)*

theater since the Municipal Council would not agree. Western women living in the Settlements regularly went to the theater, and this set an example for Chinese women. Officials thus directed their efforts toward banning Chinese operas regarded as obscene and keeping female performers off the public stage.[122]

The cultural climate in the Foreign Settlements continued to be very relaxed on the issue of women in public places. In the midst of concerted efforts by Chinese authorities to ban women from the theater, there are reports that Western and Japanese performers were invited to the Dangui Theater (Dangui Xiyuan), one of the oldest and most established Peking opera stages in Shanghai (fig. 1.34). These performances received friendly reviews.[123] The slowly rising status of opera performances as authentic Chinese cultural contributions and not just what many Westerners considered ear-splitting cacophony prompted the French Municipal Council to engage Chinese opera singers to perform in the newly opened public

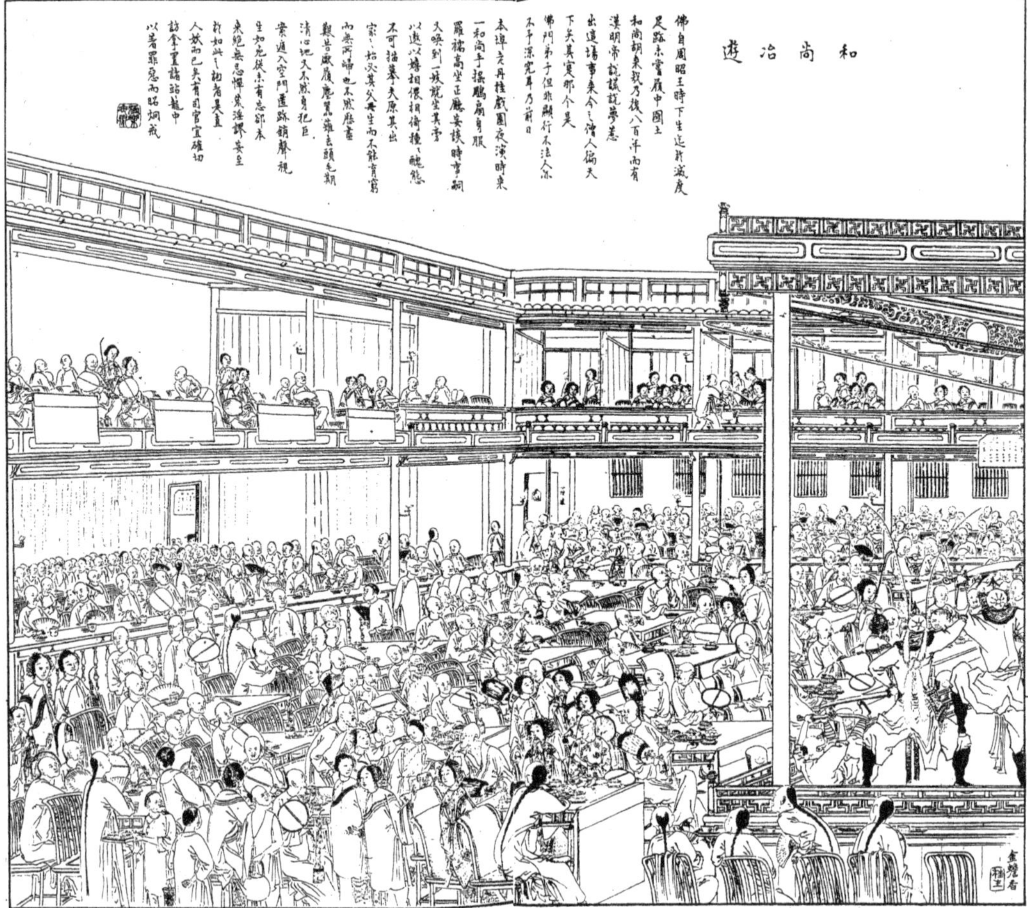

*1.34. "A monk engaging a courtesan" (Heshang yeyou). Lithograph. A monk with a fashionable feathered fan and dressed in fine silk frolics openly with a courtesan at the Dangui Theater. The illustration is evidence that men and women, the latter mostly courtesans with their maids and clients, sat together in public theaters at the time. (*Dianshizhai huabao*, no. yi, 3 [1885]: 22)*

garden in 1886.[124] Eventually, Chinese women performers became highly respected; in 1906, Chinese and Western newspapers reported that Chinese women singers had given a charity performance at the Town Hall on Nanjing Road.[125] It is not hard to see that the Foreign Settlements subscribed to a different set of social conventions; this thwarted the efforts of Chinese officials.

Huang Shiquan (1852–1924), chief editor of *Shenbao* from about 1890 to 1905 and author of many books on Shanghai, described the atmosphere in a theater of the 1880s in the following manner:

> When the night sets in, the carriages begin to arrive. The moving profiles of women, their perfumed garments, their voices and gestures, all evoke the feeling as if one were in a collective kingdom of fragrance; one's eyes are not able to move

> fast enough to take it all in and to appreciate it. When the night has deepened, there will be those courtesans who come late, and with their entrance rekindle all the fantasy and allure, congregating with their beautifully embroidered outfits [in the theater]. One can truly say that this town is the town of nightless beauties [*buye zhi fangchen*].[126]

A less flattering description, accompanied by an illustration (fig. 1.35), was published in 1909 in *The Illustrated Daily* (Tuhua ribao):

> Shanghai has a forest of theaters; when the performances come to an end, men and women in their brightly colored costumes are crowding like a swarm of bees to get out. And at the same time, carriages, rickshaws, and sedan-chairs block the road. The scene is a total mess. But what is most terrifying is that at such times vagrants and thieves mix with the crowd in order to steal. One cannot be vigilant enough. Therefore we present this illustration.[127]

From the 1870s onward, courtesans began to give public performances in storytelling halls and theaters, and the Maoer opera troupe, with its all-female cast, became a Shanghai landmark. Illustrations show that women also were in the audience during these performances (fig. 1.36).

Shanghai courtesans were rather inventive in developing new features that would entertain and set tongues to wagging. One was role inversion. On such occasions, the courtesan invited her favorite client to a restaurant or the theater as her guest. This extraordinary practice was promptly reported in *Entertainment*:

> This year, most of the famous courtesan stars invited their clients to the Yangxian teahouse—a theater—for a treat. The reason they went to this theater was that the usher [*anmu*] was very good at courting [the courtesans]. Therefore they like to go there. On the 24th, Jin Xiaobao was the host to her client, on the 25th, it was the turn of Xie Qianyun and Hu Xiaobao, and on the 26th, it was Lu Lanfen's. Each one of these invitations cost [the courtesan] anywhere from ¥40 or ¥50 to ¥70 or ¥80.[128] This year, business is not so good [for the courtesans], and although they want the event to go off with some class, much thinking had to go into it.[129]

The occasion was quite costly, but to act as host to a client no doubt was part of the public persona of a "grand courtesan." The practice is another sign that courtesans looked upon themselves as professional women who, in a bold imitation of the habit of reciprocal hospitality in the business world, treated their clients to dinner or an evening at the theater.

These public activities set Shanghai courtesans apart from courtesans in other cities. During the Qing period, courtesans were seen in public only when riding in the pleasure boats known as "painted boats" (*huachuan*, or *huadeng chuan*), for which Suzhou and Yangzhou were famous.[130] These courtesans, while sometimes in public view, were not really in the public realm. Before they moved to the Foreign Settlements in the 1850s, courtesans in the walled city participated in a lively enter-

外科新藥黑鬼血白鶴涎之能力

上海中法藥房新發明外科二藥。一名黑鬼血外治極效。無論癰疽發背對口搭手。以及瘰疬惡瘡無名腫毒一切凡未潰者。以毛筆醮敷患處無不立愈。每瓶售洋五角一名白鶴涎乃內消聖藥。善解血毒熱毒風毒火毒濕毒痰毒並山嵐瘴癘等毒。服之毒退病消永無後患。每瓶亦祗售洋五角。有疾者外以黑鬼血塗治。內服白鶴涎退消。竊謂外科當無不治之症。況厥價極廉。病家當樂於購試也。

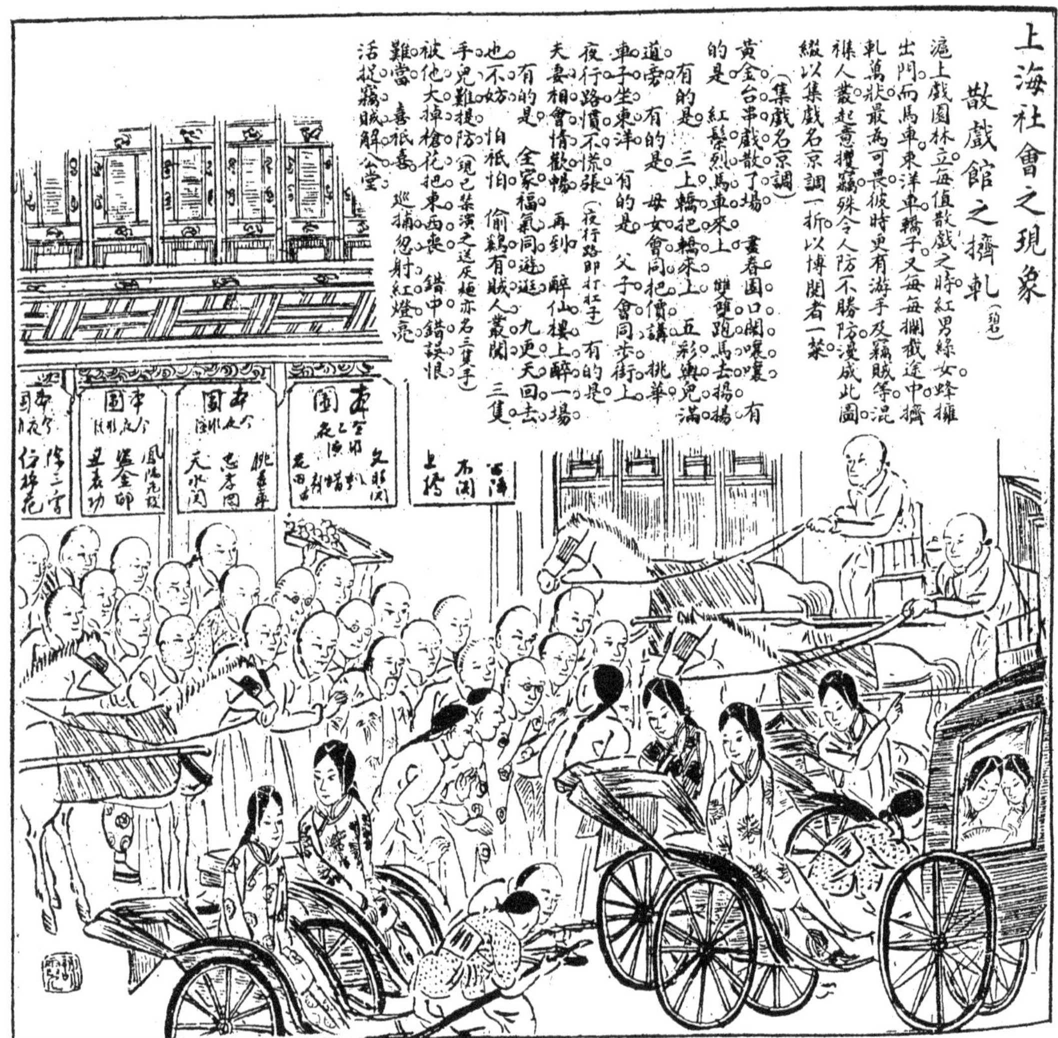

1.35. *"Events in Shanghai society: The crowded chaos after the end of the theater performance" (Shanghai shehui zhi xianxiang: San xiguan zhi jizha). Lithograph. Outside, theatergoers are busy being seen as well as looking at others.* (Tuhua ribao, *no. 29 [1909], 7)*

1.36. *"Illustrations of Shanghai Fun: Attending an opera performance by the all-female troupe in the Yu Garden near Jing'an Temple" (Haishang kuaile tu: Jing'an si Yu Yuan kan maoerxi). Lithograph. The theater performance is attended by a mixed audience of males and females. The theater features a traditional stage with Western-style windows. (Hushang Youxizhu,* Haishang youxi tushuo, *1898, 7)*

tainment scene that even included public performances by singers and storytellers in the different gardens in town. Their presence was an irritation to at least some members of the gentry, however, as well as to the Qing officials in charge, and eventually such performances were banned altogether.[131] In order to prevent the contamination of morals that would result from courtesans going public, courtesans from the Settlements were even banned from the gardens in the walled town. According to Zou Tao, the courtesans tried to circumvent this ban:

> When the courtesans want to enter these gardens, they have to imitate women from good families by being unadorned and without extravagance in their dress and makeup. Outfitted in this manner, they radically depart from the accustomed way of the courtesan houses. As the women from elite families normally would imitate the sumptuous clothing fashions of the courtesans, this is really peculiar, since their dresses are inverted, and high and low trade places.[132]

Appearing publicly in broad daylight under such conditions was risky and did not become part of courtesan life in the walled city.

The successive Shanghai Municipal Councils—the Chinese name, Gongbuju (Bureau of Public Works), signaled that its responsibility was Shanghai's infrastructure and public order, not the policing of its morals or beliefs—elicited admiring talk in every language and dialect. Contemporaries noted that it was this attitude among the foreign authorities that fostered and protected the daring actions of Shanghai courtesans.[133]

The Municipal Council also created the physical conditions that made the courtesans' forays feasible. From the 1860s onward, the roads in the Shanghai Settlements were paved, the ground in the *linong* alleys was covered with plank wood, and there were even well-maintained paths in Zhang Garden. Public defecation and urination were prohibited, and transgressors were fined. In comparison, the thoroughfares of Beijing's Chinese section outside Qianmen, where theaters and entertainment establishments were located, were a muddy mess, with rain, earth, and animal as well as human excrement each contributing a share. Shanghai visitors to Beijing were shocked by the state and the smells of the public spaces in the capital, which they said were enough to sicken people with weak constitutions. In the capital, it was impossible to enter some courtesan quarters on a rainy day without being muddied.[134] In contrast, the clean streets of Shanghai provided a high-status ambience for the courtesans' public appearances.

The degree to which Shanghai courtesans were actually designing their own roles and controlling their own destinies can be seen from their choice of private lovers. They often selected opera singers, who could not be their clients. The taboo against this type of liaison was of long standing and had, up to that time, been supported by the courtesans, who saw the singers as being of a clearly inferior social station.[135] This practice was reported in the entertainment newspapers and featured in late Qing Shanghai courtesan novels. Courtesans went to the opera house not only to show off the newest hairstyle and costume, or try to attract potential clients, but also to study the handsome opera singers.

An otherwise admiring biography of Hu Baoyu points out the one defect of this formidable courtesan, namely that she was responsible for starting the trend among courtesans of openly taking opera singers as lovers.[136] Around 1873–74, Hu Baoyu fell in love with the Peking opera singer Shisan Dan. When he left Shanghai for Beijing, she abandoned her business in Shanghai and followed him. After he fell out of love with her (or the other way around), she had to come back to Shanghai and reopen her business, and the news of her return and doings again made headlines.[137] Her business soon became even more prosperous than before.[138]

Apparently, Hu Baoyu resumed attending the opera so as to select a lover for herself. *Shenbao* reported on November 11, 1878, that, under the pretext of a dispute over a reserved theater box, Hu Baoyu had gotten into a fight with Li Qiaoling, another famous courtesan of the time, over a Peking opera star.[139]

The irritation and ambivalence the courtesans engendered among the city's men of letters had less to do with their lifestyle or outrageous fashions than with their public manners. In literati eyes, these manners threatened the traditional class and social boundaries. Even those with manifest hostility toward the Qing government and some of its conservative officials were troubled by the courtesans' irreverence toward symbols of authority. It was one thing for an upper-class lady to dress like a courtesan, but it was an entirely different matter for a courtesan to dress and behave like a grand Qing official. The language of *Entertainment* varied between irony, disbelief, and amused shock in this front-page story:

> Among the courtesans in Shanghai, the *changsan* rank highest. When one of them is called to appear and entertain at a banquet, she will ride in her grand blue woolen-cloth sedan-chair with her manservants holding the lanterns in front and her maidservants following behind. When reaching the front door of the dwelling, these will cry out loudly, and immediately people will come out to welcome her. After having taken her seat at the banquet, she does no more than offer one round of wine to those seated and sing one song, and then she hurries off to the next engagement. Her busy social schedule is no different from that of an official. There was a Mr. X who came to Shanghai for the first time from East Zhejiang. Yesterday, as he was walking by himself on Si Malu, he saw in front of him a grand sedan-chair speedily coming toward him with imposing pomp. The cries of the sedan-chair carriers were swollen with arrogance. In front of the sedan-chair were big lanterns, on which was written in bold characters "Magistrate on duty." Mr. X hurried to move out of the way, thinking this must be an important official with no less than "blue top" or "crystal top" ranking.[140] When he looked closely, [he saw] it was an exquisite beauty, leaning on her *pipa* [four-stringed lute]. He was shocked and exclaimed: "But this is a [lowly] prostitute! How could she claim to be 'Magistrate on duty'?" After a while, he realized that the sedan-chairs crisscrossing in front of him all had "Magistrate on duty" written on their lanterns.[141]

The courtesan's search for notoriety was specifically targeted to reach those who might have the means to lavish attention on her. Her behavior, her manners, and her dress also reflected the potential client's desires: he was looking for something unique in Shanghai, an experience he could not find anywhere else. To be outrageous, iconoclastic, and amusing was the name of the game in the world of Shanghai entertainment. In 1867, the *North China Herald* had already noted that wealthy merchants from Jiangsu and Guangdong or curious tourists from the gentry class congregated there to find, with and through the courtesan, the grand flavor of this unique city.[142]

Courtesans constituted one of the largest groups of money-making enterprises in the Settlements, but their precise share of the annual revenue is difficult to determine. According to Christian Henriot, the French Settlement received a very substantial part of its revenue from "vice"-related activities; in 1862, more than 42 percent was derived from prostitution, although amounts dropped suddenly after that year, for reasons that are not clear.[143] The annual reports of the International Settlement's Municipal Council contain no statistics on courtesan houses; nevertheless, it is possible to estimate the relative importance of entertainment-related business in the economic life of the city. In 1876, the combined license fees of Chinese theaters, liquor sellers, opium dens, wine shops, and entertainment enterprises amounted to about 20,000 taels, which was a third of the Municipal Council's total income excluding the general property tax.[144] In the 1893 report, license fees from "native sing-song houses" were added; there were thirty such houses in the Settlement, and the fees came to 780 taels. From these accounts, it seems that courtesan houses were not taxed beyond the property fees but were instrumental in developing businesses that generated sizable income for the city at large and for the Municipal Council.

Top-ranking courtesans saw themselves as businesswomen and used name cards that resembled modern-day business cards. Small calling cards served as invitations to banquets at the courtesan houses, and rather over-size name cards were carried by the courtesans themselves.[145]

Ascertaining the personal financial assets of the top courtesans is likewise difficult.[146] They seem to have been always in debt, yet they were also big spenders. Their true capital was not financial or cultural but consisted of personal celebrity. In fame, Hu Baoyu was seen as equal to one of the richest Shanghai compradors, Hu Xueyan, and to the famous Shanghai painter Hu Gongshou; the three were known as the "three Hus of Shanghai" (Shanghai san Hu).[147] In middle age, Hu Baoyu accompanied her niece, courtesan and opera singer Wu Yuexian, to Hankow for a performance at the Yiyuan Theater. Even there, Hu Baoyu's notoriety was such that large numbers of people came to the theater just to see the legendary Shanghai courtesan.[148]

As a new breed of independent professional, Shanghai courtesans also left behind the traditional courtesan's tie to a single locality and took their fashions and manners across the country. Their adventures were, however, limited to the Foreign Settlements, the most important among these being Tianjin, Hankow, and Canton. There, they enjoyed a certain degree of business protection. Correspondence between courtesans outside and within the Foreign Settlements, published occasionally in the courtesan guides, indicates a preoccupation with finding out what opportunities were available in these Settlements and whether visits could be arranged.[149]

Courtesan letters offer a sense of the independence with which some of these courtesans managed their business. Even though some letters might have been written by professional letter writers, the matters discussed reflect the courtesan's particular concerns.[150] A letter sent by Liu Suqing from Hankow to Zhang Lanxiang in Shanghai is instructive here:

> After we parted, I went to Hankow, where I arrived on the 18th. At the moment, I have found temporary shelter in a few rooms under the roof in Taoyuan Fang. The monthly rent is ¥32. It is extremely hard to economize with the daily expenses. However, none of my clients here belongs to the class of big spenders, and although I have had a good number of them and have no time to rest day in and day out, I have earned very little. My outward extravagance has no substance to it, and it seems inevitable that things will come to a bad end. I would like to return to Shanghai immediately, but there are bills to be collected [and I fear that they would not be honored if I am not here]. I have therefore resolved to stay until the Yuanwu [festival, when customarily debts are collected], and I will have another look after this. [Lanxiang,] my sister, by no means try to come to Hankow. What is here is only an empty name. There is no profit to be made.[151]

In their own narratives and in those of others, Shanghai courtesans figure primarily as urban professionals. These letters indicate that they had business connections with other courtesans in these protected niches. None of the top-ranking Shanghai courtesans ventured to Beijing for business before 1900. Lin Daiyu's trip to Tianjin in that year, which she described in a memoir, almost ended fatally.[152] Only after the Boxer Uprising (1898–1900) did courtesan establishments dare to move to Beijing. The first courtesan to do so was the famous Sai Jinhua.[153] The connections she had established in the capital as the concubine of a high official allowed her to find protection and patronage for such an enterprise.

Shanghai courtesans were eager travelers and seemed at ease in these ventures. Their motives were to assess the potential for profitability, to make money, and to gain fame, much the same reasons that Peking opera stars were touring at the time. While courtesan travels in the late Ming might have been inspired mostly by the desire to view the grand sights of the country, Shanghai courtesans at the end of the Qing seemed to be much more concerned with exploring business opportunities. Their travels inevitably became news items that in turn reinforced the courtesans' attractiveness.

The need to create news and stay in the public eye is also visible in the calculated flurry of gossip surrounding the "change of residence" (*diaotou*) of a Shanghai courtesan. Newspapers took the occasion to introduce the new patron who had financed the upward move and furnished her new quarters.

The Shanghai courtesan thus transferred an exclusive indoor entertainment to the public realm. At the same time, she transformed herself from a local to a national figure, from an entertainer for the few to the prototype of the mass entertainer. She set the trend for a certain style of behavior for big-city women and charted the path toward a new, modern mentality. Her cosmopolitan life was inextricably linked with the city's action, power, and money. She was the city's first celebrity, its star, its cultural icon. Her way of relating to urban space and expressing a particular kind of modern female independence would develop into the very style that commonly identified the women of this cosmopolitan center. In short, she was the model for a new type of city woman.

The Photograph and the Fading Image

Always obsessed with image and novelty, Shanghai courtesans were instrumental in making photography fashionable in town (figs. 1.37a, b).[154] Courtesans had their pictures taken as gifts for clients, as souvenirs, or as reminders to clients to visit them again on subsequent trips to Shanghai. As might be expected, Shanghai photography studios were located mostly in the cultural and entertainment district around Nanjing and Fuzhou roads. The business benefited both courtesans and studios. Under the heading "Having a photograph taken," an 1877 guidebook states:

> Westerners have the technology of photography. It can capture the image of a person entirely through liquid chemicals and reveal it on a square inch of paper. The spirit and features are absolutely true to life. Without exception, the courtesans compete to have their photographs taken. They hang these on the walls [of their rooms] or present the photos as a gift to clients. Recently, these photographs [of the courtesans] have circulated to other provinces, and you can see them everywhere. As for the few very famous courtesans, their photographs are kept by the studios; from the glass negative, they print for the customer those he chooses. From this, the studios can continuously make a profit.[155]

Photography was popular with the Shanghai courtesan because it fit with her desire to increase her public recognition. Personal access to the leading courtesans had been and continued to be the exclusive privilege of clients who had been properly introduced and had gained favor. By using photography, the Shanghai courtesan shifted from generic beauty to individualized person.[156] Initially, she offered her image to a client as a gift and memento. After photography studios discovered the commercial value of these photographs, the courtesan did not retreat into seclusion but boldly cooperated, making the studios, like the entertainment papers, her unpaid public promoters. Direct access remained as restricted as ever, but the increased public recognition lent status even to the client who was seen in her company, aware that many onlookers would recognize the woman at his side. Photography offered a tantalizing glimpse into an exclusive realm and also maintained a distance that was measured not in physical terms, such as the courts and walls that separated the courtesan from the street, but in terms of the difference in status that divided the rising star from her admirers.

The new technology helped spread the image of the courtesan. Cultural products

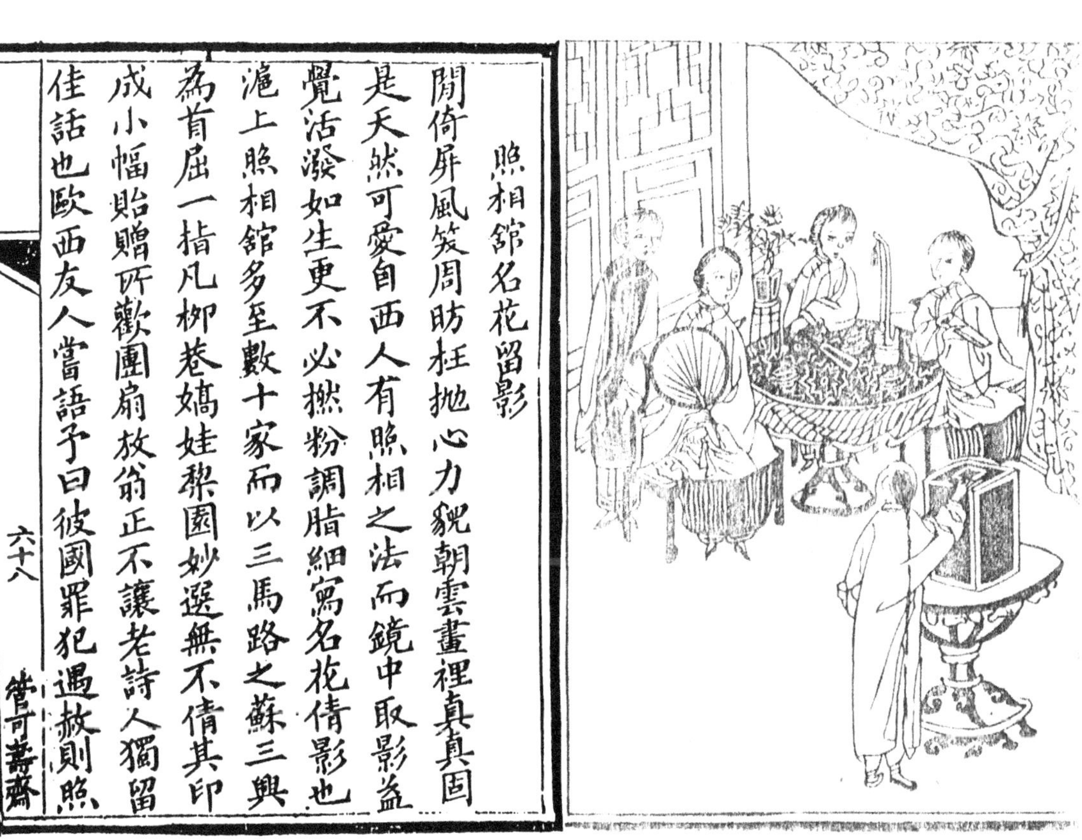

照相館名花留影

閒倚屏風笑周昉枉拋心力貌朝雲畫裡真真固是天然可愛自西人有照相之法而鏡中取影益覺活潑如生更不必撚粉調脂細寫名花倩影也滬上照相館多至數十家而以三馬路之蘇三興為首屈一指凡柳巷嬌娃梨園妙選無不倩其印成小幅貽贈所歡團扇放翁正不讓老詩人獨留佳話也歐西友人嘗語予曰彼國罪犯遇赦則照

六十八

管可壽齋

*1.37a, b. "In the photography studio, the famous flowers have their pictures taken" (Zhaoxiangguan minghua liuying). Woodblock print. The text on the left (a) explains that Shanghai courtesans love to be photographed. The illustration on the right (b) depicts the scene. (*Shenjiang mingsheng tushuo*, 1884, 68)*

1.38. Shanghai courtesan. Photograph, 1890s. (Courtesy Régine Thiriez, Paris)

of Western origin, such as photography and the tabloid newspaper, linked up with the big-city Shanghai courtesan to create a new figure, the modern celebrity or star, and with it an entire range of fresh commodities and business options. The cult of the star was made possible by photography and seems to have begun with the fad of collecting courtesan photographs. For example, a letter published in 1897 in *Entertainment* extended best wishes to the top courtesan Jin Xiaobao on her move to new quarters. The writer said he had never seen her in person but had her photograph in his collection.[157]

Courtesans were not simply objects to be photographed. The photograph was a collective product, involving the photographer, the subject, and, as silent partici-

1.39. Courtesan, Tianjin(?). Postcard from a studio photograph, around 1900. (Courtesy Régine Thiriez, Paris)

pants, her costume and the props in the studio. The courtesan chose the costume, which might be a man's outfit or a theater costume, her facial expression, and the direction of her glance. Often, a final choice would be made from among different photographs. In photographs of women who appear to be courtesans, the gestures and facial expressions, often even the costumes, speak a language of self-assertiveness. The courtesan sitting with her legs crossed and head resting on her hand projects a self-assurance that defies the standard female pose in photography (fig. 1.38). In another photograph, which, from the bindings around the ankles, is likely a photograph of a Tianjin courtesan emulating the Shanghai style, the courtesan reclining on a couch openly challenges the viewer with her crossed legs, self-assured smile, and straight gaze into the camera (fig. 1.39). Timothy J. Clark has argued that Edouard Manet's Olympia is one of the figures of modernity, articulated through the image of the desirable body of a courtesan who refuses to be a submissive woman. Availability is not part of her image.[158] The photographs of the Shanghai courtesan display some facets of this new look. Without intending to offend, the pose of these women challenges the viewer's assumptions regarding the signs of desirability.

One studio, Yaohua, spotted the chance by joining the alliance between *Entertainment* and the courtesans. It openly courted the courtesan business and was at the forefront in exploring this market in the 1890s. The studio produced glue-

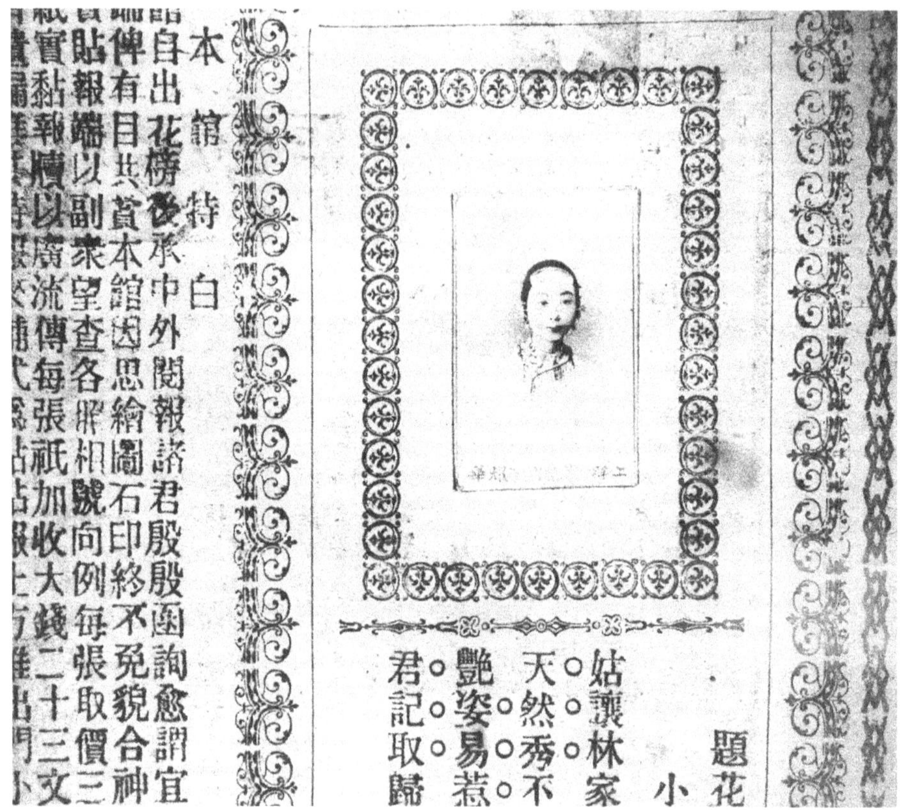

題花
小
姑○讓○林家
天○然○秀○不
艷○姿○易○惹
君○記○取歸

1.40. Hua Lijuan, a Shanghai courtesan. Photograph by the Yaohua studio, Shanghai, 1898. Hua Lijuan had taken second place in Entertainment*'s flower competition of 1898. To publicize the event, the newspaper offered glued-in photographs of the top three contestants. (*Youxi bao*, Oct. 3, 1898, 1)*

in photographs of winners in the annual "flower competition" (*huabang*) (fig. 1.40). The photographs were used to promote the studio, the event, and the newspaper itself.[159] All parties were very much aware of the high value of publicity for their business.

Yaohua was founded during the 1880s by Shi Dezhi (at the time transcribed Szu Yuen Ming), an electrician turned photographer; another photographer, Qu Yanting, was also involved for a time. By the 1890s, it had become one of the four most famous Chinese-run studios in Shanghai. Yaohua was divided into East Yaohua and West Yaohua in 1900. East Yaohua was located at Ball Court, across the street from the foreign luxury shop Hengdali, with Shi Dezhi as the photographer. West Yaohua was at 42 Nanking Road, near the racecourse, with Shi's oldest daughter as the photographer. She had received her education at a French school in the French Settlement. An article in *World Vanity Fair* (Shijie fanhua bao), another of Li Boyuan's entertainment papers, praised Shi Dezhi for teaching his daughter to be a photographer so that women who would rather not be in the company of men from outside their families could have their pictures taken.[160] Her studio advertised this convenience.[161]

Shi Dezhi was extremely interested in lighting effects and published a detailed article about the scientific aspects of using light in photography. (He also stressed that his excellent understanding of the art was enhanced by the superior German-made equipment in his studio).[162] The glued-in photograph mentioned above (see fig. 1.40) suggests that he was able to do very subtle work, and he was famous for his portraits of women.[163] Hoping to capture the courtesans' business and share in their star status, Shi advertised in *World Vanity Fair*, promising half-price portraits for courtesans who came to his studio.[164] This strategy highlights the courtesan's commercial value both as the object shown in entertainment papers and at photography shows and as the agent that spread the studio's fame.

By the 1900s, the top-ranking Shanghai courtesans were undoubtedly the most photographed group in the entire Empire. Their images were widely accessible, not only as portrait subjects but as elements in commercial postcards (figs. 1.41a–c).

Photography made the image of the courtesan reproducible and thus marketable on a large scale. In this process, the courtesan star was increasingly freed from the necessity of being visible in public. The power to renew and transform her own image as the city's advertisement, however, was lost along the way. The person who represented the city's spirit of change was made redundant by technology. The camera took over and began to select its own models according to different criteria.

Commercialization also brought specialization. The role the courtesan once played in the marketplace was subdivided into new professions. Advertising, orig-

1.41a–c.

(a) Postcard from a photograph by the Yaohua studio, about 1900. To each side of the mirror behind the men are enlarged courtesan photographs, which date, judging by the fashions, from the 1890s. Photographic enlargements came into vogue at this time as advertisements for studios. (Bian Yuqing, Shanghai lishi mingxinpian, *134)*

(b) Postcard from photograph, between 1905 and 1910. On the left is the Lao Baohua studio, with an enlarged photograph of a courtesan attached to the banister where it could be seen from the street. The text on the large streamer reads "Fine photographs, enlargements all sizes." (Courtesy Régine Thiriez, Paris)

(c) Postcard from a photograph of a Shanghai store for household goods, 1910s. The enlarged half-length picture of a woman on the right likely shows a Shanghai courtesan. This photograph indicates that images of Shanghai courtesans were very much part of the urban milieu by this time. Such exposure greatly increased the public impact of courtesan fashions. (Bian Yuqing, Shanghai lishi mingxinpian, *129)*

inally found only in newspapers, took on other forms, such as glossy full-size calendars featuring cigarette advertisements with beauties (fig. 1.42). These no longer advertised courtesan entertainment but promoted other goods, which their producers sought to associate with leisure, chicness, beauty, and modernity. The image of the "female student" (*nü xuesheng*), with her purity and innocence, began to compete with the provocative sensuality of the courtesan. Fashion drawings borrowed features from the traditional painting motif of the "beauty" (*meiren tu*) in depicting current fashion. Professional fashion models began to appear. Some of the earlier women's journals, such as *The Ladies' Times* (Funü shibao) of 1911 (later *Ladies' Journal* [Funü zazhi]), and one of the first photographic magazines, *Young Companion* (Liangyou huabao), of 1926, had special fashion columns. The beauty contest for "Miss Shanghai" (Shanghai Xiaojie) replaced the courtesan flower competitions.[165] The film industry created a new type of public personality, the film star (fig. 1.43). The image of the courtesan as the preeminent celebrity and representation of cosmopolitan Shanghai was eventually replaced by that of the star of the silver screen.

Technical innovations, business interests, and the new "civilized" notions that became the fashion among intellectuals in the context of the May Fourth project fundamentally transformed the relationship between the Shanghai courtesan and her environment. The concept of entertainment changed. With the opening of movie houses such as the Hongkew Movie Theater (Hongkou Dianyingyuan) in 1907, the rise of amusement parks and entertainment centers such as Great World (Dashijie) in 1917, and the mushrooming of coffeehouses, dance halls, and clubs in the city a few years later, high-ranking courtesan houses and the courtesans themselves faded from public view, although their business continued.[166] Even the streets that they had dominated with their grand carriages and sedan-chairs were taken over by electric streetcars, which first appeared in 1908.[167] As the "movie star" (*mingxing*) appropriated the arena of glamorous public performance, and high-class call girls or "social flowers" (*jiaoji hua*) such as the ones eternalized in Cao Yu's play *Sunrise* (Richu) made their appearance, the courtesans assumed a more culturally traditional guise in this modernizing world, only to be lumped into the tragic category of sex slaves in the May Fourth vision of the Chinese past.

Of course, Hu Baoyu did not introduce the electric fan to Shanghai, nor was Lin Daiyu the first to use an electric door bell.[168] Foreigners were the ones who introduced these gadgets to Shanghai. The courtesans did, however, bring these innovations to public attention and into the mental reach of other Chinese. In the public perception, the new Western things were associated with her image. The courtesan personified acceptance and glorification of Western civilization as embodied in material goods by inserting them, through this association, into traditional notions of wealth and prosperity.

The dilemma of Shanghai Settlements culture is marked by the uneasy shifts between glorification of the Shanghai courtesan as the ultimate symbol of the city's prosperity and modernity and ridicule of her power and influence. The contradiction pits traditional cultural assumptions against the new opportunities offered by

*1.42. Feminine beauty became a motif in calendars with cigarette advertisements put out by the British-American Tobacco Company, 1915. (*Duhui modeng*, 1)*

1.43. *Magazine cover featuring the motion picture* The Celestial Being in Cloud-Dress. *(*Qing qing dianying, *4th year, no.* 8 *[1937])*

the Shanghai Settlements. Men of letters, who entered careers in Shanghai's newly founded newspaper and publishing businesses, used the meaning traditionally assigned to the image of the courtesan in their representation of the city. Like these men, the courtesans found new opportunities in Shanghai, and this led to behavior that did not fit traditional expectations. The conflict between the fusing of traditional cultural values and the commercial life of the Shanghai Settlements constitutes the basic structure of what might be called the Shanghai Settlements culture. The Shanghai courtesan's capacity to represent this new city and simultaneously explore the traditional cultural trope with which she is associated attests to the development of this culture and the type of personality that goes with it. As the guidebooks and newspaper articles suggest, the Shanghai courtesan skillfully blended traditional cultural norms with Western elements, creating a kind of dynamism that can be understood only in the context of Shanghai's rise as a cosmopolitan center. To be successful in her business, the Shanghai courtesan had to maintain, and even insist upon, certain traditional assumptions about her; at the same time, being successful also required her to continuously "establish the new and unusual" (*biaoxin liyi*), thereby fulfilling the expectation that she was the very embodiment of Shanghai's uniqueness.

The seemingly inordinate attention given to courtesans of the late Qing by the new class of urban intellectuals calls for more than the simple explanation that these lonely and slightly disoriented men were longing for comfort. The mythicizing of the Shanghai courtesan is similar to the phenomenon by which courtesans of the late Ming were able to capture the fantasies of an entire generation. The late Ming marked the end of a long century of cultural renaissance in the Jiangnan region and was suffused with celebratory nostalgia for past glories that had fallen into ruin. The courtesans of late Qing Shanghai captured the fantasies of another generation by looking in the exact opposite direction, toward the future. In their brazen espousal of the urban and the modern, the courtesans captured and lived the spirit of a new era, and the intellectuals explored their own uneasy confrontation with its fascination and challenges through their depiction of these women.

While Chinese men of letters were dealing with the idea of change and changes in ideas, Shanghai courtesans were spearheading the advent of a new urban culture in their lifestyle, business conduct, and social and sexual relations. The intellectuals' ambivalence toward Western social values and material culture reflects the threat these values, culture, and their accoutrements—such as trade, commerce, and public manners—posed for the traditional hierarchy and the intellectuals' elevated position in it. The courtesan, being relatively free of constraints and marginal in her social position, maintained tradition only when it was advantageous to her business. In no way ideologically motivated, she translated the rights the Settlements granted to the individual and to commerce into gesture, freedom of movement, costume, and interior decoration. In so doing, she transcended the boundaries between East and West without perceiving this act as either major or disturbing. In the pursuit of personal fame, she helped usher in a new type of big-city mentality that was a unique product of the Shanghai Settlements. In the long run, the business practices of the Shanghai courtesan set the stage for a particular kind of commercialized world of glamour. Even the concept of entertainment itself was largely defined during the late Qing as the city's multicultural makeup was synthesized in her figure.

In modeling modernity, sexual relationships are an important component. The Shanghai courtesan of this time had a main patron with whom she had sexual relations. At the same time, she might also have a private lover. However, even in this realm, where the courtesan was eager to distinguish herself from a prostitute, the top courtesans were never reduced to being objects in a sex market but pushed for new urban arrangements. Some refused to assume the role of concubine under the first wife's control in a large household outside Shanghai and insisted upon a nuclear relationship in separate quarters in Shanghai; others boldly picked opera star lovers regardless of the scandalized reaction from clients and journalists. All this was instrumental in creating the space into which other women could move and in providing behavioral models they could adopt.

At the time, there already were some who saw a possible positive side to the influence of the Shanghai courtesans. Zhan Kai, a sojourner to Shanghai and an open advocate of women's rights in public affairs, was sympathetic to the efforts of the Shanghai courtesans to go public in their role as entertainers. In 1906, he wrote: "Today, well-educated young women from good families imitate the Shanghai courtesans everywhere in their dress and ornaments. But in this time of burgeoning female learning, even young women who have fallen into the courtesan profession know to better themselves and cultivate their character [by getting an education]. It would definitely be wonderful for the future of women if their influence were as strong in this area [as it is in fashion]."[169]

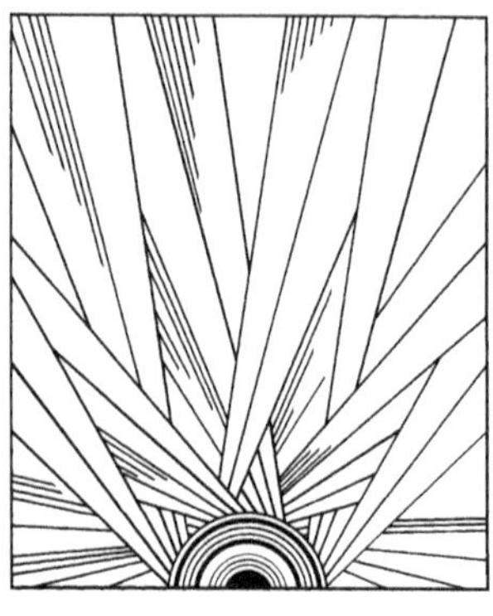

2 *Shanghai Love*

New Rules of the Game

The Shanghai courtesan's new social position, gained after she moved to the Foreign Settlements, was rapidly translated into an elaborate set of new rituals. These rituals recast the decorum of the relationships between all parties—client, courtesan, courtesan house, and different ranks of courtesans. Some had roots in older rituals; others were new. They created an order for a world of courtship that was separate from so-called normal life and was new in that they reset the balance in the courtesan-client relationship. Much of the initiative for this development came from the Shanghai courtesans who stood to benefit the most. The process offers a unique glimpse into the inner workings of the Shanghai courtesan world and, more important, into their new self-assessment.

This swift and dramatic shift called forth a plethora of insider narrations, courtesan handbooks, and guides published from the 1870s and well into the 1900s. They were part of a rapidly growing literature on Shanghai courtesans that ranged from diaries and travelogues to brush notes, bamboo twig ballads, and novels, which offered introductions to the courtesan world, personal records, and commentary. This literature grew as the Shanghai Settlements developed into China's principal trade, print, and entertainment center. Depicting the courtesans as one of the extraordinary sights of the Settlements expanded the image of commercial Shanghai by making it also appear as the "big playground" (*youxichang*) of entertainment. Here, one could experience all that was exotic, modern, foreign, and titillating. These records presented the rituals as something unique and thus helped to create and spread the reputation of the Shanghai courtesan and her theatrical world of love and, with it, that of the Shanghai Settlements themselves.

Two recent works have dealt with some of these rituals. In *Dangerous Pleasures*, Gail Hershatter describes these rituals in detail and reads them as a cultural play set up by men for their own pleasure. Invoking a "commonsense understanding" that clients made the rules in the courtesan houses, she sees the handbooks on courtesan entertainment as only recording "what men felt they needed to know about, as well as how they wished to order and remember, an elite practice situated in the rapidly changing commercial environment of a Foreign Treaty Port."[1] My analysis of the guides and other narratives suggests instead that the ritual structures they describe for the Settlements were quite new and unique. Given this realization, the question then arises as to what motivated these changes and in what way they changed the client-courtesan relationship.

Christian Henriot, in *Prostitution and Sexuality in Shanghai*, analyzes the rituals primarily in terms of their financial implications. While he touches on their cultural and social functions as status signals for the elite clients of the courtesans, he emphasizes the primacy of sexual gratification. The emphasis placed on these rituals in our sources suggests, however, that, especially for the high-ranking courtesans, cultural entertainment adorned with *qing* (sublime love), not sex, was at the core. In Chinese elite society, men and women shunned public contact, and the interaction between courtesan and client was the exception. In this fragile space of the exceptional, ritual had always served an important function. Through ritual, roles were played out and hierarchies were established. Again, the question is, what was the motivation for change and in what way were the rules of the game reset.

Courtesan Hierarchy and Ritual in the Walled City

One of the earliest and richest records of the Shanghai courtesan world comes from the hands of Wang Tao (1828–1890), among the most highly appreciated writers of social and cultural reportage at the time and member of the first generation of Chinese journalists.[2] The early sections of his *Record of Visits to Courtesan Houses in a Distant Corner by the Sea* (Haizou yeyou lu), which has a preface dated 1860, mostly refer to the courtesans in the walled city of Shanghai before the Taipings reached the Shanghai area. Ritualized behavior there was little developed. In contrast, the subsequent *Appendix to "Record of Visits to Courtesan Houses in a Distant Corner by the Sea" (Haizou yeyou lu yulu)*, written in 1878 while the author was in exile in Hong Kong, deals with courtesan life in the Shanghai Foreign Settlements and describes an elaborate set of rituals they practiced there. One may argue that the paucity of details on courtesan rituals in the walled city before the 1860s reflects the assumption that they were all too familiar to his readers. A comparison of the two works, however, shows that the elaborate descriptions in the latter work were due to the development of a new and rich set of rituals expressive of a new hierarchy among the courtesans in the Settlements as well as a change in their relations with clients.

Wang Tao notes three main classes of courtesan and prostitution establishments in the walled city: the "lodge" (*tangming*), the "straw platform" (*caotai*), and the "private residence" (*siju*).[3] The lodges, which he describes as the most popular and grand in setting, were divided into *tangding* at the top and *tangdi* at the bottom. They might house thirty to fifty women, who were ranked primarily by the quality of their musical performances. There were at the time about ten such lodges. The straw platforms were lower in rank, cheaper in price, and readily provided sexual services. Of the private residences, Wang Tao states that there were no less than three hundred. These were small operations that lacked the kitchen facilities for banquets but ordered food from outside and in general provided a cozy atmosphere. Outside of this hierarchy were exclusive houses opened by "famous ladies" (*mingyuan*) who called themselves "[ladies] residing in their homes" (*zhujia*); they did not deign to sing or personally serve guests but had their maids perform these duties. Wang did not specify the kinds of services these establishments provided.[4]

Except for the houses of the famous ladies, one could simply enter these establishments and be entertained. Wang's accounts of his own visits to courtesans confirm this general observation. The ritual he notes is service oriented and not personal. When a client entered a courtesan establishment, the madam of the house came out to greet him and offer fruit and tea. This establishes him as a welcome customer. If the town's hooligans (*liumang*) feel snubbed because this ritual is not performed for them, "they would call on their friends and make trouble. The courtesans detest them, and call them *chahui ke* [tea guests]." The courtesans were extremely fearful of these men, who, if irritated even slightly, would bring their gang and might even kidnap a courtesan, which they called "uprooting the courtesan" (*ba guanren*).[5] Courtesan houses could buy protection against the gangs by paying bribes to none other than the magistrate's chief servant, who was called the "support chief" (*chengtou*). In the legal limbo in which courtesan houses operated, the yamen underlings seem to have taken the law into their own hands. The distribution of the money among gang members was called *heigui* (black rule).[6]

There were also different types of female storytellers and singers in the walled city. They were classed according to their specialty, the highest being those "good at reciting" (*pingshu*) or "good at singing" (*changqu*). Ranking below them were singers who performed "flower-drum plays" (*huagu xi*) or were skilled at "telling stories of retribution" (*shuo yinguo*). As they performed in public, they were constantly threatened with being banned by the authorities for singing lewd songs.[7]

Wang Tao's account is largely confirmed by Mao Xianglin, a contemporary of Wang Tao's and a native of Shanghai. His *Record of Leftover Ink* (Moyu lu) sketches in anecdotal form the hierarchy and rituals among the courtesans in the walled city. He deviates from Wang only in viewing the houses of the famous ladies as of the highest ranking, but he describes them in much the same way as does Wang Tao.[8]

A very early account of courtesan entertainment in the walled city is *Yuefu Poems on Traveling in the Bitter Sea* (Kuhai hang yuefu), written around 1855 by Yao Xie (1805–1864). The 108 poems in this work are devoted entirely to Shanghai courtesan and prostitution entertainment prior to the development of the Foreign Settlements.[9] It begins, like many guides, with a general warning about the evils of lust and the craftiness of the courtesans but then proceeds to map procedures in courtesan houses, with ample details on life, rituals, and business strategies.[10] As his poems offer much unique information about the rituals practiced in the lodges, they provide a point of comparison by which to identify later changes.

According to Yao Xie, the lodges were more like traditional brothels, offering sex, food, and entertainment all under one roof. The most renowned of these were the Baohe and the Shuangxiu, with about thirty to fifty women each. Half of the women offered the core services of the house; the other half, those below thirteen and above thirty years of age, were called "associates of the lodge" (*peitang*), and their duty was to provide general entertainment. Barefoot male house attendants (*waichang*) probably doubled as security guards. The customer was referred to as *chuang men tou*, which means "head banging at the door." He was at liberty to visit such a lodge without introduction whenever he pleased. Upon his arrival, he would be welcomed by an older female house attendant, the *yiniang*, with phrases of endearment such as "Have we received you before?" followed by a polite inquiry into his ancestral home and surname. All the prostitutes, young and old, would gather, trying to catch the eye of the newcomer (poem 3).

Once he had made his choice, he was invited into the woman's room. The role of these women was midway between courtesan entertainer and prostitute. The courtesan called the client her "god of wealth" (*lutou pusa*) and referred to herself in a deprecating manner as a "village servant" (*xiangxia guanren*). After he ordered a "banquet" (*duanzheng*), the courtesan humbly thanked him for bestowing this honor upon her and then set about making the necessary arrangements (poem 4).

Candles (referred to as "oil sticks" [*youtiao*]) were lit, fresh tea was brewed, and a tray with opium sufficient for three pipes was brought out. One half of a yellow pear and four *qian* of black melon seeds were offered to the statue of the God of Wealth (for bringing the customer), an offering called "the yellow and the black." The courtesan personally served the client a special "melon edge" teacup with cover, the "intimacy tea" (*ti ji cha*). This was followed by small talk (poem 5).

A round table symbolizing "union" (*tuanyuan*) was set up and prepared for the banquet. The customer (perhaps with his friends) and the courtesan(s) took their places. Wine was served and dishes were offered; if food seemed lacking, new orders were given. Then a drinking game such as "thumb fighting" (*muzhan*) might be played, with the banquet host throwing two silver dollars into the tray on which the candles stood. This was for the servants. A cry "The master is here!" (Xiansheng dao) announced the arrival of the courtesan singer. Her performance included northern and southern tunes sung in a mixture of northern and Suzhou dialects. She played the "three-stringed lute" (*sanxian*), or a drum, and was accompanied by a two-stringed *huqin*. Finally, rice was served, signaling the end of the meal, and the courtesan asked the client in a ritualized manner to forgive the inadequate entertainment (poem 6).

When a customer left the house after the banquet and did not spend the night, the house recorded his visit as an "empty engagement" (*kongju*), at a cost of only two dollars. (Yao does not mention the price of a "full engagement.") Every effort was made to avoid such empty engagements. As the customer tried to leave, he was "dragged" back into the house and put into the prostitute's bed, where she began sweet-talking him (poem 7). Some time later, she excused herself and returned to duty at another banquet. Only when that banquet was over did she come back to bed. The next morning, the client was given a hard pancake for breakfast and was expected to leave (poem 8).

To sum up, higher-class lodge courtesans in the walled city had already ritualized some practices in conducting their business. The client could enter without introduction but could make his choice only after being formally greeted and introducing himself. The courtesan served him tea in a special cup as a token of acceptance. The client gave a dinner party at the house, accompanied by the courtesan, and courtesans who specialized in music entertained with performances. The client could opt for these social and cultural entertainments only, but the establishment was eager to secure a full engagement including sexual services. Still, even the chosen prostitute continued to have other entertainment duties, but she would attend to them only after the client's dinner party was over.

From these accounts, it is clear that the particular hierarchy among courtesans in the Foreign Settlements did not exist at this time in the walled city. There were ritualized forms governing the lodges, but courtesan business was confined to courtesan houses, so there was no need for ritual control over behavior in the public arena.

The Shanghai Settlements and the New Courtesan Hierarchy

From the 1850s to the 1880s, after the move from the walled city to the Settlements, courtesans created new categories for themselves and established a distinct hierarchy among them. Initially, the *shuyu* were at the top. They were professional storytellers, each performing in her own quarters. They definitely did not offer sexual services. Eventually, another group, the *changsan*, moved into the top category and partly took over the functions of the *shuyu*. Between 1870 and 1890, the *changsan* spearheaded the quest for the new and consequently were identified with and caught the fancy of this booming metropolis. Records show that early in the 1860s, encounters between client and *changsan* were less formal than they later became and that sexual services were explicitly part of their business.[11] By the 1880s, this earlier "three dollar" service had disappeared along with the explicit offer of sexual services.[12] In the 1890s, the *changsan* added the role of public performer and sang at storytelling halls under exclusive contracts.[13]

A level down from the *changsan* were the *ersan*, and beneath the *ersan* were the *yaoni*. The *ersan* category faded away in the 1880s, as many scholars have noted. Wang Tao's 1878 appendix describes this ranking of courtesans as unique to the Shanghai Settlements; eventually, the new hierarchy replaced the old one.[14]

The contrast between the two ranking orders of Shanghai courtesans was also depicted in numerous bamboo twig ballads of the period. Yuan Zuzhi (1827–1902), a grandson of the famous Qing poet Yuan Mei (1716–1798), who was considered an "old Shanghai" by contemporaries, wrote some of the earliest surviving Shanghai bamboo twig ballads. He had lived in the walled city since the 1850s and moved to the Settlements in the 1870s.

His "Bamboo Twig Ballads on the Northern City of Shanghai" (Hubei zhuzhi ci), published in 1872, for example, gives a detailed comparison of the walled city and the Settlements, in which he notes the new types of courtesans and their business locations:

> *Fu* [wealth], *gui* [rank], *rong* [glory], and *hua* [splendor] [elements in the names of lanes where the most famous courtesan houses in the Settlements were located] are all good omens indeed; to divide the beauties among [as many as] ten houses cannot even be considered exaggerating!

> Why should there be any need to still mention the courtesans in [the single] Ding family lane [in the walled city]; as flowers with "three" feet in diameter [*changsan* courtesans], they [the courtesans in the Settlements] can be proud of who they are.[15]

The commentary reads:

> Zhaofu, Zhaogui, Zhaohua are all names of lanes [*linong*]; together with Riqiu, Jiu'an, Tongqing, Shangren, Baihua, and Zhuxin, these are the [ten] lanes where the top courtesan houses [in the Settlements] are located; they are commonly regarded as *bansan ju* [the *changsan* courtesan establishments]. Ding Family Lane refers to the prosperous spot in the walled city where in the past the Suzhou courtesan establishments were located.

He goes on to describe the *ersan ju*, the *yaoni*, and the *xiansheng*, the women storytellers who performed in public.[16] The first two terms have not been convincingly explained. As *ersan ju* means "two/three services" and *yaoni* "one/two services," both seem to contain numbers as long as they are not words in different dialect for which random characters have been assigned. There is speculation that the new hierarchy of courtesans as well as the terms used for its categories were linked to the policies of the foreign authorities governing the Settlements. The services of *changsan* cost three dollars and those of the *yaoni* cost two dollars; these prices were set by the Municipal Council in the early 1860s to prevent random pricing by courtesan houses.[17] Despite the lack of any historical source for this assertion, the unique phenomenon of Settlements courtesans being referred to by the price a customer had to pay lends it some plausibility. This custom reflects the commercial spirit of the city and at the same time signals a complex response by clients toward the courtesan's new freedom to make money in the limelight. The courtesans themselves never used these demeaning terms. The *changsan* referred to themselves in words related to learning, as *jiaoshu*, which translates loosely as "book editor" or "proofreader," and *shuyu*, which means "book lodge," while the *yaoni* called themselves by the name of their house.[18]

The new types of courtesans pioneered new forms of entertainment. Chanqing Sheng, or Yuan Zuzhi, in his 1872 "Sequel to 'Bamboo Twig Ballads on the Northern City of Shanghai'" (Xu 'Hubei zhuzhi ci'), notes that he found the Settlements so much changed since his visit of ten years before—when he wrote the first set of ballads—that he felt prompted to write a sequel. He gives many details about the new types of courtesan entertainment then in vogue, such as going to the "singing hall" (*xiguan*), listening to courtesan performances, visiting the "theater" (*xiyuan*), inviting a courtesan for companionship, or listening to "female storytellers" (*shuoshu nü xiansheng*). He elaborates on the courtesans' public behavior, noting that they rode out together in Western-style open carriages around four in the afternoon, "dazzling and bewitching those who saw them,"[19] and that a courtesan had spotted an acquaintance among hundreds of people in a theater and sent a servant over to fill his pipe. What he noted falls neatly into the realm of the courtesan's new range of public activity. In this realm, the female storytelling hall, with its public performances by women, probably stands out as the most important feature.

2.1. "Female Storytelling Hall" (Nü Shuchang). Lithograph. The kerosene lamp, shining down from a tall pole in this illustration, transformed night into day in Shanghai. (Dianshizhai, Shenjiang shengjing tu, *2:30)*

Legend has it that the first such hall in the Settlements, Yeshi Lou, which took its name from the best-known garden in the walled city, was opened by one of the top courtesans in the 1870s. The venture proved so successful that others followed suit, and teahouses and storytelling halls that had hitherto been the domain of male singers began to invite the *changsan* and *shuyu* to perform. These halls were first called *nü changshu chang,* later *nü shuchang.*[20]

Images showing the architectural arrangement of female storytelling halls of the 1890s confirm that Shanghai courtesan entertainment was performed in part in buildings that were open to public view. The elaborate courtesan rituals developed during this period in the Shanghai Settlements should be seen in this context. What had once been a largely exclusive, indoor, and private entertainment was now open to the public and to the public gaze (figs. 2.1, 2.2a, b).

The paucity of details notwithstanding, the information provided by Yao Xie suggests that the rituals developed in the Settlements had antecedents in the Jiangnan area.[21] Courtesans moving into the Settlements from historically prosperous towns such as Suzhou, Yangzhou, or Ningbo might have brought some of these ritual elements with them. In forming a new life and a new community, the courtesans must have mixed and selected social rituals until they created the forms described in the guides. This process is hard to document in detail. There is no question, however, that the rituals described in the guides reflect the courtesans'

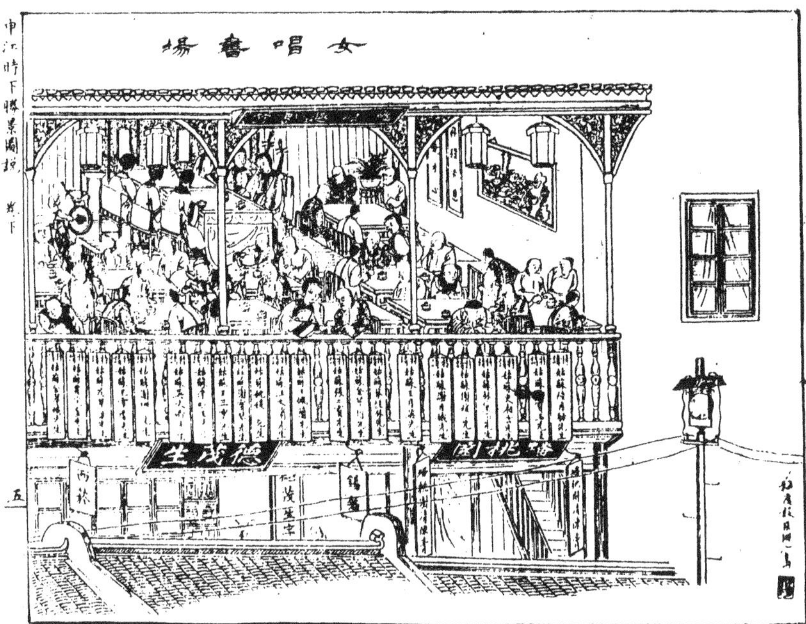

2.2a, b.

(a) "Female storytelling hall" (Nü changshu chang). Lithograph. The open architecture of the Paradise Fun Storytelling Hall (Taoyuan Qu Shuguan) allows courtesans and clients to lean against the banister and look down onto the street below. The street lamp confirms the location as Shanghai. (Meihua'an Zhu, Shenjiang shixia shengjing tushuo, *2:5)*

(b) Postcard from a photograph of the Paradise Fun Storytelling Hall, late nineteenth century. The postcard shows a similar scene with a female figure sitting close to the banister. (Private collection, Los Angeles.)

new environment and their reaction to it. The courtesans are presented as among the Settlements' unique features and contributed toward resetting social relationships in this immigrant society.

Ritualized Regulation of a New Type of Social Intercourse

The new rituals governed access to the courtesan, forms of courtship and separation, and financial obligations. The Shanghai courtesan handbooks are the most important sources on the new rituals governing the courtesan world. These handbooks, which began to appear around the mid-1870s, differed from the traditional courtesan guides, biographies, and descriptions of local courtesan entertainment.[22] The earlier sources were organized within biographies of top courtesans, but the Shanghai handbooks were written mostly in the form of itemized dictionaries. They followed an unlikely model, the Qing administration handbooks, and gave short explanations with no particular system governing the sequence of the entries.[23] They were for easy reading, not for quick reference. The rules and rituals are presented in a matter-of-fact style, mostly without commentary.[24] They show a ritualized courtesan-client "play" that assumes equality between the participants, which must be read against the steep differential that prevailed outside the Settlements.

The majority of these authors remained anonymous. Judging from the penname of the author of the 1877 *Miscellaneous Notes on Shanghai Flowers* (Haishang yanhua suoji)—"He Who Gives Directions to Those Who Don't Know Their Way Around" (Zhiyin Mituren)—their professed motive was to alert the newcomer to the seductive dangers of the Shanghai courtesan.[25] The early guides treat rituals, customs, rules, and business practices under the general heading of what the customer needs to know. By the 1880s and 1890s, the tone of the prefaces had changed, and the *Illustrated Record of Shanghai Courtesan Entertainment* (Haishang qinglou tuji) of 1892 jubilantly extols Shanghai: "The establishment of the Foreign Settlements has transformed, in the shortest time, the utterly insignificant place that once was Shanghai into one of China's greatest cosmopolitan centers, where the local fashion is that of extravagance and the flourishing courtesan entertainment is number one under Heaven."[26]

The detailed descriptions in the guides imply readers unfamiliar with the milieu. At the same time, their obsession with "the extraordinary" or "the fantastic" (*qi*) undermines the credibility of the high moral purpose often stated in the prefaces. Despite their descriptive stance, they should be read as reflections of the normative aspect of the new courtesan ritual rather than as actual practice in the courtesan houses, which would necessarily be mediated by the complexity of life and human relations there.

Rituals varied in content and elaborateness depending on rank. While the handbooks dealt with all aspects of courtesan life, their main focus was the upper-echelon courtesan, with her high visibility and impact, elaborate set-up, and jealously guarded position in the hierarchy.

The guides discuss these rituals in fixed terminologies. The habit of plagiarism certainly played a role; however, this consistency also signals the stability of the rituals. Wang Tao calls them "rules" (*guili*), and the 1904 novel *Idle Talk in Languid Moments* (Fupu xiantan) uses the term "proper manners" (*guiju*).[27] Only by the 1920s did specific categories such as "customs" (*suli*), "regulations" (*dingli*), and "rituals for festivals" (*jieli*) make their appearance.

The rituals governed social, economic, and religious aspects of courtesan life and established the codes that enabled indirect communication between courtesan and client. They regulated the client's financial obligations and described the practices by which courtesans tried to secure the benevolence and protection of the gods. By far the most elaborate set of rituals regulated social interaction between courtesan and client. This includes the client's access to and meeting with the courtesan, his courtship of her, and her acceptance or rejection of his advances.[28]

Meeting

A person who wished to meet a high-class courtesan had to be formally introduced by a well-established patron of her house. The houses of top-ranking courtesans were not walk-in establishments, and those who called without introductions were turned away at the door. Introducing a new guest enhanced the prestige of a patron but also made him the newcomer's guarantor. During the 1880s, he was even responsible for the new client's unpaid debts during the first season.[29] The introduction could take the form of *da chawei*. Given the complex rituals involved and the awkwardness of rendering the Shanghai dialect in Chinese characters, translation of these terms is sometimes unhelpful. *Da chawei* means to pay an afternoon call on the courtesan accompanied by the patron who provided the introduction (fig. 2.3). The visit was to be short, and the prospective client and patron were not to arrive too early, since a courtesan went to bed in the early morning hours, but also not too late, because then she would be busy with dressing, putting on makeup, and preparing for her evening duties. During such a visit, tea and opium were served free of charge.

The other way to become acquainted with such a courtesan was *jiaoju*, in which a patron summoned a courtesan to entertain his friends at a restaurant, theater, or storytelling hall (fig. 2.4). The *jiaoju* ritual was not a new one as it is mentioned in Yao Xie's poem collection *Yuefu Poems on Traveling in the Bitter Sea*. During the earlier period, however, *jiaoju* meant simply calling a courtesan to provide dinner entertainment. The ritual was reinvented in the Foreign Settlements and took a variety of forms reflecting the migration of entertainment into the public realm. In the most common, the name and address of the courtesan were written on a slip of red paper known as *jupiao*, and a messenger carried the note to her house. A new client had to ask a friend to call on the courtesan on his behalf, a mediation called *jieju*. After the new client had met the courtesan and had been acknowledged by her, he could visit her on his own or call for her services. The *jupiao* appears to be a Settlements innovation. At one time, courtesan houses were government institutions, and clients had to buy bamboo slips from the yamen that entitled them to the services of courtesans at private banquets; the *jupiao* grew out of this system.[30] The client's handwriting on the *jupiao* provided a dependable record for accounting. In

2.3. "Hong Shanqing makes the match in Juxiu courtesan house" (Hong Shanqing Juxiutang zuomei). Lithograph. A new client is introduced by an established patron. At this first meeting, a very young courtesan (referred to as "virgin" [qingguanren]*) is brought forth to meet him. (Han Bangqing,* Haishang hua liezhuan, *1894)*

震寰藥廠
愛理士紅
衣補丸
大補
血氣
今分行在
上海四川
路一百十
四號洋房
批發各埠
均有寄售
每瓶洋一
元二角
每半打洋
六元

2.4. *"Sights of Shanghai courtesan houses: Entertaining at banquets without pause" (Shanghai quyuan zhi xianxiang: Chenghuan daiyan wu xianxia). Lithograph. These courtesans have been called to attend a dinner party at Yipinxiang, a Western-style restaurant. Note that clothing styles have changed greatly from the 1880s (see fig. 1.1). (*Tuhua ribao*, no. 249 [1910])*

the Settlements version of the *jupiao*, the nature of the transaction had changed from officially granted access to a courtesan who had no say in the affair to a contractual arrangement between the client and the courtesan, with the latter having quite a bit of choice and independence.

The top courtesans' insistence on the formal introduction of a potential new client by a patron of good standing ensured that the newcomer had the requisite cultural and financial capital at his disposal, secured a guarantor for the newcomer, and put pressure on him not to embarrass his friend with improper behavior. The patron would have communicated the rules and rituals governing the courtesan establishments to the newcomer. This step resembles the introductory stage of matchmaking, which leaves room for rejection by both parties. Against the backdrop of public segregation between the sexes in Chinese society, this very urban and typically Shanghai innovation contributed significantly toward developing the behavioral rituals of modern love.

Courtship and love between courtesan and patron certainly did not begin with the Shanghai Settlements; it had a long history. In offering protection to these new forms, however, the Foreign Settlements became a special space for love. In China's old capital and in commercial cities, courtesan entertainment had flourished under the wary eyes of the country's officials, but in the Foreign Settlements, the shift in power favored the courtesans. Even powerful members of the elite had to play by the new Shanghai rules of the game. The ritual of courting a *changsan* reflected this change in power dynamics.

For the *yaoni*, the courtship ritual clearly resembled that of the lodges in the walled city, in that a client could go to their house without introduction. The fabulously furnished houses of the top courtesans, with their one or two residents, were identified only by a simple sign with a name plus the term *shuyu*, which was used for such houses, or had no recognizable sign at all. *Yaoni* houses, in contrast, bore signs with the "hall name" (*tangming*), reading "so-and-so *tang*." In the early years, *yaoni* names were not posted, but by the 1890s, they were written on small pieces of paper attached to the frame of the main gate. The number of *yaoni* living in such a house ranged from ten to as many as forty, and the business premises might comprise up to one hundred rooms.

As soon as a new customer walked in, a male servant would cry out "*yicha*," and all the courtesans who had no client at that moment came into one room where the customer could choose from among them (fig. 2.5). The top-ranking *yaoni* never appeared during this first round of viewing; only if the customer refused to choose and the servant called out "*yicha*" for a second and a third time did the more sought-after courtesans enter the room. As the guidebooks point out, however, the new client also needed an introduction before he could meet the very best among the *yaoni*. After he made his selection, the courtesan took the guest to her room and served tea.

The difference between the *changsan* and the *yaoni* rituals for meeting new clients is significant. It indicates that the *changsan*, in line with their ranking, placed more emphasis on their service and their standing in terms of culture, as they inevitably were better trained in the performing arts. A courtesan could rise in rank, but the

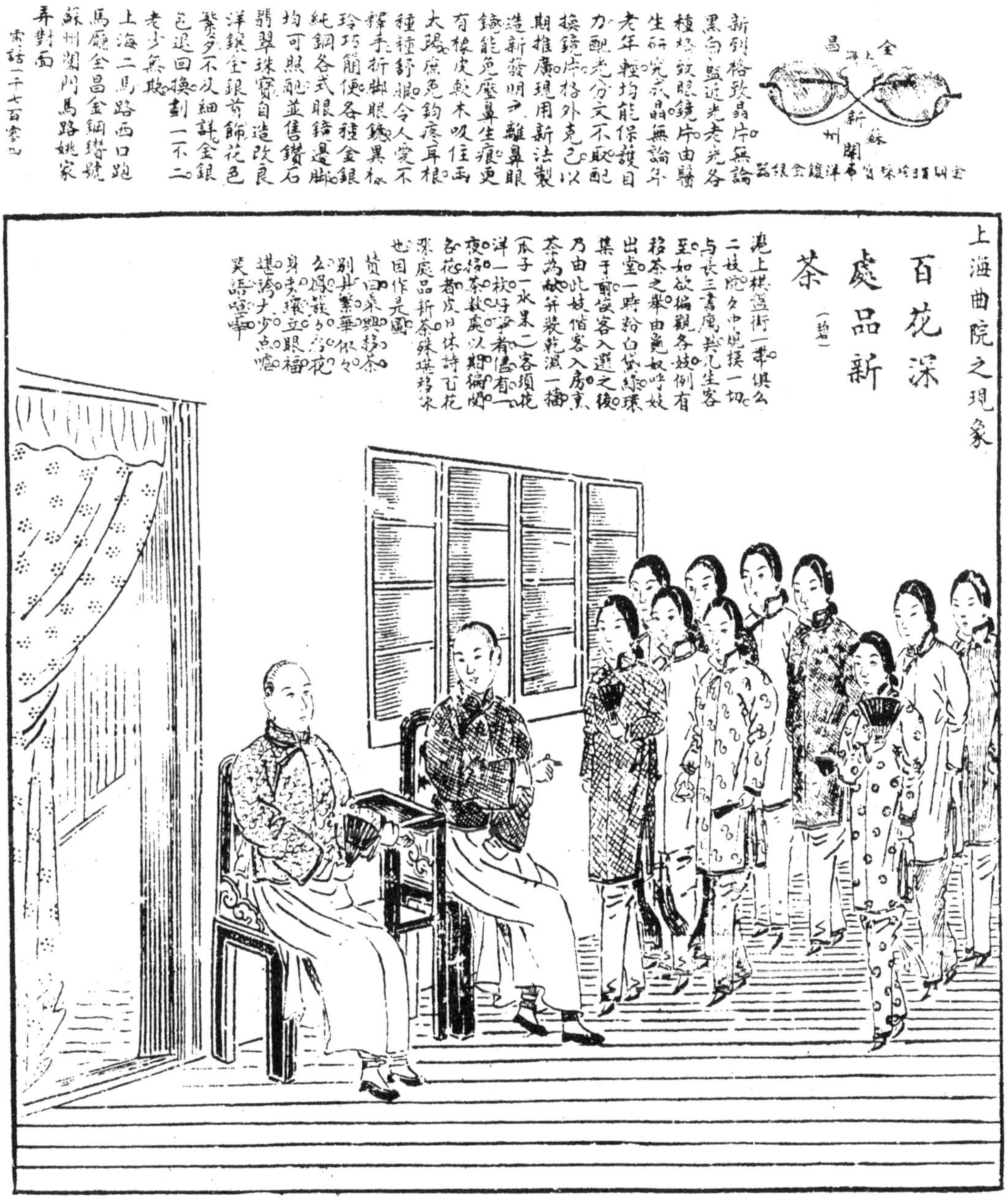

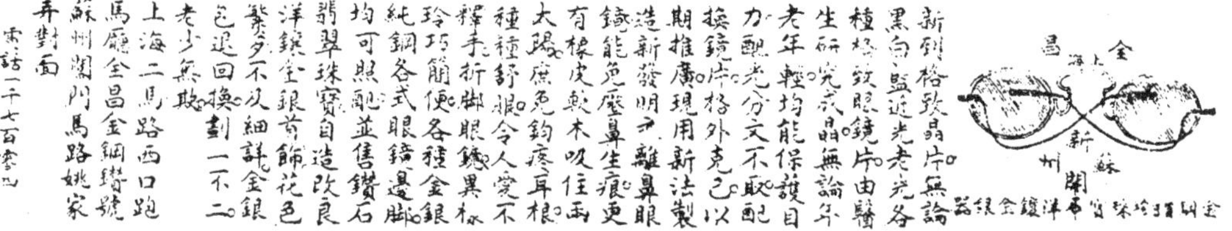

*2.5. "Sights of Shanghai courtesan houses: Amidst a hundred flowers tasting the new tea" (Shanghai quyuan zhi xianxiang: Baihua shenchu pin xin cha). Lithograph. Courtesans of a yaoni house meet new clients. Each client will then choose a courtesan who strikes his fancy. (*Tuhua ribao*, no. 282 [1910])*

difficulties were numerous, and the change in status might not be profitable. The move from *yaoni* to *changsan* rank hinged on several factors: entertainment skills such as singing and conversation, for which most *yaoni* had no training; financial backing from a wealthy patron; a loan from the madam of a *changsan* establishment or the use of one's own savings to join such a house; and, finally, willingness to assume greater financial responsibility. Being a *changsan* was costly, and not only for clients. The *changsan* had to pay a percentage of her earnings to the house, and the house normally gave the courtesan a large loan. This upward move is fictionalized in novels such as *Biographies of Shanghai Flowers* (Haishang hua liezhuan), by Han Bangqing.[31] *Changsan* prices signaled exclusiveness. Their inaccessibility marked the level of their cultural capital in the context of role-play based on the "talented scholar and beautiful lady" (*caizi jiaren*) motif, which defined the particulars of their courtship.

In the Settlements, the *jiaoju* routine for the first encounter with a *changsan* superseded the welcome of a new guest by the madam or older female maid that had been the practice in the walled city. Additionally, in the Settlements, the top-ranking courtesans often owned their establishments.[32] Since the courtesan business had expanded into a city where many other entertainment venues were located, the first encounter frequently took place in a public setting such as a theater or a storytelling hall. Under these conditions, the motif of the modern lover supplanted the role of the beautiful lady who was supposedly shielded from public view. The city became the stage for a performance by client and courtesan, with onlookers passing judgment on the unfolding affair. It was a stunning sight for people who were not used to seeing couples mixing freely in public, and depictions found their way into novels and illustrated guides, touted as among the city's extraordinary attractions.

While clients were drawn to the city by the reputation of the Shanghai courtesan and the romantic image of the city itself, they might also have expected not so much to experience the new as to experience the past. They may have wished to recapture the myth of the legendary love affairs between the grand courtesans and brilliant scholars of the past. What they found, however, was the new. The grand courtesan of Shanghai was not the grand lady of the past. Courtship and love with the Shanghai courtesan meant acting within a ritual framework that resembled the past in its quaintness but was in fact designed to accommodate a novel type of courtship and new power relations.

Courtship

For the top-ranking courtesan, a sexual relationship was a favor bestowed on only one patron at a time. It was discreet and was not allowed to interfere with other duties. Much like Japanese geisha, the *changsan* and *shuyu* provided primarily cultural entertainment.[33] Sex might be a favor for a client who was willing and able to rise to the challenge of becoming a patron. The majority of the courtesan's revenue came from banquets given at her house by clients. The first step in beginning a courtship (*pan xianghao*) with one of these women and becoming her recognized patron was to "ask for her company" as we have seen in the *jiaoju* ritual.[34] The services involved all had their own names, such as *paiju* for card games, *xiju* for theater visits, and *jiuju* for drinking games. A courtesan might be called by different clients at the same time, and this part of her professional routine was called *zhuanju* (going from one appointment to the next), with some delay allowed between clients.

By far the most important favor a client could do to secure his position with a courtesan was to give a dinner party at her house and invite his friends, a ritual called *bai taimian* (fig. 2.6). This costly gesture was taken as a sign of particular attachment. Such a dinner party also gave the courtesan face in her community. Her role was to entertain by singing, conversing, and pouring wine for the client. She herself only drank some liquor but did not join in the dining. When the banquet was over, the client and his dinner guests were invited to the rooms of the courtesans who had been their dinner companions and were served tea before departing; this was called *xie taimian*. If and when a client had hosted many such banquets and had moreover given her an expensive gift, the courtesan might invite him to stay overnight after a banquet. The gift, which in the courtesan's language was called "soliciting a little precious" (*chao xiaohuo*) would be referred to by the client as "let the ax take hold" (*zhuo futou*). It usually consisted of a pair of gold bracelets and a length of silk. From that moment, the client was considered to be the patron of this courtesan, and their behavior toward each other was that of "partners in life ad interim" (*lushui fuqi*), with numerous commitments from both sides and a heavy and largely incalculable financial responsibility for the patron.[35]

As conspicuous consumption became a dominant feature of Shanghai culture, the ritual of *bai taimian* took on ever more elaborate variations. In the 1890s, it became fashionable for a client to show clout and impress his favored courtesan by putting on a second banquet immediately after the first, a practice called "double the banquet" (*chi shuangtai*). Another option was "giving two banquets" (*fan taimian*), a second banquet at the same house or at another one. The banquets might continue throughout the night, with three or four in succession (fig. 2.7). A client could also call for two courtesans to be his companions, a double call known as *shuangju*.

As long as the relationship remained within the realm of entertainment, prices for the courtesan's services were clearly defined. If the relationship became one between lovers, however, it was supposed to be exclusive for both parties and was financially much less clearly defined. As the *changsan* were considered entertainers and not sexual partners, they had public functions to perform, and the new *zhuanju* ritual, in which courtesans went to several appointments in one evening, prevented a client from having exclusive rights to a courtesan, even if she was his lover.[36] So it often happened that a patron held a dinner party at his lady's house, but she might be attending other parties. If he wanted her company, he had to summon her, just like her other clients. Business etiquette required that she heed all incoming calls, as long as the customer had been properly introduced. The patron's gratification came late in the evening when the courtesan returned from her duties. This signaled the development of a formal separation between the courtesan's professional and private lives. Still, the patron's role-playing as "lover" was very much part of her business arrangement.

購服艾羅補腦汁須知

艾羅補腦汁。為補腦唯一無二之聖藥。中國由上海中法大藥房發行。每年銷數最廣。活人無算。曾在中西官署立案禁止冒戳。丁未夏。並呈農工商部化驗有案。無如偽牌襍出。防不勝防。請查閱新證書冒牌戳牌之歷史便知。為此謹告購藥諸君。須細認艾羅各仿單及瓶上艾羅醫生良葯之一字樣。以免魚目混珠為要。 中法大藥房啟

2.6. "Sights of Shanghai courtesan houses: At midnight, the moon is high and the music rings" (Shanghai quyuan zhi xianxiang: Ye ban yue gao xuansuo ming). Lithograph. A patron throws a dinner party in a courtesan's quarters. She accompanies herself on a pipa. *To the side, musicians are playing, a practice that developed early in the twentieth century. (*Tuhua ribao, *no. 238 [1910])*

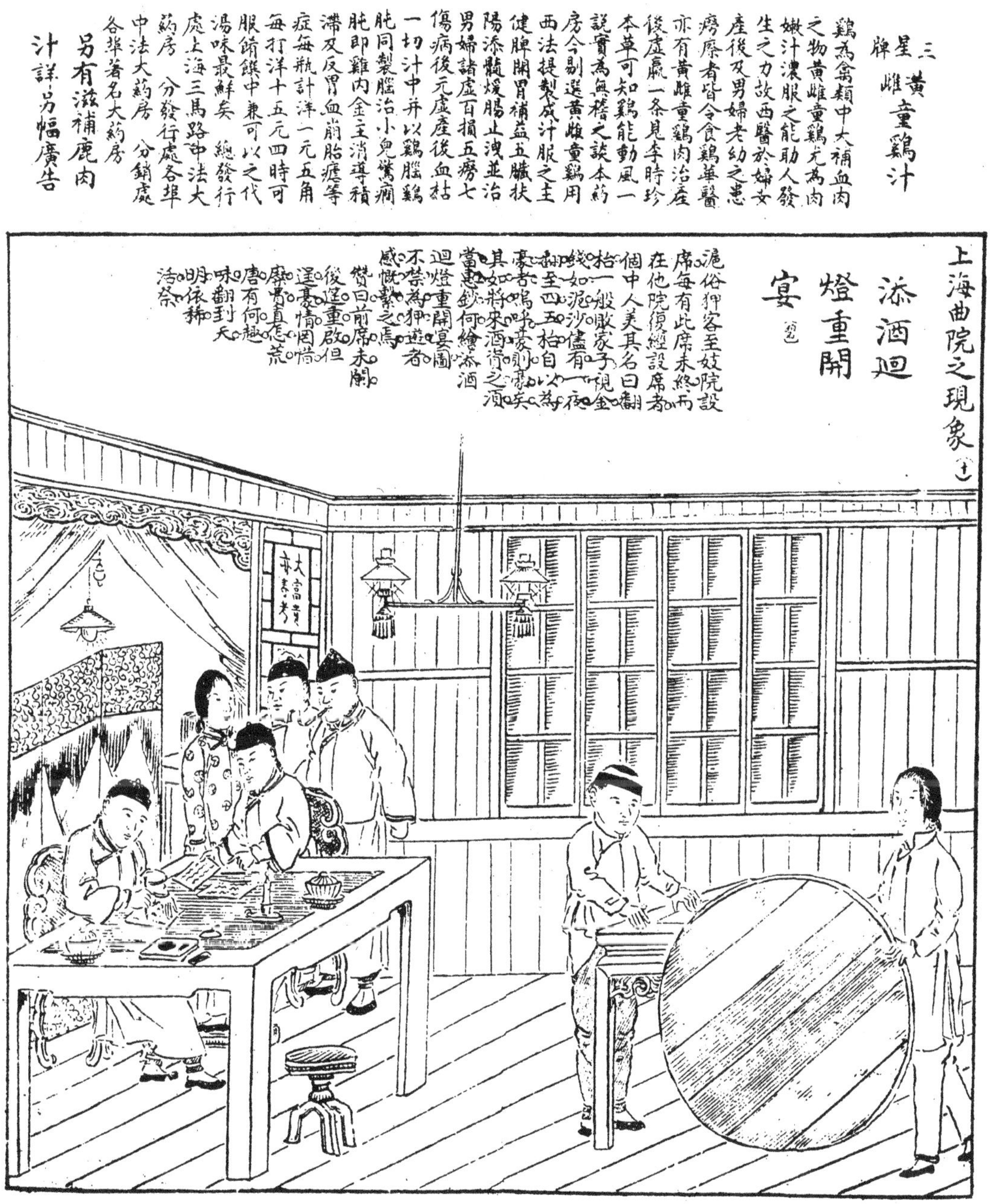

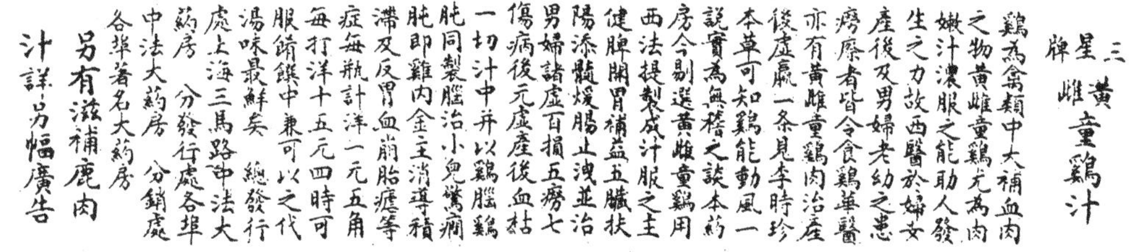

上海曲院之現象（十）

添酒迴燈重開宴

2.7. *"Sights of Shanghai courtesan houses: Filling the wine, turning up the lamp, having another banquet" (Shanghai zuyuan zhi xianxiang: Tianjiu xun). Lithograph. The client who chose to practice the ritual of* fan taimian *must pay for his second order in advance. (*Tuhua ribao, *no. 229 [1910])*

The *jiaoju* and *zhuanju* rituals reinforced the Shanghai courtesan's identity as a professional entertainer. There was much controversy attached to these practices. Visitors to the city were surprised to see a courtesan arrive at a dinner party, stay for only about ten minutes, sing one song, and then excuse herself. Conflicts arose when a client had to wait for what seemed to him an excessive amount of time or sometimes even in vain. The disputes spilled over into the entertainment newspapers. The true private life of a courtesan, however, which marked the transition to new and modern urban roles, developed with the fashion among courtesans of choosing opera singers as lovers, a practice much decried by literati at the time.[37]

The increasingly clear separation of private and public roles did not preclude playing on older motifs. Shanghai courtesans adopted names from Cao Xueqin's *Dream of the Red Chamber* (Honglou meng) so as to fill out the "talented scholar meets beautiful lady" trope of romantic love.[38] They might also stage themselves as husband and wife, with the maids in the courtesan establishment calling the client "brother-in-law." Both scenarios were popular in the *changsan* establishments in Shanghai, since most men there were far away from their homes and families. In the "family" trope, the courtesan played the wife and provided the patron with a house where he could relax and receive friends. In the midst of all this, she continued to be a professional entertainer. If the courtesan agreed, a patron could make her his concubine; she would then have the name-sign removed from the front door (fig. 2.8).

The Economy of Love

A courtesan who was invited to join a house was considered a business partner. The house "set her up" (*daidang*) by advancing her the considerable sum of two hundred or three hundred silver dollars with which to buy dazzling new clothes and furniture. The advance came with high interest, which the courtesan had to pay when accounts were scheduled to be cleared. For comparison, the monthly income of a journalist during the 1880s and 1890s was between fifteen and forty silver dollars. If the courtesan wanted to leave, she had to repay the sum in full.

When a courtesan was very successful, she moved to a higher-ranked room in a ritualized process called *diao fangjian*. Sometimes, this meant leaving a noisy ground-floor room for one on the more secluded upper floor, where her window might also have a view. To "make it an occasion" (*zuo changmian*), her clients held a dinner party in her honor at the house.

A courtesan who decided to leave the house had to "redeem herself" (*shushen*) from the madam by paying outstanding debts if she was a business partner or paying her own ransom if she had been sold to the establishment. She could obtain her freedom if her patron agreed to marry her and pay the agreed sum "in her stead" (*daishu*); or she could "buy her freedom" (*zishu*) if she had accumulated enough savings. She also could borrow money for this purpose. Many courtesans who bought their freedom intended to open their own houses and become madams in their turn.[39]

The *changsan* changed residences often (fig. 2.9). The move, called *diaotou*, had a ritualized routine. It both advertised and renewed the courtesan's business, giv-

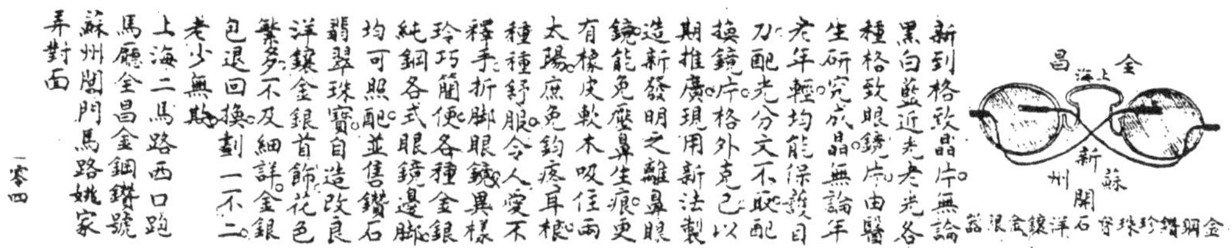

上海曲院之現象

從此蕭郎是路人

2.8. *"Sights of Shanghai courtesan houses: From now on, the young man is her companion" (Shanghai quyuan zhi xianxiang: Congci xiaolang shi lu ren). Lithograph. When a courtesan agreed to marry a patron, the wooden name-sign was taken off the front door. The manservant who performed this ritual generally received between twenty and one hundred dollars for the service.* (Tuhua ribao, no. 301 [1910])

ing it a new face. The move might take place for a variety of reasons: business was going well or was not going well; the courtesan decided that her house needed a shake-up; or a new patron wanted to add glamour to the image of his favorite by providing her with a new set of furniture. The courtesan's most intimate clients celebrated the move by giving dinner parties in her honor. At this time as well, clients brought their friends and introduced new customers to her house.

Romantic attachment between a courtesan and a client was a potential source of conflict between a madam and a courtesan in her house. The madam saw such a development as undesirable since it might have a negative effect on the courtesan's professional attitude and lead to financial losses, as these attachments often resulted in encounters with the client that were not registered in the account books. In some cases, instead of paying for services, the client became a "graciously subsidized client" (*enke*) of a courtesan who would "steal visits" (*touju*) with him. Here, the interests of courtesan and madam were in direct conflict. The courtesan was able to get away with such an affair only if she remained financially successful as an entertainer.

Although money did play a central role in the high-ranking courtesan establishments, as in any business enterprise, open discussion of prices would have undercut the high cultural profile and status of the business. More specifically, it would have undercut the identification with the romantic love role-play and the pleasures derived from it. Many efforts were thus made to relegate monetary matters to an implicit subtext familiar to and binding on all sides. The guidebooks played an important part in developing familiarity with this code, especially among potential clients.

Prices for services were preset, and costs incurred by the client were registered with the house each day and collected three times a year; the routine, called *sanjie*, was based on the dates of the dragon boat festival (*duanwu*), on the fifteenth day of the fifth lunar month; the mid-autumn festival (*zhongqiu*), on the fifteenth day of the eighth lunar month; and new year's eve (*chuxi*). A short-term visitor gave the name of his lodging to the courtesan house, and the bill was collected before he left the city. This system seems to have worked at least up to the turn of the twentieth century, when it was still possible to verify a client's whereabouts. For the sake of discretion, the client could also send a servant to the house to pay outstanding debts at the accounting office.[40]

Clients who did not pay their debts and broke their implicit contractual agreements with the house were considered to have "set their bills adrift" (*piaozhang*). Their names quickly circulated among the courtesan establishments, and they were shunned.

The houses were increasingly run as modern business enterprises, with different types of investments as well as checks and balances. A courtesan who belonged to the madam of the house or was a business partner who did not own the house received a percentage of the income generated by her services. Houses made efforts to attract outstanding courtesans, who were called *keshi* (master guest) by the madam and referred to themselves as *huoji* (business partner). Courtesans going it alone were called "residents" (*zhujia*).[41]

The financial relationships among the madam, the courtesans, and the various

艾羅花露水

滬上發行之花露水多矣。而艾羅花露水。乃艾羅醫生所創製。以百花之液釀成。不特香氣穠郁。沾衣如麝。且盥洗時滴用少許。功能辟暑祛濕。有益衛生。臨卧時。於帳中洒用少許。一切臭穢之氣。化為烏有。出門人用之。兼能辟除瘴氣。誠非尋常花露水可比。每瓶價洋六角。購者希認瓶上艾羅仿單。庶不致誤。總發行上海三馬路中法大藥房。

*2.9. "Sights of Shanghai courtesan houses: Gathering mud, last year's swallow builds a new nest" (Shanghai quyuan zhi xianxiang: Xianni jiu yan lei xinwo). Lithograph. This courtesan is moving from one establishment to another. Note the wooden boards bearing the courtesans' names above the main entrances in the background. (*Tuhua ribao*, no. 297 [1910])*

types of servants were another possible point of conflict; as a consequence, many efforts were made at ritualizing and formalizing the core procedures. Although the relationship between the madam and the courtesan was clearly an economic and contractual one, it had many layers, with emotional attachment and social obligation playing important roles.[42] While the guides depict the hierarchy in the courtesan house as clearly established, the actual power dynamics rested on a series of checks, balances, and, above all, soothing rituals. Ritual became a potent means of maintaining the different levels of relationships in courtesan establishments in a manner that did not disturb their core purpose.[43]

As a courtesan was responsible only for contributing a set minimum to the house, the madam left her relatively free to devise her own strategies for promoting business. This arrangement fostered a spirit of ingenuity and independence among the courtesans and provided them with crucial business experience. In this way, they managed to acquire surprising levels of control over rituals in the Settlements, and the madams had little to say in these matters. Late Qing sources often mention (and complain about) the exceedingly high opinion the top courtesans seem to have had about themselves and the arrogance resulting from it.[44] The independence of these women was also reflected in the advertisements they placed in entertainment papers, announcing, for example, that they were buying their freedom and setting up their own businesses. Judging from the frequency of such advertisements, placed mostly on the front pages of *Entertainment*, events like this were no rarity.[45]

Foreign Courtesans and Prostitutes

Foreign prostitution and courtesan establishments had their own, more modest rituals. Personal writings as well as city and courtesan guides reveal that foreign women had worked in this field since the early days of the Foreign Settlements. Wang Tao writes that during the 1850s, Western prostitutes operated from boats on the Huangpu River near Hongkew and the American settlement. "If a Chinese is able to speak a bit of a foreign language [probably English], he can change his clothes [to Western clothing?] and go there. One visit is at most twenty dollars. These are truly beauties from the West. One should not be stingy and forfeit the experience of this wondrous fragrance [*qifen*]."[46]

The guides differentiate among Japanese geisha, Japanese prostitutes, and Western prostitutes and report in more detail on the Japanese establishments.[47] Accounts of emotional attachments between Chinese clients and foreign courtesans were often included alongside introductions to the particular ways of these establishments.

Encounter with the Japanese Geisha

There were two kinds of Japanese establishments: *yiji*, or those with geisha, and *seji*, or those with prostitutes. The geisha specialized in singing and dancing. One guide claims that although they were outstanding beauties, they were as cold as ice; nothing in their behavior suggested that they were in the courtesan business.[48] According to one guide, the first foreign prostitutes in the Settlements were Japanese. Like the Cantonese, they were active in the Hongkew area and were patronized by Westerners. In 1880, Sansheng Lou opened as a teahouse and Sino-Western restaurant and hired three Japanese geisha to serve tea. With this exotic feature, the place was an instant sensation. Many more such establishments then opened with Japanese geisha who had learned a few words of Chinese. Even Shanghai's Chinese courtesans were curious and asked their patrons to summon these Japanese geisha to serve at dinner parties so that they could see these newcomers for themselves.[49] By the mid-1880s, there were more Japanese geisha than Japanese prostitutes. Their services consisted of greeting the client and singing songs while playing the samisen.[50]

The most publicly accessible place for Japanese geisha entertainment was the Japanese Dongyang Chalou (Beauty, Satisfaction, and Long Life Teahouse) (fig. 2.10). Upon entering the teahouse, a customer would see numerous geisha from whom he could choose. After he had made his decision, he could select service in the common tearoom or in a private room, where a tea ceremony was performed. If the client did not finish the tea cakes, they were put into finely shaped boxes that were wrapped in beautiful paper so that he could take them away. The service in both rooms was the same but cost less in the common tearoom. The price for a private room was one silver dollar (Japanese *fannu*), and the tea came to one hundred copper coins. In the common room, tea cost one *sikaiyang* (a quarter of a dollar), and service was forty copper coins. If the geisha was not too busy, she would flirt with the client and provide musical entertainment.[51] The costume worn by these women, the flowing Japanese kimono with narrow sleeves, is described as close to the fashion of the Six Dynasties.[52] This range of service required no introduction.

There are records of strong emotional attachments between Chinese patrons and Japanese geisha. One story tells of Sansan, a geisha who came to Shanghai from Nagasaki in 1882 and was very popular. She was honored with the title "exotic flower." But as the story goes, she did not care about money and loved only the "master from the Settlements," Chengbei Gong, a Chinese man of letters, with whom she talked passionately about the meaning of certain Chinese characters. The signs of deep feeling between them were described in these words: "as incense was burning and tea was brewing, they would sit at leisure and gaze at each other speechlessly."[53] In the literati world, the love of learning rather than money was a well-established trope.

In a Japanese Brothel

Japanese prostitutes wore wide-sleeved garments and stood by the doors of their brothels. They usually offered only sex and did not sing or play musical instruments, although one guide notes that the Japanese geisha Huaxian, Dayu, Shanshan, and Lanxian were excellent singers and were also available for sex. Sexual services cost as little as two hundred coins.[54] The lower-ranking teahouses were in fact brothels, and the client could purchase sex as well as tea.[55] Tea cost one Japanese *bukui yang*, and sex one silver dollar. Zou Tao (1850–1931), who provides much precious information about the 1880s, considered this price very modest.[56] No introduction was needed to enter the "Japanese brothel" (*Riben jiguan*). A client could purchase sex

2.10. "Japanese teahouse" (Dongyang chalou). Lithograph. In this "Beauty, Satisfaction, and Long-life Teahouse," as in other such establishments, the price for Japanese-style tea, two jiao *per person, is written on the side of the door. Most of the clients are apparently Chinese, with the exception of a Japanese man seated at the left corner. (Dianshizhai,* Shenjiang shengjing tu, *1:24)*

even on his first visit. Entering the room of a lower-ranking prostitute "cost one silver dollar [*yangfu*]. If the client was a longtime customer, he could return to the house two or three times on the same day without being charged. Only when he came back on the next day did he have to pay again. But each time, he paid two *jiao* for the tea ceremony; this could not be avoided."[57]

Sexual services from a higher-ranking prostitute cost two silver dollars. This was the same price as having the courtesan accompany the client to the theater or to dinner parties, a service referred to as *shangju*. The Japanese women did not follow the practice of high-ranking Chinese courtesans who joined one client but then answered a call from another. Instead, they stayed with one client the entire time. These prostitutes accepted clients regardless of whether the men were known to them or not. There was therefore nothing inappropriate about hiring a few prostitutes at the same time. Unlike the Chinese system, arrangements for Japanese prostitutes permitted them to work simultaneously in different houses.

The language barrier reduced entertainment in the Japanese houses to the very basics, with the tea ceremony and simple musical performances as the main features. The more refined rituals and entertainments of the high-class geisha establishments were out of reach or beyond the comprehension of Chinese clients.[58]

Zou Tao, who seems to have spoken a little Japanese, reports that the Japanese women came mostly from Kobe, Nagasaki, and Osaka.

Visits to Western Houses

A Register of Shanghai Beauties (Haishang qunfang pu) also mentions Western establishments. In the early years, the 1860s, they were located north of Yangjing Bang. The Western prostitutes were said to be extremely bold and extravagant, and a Chinese client had to pay fifty dollars (*bing*) for a visit.[59]

These houses did not require introductions. The guidebook warns that the entertainment as well as the expected mode of behavior were very different from those of comparable Chinese houses. Upon entering, the client was served coffee with cake. A piece of uncut meat referred to as "big slabs of food" (*dacai*)—later a synonym for Western food—was often served cold and had to be handled with knife and fork. The dinner consisted of ten courses and was accompanied by the women playing music, singing, and dancing, which, in the guide's words, "could be very enjoyable." The only real cultural problem seems to have been the cool or cold bath with perfumed soap that was required for clients who wanted to have sex. This was mandatory for all customers, and in all seasons. One writer comments: "It must be said that Westerners have a hot constitution and are close to nature; Chinese, on the other hand, are very different, which makes it quite easy for them to get sick. Thus, after the first try, many among them will be afraid to return to this extraordinarily exotic place. Only the Cantonese love going there often."[60]

The biography of one of the American girls, Mei Feier (Mayfair?), includes the tale of a young Chinese who tells the story of Mei Feier and himself. He shows the narrator a glass print of a photograph of a beautiful young Western lady and a handsome young Chinese with happiness in their faces. "This is *the* famous Mei Feier with whom I was in love, and the young man is myself, years ago. Life is like a dream! Mei Feier has died, and I have abandoned the field of amorous affairs [*huanchang*]." When the narrator looks at the back of the picture, he is horrified to see a drawing of a skeleton embracing an emaciated client reclining on a Madame Recamier chaise longue. The words "One misstep turned into an eternal regret; when turning back, a hundred years have passed" are written along the side. The young man then says, "This world of love is but emptiness." The man used the two sides of the photograph to remind himself of this lesson.[61] The scene refers to a famous episode in *Dream of the Red Chamber*.[62]

Commercial Port City, Immigrant Society, and the Role of Ritual

The Shanghai courtesans' strong ritual control over their environment, described in these narratives, is confirmed by late Qing fiction in which courtesans figure prominently, such as Han Bangqing's *Biographies of Shanghai Flowers* (1892–94), Zou Tao's

The Shadows of Heaven and Earth in Shanghai (Haishang chentian ying; 1896), and Sun Yusheng's *Dreams of Shanghai's Glamour* (Haishang fanhua meng; 1903–6). These novels describe ritual play in detail, but the dominating figure is the brilliant or cunning Shanghai courtesan who engages in the game of courtship while she keeps her eye on business.[63] The nearly daily attention given to these top courtesans even in the most important daily of the time, *Shenbao*, shows the marked difference between them and the lower-ranking courtesans.[64]

One's view of the amount of control the top courtesans exercised over their business and the extent of their responsibility for initiating the ritual practices depends to a degree on one's perspective. Hershatter claims that the male customer was in control, yet courtesan houses operated very much as interactive and interdependent businesses. To assign absolute power to the madam or the client not only would be a gross simplification that disregards the prevalence of formal or ritualized contractual relations but also would reduce to an exceedingly primitive level the complexities of cultured "play" and its crucial importance for the success of the entertainment and thus for the entire enterprise. Ritual play was based on make-believe freedom of choice. The Settlements' top courtesans managed to create ritual capital for themselves that enabled them to match the financial capital of their clients. This constructed equality was a key attraction of their new-style entertainment. The courtesans were active agents in developing and enacting the ritualized new relationships and in promoting the notion that their services were professional entertainment. In this way, they wielded considerable power, while their clients' traditional cultural and social authority was inoperative in the Settlements environment. In addition, many clients were in the weak position of transient visitors who had to adapt to unpredictable rules. The *changsan* were not shy about the business aspect of their lives, referring to their entertainment service as "doing business" (*zuo shengyi*) and to themselves as "businesswomen" (*shengyi lang [shang] ren*).[65]

The courtesans' high degree of control over ritual does not imply that they were free or had taken up their profession voluntarily. Once a courtesan was in the business, however, Shanghai gave her the freedom to devise structures, such as rituals, that ensured both financial success and personal fame.

Once in place, the new ritual arrangement remained stable because the top courtesans supported its maintenance and enforcement inside the Settlements. Comparison of early records with city guides from the 1930s and 1940s shows very little change over time.[66] In the late Qing, *The Illustrated Daily* (Tuhua ribao) devoted an entire column of detailed, illustrated literary reportage to these rituals; it depicts the main body of these rituals as intact with only minor changes.[67] In this case, preserving the rituals might have been a conservative business strategy for adjusting to new circumstances. As Shanghai grew into a cosmopolitan industrial center in the twentieth century, and with the rise of the movie industry and its film stars, Shanghai courtesans maintained the attractiveness of their entertainment by embodying the "old tradition" much as the geisha do in modern Japan.[68] The courtesans' pivotal role in keeping the soft-tuned southern *kun* opera tradition (*kunqu*) alive in Shanghai supports this view.[69]

The Business of Love and Its Emotional Cost

The protective ritual frame in which the Shanghai courtesan staged her business of love suggests the potential for emotional stress and strain in her work. As has often been noted, the predominance of male voices in the transmission of tradition makes it difficult to document the thoughts and feelings of women. However, a very rare and hitherto overlooked source, a collection of courtesan letters, helps to remedy this deficit, at least in part. These letters are included in the 1898 courtesan guidebook *An Illustrated Introduction to Shanghai Entertainment* (Haishang youxi tushuo) under the title "Letters by Famous Shanghai Courtesans" (Haishang minghua chidu). The twenty-five undated letters include three written by Shanghai courtesans to courtesans living and working elsewhere, ten to clients who had left Shanghai, four from clients who had left Shanghai, three from Shanghai courtesans to other Shanghai courtesans who had traveled to other places (usually other treaty ports) to try their luck, two from courtesans elsewhere writing to Shanghai courtesans, and a letter from a Shanghai client to a *changsan* courtesan along with her reply. Some might have been written by professional letter writers, but there are clear indications that some are from a courtesan's own hand, as one of the responses expresses delight at seeing her handwriting.[70]

These letters resist any attempt to create a simplistic and unified scenario of the courtesan's life and emotions. Even though they are not representative in any statistical sense, and much of the language contains familiar stock phrases, these letters nonetheless reveal the courtesan's concerns as expressed in her own voice.

The emotional cost of being a courtesan looms large in these letters. Lin Daiyu, one of the four grand courtesans of Shanghai, wrote to a Lady Green Lute, Lüqin Nüshi, who was residing in east Hangzhou, about her own loneliness upon being without a home or a lover. The context of the letter suggests that the recipient was a Shanghai courtesan who had married. In the title given by the editor, Lin is referred to by an honorific used frequently for Shanghai courtesans, "beautiful eyebrow historian" (*meishi*), and her correspondent, who has left the courtesan business, is called "lady historian" (*nüshi*). The print in the 1898 guidebook reproduces the very formal graphic layout of the letter, which is patterned on memorials written to the court. In these memorials, a new line starts each time the court is mentioned. The line beginnings have three levels: the lowest is for referring to oneself, the middle is for the dynasty or a member of the imperial family with a rank such as prince, and the highest is for the emperor. The arrangement is reproduced below using indents.

> In [my] fond memory, since
> [you] departed [in fall] as the blossoms of the chrysanthemums burst
> forth by the fence to this day [in early spring] when [I] receive your letter
> as the plum blossoms open on the hills, a myriad strands of
> feelings have bound us together although a long journey lay between
> us, [I] wish,

Your Excellency, [my] beautiful and virtuous older sister, may be adorned with high standing and may enjoy (Heaven's) protection!

[You] have [now] moved into the chambers [of a wife].

[Even] with simple cloth and thorn hairpins, [yours] is a place where the heart loathes the loud luxuries [of being in Shanghai as a courtesan];

[Even when] pulling the cart [yourself] and drawing up the water jar [yourself], [yours] is a homestead where the body rests in peaceful bliss.

Older sister, as [you] are happy to have a family, how could I not congratulate you?

As for me, the worries of spring just over, I am already discarded like a fan in fall. I left the Han waters [Yangzhou] lightheartedly but arrived [back] in Shanghai with a heavy heart. The sisters who had in former days been in the gay houses have vanished like stars in the morning light. I sigh that my life should be so unfortunate, adrift in endless trouble. Looking back, all seems like a dream. But what is the use of regret? Even if I return [to Yangzhou?], I no longer have a home. Furthermore, to stay too long at a place that is not home is no solution in the long run. So I resolved to find a temporary shelter to at least get out of the wind and rain. At the third watch, however, the cold moon glances from the sky on my solitary sleep, and the cock crowing in the early morning only increases my sadness. When life has come to this, you can guess my feelings. I have time and again thought to disappear into the door of emptiness [of Buddhism] and to redeem the sins I have committed in another life, but the sisters have strenuously remonstrated with me, saying that as the Buddha's notion of repentance in the end belongs to nothingness, how could it make undone what we already have done? Even if I decide to marry, in theory this is an urgent matter, but in practice it should not be done hastily. I do not know what karma still awaits me on the rocks of past, present, and future. Therefore all I can do is to wash away all the makeup, stop dreaming about the untenable, and calmly wait for the one who is fated for me. After love is established, only then can I leave my vocation.

I recall the flowering mornings and moonlit evenings when with the incense of the candles fading away I was sitting together with you, my virtuous older sister, and we were sharing our secrets contemplating and discussion [of life's] bitter and happy [moments]. While it has been only one year, it is as though we are in another epoch.

I hope I can steal [some luck] from providence, so that there is a possibility of my meeting you again. [After all,] the water of the river and the drifting cloud have their own way of going and returning. I only hope [you] take care. Furthermore, please eat a bit more. If you can manage, I beg to hear from *you* [again]. I wish *you* peace in the women's domain.[71]

The letter reflects the strong bonds within the courtesan profession that are also seen in other such correspondences. It is dominated by the question of the long-term prospects of courtesan life. This was a profession for the young. A courtesan needed to secure a future for herself while she was young and attractive. Marriage was the respectable way out. Lin Daiyu married several times but eventually returned to her old profession. As the standard story went, she resorted to marriage as a way to clear her debts.[72] In the letter, she responds to advice from other courtesans urging her to try to get married by emphasizing the difficulty of this endeavor. As she puts it, she could only trust fate to help her find the man of her heart. Lin Daiyu was a very capable entrepreneur and among the first courtesans to stage herself as a star; she remained in the business for most of her life. The stakes were high, however, and so was the emotional cost. As the letter shows, the life of a professional courtesan could be extremely lonely, especially as other women with whom she had started out and who had become close to her married and moved away.

The question of the future also dominated other Shanghai courtesan letters. Wang Shanbao asked another courtesan, Zhou Yueqin, who had married, to help her find out more about a client who was waiting for an official post and had proposed marriage. She was to be a concubine, she informed her friend, but this should still be regarded as a noble act on the client's part since it would result in a change in her life circumstances comparable to "the sudden shift from being in the ten thousand *zhang* of the fire pit to being amidst clear and cool [tranquility]." As for becoming only a concubine, she declared that it was still better than remaining in the "filthy [world] of 'mist and flowers' [prostitution]."[73] Although the terms used are standard tropes, they nonetheless convey Wang Shanbao's genuine desire to leave her profession. She sought very specific help from her friend. She wanted Zhou Yueqin to talk to her husband, who was acquainted with the suitor, and ask him about this man's character and trustworthiness. Wang Shanbao had met this client not long ago, and they had fallen in love at first sight, but as he belonged to the world of officials, she had no way of checking his background.

The suitor's reliability was of great importance. Courtesans were not inexperienced young girls; they were accustomed to luxury and entertainment. If Wang Shanbao married a scoundrel who might not have the means to support her, it would cause her more suffering. The courtesan Chen Yuqing mentioned in her reply to Li Peilan's letter that although Li's desire to get married was commendable, "nowadays young men are so pompous and unsubstantial that one has to be on one's guard."[74]

The issue of emotional attachment between courtesan and client was another dominant theme. Time and again, these letters mention the distress that accompanied separation. A letter from Zhu Wenqing to her client-lover He Lifu, for example, shows the courtesan overwhelmed by the suffering of separation. It reads:

> Lifu, Your Excellency, [my] kind older brother, two months we have been living together, our love closer than bone and flesh; spending the days and nights together, our feelings and desires were united. Unfortunately you had to depart so suddenly;

> this took *me* completely by surprise. The few words you said to me before leaving made me sob uncontrollably; inside, I was cut
> to pieces, so much so that all I wanted was to stay the reins of your carriage. After I saw you off to the steamship, I broke down, tears streaming. Because I was afraid of being laughed at by the bystanders, I could not "thrice sing [Wang Wei's farewell song] Yangguan"
> for you and personally hand you the horsewhip. In fact I am so overwhelmed by darkness that my swollen eyes are like those of Ping'er [a character in *Dream of the Red Chamber*]. After you left, I sat alone in my shadow and could neither eat nor sleep in peace. When I recall
> *your* voice and your looks, sadness wells up in me. Our love connects us with ten thousand threads; I am pining away. [I tell myself,] do not dream where the thousand mountains [separating us] might again interlock; another time if
> we meet with good fortune, we will again resume our destiny set in our previous lives. You should know, however, that this unfortunate person looks haggard in the mirror from grief for
> your sake. When [I] do not see my beloved, a single day is like three autumns. The colors of spring are disturbing me; I am feeling so weak that I might be getting ill.
> My older brother, how are you these days? Please let me know in detail the situation after your return so as to forestall this young girl's longing thoughts. I especially wish
> Your wife's well-being. If you are not offered an office, could I dare hope you will come [back] here?[75]

The expression of emotional attachment seems to imply the desire for marriage, although it is quite clear that the would-be official already has a wife. Since at the time most marriages were arranged by parents and took place when the future bride and groom were still teenagers, very few young men of good family would still be unmarried when they traveled to Shanghai.

In another message, the courtesan mentioned that she was very much comforted by the love letter she had received from her client and saw it as auspicious that he had asked her to send him her photograph.

> You have asked for my photograph; a short while ago I still had twelve prints in my house, but they have all been snatched away by others at one time or another. But as you honored me with your love, I will certainly try to relieve you of your suffering [of missing me] with my unworthy looks by going especially to the Xinchang [photography] studio and ordering the photograph to be reproduced and enlarged to three inches. . . . I am only afraid that after we reconnect in our love, you will be surprised that the bloom has gone from [my] face, as in longing for you, I have lost weight and my face has become haggard.[76]

She ended the letter with the news that she would be moving and would write to him once she had settled into her new place. Although he is not there with her, business goes on as usual, and other clients are snatching up her photographs. She also tells him that she envies a courtesan, who had debts "like a mountain" and "left the bitter sea" by running off with a client and could not be found.

The collection also contains love letters from clients to courtesans. In one, the client wrote that after returning to Suzhou, he longingly recalled how he and the courtesan spent the last spring together and could think of nothing but her with the return of spring. The last spring had been full of love, but this spring, there were only tears. He went on to write that she surely must be weeping, too, and told her that he was waiting for a letter.[77] Another correspondent apologized for his tardy letter and explained that there was so much business waiting for him when he got home that he had only just found a quiet moment in which to write. He thanked the courtesan for bestowing her favors on him, a person of no real talent (using terms that recall Jia Baoyu in *Dream of the Red Chamber*). The honor was all the greater because she was such a famous courtesan. With the letter, he sent a present of two rolls of silk and two earthen jars of wine-pickled eggs and asked her to confirm that she had received them so that he would not worry.[78] The question of marriage never comes up in these letters from clients; instead, they stress love and longing.

The close connection between love and business comes through in some of the letters. The amorous affair was part of the courtesan's business, and at times it was merely the outer form of a business transaction. A letter written by Zhu Moqing to a former client who had returned to Suzhou says:

> After your departure from Shanghai, winter arrived quickly; chilling weather was brought by snow and wind, and business gradually dwindled. Earlier you had told me that you would be back soon, so I waited in my house for you and gazed anxiously till I could not strain my eyes any further. But as you did not show up, I came to the conclusion that you must have been very busy and could not spare the time.
>
> [But] the desires of spring among the empty covers quite wear me down. Before you left, your bill for dinner parties and other sundry costs had come to fifty-four dollars. You agreed that once you had reached Suzhou you would pay the bill. My own debts are like a mountain, and furthermore I have very little savings and am not able to advance the money to the house on your behalf. At the same time, the madam has been mumbling about this debt of yours day and night to my unending distress. I hope, my older brother, once you receive this letter, you will for my sake do all you can to raise this money and send it, so that I, the ill-fated [young woman], will not have to suffer on your account without cause.[79]

Courtesans often used letters to collect past-due debts from their clients. In one such letter, the courtesan was rather sarcastic about a Shanghai client. He appeared, she wrote, to have enjoyed himself so much in her bed that he should at least be willing to pay his debts. She sent her old servant with this letter to collect the money.[80]

Business opportunities were another big topic in these letters. Inquiries were addressed to Shanghai courtesans who had traveled to other treaty ports, with Hankow being the most frequently mentioned place.[81]

These letters fit within the literary conventions and letter-writing formulas common at the time, yet they nonetheless offer a lively picture of the courtesans' emotions and concerns and at the same time reveal their pragmatism and business acumen. The courtesans explained their situation in life as fated. Collectively, they adopted a language that conveys their wish to leave their stressful circumstances; however, entertainment newspapers reported at this very time that many Shanghai courtesans who had married were ending their marriages and returning to the city to resume their old profession. The reasons varied, but the difficulties they experienced as concubines living in close quarters with extended families and under the control of first wives seem to have outweighed those of being courtesans in Shanghai.

Securing Divine Assistance

The courtesan translated her anxiety about her uncertain fate into many efforts to gain divine assistance. Courtesan holidays often coincided with religious festivities. The seasonal rituals conducted in entertainment houses frequently imitated or simulated those of regular households in an effort to convey a sense of normalcy. These conventional celebrations were also the moments during which the courtesans were most acutely reminded of the contrast between their life and the lives of other women with husbands, children, and homes. Although some had consciously chosen this life, they felt the pangs of deprivation and loneliness at such moments, and their rituals helped to provide some psychological succor.

One of the main courtesan rituals was "offering incense at the crossroads" (*shao lutou*), performed to worship "the God of Wealth coming from the five roads" (*wulu caishen*); it was also known as "receiving the God of Wealth" (*jie caishen*). The service, during which paper money was burned for the god, was usually performed in courtesan houses when debts were being paid, when a courtesan moved to a new establishment, or on a courtesan's birthday (fig. 2.11). This ritual thus might be performed as often as once a month. If business was good, the courtesans offered thanks; if not, they prayed for future prosperity. If a courtesan had just moved or was marking her birthday, she would pray for good fortune. For these occasions, clients were supposed to hold banquets at the courtesans' houses. The houses would be filled with well-wishers, and the parties often continued through the night. The *shao lutou* ceremony was divided into two days. The first day, when the house was cleared of all music playing, was known as *qing lutou*, and incense and paper money were burned. Each courtesan burned her own pair of large incense sticks on the worshiping altar, and after midday, she took them back to her own room along with some ashes from the main cauldron as an omen of good business. Music rang out the next day, which made it the day of *xiang lutou*. The courtesans did not sing on this day; instead,

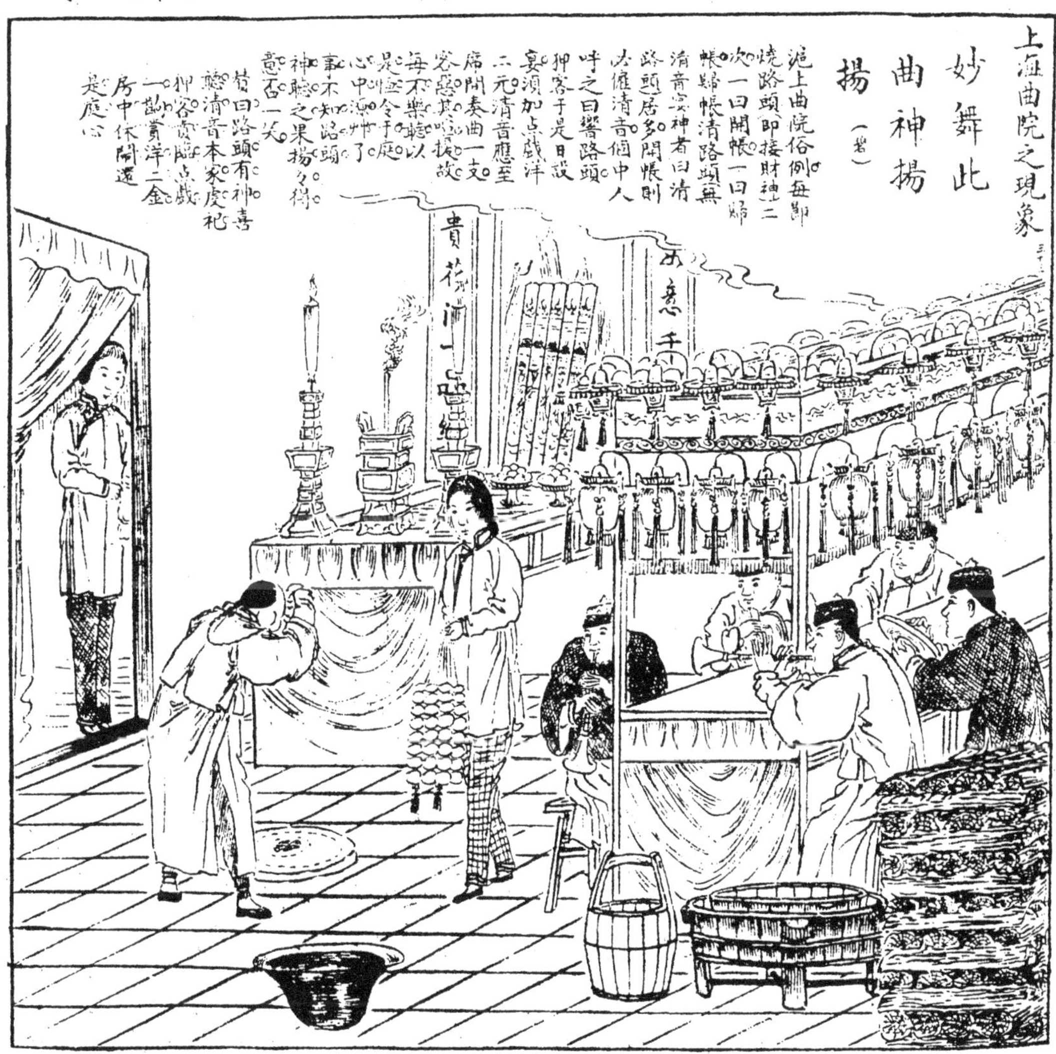

2.11. *"Sights of Shanghai courtesan houses: If this is well performed, the god will be elated" (Shanghai quyuan zhi xianxiang: Miao wu ci qushen yangyang). Lithograph. The* shao lutou *ritual linked an appeal to the God of Wealth with the collection of debts, indicating the courtesans' uneasiness regarding their clients' financial reliability. (*Tuhua ribao, *no. 262 [1910])*

the house hired four musicians, and guests could request performances of their choice of operas. If there were no guests, the courtesans chose their own favorite operas for the musicians to play in the evening. This was called "cleaning up the room" (*sao fangjian*).

The courtesans also frequented the city's temples. One major place of worship was Chenghuang Temple in Shanghai, the temple of the city god, but they also went to other temples, depending on their regional background. During the 1870s, the city's Suzhou courtesans worshiped at Shi Temple in the walled city, while the Cantonese courtesans worshiped the god housed in Hong Temple (also known as Situ Temple).[82] By the 1890s, Yi Temple had become the preferred temple of the Suzhou courtesans, and, by the beginning of the twentieth century, the sites of worship also included the wall altar of the God of Wealth on the Rue du Whampoo, which went by the Chinese name of Yanghang Jie, or Road of the Foreign Companies (fig. 2.12).[83] Courtesans also observed various religious rituals in their homes (fig. 2.13). During their worship, they would ask for fortune sticks (*qiuqian*), and would take home the messages for their clients to interpret.

In the 1890s, the practice of "reciting (precious) scrolls" (*xuanjuan*) became popular in courtesan houses (fig. 2.14). For this ritual, an establishment hired five or six reciters, who chanted from dawn to dusk, seated in a circle and dressed in nondescript garb that seemed neither Daoist nor Buddhist to contemporary elite observers.[84] Buddhist icons were included among various other objects of worship. This ritual was generally performed for birthdays or when a courtesan was sick.

Most of the early guides noted the Shanghai courtesans' passion for praying in temples. The new city was unsettling for most, but it must have been even more so for the courtesans, since their subsistence depended on their success as professional women in an ill-defined realm. The gods to whom they prayed were related in one way or another to the God of Wealth. As women who worked outside a traditional family structure, and who often found themselves in uneasy emotional and social situations, they might have felt the need for a particular kind of heavenly support. Finding patrons who might become husbands seems to have been a dominant motif in their prayers. Appeals to the deities must have appeared as the one sure way of finding real, long-term prospects through their professional specialty of emotional engagement.

The rituals of the Shanghai courtesans developed over time. Some were rooted in older practices, but new rituals arose to define the courtesan hierarchy that began to develop in the Foreign Settlements. Comparison of the early depictions of the 1850s and 1860s by Yao Xie and Wang Tao with the narratives and handbooks of the later Qing period makes clear that the basic routines and rituals were established during the 1860s and 1870s after the courtesans moved to the Settlements. The early bamboo twig ballads offer insight into some of this process. Writers such as Zou Tao and the illustrated Shanghai courtesan and city guides provide much information on the 1880s. The new rituals and routines in the Foreign Settlements also included some direct imports from the Western lifestyle, such as riding in an open carriage.[85]

日光月光鐵丸之妙用

日光鐵丸。治男子先天不足。後天失調。血分大虧。神經受損。肌體尪瘠。筋骨痠疼。以及元陽虛弱。嗣續艱難。一切。月光鐵丸。治婦女體氣衰弱。經水不調。血漏血崩。五色帶下。並抑鬱多病。艱於孕育症。二丸俱有奇效。中上海中法藥房。及各埠中法藥房。發行。每瓶價洋一元二角。

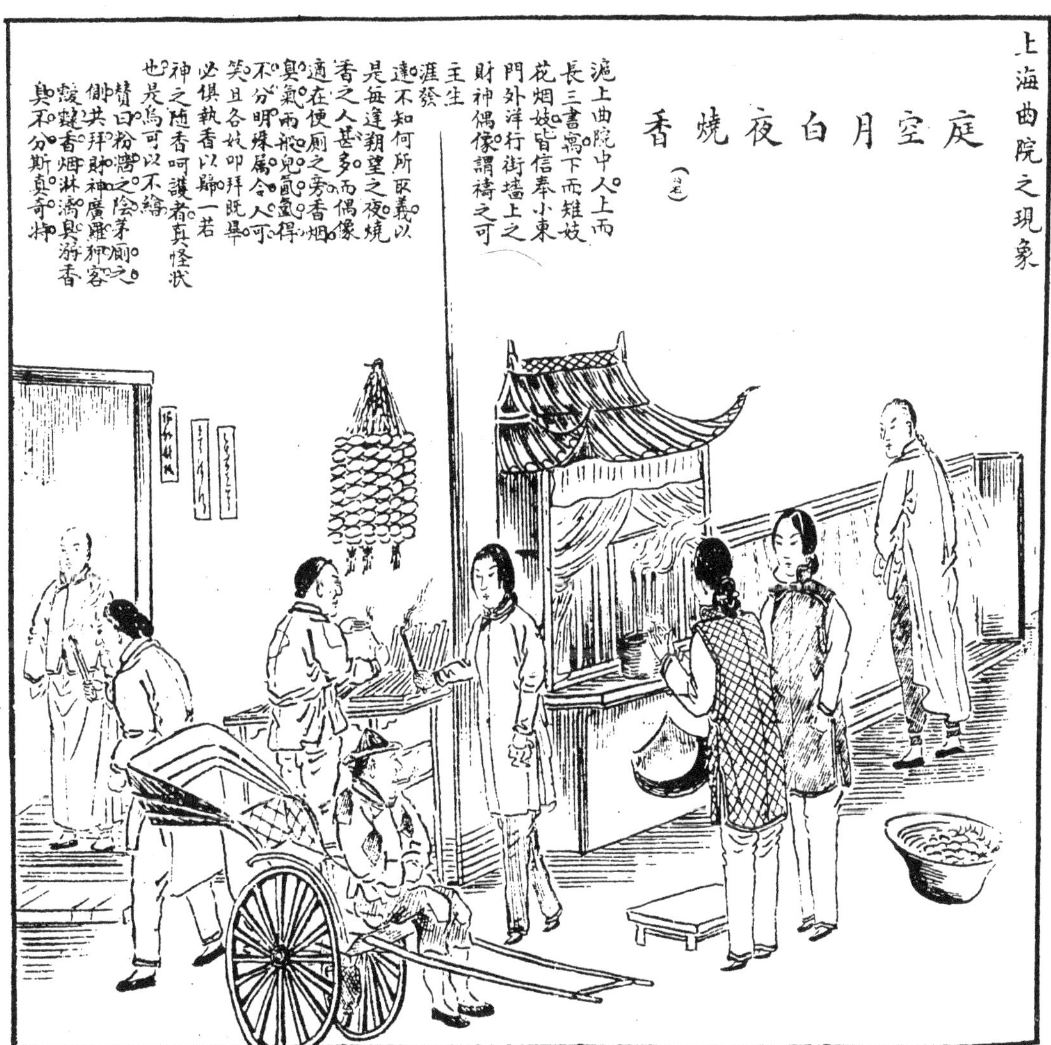

2.12. *"Sights of Shanghai courtesan houses: When the sky is empty or the moon is full, incense is burned at night" (Shanghai quyuan zhi xianxiang: Ting kong yue bai ye shao xiang). Lithograph. At the wall altar to the God of Wealth in the French Settlement, the class differentiation between courtesans and lower-ranking streetwalkers (*yeji*) breaks down as the incense is shared by all. The site of worship is next to an open public toilet, making the place quite a combination of sights and smells. (*Tuhua ribao*, no. 251 [1910])*

2.13. *"Sights of Shanghai courtesan houses: Moon on the ground, clouds as steps, pray to the immortals from the [heavenly] caves" (Shanghai quyuan zhi xianxiang: Yue di yun jie bai dongxian). Lithograph. This ritual on the nights of the new moon and full moon (*shuowang*) was aimed at better business opportunities. All courtesans of the house had to participate in order to bring about the desired effect. Incense, three fresh eggs, smoked tofu, and sesame seed cakes were offered to the god. (*Tuhua ribao*, no. 96 [1910])*

永濟堂治毒章程

本堂延醫設局送診下疳諸瘡結毒魚口便毒淋濁等症以補諸善堂之未備歷有多年茲因他醫治療不善愈後常時復發久不收功之症殊多爲此另增各種靈藥謹將病 列后 一治毒攻巔頂頭痛如劈朝夕不安 一治毒攻頸項形如瘰癧 一治毒攻頭面破腦穿鼻 一治毒攻咽喉白腐痛爛不能進食 一治毒攻四肢骨節擊痛成爲梅瘋艱於步履 一治毒攻身上燥則如癬 一治毒攻肌肉周身紅瘢 一治毒攻肛門沿肛痔瘡癢不可忍 一治毒攻陰囊濕癢出水以及潰爛不斂 一治毒攻筋骨色白堅腫形如陰疽 一治毒攻玉莖久爛不斂龜頭生瘰形如雞冠花 一治毒攻手足層々起皮致患鵝掌瘋 一治魚口便毒成管久不收功 以上上諸症如百治不效可至本堂請林君渭川醫生治之 一如煎藥不便本堂派人代煎限時赴堂飲服

上海三馬路胡家宅寶和里衖馬路朝北石庫門內便是

永濟堂董事 黄育麟 楊燕貽 周兆水 張渠卿 全啟

2.14. *"Sights of Shanghai courtesan houses: The red candle brings back the shadow, and the immortal's apparition comes near" (Shanghai quyuan zhi xianxiang: Hongzhu ying hui xian tai jin). Lithograph. This ritual took place in the courtesan house although the courtesans were not directly involved in the ceremony. The patron was expected to show his devotion to his favorite courtesan by giving a dinner party that evening.* (Tuhua ribao, *no. 264 [1910]*)

Ritual development was closely linked to growing demand for courtesan entertainment. The refinement of the rituals was a response to the steep increase in male newcomers, often wealthy and cultured, to the Settlements.[86] The top courtesans could afford to be more selective and tended to strengthen their ritual protection. The greater demand for high-level courtesan entertainers and prostitutes created the need for a clearer definition of ranks and the services associated with them; this need was especially evident for the top-ranking *shuyu* and *changsan*. The *changsan* also sought to elevate their professional position above that of the *yaoni*, so as to compete with the *shuyu*. By the 1890s, they had achieved this goal.[87]

The rituals, which defined the roles of all participants and their abstract means of enforcement, signaled the new identity assumed by the top courtesans in the Settlements in silently encoding situational equality between courtesan and client and greatly restricting the latter's leeway. They might be read as the courtesans' efforts to assert their own powers by increasing their ritual control over their environment and especially over their clients. The power of these ritualized relationships—which are different from religious ritual, with its assumed automatic powers, and from the less consciously constructed rituals of everyday life—came from their social acceptance as well as from their capacity to shield the fiction of romantic love from the potentially unpleasant onslaught of harsher realities. Although realities continued to assert themselves, the courtesans tried to regulate the conflict-ridden and socially untidy structure through rituals. Economic relationships in the courtesan business relied heavily on informal means of enforcement, not only because the entertainment business was legally ill-defined, but also, as Henriot has pointed out, because its success depended on providing ease and pleasure without disturbing clients with monetary matters.[88]

This set of rituals distinctly inscribed itself into the relative stability of the Shanghai Foreign Settlements environment. The open city space, which allowed for public entertainment and performance, demanded ritualized defenses and provided the option for new forays. The courtesans pioneered emulation of Western women and their much freer public manners and gradually made this behavior fashionable among Chinese women of style.[89]

While the Settlements milieu, which shielded all Chinese residents from the magistrate's and *daotai*'s interventions, was necessary for the flourishing of Shanghai courtesan entertainment, the cultural and social acceptance of new routines and rituals was of equal importance.

Chinese immigrants to Shanghai brought their regional cultural habits and preferences with them and entered into social networks that often had a strong regional character. At the same time, they were highly aware that they had entered a setting unparalleled in its urban and Western character and its political institutions. Their willingness to accept the rules of the new place and to assume new roles within it is visible in the ease with which the Municipal Council's rules and regulations were adopted. The city gradually imposed urban styles of behavior and social networks determined more by professional ties and less by regional affiliation.[90] The rituals of the courtesan house did not have the authority of the official traffic rules enforced by fierce-looking Sikh policemen, yet they were part of the exotic and fascinating otherness of Shanghai.[91]

Certainly, in the real life and business of the Shanghai courtesan, her clients' wealth and power continuously spilled over into attempts to attain unchallenged control over her. Madams constantly tried to squeeze more money out of even the top courtesans, nor did they sit idly by when one of their best performers went off to set up her own establishment. Finally, the courtesans did not fail to vie with one another over the most prosperous and elegant clients. Their ritual constructs must be read against this background as attempts to guard the core of the entertainment business from such disturbing conflicts, to secure its success, and to reflect the new status of the top-ranking courtesans in the Foreign Settlements.

The great variety and continuous production of Shanghai courtesan handbooks make the city a unique phenomenon among urban centers on Chinese soil. The courtesan records written during the seventeenth to mid-nineteenth centuries were mostly written in *biji* style and were modeled after the early Qing work on courtesan entertainment in late Ming Nanjing, *Random Notes on the [Pleasure Quarters by the] Wooden Bridge* (Banqiao zaji), by Yu Huai (1616–1696). These works, however, consist largely of biographies of courtesans, poems written by clients for particular courtesans, and courtesan addresses. There are no elaborate descriptions of roles, rituals, and proper behavior, especially for clients.[92] While rituals most likely existed, they were either considered too trivial or too familiar to warrant description.[93] The Shanghai guidebooks, in contrast, assumed that the reader needed this knowledge, which was otherwise inaccessible to him, and held out the hope that he might not make a fool of himself in this strange city if he bought a copy. At the same time, the entertainment, information, and gossip contained in these books made them attractive to other readers, including women.

3 *Playground Shanghai*

Reenacting *Dream of the Red Chamber*

In the new courtesan hierarchy that developed in the Foreign Settlements, the highest ranks had elevated themselves to the status of professional cultural entertainers and reset the ritualized client-courtesan relationship to reflect the enhanced stature of the top courtesans and the insecurities of clients who were newcomers to this foreign environment. Within the framework of the developing rituals, a variety of richer and more specific scenarios played out. The Foreign Settlements, with their wealth and exoticism, could be conceptualized as a shielded place for love. Exploiting the tensions between traditional assumptions about entertainment and Shanghai's open pursuit of moneymaking, the Shanghai courtesan played the game of simulating tradition and modernity at the same time. Within the openness of an immigrant society, the courtesans—in an unplanned, collective, and contradictory process—explored the effectiveness of a variety of theatrical strategies. From early on, the creative energy of the top courtesans seems to have settled upon a master scenario that linked all these aspects together. It was drawn from the novel *Dream of the Red Chamber* (Honglou meng), by Cao Xueqin.

Donning a Name, Playing a Role

Courtesans, adopting the fashion for pen names among men of letters, took professional names for themselves. With these names, which often alluded to a past beauty praised in a poem, each sought to indicate to herself and to potential clients the woman she wanted to be. The names were thus a program for self-staging. A courtesan would change her name if she set out to stage herself as a different persona. The same time span that encompasses the shift in hierarchy and ritual also includes a sudden, dramatic shift in the names adopted by courtesans.

From the 1860s and well into the twentieth century, it was the fashion among Shanghai courtesans to adopt the name—or elements of the name—of one of the characters in *Dream of the Red Chamber*. Five courtesan handbooks for the Foreign Settlements published between 1861 and 1892 provide precious evidence. Baoyu Sheng's *Poetry in Couplets Found among the Flowers* (Huajian yingtie), of 1861, presents ten chapters containing a collection of poetry couplets written for courtesans. The pen name Baoyu Sheng, with the "Baoyu" from Jia Baoyu, indicates the author's affinity to *Dream of the Red Chamber*. In the first two chapters, he lists 108 such couplets together with the names of the courtesans. The book begins with four dedications to a courtesan called Baoyu, the first known use by a courtesan of a full name from *Dream of the Red Chamber*. An additional 29 names have one character that relates to the main characters of the novel, among them 12 with *yu* and 6 with *bao*. This means that about 27 percent of the names have elements derived from *Dream*.[1] Wang Tao's *A Supplement to "Record of Visits to Courtesan Houses in a Distant Corner by the Sea"* (*Haizou yeyou* fulu), with a preface dated 1873, contains 60 courtesan biographies; 32, or more than half, of those courtesans took parts of their professional names from the names of the women in *Dream*, with one, Hu Baoyu, again adopting the name of the young male protagonist.[2] Among the 12 victorious participants in the courtesan competition he documented, 6 had such elements in their names. Wang Tao's 1878 second sequel, *Appendix to "Record of Visits to Courtesan Houses in a Distant Corner by the Sea"* (*Haizou yeyou lu* yulu), has the biographies of 23 courtesans, among whom 10 took one or two characters in their names from *Dream*.[3] Of the 100 courtesans listed in the 1884 *Register of Shanghai Flowers* (Haishang qunfang pu), 5 took their full names and another 26 took parts of their names from the women in *Dream*, resulting in a proportion just below a third.[4] Of the 122 courtesans with biographies in the *Illustrated Record of Shanghai Courtesan Entertainment* (Haishang qinglou tuji), published in 1892, 8 took their full personal names and another 21 took one element of their names from *Dream*.[5] In other words, between 25 percent and 50 percent of the top Shanghai courtesans in the Foreign Settlements of the period were signaling a link between themselves and the personae in *Dream*.

Wang Tao's earlier *Record of Visits to Courtesan Houses in a Distant Corner by the Sea* (Haizou yeyou lu), with a preface dated 1860, deals only with courtesans in the walled city of Shanghai. His thirty-nine biographies may be used to determine whether this fashion predated the courtesans' move to the Foreign Settlements. Not one courtesan took her full name from *Dream*, and only 4, that is 10 percent, used elements from the novel in their names. While later courtesan guides contain biographies of courtesans whose names do not allude to the women in *Dream* but nevertheless include anecdotal evidence of their familiarity, if not obsession, with the novel, Wang Tao's *Record of Visits* does not offer even this kind of supplementary evidence.[6] Furthermore, a check of nineteenth-century courtesan biographies for other towns such as Beijing, Canton, Nanjing, Suzhou, and Yangzhou shows that courtesans there did not take names from *Dream*. The fashion thus was particular to the Shanghai Foreign Settlements.[7] The decisive indicator of the new scenario is the use of elements of Baoyu's name. With the increase in novel-related names, elements that had been popular in courtesan names in the Shanghai walled city during the preceding decades, such as *fu* (happiness), *xi* (joyous), *jin* (gold), *feng* (peacock), and *xian* (immortal), receded. In other words, there is clear, hard evidence that since the 1870s, it was a particular fashion among courtesans in the Shanghai Foreign Settlements to suggest with their professional names that they staged their personae in the context of *Dream.* This cries out for an explanation.

Role-playing by assuming the personae of famous lovers of the past or of characters from romance novels, plays, or poems was part of both ritualized flirtation and courtesan entertainment in many parts of the world. In Edo Japan, geisha often turned to novels such as *The Tale of Genji* in their attempts to create playful settings for encounters with their clients. They tried to evoke a world of fantasy and wonder, completely separate from the familiar world of their clients' daily lives.[8] Similarly, throughout the seventeenth and eighteenth centuries, the nobles of western and central Europe were inspired to reenact the Arcadian "shepherd and shepherdess" love scenario of the pastoral novel *L'Astrée*, by Honoré d'Urfé (1568–1625). The role-play took place in the make-believe Arcadia of their gardens and parks, and the festivities sometimes lasted for weeks. *L'Astrée* also inspired an endless series of translations, sequels, and imitations.

Wang Tao writes that role-playing was an integral part of Chinese courtesan behavior; in his own words, "'Playing the game according to the occasion' has been highly fashionable among the courtesans" (Fengchang zuoxi, yi shengchuan yu goulan zhong).[9] While the complex relationship between play and business was always present, the double roles of performer and businesswoman were compartmentalized by the rituals governing the courtesan's professional life. The courtesans received strict professional training when they were young girls. Apart from the obvious skills of singing, playing the *pipa*, and conversation, they had to be prepared to act as companions on different types of social occasions. Their lessons included the art of moving their eyes, mouths, faces, and bodies so that they could vary their roles and entice potential clients.[10] Their training enabled them to act in ways that fit a given situation.

The traditional master narrative into which Chinese courtesans inscribed their relations with their clients had been the "talented scholar and beautiful lady" trope that informs many Qing love novels. Although *Dream of the Red Chamber* has been justly described, since Lu Xun's *History of Chinese Literature* (1925), as the highest achievement of this tradition, it attained its position by radically rejecting many of the genre's orthodox foundations. By choosing to play out characters from *Dream*, the top courtesans wrote themselves into a high and familiar cultural register and at the same time claimed the freedom to do something utterly unorthodox and new.

Dream of the Red Chamber *as the New Shanghai Scenario*

What made *Dream of the Red Chamber* so special and so fitting for the new situation? Cao Xueqin's novel was the most widely read and, above all, the most highly admired novel in the late nineteenth and early twentieth centuries. It relates the story of a group of young women, most prominent among them the frail Lin Daiyu, and one young man, Jia Baoyu. They are all related through family ties. Shielded from the worries of the world and oblivious of the slow decay of their family, they live in seclusion in Daguan Yuan (Great Prospect Garden). This garden is described as the "peach [blossom] garden beyond the confines of the common world" (*shiwai tao yuan*), an allusion to the idyllic and peaceful land of peach blossoms described by the poet Tao Yuanming (365–427). Daguan Yuan is a place of love and peace. There are no visible structures of authority, and the young people living there treat one another as equals, disregarding gender and hierarchical differences. They live with their maids in different parts of the garden in dwellings endowed with poetic names. Each young woman has a distinct character, personality, and fate, offering the reader a wide spectrum of possible identifications. Jia Baoyu also chooses to live in Daguan Yuan since he cannot bear to be separated from his female relatives. The only pursuit in this garden is of *qing*—sublime love, in all its complexity and intricateness. It enters into the protagonists' names through puns, such as *qing* (an honorific) and *qing* (sublime love) or *yu* (jade) and *yu* (desire) and finds expression in the poetic outbursts of the highly gifted residents of the garden.

Jia Baoyu's commitment to "true emotions" (*zhenqing*) and his rebellion against the traditional Confucian career path set out for him made him into a much admired—and much criticized—role model for young men who were looking for an alternative set of values in the waning years of the Qing and beyond. He represented the perhaps unlived but dreamed about life of a talented rebel and romantic hero, an appealing option even for those who assiduously plodded along through the imperial examinations, and he offered a satisfactory high-register role model for literati of the late Qing. Many literati had been frustrated in their attempts to enter the clogged ranks of officials and were settling into the Foreign Settlements in Shanghai to "plow with their pens"; they were to become the first Chinese urban intellectuals. Jia Baoyu showed that a person who was living out his "true" feelings would not be tempted to engage in the sycophantic flattery required for an official career.

Lin Daiyu—beautiful, sensitive, and gifted—became the emblem of the romantic female to be loved and pitied. The fated and tragic passion between her and Jia Baoyu, which attained a stature in China similar to that of the love between Romeo and Juliet in Europe, is cut short by the family. Jia Baoyu is married off; Lin Daiyu dies of grief.

No other novel has had a comparable impact on Chinese society. Ever since it circulated in manuscript form and was published in the late eighteenth century, it has been a prime source of popular literary and dramatic productions. The novel helped to shape the understanding and lent form to the articulation of romantic love in the midst of a still overpowering Confucian environment. *Dream of the Red Chamber* evoked a plethora of sequels and imitations that appeared mostly in the Foreign Settlements' print market, which sprang up after the Taiping Rebellion to replenish the burned-down cultural storehouses of the elite and provide the new urban classes with entertainment and knowledge.[11] In an 1896 novel, Zou Tao generalized his experience in Shanghai in scenes depicting clients and courtesans reading and discussing *Dream of the Red Chamber* together.[12] By the 1920s, in a political context, many members of the elite were calling for a muscular patriotic commitment to strengthen the nation; but a survey of reader preferences among middle-school students—candidates for the next generation of the elite—showed that *Dream* still remained their most beloved reading matter by far.[13]

Familiarity with this novel came to form a cultural residue shared by men and women of the traditional elite, of merchant families, and eventually of the new urban classes. *Dream* provided the dominant literary trope for articulating abandonment to love and fashioned many lives and lifestyles into living quotes.[14]

According to contemporaneous courtesan guides, personal diaries, newspaper reports, and literary works, courtesans' potential clients came mainly from three interlocked segments of society—merchants, men of letters, and officials. They were either short-term visitors or long-term sojourners and behaved as such. Not until the turn of the twentieth century did the first members of this group describe themselves as Shanghainese; before that, they considered their ancestral seat to be their real home. These men were attracted to the Settlements from all over China and even the world. While the particular needs of each kind of clientele differed, all clients had one thing in common: they were seeking comfort as well as adventure. Many of Shanghai's most extravagant features were directly linked to its unique juxtaposition of Western accoutrements and largely Chinese inhabitants. Shanghai was the place for those who wished to see the West without going overseas and to participate in Chinese conspicuous consumption—if one was not reduced to being an envious witness of it. The city itself might thus be counted as playing an active part in inspiring this scenario. While providing the ever more attractive setting of a fantasyland, it was an actor on its own stage, playing *qi*—"the extraordinary," the "West," and the ultimately and ever "new" on Chinese soil.

Judging from the portrayal of the city and the courtesans in late Qing city guides and from the behavior of the courtesans themselves, the clients sought the company of these women in order to experience full access to the city's glories and to feel for the moment that they were a part of it.[15] This gave the courtesans enormous leverage.[16] They inscribed themselves into the plot as brokers and intermediaries for the great Chinese encounter with this particular West, helping the visitor and sojourner to overcome feelings of alienation, insecurity, or threat.[17] Even if the visitor might first turn to friends from his native place, diaries of visitors as well as the Shanghai novels that generalized these visitors' experiences tell us that they explored the city primarily with courtesans.[18] The strategy that proved most effective in satisfying the courtesans' many different requirements—enhancing their status, controlling client behavior, achieving the ease of mind essential for entertainment, and establishing the trust and the sanctions that would prompt a client to pay his bills—was to play with the notion of the city as an entertainment theme park, an imagined world made visible in print and lifestyle. The courtesan offered her client the possibility of playing what might appear to be contradictory roles, ranging from the traditional man of letters to the Western dandy. The mental construct of a luxurious, outrageous, romantic, and sadly transitory love, which was familiar to all potential participants, became the dominant theme.

Under these conditions, the courtesan needed a role model that provided her with a culturally legitimate trademark. It had to correspond to real as well as imaginary desire and to her new status and place Shanghai's singular environment within the collective Chinese imaginaire. *Dream of the Red Chamber* was uniquely suited to meet these requirements.

As the novel was known to courtesan and client alike, both could draw on it and be certain that their words, acts, and jests would be perceived in the proper context. The young people in the novel do not spend their time pining about love but engage in an endless flurry of poetry competitions, games, and personal dramas. These scenes offered rich opportunities for sophisticated and entertaining role-playing.

The novel allowed the courtesans to choose a persona from any one of twelve very different young women, and they could switch—or even change to Jia Baoyu—if they wanted to present a new face. No matter which character they chose, they operated within a very high cultural register that corresponded to their new aspirations. In addition, the novel's emphasis on "true" feelings of sublime love, which did not include sexual relations, tied in with the elevated cultural stature the courtesans strove to attain.

Unlike the variety of roles provided for the courtesan, however, the client's single option was the character of Jia Baoyu. He would be wooed and pampered by the young ladies, but they ran Daguan Yuan according to their rules, and he was happy to abide by them. Recalling that Jia Baoyu considered these young women his superiors countered a tendency among clients to see themselves as the ones in charge. At the same time, the client had the satisfaction of slipping into the guise of a rebel and romantic lover. In this assignment of roles, the courtesan found a playful yet clearly circumscribed expression of the new power relations she hoped to establish that also offered an attractive role to the client.

And finally, the tragic end of the love between Lin Daiyu and Jia Baoyu added drama and emotional depth to the predictable real-life outcome of the client leaving Shanghai and his beloved to return to his family or to be married. The point of the play was to experience sublime love in the face of insurmountable obstacles by suspending one's real-life identity and entering an imaginary stage that utilized props, quotes, and roles taken from *Dream*. The players could be two, or a group, assuming their roles for a single evening or a longer stretch of time. The relationships between courtesan and client were played out as those of lovers, but sex was not mandatory, and marriage was neither a normal nor a necessary result, even though it remained a latent possibility. In the novel, Lin Daiyu and Jia Baoyu are fated to meet through events in prior incarnations, which instilled in them a deep emotional attachment that requires no further explanation or justification. It operates like the love potion inadvertently drunk by Tristan and Isolde. The play between courtesan and client was not about fulfilling social obligations of producing offspring to continue the ancestor service but to live out this predestined emotional attachment.

Choosing a Dream *Role*

While contemporary accounts offer ample evidence for the pervasive use of *Dream of the Red Chamber* in the sense sketched above, they do not go so far as to conceptualize the reenactment of the novel. The burden of proof has to be shouldered by the documentation gathered from a wide array of sources and from the analysis given here.

To return to the courtesans' names, either in full or in part, many courtesans adopted the names of characters in *Dream of the Red Chamber*. One of Shanghai's legendary courtesans did much to make this fashion take root. This courtesan, with the family name Hu, boldly became known in the 1870s under the name Lin Daiyu, the heroine of the novel. A decade later, she playfully decided to change her name, the gender of her role, and, consequently, her costume. Taking her name from Jia Baoyu, she called herself Hu Baoyu and often dressed in male outfits.[19] The name Baoyu, with the meaning "embracing desire," could be used by both sexes in the literal sense of the translation. Another one of the four top courtesans of the 1880s assumed the name Lin Daiyu, which had then become available. Among these four courtesan stars are also Zhang Shuyu and Jin Xiaobao (playing on the words *yu* and *bao*).

Examples of complete personal names taken from the novel include Lu Daiyu, Li Daiyu, Su Daiyu, Xue Baochai, Xiren, Qingwen, Xiangyun, and Xichun. Other courtesans followed Hu Baoyu's lead and became Shen Baoyu, Li Baoyu, Jin Baoyu, Ru Baoyu, and Lin Baoyu. Examples of courtesans adopting a single name element are Xiao*bao*, *Bao*er, Wen*bao*, Ai*bao*, Xiu*bao*, and Wen*yu*. Another borrowed element was *qing* from the name of Keqing, one of the novel's twelve main female characters. Examples are Yu*qing*, Yun*qing*, Xiang*qing*, and Rong*qing*. These professional names were often written on the doors or lanterns of courtesan establishments.[20] They served to advertise the playfulness of the entertainment offered, and a courtesan might use it to convey a sense of the type of person a client might expect.

Role identification also became a public cultural spectacle in Shanghai. From the 1870s onward, Shanghai literati held numerous courtesan competitions with *Dream* as the basic theme. The top twelve were awarded the rank of the twelve beauties in the novel, who were known as the "twelve golden hairpins" (*shier jinchai*). Beneath this "main group" (*zhengben*) was another group of twelve, the "supplement" (*fuben*), and below this, a third, the "secondary supplement" (*you fuben*). The ranking and biographies of these thirty-six courtesans were published in a book.[21] Other literati compiled lists matching the characters of individual courtesans with the beauties in the novel. Courtesans favored these rankings and listings as an effective and dignified means of spreading their names among a cultured, wealthy clientele.[22]

This role-playing continued long after the peak of this fashion had passed. As late as 1928, Bao Tianxiao and Bi Qihong, both prominent journalists and novelists, initiated a revival of *Dream* role-playing. Through the entertainment paper *Crystal* (Jingbao), they promoted four up-and-coming young courtesans—Hongqian, Tanchun, Wanchun, and Yunlun—as the "Four Small Golden Diamond Cutters" (Si Xiao Jin'gang), in emulation of the Four Great Golden Diamond Cutters of the late Qing. They organized a courtesan competition and invited Pang Binghong (Shubo), who had been an assistant to *Entertainment* (Youxi bao) editor Li Boyuan, to match the winners with the main female characters in the novel. This proved unnecessary in the case of Tanchun, whose name was taken from the novel.[23]

There is rich supplementary evidence that even among courtesans who did not borrow a name from *Dream of the Red Chamber*, the novel was a constant point of reference. Some courtesans referred to it as their sacred book, which informed their fantasies. Li Qiaoling was known to read the novel often on her own and to compare herself with Qingwen, one of the twelve main characters, who is admired for her passionate temper. Eventually, she was bold enough to marry the Peking opera star Huang Yueshan, although opera singers were outcasts. In 1878, she opened an opera house with him, which they appropriately called Daguan Yuan.[24]

Yue Qing, who was no mean literary talent herself, loved to read the novel, at times with her patron, the literary man Zou Tao. When going through the episode in which Daiyu buries the fallen petals—a metaphor for her own short prime of a flower—and Jia Baoyu secretly listens to Daiyu singing, "she would sit in silence and let the tears pour down her face." This, the author commented, proved that Yue Qing was "sensitive and full of feelings" (*duoqing*).[25]

A Shanghai courtesan answering a letter from her departed patron declares that she intends to welcome him on his planned return by "setting up the small table, letting the incense burn, and sweeping the sitting mats; . . . seated face to face, we will drink hot wine or tea and talk love as in the novel *Dream of the Red Chamber.*"[26]

In a fictional account drawn from his Shanghai experiences, Zou Tao has a courtesan evoke the association between her own fate and that of *Dream*'s romantic heroine. Although she is doomed to sadness because of the inequities of her profession, she might still hope to find men with enough feeling to be sympathetic and become her patrons.[27]

In real life, the role identification could be highly specific. When top courtesans and the editor of *Entertainment* discussed setting up a charity for the establishment of a burial ground for courtesans without families, the natural language for conceptualizing this enterprise was the *Dream* scene in which Lin Daiyu buries the fallen flower petals. "Flower" being a standard term for courtesans, the parallels were obvious, and the responsibility for chairing the group quite naturally went to the courtesan who was known at the time by the name Lin Daiyu.

Fashions and Interior Decorations

As in any performance, costume was vitally important in conveying the notion of play and signaling status. The Shanghai courtesans wore costumes that set them apart from normal life. They loudly proclaimed their performances and invited their clients to join them in an atmosphere of play. Extravagant costumes such as a robe embroidered with the descriptions of all the inmates of Daguan Yuan are mentioned with awe.[28] Courtesans also wore imitations of stage costumes from the increasingly popular Peking opera adaptations of *Dream of the Red Chamber.*[29] Hair ornaments, the cut and color of the garments, and the kind of shoes—all could enrich the performance with allusions to the novel. This fascination with the novel in no way prevented the courtesans from being eclectic, and their frequent adoption of stage fashions taken from men's outfits also enhanced the performance aspect (figs. 31a, b).[30] For example, the big boots worn onstage by martial arts heroes became high fashion among courtesans.[31]

The stage effect was particularly powerful in these unusual outfits because the

小妹

3.1a, b

(a) "Xiaomei" (Xiaomei). Photograph. Shanghai courtesan Xiaomei in stage costume. (Haishang jing hong ying)

(b) "Lanqiao Bieshu" (Lanqiao Bieshu). Photograph. Courtesan Lanqiao Bieshu in stage costume. (Haishang jing hong ying, 1913)

courtesan, who was supposed to be the lady pining away for love, donned a heroic and martial costume, switched roles, and took over the male part of the "talented scholar of many loves" (*duoqing caizi*), confidently strutting about and displaying a playful authority.[32]

Costumes such as these required display, and the horse race offered an appropriate occasion. Here, spectators could witness the spectacle of clients paying their respects to courtesans of their acquaintance. "Truly a great sight," marveled Huang Shiquan in the 1880s.[33] The public was not always appreciative, however, of this fashion of wearing men's clothing in public. A decade later, *Dianshizhai Illustrated Magazine* (Dianshizhai huabao) ran the story of a courtesan who went to the horse race in men's clothes and was harassed by local hooligans even though she was accompanied by two clients (fig. 3.2).

At the time, cross-dressing had another implication. Much as probably was the case in Venice, with its strong presence of male homosexuality,[34] the courtesan was reacting to the prevailing fashion among wealthy and powerful men of taking male lovers (most often young opera singers) and by means of her costume incorporated the fad into her own play. The relationship in the novel between Jia Baoyu and another boy, Qin Zhong, provides the model for this exploration of *qing*. The courtesan's cross-dressing added titillation and double-entendre to the game.

The interior decoration of the courtesans' chambers was carefully designed to create the right atmosphere, set off the world of fantasy from that of reality, and make sure all the status markers for the courtesans were in place. Again, elements from *Dream* were used. Like their counterparts in the novel, the rooms in the courtesan houses contained strange and wondrous things. The client could expect to find brilliant gas or kerosene lamps, which at the time were used only in the most luxurious houses and hotels in town.[35] Chinese as well as Western paintings hung on the walls, and Western furniture, clocks, and mirrors shared space with expensive Chinese-style furniture.[36] Lin Daiyu went a step further. Like the heroine of the novel, she kept a parrot, and one that had been taught to speak.[37] Within such an environment, both courtesan and client could ease into playful acceptance of their novel roles.

Photography was popular with Shanghai courtesans, and the pictures offer a rich archival record of their staging of their *Dream* personae.[38] Figure 3.3 shows a courtesan reclining on her Western-style sofa in a fantasyland studio scene, wrapped in luxury and desirability in gardenlike surroundings that recall Daguan Yuan. The garden motif appears frequently, evoking themes from the novel (figs. 3.4, 3.5).

The mirror is an even more poignant motif of the novel. It appears frequently, each time expressing the notion of illusion versus reality. In one scene, a lovesick young man receives a mirror from a monk who is trying to save his life. The image of a beautiful woman, one of the women in *Dream*, is on one side, and a death's-head is on the other. The monk's instructions are to avoid looking at the woman because this will lead to death, while looking at the skull will lead to life. The young man cannot resist the beauty and dies as a consequence.[39] In another scene, Grandmother Liu arrives from the countryside. She enters Baoyu's private chambers by mistake

*3.2. "Changes in the world of women" (Jinguo bianxiang). Lithograph, illustration by Zhang Zhiying. Local hooligans harass two courtesans attending the Shanghai horse race dressed in men's clothing. They surround one of the courtesans and pull off her hat, whereupon her braided hair comes tumbling down. Men wore their hair in queues during the Qing period. (*Dianshizhai huabao, *no.* shu, *10 [Oct. 1891]: 77)*

3.3. Reclining courtesan surrounded by flowers and plants, evoking the garden motif. Postcard, Shanghai, around 1900. (Courtesy Régine Thiriez, Paris)

and sees an old lady surrounded by beauties in an unfathomable setting of eroticism and luxury. She steps forward and promptly runs into something: it is a mirror, an object she has never seen before.[40] The old lady she saw is her own reflection, and the beauties are life-size portraits hanging on the walls. In both these scenes, the mirror highlights the themes of illusion and the unreliability of our senses. Such an illusion is infinitely powerful; it can enlarge the realm of the imaginary and cause the beholder's death or conjure up the utter pleasure of wonder. In figure 3.6, the courtesan is seated in front of a mirror. The illustration emphasizes the woman's pear hair ornaments. There obviously is no danger in seeing the other side of the mirror here. The courtesan is surrounded by potted plants and flowers against a background of garden scenery. The composition creates a land of fantasy and highlights the notion of "reflection" (*ying*). It conveys a sense of the "illusory" (*huan*), which is the very theme of the game. The double image blurs the distinction between "true" (*zhen*) and "false" (*jia*) and between "real" (*shi*) and "illusory" (*xu*).[41]

This self-presentation made the best of the earlier literati's idealized depiction of courtesans. The novel's theme enhanced this portrayal by adding the dream element. *Dream of the Red Chamber* was largely responsible for the creation of the dream motif within the romantic representation of the female. In a poem dedicated to Hu

小林黛玉現名小紫鵑與黛語樓合影

3.4. "Lin Daiyu Junior, now with the name Zijuan Junior, takes a photograph with Daiyulou" (Xiao Lin Daiyu, xian ming Xiao Zijuan yu Daiyulou heying). Photograph, 1917. With an idyllic garden motif as backdrop, these courtesans, who took their names from Dream of the Red Chamber *(Honglou meng), pose in a leisurely manner. (Xin Shijie Baoshe,* Huaguo baimei tu, 1918*)*

張書玉十七歲時影

3.5. "Zhang Shuyu at seventeen" (Zhang Shuyu shiqi sui shi ying). Photograph, around 1890s. The famous Shanghai courtesan Zhang Shuyu poses in a garden setting. (Haishang jing hong ying, 1913)

3.6. Courtesan in front of mirror. Postcard, Shanghai(?), around 1900. (Courtesy Régine Thiriez, Paris)

*3.7. "Liu Jinzhi" (Liu Jinzhi). Copperplate engraving. The courtesan Liu Jinzhi is portrayed in a stagelike setting. (*Jingying xiaosheng chuji*, 1897, 47, courtesy Columbia University Libraries, New York)*

Baoyu, a client refers to her house as the Red Chamber and claims that being with her was like entering the realm of dream, where it was hard to distinguish the real from the illusory.[42] Many illustrated guides to the Shanghai courtesan world show this influence. Figures 3.7 and 3.8 are from *Mirror Reflections and Flute Sounds, First Collection* (Jingying xiaosheng chuji), which alludes to *Dream* in the images used in the title. The etchings in the album are based on photographs of courtesans. The courtesan in figure 3.7 is framed in the window with the curtains pulled to both

3.8. "Wang Youjuan" (Wang Youjuan). Copperplate engraving. The courtesan Wang Youjuan is reflected in the mirror she holds in her hand. (Jingying xiaosheng chuji, *1897, 28, courtesy Columbia University Libraries, New York)*

sides in a manner that strongly recalls a stage. In figure 3.8, the courtesan herself becomes a charming "illusion" (*yinghuan*), shown as a reflection in a mirror and surrounded by the delicate luxuries of her dress and furniture. The courtesan in figure 3.9 reclines on a couch, eyes closed, with a book in her hand and a maid and a child behind her. The dream and fantasy language of the scene is completed by the sweeping curve of the curtain, a metaphor for exotic luxury and also a standard studio prop used to filter light.

3.9. "Gu Lansun Junior" (Xiao Gu Lansun). Lithograph, copy of a painting by Wu Youru. In the tradition of Suzhou New Year's paintings, Wu Youru often painted or illustrated Shanghai courtesan figures with a child. (Huayu Xiaozhu Zhuren, Haishang qinglou tuji, *1892, 2:18)*

*3.10. "The architecture of Shanghai: Zhang Garden" (Shanghai zhi jianzhu: Zhang Yuan). Lithograph. (*Tuhua ribao*, no. 10 [1909])*

In playing this game, the courtesans helped to create the image of Shanghai as the "world's playground" (*shijie youxichang*). Shanghai's Western-style prosperity became part of their exterior as well as interior decoration. They customized the ambivalence of *Dream of the Red Chamber*, making this interchangeability, of the true and the illusory, the *specialité* of the city. The public Zhang Garden, which was most often frequented by courtesans and their clients, is portrayed in figure 3.10 as a fantasyland, with Western-style architecture, Chinese landscaping, and men and women freely taking tea together on the second floor of the teahouse.

It is not hard to see the connections between eighteenth- and early-nineteenth-century illustrations of *Dream of the Red Chamber* (figs. 3.11–3.13) and late-nineteenth-century depictions of the Shanghai courtesan.[43] The overall arrangement and composition of the illustrations are remarkably similar. The differences, however, are equally striking. Illustrations of the novel emphasize the characters' emotions and pay particular attention to their inner moods. In contrast, the illustrations of Shanghai courtesans seem intent on conveying the wealth and luxury of the Shanghai Foreign Settlements. As a result, the images in these later illustrations appeal to the viewer, whom they draw into their dreamworld. These illustrations show the extent to which both courtesans and illustrators knew that Western and luxurious furniture had the power to provoke interest and admiration. Used in conjunction with a high-register traditional literary motif such as that of *Dream of the Red Chamber*, the illustrations managed to create a new image of prosperity that belonged to Shanghai alone.[44]

Next to the mirror, the most important decoration in the courtesan house was "poetry and calligraphy" (*wenmo*). These trappings of literary refinement confirmed in a satisfying manner the elevated cultural status of the entertainment provided there. In a sign of mutual respect and admiration, courtesans in the most prestigious houses would ask men of letters who styled themselves as "protectors of flowers" (*hu hua shizhe*) to provide the text and the calligraphy for poems that played on the name of the courtesan living there and inevitably had *qing*, or sublime love, as a theme.[45]

Songs

Singing was prominent among the entertainments offered by the courtesans. They sang at parties in courtesan houses and at restaurants when wealthy patrons entertained friends. Once again, themes from *Dream of the Red Chamber* are pervasive. The songs invoked the novel's familiar tragic love scenes, and while the story's setting is Beijing and the language is the northern dialect, the songs were performed in the soft and lyrical Suzhou dialect that was adopted as a professional standard by high-class courtesans at the time. The novel *Dreams of the Wind and the Moon* (Fengyue meng), by Hanshang Mengren, first published in Shanghai in 1883, has a scene that takes place in Yangzhou and is one of the very few indications that *Dream of the Red Chamber* was popular among courtesans in other areas. As courtesans outside the Foreign Settlements were prohibited from appearing in public, and in *Dreams of the Wind and the Moon* their profession is outlawed shortly after the Yangzhou scene, there is no evidence of collective and public role-playing based on *Dream of the Red Chamber*; however, a courtesan assumes the persona of Lin Daiyu thinking of Jia Baoyu as she performs this song:

> Because of you, I suffer lovesickness;
> Because of you, I suffer lovesickness; (sings with a sigh);
> because of you, I am [only] lazily leaning on my dressing table [with no
> desire to put on makeup]; (sings with the emotion of grief for the past);

3.11. "Miao Yu" (Miao Yu). Woodblock print, 1900s. This illustration of one of the main female characters in Dream of the Red Chamber *(Honglou meng) appeared in an eighteenth-century edition of the novel. (*Cheng bingben xinyuan quanbu xiuxiang "Honglou meng," *37)*

because of you, my dreams are often circling around Mount Wu [for a rendezvous];
because of you, sorrow has been added onto my brows; (sings with a sigh);
because of you, I have become thin and wasted;
because of you (sings with sorrow), because of you, when can I pay off this debt of love?[46]

3.12. She Yue, another character from Dream of the Red Chamber *(Honglou meng), illustrated by Gai Qi (1774–1829). Woodblock print. (Gai Qi,* "Hongloumeng" tuyong*)*

In keeping with the important place poetry has in *Dream of the Red Chamber*, where it serves to express feelings and display cultural skills, clients regularly wrote poems to courtesans; in some cases, courtesans responded in kind. Within the Shanghai environment, these poems could be sent to the papers for publication. Both the main Chinese-language paper in Shanghai, *Shenbao,* and *Entertainment* printed a fair amount of such poetry, and various collections were published.[47] The poems show the intricate links among emotion, literary trope, and performative stance that were woven in the environment and with the language of the game.

3.13. Shi Xiangyun, a main character from Dream of the Red Chamber *(Honglou meng), illustrated by Gai Qi (1774–1829). Woodblock print. (Gai Qi,* "Honglou meng" tuyong*)*

Poems exchanged between the courtesan-poet Chen Yuqing and her patron Lunqiu created a considerable stir when they were published in *Shenbao*.[48] The dominant theme is the deep understanding between the "lover of flowers" and the courtesan as tragic beauty. In the last count, Lunqiu can only love her, as he lacks the power to protect her.[49]

Among the courtesan-poets, Cheng Daixiang should be mentioned. In the following example, she compares herself to Lin Daiyu, and her poems with those of Lin:

I burn my poems as my life draws to a hasty close; in the next life [I hope I will] not again have such *qing* [sublime love].
You said [if I] pitied you, it could only be through the image of a shadow; I will have a portrait of you made and pity you thus.[50]

The poem alludes to the famous last scene before Lin Daiyu's death, when she burns the poems she had written to express her love for Baoyu.

While this use of poetry is a direct echo of its role in the novel, the language and images often allude to *Dream of the Red Chamber* as a metaphor for the present. A poem written for Hua Rongqing serves as an example:

Coming upon the Red Mansion, I know that this is your home.
The sleeves filled with dance and the fan turning with song vie for elegance and brilliance.
Why should I look up other famous names when all this beauty is before me united in the name of "flower"?

Talking of the past, I will never forget the time when you asked me about the [difficult] words (in *Dream*).
We cut paper to write poems similar to those in *Dream*.
What you said when holding my hand will be listed in my book of poems about enraptured [love] and separation.[51]

Both the writer and the courtesan are shown as sensitive and full of feelings, and they share the sorrow of inevitable separation.

It would be an exaggeration to assume that the references were exclusively to *Dream of the Red Chamber*. In fact, the novel's poems themselves open up a rich array of links to traditional poetry. A letter by the Shanghai courtesan Lu Xiaobao to a Mr. Keyi who resides in Zhehu provides an example. It shows the frustration of a courtesan who has literary talent. The letter begins by paraphrasing the lament of the ancient minister Qu Yuan in "Encountering Sorrow" (Lisao), a poem about the king's refusal to heed his advice, as an allusion to the sad fate of a courtesan without a patron who understands her.

When I express my lofty ideals in poetry, I am ashamed that I follow the path of a "woman in a spring mood."

The letter continues:

How should the heart know itself? When I recite poems, they are most often those by Dong Lang.[52] Yesterday, I happened to play with my brush, and like thread being pulled from the lotus, I used [Dong Lang's] "The fallen flower" as rhyme and composed a new poem. . . . I regret only that I met you so late and did not have the chance to bring out for you all that has been stored up in me. I tasted all at once the mixture of bitterness and sweetness.

Lu Xiaobao then relates that someone who admired her poem wanted to publish it in *Shenbao*, but she feared that it would cause gossip and jealousy instead of bringing her recognition. She asks the client to send her his own poems, as they are sure to be appreciated and passed around among the courtesans; above all, she would like to answer them in kind.[53]

Summing up the many years during which this game prevailed in Shanghai entertainment circles, the compilers of *A Photographic Record of Shanghai Flowers* (Haishang hua yinglu), published in 1915, include an item titled *Verses from the Courtesan Houses* (Qinglou yunyu). In their work, they address the changes in the meaning of the novel's dream metaphor in the entertainment world. They were the only contemporary writers to make the explicit claim that there was a veritable "*Dream of the Red Chamber* addiction" in the courtesan houses:

> Since Cao Xueqin published his novel *Dream of the Red Chamber* with the intention of rousing the world from its obsession with emotions, who would have anticipated that those men and women most deeply involved in emotions would fail to understand that he was using a metaphor [that this was all but a "dream"], and that they would, just the opposite, be completely poisoned by *Dream of the Red Chamber* and become even more obsessed [with emotions]! There is one high-ranking courtesan who also loves discussing this novel, and she holds that Daiyu's emotions are true but Baozhai's emotions are fake, that Xiaohong's emotions are obsessive while Yuanyang's emotions are intense. . . . According to this, we also have a *Dream of the Red Chamber* addiction in the courtesan houses.[54]

With her name associated with this novel, the Shanghai courtesan offered a scenario for game playing that provided a framework of play rather than a strict code. Certain elements, however, were firmly set. By taking her professional name from the repertoire of names in *Dream of the Red Chamber* and by other references to this novel, the courtesan suggested in a playful and unambiguous way the particular roles she and her client were to assume. The message was not lost on the clients, all of whom, as literati, were connoisseurs and devotees of the novel. The courtesan advanced an implicit demand for equality between the client and herself in their roles as lovers and for the client's respect in emulation of Jia Baoyu's worship of the young women.

Playing Baoyu

Baoyu's family name is Jia, a pun on another Chinese character also pronounced *jia*, which means "make-believe" or "fake." The figure Zhen Baoyu, whose name puns on *zhen*, meaning "true," also appears. While this dichotomy was not played out in the Shanghai environment, the client who took the name Jia Baoyu, "Make-believe Baoyu," indicated an involvement as deep as that of the novel's Jia Baoyu but signaled an awareness that, somewhere, there was his "Real Baoyu," ready to go back to his real-life responsibilities. Literati sometimes assumed pen or studio names alluding to the novel and their own counterparts when publishing about the courtesan world. An example is Haishang Baoyu Sheng (Mr. Baoyu from Shanghai), who in addition used the studio name "Tower of Borrowing from *Dream*," Jiemeng Lou.[55]

Zou Tao (1850–1931) is a fine example of a person who went far beyond taking up the part of Jia Baoyu for a short period and instead nearly merged his real life with the role. He moved to Shanghai in 1880 and lived there for the next four decades. A novelist and newspaper editor, he wrote a courtesan guide and also a courtesan novel, *The Shadows of Heaven and Earth in Shanghai* (Haishang chentian ying). He chose the pen name Attendant of the Xiaoxiang Studio (Xiaoxiang Guan Shizhe), quite consciously styling himself as an admirer of Jia Baoyu, whose studio bears the same name in the novel.[56] As his pen name signals, Zou Tao was a devoted patron of the courtesans and a lively actor in the dreamworld of emotions. At one time, he was the patron of Yue Qing, who loved to recite from *Dream*.[57] As he later confessed, he was young then and quite obsessed with *qing*:

> I was offered a job in the navy, but there was in me such a persistent attachment for a Shanghai courtesan that I left my new post and returned. . . . [During this period of my life,] the most important thing for me was *qing*; thus I gave myself the name Xiaoxiang Guan Shizhe. But in this mortal world of dust and common concerns, [I] failed to meet [her whom I can love]. When I retreated from this world and reflected upon it, I came to the conclusion that I must overcome my own desires and dissociate myself from this world.[58]

A more detailed picture of Zou Tao's personal life and his commitment to *qing* is provided by a vivid narrative from the hand of Zhan Kai, a close friend. As it shows the *Dream*-patterned dynamics of the relationship between patron and courtesan as well as the lifestyle lived by Zou Tao, it is therefore quoted here in full:

> My friend Master Zou [Tao] was a born devotee of emotional attachment [*qing*]. As he grew up, he discovered that among the novels there was one called *The Story of the Stone* [alternate title of *Dream of the Red Chamber*]. Besotted by its utterly invented story, he became obsessed with *qing* [*qing chi*]. At first there was Su Yunlan from the courtesan house, who had a smattering of knowledge of literature. When she met Zou and asked him about Chinese characters [in *Dream*, she did not know], he immediately went mad with joy, believing that a Xie girl[59] had come alive again or a Ban Zhao [the Han dynasty woman scholar, author of *Commandments for Women* (Nü jie) and coauthor of *Hanshu*] had been reincarnated and that he had met them in the person of Yunlan. Therefore, he became very close to her and pledged to remain loyal to her to his last day. Zou, however, possessed nothing, his home was but bare walls, and while he wanted to buy Yunlan's freedom [*tuoji*], sadly enough, he did not have the means.
>
> Thus he traveled over thousands of miles to southern Chu, where he became a Commissioner of Education; only years later did he manage to come back with the necessary funds. Before he had even settled on a place to stay, he went right over

> to knock at the door of Ms. Su. When he entered, the face there was utterly unfamiliar to him, and everything had changed: Yunlan had carried her *pipa* to another boat. He returned heartbroken, as though his wife had died. Since then, his obsession has become ever deeper. Eventually, to soothe his mind, he wrote his novel *The Shadows of Heaven and Earth in Shanghai*, based on the story of their love and separation. I met Zou in Shanghai in the spring of 1897, and we spent a lot of time together. Each time I directed my steps to a courtesan house and invited him to come along, he firmly refused. When friends wondered about this and asked him, he would sigh: "I, too, am aware of the great number of beauties here. But how could any of them be a match for Su Yunlan? Going there with you would only confuse my heart." And thus, he never went. I therefore beleaguered him to tell me all about her. He told me all in greatest detail and even got out the letters she had sent to him to show them to me. She wrote an upright and refined hand, and her style was so easy and pleasant that one just could not let go. After I had read them, Zou put them away like treasures.[60]

The story continues with Zou falling in love with another courtesan, whom the narrator in due order compares to the "martial" You Sanjie in *Dream of the Red Chamber*. This detailed narrative of Zou Tao's emotional makeup reveals that his love life was very much borrowed from that of the fictional Jia Baoyu. Although he may be said to have come close, in terms of literary talent and addiction to *qing*, as a Shanghai man of letters plowing with his pen, he certainly lacked the family wealth that supported his model. Zou also seemed to live in a dream of passion, however, and the Shanghai Foreign Settlements became his dreamscape as the novel's Daguan Yuan had been for Jia Baoyu. He became the uncontrollably idealist lover. Like his counterpart in the novel, he defied social convention.[61] He was willing to follow the rules imposed by the courtesans with whom he was entangled and to tolerate all of their whims. He did not fall out of love with Yunlan when he discovered that she had "carried her *pipa* to another boat" (become involved with another main patron, whom she married, only to return later to her profession), and he did not get angry when another courtesan lost interest in him after he had scraped together all the money he could and given it over to her. The sympathy and devotion that marked his descriptions of courtesans in his guide reflect this Jia Baoyu attitude. Zou Tao came to feel that he had played too much in earnest and that this had led him to remain in the city for his Lin Daiyu, a decision he later deeply regretted.[62]

An 1896 feature story published in *Entertainment* further fleshes out the *Dream* scenario. It details the encounter between a Mr. Zheng and Xie Tianxiang, who had been groomed in the arts of entertainment since early childhood in a Shanghai courtesan establishment. When she had grown into a young woman, the madam of the house finally persuaded her to begin meeting clients:

> Before Tianxiang became famous, there was a gentleman named Zheng who was full of fantasies. He was talented and prided himself on a lifestyle of drinking with the courtesans. Yet, although he traveled far and wide and met with those in

> the highest circles, he regretted not having met the true beauty [who could win his heart]. One day, he was brought into the presence of Tianxiang, who, with her delicately arched eyebrows and full cheeks, was an outstanding beauty. Zheng was delighted but said nothing at the time. Secretly, he found out who she was and where she lived. Pretending that he was drunk, he went straight to her house [that same evening] and approached Madam Zhao [of the house] directly. Tianxiang, who had just returned, heard that someone had barged into the establishment [without proper introduction] and was told that a Mr. Zheng wanted permission to meet her. As Tianxiang knew of him and his literary talents, she was extremely pleased when she heard that he had come. "I like to be by the side of refined scholars," she declared. "Today's [meeting] is fated for us by Heaven." She immediately asked to meet him. When the madam brought Tianxiang to make the introduction, she also brought two other younger courtesans of the house, Shiquan and Baoyun. [Upon seeing them come in,] Zheng hastened to meet them and sat down only after all were seated. He inquired in detail about the story of their lives and showed all signs of extreme attentiveness to their feelings. After a while, some wine was brought; the madam took her leave and ordered the courtesans to serve Zheng without delay. Thus Tianxiang came forth holding a wine cup. She moved with grace and delicacy on her tiny feet, as though a gust of wind could have carried her off. As Zheng examined her closely, she [felt embarrassed and] turned her face to the side. Her face, which was full of light, took on a pink hue, and she looked delicate and refined. After she sat down, Zheng inquired after her age; she answered that she was fifteen. When he asked Shiquan, she was too shy to answer. Tianxiang smiled and tugged her sleeves. "Why do you always make it difficult for me by using *Dream of the Red Chamber* to test my knowledge, and here we have in Mr. Zheng one of the most learned and cultured men, and you do not test him?" [Shiquan] laughed but could not say a word. Whereupon Zheng began quizzing Tianxiang [on the novel]. Her responses were quick and succinct and showed her unending wealth of knowledge.[63]

Tianxiang accepted Zheng as her patron and lover. Their relationship lasted for a long time. Later, the madam tried to break Tianxiang's loyalty to Zheng by demanding that Tianxiang go with a rich merchant. Tianxiang refused. But Zheng realized the madam was not going to be satisfied with him as a patron because he was not wealthy enough. Thus, he retreated from Tianxiang, promising that they would be together eventually.

Dream of the Red Chamber provided the framework in both establishing a common ground and identifying the roles of the potential players in this story. Zheng's Jia Baoyu–style attitude of extreme attentiveness to the young women, including his retreat from Tianxiang so as not to block her career, is highlighted and idealized. This behavior was shaped by that of the characters in the novel, and both Tianxiang and Zheng prided themselves on their intimate knowledge of the plot and the characters.

Courtesan and client engaged in a delicate balancing act as they established their roles and the rules of this game as the basis for their interactions. In the above cases, the client was a man of letters. His cultural capital was important and even instrumental in lending the game legitimacy and sophistication.[64] The courtesan required an articulate partner who was capable of acknowledging and accepting the element of fantasy and the basic rules of the game on which the atmosphere of culturally sophisticated play depended.

The majority of the courtesan's clients, however, were wealthy merchants and powerful officials. They left the accoutrements of power behind as they slipped into the role of Baoyu but retained the cultural equipment the game and its scenarios required. As a consequence, their identities of merchant and official were regularly underreported in the courtesan literature. In order to give the game cultural clout, literati skills were essential. The framework provided by the novel established basic role assignments for all participants, whatever their "real-life" positions might be. The scenarios attempted to impose a mode of behavior and offer a framework, and in this sense, they were normative rather than descriptive. In assigning the role of Jia Baoyu, the courtesans strove to control and reshape the behavior of their clients in this new Shanghai environment, but their effort must be read against the spontaneous behavior of wealthy merchants and mighty officials who were confident of their standing and power. The literati Zou Tao and Zheng therefore do not represent average client behavior but rather are among the very few examples of a client who disappeared fully into his role of Baoyu. The success of the Shanghai courtesans provides ample documentation that the fun offered easily compensated for the possible irritation of having to slip—if playfully—into the role of a man who thinks women are vastly superior to men.

Games

Playing *Dream of the Red Chamber* in Shanghai involved a convivial flurry of banquets, visits, rides, operas, and parties at all of the best Chinese and Western restaurants. *Dream* role-players also spent much of their time at various games that provided cultured, sophisticated, and amusing models for passing the time and showing off their acumen.

Drinking games, card games, word play, and poetry contests from the novel were important, regular components of Shanghai courtesan entertainment.[65] One of the most popular was a poetic drinking game played with cards, each of which bore the picture of one of the novel's main characters. The game required considerable literary knowledge and poetic skill.[66] The two parties took turns writing the rhyming lines so that the resulting poem, composed of "linked lines" (*lianju*), was authored by both. These games offered the opportunity to engage in ritualized flirtatious banter, exhibit cultural skills, and reinforce the cultural ambience of the occasion.[67]

The plan for a dice game based on the novel notes the hundreds of characters and all the famous sites in Daguan Yuan according to their relative importance (fig. 3.14). The dice are cast to place the player and determine his or her fortune.[68] Motifs from the novel were used for illustrated writing paper, in letter-paper designs, on painted lamp shades, and in "picture storybooks" (*lianhuan huace*).[69] Publishers produced numerous high-quality illustrated albums featuring the twelve beauties of the novel. Lin Daiyu burying the fallen flowers was a favorite (fig. 3.15), as were scenes from the novel depicting the relationship between Baoyu and Daiyu (fig. 3.16).

The Shanghai publishing house Shenbaoguan was quick to recognize the market for books explaining these games. In 1877, it brought out *Mad Talk: Four Kinds* (Chishuo si zhong), a set of four works designed to heighten appreciation of *Dream of the Red Chamber*. The first work, *The Essence of "Dream of the Red Chamber"* (*Honglou meng* jingyi), by Huashi Zhuren, offers terse interpretations of characters and scenes in the novel that are often radically different from the standard ones. The second, *A History of "Dream of the Red Chamber" Drinking Games* (*Honglou meng* gongshi), is a handbook, with detailed explanations of the rules of these games and a step-by-step guide to playing them. It is implied that they were played between females (courtesans) and males (clients), each side with its assigned rewards and punishments. For example, if the female who played Lin Daiyu lost a match but was then able to recite the poem Daiyu said when burying the fallen blossoms, she was exempted from punishment (drinking).[70] The other two, *Assorted Songs on "Dream of the Red Chamber"* (*Honglou meng* zayong), by Pinghu Huangjintai He Lou, and *Regulated Verse on "Dream of the Red Chamber"* (*Honglou meng* pailü), by Xu Qingzhi, are collections of poetry based on the novel and provide models for poetic themes and rhymes to match.[71]

Shanghai as Daguan Yuan

In *Dream of the Red Chamber*, the young women and Jia Baoyu play out their lives in Daguan Yuan, a realm cut off from the values and concerns of the outside world. This offered a powerful metaphor for the Shanghai Foreign Settlements, with their paradisial luxuries, their enclave position on the edge of the vast lands of Qing orthodoxy, and their peacefulness in a China that had just undergone the most devastating and murderous civil war anywhere in the nineteenth century. When the Daguan Yuan opera house opened in 1878, the link between the fictional garden as a theater of the unreal and a real stage became explicit.

In this reading, entering the Shanghai Foreign Settlements was like "entering the realm of dreams" (*rumeng*). Shanghai was the "realm of dreams" (*mengjing*), and what went on in this realm was "play" (*youxi*).[72] The Shanghai publishing industry was instrumental in the creation of this image. It helped to transfer the cultural concept of a secluded garden to an urban center by emphasizing two dominant themes: the motif of the dream as counterpart to reality and the notion of play as a light theatrical performance. Through a variety of publications about the city, it aided in developing the association between Shanghai and *Dream of the Red Chamber* and promoted the idea of Shanghai as the world's playground. Men of letters who had become journalists used their position to develop and consolidate this image of the city. City guides of the 1880s and 1890s such as *Shanghai's Prosperity Illustrated* (Haishang fanhua tu), Zou Tao's *Shanghai City Lights* (Haishang dengshi lu), *Famous Shanghai Sites, with Illustrations and Explanations* (Shenjiang mingsheng tushuo), and Hushang Youxizhu's *An Illustrated Introduction to Shanghai Entertainment* (Hai-

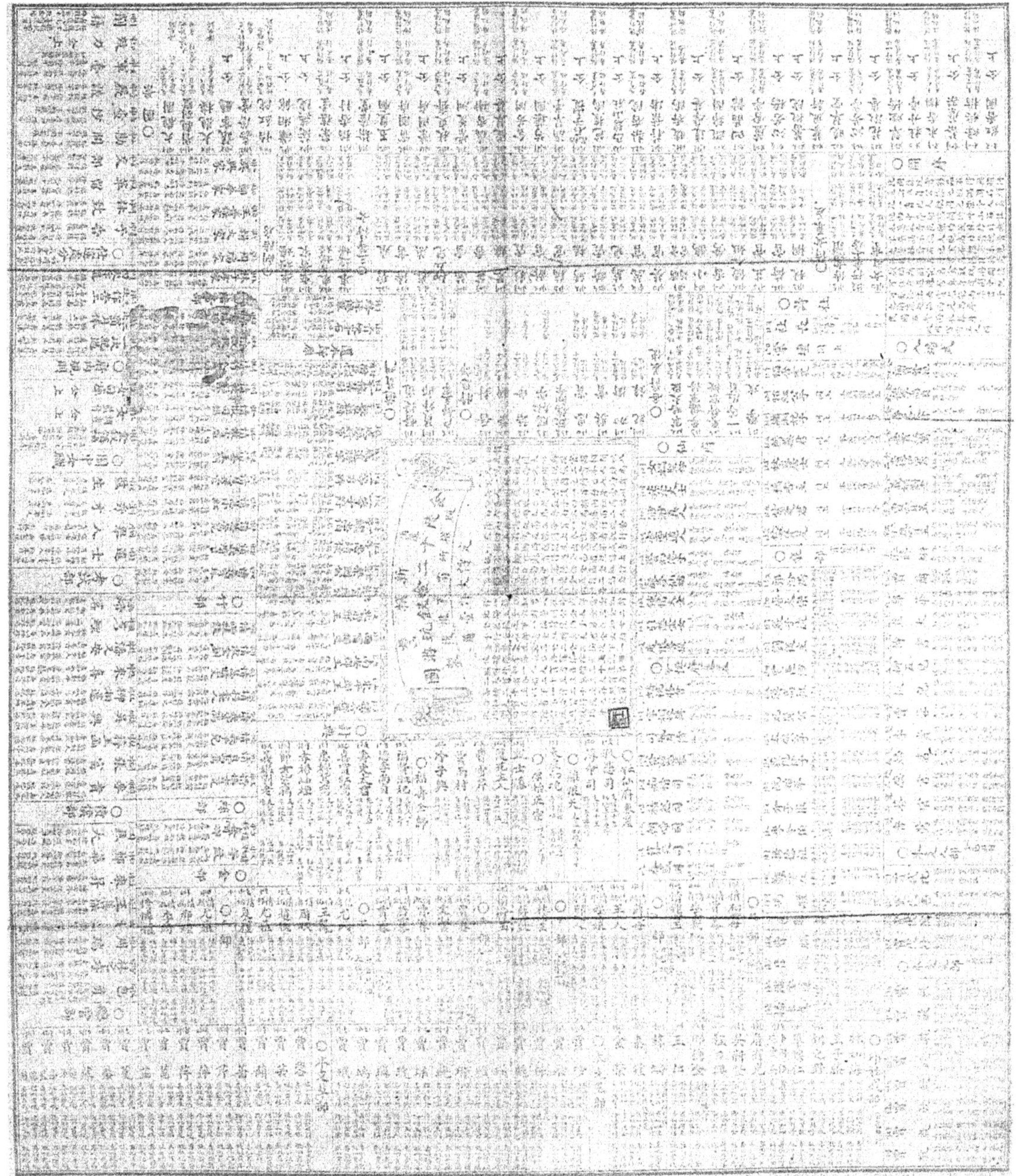

3.14. "Game Plan of the twelve golden hairpins from Jinling" (Jinling shier jinchai wanyou tu). Nineteenth century. The plan of the game is based on Daguan Yuan, the park in Dream of the Red Chamber *(Honglou meng). (Wang Shucun,* Minjian zhenpin tushuo "Honglou meng," *103)*

3.15. [Lin] Daiyu, the main female character in Dream of the Red Chamber *(Honglou meng), depicted by Zhou Muqiao. Lithograph, Shanghai, 1926. The illustration, which first appeared in* Flying Shadows Studio Illustrated *(Feiyingge huabao), shows the famous scene in which Lin Daiyu buries fallen petals. (Wang Shucun,* Minjian zhenpin tushuo "Honglou meng," *259)*

3.16. *"In Lin Daiyu, awakening from spring languor, rise the stirrings of love" (Xiaoxiang guan chun kun fa you qing). Lithograph, Shanghai, late nineteenth century. Jia Baoyu, standing outside Lin Daiyu's bedroom window, overhears her musings. (Wang Shucun ed.* Minjian zhenpin tushuo "Honglou meng," *347)*

shang youxi tushuo) portrayed the city as a paradise decorated with exotic Western customs and merchandise that could be enjoyed in conjunction with the rituals and roles invented by the Shanghai courtesan. These illustrated Shanghai city guides, courtesan guides, and other descriptions of the city made this the dominant image of Shanghai beginning in the 1870s.

Again, Zou Tao offers a fine clue. His courtesan novel *The Shadows of Heaven and Earth in Shanghai*, published in 1896, took *Dream of the Red Chamber* as its model. It features a garden, standing like an oasis in the midst of the commercial city. Zou Tao places Shanghai courtesans and their clients, instead of the lovesick young people in Cao Xueqin's novel, in his literary replica of Daguan Yuan. These talented and outstanding courtesans include an American and a Japanese woman, and there is a hero who is attached to the courtesan heroine. The characters are all living in the garden, which is run according to the rules they have devised. Emulating the events that took place in Daguan Yuan, the courtesans organize poetry societies, hold poetry contests, and create word games that play on the names of the famous characters in *Dream*. Love between courtesan and client is the dominating theme, and both parties are morally upright and emotionally devoted. Although all the male protagonists are educated men, very few make their living with words; they are merchants, military men, and officials.

The identification of Shanghai with *Dream*'s Daguan Yuan rested on the images of dreamscape and big playground. A Shanghai was presented that offered many levels of pleasure. Much as Walter Benjamin described the Paris arcades as the specialty of this "capital of the nineteenth century,"[73] playing with courtesans was touted as Shanghai's exclusive specialty. Promoting the city as a big playground and land of fantasy outside the harsh confines of the real and the necessary encouraged a particular mind-set. Here, one could forget worldly concerns and, as in a dream, play the part one desired without fear or consequences. This dreamland promised the absorbing experience of pursuing one's deepest desires, of throwing oneself into boundless sensual pleasures and fantasies come true, of displaying one's wealth and status, and, finally, of indulging in outrageous behavior.

Shanghai was well suited to support such an interpretation. The presence of Westerners, who both lived in and administered the Settlements, was seen as an essential component of the city's exotic makeup. Its physical appearance, notably its Western architecture and street arrangements, became the playground's basic scenery, and the abundance of Western material culture acted as decoration. And finally, through its successful promotion of commerce and trade, Shanghai had the wherewithal to take on the role of a Chinese dreamland, free of the social constraints prevailing elsewhere.

Explicit uses of Daguan Yuan imagery point to enclaves within the Foreign Settlements, such as the opera house or the park in Zou Tao's novel, which could interact in a narrow sense with the courtesan houses. In contrast, the Island of Immortals image referred to the Shanghai Foreign Settlements as a whole, where courtesans were venturing into the public realm, expanding their field of action, and increasing their visibility and recognition. The public spectacles they offered transformed the entire city into *Dream*'s Daguan Yuan. Zou Tao again found an apt

3.17. "Only when looking very far does it become clear" (Shi yuan wei ming). Lithograph, illustration by Zhou Muqiao. This illustration was published in Flying Shadows Studio Illustrated *(Feiyingge huabao) in 1890. It depicts a Shanghai courtesan gazing curiously with binoculars at the culturally mixed urban landscape. (Wu Youru,* Wu Youru huabao, *3b:14)*

image to express the link between Shanghai and Daguan Yuan. In his *Shadows of Heaven and Earth in Shanghai*, the courtesans adapt Western science for their purposes and construct a balloon in which they float out of their garden and into the larger Daguan Yuan of the metropolis.[74]

The courtesan became part of the city's self-staging as a marvelous playground. In figure 3.17, one of the courtesans gazes with intense curiosity at Shanghai's unique landscape, while another views it through a pair of Western-style binoculars. Both direct their attention toward the steeple of the Holy Trinity Church, considered by many to be one of the wonders of the Foreign Settlements. In this fascinated gaze at urban Shanghai, the cityscape and the courtesans join in conveying the arcadian associations of *Dream*. Modernity here is but an aspect of the exotic show.

Even less exuberant city guides stressed Shanghai's "dreamlike prosperity and extravagance" (*fanhua rumeng*).[75] The dream metaphor dominated even the titles of the city guides.[76] In the original Buddhist context, "dream" refers to the essential unreality of all that exists, including the most dearly held feelings. *Dream of the Red Chamber* transformed this concept into a rich metaphor for a life engulfed in emotions that were absorbing even though in the last count they might be "empty" (*kong*) in the Buddhist sense. In the process, the term "dream" changed in value, denoting not the ultimate emptiness of reality but a transitory time-space separated from the pettiness of daily concerns and remembered with nostalgia. Eventually, works about Shanghai entirely abandoned the Buddhist associations and became paeans to the city's dreamlike extravagance, with the courtesan and her establishment at the center. The "red dust" (*hongchen*) of the world of suffering becomes the aspired goal. But even in this inversion, the original Buddhist connotations of the novel were not entirely lost. The emptiness of the world of karmic retribution erased the difference between the rich, male, and mighty clients and the courtesans who served them, replacing it with the overarching notion of fated suffering. The courtesan became the embodiment of the Shanghai dream in all its allure and ambivalence. Beginning in the 1890s, novels about Shanghai again reread the dream in this Buddhist sense and reinterpreted the Shanghai dream of the 1880s as a nightmare.

Business concerns were never entirely forgotten. Even in the fictional Shanghai of Zou Tao's *Shadows of Heaven and Earth in Shanghai*, as readers are informed in no unclear terms, the courtesans' market value rose tremendously after they created the garden and moved into their houses. These courtesans are shrewd about money. The novel details the price for each house in the park—the American and the Japanese courtesans pay a higher monthly rent, but no down payment is needed. All transactions are formalized by signing contracts. Sections of this garden are sometimes open to visitors for a fee.[77]

Shanghai courtesans understood *Dream of the Red Chamber* quite well. Behind the seemingly easy life of the inmates of Daguan Yuan, the question of money was ever present. Courtesans did not intend to travel down the same road taken by their models in *Dream*.

Rejected Options

The particularity of the *Dream* theme is highlighted by the rejected options. The "talented scholar and beautiful lady" motif that had been so popular during the seventeenth and eighteenth centuries was an earlier and unsuccessful option for conceptualizing the courtesan-client relationship. While *Dream of the Red Chamber* is the finest example of this motif, the novel was written partly as a reaction against it. Jia Baoyu's unmanly preference for living with the young women in the secluded garden instead of going for a career did not sit well with the "talented scholar" model. More important, the novel departs from the tradition of this motif through its tragic ending, which does not lead to marriage for Lin Daiyu and Jia Baoyu. This ending enhanced the character of playful suspension of disbelief in the *Dream* scenario as it cut the link with marriage and offered a sad and tragic role for the courtesan after the client's departure.

Works such as the thirteenth-century *Romance of the Western Chamber* (Xixiang ji), attributed to Wang Shipu, and *Peony Pavilion* (Mudan ting), by Tang Xianzu (1550–1617), which had the potential to attain a cultural status and popularity comparable to those of *Dream*, were rejected because they broke with traditional notions of proper behavior. Some late Qing courtesan novels explicitly made this point in discussions that criticize these works for overemphasizing the role of sex in romantic relations. *Dream*, in contrast, stresses the emotional and romantic aspects of relationships, which interacted well with the separation of entertainment and sex that characterized Shanghai courtesan high culture and also elevated the cultural status of courtesan entertainment.

The late Ming model was also rejected. This option was based on examples from the early Qing, when grand courtesans and outstanding literati attained legendary status for their brilliant literary accomplishments and patriotic opposition to the Manchu invasion. For Shanghai sojourners of the late 1800s, the establishment of the Foreign Settlements was not equivalent to the Manchu conquest, and no one (yet) aspired to the role of the patriotic hero opposing Western encroachment. No courtesan donned the guise of Li Xiangjun, the loyal courtesan of the late Ming portrayed in the drama *Peach Blossom Fan* (Taohua shan), nor were Shanghai men of letters taking on the roles of the politically active scholar-official statesmen of the Donglin Academy. These roles seemed politically out of place and certainly were not suitable for leisure hours in the big city. Here, *Dream* had a unique advantage over the late Ming model: it was not set on the grand stage of national politics, and its theme was not national salvation but the intense pursuit of emotional fulfillment.

Literati, Courtesans, and the Publishing Industry

It was no coincidence that the intellectuals of the Settlements found *Dream of the Red Chamber* and its hero Jia Baoyu appealing. By promoting and reenacting this most famous novel about rebellion against the established paths of an official career and orthodox social relationships, they were offering a new interpretation of their own selves. They could play the highly satisfying traditional role of the "talented scholar of many loves" who defies the traditional social order. They might still aspire to success in the higher examinations and even pursue an official post; by casting themselves as Jia Baoyu, however, they signaled that they had seen through the shallowness of the novel's "true" Baoyu, Zhen Baoyu, with his dogged adherence to officially prescribed values and career orientation. Playing their own make-believe Baoyu, Jia Baoyu, as one with true feelings, they balanced their new identity as members of a rising professional class by becoming partners for the courtesans, using their literary and cultural skills to develop Shanghai's Daguan Yuan theme. This cultural capital ensured that *Dream* role-playing qualified as upper-register cultural behavior, and their persona of the talented, emotional young nonconformist gave them a symbolic version of the prestige they often lacked in real life. At the same time, they could still claim the flattering identity of "protector of flowers" (*hu hua*) even if Shanghai courtesans were by then operating as fairly self-confident businesswomen and did not appear to need protectors. And although the role of Jia Baoyu was reserved mostly for officials and merchants, the intellectuals' literary skills represented a currency of comparable validity that gave them equal status in this dreamworld. Zou Tao offers a fine image for the equivalence of cultural and financial capital: the client who arrives at the gate of Daguan Yuan must either pay ten silver dollars or write a poem that is judged worthy of acceptance by the courtesans who live there.[78]

Within this role-playing environment, however, the literati became part of the entertainment itself. Their conversation and poetry, as well as their private flatteries and public adulation, provided entertainment for their readers and lent cultural clout to the leisure hours of the wealthy and powerful. Thus, for quite a few of these men, participation in such dreamy pastimes had its own economic meaning. By helping to present Shanghai as a center of high-class entertainment, they also helped to create a job market for themselves. In their oversize Jia Baoyu dresses, they were on their way to becoming cultural salarymen.

Their partnership with the publishing industry was responsible for the popularization of the *Dream* theme. Shanghai book publishers actively promoted writings related to the novel, with Shenbaoguan taking the lead. Ernest Major, the manager and majority owner of this publishing house, had the provinces scoured in search of quality sequels to the original so that he could offer them to a market craving variations on the theme. *Another Dream of the Red Chamber* (Honglou fu meng), published in 1876, and Guichuzi's *A Sequel to "Dream of the Red Chamber" (Honglou meng* bu), published in 1879, are some of the results.[79] Literati also wrote novels emulating the *Dream* model, and these were also promoted. Among them is Yu Da's *Dream of the Green Tower* (Qinglou meng), published by Shenbaoguan in 1878. This novel is the first to describe the relationship between client and courtesan through the "talented scholar and beautiful lady" trope.[80]

The market was not restricted to wordsmiths. Many *Dream*-related novels were published with superb illustrations. By far the most popular reflection of public fantasy and recognized models were "New Year's paintings" (*nianhua*), which were purchased by many Chinese families as decoration for the coming year (fig. 3.18). These paintings were instrumental in familiarizing the general public with the novel's theme, important scenes, and characters and their relationships.[81]

Not everyone, it should be said, emulated *Dream of the Red Chamber*. Han Bangqing, for one, did not even mention the novel in his *Biographies of Shanghai Flowers* (Haishang hua liezhuan), perhaps because of his aversion to the overtly sentimental and self-aggrandizing use of the novel.[82] Others, such as Wu Jianren, later employed the trope ironically by writing not a sequel but a science-fiction variant in which Jia Baoyu is dropped into the midst of modern-style Shanghai corruption and is transformed into a well-informed urbanite.[83]

Moving toward Urban Modernity

Emulating characters and even living out storylines are not new in China but are stock features in the country's cultural tradition and make up a principal tool for educating the young.[84] Shanghai's contribution was the newly collective nature of the drama or game that included the city. Unbeknownst to those involved, the novel's reenactment became a dress rehearsal for the modern urban romantic relationship.

3.18. “Celebration of the moon festival in Dream of the Red Chamber*” (*Honglou meng *qingshang zhongqiujie). Hand-colored New Year’s woodblock print, Tianjin, Yangliuqing, nineteenth century. This New Year’s print shows the layout of a part of Daguan Yuan. (Wang Shucun,* Minjian zhenpin tushuo “Honglou meng,” *39)*

Dream of the Red Chamber pitted free partner choice against the social order represented by the traditional family structure. Family intervention caused the lovers' unhappy ending. Against this background, the reenactment of Lin Daiyu's and Jia Baoyu's love simulated a new and modern social order in which love relationships were acted out without interference from the family. Yet, because the game fit the Chinese concept of *youxi*, which includes the notion of impersonation, this radical step toward modernity appeared harmless. The relationship between men and women was transformed through an innocent public amusement that was confined to a very particular urban enclave and did not seem to warrant explosive social reactions. The Shanghai courtesan's *Dream* world became the training ground for new forms of urban love. The courtesans certainly had a hand in opening this space, with their public parades of flirtatious behavior and daring couples-based living arrangements. In this space, a bourgeois culture built on the romantic duo first found a stronghold and spread to other urban centers by way of Shanghai's fame and media. In a very real sense, as was often reported, for example, in *Dianshizhai Illustrated Magazine*, Shanghai became a natural haven for lovers when family pressures became too oppressive.[85]

By the same process, and equally behind the backs of all participants, the courtesans' inclusion of the city's Western features into the Island of Immortals and Daguan Yuan scenarios was instrumental in providing for their cultural and social acceptability first in the Foreign Settlements and then throughout the country. Shanghai's move to become the world's playground is the story of China's move to modernity, written not in the capital letters of the reformers' proclamations but rather between the lines.

As the relationship between courtesans and their clients were recast to resemble those of Jia Baoyu and his female relatives, the Daguan Yuan of *Dream of the Red Chamber* became the signature for the new Shanghai. With great ingenuity and creativity, Shanghai courtesans drew on the wide familiarity with the novel that existed among their potential clients and within their own ranks to come up with the imagery, plotlines, and cast of characters capable of accommodating their envisaged new interaction with their clients and with the city itself. The success of this daring enterprise hinged on their relentless pursuit of novelty within this open framework and the fun and entertainment they were able to generate in the process. The benefits to the courtesans were multiple. As they goaded their clients into taking on the role of a talented and pampered young man who loved to indulge women's whims, they reserved the more powerful roles for themselves and strengthened their position vis-à-vis the courtesan houses. They also succeeded in separating their role from the sexual services associated with prostitutes and the lower ranks of courtesans.

These courtesans were, among other things, professional women. The *Dream* play offered a dense and fanciful scenario that sidelined the potentially irritating fact that these relationships were commercial in nature, and the luxurious environment of Daguan Yuan indirectly justified the high charges. The endless flow of gifts described in the novel subtly challenged the modern Jia Baoyu not to restrict his attentions to the regular payment of bills. Much of the wealth accumulated by courtesans who were not also madams came from this source. Sex itself became a form of return gift that signified emotional attachment or gratitude. With this dual financial structure of gifts and billed transactions, a game horizon was established that was based on apparently spontaneous interactions, surprisingly equal relations between the sexes, and rich cultural associations, all of which contributed greatly to the success of the enterprise. The separation of the strictly financial aspects of the entertainment from the entertainment itself, with the gift culture as part of the game and occasionally even the option of direct replacement of financial capital with cultural capital, must be counted as a brilliant and culturally very successful business strategy.

The scenario offered clients a make-believe traditional environment in the heart of this money-obsessed city, in which to play out one part of their cultural persona. There was no museum spirit in this semblance of tradition; it was dominated by the notion of *qi*, or "the extraordinary," and lived on its capacity to absorb an endless variety of new and dramatically modern elements, such as Western technology and urban behavior, into the dreamscape.

It is not surprising that these conscious models for role-playing should have been devised at this time in Shanghai, nor is Daguan Yuan the last such model. At the turn of the twentieth century, young intellectuals such as Liang Qichao sought role models other than Jia Baoyu and found them in the fiery Italian nationalist reformer Giuseppe Mazzini (1805–1872) and similar men. The response to the challenges of life in the Shanghai Foreign Settlements was more conservative. It created a space for the exercise of traditional cultural skills and private enjoyments and integrated Western elements into the traditional categories of the surprising, the entertaining, and the interesting, thereby defusing their potential for upsetting cultural prejudices and preferences. At the same time, the response was very modern and extremely Shanghai in its unabashed commercial orientation. The make-believe nature of the *Dream* scenario allowed for a playful trial of fixtures, features, and modes of behavior that otherwise would have run into a cultural wall.

4 *Image Makers*
The Settlements' Men of Letters and Shanghai Print Entertainment

The fame of the courtesans and the city itself was the product and the first triumph of modern Chinese media. These media themselves developed in Shanghai, and manning their desks was a new group: urban intellectuals. Once members of the traditional literati class, they had been attracted by the city's opportunities and its openness for change.

From 1840 to 1911, the Shanghai Foreign Settlements were the only place on Chinese soil where one could publicly stage one's passage from a traditional to a modern lifestyle. This transition took varied routes. The city itself was evolving, and each generation of sojourners coming there had different motives. Still, the existing Settlements, with their framework set by the foreigners rather than the traditional gentry, exerted a powerful influence on the immigrants.[1] They provided the public arena in which these new lifestyles played out and set the margins within which the new urban culture unfolded.

Shanghai did not just consist of bulky foreigners busily engaged in making more money, Chinese compradors doing the same, and eventually a crowd of hotheaded reformers or revolutionaries plotting the fate of the nation. Its success was in fair measure due to its development into a true urban center, with all the diversity and dynamics this involved. A new industry, entertainment, sprang up that greatly enhanced the city's appeal for merchant, traveler, and wealthy retiree alike, and the rapid development of a commercial information and publishing industry offered many options for employment and public articulation to men of letters. The Jiangnan area at the mouth of the Yangtze River around Shanghai had long been famed for its excellence in education. The devastation of the recent civil war had destroyed much of the educational infrastructure and created a pool of educated men in need of jobs and a role.

Shanghai fascinated these men with its energy, thrilled them with its newness, surprised them with its comfort, and revolted them with its unabashed public pursuit of money. Brought up to believe that their role in the community was to be moral leaders, they were making a living in Shanghai with their literary skills, often working for foreigners, and felt increasingly marginalized. With the loss of their traditional role came the task of defining themselves and the meaning of their existence in a place that showed China's weakness as well as its cosmopolitan modernity. Shanghai was also an ideal hiding place where a man of letters could perpetually play the role of the "guest" (*ke*). As an outsider, he was not responsible for the community's moral standards. As he reenvisioned the city as a place of entertainment, his qualms about his own active role in it subsided.

For many of them, the new media were their daily bread, and the new literary genres their contribution. Many literati had come to Shanghai to find a way to make a living with their only capital—their education—and the new media offered them a chance. In an ironical and self-pitying way, they said they were "peddling words for a living" (*mai wen wei sheng*). In the same way, courtesans during this period were "peddling smiles for a living" (*mai xiao wei sheng*). Men of letters were the middlemen between foreigners and Chinese on all intellectual matters—values, procedures, and perspectives—fulfilling a function similar to that of the comprador in the world of business. At the same time, they acted as intermediaries between Shanghai and its Chinese visitors and sojourners. They lived on different and often conflicting planes, torn between accommodation and anger.

Between the 1860s and 1890s, these men of letters were most likely to find employment with newspapers, publishing houses, translation bureaus, and, eventually, new-style schools. These institutions were commonly owned and operated by foreign missionaries or merchants. The London Missionary Society Press, for example, where Wang Tao lived and worked when he first came to the Settlements in 1849, was founded by the English missionary Walter Henry Medhurst in 1843, the year the Nanjing Treaty was ratified. *Shenbao*, the most important early Chinese-language newspaper, was founded in 1872 by the English businessman Ernest Major and some silent partners; Major also managed the Shenbaoguan publishing house and *Dianshizhai Illustrated Magazine* (Dianshizhai huabao).[2] Another example is the Chinese Polytechnic Institute (Gezhi Shuyuan), which was founded in 1876 by Sir Walter Henry Medhurst, the English consul general and son of the missionary, for the purpose of popularizing Western science in China.[3] By the turn of the twentieth century, many Chinese-owned printing houses had followed in these tracks. As the center of the print, educational, and leisure industries, Shanghai came to dominate the market in knowledge, ideas, information, and entertainment.

The rise of print entertainment was part of this development. From its earliest days, *Shenbao* carried literary tidbits such as bamboo twig ballads, poems to courtesans, and entertainment news, but by the mid-1880s the growth of the market made independent entertainment publications such as illustrated magazines and guidebooks to the courtesan world commercially viable. By the late 1890s, tabloid entertainment papers and literary journals joined these publications. All were defined by a combination of Chinese and Western technical, literary, and artistic features. The Shanghai courtesan loomed large in these new forms of print entertainment. Through her, the man of letters explored the dimensions of the city and his own role within it.

Taking salaried jobs in the new media and institutions of the Foreign Settlements marks the transition from men of letters to urban intellectuals. They were the backbone of intellectual life in the Settlements, and as they applied their skills to new ventures, new genres and media made their appearance. The work situations of these men in institutions and enterprises with rigid time schedules compelled them to adopt an entirely new lifestyle characterized by an often uneasy mixture of time and monetary constraints on the one hand and the grand stance of the man of letters on the other, tempered by the triumphs and anxieties of someone offering his skills on the open market. Their mode of accommodation set the parameters for the development of a particular urban Shanghai lifestyle.

Some of the most popular new forms in print entertainment were urban hybrids. The new tabloids, for example, published traditional poetry, newspapers inserted the old form of the bamboo twig ballad into an altogether different setting, and periodicals started serializing novels. Their new environment, the technology with which they were printed, and the way in which they were packaged and marketed created a subversively titillating mixture of the familiar and the new that became the hallmark of Shanghai cultural production for this period.

Urban hybridity characterizes the mentality of the Settlements' men of letters. Despite the occasional case of resentment about salaried work under foreign management, these feelings were personal and not political. They did not see the Settlements as an imperialist imposition, and although, objectively speaking, the Settlements might be seen as such an imposition, this definition would be of little use in understanding the attitudes of these men. Their focus was on retaining some of the markers of the lifestyle of traditional men of letters while pursuing their new occupations (fig. 4.1). The same man might spend money and time attending a dinner party at a courtesan house, or drinking wine and composing poetry with friends in their private garden, but on the same day or late at night, he would be writing his newspaper

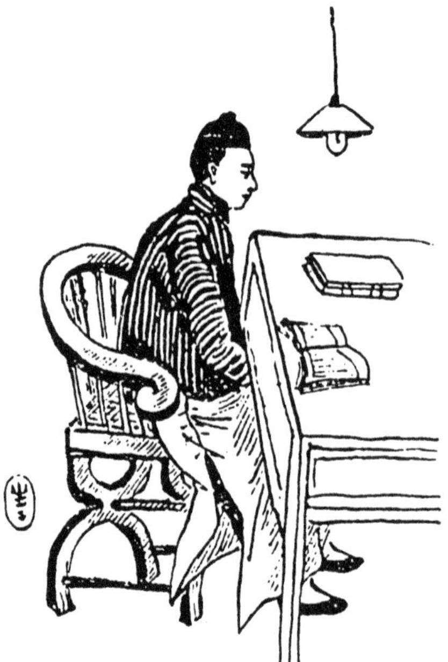

*4.1. This scholar wears the outfit of a typical educated man in Shanghai at the turn of the twentieth century. He sits under an electric lamp on an armchair that mixes Chinese and Western styles. The small format of the book was made possible by the use of movable metal type. Lithograph. (*Xiaoshuo huabao*, no. 2 [1917])*

article or segment of his novel for the morning paper. He would, in other words, write his daily quota—ironically referred to as "filling in the printed squares" (*pa gezi*), because payment was based on the number of characters written.

The Western concept of time was crucial in shaping the lives of these new intellectuals and the process of their literary production. While the rest of the empire observed the lunar calendar and structured the year according to a variety of religious and astronomical precepts, Shanghai quickly adopted a pattern that separated the working day from the leisure evening and adopted the week as a unit, with Saturday night and Sunday as times of rest. This pattern spread from the Western communities to other segments of the Shanghai population. With the artificial daylight supplied by kerosene, gas, and electric light, evening developed into a particular space for entertainment. Newspapers and periodicals operated on rigid deadlines, which meant that these men performed much of their literary and journalistic work under time constraints. The new time frame for leisure suddenly made it important for a man of letters to be on time (fig. 4.2).[4]

Shanghai Courtesans and the Settlements' Men of Letters

Literati who moved to the Foreign Settlements were enthusiastic about many of the city's physical features but quite shocked by its open and blatant commercialism. This was a city for merchants, set up to make money, and its residents were not shy about displaying their new wealth. The Shanghai courtesan came to represent this city in the most public and outrageous way, and in this role, she seemed unimpressed by the Shanghai stature of the men of letters, who had been among the courtesans' traditional key patrons.

Courtesans and literati were linked by a long tradition of mutual sympathy and love. At the highest level, this had become established and almost institutionalized by the fact that young scholars would spend long months in the capital, far from their families, to prepare for the triannual Imperial Examinations. As a consequence, the capitals of the past boasted the largest and liveliest courtesan quarters in the country. In many cases, entertainment districts sprang up close to the centers where the young men were studying, and there, the scholars spent much of their free time and their families' fortunes.[5] The same pattern held true in the provincial capitals where the lower examinations were held. The love and passion that ensued were epitomized by the legendary relationships between the grand courtesans and the talented men of letters of the Southern Capital, or Nanjing, during the late Ming period. This legacy was a powerful element in the cultural makeup of Jiangnan literati. It came with nostalgia for the past and laments about the irretrievable loss of these grand and passionate times.[6] Yu Huai (1616–1696) was the first to articulate these emotions in *Random Notes on (the Pleasure Quarters by) the Wooden Bridge* (Banqiao zaji), published in 1654, which recorded memoirs of courtesan entertainment during the last decades of the late Ming in Nanjing.[7] During the nineteenth century, interest for this work revived and many authors explicitly copied its style. They did not restrict themselves to remembrances of historical Nanjing, which was referred

艾羅花露水

滬上發行之花露水多矣。而艾羅花露水乃艾羅醫生所創製。以百花之液釀成。不特香氣穠郁。沾衣如麝。且盥洗時滴用少許。功能辟暑袪濕。有益衛生。臨卧時。於帳中洒用少許。一切臭穢之氣。化爲烏有。出門人用之。兼能辟除瘴氣。誠非尋常花露水可比。每瓶價洋六角。購者希認瓶上艾羅仿單。庶不致誤。總發行上海三馬路中法大藥房。

上海社會之現象（五）

報館記者之夜來忙（碧）

自同治年西人美查君創設申報。爲上海有華字報紙之始。逮後滬報新聞報等踵起。今則報界更形發達。惟各報館之記者。其筆墨之忙。每在夜分。埋頭燈下。況猝異常。蓋以各處訪稿之至。半須零晚始達之故。然而記者苦矣。作報館記者夜來忙圖。并繫以傳。（報館記者傳）（仿五柳先生傳）記者。不知何許人。亦不詳其姓氏。館中掌記述。部因以爲號焉。率直敢言。不避權貴。好磨夜。不求甚早。每有所聞。便欣然序稿。性嗜爽言。事不稍曲諱。政府知其如此。乃定律以限之。展閱輒駭。期在必守。既守。而喋其奈任情。阿訣。終歲勞然。無間寒暑。燈前桌上。稿件盈尺。紛如也。常箸論說自娛。頗適己志。開通社會。以此自期。贊曰。時人有言。不切切於勢要。不急急於利祿。其言茲若人之傳乎。燃犀鑄鼎以竟其志。瑪志尼之流歟。加富爾之流歟。

*4.2. "Sights of Shanghai society: The late-night 'frenzy' of the newspaper journalist" (Shanghai shehui zhi xianxiang: Baoguan jizhe zhi ye lai mang). Lithograph. (*Tuhua ribao, *no. 23 [1909])*

to as Qinhuai, but dealt with contemporary courtesan entertainment in towns such as Yangzhou, Suzhou, Chaozhou, and Nanjing after the Taiping Rebellion.[8]

In this manner, the literati established a late Qing trope in which, through nostalgic remembrance of courtesans of the late Ming, men of letters were mourning their own loss of glory and power. Shanghai was the natural home for this trope. However, while both men of letters and courtesans were seeking patrons in Shanghai and thus seemed again to have much in common, things were not the same as in the Nanjing of old. Courtesans were not only thriving in Shanghai but becoming professional entertainers and businesswomen. They no longer fit the former cultural profile, and in their world there was no place for late Ming nostalgia. The men of letters had a much harder time adjusting their cultural and social personae to these changed circumstances and found their loss of status with the courtesans unsettling.[9]

The relationship between the men of letters and the courtesans changed quickly, shifting from the cultural memory of mutual sympathy to a more businesslike arrangement. As the literati found work in Shanghai's print market, they became the makers of the courtesans' public image on the basis of and beyond the public self-staging of these women. In this context, intimate familiarity with the courtesan world became an asset for both sides. Perhaps these men were inspired to seize the opportunity by the example of the courtesans' unabashed commercial spirit and their aggressive use of public space.

At the center of the city's blossoming entertainment industry, the image of the courtesan loomed large. A new topos was created: Shanghai and its courtesans, or "city and courtesan." It replaced the old "beauty and fallen dynasty" topos in which the beauty or courtesan, whose beauty would fade, stood for the fragility of the dynasty, which was fated to fall in the end. Its most influential use for the demise of the Ming was in Yu Huai's *Random Notes*. The "city and courtesan" topos gave the courtesan a definite Shanghai locale and associated her not with fragility but with the spectacular public display of wealth and comfort. A third party, the narrator, was a silent but crucial element in the narrative structure of both old and new topoi. Through this narration, the old literati as well as Shanghai's new intellectuals tried to come to terms with their own identity. In the Shanghai case, their publishing work reconnected them in a new way with their traditional role as the admirer and protector of the courtesan. They were now selling her image. The irony was not lost on writers and editors. The courtesan was chosen not because her frailty needed protection but because of the celebrity attention her presence in the public realm was receiving. The subject sold. The public's desire to know more about these women made them highly marketable characters, and the image of the Shanghai courtesan was widely popularized and commercialized throughout the Qing empire beginning in the 1880s.

This image offers the most detailed narration of the city and also of the struggle of the Shanghai men of letters to come to grips with their own role. Exploring genres familiar to them such as brush notes, *chuanqi* (or stories about the extraordinary), courtesan guides, novels, and poetry as well as adopting new forms of Western origin, such as entertainment newspapers and illustrated magazines, the image makers flooded the market with courtesan tidbits. They offered the public, for a mere seven cents, daily details about a once exclusive world. Both for the visitor about to embark on his own exploration of the town and eager not to appear a country simpleton, and for the armchair reader looking for an adventure without risk, these publications were appealing. By this process, a taste and a set of values that once had been characteristic of an exclusive elite were popularized within an emerging mass culture.

The Shanghai intellectuals' search for identity took the form of reinventing their traditional relationship with the courtesan. Yet neither they nor the courtesans are the trope figures from the past. By examining the literary and entertainment forms used by these men together with their own experiences with Shanghai courtesans, a fuller picture of their search for self-identity emerges.

The Settlements' Men of Letters and Their Courtesan Guidebooks

Courtesan guidebooks were prominent among the new print products about Shanghai courtesans that began to appear in the 1870s. These include *Miscellaneous Notes on Shanghai Flowers* (Shanghai yanhua suoji; 1877), by Langyouzi; *A Record of Comments on Shanghai Flowers* (Hushang pinghua lu; 1881) and *Collection of Poetry on Shanghai Beauties* (Hujiang yanpu; 1883), by Liangxi Chilian Jushi; *A Register of Shanghai Flowers* (Haishang qunfang pu; 1884) and *Pearls Forgotten in the Vast Sea* (Canghai yizhu lu; 1886), by Xiaolantian Chanqing Shizhe; and *Shanghai City Lights* (Haishang dengshi lu; 1884) and *Flowers from the Spring River* (Chunjiang huashi; 1886), by Zou Tao. First published as block prints, and since the 1880s by means of lithography, these guides, some of which were illustrated, presented Shanghai together with its courtesans as a place of unique and exotic splendor. In writing for these guidebooks, authors wielded their brushes like the literati of old, assuming the connoisseur's role, and thereby linked the past to their lives in the Foreign Settlements. Shanghai increasingly attracted sojourners as well as tourists.[10] The number and quality of these guides signal the attraction of the city's courtesan life for these newcomers and their eagerness to learn how to move about in this world.

These works thus also had to explain Shanghai. By exploring the theme of Shanghai through the traditional literary genre of biographies of local beauties, writers situated the city within the legendary landscape of the rich Jiangnan commercial centers. They described it with a newly fashionable term, *qi*, which means "the extraordinary," "the fantastic," and even "the exotic," a word in the highest register of surprise and appreciation that also encompassed the outlandish aspects of the Foreign Settlements. Formerly, little attention had been paid to a mutual embodiment of the courtesan and the city's splendor. The Shanghai guides cast Western material culture as well as courtesan entertainment into the same category of unfathomable wonder.

Shanghai courtesan guides range from straightforward instruction to *biji* type narratives. They skillfully accommodate the traditional "praising the flowers and engaging the moon" (*shanghua nongyue*) and the demands of the print market, enlarging the picture to describe the city as one grand place of entertainment. Huang Shiquan, a journalist and writer on Shanghai entertainment, testified that these works were so profitable that they were much sought after by publishers.[11] In the process of gaining stature, however, the city as well as its courtesans took on a more ambivalent image. As the intellectuals began to reevaluate the city—and their own role in it—they ended up effecting radical shifts in public opinion.

Wang Tao

The man who personifies the Settlements' men of letters during the decades from 1850 to 1890 is Wang Tao. His writings include the first account of courtesan life in the Foreign Settlements and are among the earliest descriptions of life there. Although there is a substantial body of scholarship on him, his writings on Shanghai courtesans have been largely neglected. Christian Henriot was the first to begin to remedy this situation.[12]

Upon arriving at the London Missionary Society Press in 1849, Wang Tao assisted Medhurst with his translation of the Bible.[13] He initially lived without family, alone, according to one of his biographers, "in a solitary cottage beyond the Chinese city in a spot that in a few years was to become the heart of a busy commercial district, but at this time still was a stretch of desolate grave-mounds which came almost to the door of the house."[14] Because he worked for foreign missionaries, the literati community in the walled city regarded him as a man who had forfeited the self-respect of a scholar for the sake of regular wages and shunned his company.[15] His diaries reveal that during his early years in Shanghai (1849–63), he felt lonely and socially isolated. He spent most of his time after work drinking with a few friends and visiting courtesans. Most of his friends also worked for foreigners but yearned to become Qing officials.[16] Together, Wang Tao, Li Shanlan, and Jiang Jianren were known about town as the "three outrages of Shanghai."[17] They reportedly trotted about the streets singing loudly after drinking bouts, created a rumpus in a wineshop, where they smashed things to pieces, and were heard letting out long howls by the riverside. With this behavior, they defied the gentry for isolating them and expressed frustration with their unfulfilled dreams of grandeur.[18]

Wang Tao's worthy occupation of translating the Bible was in some contrast to his literary work at the time, *Record of Visits to Courtesan Houses in a Distant Corner by the Sea* (Haizou yeyou lu), which only came out two decades later, in the 1870s, with a preface dated 1860. In this highly personal account of courtesan entertainment in the walled city, Wang Tao mentions that he wrote the work during an illness in the winter of 1853 at a time when the walled city had fallen to the Small Sword Society.[19] He laments that this calamity destroyed the old city and with it the courtesans and beauties he describes. He reports, however, that after the fall of the walled city, a new and more prosperous courtesan life sprang up in the Foreign Settlements.[20] Wang Tao explicitly modeled his *Record of Visits* on Yu Huai's *Random Notes*. In mourning the demise of the Ming dynasty, and the ineptitude of the literati efforts to prevent it, Yu had recalled the grandeur of the courtesans and their quarters in the Ming dynasty capital of Nanjing. Wang Tao evokes a similar sense of loss by modeling his work, a memoir on the past courtesan life in the walled city, after Yu Huai's. The destruction Wang Tao deplores, however, was caused by internal rebellions, and there is no indication that he linked it to the foreign presence in the Settlements.[21] In his sequels (prefaced 1873 and 1878), *A Supplement to "Record of Visits to Courtesan Houses in a Distant Corner by the Sea"* (*Haizou yeyou* fulu) and *Appendix to "Record of Visits to Courtesan Houses in a Distant Corner by the Sea"* (*Haizu yeyou lu yulu*), both of which deal with courtesan life in the Foreign Settlements, the tone was quite different. Then in exile in Hong Kong, he expressed his longing for the glories of the Shanghai Foreign Settlements through nostalgia for its courtesans.[22]

The first work, *Record of Visits*, contains mixed emotions. Written after the destruction of courtesan entertainment in the walled city brought on by the Small Sword Uprising, the book is focused on remembrance. In his preface, Wang Tao laments the passage of time and the losses brought about by war. "What are now crumbled walls and collapsed chambers were once home to the sounds of music and the color of wine." The place is still there, but all beauty and life had disappeared from it. In contrast, the refugees pouring into the Foreign Settlement had, as he wrote later, transformed "what once had been wilderness and gravesites into a scene of 'powdered features and fragrant oils.'"[23]

In the first part of the work, Wang Tao describes traditional courtesan entertainment in the walled city with enthusiasm and pride.[24] The next two parts are devoted to stories of individual courtesans and highlight their passionate affairs with men of letters. The close link between the literary activities of these men and their personal lives is highlighted by Wang Tao's account of his own love affair with Liao Baoer.

Liao Baoer had once been the concubine of a wealthy man. After he lost everything through gambling, she became a courtesan. Wang Tao was introduced to her by a friend, and they immediately liked each other. Wang writes that up to that time, he had not experienced deep love. His narrative switches between scenes of passionate encounters and blissful tranquility. It tells of Baoer's obsession with flowers, cleanliness, and the art of tea making. The lovers were finally separated when Baoer's husband showed up and demanded more money for gambling. Wang Tao describes his sense of loss in the following words:

> As Baoer then moved to a new place, and as Honghong [the friend who had introduced him to Baoer] had gone back to Xishan, I did not know where she had moved to; as I had no news of her, the end became permanent. One day, when passing by her old dwelling, I saw that the swallows' nest was still there at the gate with little ones sticking out their heads, as though in some way we knew each other. The silk gauze on the window remained closed as it had been; all around there was nothing except quiet solitude. . . . I wandered around for a long time without having the heart to leave. Now, both she and her home are far away, and my heart grieves without hope.[25]

This celebration of a beauty combined with the description of his emotional attachment conveys a deep sense of loss that resonates with the writings of banished literati of the past. For Wang Tao, working in the Settlements added a new dimension to the loneliness and isolation and intensified his self-pity.[26]

The image of the man of letters who was at once self-pitying and self-possessed had to find a metaphorical expression. In traditional painting, the literati often defined themselves through the qualities associated with the pine tree or bamboo; occasionally, they also used a Buddhist emblem, the lotus, which they shared with the courtesan. Growing in all its purity out of the mud, the lotus became the metaphor for inner purity in the midst of squalor. With the courtesans, the image also evoked the often repeated biographical trope that they had not become courtesans because they loved the mud but because they had grown up in impoverished circumstances and could not help it. Throughout *Record of Visits*, Wang Tao strikes the grand and benevolent pose of "protector of flowers," a role that was altogether different from what he deemed to be a demeaning job at the Missionary Society Press.

In his story about Baoer, Wang Tao revealed his sense of powerlessness: the protector was in fact as weak as the flower. By describing the courtesan's lot, Wang dealt with his own helplessness. In this case, the role of protector did not imply strength but instead reflected self-pity and self-mockery. As powerless as the courtesan, Wang must sell himself for a living, and like the courtesan, he needs a protector, a patron who recognizes and cherishes his true value. Yet, in his self-assigned role as the protector, Wang Tao also enjoyed a sense of power. In visiting the courtesans and writing about them, he had in fact promoted them, making their value known to the world. As the protector and promoter of the lotuses growing in the mud of Shanghai, the man of letters achieved a kind of psychological balance.

Among Wang Tao's stories of Shanghai courtesans, published in 1884 after his return from exile, the biographies of Mei Jun and Li Xiujin, written in the *chuanqi* genre, may serve as examples of a newfound self-confidence. In these stories, Wang Tao clearly tried to create the image of the Shanghai courtesan according to the ideal of the late Ming heritage. By reestablishing this ideal in his stories, he at once elevated the stature of the Foreign Settlements as well as his own role in it. These stories are part of the collection titled *Miscellaneous Records of a Shanghai Recluse* (Songyin manlu) and serialized in the *Dianshizhai Illustrated Magazine*.

Mei Jun's story begins:

> Mei Jun, also known as Mei Xian, is an extraordinary beauty among the courtesans. She is known to have a "biting of the arm" love pledge with Huaying Ciren from Qianchuan. A tea or dinner party without her presence is no fun. Her disposition is graceful and gentle. Hidden beneath her dress, her feet are unbound but naturally small. When they are being caressed, they send out a soft fragrance that is enough to dissipate all will power and send one into ecstasy. She is of small stature like Li Xiangjun [a famous courtesan of the late Ming], petite like a swallow to the point of evoking compassion.
>
> She lives at Dingan Lane in the North Town [that is, the Shanghai Settlements]. Her three-room house is laid out with refinement; the decoration of the rooms is sumptuous without vulgar bombast; the silk screens and bamboo curtains, the pre-

cious *ding* [bronze sacrificial vessel] and the incense burner are all arranged in the most exquisite fashion. Upon entering her rooms, all earthly desires dissipate. The honorable Huaying Ciren called her house "the tower of four sounds and four shadows," a description other men of fashion have adopted. Outside her door, carriages line up, but she is so dearly attached to Huaying Ciren that they are almost never seen apart; even such a suggestion would make them pine for each other. Her self-esteem is so high that even when called upon by clients who have been introduced, she never goes out to attend banquets. Yutaosheng from Songbei [Wang Tao himself], with all his experience in the business of "wind and moon" [having relationships with courtesans] was all taken by her upon their first meeting. He changed her name to what it is today, with Mei Jun as her name and Mei Xian as her professional name [*hao*], and with this her fame rose even higher.[27]

Wang Tao continues with Li Xiujin's biography:

Li Xiujin also was outstanding at that time. She was of a voluptuous [beauty] with silky [skin] and a full [bosom]. At one time, she resided in Juan Lane, and her place was busy with the comings and goings of admirers. Among them, Mr. Qian from Chu'an was most devoted; he tried to buy her freedom but in the end lacked the necessary means. When Yutaosheng from Songbei [Wang Tao himself] met her at Shen Gardens, she smiled [at him], evoking a sense of true feeling. They rode back in the same carriage, and he immediately paid her a call. Xiujin personally prepared the tea and arranged the tea set; her sweetness and enchanting [disposition] were something he had never experienced before.

Her sister Caixi lives next door to her. Caixi is older, but her grace and demeanor are peerless. A Weiheshang from Jinling is known for his upright purity, but upon meeting Caixi, he was so captivated that he offered her all he had on the spot—one hundred pieces of gold that he had just received for the sale of his literary works. He then wrote for her the words [with a pun on the elements *cai* and *xi* in her name] "As [your] unique talent [*cai*] opens [my] horizon, tenfold happiness [*xi*] spreads over [my] brow." With this, her fame instantly rose. Caixi has great judgment. Although a courtesan, her temperament is that of open forthrightness, her character is upright and chivalrous, and her mind is detached [from material concerns]. Whenever she meets with a *wenren* or a brilliant scholar, she goes to the extreme with pity and love, accompanying him with all the care and respect she can offer from the bottom of her heart, and never haggles over money. But when she meets a rich merchant, she would have him break the bank before letting him off.

. . . Caixi especially loved Yutaosheng [Wang Tao], so that it often happened that he was accompanied by both sisters . . . ; but his real love was for Xiujin only.[28]

Wang Tao went on to quote his own poems for these courtesans and praise their musical performances. The stories of Mei Jun and Li Xiujin had dramatic endings. Mei Jun could not marry the man she loved because her mother wanted to extract more money. When news came that the young man had left Shanghai in anger, Mei Jun broke down and refused to eat until her mother gave in. Together, they hired a boat to chase after the young man, and in the end the lovers were reunited and married. Li Xiujin for her part was in love with a poor scholar. He eventually established a career for himself and was given the official post of *taishou*. He then returned to Shanghai disguised as a poor, broken-down man. Upon hearing his sad story of failure, Xiujin wept and presented him with her savings of five hundred pieces of gold to encourage him to go on with life. Only then did he reveal his true circumstances, and they were married.[29]

Wang Tao's portrayals of courtesans during these two periods of his life are revealing. Liao Baoer, the courtesan described in his first work, *Record of Visits*, is a refined but weak character and is not able to break free of her gambling husband, who is now living off her income; she is capable of passion and love but will not act to defend them. This image suggests an equally weak self-image on the part of the writer. In contrast, the later depictions of Mei Jun, Li Xiujin, and Caixi show spirited and strong-willed courtesans who clearly appreciate men from the literati class and are steadfast in their devotion. While they have gained a much greater and modern say in their lives and loves, they still manage to live up to the ideal past.

As in Yu Huai's *Random Notes*, the narrator is personally involved, and his nostalgic reflections carry a commitment to write down the stories of these courtesans so that they do not vanish along with their bloom. These women are extraordinary in beauty, refinement, talent, and character. They are capable of profound feelings and true devotion, and they alone seem able to "deeply appreciate and understand" [*zhiyin*] the men of letters, whom they treat quite differently from their powerful and wealthy clients. In return, the men of letters place their literary talents at the courtesans' disposal, dedicating couplets and poetry to them, which, as Wang Tao proudly states, are instrumental in the courtesans' rise to fame. Here, however, the similarity to Yu Huai's work ends.

The earlier image of the man of letters as a lover who himself needs support and comfort disappears in later narratives in which the writer exudes self-confidence and a sense of control. What has changed? Shanghai changed, and with it the intellectuals' social position. The Shanghai Foreign Settlements began as a small outpost in the 1850s and by the 1880s were on their way to becoming a world-class cosmopolitan center. Leading the country in trade as well as in cultural production, the Settlements could offer men of letters respectable positions and social clout, and they increasingly defined themselves not just in a deficient mode compared to other gentry but as members of a new urban class with its own standing. It would take a few more years, but by the 1890s, they would claim, from Shanghai, to be the natural ideological leaders of the nation. The decade of the 1880s marked the height of a honeymoon relationship between the intellectuals and the city. Wang Tao's later stories affirm Shanghai as equal to the grand centers of the Chinese past, and its courtesans and men of letters as worthy of such an eminent place and momentous time.

This self-assertiveness can be seen in Wang Tao's later stories, which stress the central position of the man of letters. They abandoned the "beauty and fallen dynasty" topos that dominated Yu Huai's *Random Notes*. While the courtesans are still the focus of these stories, the writer himself now also takes center stage as a strong character who relates his personal experience. The biographies of Shanghai courtesans thus ended up aggrandizing the Shanghai men of letters. The moral qualities these writers praised in the courtesans reflect their own self-assessment. In this way, they were reinventing themselves. The departure from Yu Huai was the natural outcome of life in the Settlements. The Shanghai of the 1880s was not a dead capital from the past, its intellectuals were not traditional literati, nor were its courtesans the fallen petals that symbolized the transience of a dynasty.

Perhaps Wang Tao's shift from the *biji* genre used by Yu Huai to the *chuanqi* form in his *Miscellaneous Records of a Shanghai Recluse* also has to be seen in the context of his loosening the associations with Yu Huai's work.

Zou Tao

The writer who inherited Wang Tao's quandaries as well as his passion for the Shanghai courtesan was Zou Tao. He came to the city in 1880 and lived there off and on for the next forty years.[30] He left an impressive oeuvre on the Shanghai courtesan that includes at least one set of biographies, two guides, and a novel as well as numerous prefaces to courtesan-related works of the period.[31] Zou Tao's writings provide extremely valuable and unique access to the attitude and mood of the Settlements intellectual during the 1880s.

Zou Tao's brush notes are based on the personal experiences of the author and his friends. As in other Shanghai works of this genre, the city figures prominently. In the opening of *Flowers from the Spring River*, Zou Tao gives a personal account of his move to Shanghai and his motives in writing about its courtesans:

> In the winter of the year *xinxi* [1881], I first came to Shanghai to become editor in chief and political commentator for the *Yi* newspaper [*Yibao guan*, short for *Xujiahui "Yiwen lu" guan* (Xujiahui office of *News of Benefit*)], the *Yiwen lu* [News of benefit]. In my leisure hours, I always went with two or three close friends to visit the courtesans. I had no intention of living a life altogether spent on wine and women but wished only to dispel my sad moods. My visits to the courtesan houses were, much like those of [the Tang poets] Fanchuan [Du Mu] and Jiangzhou [Bo Juyi], my way of bitter weeping. Thus I came to meet so many [courtesans] and began to know their disposition. [Their houses are located] on San Malu [Hankou Road] and Si Malu [Fuzhou Road], between Shi Lu and Qipan Jie. I will write a few lines even about those I have met only once.[32]

With these opening words, Zou Tao states that he came to Shanghai to work for its first Chinese-language Catholic newspaper. In 1852, Li Di (Wenyu), who had joined the Catholic Church in 1861 and later became a priest at the Jesuit mission at Xujiahui on the east side of the French Settlement, had founded this bimonthly, later weekly, paper after receiving permission from the Church. It was meant to serve Chinese Catholics and consisted of leading articles, translations from foreign papers, social news, excerpts from the *Peking Gazette* (Jingbao), church news, articles on natural science, and literary contributions.[33] Zou Tao became its editor. In his autobiographical writings, Zou never mentions the Church, but his appointment as editor in chief at *News of Benefit* suggests that he was a Catholic. His employment as a teacher at the Catholic girls' school Qiming Nüshu from 1906 to 1923 also supports this conclusion.[34]

Zou's contact with the West and Westerners was not restricted to this paper and its church sponsors. A Ying reports that Zou wrote for the first Chinese literary journal, *The Universe* (Yinghuan suoji); this journal was published under changing titles from 1872 through 1875 by Ernest Major's Shenbaoguan in Shanghai.[35] Zou had a close relationship with Wang Tao after the latter returned from his Hong Kong exile and with Huang Shiquan, who, after a stint at *News of Benefit*, became editor in chief of *Shenbao* in 1885. Foreigners, and the Chinese men of letters who were working with them, were a major element of his social environment.[36]

Very much like Wang Tao, Zou Tao described his distress at being in this city in the language used by scholar-officials of the past who had fallen out of favor with the court and found themselves living in some miserable place far from the capital. Comparisons with Du Mu and Bo Juyi must have given him some comfort, but the passage signals that the storehouse of traditional tropes held little with which to accurately describe his new situation. In the 1880s, the Shanghai Foreign Settlements were certainly not a backwater outpost but a thriving city of national importance that set out to challenge Beijing's primacy, and Zou's talents were appreciated by a fast-growing media industry. Judging from his autobiography, Zou Tao was very much bound to the literary and social identity of a traditional man of letters. Life in the Foreign Settlements triggered within him a deep sense of frustration and dissatisfaction, with the times and with himself for his inability to attain a higher ranking in the Imperial Examinations on which he still pinned his hopes. As he wrote in the opening lines of *Flowers from the Spring River*, his encounters with courtesans, and his writings about them, offered a way to link up with the past and the cherished literati ideal.

Zou writes that his family had lived in Wuxi and lost all during the Taiping Rebellion. Only after considerable difficulty and sacrifice by the clan was he given the chance to study in Suzhou.[37] He managed to pass the lower-level Imperial Examination, but his first job was not with the state but with the Catholic newspaper in Shanghai. He was by then thirty-two years of age. As it was the practice of the newspapers at the time to offer their journalists and editors living quarters on the floors above the business premises, he probably lived in the French Settlement, where the *News of Benefit* offices were located. In 1884, he bought a house for his family in Xujiahui, near the Catholic mission, and moved his parents there as well.[38] He was employed twice by Qing officials in the capital, but each time he resigned and returned to Shanghai. His only foreign trip was to Japan. The hero in his novel *The Shadows of Heaven and Earth in Shanghai* (Haishang chentian ying), who traveled to Japan and was very impressed by the Western science he found there, bears a close resemblance to the author. The novel is related to Zou's life in another way. Many of his friends mention his connection with the Shanghai courtesan Su Yunlan. Wang Tao revealed in his preface to Zou's *Shadows of Heaven and Earth in Shanghai* that this novel was based on her life.[39]

At another time, Zou Tao was deeply involved with the courtesan Wu Qinxian. He would hold dinner parties at her establishment with friends and would while away his evenings drinking and composing poetry. She wanted to marry him, but they separated regretfully, and Wu sent him her photograph as a parting gift. Zou could not get himself to forget her and said that whenever he took out her photo, he would be lost in thought. He wrote poetry to dispel his longing.[40]

Zou's active patronage of courtesans meant that he practically lived in the courtesan houses.[41] He liked the courtesan house better than the theater, often missing a good show for the sake of visiting his favorite courtesan of the moment. Among his lovers, however, there was also an opera singer. The openly intimate and free manner with which the two men related to each other became a source of mirth among his friends. His contemporaries also noted that his most favorite courtesans would not have biographies in his courtesan guides.[42]

Zou described the courtesans with a sympathy and devotion that reflect his lifestyle and attitude. Each entry in his *Flowers from the Spring River* begins with the courtesan's name and address and includes a very personal account of her fate (a kind of *qingshi*, or history of love). Writing largely in the style of traditional courtesan biographies, Zou praised her temperament, her looks, her skin, her particular entertainment skills, and, in some cases, her poetic talents and capacity to experience deep feelings for gifted literati. The following introduction to his biography of Yao Qianqing may serve as an example:

> In my viewing of the Shanghai flowers, I found Yao Qianqing the most beautiful! Born in Qingchuan as the seventh child, her beauty is of luxuriant brilliance, vivid and elegant like that of an immortal. She is recorded in *Anecdotes on Courtesan Rituals* [Zhangtai jijiu qian shi][43] and an illustration of her can be found in *Illustrated One Hundred Beauties of Suzhou* [Wumen baiyan tu].
>
> In 1880, she moved to Shanghai. After many changes, she now lives in Puqing Lane off Shi Lu. The *daotai* Ma Meishu is very much taken with her. Whenever he comes to Shanghai on official duty, he is sure to visit her, lingering under the blossoms and unable to take his leave. He planned to offer ten thousand dollars to free her from being a courtesan and to "build her a golden room" so as to keep her in style. Another military official also wanted her for the price of "a bushel of pearls." She refused them both because her mother sees her courtesan profession as a gold mine. Qianqing, however, has the eyes of true perception [*huiyan*] in choosing a partner for life. Thus, her deep feelings are directed toward someone else.
>
> In fact, Qianqing and Mr. Li Yuxian from Zhongzhou, with the pen name Er'ai Xianren, are attached to each other [*xiangqi*]. Late at night after wine and food are served, they often will confess their true feelings to each other.

To end his story, Zou quotes one of his own poems for Qianqing and adds,

> as a courtesan, you have created a new legend for having the most tender affections for the talented [man of letters].[44]

Zou Tao's reaffirmation of this age-old affinity between literati and courtesans goes back to Wang Tao's *Record of Visits*. By choosing the *biji* narrative form "biography of the flowers" in Yu Huai's tradition, with the focus on the courtesan rather than on himself, he opted to portray the present in the shadow of the past and follow the tradition of leaving a record of the "extraordinary courtesans of their times." The narrative stance is that of pitying the flowers. In this tradition, it is next to impossible to give a critical account of the courtesans or the city. The images of cultural refinement and sensitivity suggest unbroken continuity with the past.

The genre, however, is not completely oblivious of the new. Zou Tao subtly challenged this dominant image in his biography of Hu Baoyu by presenting not the shadow image of the past but the new image of a savvy big-city professional:

> Hu Baoyu resides in Yuxiu Lane. She is almost thirty. Together with Li Peilan and Li Qiaolin, she reigns supreme. Although getting on in years, she is still superb in courtesan entertainment and a true professional in the affairs of love. She once had a relationship with the martial *dan* [female impersonator] Hei'er. Every day that Hei'er performed, Baoyu would go to watch him, and after his performance was over, she would flutter away. The details have been recorded in [Wang Tao's] *Record of Visits*.
>
> She once had a Westerner as a customer and received a huge sum of money for her nightly services. Thus, she became affluent and considered pearls and hummingbird feathers as no better than refuse.
>
> Some might scoff at her licentiousness, but they do not understand that in the business of love and sex, all is but illusion. Wealthy merchants might own ten thousand pieces of gold, but without a single elegant bone in their bodies, they know just to "climb onto a sun platform [pun on male gender] in search of heavenly ladies from the high Tang" and strive for the "clouds and the rain" [means sexual relations]. How could they just "sit opposite each other [lovestruck and] oblivious of words"? If they are not able to satisfy their desires, there would be no end to her being slandered by their vulgar words. How could she then set herself apart as superior to the other [courtesans]?
>
> Some say that her surname is actually Pan and that she is the offspring of the bandit [Small Sword Society leader] Xiao Jinzi. However this may be![45]

In Hu Baoyu, Zou created the image of a courtesan whose success was not based on her relationship with men of letters. On the contrary, this figure is different in every way from the ideal image: she chases after opera singers as lovers, she spends nights with a Western client, she is willing to accept customers who are more interested in sex than in refinement. She can afford to not care about money; she is rich, perhaps even wealthier than the author. Zou does not condone her lifestyle and business strategy, but he states quite bluntly that there is a market for sex and that Hu is good at it. Through his description of Hu Baoyu, Zou articulates some resentment toward the city's merchant class and the commercialized values of the city itself, which reflect only the most rudimentary human desires.

Zou Tao lived a paradox. A member of the first generation of Shanghai professionals in an area of Western-style public communication, he spent his spare time among courtesans, writing guides, stories, and their biographies. The simile of traditional literati pursuits was undermined as much by his real life as a journalist as it was by the Shanghai courtesans who had moved out of their traditional roles. In this respect, the Settlements intellectual and the Shanghai courtesan both agreed on the need to maintain the simulacrum of traditional forms associated with a high and emotionally fulfilled life in the midst of the metropolitan bustle. Zou Tao wrote his books not in the developing style of reportage and editorial but in the language of the protector of flowers.

Wang Tao's and Zou Tao's writings were instrumental in making the Shanghai courtesan the dominating figure in print entertainment for years to come. Through her image, this new and extraordinary city became accessible. Although Zou was actively involved, and even instrumental, in creating the particular literary style and lifestyle of the Shanghai Foreign Settlements, a sense of ambivalence remains present in his writings; his feeling of being "a scholar who cannot realize his career ambition" (*shiyi wenren*) shows up in his intense devotion to the theme of the Shanghai courtesan. Yet, from his own accounts, and judging by his life circumstances in Shanghai, it seems that no other place and career attracted him as much as this city and his life there—and that he loathed himself for it.[46]

Bamboo Twig Ballads

In the representation and popularization of the image of the Shanghai courtesan and courtesan entertainment, no genre was more powerful than the "bamboo twig ballad" [*zhuzhi ci*]. A popular form of doggerel, these ballads were much loved by ordinary residents and Shanghai men of letters during the late nineteenth and early twentieth centuries. This was not unique to Shanghai. It dates possibly as far back as the Tang dynasty but was most widely used in the nineteenth century.[47] The 1879 preface of *A Record of Essential Aspects of the Capital City* (Zengbu dumen jilüe), by Yang Jingting, claims that the genre primarily records unique social phenomena and changes in local customs, but the ballads also touch on the natural beauty of and historical change in a place and contain criticism of contemporary politics.[48] Shanghai, with its flurry of things unique, extraordinary, and shocking, was a natural candidate, and the genre took a new turn, with ample references to Shanghai courtesan entertainment.[49] Shanghai bamboo twig ballads were published mostly in newspapers, and the genre moved from being an anonymous to being an authorial medium with well-known literati willing to sign their pen names. The plethora of surviving Shanghai ballads is proof that topic, medium, and author combined to give these works a new status and cultural profile.

From its earliest days, *Shenbao* published such ballads, and most later papers followed suit. The ballads formed one of the earliest literary supplements of Chinese newspapers—although it was not yet termed a "supplement" (*fukan*)—and this forum contributed to the ballads' widespread use in Shanghai.[50] They offered the urban reader some light literary diversion mixed with the self-congratulatory pleasure of having visitors admire his city. Selections appeared in book form, and even Western entertainment papers such as *The Shanghai Evening Courier* occasionally carried translations of these quaint Chinese items.[51] The ballads are a precious if little-used source of information on the things Chinese visitors considered most remarkable in the Shanghai Foreign Settlements (called "Yangchang" in the poems).[52]

The ballads generally brim with enthusiasm about the International Settlement. They address a wide range of topics, describing stunning sights, sounds, and fashions. The following excerpts from *Bamboo Twig Ballads on the Foreign Settlements* (Yangchang zhuzhi ci), published in *Shenbao* on April 27, 1874, may serve as an example:

Opening Words

After the signing of the Peace Treaty, five ports were opened [for trade];
soon warships began to enter Wusong [Harbor].
But now after thirty years, both scenery
and prosperity are altogether incomparable.

Foreign Building

With richly colored iron flanking and stone balustrades,
it rises straight to the clouds, four or five levels high.
Suddenly I hear right over my head the whistle of the [wind],
mistaking it for the sound of a flute piercing the clouds.

Steamship

It travels over the seas and rivers without the aid of sails,
relying [on its steam engine], it can traverse even gigantic waves.
With the steam soaring a hundred feet it travels thousands of miles;
it needs only the nimble turning of the wheels.

Foreign Newspaper

Extraordinary tales about foreign lands are a rare [commodity];
with lightning speed, the lead type is set.
No matter whether near or far, all is clearly said;
even for the trade news on foreign goods, one must depend on it.

The Grand Automatic Chime Clock

When it strikes twelve o'clock, it is heard far and near.
The clock is housed in a towerlike building;
the sound of the bell wakes people up from a daze.
This is not just an extraordinary sight, but serious business.

Police Station on Qipan Road

Like a checkerboard, this street has many crossings.
Western custom greatly detests [public] defecation;

Beside the road are clean urinals.
In the police station, the laws prohibiting [public defecation] are strictly enforced.

The Courtesan House

The best [of the courtesan houses are represented by the] four words *fu* [wealth], *gui* [rank], *rong* [glory], and *hua* [splendor] [and are located in the lanes going by these names].
The famous courtesans, with beauty that can bring down a kingdom, all hail from Suzhou and Yangzhou.
With smiles, their maids greet the arriving visitor;
It is a place where courtesans perform their pure [southern] tunes.[53]

Characteristically, courtesan entertainment was an integral part of this mosaic of the city. As indicated in the first line of "The Courtesan House," the best of the courtesan establishments in the Foreign Settlements were known by the name of the *linong* in which they were located. In such high-class houses, singing was one of the most important entertainments. While Peking opera was offered in the theaters, the clients came to these houses to enjoy melodies from the south, *kunqu*.

Courtesan entertainment was thus a worthwhile topic for these ballads, together with other extraordinary items such as Western-style carriages, wine shops, a road-sprinkler cart, the horse race, theaters, photography, opium dens, gas lamps, and the Western-style bar. While it is difficult to identify the authors behind the pen names, the prefaces state that they were men of letters who happened to tour Shanghai or had come for business, often more than once. For them, the city was so strikingly different from anything in their experience that they felt prompted to record their impressions in the genre best suited to the purpose. The following couplets were collected in "Bamboo Twig Ballads on Shanghai Courtesan Entertainment" (Hushang qinglou zhuzhi ci):

Where on the morning of New Year's day can one [make one's wishes known by] offering incense? It is better to go early to visit Hong Temple.
By late afternoon, the place will be full with the carriages [of the courtesans], all of them in competition with their pomegranate [red] skirts.

With five different types of flowers to adorn the horses' heads, by evening all will have congregated at the racecourse.
Who among the chauffeurs, one must ask, is the most outstanding?
The collective judgment of the bystanders at the racecourse was: Those of the Four Great Golden Diamond Cutters.

Everywhere one can hear the calls of the house servants as they deliver gift plates [from the courtesans] to the clients.
Only as the time comes near for the courtesan [to pay her bills to the house] does she start to worry.

This year, there could be a lot of bad debts [by clients], and how could one
find out where they have gone to hide?

The [female] storytelling hall is crowded with *jiaoshu* [courtesans].
[On the street,] many of the passersby raise their heads;
this caused all to stop to listen. By paying two *fanbo*, one can enter Apricot
Blossom Hall.

In the deep quiet night, the rouge on the lips is sweetest; by now, the moon
is up the short wall.
Coming to Yu Garden and stationing [themselves] in the carriage counts [for
the courtesans and their clients] half as business and half as cooling down.

With anxiety and dread as New Year's eve approaches ever closer, [the maid]
A Bao just returned from collecting debts [from clients].
Together they try to anticipate who will show up once morning comes, to
open the New Year's fruit plate offering.[54]

The short vignettes in these poems indicate what the authors considered fashionable and new with the Shanghai courtesans. The women dressed in red, a color forbidden to them by Qing sumptuary laws, and they competed with one another at the horse race by adorning themselves, their horses, and their chauffeurs. The poems also reflect in a sympathetic manner the courtesans' worries about clients paying their bills, because the courtesans themselves must pay the house, servants, jewelers, tailors, and restaurants. Financial pressure on the courtesans was immense, and their anxiety was highest during New Year's, when bills were due. Thus, their need for divine protection, expressed especially during holidays. These poems take the tone of the knowing insider who describes the scene with sympathy and at the same time maintains a bemused distance.

Yuan Zuzhi (1827–1902) was one of the most prolific writers of bamboo twig ballads. He published under the pen name Cangshan Jiuzhu and wrote hundreds of poems. Handwritten copies were passed around, and many were published in *Shenbao*.[55] Yuan, the grandson of the famous Qing poet Yuan Mei (1716–1798), was a native of Hangzhou. He had come to Shanghai with his older brother when the latter became the local magistrate in 1853. A few months later, his brother was killed during the Small Sword Uprising. In the 1870s, Yuan Zuzhi became an official in the local government. When he retired, he lived in the walled city, looking forward to a quiet life of few cares, but in 1881, he moved to the Foreign Settlements.[56] Perhaps he was invited to work for a newspaper, as he is known to have done.[57] He built a house near Fuzhou Road, which became famous under the name Willow Towers (Yangliu Loutai).[58] It soon became the gathering place for the city's best-known new men of letters; people such as Wang Tao and He Guisheng used to go there to drink and recite poetry.[59] Among the regular guests was the Japanese Shibata Yoshiku, with whom Yuan maintained a close friendship over many years.[60] Willow Towers was also the home of the Kui Garden Poetry Society (Kuiyuan Shishe), which Yuan himself had organized. Some of the other members of this society also wrote and published bamboo twig ballads in *Shenbao*. The tight connection between the press and writers such as Yuan Zuzhi was very much the norm at the time.

Yuan Zuzhi was considered a lone master of bamboo twig ballads. He was also known as a great patron of the Shanghai courtesans. He wrote much about them, in both bamboo twig ballads and rhymed couplets.[61] His relationship with Li Sansan was legendary.[62] Zou Tao commented that Li certainly was one of the courtesans whose fame was made through promotion by a man of letters.[63]

Li Sansan was the daughter of an official (*taishou* rank) and his concubine. After the official's death, the concubine was thrown out by the main wife and moved to Suzhou with Sansan. Xiaolantian Chanqing Shizhe, the author of *A Register of Shanghai Flowers*, who claimed to know the mother and daughter personally, wrote that Sansan's mother had little ability in managing their household. She spent much money inviting courtesans to the house for dinner parties and often stayed at courtesan houses herself. Thus, all her fortune evaporated. When the Suzhou magistrate banned courtesan entertainment, she found the boredom unbearable, hired a boat, and moved to Shanghai with her daughter. As money finally ran out, the mother established Sansan, who was then sixteen years old, as a courtesan. Sansan's beauty and charm made her a success. Her staunchest devotee was Yuan Zuzhi. To promote her, he wrote a series of sixty rhymed couplets.[64] He and two other friends launched a poetry event at *Shenbao* on Li Sansan's behalf. Eighty people ended up entering their dedication poems. As a consequence, she became nationally known, and visitors from all over the Empire came to seek her out. Clearly, the poems and ballads of these men of letters were instrumental in establishing her fame.[65] She went on to win second place in the courtesan contest of 1882.[66]

Yuan wrote this poem to her:

1

Courtesan entertainment here [in Shanghai] matches [= is superior to]
  that of all other cities in Jiangnan,
Exuding a myriad different hues, which visitors are at liberty to explore.
After visiting the thirty-*li* [stretch of] courtesan establishments,
There is no one who does not mention Li Sansan.

2

In search of spring, [my] heart is already intoxicated;
In a drunken state, [I] enter among the flowers and compare the loveliness
  of the different butterflies.
After a thorough survey of their variety,
All of them pale compared to Li Sansan.

3

[Her] beauty, which radiates all over with its subtle fragrance,
Without doubt overwhelms all competition.
[I] would like to cast one hundred thousand golden bells
[So that I can] provide the most secure protection for Li Sansan.[67]

All the poems in Yuan Zuzhi's *Songs of Shanghai* (Haishang yin) are dedicated to courtesans.[68] When Li Boyuan's newspaper *Entertainment* ran its first flower competition in 1897, Yuan wrote the guidelines.[69]

Although Yuan was one of the resident writers, he at times criticized the reckless fashion of conspicuous consumption, especially on courtesan entertainment, among Chinese visitors and residents of the Foreign Settlements. His criticisms were mostly directed at the clients, not the courtesans:

1

When visitors come to Shanghai, their enthusiasm immediately runs wild;
Even a miser will want to show off.
Four dollars in hand call a courtesan to keep one company with drinks;
with eighty cents, one can disappear into the theater.
If one looks only at their dresses and furs, indeed they are gay and pretty,
but when one judges what they are after, it is perfectly frivolous.
Their only concern is with the three festivities [when bills are collected];
there is no place to hide, and who is going to pay the debts?

2

Socks from Canton, shoes from Beijing, this is the fashion of the day.
All wrapped and tied up à la mode, the young man looks stunning.
At the Dangui Theater, he calls for the courtesan,
and at the Tongxin Teahouse, he is again accompanied by a beauty.
[On the street,] he sits high up on his sedan-chair with its blue coating;
[in the storytelling hall,] he proudly writes his requests for arias on the
little blackboard.
Just when he plans to "call home the soul" [return home], he
breaks down and loses all
on this [entertainment] street of Baoshan, which he tried to work through
[from one end to the other].[70]

In the hands of men like Yuan Zuzhi and in media such as *Shenbao*, these Shanghai ballads became a defining element in the Foreign Settlements culture and were one of the earliest indigenous forms for articulating public opinion. By opting for this form of poetry, the Settlements intellectuals used a medium with roots in the past that was yet very much suited to the new circumstances through its capacity to narrate an individual's opinion on all that was new about the Foreign Settlements. These poems are similar to the *yuefu* poems of the Tang, a type of ballad used for social commentary.[71] They appear to have reached many readers. In the preface to his collection of bamboo twig ballads, Yuan claims that people who wanted to know something about the Foreign Settlements read the ballads with great relish when they first appeared in the papers.[72] The large number of such ballads and their accessibility and popularity made the genre important for the new literary and entertainment market and offered their authors a new way to shape public opinion about the city and its courtesan entertainment.

Publishing in the papers helped the writers to become publicly known and even, as was the case with Yuan Zuzhi, to gain a kind of celebrity status. It was a new way to shape and explore their public persona. The medium allowed them to reach readers at all levels quickly and regularly, and this shift in the medium transformed the message. By not only commenting on fashions and trends in the Foreign Concessions but publicizing their personal appreciation of courtesan entertainment and their devotion to individual courtesans, they transformed a central theme of elite culture into a subject for mass consumption and replaced the elite connoisseur with a voyeuristic public.

Making the Image of the Urban Beauty

The topic of the courtesan also evoked interest in the print industry, Shanghai's growth industry par excellence. It took up the literary elaborations of the courtesan image and often matched them with illustrations in the new medium of lithography. Bona fide literati were willing to enter this market with products for popular consumption, for example, Wang Tao, whose *Miscellaneous Records of a Shanghai Recluse* was serialized in *Dianshizhai Illustrated Magazine*. Artisans without the cachet of men of letters also entered this market. Perhaps the best example is Wu Youru and the group of lithograph draftsmen who filled the pages of this magazine.

In the image of the courtesan figure, a particular Shanghai urban sensibility formed and became visible. The figure of the "beauty," or *meiren*, which had been associated with cultural refinement in the exclusive setting of long-established cultural landscapes such as nature, gardens, and inner quarters, was transplanted into the Shanghai urban space. By the traditional definition, the courtesan was already synonymous with the beauty. The revolution in these Shanghai illustrations is the courtesan's position and behavior in the urban environment. Her public persona as depicted in this new setting signals the characteristics of what was to become the urban beauty.[73]

Dianshizhai Illustrated Magazine was instrumental in articulating and spreading this image. Founded and managed by Ernest Major, the magazine established an illustrated journal in the style of the *London Illustrated News, Harper's, Frank Leslie's Illustrated Paper*, and *The Graphic* among the Chinese media.[74] Designed to provide readers with entertaining illustrations and reading in their leisure time, this magazine, which came out thrice a month, was immensely popular and successful in and beyond Shanghai; it ran for a total of fourteen years, from 1884 to 1898.[75] It focused on fantastic, outrageous, and generally newsworthy events in Shanghai, China, and the world, reflecting a new type of globalized and urban aesthetics, which privileged specific, titillating depictions of the urban social environment.[76]

Shenbao had established the newsworthy status of Shanghai's top courtesans a decade earlier; their newsworthiness was most obvious when the paper felt it should report on their public behavior.[77] Eventually, this last feature became one of the favorite topics for *Dianshizhai Illustrated Magazine*. Far from unified, these new stories offer a lively and multifaceted profile of the courtesan. Her public persona was at the heart of the fascination she evoked. She was a source of titillating scandal.

*4.3. "The startling separation of the mandarin ducks" (Jingsan yuanyang). Lithograph, illustration by Zhu Ruxian. Lin Daiyu, one of the four courtesan stars of the 1890s, and one of her lovers kneel before the Western magistrate, begging to be let off. They had been apprehended while making love in her carriage. (*Dianshizhai huabao*, no.* yuan*, 11 [Nov. 1897]: 87)*

The magazine illustrated a report that a Sikh policeman had apprehended Lin Daiyu and one of her clients for making love while riding in her carriage on a secluded road (fig. 4.3). Another illustration from the magazine depicts a courtesan who has dared to appear on the street wearing men's clothes (fig. 4.4), and yet another shows two courtesans standing in their carriages to hurl insults at each other with bystanders clapping and cheering them on (fig. 4.5). On the other end of the spectrum, a courtesan is shown to be capable of grand generosity. In figure 4.6, Hong Wenlan, who is described in the text as "valiant and heroic in bearing" and well known for her "bold and generous character," sees a woman with a baby crying by the river and stops her carriage to give the woman a generous donation.

The portraits were drawn in a realistic style and illustrated the public behavior of the Shanghai courtesan as a core ingredient in Shanghai's new image. They contain an implicit expression of cause and effect. In figure 4.3, Lin Daiyu is humiliated as she and her lover beg for clemency; in its juxtaposition of Lin to the foreign

*4.4. "The desire to imitate the stride of the male" (Yuanxiao xiongfei). Lithograph, illustration by Fu Jie. This courtesan has been caught on the street in men's clothes. (*Dianshizhai huabao, *no.* le, *12 [1894]: 95)*

magistrate, the scene contrasts law and order, represented by the foreign official, with scandalous behavior. Figure 4.4 seems to have a similar message. The courtesans' misuse of the public realm is highlighted in figure 4.5, with the fighting courtesans dominating the street in their luxurious open carriages, which evoke the particular background of the Shanghai Foreign Settlements. These illustrations add an ironic twist to the image of Shanghai as the land of order and wonder by recasting its marvels in an exciting, even marginally outrageous real-life context. The city's glorious image was not fully negated, but the illustrations conveyed a sense of ambivalence and urban irony.

The vulgarization of the courtesan's image reacts to the commercialization of the Shanghai embodied by these women. Just as the earlier courtesan image was built on the values and imagined world order of the literati, the portrait of its demise shows the former refinement replaced by materialism, Western-style urban accou-

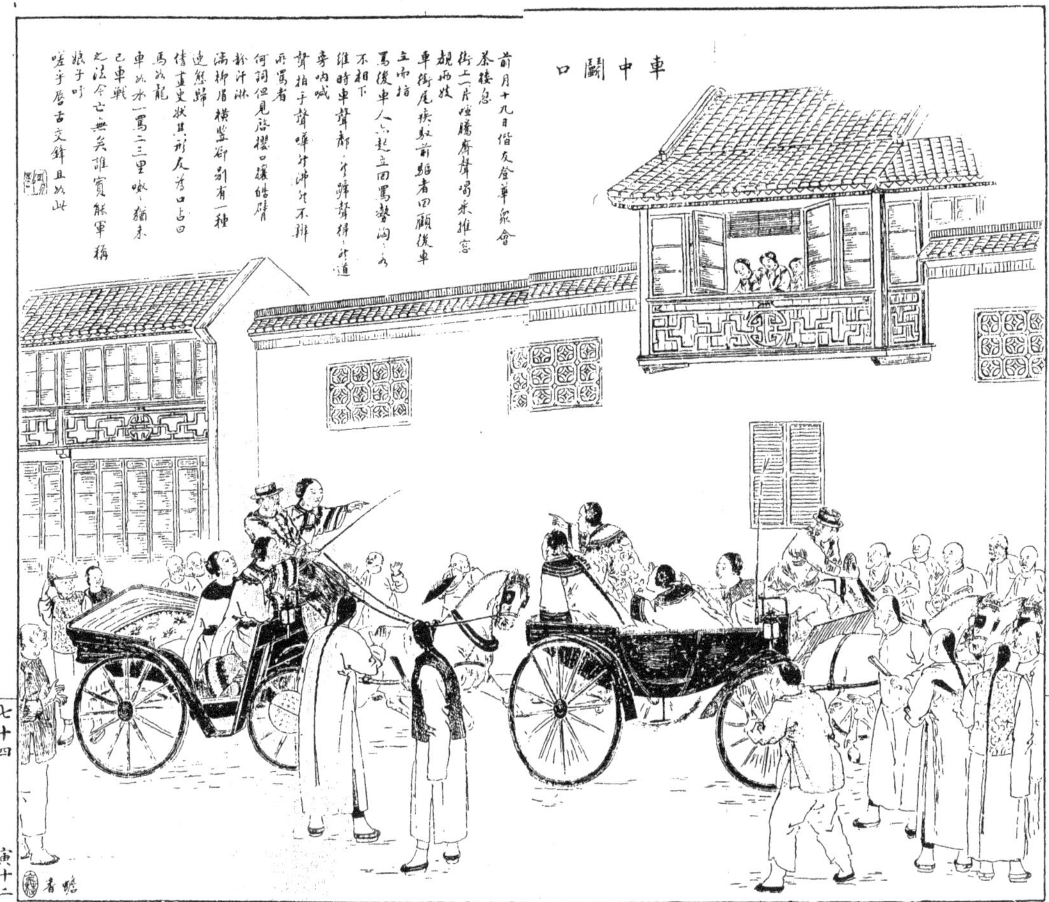

*4.5. "Fighting with words in the carriage" (Chezhong doukou). Lithograph, illustration by Jin Chanxiang. Two courtesans insult each other while bystanders clap and cheer them on. (*Dianshizhai huabao*, no.* ying*, 12 [1888]: 74)*

trements, and moral corruption. These representations of courtesans reflect the conflicting experiences of the city's commercial might and decadence. The triumph of commercialism is marked as an urban phenomenon, and it finds expression in scenes of vulgar behavior on the part of the courtesans.

The illustrations and the accompanying text emphasized the unmistakable public landmarks of the Shanghai Settlements. With the carriage alone, the locale was identified, its urban environment, which included the Western presence, was characterized, and a new Chinese urban lifestyle was shown in which unique and newsworthy, if occasionally scandalous, women had become prominent parts of the public realm.

The transformation of the traditional secluded beauty into the urban beauty thus entailed a reinterpretation of cultural symbols. The traditional dreamscape was replaced by the extraordinary as evoked by the foreign. Yet, depending on perspec-

*4.6. "A courtesan eager to perform righteous deeds" (Qinglou haoyi). Lithograph, illustration by Yun Lin. While on an outing, the courtesan Hong Wenlan stops her carriage and helps a poor woman with a baby. (*Dianshizhai huabao, *no.* li, *11 [1898]: 82)*

tive, the Shanghai urban environment was seen with quite different implications. Unlike the figures in traditional illustrations (figs. 4.7–4.9), the urban beauty in *Dianshizhai Illustrated Magazine* was shown in crowded streets and parks. Sensational reporting replaced the guides' aggrandizement of the city and its courtesans. This representation greatly changed the cultural status of the setting. The element of exclusiveness, one of the most important signs of high culture, was being erased. The public realm, although decorated with foreign things, was the property of urbanites at large. The image of the courtesan as presented in this environment was a sardonic reflection on past cultural refinement. As she began to be treated as a newsworthy personality, the courtesan's public behavior was read against the cultural assumption of what a beauty ought to be seen doing. By surrounding her with crowds and showing her behaving like a commoner, *Dianshizhai Illustrated Magazine* illustrations added a layer of irony. The beauty of the urban space thus combined *qi*, or "the extraordinary," with the new element of "the strange" and even "the grotesque" (*guai*), which traditionally was not part of the beauty's representation.

4.7. This seventeenth-century illustration exemplifies the painting motif "gazing into the distance" (wang yuan)*, a well-established trope with romantic associations. Woodblock print. (Deng Zhimo,* Sensen pian*)*

4.8. "Qushi" (Qushi). Woodblock print, by Huang Duanfu (active early seventeenth century). Courtesan and patron are depicted in an intimate and refined setting that evokes the dreamlike quality of the world of sensuous pleasures. The figure of the courtesan is both an embodiment of a culture of refinement and a symbol of an idealized social order. (Zhu and Zhang, Qinglou yunyu, *1:12)*

4.9. "Elegant banter" (Yaxue tu). Woodblock print. As a professional entertainer, the courtesan was allowed a certain degree of freedom. In this illustration, she is shown initiating sexual play by clasping the catalpa tree between her legs, evoking the notion and image of union. This elicits a smile from her patron. (Wu ji baimei, *1617, 1:11)*

Tabloids, Intellectuals, and Courtesans

Next to the lithograph illustrations, the new mass media were instrumental in creating the image of the urban beauty. They also benefited from not being bound by the conventions of established genres. The entertainment tabloid daily, known as *xiaobao*, was the unmistakable venue for entertainment news. Its appearance during the 1890s shows the degree to which the new culture of leisure had consolidated. These papers pioneered a new way of perceiving time and leisure. They were by nature urban. They brought together high and low literary and journalistic matter ranging from poetry to jokes and from gossip to fiction, and they might include a strong dose of political satire. During their early period, in the late 1890s and early 1900s, however, their main focus was the Shanghai courtesan, and they were run by some of the brightest and most innovative young men of letters of the time.

Li Boyuan (1867–1906) founded this new medium with his two papers *Entertainment* (Youxi bao) and *World Vanity Fair* (Shijie fanhua bao).[78] He decided that *Entertainment* would focus on Shanghai courtesans and that *World Vanity Fair* would concentrate on both courtesans and opera actors. In these pages, Shanghai men of letters could amuse themselves by writing about courtesans and actors in the safe haven of the Foreign Settlements and even have their fun lampooning the Qing court.

The Shanghai courtesan as a *specialité* of the city shared the papers' pages with literary works. Both *Entertainment* and *World Vanity Fair* made serialized dramas and novels into standard features. Their early fictional pieces had no political agenda. For example, *A Pair of Phoenixes Takes Off* (Feng shuang fei), a hitherto unpublished work by the woman author Cheng Huiying, was serialized in *Entertainment* starting in 1897. The installments came as loose-leaf inserts in the paper. In his preface, Li cast himself in the role of the protector of flowers who had discovered the work of this talented woman and brought it to public attention.[79] Eventually, serialized novels of social and political satire took center stage. The publication of these works constituted another Shanghai *specialité*, for only in Shanghai could such subversive works be published and find their way into the marketplace (fig. 4.10). The upper part of the page shown here has courtesan news, and the lower part has a segment of a novel. The Boxer Rebellion and the invasion of the capital by allied forces in 1900 prompted Li Boyuan to use his *World Vanity Fair* to publish even more works of this type.[80]

When Li Boyuan came to Shanghai in the spring of 1896, he was twenty-nine years old, and no one had heard of him. Within a few months, he became the most successful Chinese journalist working in the new line of Chinese-language entertainment tabloids. He set up *The Guide* (Zhinan bao) in 1896; this paper exhibited some key features of his later papers, namely a focus on entertainment news and a literary flourish in the column headings.[81] He stated that the idea for the paper came from a discussion about French entertainment papers with a Westerner, probably J. D. Clarke, the editor of the *Shanghai Mercury*.[82] In his opening statement in *Entertainment*, Li confirmed the Western origin of the concept of the entertainment

時事嬉譚

滑稽新詩

遊記

妝飾志

救時策

庚子國變彈詞

4.10. On one page, World Vanity Fair *(Shijie fanhua bao) offered news about the comings and goings of Shanghai courtesans, fashion trends, and new regulations for the city's public parks as well as, in the lower section, an installment of a political novel. (*Shijie fanhua bao, *October 10, 1902, 2)*

paper, adding that the British founder of *Shenbao*, Ernest Major, and the American founder of *Xinwen bao*, John Ferguson, were his models as editors.[83] He wanted to emulate their principles of hard work and well-researched articles based on solid evidence.[84] These certainly were lofty aims for an entertainment newspaper, but, judging from the "Correction" column on the last page of the paper, it is clear that at least in some cases mistakes were duly acknowledged and corrected.[85]

Li Boyuan's Shanghai residence also served as his business premises. He edited *Entertainment* on Huifu Lane, off Fuzhou Road, in the heart of Shanghai's entertainment district, and later moved to nearby Xizang Beilu, Yixing Lane, for *World Vanity Fair*.[86] Although he lived the hectic life of a big-city journalist, and his job made him a habitué in courtesan circles, his personal life was rather traditional, according to his second wife. He lived in a two-story house in Xizang Beilu. The top floor was occupied by his family with his mother and his first wife and, after the latter's death, his second wife and his concubine. Quite in the traditional manner, his mother arranged these marriages; she had the two women sent by boat from his hometown to Shanghai.[87] Li dutifully gave his mother four hundred dollars a month for household expenses. He dressed very simply in a long indigo blue gown and rarely wore the fashionable silk jacket.[88]

Li Boyuan was always overworked and eventually died of tuberculosis. He had reporters in the entertainment quarters of the city and the help of at least two assistants but was still extremely busy.[89] Socializing went with his profession. In addition to his newspaper work, he also organized the Calligraphy and Painting Association (Shuhua She), in November 1897, and the Shanghai Literary Society (Haishang Wenshe), also known as the Literature and Arts Society (Yiwen She), which had its own newspaper.[90] In this sense, the newspaper also became a new nucleus for a social network, with writers and readers forming a virtual society.[91]

In his desperate efforts to manage his workload, Li placed a public announcement in *Entertainment*, informing friends and readers that he would receive visitors only between 4:00 and 5:00 P.M.[92] This act was extraordinary in its radical departure from both the traditional notion of time and the lifestyle of men of letters and clearly marks the beginning of a modern attitude toward time and the work schedule of a modern industrial enterprise. As Li's day was divided between writing and the business operations of the paper in the morning and socializing in the late afternoon and evening, the 4:00–5:00 time slot was the only one available. One of his favorite places for afternoon tea was Zhang Garden, but of course he also went there on business. Most of the top courtesans showed up there with their clients, and it was the preferred meeting place for visitors and local men of letters.[93] Here, Li Boyuan met friends, cultivated the connections necessary for running his papers, and collected gossip by and about courtesans.

Profitability was a major concern. Through his advertisements, Li Boyuan demonstrated that entertainment newspapers could also offer cultural products—such as books, calligraphy, and paintings—access to a targeted readership. The serialization of novels helped to stabilize circulation. However, income from his different enterprises apparently was not sufficient to support a lifestyle such as his. When he died at age forty, he left his family nothing but his enterprise, which was loaded with debt.[94]

Ouyang Juyuan continued in the footsteps of his mentor. It is said that he did much of the actual writing and editing of Li Boyuan's papers and even some parts of his novels.[95] He arrived in Shanghai in 1898, a year after Li Boyuan founded *Entertainment*, and began sending his contributions to the paper. According to Bao Tianxiao, Ouyang was an extremely talented young man with a gift for writing very fast.[96] This might have been one of the reasons why Li hired him to work for the paper, which was published daily. Ouyang is known as the author of the novel *Idle Talk in Scorching Heat* (Fupu xiantan), published in 1904, but much of his writing did not appear under his name. Little is known about him, but he clearly was familiar with the courtesan world; at one time, he was rumored to be the lover of none other than Lin Daiyu. He wrote a preface to her account of her experiences in Beijing during the 1900 Boxer Rebellion and might have had a hand in writing the text as well. The author of the 1899 courtesan novel *Traces of the Past in the World of Shanghai* (Haitian hongxue ji) used the pen name Erchun Jushi, which has been identified as one of his.[97] He also coauthored a play with one of Li Boyuan's assistants, Pang Shubai. The subject of this work is the founding of the courtesan cemetery, in which he appears to have played a very active part. The play places Lin Daiyu at the center and makes her the heroine.

After Li Boyuan's death, Ouyang tried to take over ownership of Li's two papers, which caused some irritation among fellow newspapermen. The move was blocked by a close friend of Li's, the Peking opera singer Sun Juxian. Ouyang died very young at the age of twenty-four, of syphilis, according to some contemporaneous accounts. It was said that Ouyang's talent represented the best of the Settlements' men of letters, and his drinking and whoring the worst.[98]

Li Boyuan's entertainment papers functioned as a kind of daily guide to Shanghai's best-known attraction—courtesan entertainment. These papers also reached other cities, where readers might have enjoyed them as virtual and sometimes nostalgic entertainment, quite apart from the satisfaction of being up-to-date on Shanghai.

Li Boyuan was concerned that his papers not appear lightweight or frivolous in their reporting, although their subject matter certainly lent itself to this assumption. He expressed his anxiety and annoyance with those who considered his papers and himself frivolous. His ideal was to combine the modern sense of a journalist with the culture of sophisticated fun inherited from the *wenren* tradition.[99]

In his own dealings with courtesans, he tried to adhere to similar standards. During the early years of running *World Vanity Fair*, he became close to the courtesan-poet Li Pingxiang. According to one source, it was Sun Yusheng (Haishang Shushisheng) who first brought her to Li's attention. Li helped her to set up her own business and raised her stature by continuously publishing her poetry in his paper.[100] By reporting in detail on Li Pingxiang and her creative production, Li Boyuan attempted to establish a cultural connection to the traditional image of collaboration between the literary courtesan of the past and her patron-protector; however, the path he chose was anything but traditional. He held a special competition to promote literary talents among courtesans in 1901 and gave it the same name as the one used by the Qing court, "Special Competition with Focus on Management of State Affairs" (*Jingji teke bang*). It was an easy lampoon of the new type of Imperial Examinations, which also tested Western knowledge.[101] Predictably, first place went to Li Pingxiang.[102] Li Boyuan edited a volume of her poetry titled *Poems from the Heavenly Charms Chamber* (Tianyun ge shi).[103]

All their patron airs notwithstanding, Li Boyuan and his friends were unable to protect Li Pingxiang from being dragged before the court in the Settlements. As the editor of an entertainment newspaper, Li had no choice but to report the story in detail. But he was in a quandary, torn between his duty as a patron to shield the courtesan from public defamation and his duty as an editor to inform the reader about the sensational events involving a top courtesan. He tried to solve the conflict by adding a leading editorial to the news reports in which he presented the case as a misfortune that had befallen this courtesan. In it, he lamented her recent string of misfortunes and included among them the court case.[104] His actual reporting downplayed the case by using language full of sympathy.[105] When Li Pingxiang left Shanghai, *World Vanity Fair* ran an editorial mourning her departure: "Alas, Pingxiang has left! There is no parting banquet, no farewell drink [by the riverbank]; [she left] with little luggage and under an overcast sky; how could one not feel sad, seeing the contrast between [her] rise and fall and the quick shift in the attitude of the world from hot and cold? [I] write these plain lines as parting words for you. [I] think you will not laugh at them."[106] The sharp contrast with the sensational headlines reporting on the trial of the *dan* actor Gao Caiyun, who had been accused of taking an official's concubine as lover, shows that this stance was a conscious choice.[107]

According to reports in *World Vanity Fair*, in 1901, a man accused Li Pingxiang of being his runaway daughter. During interrogation, Li neither confirmed nor denied the relationship or the man's claim. She was sentenced to return home with her father and banned from ever reentering the courtesan profession in Shanghai.[108] Within a few days, the story about her and a Mr. Pan surfaced.[109] Later writers linked the two stories, claiming that the "father" was in fact her former lover.[110] Li Pingxiang had been born into a good family, and her parents had arranged a marriage for her with a Mr. Liu. She, however, had fallen in love with Mr. Pan and managed to convince her mother to take her on a pilgrimage and declare her dead. After the Liu family collected the coffin for her burial, she went to live with her lover in Hangzhou. There, she sold calligraphy for a living before they moved to Shanghai, where she became a courtesan. She continued to excel in poetry and calligraphy; in fact, when she was arrested, she was in the process of demonstrating her calligraphic skills to a patron. She became famous and was much appreciated by Shanghai intellectuals. She left Pan, who had been living off her. He then went to court claiming that she was his daughter. As she did not contest the claim, she lost the case. She then went to Ningbo and tried her luck there. Eventually, she changed her name and returned to Shanghai, where she lived a secluded life.

This episode reveals a new relationship developing among the courtesan culture, the marketplace, and men of letters. Li Boyuan's example shows some of the conflicts and confusion this involved. However reluctantly, the man of letters presented the courtesan, who had once been his ally and a person who could claim his protection, as a news item in the media. In moving the courtesan into the marketplace, men of letters forfeited their past privilege of exclusive access. With the entertainment newspaper, the way was opened for the mass consumption of the entertainer as a cultural product.

The glory of the courtesans, expressed in reports from the 1880s, was also gone. In these times of a perceived national crisis, they were not candidates for the roles assumed by the grand courtesans of the late Ming, with their upright and patriotic commitment. In the same move in which the Qing government was shredded by political satire, the courtesan dissolved into a flurry of news tidbits and sensational reports and reemerged as a star in her own right. This did not leave the image makers untouched. The Settlements' men of letters abandoned their aspirations to the grand, central role of savior of the nation and settled into their independent and marginal lives as Shanghai's urban intellectuals.

The Serialized Exposé Novel and the Image of the "Urban Shrew"

By the end of the nineteenth century, a new and powerful voice had joined in defining the courtesan image: the courtesan novel. Some of these novels were first analyzed as a group by Lu Xun and in recent years by David Der-wei Wang and other scholars.[111] An unexplored aspect, however, is the close link between these novels and the press. They were all serialized in the papers, and they were all written by men who made their living as journalists.

The courtesan novels link what hitherto had been news tidbits and separate biographies into an overall narrative. In a unified form that does not share the fragmentary nature and short shelf-life of earlier narrations, they move from news item to story and claim a higher order of truth and justify this claim with realistic reporting derived not from mystical insight but from sociological observation and generalization. In this manner, they had many points in common with the French courtesan novel of the time.[112] The authors of these novels also assumed a new stance. They moved from journalists who followed disjointed daily events or jotted down biographies of courtesans to become masters of the narrative, the men with a comprehensive understanding of this urban world, capable of discerning and describing what is typical while retaining the moral stature that enabled them to make judgments that accorded with values presumably shared by their readers.

The first of these novels is *Biographies of Shanghai Flowers* (Haishang hua liezhuan), which was published in 1892. This novel has a transitional form and indicates its link to courtesan biographies with its title. It took a few more years before this new type of novel took on the character of an exposé that revealed the inner workings and dark side of the courtesan world.

The author most responsible for recrafting the courtesan image is Sun Yusheng (1862–1939), also known as Sun Jiazhen, with his first novel, *Dreams of Shanghai's Glamour* (Haishang fanhua meng).[113] Sun was born into an affluent Shanghai family and was a great patron of Shanghai courtesans in his youth; his ample insider knowledge served him well when he was writing his novels. He was, and remained, primarily a newspaperman.[114] In 1898, he founded the entertainment tabloid *Fashions of the Day* (Caifeng bao), in which *Dreams of Shanghai's Glamour* was serialized with illustrations. The paper sold for six *wen* and was in the same format as Li Boyuan's *Entertainment*, which had begun coming out a few months earlier. In 1900, Sun became an editor at the big daily *Xinwen bao*, and his next entertainment venture, *Be Happy Now* (Xiaolin bao), founded in 1901, continued to serialize the novel. His employment brought him into close contact with Li Boyuan, whose *Entertainment* offices and home were across the street.[115] In these early years, there was much experimentation with serialized fiction in the tabloids. *Dreams of Shanghai's Glamour* appeared with lithograph illustrations in the manner of Wang Tao's *Miscellaneous Records of a Shanghai Recluse* (figs. 4.11a, b, 4.12).[116] It was an instant success. After the first twenty chapters had been serialized, Sun had them printed in book form while serialization continued.[117] It is an exposé of Shanghai courte-

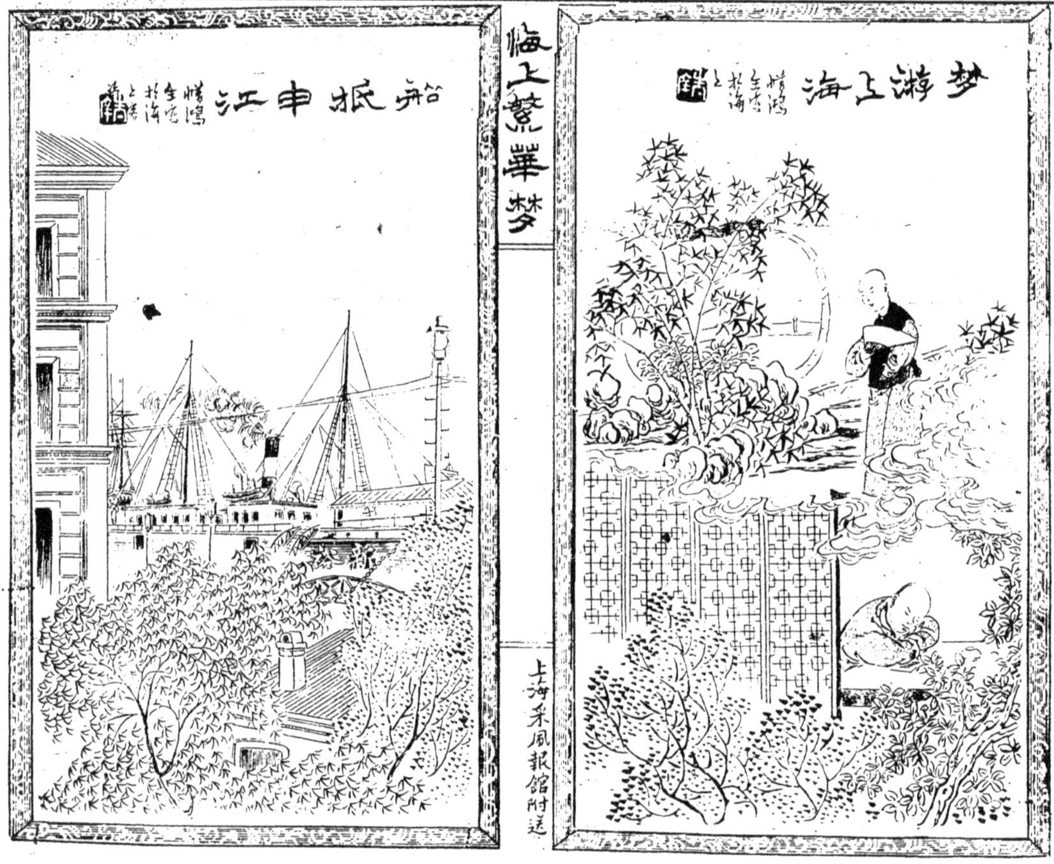

4.11a, b

(a) "A dream visit to Shanghai" (Meng you Shanghai) and (b) "Arrival in Shanghai by boat" (Chuan di Shenjiang). Lithographs. Illustrations for chapter 1 of Dreams of Shanghai's Glamour *(Haishang fanhua meng), by Sun Yusheng. The illustration on the right (a) represents the world of Suzhou. The one on the left (b) is Shanghai, which typically is represented by the steamship, Western-style buildings, and the electric street lamp over the trees.* (Caifeng bao, *July 27, 1898)*

san entertainment and describes the courtesans by and large as cunning businesswomen devoid of any true feeling.

Serialization was not just a minor feature of these novels. It had a major impact on the lives of the authors as it demanded daily installments. Later, popular authors even wrote daily installments of different novels for several papers at the same time. Unlike the *hui* into which earlier Chinese novels were divided, which closed at an unresolved point designed to create interest for the next installment, the newspapers' daily inserts were not segmented by content but by space and might break off in the middle of the action or even a phrase. The inserts were in the form of two pages in a book and eventually could be bound into a real book. The enticement for readers was to buy the paper every day.

海上繁華夢

酒我祇想了詩句沒有將字數算算不是我的心太覺粗了子靖笑道俗語說得好自搬磚兒自打脚本來有的快請一同乾了杯兒我要收令了戟三無語一飲而乾子靖身邊擺的是一碟福橘遂念了一句山中奴隸橘千頭照字點去應少牧一人飲酒少牧道人家一句詩兒是兩杯酒大哥祇有一杯却偏偏作成了我到也湊巧得緊子靖道祇算我心敬的罷如今是應你的令了少牧乾過了酒道我也是席上生風但不許用着酒饌祇許用每人身邊席上的動用器皿又要用身体上一個字又要做一個手勢兒把這句詩描摹出來說不出的罰酒說出的就此過令省得牽扯別人飲酒未知衆意可好戟三道這到有趣少翁請先做個樣兒我們瞧瞧然後可以依令而行少牧點頭稱是遂滿滿的斟了一大杯令酒立起身來將酒杯高高擎起笑嘻嘻念出一句詩來道我說的是萬事不如杯在手念完將酒一喝而盡子靖看着忽大笑道牧弟好幾年不見仍是一塊天真你們看方纔好個樣兒幼安微笑答道他本來是孩子氣慣的今日故友重逢又喝了幾杯酒自然要露出本相來了少牧也笑着道我不與李大哥和你鬬口你們請照這樣兒把令行下去就是倘行不下罰酒不饒子靖道是了待我來接將下去口中說着心裡暗想有了器皿上的字兒沒有了身体上的有了身体上的字兒却又沒了器皿上的一時性急不覺面紅耳熱起來除下瓜皮帽子搔了搔頭靈機一動把帽子吹了一吹又將頭髮捋了一捋衆人見此光景忍不住彼此大笑子靖道且莫要笑聽我過令我說的是羞將短髮還吹帽不知可算得麼少牧道大哥果然靈變怎麼從這帽子上頭竟想出這句詩來祇可惜帽子不是那席上的器皿罰酒是不能免了子靖撲哧的笑道這是我糊塗了若帽子算了器皿衣裳鞋襪却是怎麼東西本來怎能免罰如今我喝一杯安弟接下去罷說定自己斟了一杯熱酒一吸而乾不留涓滴幼安道大哥為人到底豪爽就是喝一杯酒也是直捷痛快的少牧道閑話休題安哥你說的

五

采風報館附送

4.12. Dreams of Shanghai's Glamour *(Haishang fanhua meng), by Sun Yusheng, was serialized in* Fashions of the Day *(Caifeng bao) on single-sheet inserts such as this one. Lithograph.* (Caifeng bao, *July 27, 1898)*

These serialized novels used language tailored to be compatible with the realistic language of the rest of the paper, which helped to broaden their readership. The character of the newspaper changed with the establishment of a storyline linking otherwise disjointed daily issues; arguably, the storyline in turn transformed the entire sequence of the paper and all its contents into a story of the world. It furthermore shifted the status of the reader from that of the highly esteemed customer who, the paper hoped, would buy the paper to that of the passive, enthralled recipient of his daily installment from the hands of the master narrator. Finally, it shifted the reader's reading habit by itemizing fictional segments next to news tidbits and blurring the lines between factual and narrative truth.

Novels had been successfully serialized in newspapers in Europe as a device to expand and regularize newspaper readership, allow journalists to sum up their anecdotal knowledge through fictionalized sociology, and prepare the ground for the publication of these novels in book form. Serialization was introduced into China by

Westerners who were managing Chinese-language publications. Ernest Major's first periodical venture, *Trifling Notes on the World at Large* (Huanying suoji), serialized the translation of *Nights and Days*, by Edward Bulwer-Lytton (1803–1873), beginning in 1872, and his *Dianshizhai Illustrated Magazine* regularly appended free supplements with serialized fictional work by Chinese authors such as Wang Tao from 1884.[118] In 1891–92, Timothy Richard's *Review of the Times* (Wanguo gongbao) newspaper serialized a summary of Edward Bellamy's *Looking Backward*, and Liang Qichao's *Circumstances of the Time* (Shiwu bao) did the same with translations of Arthur Conan Doyle's Sherlock Holmes pieces in 1896.[119] The first Chinese novel to come out in this form was *Biographies of Shanghai Flowers* in 1892, although it was not actually written in installments, and the paper in which it appeared consisted of little else. The entertainment tabloids of the late 1890s were instrumental in making the serialized novel a regular and important newspaper feature and in consolidating the literary segment of the newspaper that eventually developed into the *fukan*, the literary supplement.

Yuan Zuzhi's bamboo twig ballads of the 1880s already exhibited signs of irreverence toward the courtesans, and Sun Yusheng's *Dreams of Shanghai's Glamour* created the first fictional character of the corrupted and corrupting courtesan. In this novel, the image of the courtesan is characterized by full estrangement between the authorial voice and its protagonist. The image of the Shanghai courtesan has gone from the flower to be pitied and the lover whose loss is to be lamented in Wang Tao's and Zou Tao's writings, to Li Boyuan's talented courtesan stars as public personalities, and now to the urban shrew. She is a new breed of cunning urban female who uses traditional assumptions about her as a cover so that she can get as much as possible from her naive patron. The authorial voice appears as the true hero: he is the one who coolly sees through the games these women play.

Liang Qichao's grand claims for the political novel, made at the turn of the twentieth century, as the most important tool for "renewing the people" have all too often been repeated and credited for elevating the novel to the position of premier literary genre. In fact, there was very little actual novel writing to flesh out his promise. Without any such grand words, the courtesan novels were unobtrusively at work to actually do what Liang claimed should be done by the political novel.[120] Instead of offering political education, they pursued their own track of urban modernity in their innovative structure, urban themes, "sociological" approach, realistic writing, and the often ironic distance of the authorial voice. They exposed the hidden side of the Shanghai entertainment world and in this manner paved the way for the political exposé novel, the first examples of which were published in the entertainment papers. The few novels that could be seriously inserted into Liang's "political novel" agenda are courtesan novels such as Zeng Pu's *Flower in the Sea of Retribution* (Niehai hua). In the end, the Shanghai courtesan novel predates Liang's claim, prefigures the rise of the novel to be the leading genre, and ends up offering the only examples for the "political novel" in a further example of a surreptitious push toward modernity occurring in an area sarcastically dismissed by May Fourth authors as one of "depravity."

The close connection between entertainment business and literary *xiaobao* was eventually cemented with the founding of the Great World (Da Shijie) entertainment park, in 1917, the name of which continued the cosmopolitan claims already visible in the titles of earlier Chinese-language newspapers and periodicals. The business tycoon Huang Chujiu hired Sun Yusheng as his consultant to help him develop a concept for this first theme park in Shanghai. Sun had been to Japan and seen the amusement facilities atop tall buildings in Tokyo and Yokohama, and Huang immediately seized on this idea.[121] Sun also created and edited a daily paper for Great World. This was to be one of the theme park's features and would also serve as a news bulletin announcing events as well as an entertainment paper with literary works and cartoons. The paper's English subtitle was *The Great World Daily News.* It sold for one copper apiece. It featured many of the best writers of the day, and three fourths of its content was composed of literary works, all of which were serialized.[122] Under his pen name Haishang Shushi Sheng, Sun Yusheng serialized his exposé novel *Dark Shadows behind the Scene* (Heimu zhong zhi heimu) over a period of three years.

Dreams of Shanghai's Glamour started a subgenre of exposé novels on the Shanghai courtesan. These novels represented a sea-change in the way writers thought about Shanghai, its courtesans and, most important, their own role in the city.

As Shanghai became the print center of China, the demand for talents to operate within this rapidly expanding market intensified.[123] New openings in the writing professions and in advertisement, photography, calendar painting, and illustration drew young writers and commercial artists to Shanghai. The development of the different kinds of print entertainment also generated new ways of living in a market fueled by the rise of urban leisure. The writers, journalists, painters, and illustrators were stimulated by the particular multiethnic culture of the Shanghai Foreign Settlements and their blunt commercial orientation.

They saw and sensed the marketability of the unique figure of the Shanghai courtesan. The first generation of the Settlements' men of letters had brought the subject of their relationship to the courtesan into the commercial print market. As newspapers and illustrated magazines came to dominate the image making of Shanghai and, with it, of its courtesans, the narrative shifted from the individual voice and experience to that of a collective or popular one. A new image of the courtesan emerged with the illustrated city guides and *Dianshizhai Illustrated Magazine,* in no small way as a reaction to the self-staging of the Shanghai courtesans themselves. Shaking off her stereotyped image of frail beauty, she transformed herself into the savvy urban female professional, marketable in her public persona and modern in her sensibility. With this image, the new print media made the courtesans into the utterly adapted personalities of a coming urban and modern society.

The Foreign Settlements were undoubtedly the most receptive place for the exploration of new forms of entertainment. The development of various kinds of print entertainment was fostered by a rising demand for urban leisure and the ability and willingness of the Shanghai print industry to take note of this new market and devise relatively inexpensive and attractive media products with which to explore it. In form, print entertainment replaced the traditional interactive character between the entertainer and his or her client, be it in the theater, in the storytelling hall, or in courtesan entertainment; it largely treats the reader as a passive consumer. To a degree, however, the media actively involved the reader as a writer of letters or a voter in courtesan contests. These media provided readers with a form of public intimacy in which they were entertained and informed about persons, events, and sentiments without the cost or risk of getting involved in person, yet they could be secure in the knowledge that, as members of the public, they were absorbing and judging the same news as were other members of the public but would do so privately.

Shanghai's print entertainment was successful because it integrated Western forms of literary publication with up-to-date news presented from a perspective adapted to largely traditional values. As leisure became a regular part of life for broader segments of the urban population, there was a constant and growing demand for ever new products to fill this time slot. Shanghai, as the first modern urban center on Chinese soil, was the largest cohesive market for these products. Its independence from the moral agenda of Chinese officialdom and its commercial orientation combined to create an open space for new forms of literary publication. It thus became the natural center for the development of modern Chinese print entertainment and attracted the needed talents in the process. Here, men of letters found their skills employable, the life circumstances demanding but attractive, and the environment conducive to exploring new urban social roles. If they had at one time entertained the idea of becoming moral and social leaders through the Imperial Examination system, they found that as journalists and editors in Shanghai's print marketplace, they had a platform on which to publicly play this role in a different context. While the entertainment aspect secured the commercial viability of their products and allowed them a culturally satisfying role, these men and their products maintained a critical edge. The pun on *hua*—which could be either "flower" or "China"— even lent a double meaning to the self-assigned role of these men. In "protecting the flowers," they were living out their grand ambition to serve the country. As they were not given official positions in which to live out this purpose, however, they played the role symbolically and, in part, ironically through their relationship with the courtesan. Furthermore, the same papers that published courtesan news serialized novels of social and political criticism and satires lampooning Qing policies. These men found an acceptable compromise between the need to make a living and their desire to play a public role. As they became more self-assured in their new roles, they found the courage and the freedom to treat their city and themselves with a distinctly urban sensibility, which included a solid dose of humor and self-irony.

In the four decades from the 1860s to the beginning of the 1900s, these men brought to the market a literary and aesthetic taste that was once the exclusive cultural realm of the literati. The commercialization of this taste and its subject matter, the courtesan, made the courtesan the most popular theme in late Qing literature. On one level, the narration of the courtesan took on the symbolism of the past, although the beauty's fate no longer reflected on the falling dynasty but instead symbolized the city. On another level, the narration of the courtesan was the Shanghai men of letters' reflection on their own role and fate as they were in the process of becoming urban intellectuals. Efforts by widely read writers such as Wang Tao and Zou Tao, who themselves were fully involved with the new Shanghai media, to maintain the idealized cultural memory of the grand love between the man of letters and the courtesan show a persistent nostalgia for a past in which both the courtesan and the protector of flowers were in need of patrons and each other. Such efforts also highlight the unwillingness of these men to part with their traditional cultural and status-related accoutrements even under the dramatically changed circumstances of their professional lives.

The rapid development of the Settlements created new circumstances and opportunities for both courtesans and men of letters. By the late 1890s, men such as Li Boyuan and Sun Yusheng were distancing themselves from the idealized image of the courtesan and themselves. In doing so, they left behind the traditional pose of the man of letters. Simultaneously, courtesans and men of letters assumed a new stance, becoming independent professionals. The process continued, and another decade later, the idealizing glow is gone from the courtesan as well as the city. The man of letters has turned into the salaried big-city critic. In his reflections on the self-confident and outrageous behavior of the top Shanghai courtesans, who had long ceased to be flowers in need of protection, and on the city, which had gone from paradise to metropolis, he again expressed his thoughts on his shifting identity.

5 *The Public Flower of the City and the Media Star*

The Shanghai courtesan prefigures many of the features of the urban new woman of the 1920s and 1930s. At the same time, she is at the origin of the period's blossoming star culture. Film and theater stars but also politicians and intellectuals followed in her tracks, vying for a prominent place on the public stage.

Conditions for the courtesan's move from public figure to star were in place by the late 1890s. Shanghai's entertainment industry together with its wealth and Western features attracted well-to-do Chinese sojourners and visitors in steeply rising numbers. They in turn formed a market capable of sustaining not only courtesan services, theaters, hotels, and restaurants on a grand scale but also a new print product, the entertainment paper.

Li Boyuan's tabloids became one of the main features of Shanghai print entertainment. After he had shown the way, a whole range of such papers sprang up, with as many as thirty to forty in publication before the end of the Qing.[1] These papers, most of them dailies, capitalized on the expanding leisure-reading market and were beginning to reach sectors of the populace that were eager to join the formerly exclusive world of play and engage in new forms of urban leisure.[2]

Entertainment (Youxi bao) and *World Vanity Fair* (Shijie fanhua bao) were highly popular with readers, and sales were good. *Entertainment* sold for five *wen* a copy in 1897, and the price was raised to seven *wen* in 1899. Its circulation was about five thousand to seven thousand.[3] The papers also had considerable influence on a national scale, with an initial distribution network that included Beijing, Tianjin, Hankou, Hangzhou, Suzhou, Nanjing, Ningbo, Songjiang, Changzhou, and Wuxi. Demand was strong enough that cities such as Suzhou, Wuxi, and Changzhou increased their sales points from one or two to three or four within a few months after the paper was founded.[4] Letters from readers in the Jiangnan region, Tianjin, Beijing, and even Southeast Asia confirm that the paper was widely read.[5] The fact that both papers ran for more than ten years attests to their success, especially compared to the much more modest life spans of other papers.

The flourishing of entertainment papers at this time might not fit the political master narrative of China's development, which uses the Sino-Japanese War in 1895, the Hundred Day Reforms in 1898, and the Boxer Rebellion and the occupation of Tianjin and Beijing by foreign troops in 1900 as key markers. Nor would it fit the master narrative of newspaper development, with its focus on political advocacy papers such as Liang Qichao's *Shiwu bao* (1896), *Qiangxue bao*, and *Zhibao* as well as the papers published by Chinese students in Japan. The sudden popularity of entertainment papers confirms that society was moving at different, and sometimes seemingly incompatible, levels. These different levels actually interacted closely, even if their stories are not told in the same breath.

The entertainment papers learned from their Western and Japanese predecessors as well as their readers' reactions that catching and holding a reader's interest in their "unnecessary" news required persons and events of some sensational interest.[6] The courtesans were their first and natural choice, given their singular prominence and notoriety in Shanghai, their key role in Shanghai entertainment, and a readership that had been familiarized with the names and attractions of the most prominent courtesans through the courtesan guides. The most renowned male opera singers were a second choice; they mostly gained attention as the courtesans' lovers but soon gained enough notoriety in their own right. By the beginning of the twentieth century, some entertainment papers such as *World Vanity Fair* put them on a par with courtesans. One group that definitely did not qualify, although some of its members might have liked to see themselves on this stage, was that of the new urban intellectuals. The market demanded individualized icons, and for this, the intellectual salarymen had little to offer. They had to resign themselves to writing the stories.

While the general tone of the paper was lighthearted and boastful of insider knowledge, it could also be quite serious at times. The editorials, for example, often dealt with problems in courtesan establishments, such as prices, poor service attitudes, or mistreatment of courtesans by their foster mothers or the magistrate.

The arrival of the entertainment papers created its own dynamics. They not only were making use of the top courtesans' prominence as public figures but in the process unwittingly lifted the standing of these women, increased their name and face recognition, and pushed them toward national star status even though the reporting was often spiced with criticism and satire. In fact, this mixture of adulation and ironic distance remained a standard fixture of the tabloid press.

These newspapers furthermore needed events on which to focus attention, and if these were not forthcoming, they would create them. The courtesans in their turn quickly spotted the opening. They made fullest use of the entertainment papers for their own benefit and obliged with events of their own staging. There was some tension, as courtesans were willing to comply to a degree with the papers' agenda but were also attentive to their own interests.

The new format—with its juxtaposition of political satire, literary effusion, and hot news about Shanghai courtesan stars and starlets—reflected and promoted a shift in the order of things. The idealized image of the courtesan of the past was replaced, in a general literary mode of adulation, mirth, and irony, by what might be called the "urban flower."

The Four Great Golden Diamond Cutters

The Shanghai Foreign Settlements had long been associated with the names of legendary courtesans such as Hu Baoyu and Li Sansan.[7] Shanghai's fame as a place of grand courtesan culture, however, unfolded only with the rise to national prominence of the Four Great Diamond Cutters, namely, Lin Daiyu, Lu Lanfen, Jin Xiaobao, and Zhang Shuyu. The term, coined by Li Boyuan, appeared first in *Entertainment*.[8] It is derived from the name of the mighty Buddhist gods who guard the dharma against evil spirits on all four sides.[9] *Entertainment* wrote later about its origin:

> The term "Four Great Golden Diamond Cutters" was first used in the world of Shanghai courtesan entertainment two years ago in an article in our paper titled "The Four Great Golden Diamond Cutters visit the Zhang Garden." It was at the time based on the fact that Lin [Daiyu], Lu [Lanfen], Jin [Xiaobao], and Zhang [Shuyu] often visited the Garden on the same day. They go to the back of the Dayangfang [Western-style restaurant in the Ankaidi (Arcadia) building] and sit down two on each side [of the door]. As a joke, it was reported as news with that title. Initially not much thought went into the matter. However, [after this article appeared,] the courtesans' patrons at once began to use the term for these four as an honorific.[10]

Entertainment expressed pride in its influence with readers in another article:

> During the end of fall and the beginning of winter 1897, an article titled "The Four Great Golden Diamond Cutters visit the Zhang Garden" appeared [in this paper]. At the time, the term was coined quite playfully. Unexpectedly, it was read widely and praised as being evocative. As a consequence, the names of the four top courtesans Lin, Lu, Jin, and Zhang became known even to women and children, and their notoriety increased tenfold. This also shows how popular our paper is, and how many readers have been inspired by it.[11]

Identifying the courtesan stars by name was instrumental in developing their public personae. Readers' letters about Shanghai courtesans, sent from Shanghai, Beijing, and other centers, make clear that this new cultural game with the Shanghai courtesan as the star held a wide and powerful appeal. The public response sparked by the random quip about the Four Great Golden Diamond Cutters showed Li Boyuan that there was a market for such material. The new term had an ironic tinge, transforming the frail and transient flower into a tough substance, which "even the fire at the end of a Kalpa cannot demolish."[12] Such women hardly needed protection. Some had been in the business for nearly twenty years and had not lost their powers. The irony in the paper's voice reflects a loss of control and, at the same time, reasserts a certain independence. The demise of the Hundred Days Reform was certainly a key factor in convincing men such as Li that the literati had failed in their last effort to save the imperial state.[13] The similarity in attitudes displayed in the paper's satires on officialdom and in its reports on courtesans showed the loss of standing experienced by the men of letters yet reasserted their new role as urban intellectuals.

On their way to stardom, the Diamond Cutters provided *Entertainment* with endless opportunities to report on their every move. The paper covered birthday parties given in their honor; the opening of a new house; the ups and downs of their relationships with clients; their travels; the outfits they wore on particular occasions; and their friendships and fallings-out with one another. It regularly published biographies, letters, essays, and poems about these courtesans written by their admirers. In this way, it effectively put them in the limelight and promoted their public perception as trendsetters in fashion, manners, and business. News often took the form of high-profile front-page editorials, making the Four Great Diamond Cutters the most talked-about people in the city. They became legendary enough to provide the theme of a new opera and a novel in 1898.[14] The paper thus became the medium that translated their public self-staging in the city into national news.

The courtesan stars would not miss occasions such as the three-day spring and fall races, which offered opportunities for a great public display of their style and allure; these occasions were prime news for *Entertainment*, filling its pages with numerous reports and commentaries. The competition among the Four Great Diamond Cutters caused quite a stir. The writer of an 1899 editorial commented sarcastically, "While the Westerners compete with horses, the Chinese compete with money" (Xiren saima, Huaren sai qian). The race might have been the occasion, but the Diamond Cutters were the event. The same writer noted that, already during the previous races, "the four Diamond Cutters had been more determined than ever to show off more than anyone else with careful attention paid to an ostentatious exhibition of wealth. The horses drawing their carriages were decorated with many-hued silk sashes and bows, while their coaches were decked out with brightly colored uniforms especially designed for the occasion. Each day [during the race], when the sun was going down, the four would come to the racecourse and stop their carriages to 'have a look.'"[15] But in 1899, the paper reported, things had gone even further. It then offered, under the heading "Rich Attire Dazzles the Eye," a detailed description of the fashionable outfits worn by the four that even included comments on the manner in which they had decked out their chauffeurs.[16]

The report for the next day went on to compare the "competition about horses" (*saima*) with the "competition about humans" (*sai ren*). In the latter, the four stars engaged in a "competition over coachmen" (*sai mafu*), as to whose was most chic, and a "competition over patrons" (*sai xianghao*), to determine the most elegant.[17] After descriptions of the courtesans' outfits, the style and adornments of their carriages, and the garb of their coachmen, the reader also learned how the courtesans' lovers and patrons approached them to pay their respects.

> Because of the horse race, the Zhang Garden has recently attracted large crowds. Men and women are mingling in an improper fashion, having fun without restraint, and all this in full public view. This truly is a *pañca vārṣika* [Buddhist term for the quinquennial assembly for having all things in common and for confession,

> penance, and remission]! When a visitor sees the courtesan with whom he is on intimate terms, he will surely come forward and chat with her. When a courtesan sees a familiar client, she will nod and greet him. Yesterday, around four or five o'clock in the afternoon—Lin Daiyu only arrived later—when visitors were already dispersing, one saw numerous rich clients coming one after the other to the place where Lu Lanfen and Jin Xiaobao were sitting, to drink tea and chat with them. Seen talking with Zhang Shuyu were also one or two men of refined appearance who looked as if they worked for a foreign firm. There were in addition countless other courtesans who were either sauntering around with clients or were treated by clients to drinks and food. In this public place where the crowds gather, they can be quite proud [of their success].[18]

The reports focused on the show aspect. The horse race was an important opportunity for courtesans to be seen at their best and to signal their growing stature through ever more conspicuous display of their fashion and connections. Reports in Li Boyuan's papers, with their increasingly national distribution, enlarged the stage immeasurably. They heightened the attractiveness of Shanghai entertainment in general and that of the courtesans' offerings in particular and gave patrons some additional clout and notoriety. The top courtesans were close personal acquaintances of Li Boyuan and his very able coeditor Ouyang Juyuan, and, well aware of the importance of the newspaper coverage they received, they made sure that the papers had something to report.[19]

The four stars' power to set trends among courtesans as well as among a widening circle of fashionable married women was reflected in and reinforced by many of the papers' reports and commentaries. The four courtesans' visits to the Arcadia were quickly emulated by other courtesans.[20] To demonstrate one's ambition to become a courtesan star, one had to ride to the Zhang or Yu Garden in an open carriage, dressed in the most expensive and fashionable clothing. As conspicuous display of expensive and gorgeous fashion was the trademark of the four, this was the area in which one had to compete with them. The author of the 1898 novel *The Sensational Biographies of the Four Great Golden Diamond Cutters from Shanghai* (Haishang mingji Si Da Jin'gang zhuan qishu) wrote that staging oneself as a courtesan star meant adopting a lifestyle of conspicuous wealth and splendor.[21] In so doing, some courtesan upstarts even succeeded in having it said that they dared "compete with the Diamond Cutters" (*sai Jin'gang*).[22]

Reporting on the four stars alone would not suffice; new stars were rising, and starlets were trying to attract attention. Li Boyuan's papers made sure to stay abreast of the newest developments so that readers could display their fashionableness, knowledge, and taste. Under the rubric "News from the Flower World," *Entertainment* reported the activities of all those who might have some standing in the courtesan business. *World Vanity Fair* had different special columns, including "Daily Notes on Flower Viewing in Shanghai" and "Main Theater Events" and covered miscellanea under "Tidbits from Trips through Shanghai" or "Anecdotes from Playing in the Gardens." These reports set a new pattern by itemizing events in Shanghai courtesan entertainment in connection with their urban environment.

For example, "Daily Notes on Flower Viewing in Shanghai" reported as follows:

> Lin Daiyu sends a telegram:
>
> On the seventeenth at 6:30 P.M., Lin Daiyu sent a telegram by night express to Yangzhou. For what purpose is not clear. Some say it was sent to Lin Ruhai, the Salt Transportation Envoy for the two Huai rivers.
>
> Zhu Ruchun is not planning on getting married:
>
> Only two days ago, there was news that Zhu Ruchun had married. This is just baseless rumor. In fact, two more young [courtesans] will be "entering her household" [*jin men*] on the twentieth of this month,[23] one called Zhu Yichun and the other Zhu Meichun; together with Zhu Fenchun, who has been there for quite a while, they will be a foursome in the business.
>
> He Airong is moving [her business] premises:
>
> He Airong of Huixiu Lane actually is a courtesan without a business sign hanging outside [*gua paizi*]. Now we hear that she is moving her business premises. The new location will be at Laji Bridge. Perhaps it will [again] be a *zhujia* establishment. . . .[24]
>
> Li Jinhua is looking for "Little Deer":
>
> Two days ago during the evening, Li Jinhua of Yingchun Lane was leaving her house on the shoulder of a *xiangbang* [male servant] to look up and down the streets. When she saw someone she knew, she would ask if they had seen Xie Xiaolu [Little Deer]. When asked what was the matter, she said that Little Deer [a client] owed her the money for one dinner party and fourteen calling services [*ju*] and had not come to clear his debts on accounting day [*jie*]. As a result, the debts have made him disappear altogether, and she had no idea what could be the cause. . . .
>
> Jin Xiaobao and Zhu Ruchun curse each other:
>
> On Sunday night, Jin Xiaobao arrived at Guanxian [Theater] to see Zhu Suyun's performance. During a pause [in the program], Zhu Ruchun also arrived. This is truly [as the old saying goes] "enemies are bound to meet face to face," and the two sides soon began to throw curses at each other. "Wala . . . wala . . ." they made a fearful row. It was only due to the persuasive powers of an employee of the theater, who had come up the stairs [to their boxes] to make peace between them and to convince them to leave, that they did not get into a fistfight, which was sure to come. . . .[25]

These reports, written partly in the Shanghai dialect, are interspersed with puns and insider jokes. With the famous courtesans in the high register of the flower world, the lesser courtesans, identified by their *linong* addresses, supplied lively and intricate detail. The difference between this new literary genre of reporting on the daily activities of the courtesans and her traditional depiction could not have been greater. In these news reports, the grand was made trivial, the sentimental banal, and the cultural attributes and skills that were the accoutrements of the outstanding courtesans of the past appeared hollow and were replaced with petty concerns.

This deconstruction of the traditional image of the grand courtesan, however, was never condescending. There was ambivalence in the viewpoint and judgment. The outrages of the Shanghai courtesan star were represented with a mixture of admiration, disbelief, and sharp disapproval but never with contempt. This type of reporting helped to transform the image of the grand courtesan of the past to that of the outrageous yet savvy courtesan star of the Shanghai Foreign Settlements. In providing daily encounters with the Shanghai courtesan, the papers created a sense of familiarity and even affinity with that world in their readers, which in turn became the environment in which the new star culture thrived.

The most important new development signaled by the rise of the courtesan star was the new cultural powers of the media. They reached far beyond the political class addressed by the political papers of the time. In their reporting on the stars, the entertainment papers began to articulate a new value system for public behavior that resulted not from some supreme discursive power associated with political or intellectual authority but from the recognition of the Shanghai courtesan's strength and a compromise with the courtesan culture prevailing in Shanghai at the time. In this compromise, the courtesans interacted with the media in a way that helped to explore the Shanghai and national entertainment markets but left the newspapers' men of letters little power to dictate and control the agenda. The ironic and occasionally sarcastic overtones in the reports seem to indicate an uneasy awareness of the true power relations in this compromise. From the margins of society, the courtesans came to occupy center stage, and through the media, their stardom eclipsed the earlier fame of nationally renowned men.

The share of the entertainment papers in the making of stars is exemplified in the careers of Zhu Ruchun, who won third place in the flower competition of summer 1897, and Li Pingxiang, whose talents as a poet have been mentioned. They received almost daily coverage for many years in *Entertainment* and then *World Vanity Fair*. The papers even followed Zhu Ruchun through her marriage, troubles with her husband's family, divorce, and the reestablishment of her courtesan business. During all this time, readers wrote letters inquiring after her whereabouts, poems were dedicated to her, and articles were written defending her return to courtesan life after marriage.[26] Li Pingxiang's stature as a public personality was entirely the creation of *Entertainment* and Li Boyuan. During her trial, the daily reports were supplemented by readers' letters and inquiries about her whereabouts.

Flower Competition

From the time *Entertainment* was founded in 1897, Li Boyuan staged events designed to heighten the public profiles of the courtesans along with that of his newspaper. The most important such event was the "flower competition," or *huabang*, for promising young courtesans. *Entertainment* made these competitions into a playful, public event. Readers were to cast their ballots on a form published in the paper and often included a poem or piece of prose in praise of the candidate they were supporting. These were then published in the paper. The courtesan who received the most votes was the winner. In what must be understood as a satiric jest, Li Boyuan stated: "The competition held at this time will be modeled on the Western democratic voting [system]. The result is based on the number of 'write-in' votes [for a particular courtesan]."[27] By utilizing both this "democratic" practice and terminology from the Imperial Examinations, the paper poked fun at the court's method of choosing its officials.[28] In the flower competition, however, the men of letters, normally the sorry objects of the examination process, were in control of the selection. The competition increased its appeal by lampooning the examination system, the hurdles of which Li himself had unsuccessfully tried to overcome.

> When the country holds its Imperial Examination, all hinges on the preferences and abilities of one or two persons who are to judge the strengths and weaknesses of tens of thousands of candidates. Those who are chosen are but one tenth of that number, leaving a few thankful and most in hatred.
>
> What I am proposing today [will be considered] either as being unbiased or as being prejudiced. If you understand me, well and good; if not, I don't care a bit. As I have no preferences with regard to people's choice [in the vote], why should I constantly be concerned whether I will be praised or despised?[29]

In using the public ballot instead of the "one or two" imperial examiners, with their preferences and limited abilities, Li Boyuan gave vent to his discontent with Qing officialdom. In openly contrasting the two systems and events, he made sure that the satire was not lost on his readers. The courtesans chosen in this process represent a complex public accommodation and compromise between the varying preferences of the voters and the candidates standing for election at a given time, with the minority and the majority accepting the votes of the other side as being in good faith. According to Li Boyuan's argument, the resulting courtesan star was the product of democratic principles and popular consent, not of the preferences and judgment of one or two leaders of opinion among the literati.

A Short History of the Flower Competition in Shanghai

Flower competitions had been popular among literati from the lower Yangtze region as occasions for displaying their sense of fashion and taste. The mocking use of terminology from the Imperial Examination system is already found in the name of these competitions, *huabang* or *yanbang*, as *bang* is the term used to refer to the examination competition. Winners of the flower competition were given the honorary titles of the top three graduates of the Imperial Examinations—*zhuangyuan*, *bangyan*, and *tanhua*. The habit of using these honorific titles is first documented for the late Ming. During the early Qing, however, the practice was regarded as a high crime punishable by death.[30] Matching the top-ranking courtesans to different types of flowers, already a highly popular practice during the late Ming, continued to be in vogue during the Qing. From the similarity of the titles awarded to the winning courtesans in late Qing Shanghai to those used during the late Ming, it is clear that the Shanghai literati were well aware of this tradition.

According to brush notes and other records, the procedure in the past was for a renowned and well-respected man of letters to hold such a competition among the local courtesans, serve as the judge, and make the results public in an appropriately literary manner.[31] Sometimes, a collection of poems written for local courtesans, although not necessarily written for the occasion, would be attached.[32] Occasionally, these tasks were divided between the sponsor and his friends, with the sponsor making the selections and the friends writing the poems.[33]

Flower competitions benefited from the protection afforded courtesan entertainment in the Foreign Concessions, where they had flourished since the 1870s. Records of these competitions, however, are far from complete.[34] Wang Tao, who was the judge and co-organizer of a flower competition in summer 1882, left a sketch of some earlier competitions.[35] One of the earliest was organized and judged by a Gangzhai Zhuren in 1868. It included the very substantial prize money of one thousand silver dollars, and first place went to Li Qiaoling, whom Wang Tao introduced in great detail.[36]

During the 1870s, a Mianchi Daoren selected twenty-four outstanding Shanghai courtesans, matched each with a particular flower, and wrote his *Illustrated Appraisal of Twenty-four Courtesans as Flowers* (Ershisi nü huapin tu).[37] Huamei Louzhu and friends organized a follow-up and produced the *Sequel to Appraisal of Flowers* (Xu huapin). Li Peilan took first place in this competition.[38] As in former days, comments on each courtesan appeared under her name.[39] Another competition, held in 1877 by Gong Zhifang, resulted in *The 1877 Shanghai Competition among Immortal Flowers* (Dingchou Shanghai shuxian huabang).[40] Each of the twenty-eight victorious courtesans was matched with a particular type of flower, and they were furthermore grouped into classes. The top three candidates in the 1877 competition were evaluated as follows:

> First place: Rank: elegant [*lipin*]: Wang Yiqing,
> peony.
> She alone dominates with
> unsurpassed elegance and intellectual brilliance;
> [her music is like] the fragrance that seems to
> come from afar, and with it comes the ease of spirit
> that is unique to her.
>
> Second place: Rank: refined [*yapin*]: Li Peilan,
> cherry-apple.
> She is the red-colored hue that lights up
> half the sky; as the white crane, she appears out of
> the clouds.[41]
>
> Third place: Rank: harmonious [*yunpin*]: Hu Sujuan,
> apricot blossom.
> She is the [blossom] that meets the new willow [standing] against
> the wind; underneath, her petals hide the tender oriole.[42]

Of interest in this competition is the emphasis on the courtesan's musical accomplishments rather than her appearance. During different periods of Chinese history, courtesans were appreciated according to different criteria. Although there is no one standard governing any particular period, there are general tendencies, such as the emphasis on cultural sophistication during the Song period, on singing during the Yuan, on literary achievement during the Ming, and on beauty during the Qing.[43] In addition to beauty, these Shanghai competitions of the 1870s also considered other attractions. This emphasis on character and skill is also evident in the use of *Dream of the Red Chamber* (Honglou meng), by Cao Xueqin, as the basic format for the competition; the top candidates were ranked according to the novel's major female characters, who, while certainly beauties, also have education and literary accomplishments.[44] Some competitions included a ranking of "female storyteller" (*tanci nüzi*), which further stresses the point.

For the 1880s, when Shanghai became the publishing center of China, records of flower competitions are more complete. Competitions were held in the spring, summer, and fall of 1880–83, 1888, and 1889 and were recorded in publications such as *A Record of Comments on Shanghai Flowers* (Hushang pinghua lu) and *Collection of Poetry on Shanghai Beauties* (Hujiang yanpu), both by Liangxi Chilian Jushi; and *Illustrated Record of Shanghai Courtesan Entertainment* (Haishang qinglou tuji), by Huayu Xiaozhu Zhuren.[45] The language is closer to that of the Imperial Examination system, with the top candidate given "first in the top tier" (*yi jia yi ming*) or "first in the top tier of the [new] special examinations" (*teke yi deng yi ming*). Short comments follow each name. Among the top-ranked candidates, some, such as Yao Qianqing, Hu Baoyu, and Li Sansan, went on to great fame. They gained public stature to the point that their lives later became the subject of novels.[46] Although similar in form to those of the 1870s, commentaries of the 1880s convey a different emphasis, with personal appeal and physical beauty highly valued.[47] The three winners of the spring 1881 competition were described in the following terms: "First in the top tier: Zhang Baozhen, gentle and serene, chaste and calm. Second in the top tier: Zhou Xiaocui, lovely and charming, lively and vivid. Third in the top tier: Zhou Yaqin, a fairylike beauty, the spirit carries far."[48]

Records are sketchy for a competition held in 1890 and another in the spring of 1891. The source mentions only that Zhou Xiaohong won third place in the 1890 competition, and Hua Cuifang won third place in 1891. During the period when *Entertainment* was holding its competitions, a Nangyue'an Zhuren also organized a competition in 1897, and a Yanshan Taishou Sheng held one in 1898.[49] In all the competitions of the 1880s and 1890s, one man appears to have been the final judge. His name sometimes appeared in print with the record of winners in his competition.

As lithography and other new printing technologies became popular during the 1880s in Shanghai, illustrated courtesan guides and connoisseur books flourished. They do not record formal competitions but represent independent selections. Examples are Zou Tao's *Illustrated Commentary on One Hundred Flowers of Shanghai* (Shanghai pinyan baihua tu), published in 1884, and the copperplate print *Mirror*

Reflections and Flute Sounds (Jingying xiaosheng chuji), published in 1887.[50] As the titles of some works suggest, the scale of courtesan selection and critique had enlarged to incorporate further refinements. New class differentiations were introduced. *Illustrated Commentary on One Hundred Flowers of Shanghai* grouped the courtesans into five new classes: "supreme" (*gaopin*), "beauty" (*meipin*), "unusual" (*yipin*), "alluring" (*yanpin*), and "fine" (*jiapin*).[51] Each class included twenty candidates, who in turn were assigned a particular flower. New ways of linking illustration and text were introduced. *Mirror Reflections and Flute Sounds* did not print all the illustrations at the front of the volume as had been done earlier but put illustration and biography side by side. As illustrations were based on photographs, the generic image of the beauty was replaced by the individual courtesan who was linked to her particular features.[52]

It is difficult to judge the effect of these competitions on the fame and prestige of the courtesans. According to the authors of these events and the literary productions that accompanied them, the victorious courtesans became famous and their businesses flourished.[53] Men of letters detailed their motives for holding such competitions in the prefaces to their publications and characteristically reiterated the traditional position that it is the duty and honor of men of letters to appreciate, promote, and protect outstanding courtesans so that they do not pass away without their names recorded and their fame spread.[54] At the same time, these competitions and publications had an extraordinary effect on the image of Shanghai urban culture. They contributed to an image of prosperity and wonder that did not depend on firsthand experience but could exert its influence far beyond the confines of the Foreign Settlements. They signaled the beginning of the city's self-aggrandizement and self-promotion as a tourist center that one simply had to visit.

From the 1860s to the 1890s, two changes occurred. The courtesan competitions were no longer staged and judged by a single man with perhaps a few collaborators but increasingly involved the public. The same drift toward collective authorship is discernible in the books that recorded and celebrated these events. The latter development might be due in part to the development of Shanghai's print industry, with its focus on gaining a broader market. As a consequence, many courtesan connoisseur books were put together by editors out of material written by different authors. The editor continued to hold a very important position, but the list of the outstanding courtesans could come from many authors. For example, the defining feature of *Illustrated Record of Shanghai Courtesan Entertainment* is the individualized calligraphy and the signature at the end of each of the one hundred courtesan biographies, which emphasized the popular nature of the enterprise and the collective effort behind its creation. With the larger, high-quality lithograph runs and advertisements for them in the newspapers, these books reached a far wider and more diverse readership.[55]

Entertainment's flower competitions took these trends one step further with the transition from collective authorship to a public competition that offered heightened publicity. The refined semiprivate event of the past became a participatory public event. The winners rose to stardom through a popularity fueled by regular, attractive, and positive press coverage and not through the influence of a particular patron.

Entertainment *and the Development of the Flower Competition*

The first *Entertainment* competition, called an "election of flowers" (*huaxuan*), was held in August 1897. It was designed to promote younger and lesser-known courtesans, and famous courtesans such as Cai Menglan (also known as Sai Jinhua), Lu Lanfen, and Hua Tianyu were explicitly excluded.[56] The winner in the top category, with nine votes, was Zhang Sibao, sixteen years old, from Suzhou, residing in West Huifang Lane; second, with seven votes, was Jin Xiaobao, nineteen years old, from Suzhou, residing in Daxing Lane; and third, also with seven votes, was Zhu Ruchun, seventeen years old, from Suzhou, residing in Tongan Lane.[57] Of the other courtesans, 30 made it into the second tier, and another 107 into the third. Obviously, voting required personal familiarity with the courtesan and willingness to share personal preferences with the public. The numbers might seem low, but the competition demonstrates the emergence of a new way of public consensus forming as well as acceptance of majority rule.

The initial success of *Entertainment* as a newspaper was certainly closely connected with its revival of the flower competition.[58] The event's success showed the viability of integrating commercial considerations with cultural play in entertainment papers and had considerable impact on the later tabloids.

The flower competition became a regular feature of *Entertainment* during the first three years of its publication. In 1897, the paper organized at least two such events.[59] Li Boyuan had originally announced that there were to be four such events a year and that the paper would depend on reader participation for a public vote.[60]

Both readers and courtesans wrote to the paper.[61] The date when the voting results were to be announced had to be postponed several times.[62] Along with Shanghai readers, readers who had visited Shanghai and had kept in touch by subscribing to the paper also submitted votes and write-ins. Even an American presented his vote, giving the Shanghai Municipal Council as his address because, as he put it, he had no particular occupation or permanent address.[63] In the first ten days after the announcement, the paper received more than one hundred ballot letters.[64] Publication of the results produced another wave of letters, some in support and others appalled. The paper relished the publicity and reader participation by publishing many of these letters.

Li Boyuan's job certainly was not easy, and many of the letters as well as his occasional responses to them highlight the difficulty of organizing this kind of "democratic" competition. In an introductory essay accompanying the publication of the election results, Yuan Zuzhi noted the unique features of this flower competition: "The Master of Entertainment, Youxi Zhuren [Li Boyuan], foresaw the problem [of having too many unknown candidates] and devised a unique solution. When the flower competition was first announced, he asked the public for its preferences [in candidates]." As the recommendations came in, Li compiled and organized them and made notes. There were also letters of denunciation that had to be considered.

In the end, the winners were "decided on the basis of the number of votes with no other comments by the organizer, to show that no one thinks so highly of himself as to dare to take the seat of the judge."[65]

In one article, Li Boyuan quoted at length from a letter in an article that discussed the main complications. First, the letter argued, the most outstanding courtesan was least likely to be popular since she had discretion in choosing her patrons and serving clients and might fear becoming the object of envy and scorn. Second, as Li Boyuan himself had written, there were about two thousand to three thousand courtesans of the highest ranks, *changsan* and *shuyu*, in Shanghai. It was impossible to know them all and form a comparative judgment. Journalists or investigators would be subject to bribes from the courtesan houses, as had happened earlier. And even if *Entertainment* and Li Boyuan provided a public forum for an open competition, men's tastes were so diverse that such a competition could never be brought to a conclusion.[66]

Li Boyuan acknowledged all these difficulties and came up with two more. Interpreting the changes in courtesan entertainment as signs of the deteriorating quality of their services, he bemoaned his troubles as the editor who was sponsoring these competitions:

> Especially in recent years, talents have become ever rarer. Courtesans with talent, beauty, integrity, and accomplishment [the four essential qualities of an outstanding courtesan] are hard to find indeed. With reluctance, we must consider the less accomplished. In fact, I do this with deep regret at having no alternative. Who with strong sentiments would willingly accommodate [this] perverse trend that defines the [spirit of our] times?
>
> Moreover, as we are now choosing the most outstanding courtesans, what is [our] purpose in this competition? And as to the [courtesans] who are working at pleasing others, what is their purpose in [taking part in the] competition? If a courtesan has no clients because of her frightful ugliness, should one then consider her virtue as being hard as granite and her chastity as cool as frost? Or, if I may give another example, during the 1895 Sino-Japanese War, Qing officials outdid one another in fawning and flattering the enemy with abandon. Can we then accuse a courtesan of being unfaithful as she sends an old [client] away and welcomes the new? Is this not [putting things] upside down?[67]

Li Boyuan took an ironical stance in bringing up the hypocrisy of judging courtesans by standards that the highest officials of the realm had shown themselves unable to meet. Into the light banter about his quandary over the criteria for judging courtesans, he threw a political broadside against Qing officials and their lack of patriotism. Such jarring comments combined with the serialized political novel and courtesan news in the newspaper suggest a constant double-entendre. The courtesan world was just a microcosm of the polity at large, and any comment about the courtesans was also a comment about the state of the land. How could one expect to encounter, in times like these, great courtesans, and how could one judge them more harshly than one would officials? Li Boyuan responded to the letter's protestations only indirectly. His lamentation seems to imply that even in such times, one has to make a choice.

Public criticism and scrutiny became important elements in the star culture as promoted by the entertainment newspapers. In Li Boyuan's presentation, the competition became a display of the general deficiency of the times. Morality and integrity were no longer applicable criteria. To make his point, Li Boyuan raised the issue of the fashion among Shanghai courtesans to openly take opera singers as lovers. In the traditional order of things, this would have spelled the ruin of a courtesan's career, since the actor, who had the lowest social stature, was considered beneath the dignity of a self-respecting courtesan. Li Boyuan claimed that if the winner of a flower competition was discovered to have had an affair with an opera singer, she would be dropped from the list. This, he said, had not affected the quality of the outcome, since there were many other equally accomplished courtesans, but as such affairs had become so common, especially among the most accomplished courtesans, if he removed the transgressors from the list, there would be no competition at all. The competition was thus based on imperfection, and its winners were talented but flawed. If a candidate possessed three out of the four above-mentioned qualities, she ought to be considered the winner. The realities of the times required compromise, accommodation, and perspective, according to Li Boyuan.

In a reversal of fortune, opera singers during the late nineteenth century were following closely behind the courtesans on their way to stardom, and *Entertainment* later followed their lives with the same care and attention it had lavished on the courtesans. As public entertainers, opera singers, especially the *dan* singers who took the female roles, inhabited the gray area between entertainment and sexual services. Like the courtesans, they made use of the International Settlement's flourishing entertainment industry to increasingly take control of their lives. In making this choice, both courtesans and opera stars were reacting to their newly gained freedom; they knew their affairs would set tongues wagging, but they seemed not to care.

Li Boyuan's comments were meant to justify his newspaper's seemingly frivolous flower competition in a time when the climate was heating up on the grand political stage for the reform effort of 1898, but even a female impersonator could gain the upper hand compared to the man of letters and reformer by becoming the lover of a courtesan. There was little left for men of letters to do but become newspapermen and organize flower competitions. It was a way of making a living and regaining some degree of control by having a voice in the world.

The courtesans took these competitions seriously. The events were their chance to become famous throughout the Empire overnight. In the last days of the competition, with public discussions breaking out in Zhang Garden and debates being published in the form of readers' letters and letters of recommendation, the courtesan world felt the pressure.[68] On the day the results were announced, some courtesans were nervous to distraction; others kept their patrons at their sides, hoping for news of triumph. On one occasion, the wrong courtesan was notified that she had won, with pomp and ceremony, only to be disappointed when the crown was retracted and given to another courtesan with the same name but a different address.[69] Attractive marriage proposals from clients were another direct benefit of these competitions.

To highlight the power of the press to achieve results, *Entertainment* continuously publicized the marriage announcements of courtesans who had ranked in the competitions. This also signaled the paper's intention to help courtesans escape what was often described as their predicament.[70] Winning the competition meant gaining a form of cultural capital that was still recognized by society.

Judging from the increase in the paper's circulation from five thousand to more than eight thousand copies a day, the response was overwhelming.[71] For the 1898 competition, Li Boyuan went as far as to have photographic prints of the winners glued onto the first page of the paper. People lined up to buy the paper, and the photo studio tried desperately to speed up the process of making the prints.[72] This level of circulation was being maintained at least a year later.[73]

Notwithstanding his political satire and focus on marketable entertainment, Li Boyuan also tried to shape and direct the entertainment business through the paper and advocated a higher level of professionalism in courtesan entertainment. The separate competitions for different types of courtesan entertainment, each with its own set of criteria, were an important innovation and a way to shape the profession by setting standards and encouraging certain tendencies.[74]

During the next two years, *Entertainment* organized what was referred to as *yebang* (leaf competitions) for courtesans' maids, some of whom also became courtesans. Most significant, it organized a competition among music entertainers, known as *wubang* and *yibang*, of which a record survives for the summer of 1897. According to Li Boyuan, this competition was modeled after the Peking opera competitions in the capital, but again, winners were selected by ballot.[75] The *wubang* was meant to recognize and encourage performance and musical talents. Among the winners was Xiao Ruyi (second place), who had been highly praised in the paper before and after the competition for her storytelling.[76] The 1901 *World Vanity Fair* courtesan competition in literary accomplishment is another example of this kind of event.[77] The paper's persistent promotion of entertainment of higher cultural sophistication did not necessarily go down well with clients.[78] The very existence of these competitions and much anecdotal evidence, however, means that recent scholarship asserting pervasive illiteracy among courtesans of late Qing Shanghai should be read with caution.

Li Boyuan attempted to consolidate his papers' position as the national forum in which stars were made by holding a competition in Suzhou, the place from which many of the most famous courtesans had come. As the end of balloting drew near, he made a trip to this city to gain firsthand knowledge of the proposed candidates. *Entertainment* reported his meeting with candidates from a dozen courtesan houses.[79]

During these early stages in the development of the star, core features of a "star culture," which was to unfold later, were developed. The first is the promotion of local urban beauties to national stars. As the paper had the beginnings of a national circulation, participating voters came from different regions of the country.[80] At the time of the competition, a letter to the editor from Beijing reported that the paper was making the rounds in the writer's office and was read with great enthusiasm by many.[81] While the publication of this piece certainly was self-congratulatory, it reveals the inklings of a stardom of national urban dimensions to which the entertainment papers allowed courtesans to aspire. Like the scholar-officials of the past who were known throughout the country through their achievements as officials or literary men, the emerging courtesan star became a national figure by way of the papers.

Second, the competitions created for the reader the figment of a relationship with the star that included participation in the earliest public exercise of the right to vote, albeit in a flower competition.[82] The public airing of conflicting views and the equal value accorded the votes gave the reader the impression that he was actively involved in the making or breaking of a star. This involvement, with its rich helping of make-believe, was part of Li Boyuan's design for the competition, and it established the crucial connection between the paper's effort to create the star and its wish to increase its circulation and advertising value. As the paper was a commercial enterprise dependent on a notoriously shifty market, its survival hinged on its popular appeal and its capacity to establish a loyal core readership. As ideological, ironic, and decidedly marginal as it was in its application, the voting principle introduced by Li Boyuan was a commercial rather than a political device, and its acceptance might have been due to this fact.

The star is meant not only for verbal mass consumption but also for mass viewing. By having the photographs of the victorious beauties glued into his paper, Li Boyuan introduced a new notion, the individualized image of the star with subsequent public recognition as a consequence. This public availability through the image later developed in full with the movie star's peculiar mixture of personal unapproachability and ubiquitous, intimate access to her life and image.[83] The pseudo-intimacy provided by the photographs and reports offered readers a semblance of belonging to the star's world. The flower competitions enhanced this illusion and furthermore created the impression of a market-based consensus on matters of taste and appreciation. The paper's capacity to make itself the medium of both public information on the star and public articulation of this taste was crucial for its market success.

Third, the newspaper and the journalist were the new power brokers in the field of cultural production. Through the competitions, *Entertainment* established the newspaper as a new forum in which cultural authority in matters of fashion and taste could be expressed, with the paper itself a strong voice in the concert. In making the flower competition a public play and a public event, the paper positioned itself as the master of entertainment that was orchestrating the new public voice. Because of her part in the event, the courtesan on the way to stardom was required to be responsive to the new medium and supply newsworthy events that would satisfy readers' voyeuristic appetites; the medium in turn provided coverage and eventually, with illustrations and photographs, familiarized the public with her image. In the process, a courtesan's ability to perform in the limelight became a great asset.[84]

Fourth, although Li's papers freely dispensed news about the professional and private lives of Shanghai courtesans and opera stars, the flower competitions clearly separated the two realms by focusing exclusively on professional entertainment skills. During the competition itself, the paper carried hardly any news on the candidates' private lives, signaling a new and essentially urban cultural agenda. The paper was not interested in censuring individual courtesans for their selection of lovers but assigned them the responsibility for maintaining public morals by harping on the bad influence such behavior might have on the young concubines of the rich and powerful, who might seek out handsome opera singers to replace their aging husbands.[85] With the distance established between the new star and the general public came the print product that promised intimate insights into the lives of these figures. Li Boyuan's papers and the city's top courtesans thus interacted in developing strategies and discovering possibilities for a new and marketable entity in the emerging modern Chinese public sphere, the courtesan star. Far from exposing the private realm of the stars to public view and reducing the distance between the star and her admirers, Li Boyuan discovered his market in the carefully maintained distance between the star and his paper's readers. The tabloid press, which thrived on the development and deeper penetration of the star culture during the ensuing decades with their movie houses and big stages, was to follow *Entertainment*'s trajectory.

The Flower Cemetery: A Measure of the Stars' Powers

In the symbiosis between the entertainment star and the entertainment paper, both sides had no prior models to guide them. They had to craft new public roles for themselves that also addressed their mutual dependency. The creation of the charity "Flower Cemetery" (Huazhong) is a good example of the resulting interaction. The plan to open a cemetery for Shanghai courtesans who had died destitute was first brought up during a dinner party in the early fall of 1898, after that summer's flower competition. Those present thought this was an excellent idea, and Lin Daiyu was invited to join the discussion. She was chosen out of many possible candidates because of her professional name and a famous scene from *Dream of the Red Chamber* that had symbolic meaning for the courtesan world. The fictional Lin Daiyu feels pity (and self-pity) for flower petals that have fallen to the ground, and she collects and buries them. As the courtesan Lin Daiyu was the most charismatic among the Four Great Golden Diamond Cutters, she was the natural leader for such an enterprise. Given her high and wealthy connections as well as her prestige among courtesans, her participation would be essential in securing funds and acceptance.[86]

Lin Daiyu supported the proposal but felt that raising the funds was too much responsibility for her alone and suggested that the three other Diamond Cutters join in. It was also her idea to record donations in a book, for public accountability, and to publish the names of donors in *Entertainment* as a sign of appreciation. The money was to be given to a "charity hall" (*cirentang*) for safekeeping.[87]

In April 1899, seven months after this meeting, the Flower Cemetery was established on a two-*mu* (one third of an acre) lot near Longhua Pagoda southwest of the city. The ceremonial arch at the entrance bore the inscription "Charity cemetery of the flower community" (Qunfang yizhong).[88]

Success, however, had been hard to secure. At times close to collapse, the whole affair was plagued by intrigue, rumors of embezzlement, and recriminations. These problems were caused by a difference between the expectations of the courtesan stars and the journalists. The *Entertainment* agenda was very clear. It tried to use the event to promote the paper by providing its literati readers with a platform on which to stage a drama of nostalgia for the role played by their forebears, pitying the flowers. This also meant that the courtesans' role was preset: they were to be pitied. They were required to play the literati's counterpart and to help in re-creating the cultural setting by behaving with selfless dedication according to the mystique of the grand courtesans of the past. But this role Lin Daiyu and, to some extent, Zhang Shuyu and Lu Lanfen were unwilling or unable to play. This discrepancy made for some tension. Although the courtesans welcomed the publicity, they refused to be drawn into too close an alliance with the paper and to devote themselves completely to fund-raising for a longer stretch of time. In the end, it was the younger star Jin Xiaobao who was willing to take up the challenge and ended up the heroine of the story.

The first public announcement of the event came in the article "A Notice on the Planned Establishment of a 'Flower Cemetery.'" Li Boyuan spelled out his paper's idea of the basic agenda. After lamenting the inevitable passage of time, the sadness evoked by the beauty of a woman through the knowledge that one day it will be dust, and the sad condition of being a courtesan, Li Boyuan turned to the shortness of the women's bloom and the tragic end that often followed. As he put it, when courtesans died, those who were not claimed by their families were buried in common graves with no ceremony to send them to the other world or songs that paid tribute to them. Calling up examples from history, he appealed to the men of letters' sense of duty for help in remedying this situation.[89] The cemetery was to be a historical memento. The literati of the past had kept the names of the grand courtesans alive through their literary depictions. To create a cemetery for the courtesans was to create a locale for the act of remembering, a place where literature, memory, and the fate of the courtesan would fuse in the minds of literati donors.

The courtesans' view of the matter, published under the name of Lin Daiyu, reads somewhat differently from Li Boyuan's. Even though someone else might have written it for her and the other Diamond Cutters, the tone of this announcement is theirs, and it is much more down-to-earth:

> That there should be spring wind everywhere; that the fall moon should be there all year round; that the colored clouds should linger on; and that the beautiful flowers should never wither—of course this is everyone's deep longing, and how could one lack sympathy with such desire? Alas, [life] is fleeting like a short dream; one turn and it already has passed by; dark resentment piles up, and one will be overwhelmed by upsetting feelings. Sublime [love] does not last; the fragile constitution [of the courtesans] is easily shaken; while living in the realm of remorse and anguish [living the life of a courtesan], she [still] has to put on an expression of joy and smiles; [her] happiness or sadness are not within her powers, and whom does she have to share amiable [feelings] with? There are also times when looking into the mirror would increase her lamentation and arouse her self-pity. And when a devoted lover fails to show up, she realizes that there will always be many obstacles between her and the happy event [of marriage].
>
> Thus, before [even] getting rid of old grievances, new sorrows all of a sudden take root. In misery, she faces the medicine pot. All her feelings she speaks not; it

> is difficult to endure the sickness in her body, thin and emaciated, but to whom can she turn?
>
> There are also those who fall into this world of wind and dust [prostitution] through a mishap and live the fate of disaster, while the whole family sees them as the golden goose, so there is no chance for them to pay back what they owe from a previous life. She suffers daily under worries and cares. Sorrowful thoughts are stored and knotted [in her heart]; once they become illness, she goes into decline.[90]

Lin identifies the particular miseries of humiliation, stress, and loneliness as the reasons for the early deaths of many courtesans. She emphasizes the difficulties and psychological burdens of their lives. There is little moralizing, but there is a firm conviction that the courtesan is to be pitied. The question is not responsibility or their historical legacy but the conditions under which many of these women died young. The article then turns to the way in which many of the courtesans of the past were buried and remembered. Hence the need for a "flower cemetery" where the souls of the courtesans could rest and their admirers could come and "shed their tears."[91] The beauty who dies young is a literary trope of long standing that evokes sympathy and sorrow. Li Boyuan and Lin Daiyu used the metaphor in this sense.

Both sides use the traditional tropes of protecting the flowers and asking for empathy with the flowers. This rhetoric hides the fact that the protagonists' roles were all new and shows that they were rather unaware of this. The Diamond Cutters had become well-known urban personalities of high standing who now addressed the public through the medium of the newspaper. Lin Daiyu was the star with the leading role, and through the newspaper, she became the leader and organizer of a public event. Instead of writing private poems of lamentation, both the literati and the courtesans used the newspaper to argue their case and make it a public event. Communication between the courtesan stars also was transformed. They began talking to one another through the newspaper. Lin's letter to the other three asking for their support and participation was published in *Entertainment*. This put quite a bit of pressure on them.[92] Their differences of opinion were voiced through the paper.[93] It also became a forum through which the editors communicated their ideas to the courtesans.[94] The active use of the newspaper by the courtesans as a means to create publicity became a central feature in the formation of the star culture.

The fund-raising procedure set up by Lin Daiyu involved the printing of sixteen hundred Flower Cemetery account books; they were divided among the four stars, who were responsible for distributing them to the various courtesan houses.[95] At the end of the month, the books were to be collected. It is said that on the first evening, Lin Daiyu alone raised more than three hundred dollars.[96] The money needed for the entire project was estimated at twenty thousand dollars.

Entertainment and the other Diamond Cutters suggested that the first steps, such as purchasing a small plot of land, should be taken even before the entire sum had been collected, as this might take too long.[97] It appears that after a month, the fund-raising effort was losing momentum. Lu Lanfen commented in an interview that one master donation book should suffice, and that the four stars should make their own donations and only then go to each courtesan house and ask for contributions.

"We need only a few *mu* of land," she said, "since those who get married need not be our concern, and those with family members will not allow their daughters to be buried in a charity cemetery. Thus, each year, there are only a few [who die and must be cared for]. Hence the need for only a small piece of land. It can be enlarged as time goes on. . . . For the purchase of the land and the building of a sacrificial hall, only limited funds are required. If the four of us each donates two hundred to three hundred dollars, this is already more than a thousand."[98] Jin Xiaobao added: "Since we four are the founding members, we ought to contribute more so as to build up capital. Furthermore, we should host a dinner party at Dacaiguan (i.e., the most famous Western-style restaurant Yipinxiang), add to our invitation list seventy to eighty of those among our sisters generally considered most fashionable [*shimao*], and try to persuade them to help out. We are all inclined to do good and do not want others to surpass us; after [the dinner], we will hand out the donation record book, and the result will not be negligible."[99] Originally, clients and patrons were called upon to contribute funds; in this case, the courtesans took over the role of the primary donors. Perhaps the idea behind the scheme was to encourage the patrons to make good on the courtesans' pledges.

Lu Lanfen's suggestions were directed, through the paper, at Lin Daiyu as the person responsible for the initial planning of the event and for making decisions. The use of the medium depersonalized and objectified differences. Lin Daiyu, in this case, did not deign to respond through the same medium. Meanwhile, to promote their project, the four had a joint photo session with Mr. Shi, the owner of the Yaohua photo studio.[100] In an effort to associate the Flower Cemetery with his paper, Li Boyuan solicited poetry on the topic from his readers. The poems were published in the paper and then collected into a volume titled *The Jade-Hook Collection* (Yugou ji). Contributions, some from women, came not just from Shanghai but also from Beijing, Guangling, Shimen, Lanling, and even Japan. Many of the poems were addressed directly to the four stars, and quite a few rhymed on their names.[101] Some writers treated the event as a poetic theme and wrote continuously for the newspaper in praise of the four Diamond Cutters.[102] The paper even published some "inscriptions" (*zhongzhi beiwen*) that were to be engraved at the cemetery.[103]

In a January 1899 article, Jin Xiaobao answered questions addressed to her by visiting literati friends about the fund-raising for the Flower Cemetery.[104] Waiting for the money required to build a grand cemetery, she argued, was unreasonable and might jeopardize the entire effort. She had decided to take it upon herself to raise what was needed for a modest cemetery and to start immediately. She had already looked at two pieces of land. One located at the northern side of the city was at a good price but was too difficult to reach, since it was in the middle of fields with no real road leading to it. The other was on the left side of the French Settlement, but she was concerned about the Siming Gongsuo incident (in which French authorities built a road through the cemetery of a *landsmannschaft* and opened fire on Chinese protesters), which suggested that the location might jeopardize the peace and harmony necessary for a cemetery. She also had looked at a piece of land near Xujiahui (west of the city center). This she planned to purchase and then begin raising funds for the buildings.[105]

At about the same time, *Entertainment* ran an article accusing Lin Daiyu of embezzling funds raised for the cemetery by repeatedly refusing to hand over the money as agreed upon.[106] Lin Daiyu defended herself in a letter, claiming that she had not turned in the money because it was too small a sum, and that, come what may, she planned to get things moving in the spring.[107]

Lin Daiyu was famous for her extravagant lifestyle, and she was always in debt.[108] It is conceivable that she had used the money to settle debts at the end of the year and hoped to return it after the new year began, but there is no independent account of what actually happened. Li Boyuan, who had invested much energy in the affair and had proposed that Lin Daiyu be the leader, was very disappointed.[109] The rumors continued. On March 19, 1899, after Jin Xiaobao had taken over management of the project and finalized the purchase of the land, *Entertainment* again criticized Lin Daiyu for refusing to hand in the money.[110] In the end, Jin Xiaobao was given full credit for the cemetery. While other courtesans helped in raising funds to purchase the land, Jin raised the bulk through the sale of her orchid paintings, and she wrote the inscription on the arch over the entrance to the grounds.[111] The whole affair, and especially Jin Xiaobao's effort in bringing the plan to fruition, was publicized in an *Entertainment* leader.[112] Reader reaction might be gauged from an article in a Singapore paper that came out harshly against Lin and was full of praise for Jin.[113] It seems, however, that the cemetery was badly managed and soon fell into decay.[114] A few years later, around 1903 or 1904, Jin Xiaobao once again tried to establish a cemetery for courtesans, called the New Hundred Flowers Cemetery (Xin Baihua Zhong), near Jing'an Temple, but she was thwarted by the laws of the International Settlement that forbade intermediate burial in "temporary coffins" (fig. 5.1).[115]

Yet, in a *chuanqi* opera—a popular genre often used at the time for contemporary themes—commemorating the founding of the original cemetery, Lin Daiyu came out well enough. *The Jade-Hook Mark Opera* (Yugou hen chuanqi), a ten-act opera coauthored by Li Boyuan's two assistants, Binghong Shanren (Pang Shubai) and Xiqiusheng (Ouyang Juyuan), tells the entire story of the founding of the Flower Cemetery. While there is one act devoted to Jin Xiaobao painting orchids so as to raise funds, Lin Daiyu clearly is the heroine, and the surviving program notes show her inviting the three other Diamond Cutters to the Yipinxiang restaurant to solicit their contributions.[116]

In reports on the Flower Cemetery, Shanghai courtesans figure for the first time as public personalities, venturing beyond the entertainment sphere and taking charge of a charity of their own. They had contributed earlier to charity, but this was a first test of their star potential.[117] At the same time, it was a test of the power of *Entertainment*. Lin Daiyu regretted failing to live up to her assigned role in being unable to convince other courtesans to participate.[118] Jin Xiaobao, in contrast, argued that Lin's method of fund-raising was to blame for the lack of support, not any deficiency in the power of the four courtesan stars.[119] The event demonstrates that the Shanghai courtesans did accept the fact that, as stars, they had a certain public role to perform and that they understood the potential usefulness of the newspaper in this respect.

*5.1. "One hundred scenes of Shanghai: The new Hundred Flowers Cemetery" (Hubin baijing: Xin Baihua Zhong). Lithograph. Jin Xiaobao took the lead in raising funds for this cemetery for courtesans who died in poverty. She is shown riding in her carriage with a male figure, pointing out to him where the cemetery could be established. (*Tuhua xunbao*, 13 [1909]: 6)*

Star Culture and New Business Alliances

The courtesans were actively involved in their presentation in the papers and the formation of a star culture. As they became aware of this new medium's usefulness, they employed it on a more regular basis for their own business purposes.

Courtesans began making use of the paper by "advertising" (*gaobai*) their changes of address.[120] As they intended to give a boost to their business in their new quarters, these advertisements were crucial in reaching former clients who might not have known about their latest move and might also entice potential customers. They first appeared on the front page of *Entertainment*; later two and then four pages were added for these advertisements alone. The following is typical example:

> Advertising Changes of Address:
> Chen Jinlan at Xiao Jiuan has moved to Baoshu Lane.
> Lin Fengbao, who lived at Xi Shangren, has changed her name to Wen Xiuying after having her freedom bought [from the madam of the house] and has moved to West Huifang Lane.[121]

World Vanity Fair had a special column for business advertisements titled "Commercial advertisement" (*Shanghao gaobai*), and courtesans often placed their ads there. One example reads:

> Advertisement by Wen Yuanyuan: Wen Yuanyuan, who resides in Tongan Lane, is changing her name to Wen Yuyun and is moving to Huixiu Lane.
>
> Advertisement by Zhang Yuelan: Zhang Yuelan, who resides in Tong Shangren, will be moving this morning to Xi Huifang; all young lords, please come and celebrate the occasion by giving a "changing address banquet" (*diaotou taimian*); please come and patronize!
>
> Advertisement by Lu Saiying for her daughter A Bao: After the Duanwu festival, we will remain at our current address; all young and old lords, please come and patronize us as a special favor; incense should be burned *inside* the temple, and rain should fall on land which is *desolate*![122]

Shanghai courtesans also used the newspaper to address grievances such as mistreatment by the madam, unjust accusations leveled by clients, clients reneging on their debts, and disputes among themselves. This might take the form of an advertisement or of an editorial in which courtesans voiced their side of the story. Xiao Ruyi, for example, who won second place in the performing arts competition, placed an advertisement denouncing clients who failed to pay their debts on time. Li Boyuan wrote an article supporting her claim and pressuring clients to pay their bills.[123] The next day, he followed up with a front-page editorial discussing the art of her *pipa* playing.[124] This is evidence that she had moved into the star category, and her newsworthiness did not hinge on some sensational tidbit.

For the courtesan and her client, the entertainment paper functioned as a public arena in which to voice and settle their grievances with each other. In most cases, the paper played the role of mediator, as it did with the courtesan Jin Hanxiang and her client Yufeng Yuyin. On Saturday, October 2, 1897, Yufeng Yuyin complained in an advertisement that Jin Hanxiang did not show up when he called her to a dinner party, a serious breach of professional standards; he further insulted her by referring to her low origin as a prostitute. Jin Hanxiang counterattacked the next day with an advertisement accusing him of lacking compassion, since she had been overworked and overbooked that evening. On Monday, *Entertainment* published an article interviewing Li Boyuan on the matter. He defended the paper's printing of both advertisements, claiming that those who take out ads pay for them and thus have the right to free speech; it was not the paper's responsibility to judge anyone's opinion or to discriminate among them. Pressed for an opinion, he replied that the client was at fault for overreacting and trying to harm the courtesan's business prospects with his ad, although the courtesan should have thought of sending a maid to communicate with the client so as to avoid misunderstandings.[125]

With the papers' success in promoting the new courtesan stars among a broader public, the entertainment industry came to recognize these stars' business potential. Two cases might illustrate the new types of business connections and ventures generated in this manner.

In August 1899, *Entertainment* reported: "In the Storytelling Hall: Tonight the Haishang Yipin Lou storytelling hall will definitely invite the famous courtesans Lin Daiyu, Jin Xiaobao, Weng Meiqian, and Lin Baozhu . . . to come and perform onstage. We have heard that, after many invitations, they finally have all agreed to appear tonight. You, the audience, will be able to appreciate their beauty while listening to their music."[126]

The invitation to *changsan* courtesan stars, who did not specialize in musical entertainment, to a storytelling hall where the cast normally was all male, shows recognition of the attractiveness and market value of these women. Even courtesans who were not specialized *shuyu* performers were trained in singing *chuanqi* and *kunqu*, the southern opera tradition, as well as the popular Peking opera arias and were expected to perform in these styles. The storytelling halls had a chance to present something new, and they used the names of the courtesan stars to draw bigger crowds (fig. 5.2).

The next day, *Entertainment* had the story. It had not been a very successful event. Lin Daiyu had not even shown up, but this lapse was passed over in silence. Jin Xiaobao went and received thirty or so orders from the audience but left without singing. The numbers of requests for the other courtesans were reported in detail.[127]

A few days later, the situation had improved, and *Entertainment* reported excitedly on the new show:

> Follow-up report on the Storytelling Hall: The nightlife entertainments of our city are all located around Si Malu. A few days ago, the various storytelling halls began to invite famous courtesans [*mingji*] to perform onstage, and since that time, Si Malu has been crowded with visitors as soon as night falls. The sudden increase amounted to several times the original numbers, proof enough that the market is greatly swayed by the business of courtesan entertainment. For no other reason, [the early Chinese statesman and philosopher] Guanzi made the establishment of courtesan entertainments in the kingdom of Qi a government policy so as to help his state become strong and rich.[128] Thus, our paper has been investigating and reporting on this development in detail and on a daily basis. Each night [after the performance], we make our reports and print our paper, so that on the next morning it provides a feast for the eyes of our readers. Right now, we have learned that last night Lin Daiyu went onstage for the first time at the Haishang Yipin Lou storytelling hall. The leader among the flowers, this illustrious *jiaoshu* is outstanding

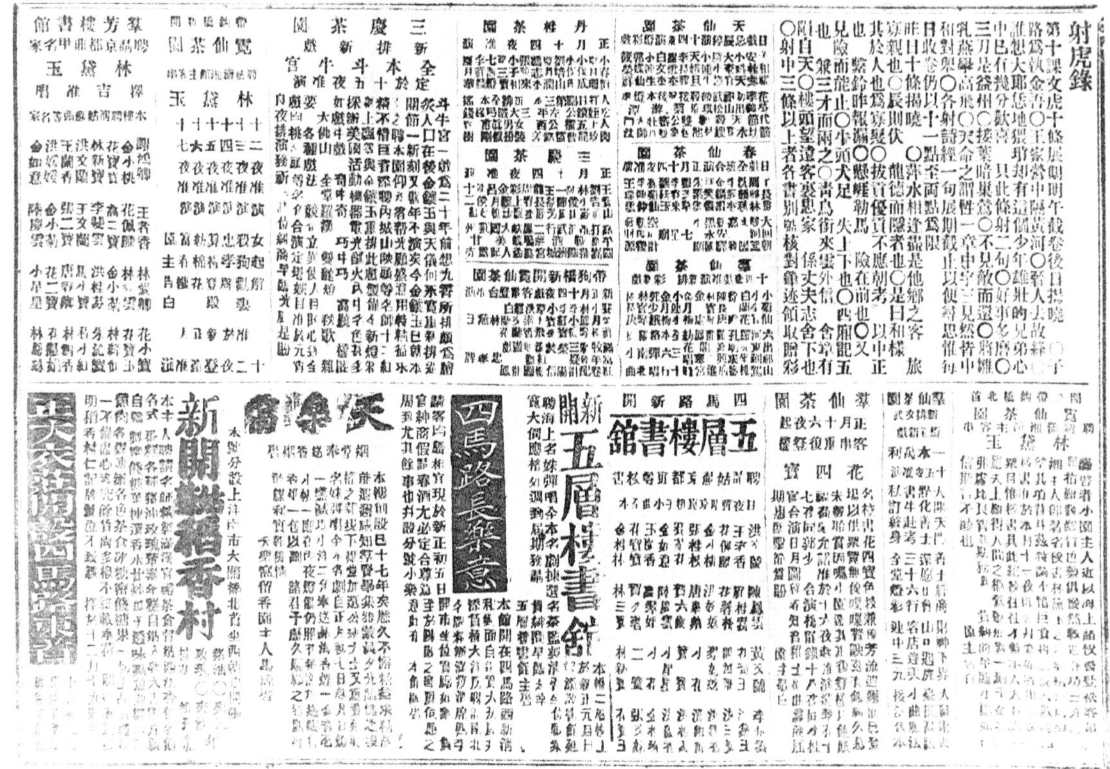

射虎錄

五層樓書館

四馬路長樂意

新開稻香村

5.2. Advertisements in World Vanity Fair *(Shijie fanhua bao) for Lin Daiyu's public appearances at two storytelling halls, Qunfang Lou and Hongxian Chayuan (upper right corner). (*Shijie fanhua bao*, Feb. 11, 1903, 3)*

in beauty and the arts, but she has long since stopped performing in public. At times, only for the sake of giving vent to refined sentiments, she would "face the moon, arrange her instruments," and sing an aria. Not long ago, she was invited to perform by the Fugui Lou establishment; it tickled her fancy, and she agreed on the spot. On this first evening, the audience requested no less than forty-five arias. The Yipin Lou storytelling hall was extremely impressed and envious, and as a consequence, they tried many times to invite her. In the end, it was impossible for the *jiaoshu* to refuse, and last night she began performing there. Those waiting to get a glance at her beauty did not know how to express their joy and feelings of luckiness. She received thirty-five requests. Other *jiaoshu* who have signed contracts with the hall, such as Weng Meiqian, are there every evening. Yesterday, she [Weng Meiqian] received twenty requests, Lin Baozhu forty-five.

. . .

We have also learned that Zhu Ruchun already appeared yesterday at Fugui Lou; she had thirty requests for arias and one for a set of *kunqu*. This shows that all those who are considered "fashionable officials" (*shimao guanren*) [meaning the courtesans] know the art of *kunqu*. This is to be encouraged among all courtesans.[129]

Li Boyuan, for one, had a very clear idea of the impact of courtesan entertainment on the Shanghai entertainment industry and on the prosperity of the city at large. For the courtesans, it obviously had not been immediately as obvious whether this exposure and public accessibility would enhance their star status, and one, Lin Daiyu, hesitated. For a fixed fee, members of the audience could request an aria from them, and this made them in a way "serve" people who might never rise to the point of qualifying for a proper introduction. In the end, it became such an event that even she decided to participate. An invitation to *changsan* courtesans from the hitherto exclusively male storytelling halls together with the newspaper publicity produced a breakthrough.

Courtesans had earlier explored the business potential of storytelling halls and theaters. Female storytelling halls featuring *tanci* singing (also referred to as *tanchang* or *pingtan*) first appeared in the 1870s at the Yeshi Yuan. As legend has it, the hall was opened by the courtesan-singer Zhu Sulan in the International Settlement, right off Fuzhou Road.[130] As public performances by female singers were strictly forbidden in the Qing Empire at the time, the hall was regarded as a sensation; it was hailed as one of the grand sights of Shanghai in the first lithograph album of the city, *Illustrated Grand Sites of Shanghai* (Shenjiang shengjing tu), published in 1884.[131] The storytelling halls proved to be such a success that by the 1890s, there were more than a dozen.[132]

Business arrangements among different sectors of the entertainment world were nothing new in Shanghai. Theaters routinely brought their daily programs to the courtesan houses, urged their customers to call for courtesan company, and introduced courtesans to new clients for a fee. This brought everyone more business.[133] The entertainment paper was a third partner. The Shanghai courtesan had become savvy enough to see this publicity as a welcome boost. For the storytelling halls, favorable newspaper reports were like free advertisements. This new joint venture of the stars, the newspapers, and the performing halls demonstrates that, by the late 1890s, the market recognized the commercial power of stardom. Shortly thereafter, and again with the entertainment papers' crucial help, some Peking opera singers joined in the race for national stardom.[134]

The experience reinforced these courtesans' appreciation of the economic value and impact of their star quality. Lin Daiyu felt confident enough to go to Hankow and open her own opera theater, where she took over the male prerogative of performing the role of the "coquettish young woman" (*huadan*). She was joined in this endeavor by Weng Zhuqian, another Shanghai courtesan star, an example of courtesans joining forces in new entertainment ventures. After the failure of this probably premature enterprise, they returned to Shanghai, and Lin Daiyu renewed her links with the storytelling halls.[135] Her name was prominently displayed in the advertisements taken out by the various halls, and, judging from these ads, she single-handedly started another wave of top-ranking courtesans being engaged by storytelling halls in 1904.[136] Lin Daiyu was active as a star performer well into the twentieth century. During the 1920s, at the age of fifty-eight, she was introduced to the Japanese writer Akutakawa Ryūnosuke as a person who "except for President Xu Shichang, is the only person who knows the political secrets of the past twenty years."[137]

The entertainment newspapers were crucial for this new trend to catch on. The storytelling halls needed publicity for their new feature, and the courtesan star needed the newspapers to interpret the event as a sensation, thereby affirming her high cultural standing and providing a boost for Shanghai commerce altogether. The papers met these expectations by treating their daily follow-up reporting on the event as a rare, exclusive treat for the public. Beyond the increased advertising revenue, the newsworthiness created around the event also helped to promote sales of the paper.

Personalities such as Lin Daiyu and Jin Xiaobao initiated a revolutionary change by moving their cultural profile from that of famous courtesan to that of "star." With public activities such as performing in public theaters and storytelling halls and participating in charity fund-raising, they created a public persona that was marked by the presence of two mutually exclusive features of the modern celebrity, high exclusiveness and perfect accessibility.[138] The former is characteristic of the person, and the latter of the image.

This shift involved a complete changeover in the courtesans' relationship to private patrons. In the past, these patrons had privileged access to the courtesans, and through them, a courtesan might attain fame and notoriety. With the creation of a new type of public realm in the Shanghai Foreign Settlements, in which courtesans were able to move freely, the power dynamics shifted. The tabloids took over the traditional patron's role of spreading the courtesan's fame, the exclusive channels of communication were thrown open, and courtesans gained a strong influence over these papers as the papers' success with the public hinged on the new stars' public performances.

The papers in their turn helped to reshape the notion of exclusive access to these stars. While the star retained a high level of exclusiveness and aloofness, she was also presented as a public performing artist and personality. The successful creation of this new public personality changed the hierarchies within the courtesan world, where the top-ranking courtesans found that it was no longer beneath their dignity to step into the limelight as *shuyu* performers but, quite to the contrary, that it added to their standing.

With the entertainment tabloid, a new medium was created that offered a public forum for the business of entertainment and its stars. Aiming to establish his type of paper as unique, Li Boyuan chose to focus on the Shanghai courtesan. The choice was a shrewd business move. It was based on recognition of the de facto stardom of the courtesan in Shanghai's entertainment world and an acute sense of its economic potential. In an ironic cultural inversion, the papers brought what had once been an exclusive literati prerogative into the marketplace; the refined culture of courtesanship and patronage was opened to the public gaze and marketed as a new form of entertainment. With the new media and Shanghai's growing national importance, the city's entertainment culture took on a new significance. The Shanghai courtesan had already become famous through guidebooks and brush notes, and the enlarged media exposure made a national pastime out of following her and her lifestyle. Strictly speaking, the entertainment newspaper did not create the star personality of the courtesan, but it did help to fashion the public star image of this personality. The Shanghai courtesan had long ago moved into the public space through her new business practices and was already occupying the symbolic space reserved for the embodiment of Shanghai's glamour. This earlier move into the public space enabled the tabloids to establish their base of reporting in the first place.

A small number of Shanghai courtesans became what one might call China's first generation of media stars. From their origins in the lowest rank of society, this group of entertainers managed to install themselves at center stage within two or three decades. They upstaged the traditional "famous literati men" (*mingren*), who had gained their fame through the high arts of poetry, calligraphy, painting, and scholarship. The courtesan's rise certainly was a fundamental challenge to the social status quo, and only Shanghai provided the environment to let this happen and to give it national importance. The new stars did their share to become nationally known by traveling to other centers of entertainment that also had foreign settlements. The Shanghai courtesans' interactions with the entertainment newspaper established the pattern for later opera and movie stars.

Both journalist and courtesan recognized the limits of their control over the image of the star. As the literati-journalists attempted to forge a compromise between traditional cultural norms and expectations and the titillating new Settlements culture, the top-ranking courtesans had to adjust to the new type of publicity they were receiving and which exposed their every move.

Despite the sharp eye and energy needed to spot the potential of the Shanghai top courtesans for becoming public stars and to exploit it by linking the paper's growth to their rise, creating these stars was also a supreme exercise in self-irony by a man of letters such as Li Boyuan. The new star was turned into a mirror of her times. In this sense, reporting on the Shanghai courtesan became a vehicle for political protest. Disillusioned with the late Qing Empire, Shanghai intellectuals of the 1890s developed a discourse in which they articulated the state of the nation through their depictions of the courtesan, hiding their scathing comments about officialdom in their ironical focus on these women. They were no longer potentially powerful officials in charge of China's fate but disillusioned members of the urban intelligentsia plowing with the pen, while the top courtesans were leaving behind their fully dependent status and becoming strong-willed urban businesswomen and national celebrities. Their paths crossed at this critical juncture and in this critical place. They realized their interdependence and, in a continuum of mutual need and alienation, contributed to creating what became a modern urban entertainment culture, with the papers and the stars as key ingredients.

An unforeseen casualty of the courtesans' public exposure and status of social stars was their former role as counterparts to the men of letters. In the Shanghai of the 1920s and 1930s, courtesan entertainment continued but consisted of other types of social and business activities. The lifestyle of the men of letters underwent the same changes as that of the courtesans, and with the development of the new bourgeois family structure in urban centers, the flourishing courtesan entertainment culture of the past decades faded.

6 *The Image of the Shanghai Courtesan in Late Qing Illustrated Fiction*

The entertainment newspapers were not alone in lionizing the Shanghai courtesan. They were quickly joined by a rich array of novels, which often were serialized in these very papers. The courtesan has continuously enjoyed a high literary status in Chinese literature. She was a major literary character in Tang dynasty poetry and *chuanqi* stories and carried on in this role in drama and novels. These works explored the rich potential of the courtesan character in their treatment of a wide range of moral and emotional themes.[1] She may be capable of unconventional yet devoted love, like the sixth-century courtesan-poet Su Xiaoxiao, a constant point of reference for the great Tang poets;[2] of grand passion, including vengeful hatred, as epitomized by Huo Xiaoyu, a literary character in Tang dynasty stories;[3] of the deep emotional and moral integrity shown by the literary character Du Shiniang in a famous late Ming story by Feng Menglong;[4] and of staunch loyalty to a fallen dynasty and the men who fought to preserve it, as was true of the courtesan Li Xiangjun, in the most famous play about the late Ming, *The Peach Blossom Fan* (Taohua shan), by Kong Shangren. In the process, she became a stock character in literature as well as in popular mythology, with the key traits of being "sensitive and full of feelings," or *duoqing*, intelligent, courageous, and imbued with sound judgment. She is the "extraordinary female" (*qi nüzi*) and the "heroine of eternal fame" (*qian'gu nüxia*).[5] Although courtesans or, more often, prostitutes have been portrayed as negative characters in traditional Chinese fiction such as in *Water Margin* (Shuihu zhuan), by Shi Nai'an, and *The Plum in the Golden Vase* (Jin ping mei), by Xiaoxiao Sheng, they were never one of the protagonists.[6]

In literary terms, the courtesan's person and station in life provided writers with a unique set of options. She was confronted with, exposed to, and offered a whole range of possibilities, contradictions, dilemmas, and choices that a young lady from a good family would seldom experience. Her marginality within mainstream society became a literary asset that enabled the writer to use *qi*, or "the extraordinary," associated with her to explore extraordinary situations and behavior. As a character with high elasticity and a license for unpredictability, the courtesan provided literature with a particular artistic stimulus.

This image of the courtesan as *qi* in the positive sense was shattered in the late nineteenth century when a group of novels with Shanghai courtesans as main protagonists portrayed a new kind of courtesan. This courtesan was neither fantastic nor romantic, neither sentimental nor idealistic. Employing realism in the broadest sense, these works portrayed her as a cunning, unscrupulous, at times base, and forever scheming woman with her eyes fixed only on her business enterprise and her own sense of power and fulfillment. These novels feature group portraits with the courtesans individualized within the group, and their particular personalities contrasting with one another. The resulting collective image is that of self-assertive women in a fully commercialized entertainment business. A forerunner might be seen in Yao Xie's "*Yuefu* Poems on Traveling in the Bitter Sea" (Kuhai huang yuefu), from the 1850s, which exposes the inner workings of courtesan establishments in the Shanghai walled city. The late Qing novel about Yangzhou courtesans *Dreams of the Wind and the Moon* (Fengyue meng), by Hanshang Mengren, first published in 1884, may be considered the precursor of this literary trend in the novel's form. Its depiction of Yangzhou courtesans is not idealized. Patrick Hanan considers it the first Chinese city novel.[7] At the center of the late Qing Shanghai courtesan novels, however, we find another and quite stunning new character, the city of Shanghai itself. Rather than simply providing the locale for the story and serving as the backdrop, as in *Dreams of the Wind and the Moon*, the city of Shanghai is an active player in these novels. The identification of the courtesans, their lifestyle, their behavior, their values, and their daily activities with this new city is an essential part of these novels' design; the Shanghai courtesan is presented as a product particular to this city. Her portrait is defined largely in relationship to it.

In these new urban novels, the city itself ultimately stands out as *qi*.[8] It becomes the implied subject, with the courtesan acting as the agent who reveals and guides the reader through its different dimensions and inner mechanism. The courtesan and the city are in a literary embrace, a form of mutual embodiment.[9]

What are the reasons for the emergence of this group of novels with their transformed courtesans and new metropolitan protagonist? In *A Brief History of the Chinese Novel* (Zhongguo xiaoshuo shilüe), Lu Xun argues that the rise during the late Qing of what he calls "prostitution" (*xiaxie*) novels, with courtesans and clients as protagonists, should be seen as a development of the "talented scholar and beautiful lady" literary motif that developed during the Qing period and had its high point in *Dream of the Red Chamber* (Honglou meng), by Cao Xueqin. It resulted from the literary exhaustion of the old formula.[10] He furthermore points out that the break with the *Dream of the Red Chamber* tradition came with Han Bangqing's *Biographies of Shanghai Flowers* (Haishang hua liezhuan), which exposed the cunning and swindles of the courtesans. While these arguments are very insightful, Lu Xun does not explain the reasons for this radical break with tradition and pays no attention to the unique feature of even this novel, the dominant presence of the city and the particular urban features associated with these courtesans. The motif of the arcadian Daguan Yuan from *Dream of the Red Chamber* did not simply disappear; it was replaced in these novels by the notion of Shanghai as a "big playground," or *youxichang*, with courtesan and client as the core inhabitants. The forceful entry of the city into these novels reflects the particular status and environment of the Shanghai Foreign Settlements.

David Der-wei Wang's recent study on late Qing fiction deals with many of the Shanghai courtesan novels studied here, in particular *Biographies of Shanghai Flowers*. He stresses the authors' attempts to make visible the contradictions of the old order by exaggerating the erotic and ethical conventions. "When social, political, literary rules are seen as conventions, then the fiction that observes them assiduously lays them bare for parody." Courtesan novels are wayward, he argues, and "to be wayward, one must disobey conventions, and truly wayward fictions may disguise their disobedience by an exaggerated observation of certain obvious conventions." Thus, the late Qing courtesan novels, to which he refers, with a term borrowed from Lu Xun, as "depraved novels," can achieve through the means of "dazzling mimicry" the equally "uncanny displacement" of the genre's traditional tropes.[11] Modernity here is seen from the viewpoint of literary structures. While the would-be modernist feature within this group of novels lies in their unintended subversion of the old forms in the manner of the old order, the question remains as to where the source for this tendency might be found. Or, using Wang's language, what is the source for this "excess," as it does not appear to be inspired by courtesan characters that now are neither grand nor virtuous?

When Wang applies his theory to novels such as *Biographies of Shanghai Flowers*, the subversion of the norm takes on a rather particular form in his argument and proceeds via the most mundane description of luxury entertainments that might otherwise have called for very flowery language. What should strike the reader as sensational appears as perfectly familiar.[12] But is this true? A close examination of these novels reveals an utterly new feature, and an obvious departure from the literary conventions of courtesan novels or stories from the past centuries—namely, the detailed descriptions of the rules and etiquette governing the inner world of Shanghai courtesan establishments. These details, furthermore, are seen from the perspective of an outsider, a visitor who comes to the city for the first time and reacts by being overwhelmed. The message is that this city is a unique place that has produced a courtesan culture unlike anything one might expect. What is being emphasized for the first time is the overarching role of the city—in this case, Shanghai—in courtesan novels. The source for the "dazzling mimicry" and exaggerated obedience to the norm to which Wang refers is the writer's helplessness in dealing with a new topos: the city. This is the key structural element that makes these novels "modern." The link connecting modernity, the city as a player, and the new identity of the sojourner articulated in interaction with the city has been noted by scholars of the European urban novel.[13] The close proximity of the city to the courtesan forms a referential and symbolic new literary paradigm.

Evidently, these novels are works of fiction. At the same time, their realistic approach—down to the insertion of real-life names, persons, and places—signals an intent to offer a portrait of the real city of Shanghai and a "sociological" study of the actions and manners of its top courtesans.

The New Urban Novel and the Genre of Local Courtesan Biographies

In their emphasis on the Shanghai locale, these courtesan novels inherit a feature from the nonfiction genre of courtesan biographies. While the role of cities, such as Yangzhou or Hangzhou, in earlier sets of courtesan biographies is largely reduced to their presence in titles (for example, *Record of Painted Boats in Yangzhou*), the Shanghai courtesan guides started to link the lives of these women directly to the city. In this manner, the late Qing courtesan novels are clearly and very explicitly Shanghai.[14]

Since the Tang dynasty, there has been a sizable tradition of a semi-biographical literary treatment of the courtesans of a given place, of which the capital was the most important.[15] While these works provide a record of all the outstanding courtesans of a particular locale, they do not single out any one of them as the embodiment of the place's vitality and prosperity. Their titles, with the place-name at the beginning and a reference to courtesans at the end, signal their genre affiliation.[16] Setting the example is *Random Notes on (the Pleasure Quarters) by the Wooden Bridge* (Banqiao zaji), by Yu Huai. Banqiao was the well-known pleasure quarter of Nanjing, and the work bemoans the demise of the Ming capital city by commemorating its courtesans; this work served as the model for Wang Tao.

Almost from the beginning of the Foreign Settlements, literature about its courtesans began to be written. Wang Tao wrote some of the earliest literary works on the Settlements, and he depicted the place through a narration of its courtesans. The Shanghai courtesan thus became the first literary character to embody the spirit of this city.[17]

Following the precedent of works by Wang Tao, works produced in the mid-1880s such as Huang Shiquan's *Record of Dream Images of Shanghai* (Songnan mengying lu) and Zou Tao's *Shanghai City Lights* (Haishang dengshi lu) were instrumental in creating the dreamscape image for Shanghai. Huang described the city in all its glories as an outstanding example of *qi*, which included Western city management, modern urban infrastructure and amenities, and the flourishing cultural and entertainment life. The Shanghai courtesan was the highest expression of this element of the city. *Record of Dream Images* contains the story of the refined and serene Li Peilan, the "mistress of the tower of beauty and fragrance," who donates three hundred dollars to the cause of famine relief; of the elegant and demure Chen Yuqing, whose fine poetry is published in *Shenbao*; and of the alluring Gu Zhixiang, whose singing brings tears to the eyes.[18] Huang Shiquan used romanticizing language to recount the courtesan liaisons of well-known Shanghai men of letters such as Wang Tao, Zou Tao, and Yuan Zuzhi. His courtesans are grand characters, outstanding professional entertainers, and capable of deep emotional attachment, very much on the level of the grand courtesans of the late Ming.[19] When he described the business side of courtesan life, he did so matter-of-factly, without offering the reader glimpses of some dark and vicious hidden side. Zou Tao also explicitly linked Shanghai's prosperity with the courtesan and thus helped to establish the literary trope of their mutual embodiment. His later novel *The Shadows of Heaven and Earth in Shanghai* (Haishang chentian ying) is among the few works to transfer the glorification of Shanghai and its courtesans to the novel form.

The mutual embodiment of city and courtesan in literary descriptions is neither a coincidence nor unique to China, or Shanghai, and has much to do with the development of real-life courtesans and their cities. The same fashion developed in sixteenth-century Venice, eighteenth-century Edo, and nineteenth-century Paris.[20] The Shanghai courtesan is not a generic type but is unthinkable without the particular lifestyle she was able to develop in the Settlements. The Settlements in their turn did not represent a generic Chinese urban center but were different from all the rest to such a dramatic, fascinating, and even disturbing degree that both the Settlements and their courtesans became literary subjects of absorbing interest.

The City and Its Metaphor

The courtesan novels emphasize their identity by placing Shanghai in their titles; in dialogue, the courtesans often use the Shanghai Wu dialect for local color. The name of the literary journal in which Han Bangqing's *Biographies of Shanghai Flowers* was first serialized, *Shanghai Sensational Books* (Haishang qishu), may be read as programmatic for this entire literary genre.[21]

The novels' chapter headings echo their titles and offer a constant flow of references to particular and often well-known places in the Foreign Settlements. Sun Yusheng's *Dreams of Shanghai's Glamour* (Haishang fanhua meng), for example, begins with a chapter titled "Xie Youan recalls his dream among the flowers; Du Shaomu comes to Shanghai to visit the courtesans." The names are puns on the Eastern Jin official Xie An and the Tang poet Du Mu, both of whom were famous for their liaisons with courtesans. Xie Youan, who lives in Suzhou, dreams of "flowers" and is warned of their danger; when he awakes, his friend Du Shaomu invites him to go to Shanghai to have some fun. Chapter 2 is titled "In the Changfa inn, the travelers temporarily take their lodging; in Jixian Lane, old friends meet again." The Changfa is a famous hotel in the Foreign Settlements. In chapter 3, "To welcome the honored guests, a banquet is given at Yipinxiang; playing his new tune, Qizhandeng performs," the Western-style restaurant Yipinxiang and the equally famous Dangui Theater with the Peking opera singer Qizhandeng are featured. In chapter 4, "Surprise encounter with a bewitching courtesan at Shengping Lou; a demonic passion is aroused at Tianlewo," the newcomers finally meet Shanghai courtesans at the city's entertainment landmarks, the Shengping Lou teahouse and the Tianlewo female storytelling hall. The subsequent chapter headings continue to place the action in the city's famous sites.[22]

Finally, the prefaces following the chapter headings forge the link between the city and the Shanghai courtesans. Sun Yusheng defines the conceptual framework of *Dreams of Shanghai's Glamour* in the following terms:

> Shanghai's prosperity ranks number one under heaven. Those who come and visit the city, however, are without exception persons wandering in a dream [*meng*

> *zhong ren*]; and the places they go to are without exception places in a dream [*meng zhong jing*]. Therefore, the red lights and the green wine are a dream illusion [*menghuan*]; the stream of carriages forming the shape of the dragon is but wandering in a dream [*mengyou*]; Zhang Garden and Yu Garden, the opera houses and storytelling halls are but enticements for one to enter the dream [*rumeng zhi di*]. The *changsan* and *shuyu* [high-class courtesans], the *yaoni* and *yeji* [lower-class courtesans and prostitutes] are but the comfortable environment retaining [the visitor] as he searches for his dream [*liuren xunmeng zhi xiang*].
>
> Shanghai's glittering facade draws the visitor into swooning dreams with the courtesans providing the lure. There is the dream of drunkenness [*zuimeng*] when enjoying the sumptuous banquets in the courtesan houses; the dream of grandeur [*hao meng*] brought on by lavish spending; the dream of beauty [*qi meng*] evoked by the attentions bestowed on the client; and the dream of pillow talk [*yi meng*] when the hearts of the client and courtesan come together; but then there is the dream of madness [*chi meng*] as the client gives his family fortune to the courtesan; and finally comes the dream of emptiness [*kong meng*] as the fleeting moment of love dissipates and all that was once dearly held flies away. In between, there are more dreams of worry, evil, hate, poison, and frightful danger.

The author concludes by reiterating that

> since there is no part of Shanghai that does not belong to the realm of dreams, those who enter it are without exception persons in a dream.[23]

The "land of fantasy" metaphor for the city came about under the impact of *Dream of the Red Chamber* and was eventually subverted. Through its contrast with the rest of China, the real Shanghai was experienced as a dream. And the city with the courtesan as its most prized emblem did its best to enhance this quality, which ended up drowning its visitors' sober senses.

From the early twentieth century onward, the juxtaposition of the realm of dreams and "hell" (*diyu*), both represented by the Shanghai courtesan, provided a standard frame for the depiction of Shanghai. The 1923 novel *Living Hell* (Renjian diyu), by Yi Hong, expresses the opposite extreme of the earlier glorification of the Shanghai courtesan world. The city is described in *Living Hell* as a place where evil congregates and gives birth to monsters, where laws are confused, and demons are formidable. The Shanghai prostitution industry is at the center of this evil world.[24]

The Shanghai courtesan thus became the multifaceted and changing metaphor for this city. She was the product of greed and openness; the freedom and splendor she exhibited represented the city's wealth as well as its hollowness. She at once embodied the dreams of heaven and the nightmare of hell.

Courtesan Novels as City Guides

The use of Shanghai entertainment landmarks to structure the plotline was a common feature in Shanghai courtesan novels. The novels were patterned on the literary structure of a city guidebook, with the courtesan herself serving as the guide. They devote much space to introducing the basic rules governing behavior in this city. The reader learned and at times was directly told what to expect, what to do, and how to conduct himself in this strange environment. Many of the city's foreign features were dealt with in great detail. This is most clear in Han Bangqing's *Biographies of Shanghai Flowers*, which explains how the foreign firefighting brigade puts out a fire, how the Sikh policemen patrol the streets, and how a police detective investigates a crime. The novel goes on to describe the different kinds of entertainment, such as opera houses, wineshops, teahouses, gambling establishments, and opium dens. Courtesan novels also mention the fanciest stores and their specialties; suggest where to dine, what to order, and how to eat it; propose the appropriate attire for certain occasions; and offer different schedules for the short-term visitor and the long-term resident. Of course, there are in addition detailed descriptions of the ritualized forms of behavior particular to Shanghai courtesan houses, ignorance of which may expose the visitor to laughter. The novels thus use their descriptions of scenes and types as a city guide and manual of behavior in literary form.

Almost all of these novels begin with a visitor arriving in the city from the country or a nearby town. This visitor acts as an identification figure for the reader and allows him to become familiar with the place without exposing himself to its dangers. According to the basic plotline, the protagonist begins as an ignoramus, experiences and survives all the lures and dangers of the city, and finally returns home.

In *Biographies of Shanghai Flowers*, Zhao Puzhai and his sister Zhao Erbao, who come in from the countryside, provide the narrative thread that allows the novel to reveal the dazzling and unique enticements of the city.[25] The novel describes the fantasies and fears of the brother and sister upon approaching Shanghai, their fascination with the city, and their pursuit of new and extraordinary experiences. Both fall victim to Shanghai's temptations, and the novel traces their gradual demise. After indulging in the ecstasies of high living, the brother descends into poverty. He becomes a rickshaw coolie and eventually the brothel attendant for his own sister, who was also quickly seduced and corrupted by the city. Both siblings pass up the chance to leave the city and escape their demise. Through their story, the novel builds up a very vivid image of Shanghai against the background of the protagonists' traditional, rural background. The novel's illustrations help readers to visualize the siblings' Shanghai experiences (figs. 6.1a–n).

Other courtesan novels elucidate the inner workings of the city by following the Shanghai courtesan's interactions with her clients. In *The Nine-Tailed Fox* (Jiuwei hu), by Menghuaguanzhu Jiang Yinxiang, Shanghai's most famous courtesan star Hu Baoyu is quoted as saying that a courtesan's business practices in Shanghai are basically not different from those of ordinary commercial enterprises. To be wooed, entertained, cheated, robbed, and played with is the name of the game.[26] The novels promised to make the reader an insider, with entertainment and thrills, at a safe distance, all provided for the price of a single book.

Precious Mirror for Judging Shanghai's Flowers (Haishang pinghua baojian), published in 1911 under the pen name Pingjiang Yinnian, is one of the clearest examples of the novel functioning as a guide. The story begins in Suzhou with a happily

(a) Arriving in Shanghai. Note the street lamp representing the city.

(b) After arrival, the visitor either stays at his own Shanghai residence . . .

(c) . . . or checks into a lodge.

(d) One of the first things to do in Shanghai is to hold a banquet at a courtesan house.

6.1a–n. Illustrations from Biographies of Shanghai Flowers. *Lithographs, 1894. (Han Bangqing,* Haishang hua liezhuan*)*

(e) Other activities are visiting courtesan houses,

(f) going to the theater, . . .

(g) . . . dining at a Western-style restaurant,

(h) drinking and eating at leisure in Shanghai's famous teahouses . . .

(i) or smoking at the opium den.

(j) Among the town's exotic features are the foreign firefighting brigade, . . .

(k) . . . the detective,

(l) and the Western-style hospital.

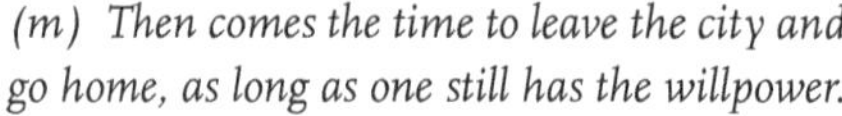

(m) Then comes the time to leave the city and go home, as long as one still has the willpower.

(n) But some stay on and lose all, including their lives.

married couple. One day, after reading *Dream of the Red Chamber*, the two decide that Zhang Xunbo, the husband, should go to the Shanghai International Settlement to experience the southern beauties for which the city is so famous. The wife's condition is that Xunbo write a detailed record of each of his encounters so that she may share his experience through reading. Obviously, Shanghai's reputation of being the place in which to live out one's fantasies and dreams was well established. Equally well established was the opinion that the place was thoroughly corrupting. Aware that Xunbo's father is of this opinion and would not agree to his son's going to Shanghai, they tell him that Xunbo intends to see something of the world by traveling to Tokyo. Tokyo had the reputation at the time as a center of Western learning for young Chinese. The large sums of money Xunbo needed for visits to Shanghai courtesan establishments were justified in part as travel expenses to this center of learning.

Accompanied by a trusted family friend who had grown up in Shanghai, Xunbo bravely takes the "modern" train, whereas less adventurous travelers such as Xie Youan and Du Shaomu in *Dreams of Shanghai's Glamour* rent a private boat. Once in Shanghai, Xunbo begins to enter into the mysteries of the city. Along with the reader, Xunbo receives his first impression of the unfamiliar urban environment on a drive through the streets.

> Riding in a grand carriage, Xunbo was first shown Da Malu [Nanjing Road], where he admired the width and cleanliness of the street. Driving along the Bund, he was overwhelmed by the imposing Western-style buildings on the banks and

> the steamships crowding the river. Turning into Si Malu [Fuzhou Road], he was dazzled by the rich and ornate decor of the shops lining both sides of the street. When he asked why Si Malu was much narrower than Da Malu, he was told that real estate was so much more expensive on this street.[27]

The next day, Xunbo begins his exploration of the various types of Shanghai courtesans. His first encounter is with a top-rank singing performer, who, however, could claim only comely beauty. As he moves upward through the courtesan hierarchy, the novel lays out in each new encounter the rules governing this world as well as its pitfalls, while Xunbo does his share by filling his notebook for his wife to read. Xunbo learns fast; as he becomes more and more skilled in the art of enjoying and surviving in this environment, he becomes increasingly cunning and even starts to play games with the courtesans. His search ends when he finds the ultimate of beauty and talent in the most acclaimed of all courtesan stars, Hua Yuanyuan. But there are hints that even this courtesan is not sincere in her feelings toward the young man. Just when Xunbo is about to fall for Hua Yuanyuan, with all the costs this would have involved, the novel ends with a telegram summoning him home with the news that his father has fallen ill. As the protagonist is dispatched, the author sends the reader home as well.

The sequence of courtesan-client encounters serves as the plot engine for the novel and anticipates the reader's own fantasy journey to the city. The jarring end makes it clear that nothing short of a threat to the life of his father can tear the young man away.

The City's Many Faces and the Group Portrait as Literary Device

These novels use the group portrait as a literary device with which to show the city's different dimensions. It had been used earlier, in *Water Margin* and *Dream of the Red Chamber.* In *Water Margin,* each of the 110 characters contributes to the dynamism of the novel, and together they form a collective image of a band of outlaw heroes. Time and again, city life provides background in this novel, but the emphasis is on individual characterization and group dynamics. *Dream of the Red Chamber* explores the common theme of emotional attachment through the individual portraits of twelve women. Daguan Yuan plays an active part by defining the boundary between the world at large and the artificial dreamscape in which these emotions can unfold.

The Shanghai courtesan novels developed their group portraits from this tradition. This literary device gave them far greater leeway in presenting diverging situations and characters in a multilayered urban environment as opposed to following a single protagonist and a single plotline. In the case of Shanghai, this device became almost a necessity in order to handle the mutual embodiment of the city and its courtesans. Daguan Yuan offered an apt metaphor and model for the challenging depiction of the city as an active and central element in the novel's structure. (In some novels, such as *Shadows of Heaven and Earth in Shanghai,* such a garden was literally created within the city.) The twelve golden hairpins from *Dream of the Red Chamber* were playfully reenacted by the Shanghai courtesans, and the notion of Shanghai as the big playground took up, and subverted, the romanticized Daguan Yuan dreamscape. The group portraits of courtesans showed Shanghai's manifold faces. In *Biographies of Shanghai Flowers*, Zhang Huizhen appears timid, humble, and loyal but calmly cheats on her new husband; Zhou Shuangyu, who seems innocent enough and capable of deep devotion, turns out to be quite a calculating operator; and Huang Cuifeng arrives on the scene, with the appeal of the grand courtesan of integrity and self-respect, and proceeds to relieve her client of a huge sum of money. The novel's losers are the courtesans who lack cunning and ruthlessness, such as Zhou Shuangbao, who is moved from the top to the ground floor of the courtesan house, and Shen Xiaohong, who falls quite unprofessionally head over heels in love with an opera singer, so that her rich client leaves her and she is reduced to poverty. For both the courtesans and the city, the novels make ample use of the contrast between glamorous appearance and hollow reality.

In Chousi Zhuren's *Sensational Biographies of the Four Great Golden Diamond Cutters from Shanghai* (Haishang mingji Si Da Jin'gang zhuan qishu), characterization and plotline are more complex. The novel features the four Shanghai courtesan stars Lin Daiyu, Zhang Shuyu, Lu Lanfen, and Sai Jinhua (later replaced by the younger Jin Xiaobao). The frame of the story is provided by a Buddhist tale of reincarnation and retribution. In the novel, the four courtesans are actually the four "diamond-hard" door guardian gods who have been reincarnated as females so as to humiliate the muscular gods and teach them a lesson (figs. 6.2a, b–6.4a, b).

The treatment of the courtesans changes sharply between the first and second parts of this fifty-chapter novel.[28] The first part depicts them with sympathy and candor and takes the traditional line of empathy with their predicament as courtesans. In the second half, the tone switches to vicious satire and harsh ridicule. By the end of the novel, the author has relegated the four stars to being the fox, the pig, the monkey, and the dog in the Buddhist hierarchy of beings.

The author announces his reasons for doing this at the beginning of the second part. He intends to reflect the recent changes in the ways of the city. This is foreshadowed in the title of the last episode of the first part: "The *mingshi* [gentlemen of renown] disperse; the customs change" (Mingshi sanchang, fengsu gaibian). Between this episode and the beginning of the second part, a whole decade has elapsed, and since that time, morals in the city have undergone a radical change. The narrator's language is blunt:

> From that time [when the first part of the novel ended], Shanghai's gentlemen of renown all went their different ways. Only the fashion of libidinous practices and degeneracy became increasingly dominant by the year.
>
> Courtesan entertainment has always been the embellishment of a world at peace. Therefore, gentlemen and noblemen all patronize the courtesans and lose themselves under the influence of music and wine. Who would have guessed that nowadays in Shanghai things would be quite different? In the courtesan establishments, nothing but salacious, lowly vagrant whores are found. Their customers are noth-

(a) Molihai *(b) Lu Lanfen*

6.4a, b

Lu Lanfen as the reincarnation of Molihai, one of the four Buddhist door guardians. Woodblock print. In (a), Molihai holds a pipa*; in (b), Lu Lanfen holds her own* pipa*. (Chousi Zhuren,* Haishang mingji Si Da Jin'gang zhuan qishu*, 1898, 3)*

> ing but those who are attracted by the foul smell and like to rake in [rather than put out]. Those who are abroad [as suitors of the courtesans] in the small lanes in the district of Si Malu [Fuzhou Road] are all opera singers and chauffeurs. As a consequence, those with any self-respect have naturally all disappeared.[29]

Respectful men are no longer patrons of courtesans as much because of the decline in the courtesans' quality as because of their open liaisons with opera singers and chauffeurs, which formerly were regarded as deplorably unprofessional. The city's men of letters were in part responsible because their poems in praise of the courtesans had made the women conceited in their glory.[30] Their ensuing gloating, pride, and haughtiness were more than any gentleman of taste and honor was willing to tolerate.

(a) Molishou

(b) Zhang Shuyu

6.3a, b

Zhang Shuyu as the reincarnation of Molishou, one of the four Buddhist door guardians. Woodblock print. In (a), Molishou holds a dragon; in (b), the dragon has become a small snake underneath the table where Zhang Shuyu is sitting. (Chousi Zhuren, Haishang mingji Si Da Jin'gang zhuan qishu, *1898, 3)*

With this shift, the men of letters, who once had a say in defining acceptable courtesan behavior, were replaced by merchants and compradors who had no cultural pretensions. This latter group fell victim to the schemes developed by the courtesans to get their bills paid and have their freedom bought from their madams.[31] The change is evoked in different scenes that depict the four courtesans calling the shots, riding high through the city and appearing in every fashionable spot. The author reserved his greatest wrath for their domination of the city's public space. To be seen in public was tolerable but to openly defy decorum was unforgivable. The author's scorn reflects the men of letters' frustration with their loss of cultural authority.

The relationship between the city and the courtesan also changes visibly in the second part of the novel. Although the city environment is quite present in the first, the close connection is established only in the second part, in which all actions by

(a) Molihong *(b) Lin Daiyu*

6.2a, b

*Lin Daiyu as the reincarnation of Molihong, one of the four Buddhist door guardian gods. Woodblock print. In (a), Molihong is shown with his magical umbrella; in (b), the magical umbrella has changed into a Western-style umbrella in Lin Daiyu's hands. (*Haishang mingji Si Da Jin'gang zhuan qishu*, 1898, 2)*

the courtesans are linked to the city's landmarks, which become stages for their performances. The implication is that courtesans could behave in such fashion only in Shanghai, where the public space was open to them and no authority prevented them from breaking the boundaries of propriety.

The City as Big Playground and the Courtesan as Its Star

With this group of novels, the Shanghai courtesan star became a major literary figure. Her character combines glamour and deceit, self-assertiveness and moral decay. Her rise to literary notoriety matches her rise to a highly visible and emblematic public personality. Through these depictions, the novels effectively demolished the myth of the courtesan heroine of eternal fame and, with it, the easy glory of the city. Characters such as Hu Baoyu in *The Nine-Tailed Fox*, by Menghuaguanzhu Jiang Yinxiang, and the four "diamond cutter" courtesan stars in Zhang Chunfan's *The Nine-Tailed Turtle* (Jiuwei gui) and in Chousi Zhuren's *Sensational Biographies of the Four Great Golden Diamond Cutters* became the chief protagonists, with the city as their showcase. In their world of endless pursuits and conquests, the dominant symbol is the city street through which the courtesan moves. Familiar with every place in the city, and always confident, she leads the reader, through her adventures, on an exploration of the inner mechanisms of this big playground. Its entertainment establishments in their turn show unexpected and perhaps unintended dimensions of power in shaping a new urban character and, with it, a new lifestyle.

Legendary in Shanghai history, Hu Baoyu was credited with developing many of the core features associated with the public persona of the grand Shanghai courtesan. The basic narrative of *The Nine-Tailed Fox* follows the trail of Hu Baoyu's love affairs (at times for business, at other times for her own fun) to different locations within the city. The city is her playground, and its public spaces are the premises for her thoroughly urban self-presentation and performance.

The theater was an excellent setting for her depiction. Sitting in her box, decked out in the latest fashions and drawing admiring glances (as well as risking some of her own), Hu Baoyu discovers the potential of the public arena and the thrill of being a public personality. The novel begins as she arrives at the Dangui Theater, accompanied by her patron of the moment, Yang Si, and falls in love with the opera star Huang Yueshan:

> After dressing in a new and fashionable outfit, [Lin] Daiyu [the name used by Hu Baoyu at the time] with her maid [accompanied by her patron] hailed a horse-drawn carriage at the street corner. Within seconds, the carriage arrived at the theater, and they were received by the theater attendant and shown to their box. There they sat down side by side. The show was already in the third act. At the time, nothing very remarkable was to be seen on stage, but then Huang Yueshan appeared. That night, he was playing the golden-eyed eagle Qiu Chen in the number "Five Heroes Meeting on Jianfeng Mountain." Daiyu was mesmerized by his style and movements. Her pretty eyes were riveted on him as she admired his lively spirit and lofty character. . . . Staring at the stage, she was not even aware that Yang Si was talking to her.[32]

After this experience, the courtesan becomes a fan of the theater. Huang could not fail to notice the beauty sitting in her box and showering him with adoring glances every night. Throughout most of the novel, Hu Baoyu has her own reserved theater box. She habitually chooses her lovers from among the opera stars, making behavior that hitherto had been shunned as utterly unacceptable into a fashion among Shanghai courtesans.[33]

The theater was the place where the courtesan could play hostess, invite her client, parade her conquest in public, and be seen by potential clients. It was here that she met other courtesans to trade gossip, exchange greetings, and occasionally have a fight. For the Hu Baoyu in *Nine-Tailed Fox*, the theater is also a means of escape. As she grows bored living in a closed house as Yang Si's concubine, she goes to the theater as a way of venting her frustrations and letting him know her change of heart. At times, when she is lonely and desperate, a visit to the theater also helps her to rediscover her desire for personal fulfillment and find the energy to go on.[34]

The city's fancy restaurants provide another public arena, where negotiations take place between courtesans and lovers, between a courtesan and a client's wife, and between courtesans themselves.[35] In *The Nine-Tailed Fox*, after Hu Baoyu's passion is ignited at the theater, she devises a strategy to win Huang Yueshan's affections. She goes to the theater daily and leaves as soon as Huang's act is over. Once their eyes meet, Huang is smitten. He invites her to dinner at the famous Yipinxiang (fig. 6.5). Hu accepts, and their love affair begins. The scene is extraordinary! In full public view, an opera star and a famous courtesan woo each other. Such a scene set tongues wagging and made Shanghai's outrageous image: only in such a place was there the space and the stage for these events.

The public parks, also a unique urban feature of Shanghai, are another public venue for the courtesans in these novels. Compared to the more exclusive restaurant and theater, the park and its teahouses made the courtesan visible to a much wider public. Like the Parisian courtesan stars of the Second Empire, Hu Baoyu understood the significance of this public space and used it time and time again to further her own purposes. In *The Nine-Tailed Fox*, Hu Baoyu decides to adopt the dress and hairstyle of the Cantonese prostitutes. She is determined to be the one who sets new fashions among the Shanghai courtesans, most of whom are of Suzhou origin. With her new bangs and clothes, she decides to test her position and estimate her influence by going straight to Yu Yuan. She chooses to sit down with her two maids at one of the park's busiest teahouses:

> At the time, it was still early; not many visitors were in the park. Although there were a few that had seen her, they only whispered among themselves. After three o'clock in the afternoon, fashionable dandies and well-to-do young men accompanied by courtesans gradually arrived. Upon seeing Baoyu leaning against the banister, sipping tea as though there were no one else around, and decked out, furthermore, in such an unusual fashion, with cut bangs as long as three or four inches covering her forehead and ending right over her brows, all the flirtatious young men cheered in chorus. Even the other courtesans began to talk among themselves. Some said it was nice, some said it was ugly, some said they wanted to learn from her, and others said doing so would only make one a laughingstock. . . .
>
> After tea, Baoyu and her maids went for a stroll in the park. This produced a great stir of excitement among the playboys, and they followed her everywhere. Some whistled as they commented on her outfit; some spoke English as they admired her fashion. There was more approval than criticism. There were discussions and clapping, and the crowd swayed as people tried to get a glimpse. Baoyu did not consider that outrageous; she increased her charms by turning to look back and bestowing a glance on the crowd with a faint smile.[36]

6.5. *"The courtesan Hu Baoyu has a rendezvous with an opera singer" (Xiangcaiguan fuyue hui liren). Lithograph. The opera singer Huang Yueshan and Hu Baoyu, accompanied by her maid, dine in a private room at the Western-style restaurant Yipinxiang. (Menghuaguanzhu Jiang Yinxiang,* Jiuwei hu, *1918, unpaginated, illustration for chapter 9 at beginning of book.)*

In traditional cities, the narrow, noisy, unpaved streets ranked low in the hierarchy. In Shanghai, however, the Shanghai Committee on Roads and Jetties—the predecessor of the Municipal Council—had promulgated, in 1845, regulations providing for wide avenues in the city center.[37] Later, the Municipal Council's tax revenue was used for drainage, pavement, and lighting; traffic regulations and police established a modicum of order and helped to cut down noise as well as restrain the habit of public urination. The grand buildings did the rest to transform this lowly thing, the street, into a panorama through which the courtesan moved, showing the city to her client and being seen. As much as in Paris just a decade or two before, riding in the horse-drawn carriage with a liveried groom on the coach box was the chic thing to do, and the novels faithfully went along. *The Nine-Tailed Fox* especially relishes such scenes. After showing off her new Cantonese-style outfit, Hu Baoyu and her maid leave the park:

> Upon seeing Baoyu getting into her carriage, the group of young good-for-nothings [*qingnian eshao*] went in pursuit. Some sat in their [hansoms?], holding the reins themselves, and some got onto their bicycles and followed her by moving their legs fast. They immediately caused a commotion by surrounding her carriage on all sides, like fish in a swirl, trailing one another. From the Nicheng Bridge down to the Da Malu [Nanjing Road] in the English Settlement, more and more bystanders stopped to look. Most of them recognized Baoyu and added a new wave of cheers. Among them was a man from the country. This was his first time in Shanghai, and he had never seen anything of this kind. He mumbled to himself, "There is so much bustle and excitement today, has some foreign queen arrived for a tour?" A bystander interrupted: "Nonsense, there is nothing of the kind! [What you are seeing] is Shanghai's most famous courtesan, Hu Baoyu!" The other was surprised. "So the stature of the Shanghai courtesan is even greater than that of officials; when she rides out in her carriage, she travels with so many bodyguards in front and behind, right and left!" Those who heard him knew that he was from the country, and they knew that it was hard to make him understand [the ways of Shanghai]. So they laughed and clapped their hands as they dispersed.[38]

For the reader in the late Qing, the city of Shanghai was as extraordinary as the behavior of the Shanghai courtesan, and both complemented each other. What at first seemed like a literary device, using the courtesan to introduce the city's landmarks, points in fact to a social reality unique to the city.

As descriptions of the urban lifestyle in these novels serve to highlight the strangeness and uniqueness of Shanghai, much attention is given to details such as the courtesans using the banknotes of the Hong Kong and Shanghai Bank, ordering a meal at a Western-style restaurant, going to have their photographs taken, appearing at the Mixed Court, going to the horse races or the circus, or furnishing their rooms with fashionable Italian or Cantonese furniture. These descriptions, with their delight in the exotic flurry, do much to balance and even undermine the original purpose of the novels, namely, to denounce the lifestyle fostered by this city.

The New Urban Female versus the "Honest Courtesan"

The novels reinterpret what traditionally had been read as the outpouring of the true feelings of highly gifted courtesans, depicting these outpourings as nothing but Shanghai-style business strategies. Traditionally, the literary skills of the outstanding courtesan had been emphasized; they allowed her to express and evoke true emotions through poetry and song. *Dreams of Shanghai's Glamour* offers a succinct counterpoise: a top courtesan's only motive for learning to read and write is her wish to extend her control over a client with literary inclinations. It also did allow her to read love letters written to him by a competitor.[39] The moving love song she sings to him at a banquet, which restores his respect and devotion, appears as but an act calculated to produce the desired reaction through the conscious use of traditional forms of courtesan articulation.[40] The literary device used is the contrast between appearance and essence. This device plays on the reader's presumed familiarity with the traditional courtesan tropes. Against this shared knowledge and appearance, the novels reveal the truth of the matter and proceed to judgments for which they rely on the implied reader's conservative values.

Under the pretense of warning readers of the pitfalls of Shanghai, the novels go into great detail about the Shanghai courtesans' deceitful business practices. At the same time, the depiction of clients in the novel has taken a steep fall. The talented scholars have been replaced by miserly and greedy businessmen, and considering their attributes, the courtesans' new behavior even appears logical. The novels, all their moralizing posture notwithstanding, are quite taken by these headstrong, glamorous, and cunning courtesan stars whose image unwittingly features a certain strength, independence, and urban self-assertiveness.

There is thus much ambiguity in the description of these courtesans, an ambiguity that mostly reflects that of the author as he is faced with an emerging character: the urban female. This character captures his imagination and yet repels him, as does Shanghai and Shanghai's style of life. The new features of this urban female come through most strongly in the figure of Gao Xianglan, in Erchun Jushi's *Traces of the Past in the World of Shanghai* (Haitian hongxue ji). This character is most unlike the standard Shanghai courtesan or courtesan star. She walks into the novel wearing a pair of gold-rimmed dark glasses (later, we learn that she dresses mostly in Western clothing), and at her side is a young lady dressed in a Western-style long dress and jacket. The occasion is a performance by the Italian circus Chiarini, another Shanghai entertainment highlight immortalized in Dianshizhai's *Illustrated Grand Sites of Shanghai* (Shenjiang shengjing tu). Without maids or male friends to accompany them, the two women walk into the large tent, find seats for themselves, and sit down. After the show, they dash off in their carriage and vanish into the night.[41] The reader follows them through the eyes of the male protagonist. Who are these women? And what are they? Only later does he learn that the young lady in Gao's company belongs to a good family, and that Gao Xianglan is a former courtesan who has become a socialite. She lives alone in a three-story house and depends for her livelihood on suitors who supply her with money. A woman of extraordinary beauty and talent, she is also sinister and cunning. While she maneuvers to get money from rich men, she takes handsome young dandies as lovers and does all this outside the traditional business structure of a courtesan.

Gao Xianglan is an intriguing and complex character, and in terms of lifestyle, she is very much the new breed of city character. She acquires great sums of money and spends them overnight; she goes out a lot and enjoys herself in public by dining in fancy Western-style restaurants, attending the theater, or driving around town in her carriage, alone or with friends. She is seen as an "independent" woman, living without family and social structures. Her friends and allies are newspaper editors and journalists. She is able to have long and engaging discussions with men of intelligence and knowledge. Gao Xianglan offers a clear example of the transition from the top courtesan to the modern Shanghai urban woman. The author who approaches her with a critical eye ends up being fascinated by her, and, in articulating his own ambiguity, he creates a powerful new literary figure.

This new image of modern, cunning, urban female characters is sometimes contrasted with that of the "honest courtesan," a fitting term originally applied to some Venetian courtesans. While Gao Xianglan's free and easy lifestyle brings her men of wealth who almost deserve to be fleeced because they are dishonest themselves, the "honest courtesan" allies herself with upright men. Her client may take on the role of the hero, as is the case with Zhang Qiugu in *The Nine-Tailed Turtle* and Han Qiuhe in *The Shadows of Heaven and Earth in Shanghai*. In both novels, the courtesans who win the heroes' love are portrayed as positive exceptions among the courtesans of the day. Zhang Qiugu is a man of letters who proves to be a "master among the flowers," with all the courtesan stars at his feet. He marries Chen Wenxian, whom he considers the only virtuous courtesan among his acquaintances. Han Qiuhe is something of a knight-errant; he travels the world and learns about new ideas and technologies from Japan and the West. He comes to Shanghai only to visit his beloved Su Yunlan, a rare courtesan endowed with culture, taste, and virtue. Han manages never to get too deeply involved, however, coming and going at will. The "honest courtesan" is a nostalgic reminder and provides the necessary contrast to the new urban character, but she does not dominate the scene, and is seldom the main character.

The independent Gao Xianglan has no patron and fights to survive through her cunning and with some help from allies; the "honest courtesan" is given the chance to have an esteemed partner whom she loves and admires.[42] The courtesans' men shed more light on the city. The clients in these novels also are presented in a group portrait. They come from many walks of life, include visitors and long-term residents, and may be merchants, officials, compradors, or provincial landed gentry. Like their female counterparts, they tend to operate on the principle of trying to get more for less. In the process, they fall victim to the Shanghai courtesans and end up either leaving town after losing their fortunes or sinking into the lower reaches of society. Zhang Qiugu and Han Qiuhe, however, are the exceptions. In these two heroes, the authors present men who not only are undefeated by Shanghai but are able to handle the city with ease. The devotion of the "honest courtesan" is proof of their success with the city. There are strong autobiographical elements in the depictions of these men.[43]

Changing Opinions of the City and Its Courtesans

Given the close symbiotic relationship between Shanghai and its courtesans, changes in views of the city are directly reflected in changing assessments of the courtesans. This is visible in the difference between literary works on Shanghai written mostly between the 1870s and the 1880s, with their very favorable view of the city, and the courtesan novels of the 1890s.[44]

The men of letters' infatuation with Shanghai seems to have cooled down by the 1890s. Shanghai had been transformed from Penglai, Island of Immortals, in the 1870s and the dreamscape of the 1880s into the big playground. In the 1880s, many authors such as Wang Tao, Zou Tao, and Huang Shiquan were also journalists, but their stories were not taken from the papers and their works were not serialized there. With the advent of specialized entertainment papers, this situation changed. The writing became more realistic, and the tone acquired an urban style. Many episodes in *The Sensational Biographies of the Four Great Golden Diamond Cutters* and *The Nine-Tailed Turtle* are based on stories published in *Shenbao* and *Entertainment*.[45]

This change in perspective reveals more about the Shanghai men of letters and their shifting self-assessment. Their values and privileged standing were under threat. As a consequence, they took a bleaker view of the city and its courtesans, which had come to symbolize for them the very embodiment of crass commercialization.

Shanghai's transformation into an industrial town, the growth of organized crime, and finally the "new culture" movement, with its disdain for the "feudal" leftover of courtesan culture, brought additional change in the image of the courtesan as well as the city. It moved from "dream" to "nightmare." While the actual capacity of the entertainment industry to attract ever greater numbers of sojourners and tourists to Shanghai continued to grow unfazed, the literary image of the Shanghai courtesan along with that of the city shifted from *qi*, or "the extraordinary," to *guai*, or "the strange," and, later in the Republican period, "the ugly" (*chou*). However, throughout all the changes in the perception of Shanghai, one element remained constant: the uniqueness of Shanghai and of its emblem, the Shanghai courtesan. Nothing else could compare.

The Image of the City in Literary Illustrations

The creation of an urban literature depends largely on the development of an urban mentality and sensibility. The Shanghai courtesan character offered the real-life option of using a familiar literary character and the manifold tropes associated with it to explore the new type of city and the new attitudes developing in the Jiangnan region. The courtesan traditionally was associated with wealthy commercial towns and big administrative centers, but their urban character was distinctly different from that of Shanghai, and the urban setting remained in the background in traditional depictions of courtesan life.[46] The Shanghai courtesan, however, was routinely described and depicted in close connection with this city's particular features. Even before the literary treatments in the courtesan novels, her relationship to the city was explored in woodblock and lithograph illustrations. The novels linked up with this heritage through inserted illustrations.

The relationship between the Shanghai courtesan as portrayed in literary text and in literary illustration is anything but simple and becomes more complex with the transformation of the courtesan image and character. Owing to differences in artistic traditions and constraints, narrative art and illustrational art moved in quite different directions, with the illustrations displaying an agenda of their own. The two modes supplement each other, but they are also in conflict. The difference hinges on the question of how to present Shanghai as an urban center with a distinct urban lifestyle through the image of the Shanghai courtesan. The new technology of lithography provided the option by which to match the fast, realistic journalistic style with a graphic equivalent in news painting.[47]

The City and Its Illustrated Icon

Wu Youru began illustrating literary texts with lithographs in *Dianshizhai Illustrated Magazine* (Dianshizhai huabao) in 1884.[48] The first was Wang Tao's *Miscellaneous Records of a Shanghai Recluse* (Songyin manlu), which was serialized as an appendix to *Dianshizhai Illustrated Magazine.* A comparison of one of his literary illustrations with a regular news illustration reveals a marked difference. The news illustration emphasizes action (fig. 6.6); it shows the fracas that resulted when an inmate of a courtesan house misidentified a policeman as an impostor. The style of the other (fig. 6.7) belongs to the tradition of literary illustration and has mood as the dominating element; there is no reference to a particular event. One representation emphasizes the theatricality of the scene at the expense of the courtesans, and the other maintains the aura of refinement of the courtesan figure.

Although different in style and depiction, the graphic arrangements of the illustrations unmistakably define the common locale, Shanghai. Figure 6.6 shows the name of Lanfang Lane, a section in the International Settlement where many courtesan businesses were located, and the unique architecture of the *linong* houses that were found only in the Foreign Concessions. The Shanghai courtesans are depicted as a group. In figure 6.7, the place is almost unidentifiable except for the name of the lane in tiny characters. Yet, one object identifies the scene as Shanghai: the street lamp, with its electric wire looming above. (A less obvious prop are the Western-style glass-pane windows, which could be pushed open from the inside.) The street lamp attests to the deliberateness of the attempt to localize the story. By adding what seems to be an alien and unnecessary object to this traditional scene, Wu Youru compelled the viewer to acknowledge the locale of the story, an unessential element in traditional literary illustrations.

The graphic arrangement shows the artist's deliberate effort in creating such a configuration. Wu Youru also used this device, simply moving the iconographic symbol of the city into an otherwise traditional scene, in figure 6.8. The intent is clear in comparing his illustration with a seventeenth-century illustration of a similar

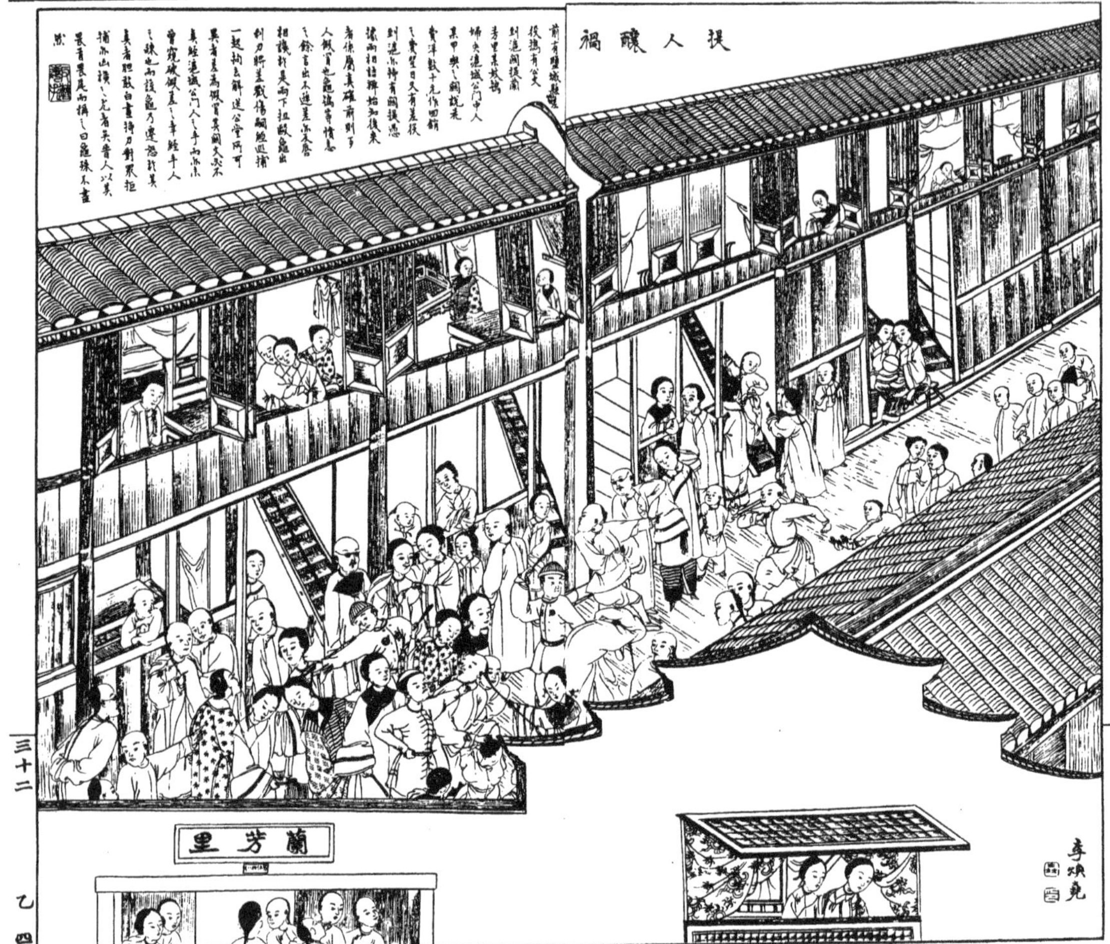

*6.6. "An arrest that led to disaster" (Tiren nianghuo). Lithograph, by Li Huanyao. This illustration accompanied the news story of a policeman who was incorrectly identified as an impostor by an inmate of a courtesan house and was beaten up as a result. (*Dianshizhai huabao*, no. yi, 4 [1884]: 32)*

theme (fig. 6.9). The lamp and its wires were added in order to highlight Shanghai as the place of the extraordinary, a category that also included Shanghai's courtesan. The way in which the street lamp cuts straight into the scene demonstrates the initial encounter between traditional and modern sensibilities. In this case, the encounter can be further substantiated. The graphic arrangement of the city and street lamp has its roots in early photographic presentations of the Shanghai Settlements such as figure 6.10, which shows the first street lamps, installed in 1882 along the Suzhou creek by the Municipal Council. In its construction of Shanghai's identity, *Dianshizhai Illustrated Magazine* helped to establish the street lamp as a trope for Shanghai. Furthermore, the illustrations established the iconographic connection between the literary figure of the Shanghai courtesan and the city.

6.7. "The joint biographies of the jiaoshu *[courtesans] Mei and Xiu" (Mei, Xiu er jiaoshu hezhuan). Lithograph, by Wu Youru. Illustration for a story in Wang Tao's* Miscellaneous Records of a Shanghai Recluse *(Songyin manlu). (*Dianshizhai huabao, *no.* yi, *23 [1884]: end page)*

6.8. "The reincarnation of Jade-flute" (Yuxiao zaishi). Lithograph, by Wu Youru. In this story from Miscellaneous Records of a Shanghai Recluse *(Songyin manlu), by Wang Tao, a loyal and devoted courtesan sacrifices her own life to save the gravely ill man who loved and had married her. (*Dianshizhai huabao, *no.* yi, *13 [1884]: end page)*

6.9. An illustrated scene from Second Collection of West Lake *(Xihu erji). Woodblock print. (Zhou Ji,* Xihu erji, *1628–44, Jujin Tang edition; reprinted in Zhou Yuan,* Zhongguo banhua shi tulu, *543)*

6.10. First streets lamps in Shanghai. Photograph, early 1880s. (Shi Meiding, Zhuiyi, *267)*

The magazine's news illustrations represented the Shanghai courtesan within the public space of the urban landscape from the outset. But the literary illustrations of courtesans in the same publication and by the same artist, Wu Youru, had to deal with a long artistic tradition in this genre in which the backdrop was the private environment of the garden or the boudoir. In the hierarchy of elements within literary illustrations, the city held no rank. It was already difficult enough to move the city into the traditional landscape of literary illustration; to move the courtesan or even a female figure from a good family into the cityscape posed an even greater challenge. Here, the traditional arrangement of the female as flower in the secluded setting of the garden or the boudoir, framed by a window or half hidden behind a portiere, or in a nature setting in the company of men, continued to have a strong impact on the artists. To move the female figure from this private "inner" realm, with its rich social and cultural associations about a woman's place in life, into a public scene, most pointedly into the street and under the public gaze, required a break not just with a painting tradition but also with everything associated with it.

6.11. Illustration from Flowers in the Mirror *(Huitu Jinghua yuan). Lithograph, by Lin Xie. The wall signifies the city. (Li Ruzhen,* Huitu Jinghua yuan*, 1888, chapter 11)*

Until late in the nineteenth century, there was almost no literary illustration showing a female figure in the public urban space, although the novels were often set in cities. The image of the city or town is tied to that of men (fig. 6.11). If a female figure was shown in an urban environment, she was shielded from direct public view by a wall (fig. 6.12) or was elevated high above the ground in a tower from which she could look out without being seen (fig. 6.13). Rare illustrations of women

6.12. Illustration from The Record of the Old Town *(Quanxiang yinshi gucheng ji). Woodblock print. The wall separates the inner and outer realms. (*Quanxiang yinshi gucheng ji, *Jinling Wenlin Ge edition, Ming dynasty; reprinted in Zhou Yuan,* Zhongguo banhua shi tulu, *664)*

in public show her in front of a magistrate (fig. 6.14) or on one side of an artificial demarcation that separates the "inside" (*nei*) from the "outside" (*wai*) (fig. 6.15). A seventeenth-century illustration not only places the female figure on the other side of a street but shields her with a curtain (fig. 6.16). In fact, she should not be seen by the door of the house at all; simply being there and looking out signals trouble. Her rightful place in literary illustration was in the garden (fig. 6.17) and in the adjacent room (fig. 6.18). Among legitimate activities, she could be shown praying (fig. 6.19) but most often was depicted engaging in playful entertainments such as making music, dancing, painting, weaving, and playing chess or simply yearning and waiting (fig. 6.20).

Traditionally, men and women were shown together only in nature or indoors (figs. 6.21, 6.22). If they were depicted together in public, it signaled impropriety and trouble. In figure 6.23, the female figure exposed to the public gaze signals the beginning of an illicit relationship. The illustration accompanies the story of the

6.13. Illustration from The Poetic Oath *(Shifumeng chuanqi). Woodblock print, by Xiang Nanzhou. (Xihu Jushi,* Shifumeng chuanqi, *Ming period; reprinted in Zhou Yuan,* Zhongguo banhua shi tulu, *853)*

6.14. Illustration from The Second Collection of Striking the Table in Amazement *(Erke Paian jingqi). Woodblock print. (Ling Mengchu,* Erke Paian jingqi, *late Ming period; reprinted in Zhou Yuan,* Zhongguo banhua shi tulu, *516)*

6.15. Illustration from The Tale of the Merchant Carriage and the Three Great Principles *(Xinkan chuxiang yinzhu Shanglu san yuan ji). Woodblock print. The demarcation separating the inner and outer realms is indicated symbolically with the brick steps. (Shen Shouxian,* Xinkan chuxiang yinzhu Shanglu san yuan ji, *Wanli period [1573–1619], Jinling Fuchun Tang edition; reprinted in Zhou Yuan,* Zhongguo banhua shi tulu, *618)*

6.16. Illustration from The Second Collection of Striking the Table in Amazement *(Erke Paian jingqi). Woodblock print. The street separates the female and the male figure who are looking at each other. (Ling Mengchu,* Erke Paian jingqi, *late Ming period; reprinted in Zhou Yuan,* Zhongguo banhua shi tulu, *517)*

6.17. "Lin Daiyu." Illustration from Illustrated Eulogies of "Dream of the Red Chamber" *(*Honglou meng *tuyong). Woodblock print, by Gai Qi (1774–1829). (Gai Qi,* "Honglou meng" tuyong*)*

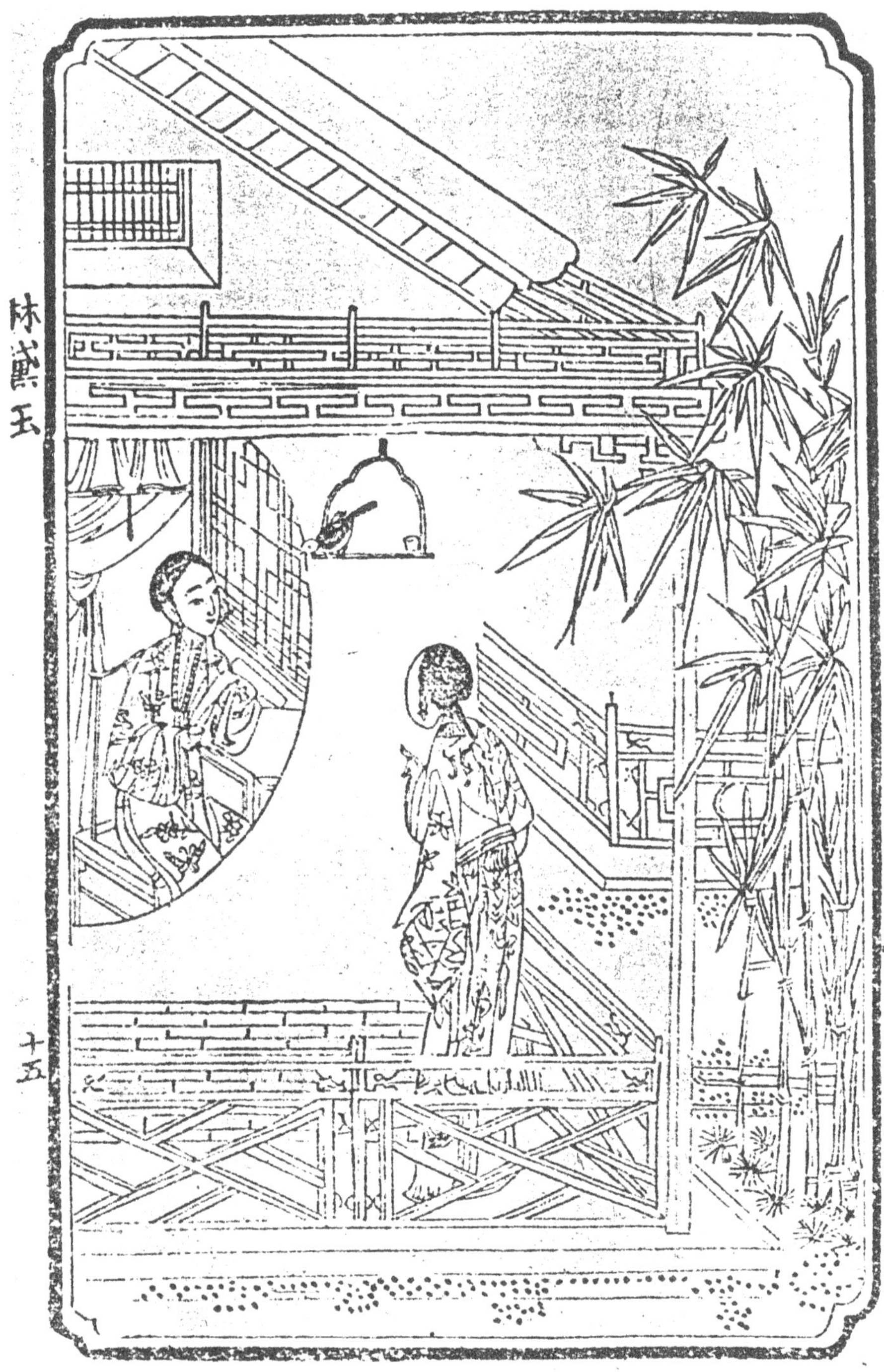

6.18. "Lin Daiyu." Illustration from Completely Illustrated "Dream of the Red Chamber," Zheng and Bing Manuscripts, Newly Compiled *(Cheng bingben xinjuan quanbu xiuxiang* Honglou meng*). Woodblock print. (*Cheng bingben xinjuan quanbu xiuxiang "Honglou meng," *eighteenth century; reprinted in Zhou Yuan,* Zhongguo banhua shi tulu, *590)*

6.19. *"Madam Liu burns incense before the moon" (Liu shi dui yue shao xiang). Woodblock print. Illustration from* A White Robe Story on Xue Rengui's Crossing the Ocean to Rectify the East *(Xinke chuxiang yinzhu Xue Rengui kuahai zheng dong Baipao ji). (*Xinke chuxiang yinzhu Xue Rengui kuahai zheng dong Baipao ji, *Wanli era [1573–1619]; reprinted in Zhou Yuan,* Zhongguo banhua shi tulu, *627)*

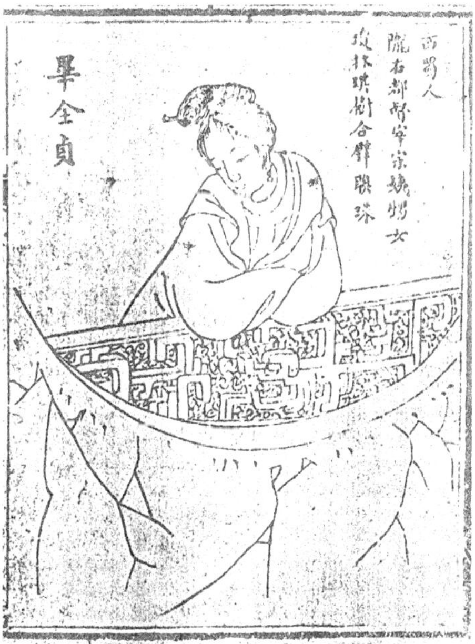

6.20. *Bi Quanzheng is the leading character in the novel* Flowers in the Mirror *(Jinghua yuan). Woodblock print, by Xie Yemei. (Li Ruzhen,* Jinghua yuan, *1832; reprinted in Zhou Yuan,* Zhongguo banhua shi tulu, *591)*

6.21. "Bidding farewell at Long Pavilion" (Zhang ting songbie). Illustration from The Romance of the Western Chamber *(Xinke chuxiang yinzhu Hualan nandiao Xixiang ji). Woodblock print. (Cui Shipei and Li Ye,* Xinke chuxiang yinzhu Hualan nandiao Xixiang ji, *Jinling Fuchun Tang edition, Ming period; reprinted in Zhou Yuan,* Zhongguo banhua shi tulu, *619)*

6.22. Scene from chapter seventeen of Flowers in the Mirror *(Huitu Jinghua yuan). Woodblock print, by Lin Xie. (Li Ruzhen,* Huitu Jinghua yuan, 1888*)*

6.23. "Wenjun at the counter selling wine" (Wenjun dang lu maijiu). Illustration from The Tale of Sima Xiangru and the Heart of the Zither *(Xinke chuxiang yinzhu Sima Xiangru qinxin ji). Woodblock print. (Sun You,* Xinke chuxiang yinzhu Sima Xiangru qinxin ji, *Wanli period [1573–1619], Jinling Fuchun Tang edition; reprinted in Zhou Yuan,* Zhongguo banhua shi tulu, *635)*

6.24. Illustration from A Tale of Chivalry *(Chongjiao Yixiaji). Woodblock print. (Shen Jing,* Chongjiao Yixiaji, *1607; reprinted in Zhou Yuan,* Zhongguo banhua shi tulu, *660)*

meeting between Zhuo Wenjun and the young poet Sima Xiangru (179–117 B.C.E.), which led to their eventual elopement. Even in this scene, however, Zhuo Wenjun is elevated above street level. A man and a woman facing each other with the curtain of the door to the street lifted signals adultery, as shown in figure 6.24. The literary illustration often replaced the text's public setting with a private space, substituting a garden backdrop for the urban environment. An example is the story "Jiang Xingge Meets the Pearl Shirt a Second Time" (Jiang Xingge chonghui zhenzhu shan), by Feng Menglong. In it, the seducer by chance sees a woman looking out onto the street, and her house is on the town's main thoroughfare. The pawnshop on the other side of the street plays an important role in the story's denouement.[49] The illustration, however, contains no trace of this urban environment and reschedules the event in nature (fig. 6.25).

Illustrators for the late Qing Shanghai courtesan novels had to come to grips with the problem of transporting the iconography of the courtesan scene, such as the lotus as the symbol of the courtesan (fig. 6.26), onto busy Shanghai streets. This was necessary not only because the literary texts placed scenes there but also because the city played such an important role in the novels themselves. When illustrated editions of the Shanghai courtesan novels first appeared in the 1890s, their images were revolutionary (fig. 6.27). Their most important breakthrough was the depiction of the female figure in the public urban space. Nature and the private realm were largely replaced by the cityscape.

Certain crucial steps had been taken a decade earlier in *Dianshizhai Illustrated Magazine*'s literary illustrations and the various illustrated albums on Shanghai. When Wu Youru added an urban background to the image of a courtesan in a traditional enclosed space in *Miscellaneous Records of a Shanghai Recluse* (see fig. 6.7), he took the first step in this revolution, but the crucial transformation came with the bold move of the female figure into the urban public space in Dianshizhai's *Illustrated Grand Sites of Shanghai* (fig. 6.28). In this work, the courtesan figure, in all her elegance, became a constituent of the cityscape. As part of the glorification of Western material culture, the female (courtesans with their maids and patrons) becomes the Chinese figure of the extraordinary, perfectly at ease with these stunning contraptions. At the storytelling hall, the theater, the horse race, and the public park, she is not a decoration within the cityscape but the highlight of its extraordinary character.

The public persona of the Shanghai courtesan could also take on a less glorious aspect. At about the same time as the luxurious illustrations were appearing in *Illustrated Grand Sites*, *Dianshizhai Illustrated Magazine* was also depicting courtesans in a distinctly lower register of style and in less flattering situations. The portraits were light-hearted in tone and showed bystanders making fun of courtesans, which invited readers to follow suit and made courtesans part of the general urban cultural amusement.

In this way, *Dianshizhai Illustrated Magazine* and *Illustrated Grand Sites of Shanghai* prefigure in both text and illustration, with regard to the city as well as to the courtesan, developments in illustrated courtesan novels since the 1890s.

6.25. Illustration from "Jiang Xingge Meets the Pearl Shirt a Second Time" (Jiang Xingge chonghui zhenzhu shan). Woodblock print, Wanli era (1573–1619). (Feng Menglong, "Jiang Xingge chonghui zhenzhu shan")

6.26. Illustration from Second Collection of West Lake *(Xihu erji). Woodblock print. (Zhou Ji,* Xihu erji, *1628–44; reprinted in Zhou Yuan,* Zhongguo banhua shi tulu, *542)*

6.27. Illustration from Biographies of Shanghai Flowers *(Haishang hua liezhuan). Lithograph, 1894. A patron and a courtesan with her maid have left their carriage to enter a shop specializing in Western goods. The scene is set among Shanghai-style buildings and street environment. (Han Bangqing,* Haishang hua liezhuan*)*

6.28. "Chinese riding in a horse-drawn carriage and on a bicycle" (Huaren cheng mache jiaotache). Lithograph, by Wu Youru. (Dianshizhai, Shenjiang shengjing tu, *1884, 2:34)*

The Urban Novel and Its Illustrations

The critical spirit of these novels notwithstanding, the courtesan continued to be treated as the grand emblem of Shanghai. An illustration for *The Nine-Tailed Fox* (fig. 6.29) inscribed her into the city as an unalienable part of its glories and amenities, along with the wide street, the fire hydrant, the gas lamp in the doorway, the French window shutters, the balcony, the glass-pane window, the suspended square painted lamps (a marker for the Shanghai courtesan house), and the Japanese-style rickshaw. The two lovebirds on the wire are a gentle reminder of the courtesan's vocation. The clear identification of the Shanghai locale and the emphasis on the particular urban character of the city mark a watershed in literary illustration. Like the novels, literary illustration had to transplant itself into the urban environment, treat the city as an integral part of the story line, and grant it an active role in the denouement.

One clear divergence, however, remains. Writers had to deal with the problem of bringing the courtesan down from her high literary pedestal without making her

6.29. "On San Malu, [Hu Baoyu] again thinks about restarting her former business" (San Malu chongsi xing jiu ye). Illustration from The Nine-Tailed Fox *(Jiuwei hu) shows courtesans traveling through the city in a rickshaw. Lithograph. (Menghuaguanzhu Jiang Yinxiang,* Jiuwei hu, *1918, 1991 reprint, illustration for volume 2, chapter 8)*

commonplace and having her lose her fictional powers in the process. Literary illustrations were concerned with safeguarding and maintaining the cultural stature of the female (or the courtesan) while resetting her image into the urban milieu. Although the novels are focused on Shanghai's contradictory character, the illustrations attempt to elevate urban landscape to the status of legitimate subjects of high art. As is evident from Wu Youru's illustrations for *Miscellaneous Records of a Shanghai Recluse*, the urban environment, and in particular the street, lacked the cultural stature necessary to evoke associations with a cultivated lifestyle. Evidently, simply inserting the female figure into an urban scene sufficed neither to make the urban environment culturally acceptable nor to show the compatibility of the female figure with such a setting. One way of remedying the social pollution of the female through contact with strangers on the street was to elevate the status of the city by emptying its streets and eliminating all references to crowds and the commercial bustle. This was the strategy used in the early illustrations of Shanghai courtesans until the late 1910s.[50] For example, in a theater that normally would have been packed with spectators, the courtesan star is depicted in near isolation (fig. 6.30). The novels' highly critical image of the Shanghai courtesan and of the city is not reflected in these literary illustrations.

There are certainly different styles and orientations in the literary illustrations, and those depicting the courtesan inside a courtesan house are done in different manner from those that show her in an urban scene. Domestic courtesan scenes in Han Bangqing's *Biographies of Shanghai Flowers*, for example, illustrate events in a given chapter. But even these scenes do not clearly reflect the scorn with which the text often handles her; true to the cultural symbolism attached to her image, the courtesan and, through her, Shanghai remain glamorous. This discrepancy ends up serving the novel in an unexpected and probably unintended way: It highlights the ambiguity in the image of both city and courtesan, with the novel deconstructing its own illustrations, and vice versa.

Given the literary and metaphorical potential of her character, it is not surprising that the Shanghai courtesan played such a key role in the novels discussed here. In their text and illustration, she left the inner realm and came to dominate the public space of Shanghai, embodying all the ambiguities of desire and money. The novels sharply set off her character against the traditional courtesan image and left no doubt about the fundamental difference between Shanghai and any other Chinese town.

A New Urban Sensibility in Literary Illustration

As part of the early modern urban art forms, both the novel and its illustrations reflect a new kind of urban sensibility. The texts show an alienation and distance that are reactions to the perceived decline of a world governed by a fixed and familiar set of values. The reader was invited to take a close look at this city, which was his or might become his, but was asked to let the novels help him to look through its glittering surface. With their extensive and realistic depictions of the city's extra-

6.30. *"Looking at* dan *actor Shisan Dan entering the stage during the evening performance" (Kan yexi Shisan dan deng chang). Illustration from* The Nine-Tailed Fox *(Jiuwei hu) shows Hu Baoyu in her seat on the second floor of a theater. Lithograph. (Menghuaguanzhu Jiang Yinxiang,* Jiuwei hu, *1918, 1991 reprint, illustration for volume 2, chapter 4)*

ordinary features, the novels banked on its lure, but they gave the reader safe distance through their exposé technique. The effectiveness of this technique hinged, however, on the traditional values even sojourners in this city continued to espouse. The city was a fascinating, strange, and disturbing sight better viewed from the distance maintained by the noncommittal voyeur. This form of modern alienated perspective was due in part to the influence of *Dianshizhai Illustrated Magazine*, which first began to depict the city as an object to be looked at. The works were created through dialogue not with the reader but with the city. The reader, therefore, was not the real addressee but the onlooker.

This sense of alienation is also very much part of some of the illustrations. They do not seem to have the reader as their direct addressee or point of reference. The scenes and the characters depicted in the illustrations are framed by urban structures, and a sense of dislocation and noncommunication prevails in human relationships (figs. 6.31–6.33). The figures are often on different physical levels, separated by structures and psychological barriers. The composition of these illustrations reflects a sense of inside versus outside, with the insiders appearing to a certain extent in control. The illustrations also exhibit a new concept of space represented largely by the alienated relationship between the individual and the impersonal physical structures of the city, where one might be the subject as well as the object, the one who observes or who is observed.

As the art of illustration of urban literature unfolded, the image of the Shanghai courtesan began to develop. She continued to be the means to evoke a feeling for the city, as demonstrated by illustrations from the 1930s (figs. 6.34, 6.35). Although the figures in these illustrations are shown without a rich urban context, comparison with the traditional image in figure 6.36 shows to what degree her body language and gaze have internalized the city environment and to what degree she alone is able to evoke the city as a whole. In figure 6.35, the female figure leans outward in the traditional pose of "looking far into the distance" (*yuantiao*), but instead of the expected mountain and river, her eyes seem to catch the invisible urban landscape, which is already encoded in her posture.

The rise of the late Qing courtesan novels is closely linked to the larger picture of literary developments during that period, with the exposé novel setting the fashion. The fact that these novels were written largely in Shanghai and about the Shanghai courtesan and carry the city's name in their titles shows the importance of the locale and in part reflects the men of letters' quandary with their identity in this city. Their traditional standing was among the first casualties of change, and through their depiction of Shanghai and its new most-favored children, the courtesan and the merchant, they expressed their sense of loss and disillusionment. Even the courtesans who traditionally needed their protection and promotion were thriving in the haven of the Foreign Settlements and had achieved the status of free agents and businesswomen in their own right. The future urban intellectuals were enticed by this city, which gave them employment and a public voice, and repelled by it as well because it did not grant them the role of arbiters of value and taste. As a consequence, they took on the image of the city they had helped to create and resorted to its deconstruction.

6.31. Illustration from Biographies of Shanghai Flowers *(Haishang hua liezhuan). Lithograph. (Han Bangqing,* Haishang hua liezhuan, *1894)*

The writers of these novels were journalists. Journalistic writing had a substantial impact on the development of the late Qing novel. The Shanghai courtesan novel has a great deal in common with the political novel of the period, which was often written by the same group of authors and exposed the corruption of Qing officialdom. Both types of novel used exposé as their core strategy. Their proximity is most evident in novels such as *Flower in the Sea of Retribution* (Niehai hua), by Zeng Pu, published in 1903–7, and *Amorous Adventures in Beijing* (Jinghua yanshi), by Zhongyuan Langzi, serialized in 1908, which target both courtesans and politicians for scorn.[51]

6.32. Illustration from Biographies of Shanghai Flowers *(Haishang hua liezhuan). Lithograph. (Han Bangqing,* Haishang hua liezhuan, *1894)*

6.33. *Illustration from* Biographies of Shanghai flowers. *Lithograph. (Han Bangqing,* Haishang hua liezhuan, *1894)*

As a literary genre, the Shanghai courtesan novel of the late nineteenth century set a trend for urban novels, with the courtesan playing a major role. Novels of this kind set in other cities followed, for example, *New Hankow* (Xin Hankou), by Hanshang Yugong, in 1909; *The New Suzhou, First Series* (Xin Suzhou chubian), in 1910, and *Dreams of Suzhou's Splendor* (Suzhou fanhua meng), in 1911, both by Tianxiao; and *Yangzhou Dreams* (Yangzhou meng), in 1915. These novels are a mixture of the urban novel, which focused on the provocative new urban lifestyle of a

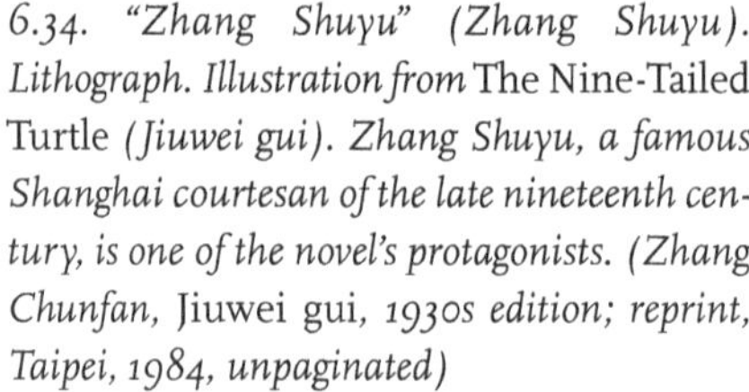

6.34. "Zhang Shuyu" (Zhang Shuyu). Lithograph. Illustration from The Nine-Tailed Turtle *(Jiuwei gui). Zhang Shuyu, a famous Shanghai courtesan of the late nineteenth century, is one of the novel's protagonists. (Zhang Chunfan,* Jiuwei gui, *1930s edition; reprint, Taipei, 1984, unpaginated)*

6.35. "Jin Xiaobao" (Jin Xiaobao). Lithograph. Illustration from The Nine-Tailed Turtle *(Jiuwei gui). Jin Xiaobao, a famous Shanghai courtesan of the late nineteenth century, is one of the novel's protagonists. (Zhang Chunfan,* Jiuwei gui, *1930s edition; reprint, Taipei, 1984, unpaginated)*

particular city, and the exposé novel, which critiqued that very lifestyle. While courtesans certainly played a major part in these novels, there was also much in the way of general social and political criticism.

The Shanghai urban novel, however, continued to dominate the scene well into the 1920s. As an inspiration, a source, and a subject, the city held a dominant position in literature throughout the first decades of the twentieth century. As the image of the Shanghai courtesan evolved from the late Qing and throughout the Republican period, becoming the "socialite" (*jiaoji hua*), the movie star, the dance-hall girl, and the prostitute, she continued to be a major literary character in describing the modern city.

6.36. Illustration from The Tale of Planting the Jade *(Zhong yu ji). Woodblock print. Female figure in a relaxed pose looking at a pair of lovebirds. (Wang Tingna,* Yumingtang piping Zhong yu ji, *1628–44; reprint in Zhou Yuan,* Zhongguo banhua shi tulu, *808)*

7 *Guides to Paradise*

Entertainment in the Formation of Shanghai's Identity

In the 1860s, Shanghai—a unique entity in the making—became the most intensely described place in the Chinese Empire. Journalists, novelists, and writers of travel guides attempted to narrate the city and define its core, partly because of Shanghai's unusual background as an alien entity on Chinese soil, but more important, because it was open to definition, and the shapers of Shanghai would influence the city's development. As people were drawn to this enclave for different reasons and with different visions for its future, their minds were far from unified in their understanding of the city's defining features. Yet for all this broad variety, the Shanghai Foreign Settlements were seen from the beginning through a limited set of conflicting but interwoven myths.

Shanghai city guides written between the 1870s and the first decade of the twentieth century are an important source for the various scenarios for the city. They offer highly conscious constructs of an imaginary place. Through a guide, the author intends to tell a particular story of the city and hopes to create a particular image of it. This image is drawn against one or several shadow images of other visions of the same place. In this respect, the guides are not language-bound. As they narrate Shanghai, their points of view and perceptions confront, echo, and build on one another. In the process of drawing up a particular image, complex questions must be answered, and decisions as well as compromises need to be made. Where is the center of town? Is it in the walled city with the district magistrate's yamen? Or in the new International Settlement, with its foreign banks and big merchant houses along the river? What is to be put into the city guide, and what is to be left out? Should the components of the Foreign Settlements be treated separately, or should the city be described as an overarching entity with different subsections? Which aspect of the city should be introduced first? What constitutes the main feature of the city? Is it trade, industry, tourism and entertainment, or education? For Shanghai, these were open questions. The guides reflect the struggle over the design of the city. At stake was control over its future, and the authority to shape it not just politically and economically but also physically, through its buildings and street layout, and mentally, through the introduction of new social and cultural values. These guides are symptoms of, and instruments in, an ongoing struggle for hegemony in defining the city.[1]

While a guide might be highly personal, it is also bound by certain genre-related and functional restraints. It is the form by which a writer or publisher presents a public and verifiably factual account of the city. By implicitly distancing itself from the courtesan guides or novels, which present the image of the city through that of the courtesan with her brazen modern ways, and from the critical and ironic journalistic stance taken by the newspapers, a guide defends the city and justifies its value, strength, and potential. Still, Shanghai guides had to mediate among an existing genre, the new type of city they were describing, and the particular information needs of the Shanghai tourists and sojourners. They also had to come to grips with an image of the city centered on entertainment and, in particular, the omnipresent courtesan. Accordingly, these guides were from the outset forced to address the question of the role of "play," or *youxi*, in the city's image.

That was not all. While it may be expected that such a rising commercial port would tout its own importance and advertise its image, the case of Shanghai was greatly complicated by the fact that the Settlements were created by foreign intervention but were not a colony and that the Shanghai Foreign Settlements were for Chinese and foreigners alike an immigrant community without a local population. This particular feature of the city provided the open space on which the battle for its definition was being fought. The Shanghai city guides thus present complex and often conflicting images inserted into ever changing master constructs.

To render their impressions of the Shanghai enclave, ethnic Chinese long-term sojourners and short-term visitors tended to use the language of Penglai, Island of Immortals, full of wonders and splendor set apart from the common world of mortals. The voyeurism of this discourse signals the fact, and the acceptance of the fact, that this place was run according to its own rules. It remained the dominant mode until the great changes in the city's makeup at the end of the century, after the Treaty of Shimonoseki, which ended the First Sino-Japanese War in 1895. The construction of this Penglai image began in the early years of the Foreign Settlements. Chinese men of letters who fled the Taipings and moved into the Foreign Settlements beginning in the 1850s created and elaborated upon this image. The development of the newspaper and publishing industry in Shanghai from the early 1870s further allowed and fueled large numbers of writings on the city produced in sizable runs.

European and North American sojourners, who represented the dominant force in the foreign community, however, had been to or knew of other modern cities such as Paris, Vienna, London, Chicago, and New York. They were not simply gazing at the Settlements but felt they were shaping them, and that shape became the subject of much controversy. While the French Settlement remained under the firm control of the French consul, conflicts within the council of consuls, which was supervising the International Settlement, all but neutralized this body and left the Shanghailanders much leeway, which they eagerly exploited. From the early 1860s, the general notion of Shanghai as the model settlement, which was to be set up and run by Shanghailanders, had come to dominate the discourse. Between the 1860s and 1900, the interaction of these different perceptions, images, and myths with the language of metaphor and narration they generated and the structures of value and power they implied laid the foundation for a collective and unique cultural enterprise.

The images thus construed were full of inner tensions and contradictions. While they talked back to other options, these rejected options continued to form images, and some of their inner ambiguities were brought into the open as history moved on. Hidden within the Penglai metaphor was the option that Shanghai might be a kind of amusement park, or later "big playground," and, still later, a "great amusement park" (*da leyuan*); this opened the way for an ironic attitude toward the Shanghai Foreign Settlements and the behavior of its men of letters. The "model settlement" language in its turn, with its high-pitched agenda of social responsibility, talked back to the often stated claim that "people in the Treaty Ports are a set of brainless pleasure-seekers."[2]

Miscellaneous Notes on Visiting Shanghai

The earliest guides to Shanghai were written by residents of the city. These guides are of particular interest since they are closely linked to the writers' self-perception. The way in which people define their city has much to do with their definitions of themselves and their roles in it. One of the earliest guides written by residents of the Settlements is *Miscellaneous Notes on Visiting Shanghai* (Hu you zaji).[3] Written by Ge Yuanxu, a medical doctor by profession and a Shanghai sojourner since the Taiping Rebellion, this guide was published in 1876.[4] During the following decades, it enjoyed great popularity. Two years later, in 1878, an illustrated Japanese translation was published, and in 1887, a second Chinese edition was issued, with Ge's friend Yuan Zuzhi as editor.[5]

The author announces in his preface that the guide is meant to assist men of letters, officials, wealthy businessmen, and merchants with their visits to Shanghai. Shanghai had become a commercial and tourist attraction, and these men did not know the new ways of this place. As the author states: "Since the opening of this treaty port, the scenes of prosperity have become more exuberant by the day. The streets are jammed with traffic, and the markets and people dazzle the eye. Shanghai has rapidly surpassed such famous towns as Canton and Hankou. There are visitors from all eighteen provinces of China and from the twenty-four countries abroad."[6]

The author takes it for granted that a guide to Shanghai is a guide only to the Foreign Settlements, where the customs and laws would be most confusing for the visitor. It is the place to which "both merchants and officials love to come for a visit." The walled city of Shanghai, with its official yamen, is "utterly different" from the rapid change and economic prosperity of the Settlements and therefore has simply been written out of this guide.[7] It was marginalized.

The Foreign Settlements, once referred to despite strenuous foreign objections as *yichang* (the barbarians' market) are politely called *yangchang* (the foreign settlements) in the guide, or simply "the northern town" (*beishi*), as opposed to "the southern town" (*nanshi*), the walled city. Ge's guide shows how the Foreign Settlements gradually usurped the name "Shanghai."

The guide's organization does not follow that of guides to other Chinese cities or that of city guides in the West; beyond a fairly random division into four sections, no other principle of organization is discernible. Set up like a dictionary, with more than three hundred entries, it presents the Shanghai Foreign Settlements as a series of distinct fragments that together form a grand mosaic of Shanghai.

The guide begins with three separate maps for the French, English, and American Settlements. The maps are followed by a new feature in a Chinese guide, depictions of the flags of all major powers present in Shanghai, including, as one among others, that of the Qing government. Except for the maps, which are also found at the beginning of earlier Chinese guides and local chronicles, the sequence in the rest of the work is free of the constraints of tradition and hierarchy.

The entry "Foreign Settlements" is followed by those for "street," "sewer," "covered well," "big bridge" (*daqiao*), "roadside trees," "Regulations governing the Settlements," "orchid exhibitions," "horse races," "Customs Office," "Mixed Court," "Guang Fangyan Language School," "Natural History Museum," "Bureau for Small-pox Inoculation" (Niudou Ju), "Municipal Council," "police headquarters" (*xunpu fang*), "Shenbao Publishing House," "Western calendar," "garbage truck," and "sprinkler cart," in happy serendipity.

The contents of the first volume might be seen as an introduction to the institutional aspects of Shanghai, with the remaining three volumes addressing life in the Settlements with a focus on entertainment and leisure. This includes courtesan houses, twenty-six of their rules and regulations, and their ritualized forms of interaction, such as "receiving clients for tea," "calls by clients to entertain at dinner parties," or "serving watermelon seeds and fruit preserves to clients." There is also a comprehensive list of restaurants and delicacies, including "Western-style pubs," "Western-style restaurants," and the names of the dishes for which different restaurants were known. There is a category for theaters that includes "foreign theaters," the "foreign circus," the "foreign magic show," "foreign shadow-plays," and "famous Chinese opera programs in the theaters." Also mentioned are a variety of "wineshops," "storytelling halls" (*shuchang*), "opium dens" (*yanguan*), and, not to forget, lists of specialty shops for Western, Cantonese, and Beijing goods.

Included in this mixed category of items, and described as a part of the general category of entertainment and leisure with its emphasis on the novel and curious, are all kinds of Western technical innovations, industrial products, and features of the Settlements' infrastructure. They become objects of curious attention, admiration, or amusement. Examples include "coach," "foot-treading vehicle" (bicycle), "tower clock," "gas lamp," "self-turning fan," "foreign fire engine," and "photography studio," all of which appear in the same series as "orchid exhibition" and "horse races."

Ge Yuanxu's Shanghai has no center of any kind, either physically or mentally. There is no sense of a political center or a seat of government. The entry for Shanghai's governing body, the Municipal Council, which ran the town and kept public order, is wedged in between an item on "released soft-shelled turtles" (which then proceeded to not only eat all the other fish in the pond but come ashore to prey on humans) and one on "inns," with a sketch of the bustling shoreline harbor and a warning against pickpockets.

This city is not dominated by any particular feature, be it trade or entertainment. Relevant knowledge about new features takes on the form of the new terms under which they come and is offered in entries that follow one after another in perfectly egalitarian fashion. Who is to say that the Mixed Court is a more fascinating tourist attraction than the water hydrant? Through this terminological itemization, the Shanghai Foreign Settlements becomes a place without physical presence. No architectural landmarks are mentioned, no building is connected to a street, and no street is introduced with its architecture. And Shanghai is a city without a past. Its origin in the Opium War is never mentioned. In this frenzy of the new and fascinating, there is no historical reference and no sense of change over time. All packed into the present, the city is a live performance of itemized and decontextualized tidbits, of games, goods, stores, teahouses, and gas lamps. Shanghai becomes a theme park of utopia, a center of voyeuristic amusement. In this park, the center is everywhere, depending only on one's choice of indulgence. Ge Yuanxu's Shanghai is constructed out of the idea of novelty and amusement. The reader is the aimless visiting voyeur playing in this harmless, timeless, fascinating, and glittering amusement park.

Explicitly modeled on a mid-nineteenth-century guide to Beijing, *A Record of Essential Aspects of the Capital City* (Dumen jilüe), by Yang Jingting, which dealt with Beijing not of the past but as it was at the time and included for the first time categories such as "fashion," "shopping," and "entertainment," *Miscellaneous Notes* nonetheless follows the breathless enumeration of the *fanhua*, the extravagance and luxury, contained in earlier models.[8] In one way or the other, however, these guides had their problems. The Yangzhou guide *A Record of the Painted Boats in Yangzhou* (Yangzhou huafang lu), by Li Dou, offers a diachronic view of the glories of the town rather than being focused on the present; Meng Yuanlao's nostalgic Kaifeng description *The Eastern Capital: A Dream of Splendors Past* (Dongjing menghua lu) was a memoir written after the city had fallen to the Mongols and did not fit with Shanghai's actual bustle; and *A Record of the Splendors of the Capital City* (Ducheng jisheng), by Guanyuan Naideweng, a 1235 guide to the Southern Song capital Hangzhou, did all the right things and would even have allowed description of Shanghai on the model of a capital, but it had fallen afoul of critics enraged by the glorification of a city that owed its ascendance to the loss of the North. In view of this type of criticism, even alluding to the Hangzhou record in a guide to Settlements Shanghai would have been highly impolitic on Ge Yuanxu's part.

The narrative strategies and the formal structure of *Miscellaneous Notes on Visiting Shanghai* are thus quite carefully calculated in their inclusions, adaptations, and silent rejections. Adopting the impersonally terse tone of the Beijing guide but fragmenting its categories, and duplicating the emphasis on *fanhua* in the Kaifeng and Hangzhou works yet keeping a distance from the nostalgic tone of the one and the compromised glory of the other, Ge Yuanxu was able to present

Shanghai without a linear or unified narrative, creating in the process greater leeway for his description of the city and making it easier for his readers to accept that description without qualms. As a result, the city has no unified core. It appears as a non-centered and non-hierarchized entity, free from a past that could weigh it down and predetermine its course.

Ge Yuanxu does not hide his admiration for the Settlements. Under his pen, Shanghai is all *fanhua*. One of the popular bamboo twig ballads included in his guide likens the Settlements to the mirage of a fantasyland.

> On the flats north [of the walled town], all wild weeds cleared;
> Millions of gold coins the ocean waves bring.
> All barren hills turned into sumptuous dwellings;
> Clearly a mirage city, with fantasy towers![9]

The flats north of the walled town are where the Settlements had grown. Here, the millions made from overseas trade converge. The much-vaunted Shanghai Western-style buildings have taken over the barren hills, and the author assures us with mock certainty that all this cannot be real but must be a fata morgana.

The foreigners are not portrayed as strange or even hostile aliens. Every item of Western life in the city is subsumed with approval and often overwhelming enthusiasm under the category of *qi*. The guide's city is filled with Westerners at a time when in fact only about 2,000 lived there amidst about 130,000 Chinese.[10] Their sheer overrepresentation as well as the absence of any concerns about their presence contrast to a degree with the second big emblem of the city's attractions, the courtesans whose inclusion the author found it necessary to justify.[11] Together, the foreigner and the courtesan stand out as markers of the city's *fanhua*.

The international character of the Settlements is portrayed not as decoration but as the very heart of the Shanghai theme park. All Chinese and foreign aspects of life, trade, and entertainment are mixed in a seemingly random manner into one condensed flurry of exoticism. The motley crowd of residents and visitors from many parts of China, Asia, and the West could view Western theater, circus performances, magic shows, and shadow plays and even "Japanese acrobats" (*dongyang xifa*), and all these in addition to the plethora of Chinese entertainment from many regions and in different languages. All these attractions become part of the city's international and metropolitan flair. Hidden in the time tables of domestic and international ship arrivals and departures and the listings of different Chinese and foreign shipping companies given by the guide is the silent but defining image of Shanghai as an international commercial center.

Still, Ge Yuanxu's attitude toward the Foreign Settlements is more elusive. By using the word *you* (here with the sense of "visit") in the title, and referring to his own sojourn in Shanghai with the words "Alas, I have been 'wandering' in Shanghai for fifteen years" (Yu you haishang shiwu nian yi), he claims nonattachment. The notion of "wandering" (*you*) is linked to Shanghai as the wonderland where no one could claim to be a permanent resident.

Shanghai as a Multiethnic Community

In 1884, Ernest Major's Dianshizhai studio published *Illustrated Grand Sites of Shanghai* (Shenjiang shengjing tu). It was the first illustrated narrative of the city and offered an integrated and idealizing view based on both Chinese and Western cultural traditions. The introduction of copper engraving, lithography, and photography opened new possibilities for highlighting Shanghai's glories; these methods also allowed publishers to present a mostly visual powerful image of the city that could compete with other views expressed in words.

Illustrated Grand Sites combines elements from Chinese travelogues, with their emphasis on the "grand sites of nature" (*mingsheng*), with features from nineteenth-century European illustrated works, which presented exotic scenes straight from the heart of the big cities or far-off lands.[12] Each illustration is accompanied by a short text rendered in a variety of calligraphic styles. The book treats the different parts of the city, including the walled town, as one entity. Selected scenes range from grand temples and elegant gardens inside and outside the walled city to street scenes in the Foreign Settlements and different types of Western-style amusements. The artist was Wu Youru, who is most famous for his work in *Dianshizhai Illustrated Magazine* (Dianshizhai huabao). The book's introduction quite explicitly states that Shenbaoguan and Major, who managed Dianshizhai, were directly involved in conceptualizing and planning the book.[13]

As a unique cross-cultural product with no precedent to emulate, the book expresses a vision that is in its own way uniquely Shanghai. This was a city with a multiethnic cultural identity. The book focuses on the blending of Chinese and Western cultures and the peaceful coexistence of Chinese and Western ways. A visionary and mover in forging this vision of Shanghai, Major succeeded in this book in synthesizing the different notions and representations of the city's success and glory into one grand visual feast, which, in spirit if not in words, blends the European notion of the model settlement with the Chinese notion of a prosperous commercial town where the entertainment industry was considered an indispensable accoutrement. Wu Youru did his part by expressing this new urban ideal through a style of illustration that combines Chinese and Western drawing techniques. In *Illustrated Grand Sites*, Shanghai's prosperity is represented for the first time through its architecture, its public spaces, and its public institutions such as the firefighting brigade (fig. 7.1).

This point of view informs the entire book. The advertisement for the book that ran in *Shenbao* claims that Shanghai's wonders are different from those of nature, which are made by heaven, because they are man's creation: "Shanghai, a nook of a place, has become the champion among all the open port cities, and it excels in ingenuity. . . . There is the monumental and the astonishing, there is seclusion and elegance; there is also extreme extravagance to intoxicate the heart and dazzle the eyes; at the same time there is also that which is far above all worldly concerns."[14] The book defines the city in high-register language as "a grand cosmopolitan center among the Chinese" (Zhongxia yi da duhui).[15]

7.1. "The Western-style fire engine" (Jiuhuo yanglong). Lithograph, by Wu Youru. (Dianshizhai, Shenjiang shengjing tu, *1884, 2:12)*

There is no division between Chinese and Western contributions. Taking the stance of the city's proud representative, the book sets out to present Shanghai's achievements as the result of cooperation and interaction between Chinese and Westerners. Although *Illustrated Grand Sites* aims to present a series of "grand sites," as the title declares, its arrangement clearly and consciously reflects a balanced view of the forces at work. It brings together two different understandings of the city: Shanghai as wonderland and as multiethnic city.

Cultural sights are at the top of the list. They are all situated in, or culturally connected with, the Chinese walled city: The Shanghai Hall of Learning, Yeshi Garden, the Inner Garden of the Temple of the City God, the Hall of the Zhejiang and Ningbo Guilds, and the Guangzhao Mountain Resort. The walled city is not simply omitted, as it was in Ge's *Miscellaneous Notes.* There is some culture to be had. By the standards of other Chinese cities in the Jiangnan area, Shanghai's offerings in this realm were quite modest. The prominence given to these fixtures in *Illustrated Grand Sites* signals an agenda, namely to offer an image of a city of which all inhabitants could be proud, as it reflected their own contributions.

The Western contribution to the city appears mostly in the technical sophistication of its infrastructure, such as the "Gas Company," the "Fresh Water Company," electricity, the railroad, the commercial steamer coming into the harbor (fig. 7.2), and, in all modesty, the Dianshizhai printing house where the book was printed. Grand buildings are depicted in order to highlight the powerful Western presence. Examples are the British Embassy, the German Club, the French Chamber of Commerce, and Trinity Church. There are no images of Western warships; instead, the book highlights Chinese military vigor and innovativeness with views of the Shanghai military drill ground (fig. 7.3), the Wusong military garrison, and the Jiangnan Arsenal.

The illustration shown in figure 7.4, which depicts the river teeming with Chinese junks and Western steamships, is a tribute to the benefits of treaty port status. In the foreground, the "model settlement" theme of foreigners and Chinese leisurely going about their business brings out the peace and order prevailing in the Settlements. The juxtaposition of the big steamship and the peaceful scene in the foreground redefines the former. Instead of representing the Western threat, it suggests the benefits brought to both Chinese and Westerners through the opening of trade. In Major's own perception, Western expansion could take different forms and perform different functions. As Rudolf Wagner has shown in his study, Major followed what may be called a "Scottish enlightenment agenda," according to which the businessman is responsible for contributing to the betterment of the society in which he happens to be living.[16] This was consistent with Major's multiethnic cultural ideal. This vision set him on a collision course with hard-core defenders of British interests.[17]

Illustrated Grand Sites of Shanghai celebrates and promotes the ideal of the public, which translated into its presentation of Shanghai as a public space. The parks, the racecourse, the Bund (fig. 7.5), the grand avenues, the buildings, the harbor, and even the foreign cemetery are all symbols of communal life. These illustrations also show the public side of life as it was lived in this city, including public administration, such as police transporting prisoners and a picture of the Mixed Court, where foreign and Chinese officials administered justice together. In this respect, there is no divide between the Chinese walled city and the Foreign Settlements. These scenes make a point of vividly depicting the life of the people on the streets and in the buildings, with foreigners and Chinese inhabiting the public space together. Most revealing, women are seen everywhere: strolling through the public parks, going to the temple (fig. 7.6), riding in open carriages, sitting in opera houses or teahouses, attending church services (fig. 7.7), and even going to the Mixed Court.

The city as a center of entertainment is not lost among the loftier concerns of establishing the image of the ideal community, and the theme of Shanghai as entertainment dominates the second volume of *Illustrated Grand Sites of Shanghai*. The book adhered to a nineteenth-century view in recognizing entertainment as part of a city's attraction but failing to notice its economic importance. As emblems of the cosmopolitan, glorious, and often sensational pastimes the city had to offer, this volume contains depictions of a Western-style billiard hall (fig. 7.8), a courtesan house, the singing hall for women performers, the opium den, the American circus, the

7.2. *"The commercial steamer coming into the harbor" (Shanglun jinkou). Lithograph, by Wu Youru. (Dianshizhai,* Shenjiang shengjing tu, *1884, 1:40)*

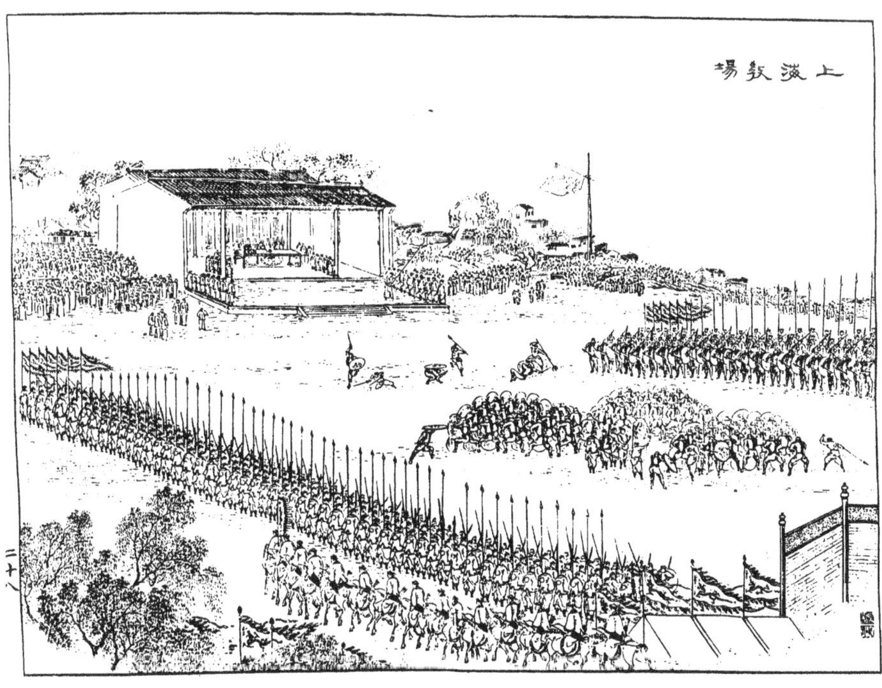

7.3. *"Shanghai military drill ground" (Shanghai jiaochang). Lithograph, by Wu Youru. (Dianshizhai,* Shenjiang shengjing tu, *1884, 1:29)*

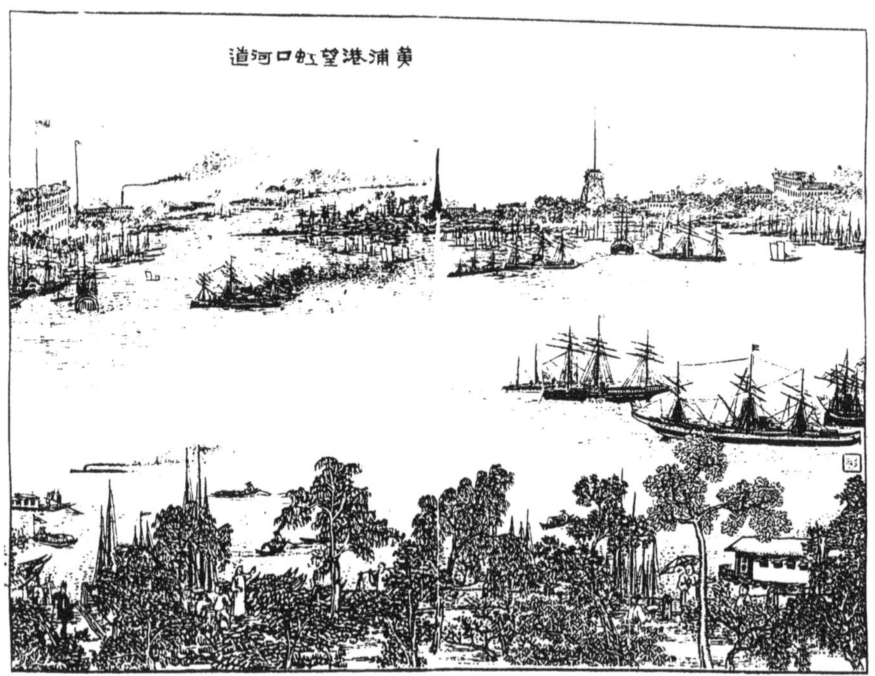

7.4. "The view of Hongkou waterway seen from Huangpu Harbor" (Huangpu gang wang Hongkou hedao). Lithograph, by Wu Youru. (Dianshizhai, Shenjiang shengjing tu, *1884, 1:38)*

7.5. "The English section of the Bund" (Yingjie Huangpu tan). Lithograph, by Wu Youru. (Dianshizhai, Shenjiang shengjing tu, *1884, 1:56)*

7.6. "Going to Longhua Temple to offer incense" (Longhua jinxiang). Lithograph, by Wu Youru. (Dianshizhai, Shenjiang shengjing tu, *1884, 1:34)*

7.7. "Preaching at the church" (Libaitang jiangshu). Lithograph, by Wu Youru. (Dianshizhai, Shenjiang shengjing tu, *1884, 2:26)*

Japanese teahouse with geisha entertainers, and Westerners engaging in innocent antics such as the bag race (fig. 7.9) and practicing gymnastics (fig. 7.10). The Chinese concept of entertainment is linked to the notions of extravagance and prosperity, which include the exotic and fantastic. The foreigners are present not as mighty imperialists but as innocent and exotic objects attracting a curious idle gaze. These scenes of merrymaking and gentle pastimes convey an overwhelming sense of ease and prosperity and carefully avoid any direct suggestion of the less pleasant aspects of being in such a commercial town.

Objects play no part in this landscape of paradise; apparently, nothing here is for sale. There is no insinuation of the consumption of things, only the consumption of sights. The buying and selling, the craving for money—these are not part of Shanghai's grand cultural landscape. In fine style, the book ends with the picture of another branch of Major's publishing enterprise, the Office for the Publication of the *Collection of Books and Illustrations Old and New* (Gujin tushu jicheng ju). Major was the main publisher of high-quality Chinese books in China by this time, with titles ranging from the first commercially available print of the Kangxi dictionary to the materials necessary for preparing for the Imperial Examinations, from the huge illustrated encyclopedia *Collection of Books and Illustrations Old and New* to novels such as the first edition of Shen Yue's *Six Chapters from a Floating Life* (Fusheng liu ji).[18] In this order of things, Shenbaoguan is producing not goods but an important part of Shanghai's cultural offerings.

Shanghai as Penglai comes alive with an array of images evoking the grand, the cultured, the refined, the playful, the exotic, and the new. The city is shown as a series of sights, with a fine balance between the extraordinary and the solemn. This is not a theme park for consumption as in Ge's *Miscellaneous Notes on Visiting Shanghai* but a paradise for enjoyment and admiration. In these urban spaces, it is the public that is being celebrated through the depiction of Shanghai residents and their contribution to the common good. Permeating these unending scenes of wonder, racial harmony, and cultural diversity, however, one might sense the Western Shanghailanders' pride in their management of this success story.

Model Settlement Shanghai: A Handbook for Travellers and Residents

The first Western-language Shanghai guide written by a Shanghai resident came out in 1903, twenty-five years after Ge's guide. Western-language introductions to the Shanghai Settlements had been produced since the 1860s.[19] The purpose of these guides was mainly to introduce the Western business community to the potential of the recently opened markets, which were seen as part of the Western sphere of influence.[20] Characteristically, these early guides tended to be all-encompassing in content, monumental in size, and luxurious in binding as well as in the number of illustrations. During the early twentieth century, with international interest in Shanghai as a tourist destination on the rise, a range of hotel and tourist guides was also produced.[21] Their outsider perspective and mostly anonymous authorship, however, contrast with the signed 1903 guide by Reverend Charles Ewart Darwent,

7.8. "Billiard hall for Chinese customers" (Huaren danzifang). Lithograph, by Wu Youru. (Dianshizhai, Shenjiang shengjing tu, *1884, 1:40)*

7.9. "Westerners' bag race" (Xiren saipao). Lithograph, by Wu Youru. (Dianshizhai, Shenjiang shengjing tu, *1884, 1:54)*

7.10. "Westerners practicing gymnastics" (Xiren xiyi). Lithograph, by Wu Youru. (Dianshizhai, Shenjiang shengjing tu, *1884, 2:58)*

Shanghai: A Handbook for Travellers and Residents to the Chief Objects of Interest in and around the Foreign Settlements and Native City. Darwent's guide is the first special Shanghai guide in English and certainly the most influential at the time.

According to his forewords in the different editions, Darwent, a minister of the Union Church, lived in Shanghai from at least the late 1890s to the late 1910s. A highly structured work, the guide is divided into five sections: Introduction; Routes with chief objects of interest (Foreign, Chinese, and Outside excursions); Public institutions; Clubs and associations; and Historical and descriptive, with photographic illustrations.

Darwent's narrative is made up of different layers. The first takes the shape of a grid of crisscrossing streets and the buildings alongside them. Within this grid, life in the Settlements unfolds. He begins with the Bund, which defines the first line in the grid. This opening illustrates one of the central themes behind his presentation:

> The first walk taken by any visitor to Shanghai will probably be along the Bund, one of the most interesting, famous, and handsome thoroughfares in the world. Forty years ago there was no footpath on the farther side, no trees, no lawns, and it was less than half its present width; and at high tides the water came up almost to the walls of the compounds by the Canton Road and by Siemens & Co.'s (Beijing Road). There was no Public Garden, and the fore-shore, when the tide went down,

> was all mud and rubbish, except where it was used by builders to store their material. Successive Municipal Councils have made it the splendid promenade that it is, and have fought against all attempts of the shipping interest to construct wharves for shipping. They have maintained and improved it as the great lung and promenade of Shanghai.[22]

Darwent's city has an orientation, the waterfront, and the emphasis is on betterment. To start a narrative of the city from the river and the Bund is very much in the spirit of Western city narrations. In the mental map of the Shanghailanders, the Huangpu River, with its protected deepwater inland and ocean access, is the reason for their presence and holds the promise of the Settlements' future. The river is the lifeline of trade; it stands for the commercial nature of the Foreign Settlements. This notion is very much reflected in the way in which Shanghai maps made by Westerners present the city. The river inevitably is shown as the key defining feature of the Settlements.[23]

All this clear commercial orientation notwithstanding, Darwent tells the history of the city's development and transformation as a history of the victorious battle of the public interest of the Shanghai settlers, represented by the Municipal Council, against narrow business concerns. Shanghai settlers built up this city in the spirit of public interest. The description thus begins with the implied argument that the city the visitor sees is the result of struggles between conflicting interests and is a city that could have looked quite different. The issue of public versus private is so important that Darwent takes it up in even blunter terms in his 1920 revised edition:

> The newcomer will observe a most striking difference between the river-front of the International Settlement and that of the French Settlement. That of the French has been captured by commerce; steamers line it, cargo and coolies litter it; it is not pleasant to promenade. That of the International Settlement is a splendid open space—save for a few launches and cargo-boats moored off it. Its pleasant grassy lawn and walks, with an unobstructed view across the open water, across which the cool breezes from the sea are wafted and borne in the heat of summer, make it of untold value to the amenity, the health and beauty of our river-front. Had commerce had its way, and had it lined the foreshore with steamers, we should not have been able to boast that our Bund is one of the handsomest streets in the world.[24]

Who will control the present and shape the future of this unique town, the interests of commerce or those of the public at large? For Darwent, the answer to this question would determine the physical appearance of the city as well as its spirit.[25] The comparison with the French Settlement reveals that this contest is far from over. Throughout the guide, the public interest remains at center stage, and Darwent tries to convince his reader to share this preference.

Darwent introduces the visitor to a whole series of public buildings and institutions on the Bund, again described from the point of view of public interest. The ensemble becomes fraught with meaning and signs. The streets are introduced as the places of public life. There is the Garden Bridge, a toll-free public bridge; the Public Garden beside the Garden Bridge; and the various public monuments erected by public subscription. The author narrates the history of these structures as resulting from struggles by the settlers to ensure that public interest should find expression in the Settlements. The spirit of the city is symbolized by the Recreation Fund, a shareholder organization created in 1863 to guard and support public welfare. It had become the financial backbone for almost all the public recreational institutions of the town. In every case, Darwent details the process through which these institutions were founded. In the first few pages of his book, the city already appears weighty, and this serious narrative tone is maintained, although in a gentler manner, throughout the guide.

Political institutions governing the Settlements together with financial and commercial businesses are presented through the buildings they occupy in this first layer of Shanghai, a layer that is markedly absent from Ge's *Miscellaneous Notes on Visiting Shanghai.* "The plastered buildings are in the Classic style; many of them are architecturally very fine. . . . It is not possible to name all the business houses [*hong*] on the Bund; but the Jardine Matheson *hong,* at the corner of Beijing Road, must be noticed. The site probably cost about $500 at the founding of the Settlement; now, probably a million would hardly buy it. It was built in 1851."[26] And as Darwent leads the visitor to face new cultural and financial institutions, the guide points to their architectural merits rather than their business activities.

The next line on this first grid of streets and buildings is Nanking Road. Set at a right angle to the Bund and forming a T with it, Nanking Road more than any other street in Shanghai reflects the power of commercial interests. But Darwent's focus is different, and he instead describes Settlements life as seen from the various community projects in the form of buildings on that road. The Municipal Council is first, with its public duties and then with its building, the Town Hall (fig. 7.11): "The Town Hall [where the Council's meetings took place] and Market built in 1896, covers an area of 43,000 square feet. The principal elevation of the Drill Hall is in red brick with Ningpo stone dressings and its heavy gables give it a very dignified appearance." The Louza Police Station "is a bold and well-proportioned building, with pointed arches and a central tower; the quadrangle is neatly kept."[27] Darwent leads the reader through the Central Police Station, the Central Fire Station, the New Health Offices, the Municipal Laboratory, and several churches, including his own Union Church, in Early English style, and the often illustrated Anglican Holy Trinity Church (figs. 7.12, 7.13).

The Chinese walled city (which Darwent refers to as "the Shanghai Native City") has a chapter all to itself. Like the Settlements, it is introduced with streets forming the narrative grid. Into this grid, Darwent writes a much fuller story of Chinese street life and also mentions his admiration for the colorfully painted Chinese architecture (figs. 7.14, 7.15).[28]

This gridlike narrative structure, which crisscrosses through the International Settlement, the French Settlement, and the Chinese walled city, creates a particular effect: Shanghai emerges as an interrelated whole. All signs, places, buildings, institutions, and people are presented in relationship to one another. As the narration moves from street to street, from district to district, no item is introduced

7.11. "Town Hall, Nanking Road." Photograph. (Darwent, Shanghai: A Handbook for Travellers and Residents *[1903])*

7.12. "Union Church." Photograph. (Darwent, Shanghai: A Handbook for Travellers and Residents *[1903])*

7.13. "Holy Trinity Church: The Cathedral Church of the Anglican Bishop of Mid-China." Photograph. (Darwent, Shanghai: A Handbook for Travellers and Residents *[1903])*

separately as something in and of itself; information on all aspects of life in the Settlements, with all the details and stories about the past and the present, remains locked into and connected with this grid.

As the guide proceeds, a second layer of the city is constructed in the form of social units marked by the sections "Public Institutions" and "Clubs and Associations." "Public Institutions" includes churches, schools, Freemason lodges, theaters and other places of entertainment, parks and gardens, the public library, the fire brigade, and the public band. The "Clubs and Associations" section encompasses national and local, literary and scientific, professional and business, philanthropic and sports-related groups. Many of these organizations appear in the first layer of the narrative as inhabitants and owners of architecture. If these institutions serve as identifiers for the physical manifestations of the community in the first layer, in the second layer, they are grouped into clusters that convey a concrete picture of how spiritual life and leisure activities are organized in the Settlements.

The result is a picture of gentility and order. In Shanghai, foreigners seem to have developed a passion for organized leisure. The variety and richness of activities of this kind are overwhelming. Darwent's guide lists about fifty institutions of the social kind, and about one hundred societies and clubs, of which about thirty are devoted solely to leisurely sports, and this for a foreign population counting some five thousand souls in 1903.[29] As portrayed, the community has fashioned its social

7.14. "Yu Yuen Gardens." Photograph. (Darwent, Shanghai: A Handbook for Travellers and Residents *[1903])*

7.15. "Two of the 'Four Brothers' [door gods] in Bubbling Well Temple." Photograph. (Darwent, Shanghai: A Handbook for Travellers and Residents *[1903])*

life and pastimes in a most exemplary manner. They go to balls at the town hall; they ride horses and play cricket at the public recreation ground; they go to the Lyceum Theater for shows; they visit the Public Garden, travel to the Chinese suburb of Nantao, stop in at the Shanghai Library, which boasted more books per inhabitant than the British Library could offer Londoners; or they visit the Public Museum.

As for Chinese entertainment, the guide's recommendation of a walk around the walled city and a visit to the Settlements' Chinese theater is accompanied by a warning not to entertain too high hopes, "only for the magnificent silk costumes of the actors, a visit is worth the trouble. The acting is done in a naïve style."[30] The Zhang Garden (which Darwent calls Su Ho Garden, based on the name of its Chinese owner) is described with loving care; it was located outside the walled city, on the outskirts of the International Settlement (figs. 7.16, 7.17).

The depiction of leisure and entertainment was a particularly sensitive issue, since this was the main point of contention in the development of a unified image of Shanghai. Darwent's wholesome presentation of leisure as practiced by the non-Chinese settlers contains his rejection of certain views about Shanghai and provides a clue to the hidden counter-text of his narrative. After his glowing report on the founding and significance of Shanghai's Public Library, he explains the reason for going into such detail: "I name [the large holding of the library] because it gives the lie to the ridiculous taunt that people in the Treaty Ports are a set of brainless pleasure-seekers."[31] The issue at stake was the identity and moral standing of the

7.16. "Chang Su Ho's Gardens [Zhang Garden], Arcadia Hall." Photograph. (Darwent, Shanghai: A Handbook for Travellers and Residents *[1903])*

7.17. "Chang Su Ho's Gardens [Zhang Garden]." Photograph. (Darwent, Shanghai: A Handbook for Travellers and Residents *[1903])*

foreign community in Shanghai. Their recreation and leisure, otherwise the natural place for debauchery, proved their mettle. Darwent's Shanghai manages to hold on to the ideal of a model community.

The notion of the model settlement originated in nineteenth-century Europe. During the second half of the nineteenth century, the term "model settlement" referred to a place where the needs of a modern commercial and/or industrial agglomeration were combined in an exemplary or model manner with the amenities of the modern age, with enlightened political institutions securing social order. It implied the peaceful coexistence of different classes (and races) in one stipulated domain and the responsibility of public institutions for the welfare of all, with the public library in these communities an important symbol. A famous example is the Eixempla (Model) section of Barcelona, which developed outside the walled gothic town around the same time as did the International Settlement.[32]

This rather clear goal becomes clearer still upon discovering what Darwent left out. Although he was a Shanghai pastor for twenty years, he mentions neither pubs nor taverns in a city sporting the longest bar in the world and does not touch upon the betting that took place during the biannual horse race or people playing billiards in pool halls. He barely notes the central Chinese entertainment district located on and around Fuzhou Road in the French Settlement, and the courtesans are not mentioned at all. Roads, which Western journalists at the time referred to as "The celestial [Chinese] 'Boulevards' of Shanghai,"[33] rate but a few words, and opium shops are remarked upon only for their architecture.[34] Under the subheading "Benevolent societies," however, Darwent comments that "the lot of certain classes of women and children in China is pitiable. From many causes, girls and women drift into prostitution: babies not wanted, unwanted daughters-in-law, poverty leading to the selling of girl children, syndicates of scoundrels who steal young girls. Opium, too, has helped."[35] He makes no attempt to convey a sense of the Chinese cultural underpinnings of courtesan entertainment as did the Dianshizhai guide *Illustrated Grand Sites of Shanghai*.

Other sources attest to the importance of betting at the horse races and billiards and to the involvement of foreigners in the courtesan world both as clients and as entertainers. But while Darwent provides information on the Shanghailanders who were committed to the public interest, unlike the "brainless pleasure-seekers," another character, namely, the shrewd, hardworking businessman of whatever nationality, is missing. In Darwent's view, the forces of commerce are a threat to the model settlement. As in Ge Yuanxu's creation of Shanghai, there is no direct mention of the economic base of the treaty port's prosperity.[36] Historically speaking, industrial, as opposed to trade and financial, enterprises were still a rarity in Shanghai in 1903. Only after the Japanese gained a written commitment in 1895 allowing them to import heavy equipment for industrial production did such establishments begin their rise in Shanghai. At this time, Shanghai's economic base was composed primarily of trade, finance, and entertainment.

Beneath the grid and the clusters lies the hard sheet of historical facts. In this third layer, Darwent presents the story of the city so as to make the central point that Shanghai as a model settlement is essentially independent. "It must be clearly understood that Shanghai has been from the beginning a SETTLEMENT, not a possession. The British Government annexed Hong Kong, which became British territory and subject to British law. The land on which the Foreign Settlements of Shanghai was created was, on the other hand, only leased to the British Government. That is proved by the fact that all the landowners still pay ground-rent to the Chinese Government."[37]

Unlike the unified picture of the city in the Dianshizhai guide, Darwent's Shanghai appears as a community with not one but many administrative and social centers. There are the various settlements, including the International and French Settlements and the Chinese walled city, which is fully under Chinese administration; there are also the various clubs and societies where people meet and socialize. Shanghai owes loyalty to no political entity or country; it is self-governed. To illustrate this point, Darwent goes out of his way to stress throughout his guide that the Settlements' governing institutions were founded and are run by the residents; in the last count, the residents themselves are in charge. The Shanghai Municipal Council is but a representative of the Foreign Ratepayers' Association, which constitutes the highest governing body in the International Settlement and, to a lesser degree, in the French Settlement as well.

The emphasis on the independence of the Shanghai Settlements, which in fact was not entirely true since the Qing government on paper held sovereignty over the territory, reflects a European understanding of the rights of cities. The public spirit highlighted in Darwent's narrative was meant in part to illustrate a Shanghai built through community initiative. The possible deterioration into a place of pleasure seeking, and the threat of being overcome by commercial interest, had been fought off by forces representing the public spirit of the Settlements.

Three Shanghai Scenarios and Three Possible Futures

The diverging representations of Shanghai—as theme park in Ge Yuanxu's *Miscellaneous Notes on Visiting Shanghai*, as multiethnic community in Dianshizhai's *Illustrated Grand Sites of Shanghai*, and as model settlement in Darwent's *Shanghai: A Handbook for Travellers and Residents*—follow different ideological orientations. These narratives of the city's actual situation imply assumptions about the place's development and the personal commitments and public values that contribute to it. While unified in presenting Shanghai as a success story, they offer different futures for the city. What roles do the Chinese and Western communities play in this city, and what role should they play? Or, to put it simply, whose city is this?

The itemized structure of Ge's description of the city reflects the inability of Chinese men of letters to claim the organizing, defining, and leading role in this success as much as the prosperous harmony presented in *Illustrated Grand Sites of Shanghai*, produced by Chinese and a Westerner for a Chinese audience, represents an effort to soothe this uneasiness. The self-righteous yet defensive voice of pride in Darwent's narrative shares Ge's sense of unease; Darwent's concerns center on control by the community of morally upright, God-fearing citizens over the city's image and its future. While Darwent shares Dianshizhai's upbeat program piece

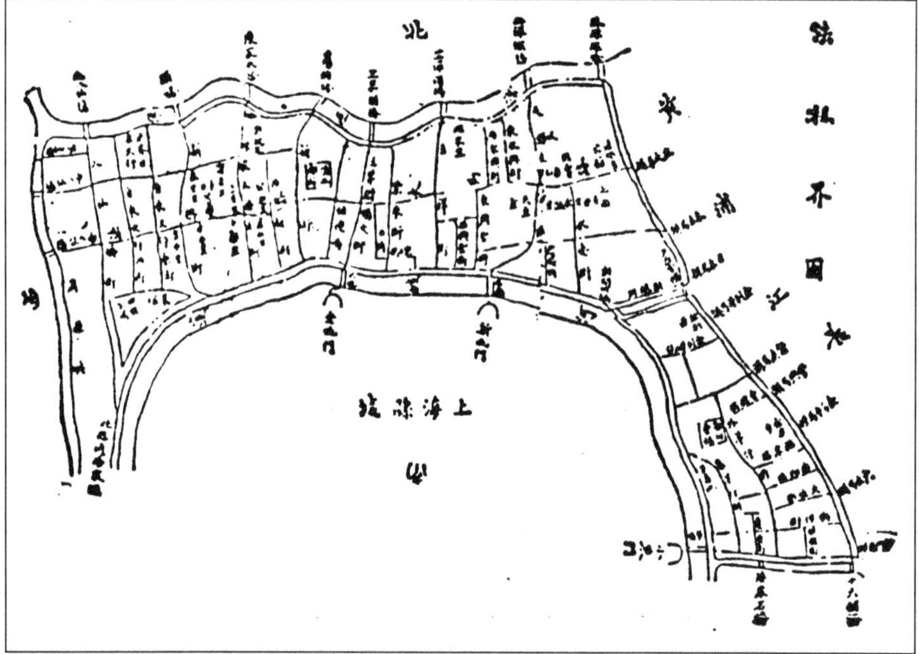

(*a*)

7.18a–c. Maps of the (a) French, (b) English, and (c) American Settlements. (Ge Yuanxu, Hu you zaji, 1876*)*

about the future of the city, with its vision of the health and prosperity of the Shanghai community depending on the cooperation of the different communities, he stresses the public interest as the measurement of a good community. The Chinese sojourners living in the Settlements are implicitly included in this "public." For its part, Dianshizhai's *Illustrated Grand Sites* makes the Western enlightenment vision of structured civilization prevailing over private interests and narrow national or ethnic concerns accessible to the Chinese reader. Its presentation of the city's future is not a morally guided one but instead insists on cultural tolerance and its importance for the city's well-being.

A visual representation of these three positions can be found in the maps that come with these guides. Ge Yuanxu presents the Shanghai Settlements in three segmental maps of the French, English, and American Settlements, printed on separate pages (fig. 7.18a–c). The map in the pocket at the end of Darwent's guide has an empty space where the walled city of Shanghai would have been shown (fig. 7.19). The Dianshizhai map of Shanghai, published the same year as its *Illustrated Grand Sites,* presents the Shanghai Settlements and the walled city as a whole consisting of different parts (fig. 7.20). These maps are highly conscious constructs. All its claim to truthfulness and reliability notwithstanding, a map by design projects an image from a particular point of view. The different maps of Shanghai, each with its emphasis on a particular segment of the factual record, are products of selective projection. Once the guides and maps with their different languages are compared, this point becomes even clearer.[38]

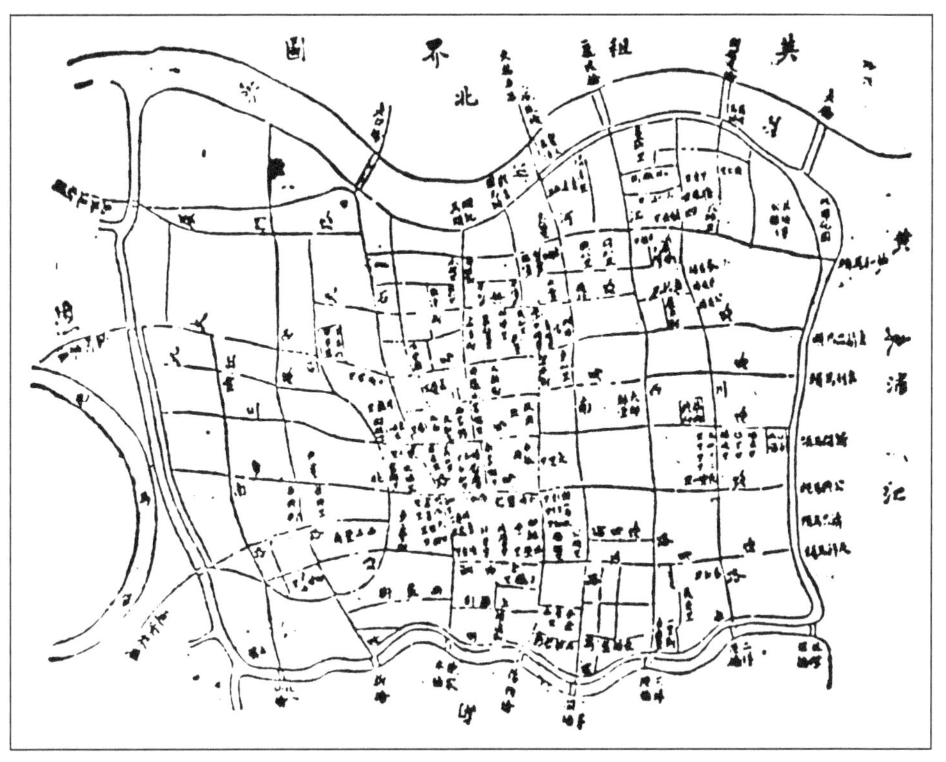

(b)

(c)

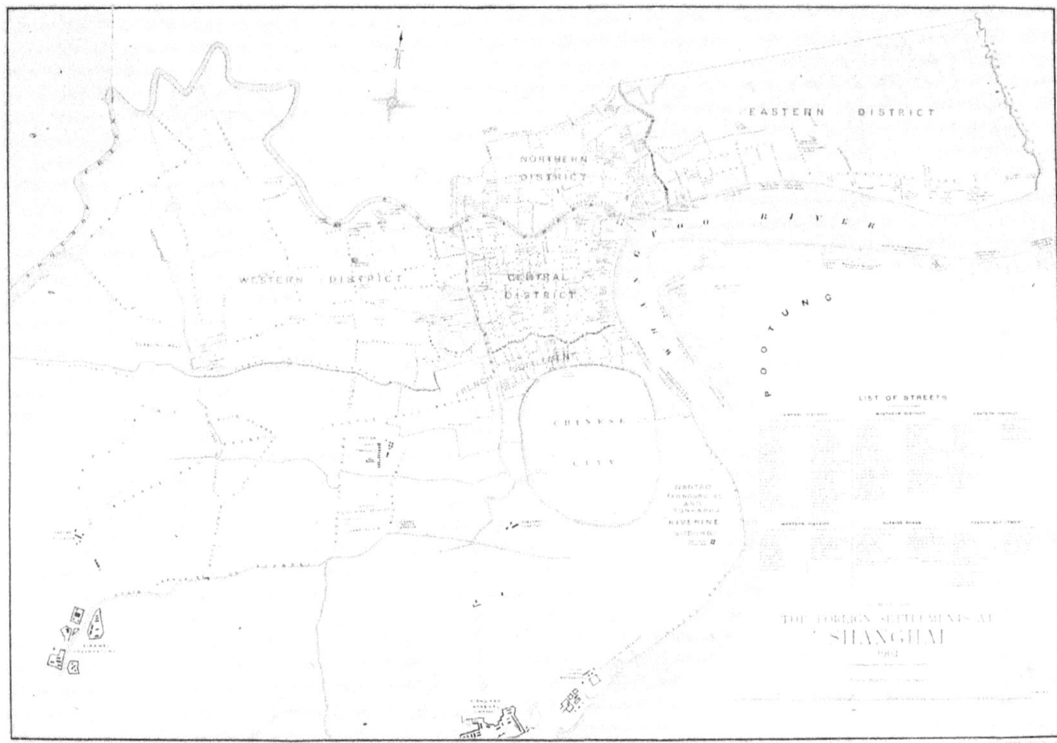

7.19. "A map of the Foreign Settlements at Shanghai." (Darwent, Shanghai: A Handbook for Travellers and Residents *[1903])*

In the different scenarios of the city, entertainment remained an exceedingly sensitive topic. Throughout all the specific descriptions and accounts of its particular aspects, each guide was aware of its potential symbolic value. Depending on the stance taken, it was overtly stressed, consciously underplayed, or used to highlight some larger point. Much of the battle over the image of the city and the identity of the community was fought over the place to be accorded to entertainment.

These three guides to Shanghai each articulate some particular core features. Their selection and representation of these features had a strong impact on the mental and cultural options for perceiving the city up to the early twentieth century. Ge Yuanxu's 1876 presentation showed the Shanghai Foreign Settlements as essentially an entertainment paradise. Its "theme park" concept very much dominated later Chinese-language guides from the 1880s and 1890s. The 1884 Dianshizhai guide, with its emphasis on peaceful coexistence and interaction among the different groups and races in Shanghai, introduced a notion too far ahead of the Chinese and Western communities to find more than a faint echo, despite the stunning quality of the illustrations and the outstanding marketing mechanism. Only much later did this vision bear fruit. The Western-language guides wavered between Major's vision of Shanghai as a multicultural community of equals and Darwent's settlers' vision of peaceful coexistence but with little interest in interaction.

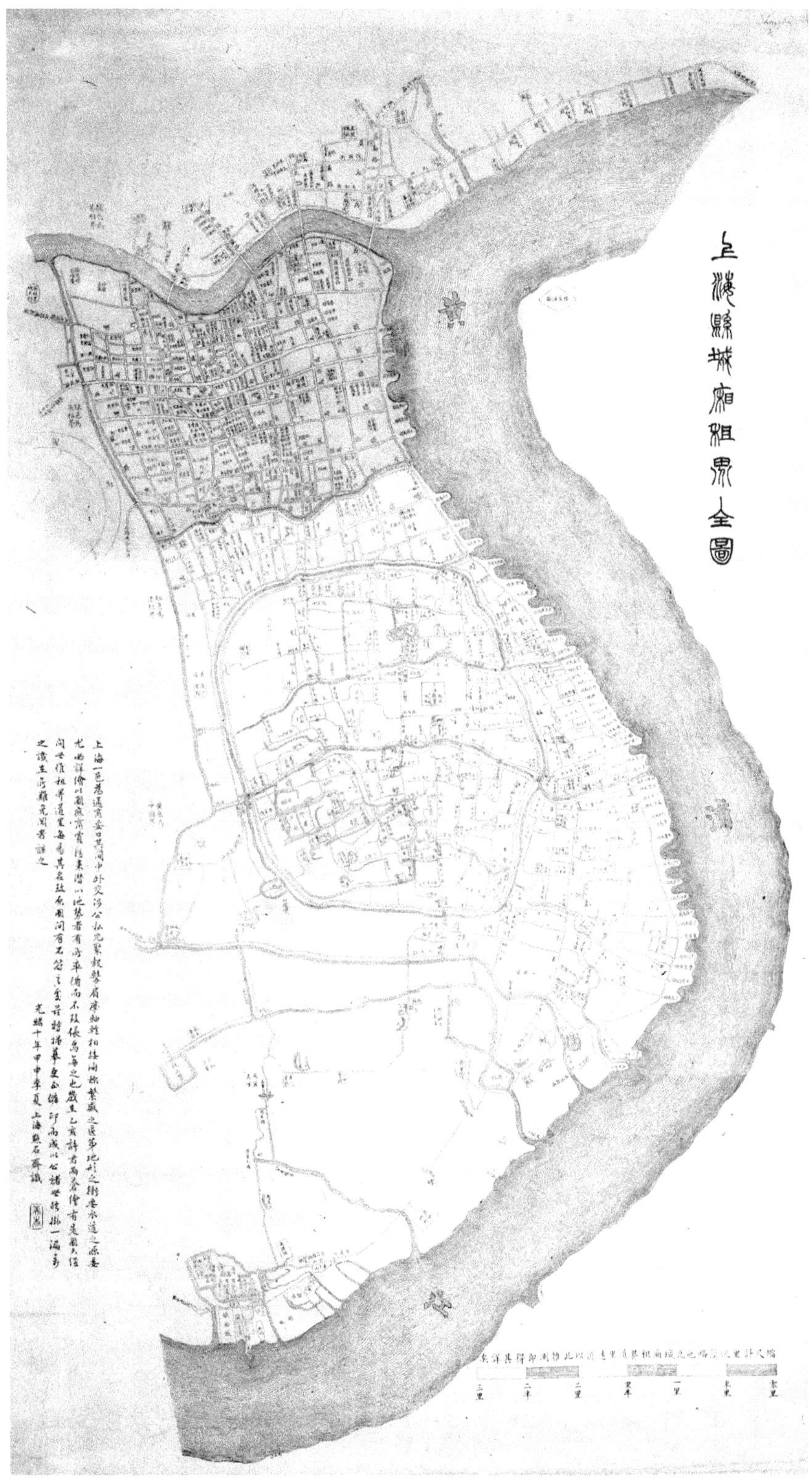

7.20. "Complete map of the Shanghai district town, its immediate surroundings, and the Settlements" (Shanghai xian chengxiang zujie quantu). (Dianshizhai, 1884)

Although other guides were published in the meantime, the turning point came after 1909 with the publication of two completely new Chinese guides that were to dominate the market with their biannual updates for the next twenty years or more. They interacted strongly—in their adoptions and their rejections—with the three currents outlined above and initiated a new level of articulation about the city as well as a new level of competition for the power to define the image of the city and its inhabitants.

Shanghai as the International Commercial Metropolis

The Commercial Press in Shanghai signaled its determination to set a new agenda in the title of its 1909 *Shanghai City Guide* (Shanghai zhinan). By using the city's official name, "Shanghai," in the title, this guide draws a hard line between itself and the previous guides, which used "Haishang," "Hushang," or "Shenjiang," terms that connote cultural rather than administrative boundaries. The second breakthrough in *Shanghai City Guide* is the new set of categories by which the city is organized, shaped, and presented. This guide combines the forms of the traditional "gazetteer" (*xianzhi*) and the Western-style directory. In its orientation and guiding spirit, it resonates strongly with Darwent's narration of the city: first and foremost, highly rational, with its solidity firmly grounded in the balance between private and public interests, and structured along hierarchical lines and by categories representing different interests. It is a modern version of Darwent's vision in its depiction of the administration but takes its own path in grouping businesses independent of their Chinese or Western ownership. What it clearly rejects, as seen from its title, is the prevailing notion of the Foreign Settlements as a site of the extraordinary or as a dreamscape as represented in previous Chinese-language guides. The fact that this guide represents the Settlements and the walled city as parts of the entity of Shanghai, however, echoes the approach of Dianshizhai's *Illustrated Grand Sites*. In this respect, it evokes the image of an international and multiethnic metropolis. Among Chinese-language guides, *Shanghai City Guide* is a watershed; its new and unfamiliar approach makes it seem almost alien. Perhaps this is not so surprising, since as early as 1903, Japan's largest publishing house Kinkōdō had bought half the shares of the Commercial Press, which also published many of the new modern schoolbooks.[39]

This new international metropolis is first and foremost ruled by laws. After beginning with geographic chapters relating the position of the city and its different segments, Commercial Press presents the city in new categories, with the title "Rules and regulations of different authorities" at the head. This section covers the larger part of the first volume of the guide. It details the different laws governing the walled city and the Settlements, leaving nothing to cultural assumptions. This city holds the larger public interest in higher regard than it does commerce and industry, and the guide conveys this message in the next section, titled "Public institutions and organizations" (*Gongyi tuanti*). It includes learning societies, schools, public libraries, museums, charitable organizations, hospitals, jails, and religious institutions. The whole notion of public versus private is thus presented as part of the institutional arrangement of a city, with the public library and museum entering this realm for the first time in a Chinese-language guide as "public" institutions. A section headed "Industry and trade" comes next. The guide structures its argument throughout on the juxtaposition of public and private. In this hierarchical and balanced vision of the city, it comes as no surprise that the section "Tourism, food, and lodging" is found at the very end. Entertainment is not part of this guide at all; it has been erased as a legitimate part of image construction. What is left is a proud, hard city. This absence marks a defensive and even helpless attitude.

Shanghai's image as a theme park was so well-established that the absence of entertainment shows the inability to come to grips with this aspect in a manner compatible with the rest of the agenda. As in Darwent's guide, information about entertainment is hidden in other categories; in this case, only a few innocent items such as theater and boat racing have been preserved within the category of "tourist information." In this spirit, even foreign entertainment is reduced to shadow plays and horse races. Courtesan entertainment, which undoubtedly was among the attractions of Shanghai, is addressed in the introduction in no unclear terms: "The number of Shanghai courtesan houses exceeds that of any other city in the country. Due to moral considerations by our publishing house, we will record only as a form of warning that which is at the root of enticement that leads to confusion. No details will be offered."[40] Under the category "local customs," the guide notes that Shanghai's character is "decadent" (*shechi*). "Ever since Shanghai has opened up to trade with the outside world, commerce has developed rapidly, but the morals have become decadent. This can be seen in the fashions of visiting the courtesan houses and gambling. Beyond these two, [the city] has no entertainment to speak of."[41] As to amusement, *Shanghai City Guide* has a mere two lines on the subject of Shanghai courtesan life, mainly warning the reader of its pitfalls. *Shanghai City Guide* was a response to Ge Yuanxu's *Miscellaneous Notes*, which portrays Shanghai as a wonderland of pleasures made up of mosaic pieces, each of which carried the tinge of *fanhua*.

In *Shanghai City Guide*, the city's *fanhua* finds its best expression in the rich and variegated economic life. A third of the guide consists of listings of commercial and financial enterprises. The variety of this list illustrates the kinds of bodies and businesses that were the real masters of the city and the main holders of its wealth. There is no physical presence of the city other than the few copper engravings at the front of the guide. Next to the listings of businesses, the main emphasis is on the rules and regulations that maintain order in the city. The first half of this guide thus sketches how the city is governed and regulated, rule by rule, and category by category, with the narrator remaining impersonal and offering no opinion or explanation of his own. Likewise, in the chapters devoted to public institutions and to businesses operating out of Shanghai, there is little information beyond the list of enterprises, titled "Hong list," which includes the names of head managers and addresses. The guide keeps the city it is describing at a distance; the place appears foreign, well-managed, safe in its peace and order, and utterly devoted to conventional business. A sense of its power and wealth is silently conveyed through the endless lists of political and economic institutions.

With *Shanghai City Guide*, the Commercial Press presented a new Shanghai to the Chinese reader. It essentially organized the guide according to a Western concept of a city and made Shanghai into an unfamiliar entity.

In replacing the previous descriptive key of *qi* as the core of the city's *fanhua* with that of Western institutional and business know-how, here shared by both Chinese and Western business interests alike, the guide offers a first direct echo of the "model settlement" reading of Shanghai, which also dominated Darwent's guide. Although it presents Shanghai as a city with a healthy balance between public and private interests, the dominant picture is that of a model settlement of commerce.

The 1912 edition of *Shanghai City Guide* reverses course and grants entertainment a section of its own. The Commercial Press managers must have felt that the Protestant rigor of the first edition had gone too far and made the guide impractical for its real-life customers. "Entertainment is a must for any visitor to Shanghai, therefore it will be given ample coverage," reads the updated edition.[42] Under the new heading "Different entertainments" (*Gezhong youxi*), the 1912 edition lists the various Shanghai entertainments in bold letters, the first time a Chinese-language guide to Shanghai uses a separate category for acknowledging this aspect of the city's life. Shanghai courtesan establishments, including Western and Japanese houses, are introduced in detail. Unlike the model set up by *Miscellaneous Notes on Visiting Shanghai*, entertainment does not define the city but is well contained in a section that relegates it to a necessary but subordinate role in the city's life, thus prevents it from taking over.

Shanghai Tourist Guide

The legacy of *Miscellaneous Notes on Visiting Shanghai*, however, did not end with the *Shanghai City Guide*. In 1919, the *Shanghai Tourist Guide* (Shanghai youlan zhinan), published by the Zhonghua Tushujicheng press, resurrected it in a modern fashion. Both the "theme park" image and the mosaic structure of the narrative, which are hallmarks of Ge's guide and were so vehemently rejected by the Commercial Press, are reinstated in the *Shanghai Tourist Guide*.

The mosaic structure of this guide represents the city in a non-centered, nonlinear, and non-hierarchical fashion. The reader, the implied tourist, is at the center, and the city is offered to serve all needs without the imperious impositions of the *Shanghai City Guide*. To begin with, the first three sections of the *Shanghai Tourist Guide* are organized according to the needs of different types of visitors to the city. The categories include those traveling "alone," "with friends," "with family," and "as husband and wife" and considers whether the purpose of the trip is "to look up an old friend," "to gamble," "to look for education," "to buy stocks," "to purchase machinery," "to seek help from a doctor," or "to buy coal and iron." It gives specific and practical advice for these different kinds of visitors. Through the list of possible visitors and the purposes that draw them to the city, the guide shows its confidence that the city has achieved broad appeal. The visitors' needs are presented as legitimate and deserving of being addressed.

Central to this narrative stance is the host, the person who is at home and in full control of all relevant information on Shanghai. This host is not so much an individual with quaint views about the city as the emblem of Shanghai's proud yet relaxed collective identity. Much in the spirit of Dianshizhai's *Illustrated Grand Sites*, the host persona takes responsibility as well as pleasure in introducing the guest to his own place. It marks a clear departure from the stance of the "guest" (*ke*) adopted by the authorial voice in Ge Yuanxu's *Miscellaneous Notes*. Ge introduced the city with pleasure but denied any responsibility for it. The tone of the narrative in the *Shanghai Tourist Guide* exudes confidence and pride. With an insider's worldly-wise perspective, this guide admits the reader into the rich options of the city, sounding an occasional warning against potential hazards.

In this narrative, Shanghai has acquired a new attribute, a history. In typical brazenness, this history starts not with the walled city becoming a district town in the Song dynasty but with the establishment of the Foreign Settlements in 1841. When the walled city is mentioned, it is criticized for its backwardness in comparison to the Foreign Settlements. Courtesan entertainment figures prominently in this guide and is presented within a historical narrative. This approach is new for a Chinese-language guide. Shanghai is seen not only as what it is but also what it used to be. The city is described as the very process of change, and the guide as its memory.

The need for a past, which began to be articulated around the late 1910s, is an indicator of the formation of a particular Shanghai identity. In this respect, *Illustrated Grand Sites* seems prophetic. The sojourners are taking possession of their city. In this narrative of the city's past, the notion of celebration is indirectly inserted into comments on the physical appearance of the city. Shanghai's lack of the "historical landmarks" (*guji*) that fill the pages of other guides is balanced by the plethora of things that partake of *qi*, which includes the foreign with its exotic lure. Instead of old temples, the photographic section of the guide illustrates women's fashions under the headings "The transformation of women's clothing during the last sixty years" and "The various kinds of hairstyle during the last sixty years." To create a sense of history, the narrator is the Old Shanghailander, or Lao Shanghai, who comments wisely on the past in a section called "Chats on things experienced by an old Shanghai Insider." Even the notion of the "big playground" is given the dignity of a past. Under the heading "The history of sixty years of transformations in Shanghai courtesan houses," the guide details and at the same time deconstructs this notion.

The complete absence of any sense of defensiveness in the *Shanghai Tourist Guide* represents another qualitative shift from previous guides. In a silent manner, the city's identity has come into its own. This is reflected in the ability of the guide to deal with the city in both its positive and negative sides and to present its image as that of a place full of contradictions. The idea that Shanghai represents "civilization" (*wenming*) comes with a warning at the beginning of the guide. This is a place that represents civilization in its extreme forms, says the author of the introduction; its physical appearance is splendid, and its well-managed civic order is backed by the most comprehensive set of regulations and an able police force.

But, he warns, this smooth surface, which is there for all to see, hides crime and corruption. Nowhere is this dichotomy more vividly illustrated than in the depiction of courtesan entertainment. In a city ready to provide service for all needs and desires, courtesan entertainment becomes the highlight of the guide. While describing these courtesan establishments as both rich in history and vibrant in the present, however, the *Shanghai City Guide* also soberly relates what to expect in these places. In "Methods by which the courtesans entice a client," the guide warns the potential visitor against "cheating, hard bargaining, and seduction."[43]

The reintroduction of courtesan entertainment in later editions of the Commercial Press's *Shanghai City Guide* suggests pressure from the earlier guides as well as from readers' expectations. The narrative strategy of the *Shanghai City Guide* and the later *Shanghai Tourist Guide* is to absorb the earlier models and transform them. An ideological divide, however, remains between them. One offers a Shanghai with a present and a future as an industrial and commercial power; the other portrays a center of goods, entertainment, and culture. The borders, nevertheless, had become blurred. They both, although to different degrees, merge "entertainment" Shanghai and "model settlement" Shanghai into a homogenized whole around a commercial core.

Shanghai as a Foreign Country

Perhaps as a reaction to the discomfiting overall rise in confidence among Chinese Shanghai sojourners and their sense of ownership of the city, the Chinese-language *A Guide for Residents of Shanghai* (Huren baojian) was published in 1913 by the Methodist Publishing House. The Chinese author Huang Renjing (Mirror for the Yellow Man) adopted a wholeheartedly imperialist outlook, utterly rejecting Major's "multiethnic community" ideal.[44] Amid debates about the city's identity and competition to define its future character, this guide comes up with a radical version of Darwent's *Shanghai: A Handbook for Travellers and Residents.* As in Darwent's Shanghai, Westerners and Chinese are shown occupying different levels in the social hierarchy. This guide informs Chinese residents of the foreign rules governing their lives, as expressed in the English subtitle *What the Chinese in Shanghai Ought to Know.* This is a stunning departure. A guide to a town would as a rule consider its reader to be the visitor, offering to save him the trouble of having to ask around by posing as the collective knowledge of the city's connoisseurs. In the case of Shanghai, however, there was, well into the twentieth century, no such thing as an authentic citizen of the International Settlement. This changed the communication structure of these guides. They had to address both the visitor arriving for a short business or pleasure trip and the sojourner who planned to stay. The Methodist Press's *Guide for Residents* went a step further by focusing exclusively on the "Chinese residents" of the International Settlement. The aim was to domesticate not the visitor but the resident. In the English-language preface, the author states that the guide "is intended to furnish the Chinese residents in Shanghai with a knowledge of the real conditions of Shanghai and practical methods of preventing legal trouble and loss." In his Chinese foreword, he puts it more bluntly, "When one enters a foreign country one first asks about what is prohibited by law; to be cautious is one's bounden duty."[45] If the Commercial Press's *Shanghai City Guide* presents the city as an alien entity, Huang Renjing presents it as "foreign enclave on Chinese soil" and devotes his guide solely to introducing the Western laws and regulations governing the Settlements. It also describes how one should behave on the street; how to ride in a streetcar; how to order and eat at a Western-style restaurant; the traffic regulations that are in force; the need to acquire a building permit before starting construction; and the safety measures necessary in a theater. One of the most revealing entries defines proper behavior in a public park.

> Shanghai has four public gardens altogether. Among them, three are for Westerners and one is for Chinese. One of the gardens for Westerners is located by the Huangpu River, and during the week, black musicians [in fact, Filipinos] will be performing. Unless accompanied by a Westerner, Chinese are not allowed to enter. Dogs and bicycles are definitely forbidden to enter. As for the Chinese public garden, it is located at north Suzhou Road across from the public bridge. Chinese and Westerners are both allowed in. There is no music. The space is narrow and small.

This entry is followed by "The guide to visiting the Public Garden":

> Chinese who are dressed in Western-style clothing can freely enter the Public Garden (by the Huangpu) and amuse themselves; dressing in Japanese-style clothing will also be permitted; otherwise entrance is forbidden.[46]

Guide for Residents presents Shanghai as an alien city where the foreigner sets the tone. Chinese life is judged by Western standards, and only Chinese assimilated enough to wear Western clothing are given the privileges of the foreigner. The cultural divide is even more clearly visible in the depiction of Western- and Chinese-style entertainment:

> As for entertainment, there obviously are great differences between China and the West. Unmarried Westerners mostly spend their leisure and enjoyment time drinking, playing pool, going to the theater, dancing, attending races, riding horses, or going for walks. Very few ever visit the courtesan house. If on occasion it still happens, the person in question most certainly belongs to the lower classes and is looked down upon. As to those who are married, other than drinking and taking part in running competitions, husband and wife often either stroll together in the gardens or go to the theater. For these men to visit the courtesan house is unheard of. This is the broad outline of entertainment practiced by Westerners.
>
> Our style of entertainment, however, is the opposite of that of the Westerner. Other than drinking and going to the theater, all regard seeking carnal pleasures as the true pursuit of happiness. The so-called rich and civilized, with few exceptions, all have many concubines. Those who have just enough to live on, and have not the means to marry concubines, will necessarily visit prostitutes and leave their marks at the bordellos. This in big strokes is our [Chinese style of] entertainment.[47]

Guide for Residents castigates the Chinese for such immoral and wasteful indulgence. According to the author, this behavior is responsible for the weakness of the Chinese nation and the failure of its prospects! The foreign institutional and moral standards governing the Shanghai enclave are the norm and define the city's best elements, while Chinese sojourners are the problem and must be remade into inhabitants worthy of this town. This guide sees itself as contributing to the effort.

While most earlier guides deal only implicitly with the ethnic composition of the city and its relationship to the city's identity, this example shows that by the 1910s, the issue of race was in the open. *A Guide for Residents of Shanghai* reflects the notion of separation cum harmony but develops it into a narrative in which the rules set for the Foreign Settlements appear to privilege the foreigner. The guide is a response to the vision of racial equality and joint responsibility for Shanghai's achievements presented in *Illustrated Grand Sites of Shanghai*; it is also a harsh critique of the Commercial Press vision of the coming of a modern metropolis, as expressed in the *Shanghai City Guide*.

The Methodist Press narrative did not, however, go without reply. The 1919 *Shanghai Tourist Guide*, published by the Zhonghua Tushujicheng press, must be seen in this light. With the strong and prominent position of the proud host as its narrative persona, this guide connotes a sense of Chinese ownership and responsibility. While the Methodist Press guide never dominated the narration of the city, it signaled by example the lingering tension around, and ambivalence toward, the city's identity.

In the mixing and melding of images, Shanghai was continuously reconfigured. The city provoked competing representations. Its capacity to permit and sustain contradictory images demonstrates its power to absorb and attract vastly different interests into its creative force. The absence of a unified discourse on the city reflects the absence of a unified hegemonic structure, the polyvalence of the city itself, and the absence of the long corridor of a historical narrative about the city's past within which new narratives would have to move. Still, the later guides indicate the power of the earlier narratives over the city and react to their representations.

The central issue at stake was the definition of the city's key features. Because of the conflict about the city's essential character—"model settlement," "multiethnic community," or "theme park"—and the moral standards by which it was to be measured, entertainment remained a highly sensitive issue. It clearly had the potential to become the defining metaphor for the city. This can be seen in the balance Major carefully drew between the scenes marking the outward signs of the city's prosperity, of which courtesan entertainment was only one. It is also evident in the unstable position of courtesan entertainment in the Chinese guides, to the point that the Commercial Press obsessively disassociated itself from narratives of Shanghai as a place to live out backward and murky habits. The notion of Shanghai as playground became problematic once new-style Chinese commercial forces took a more active stand in defining their ideal for the city and its image. The dreamscape metaphor for Shanghai was all but eradicated by the image of the modern metropolis. In this respect, the Commercial Press talked back to what it saw as misleading representations of the city.

Beyond the contending images of the city, there remained one overall uniting factor: they all presented Shanghai as paradise, a place not found anywhere else. The city's uniqueness, the image of peace and prosperity, ignited the imagination. Even the sober Commercial Press guide reverted in its third edition to the image—first used in a bamboo twig ballad in the 1870s—of Shanghai as a secluded place where one could enjoy an easy luxurious life and beautiful and attentive ladies, possessed of a lure so great that one forgot the duties and strictures of real life in China proper.[48]

With the city rapidly becoming one of the leading financial and commercial centers in Asia and the world, the image of Shanghai as an economic force absorbed the images of the model settlement and the playground. By the 1920s, the concept of Shanghai as a cosmopolitan city of the world was easily accepted by the contending forces. All parties saw that Shanghai was primarily an economic power. Fading was the central feature of the balance between private and public interests argued by Darwent and the attitude of non-engagement expressed by Ge Yuanxu. In later guides, industrial and trade goods end up in the same category as the courtesans, the first as accoutrements to the extravagant lure of the town, and the second as a part of a tourist industry fueling much of the town's growth and attractiveness.

Metaphors for the city shifted meaning. Western-style monuments and buildings featured in the Dianshizhai and Darwent guides as signs of the healthy balance of public spirit and business interests resurfaced in photographs in later Chinese-language guides as exemplars of the exotic.[49] The metaphor of Shanghai as a dreamland reappeared as a marketing slogan promoting Shanghai and its goods.

The commercial city guides of the 1920s eventually conferred on Shanghai the title of "world's playground," or *shijie youxichang*, by using language associated with the term for their descriptions of the modern commercial model settlement.[50] This was the place where the Chinese could experience the Western and the exotic without leaving the country. In the 1923 edition of Zhonghua Tushujicheng's *Shanghai Tourist Guide*, the authors describe the city as their own place.[51] They express their pride in the city with the freedom of those who do not have to prove their authenticity. Their city was a cosmopolitan center in a Chinese environment, created by foreigners and Chinese alike.

> If a traveler asked which one of all the Treaty Ports was the most prosperous, the unanimous answer is always "Shanghai." Do you know Shanghai is the center where the most outstanding talents of all of China congregate? Here is where the enterprises of the wealthiest Chinese and Western merchants are; it is to this place that the high officials retire; it is here that famous intellectuals and elegant persons write and compose their poetry. It is so much the place to be that beauties and wanderers, knights-errant and magicians are all attracted to this city over great distances.[52]

The new take on the city also brought out a new and darker aspect. By the 1920s, Shanghai had developed into an international center of industry and business, and with it came the rise of organized crime. A new type of guide focusing on this dark side of Shanghai mushroomed, much in line with the new "muckraking" (*heimu*) novels. They sported titles such as *The World of Trickery in Shanghai* (Shanghai pianshu shijie), by Dian Gong, published in 1914; *The True Picture of [Shanghai's] Secret Underworld* (Sanjiao jiuliu mimi zhenxiang), by Shanghai Laojianghu, published in 1923; and *Key to Shanghai* (Shanghai menjing), by Wang Dingjiu, published in 1932. Looming large in these guides are Shanghai prostitution and other entertainment enterprises. The city was characterized by many different and sharply contrasting layers. The general trope most current in the People's Republic of China today originated with these guides. Shanghai was reduced to being "The Paradise of Adventurers," an image taken from the title of a book by a Western author published in the late 1930s.[53]

8 *Conclusion*

Seen from a broader perspective, the Shanghai courtesans' most significant impact on a Chinese society that valued conformity to tradition was to establish the "new" and even iconoclastic as desirable in an urban environment that became the emblem of Chinese prosperity and modernity. This happened decades before political reformers such as Liang Qichao set out to "renew the people" (*xin min*), to make them fit for modernity, and to publish journals such as *New Fiction* (Xin xiaoshuo), with a program to revamp cultural values.

This study on the entertainment culture in Shanghai during the late nineteenth and the early twentieth centuries addresses three broader issues. First, the unwitting role of entertainment as an engine of social change and modernization; second, the intertwining of entertainment with the market of this international trading center and the emerging Chinese public sphere; and third, the relationship between the actions of the courtesans as women who were gendered in a very pronounced way and a treaty port environment that has been characterized by some as semicolonial.

The claim that Shanghai entertainment played a crucial role in the cultural and social transformation of the city and China at large is a historical one. It is based on the analysis of a wide and unusual combination of historical sources including elements from material culture, such as costumes and furniture, and visual culture, such as illustrations, photographs, and maps. Three major players were involved: the Foreign Settlements of Shanghai, which provided unique conditions for the development of entertainment business and culture; the energetic and ingenious Shanghai courtesans who became aware of the opportunity offered by their unusual situation in the Settlements and used it to push for a more public role and greater visibility for themselves and their business; and finally, the newly forming group of urban intellectuals who, with their traditionally close relationship to the courtesans and their prominent position in the Shanghai print market, became unwitting partners of the courtesans in the promotion of star culture and print entertainment. The most visible outcome of this threefold interaction was the creation of a new type of urban culture in which women played a public role and Western accoutrements of urban comfort were integrated into the dreamland image of Penglai through their association with the courtesans. At the same time, the press became the platform on which to negotiate urban modernity in Shanghai and the medium by which to make it attractive and acceptable throughout the country. However, the coexistence of a packaged and ready-made modernity with the lure of a worldwide fashion and a booming, multicultural trading center does not in itself produce urban modernity. Shifts in lifestyle and values require their own conditions, trajectory, reason, and human agents.

As human agents, the Shanghai courtesans clearly stand out. In their relentless drive for the new, the chic, and the pleasant, they crafted the association between Western accoutrements and what was most desirable and extravagant, and with their equally relentless self-advertisement, they opened the public space for women. Neither they nor the journalists who wrote about them acted as conscious modernizers. The entertainment press won a market by writing about every move of their courtesan stars and joined its readers in claiming to be shocked as they overturned the social order and set a bad example for women of good families. For the courtesans, the issue was not liberation but increased freedom of movement and public presence, both of which certainly were beneficial to their business. Still, their appearance on stage as performers and in their boxes at the opera house opened the space into which women of good standing—first concubines, and then first wives—would follow. As in any study of change, a direct, hard link between the behavior of Shanghai courtesans and that of the urban women of the Republican period is as difficult to prove as the broader link between the particular Shanghai courtesan performance and the coming of urban modernity in China. For contemporaries, however, this link was evident. Whenever similar habits were adopted elsewhere, the press inevitably claimed that it was but in emulation of Shanghai.

By leaving their confined and exclusive houses and developing new public personae, the courtesans reshaped and upgraded their own identity and stature, which was reflected in their public perception. Sexuality was part of the picture and part of their public allure. Their appearances with clients in a personal relationship that was not mediated by clan or family but went by its own rules and rituals may be said to have facilitated the formation of a new public sexual culture, with men and women relating to each other in a freer manner and in public places. This impact was the greater as the top courtesans were not pushing for a larger share of the sex market but were upgrading the cultural and social standing of their entertainment services by broadening their appeal and obscuring their private relationships with their main patrons. As they moved into the role of public performers, they increasingly depersonalized their relationships with their clients. This new relationship prefigures the mass-based star culture mediated by the entertainment papers. The very fact that they continued to be courtesans with an exclusive clientele and lovers outside the public limelight made their public persona all the more fascinating. They did not attempt to loosen the exclusive confinement of their traditional business environment for the purpose of abandoning their private clientele but in order to gain a greater financial base of operations. This increased their leeway, both financially and emotionally. The exclusive clientele had to live with and learn to appreciate the fact that they were in liaisons with women whose lives were eagerly followed by a widening circle of newspaper readers. They also had to accept that the courtesans' duties required them to move from one party to the next on a single evening and that they would eventually choose their own lovers from among the pretty opera actors who were visiting from the capital. Traditional patrons from the literati class also had to come to grips with the new stance of these women. They reluctantly acknowledged their marginalization as clients and adapted to their new role as rather powerless urban intellectuals who were earning a living by producing a vast array of courtesan lore that did much to spread the fame of these women. They gradually adopted a stance of urban irony that allowed them to bemoan the impact of these women while describing their outrages in loving detail. These writings are instrumental in fortifying the case for the Shanghai courtesans' impact on urban female behavior.

The courtesans well understood the price of going public. As with the film stars of today, after the press discovered that they were sensational and circulation-enhancing news items, they could no longer choose to remain secluded and might even be made into public laughingstocks. The combination of increased visibility and press reports on their every move culminated in their image as the unabashed, notoriously attractive female in the public arena. Social upgrading and increased visibility brought greater expenses and greater risks; these in turn prompted new business initiatives, for example through well-announced trips to other treaty port cities.

There was much ambivalence toward this development. Members of the Chinese educated elite, missionaries as well as some members of the city councils, felt that the city's reputation was at stake. Yet, on what basis could they force the closure of these establishments or ban the public appearance of these women? All European eyes were on Paris, where the attractions of entertainment, and courtesan entertainment in particular, had proved such a draw for wealthy men from all over the world and transformed Paris into the financial "milk cow" of France.[1] Courtesans were allowed to exist in European big cities and were regarded as part of the legitimate entertainment business and as tourist attractions.[2]

Pivotal social changes may take place at the most unexpected levels and be led by the most unlikely persons. Numerous studies have detailed the role of leading intellectuals and politicians such as Yan Fu, Liang Qichao, and Zhang Taiyan in China's journey to modernity. Yet, while scholars like to see social change originate in the heady ideas of their peers, it moves simultaneously on many different levels, and there is no reason to a priori privilege one over the other. In fact, the normative appeals of these political intellectuals are, as a rule, just that—normative appeals to change a reality that looks quite different. But the process of social diffusion that must take place before such ideas become shared assumptions, which broadly guide actions and thus become culturally relevant, is little studied. In a true cultural history of Chinese modernization, changes and their meaning in the details of daily life certainly deserve as much attention: in the manner of clothing, in the way men and women relate to each other in public places, in the way private space is decorated, in what constitutes leisure, in the manner and gait with which women move in an urban environment, in the interaction between different ethnic segments of the Shanghai urban population, in the diffusion and adaptation of Western things and habits in Shanghai and of Shanghai things and habits in the rest of the country, and so on. They are real-life processes, not normative projects, and their acceptance stands in an asymmetrical relationship to that of the grand idea. Their impact on the acceptance of modernity deserves much further study.

Shanghai entertainment was anything but a normative modernization program. Its effectiveness as a modernizing agent lay in the fact that it was neither presented nor seen as such. Its coded lure to change was transmitted through the attractions of courtesan entertainment. This was defined by a fourfold marginality. It was outside "regular" business; it was offered by women who were beyond the purview of the "good family" and had very little to hold them back; it depended on the make-believe of role playing, which implied an eventual return to real life; and while the financial aspects of the entertainment offered were carefully kept apart, it was quite clear that the client's currency was money, not beliefs, values, or lifestyle. The client could momentarily, publicly, and without consequence slip into the role of a Jia Baoyu, shed the traditional constraints, and play at having a modern love affair with a free-spirited beauty in the Daguan Yuan of Shanghai's urban modernity. That he paid for the experience made it an exchange of goods on the market and thus secured his freedom to try, adopt, or reject. This particular brand of entertainment quickly became one of the main attractions of the town as well as one of its most important business sectors. As is all too clear today, entertainment and the money behind it have very much become the forces that shape society's desires and consciousness. At this early time, the entertainment sector was not monopolized in any manner, which enabled individuals such as the Shanghai courtesan to play a substantial role in defining both the culture and the field of play. By the end of the century, this sector had grown so enormously that it may be seen as a huge, untidy, and utterly unplanned Chinese laboratory for experimenting with urban modernity, involving sojourners, literati, tourists, and the growing leisure class of wealthy retirees. Without any call to arms, Shanghai courtesan entertainment managed to subvert the status quo and make change acceptable without giving much offense. The courtesans' insertion of urban modernity into the framework of fun, comfort, and blissful pleasure certainly helped to make it attractive and acceptable.

Most earlier studies of the early Chinese press focused on political advocacy papers such as Liang Qichao's *Shiwu bao*. More recently, the emergence of a "modern" public sphere in late Qing Shanghai has been the subject of some important studies. They have grandly expanded our understanding by focusing on the so-called serious newspapers such as *Shenbao* and on issues such as the papers' role in fostering nationalism, development of the newspaper editorial as a form of civic articulation on matters of national concern, or the development of professional journalists. In this study, the public sphere takes in an even broader swath of many different forms and layers. These include the endless variety of the courtesans' public self-staging as incipient stars and their assumption of some civic responsibilities in charitable and civic action as well as the specialized entertainment press, which also serialized many of the most important late Qing novels of social criticism. These entertainment papers and publications were patterned as much on Western models as were the serious papers or advocacy press and made use of imported technology. They entered the market with the unambiguous promise of offering access to an attractive form of high-class entertainment—the Shanghai courtesan—without the considerable costs and risks involved in closer encounters. They were market-driven in a much more radical sense than even the commercial papers such as *Shenbao*. This again allowed them an effectiveness in the public sphere that was innocent and might at times have surpassed that of their larger contemporaries. Their influence involved not only enhancing the fame of top Shanghai courtesans by reporting on their public behavior but also undoing the prestige of the Qing court by lampooning corrupt and ineffective bureaucrats in their serialized novels. They established the entertainment paper on a firm footing next to the commercial papers and provided a light version of the exercise of civic responsibility, such as casting votes in the flower competitions. The Shanghai courtesans and the entertainment papers writing about them created an extraordinary new social configuration. Although they may not have fit the classic definition of the "public sphere," in terms of influencing public opinion, they certainly had an impact.

In the triangular relationship that developed—with courtesans pushing their business onto a more popular basis, entertainment newspapers feeding on the growth of this public side, and the market responding very quickly to enlarge access to such entertainments—a new kind of market-based "democratization" of entertainment emerged. This was not political democracy but was closer to the notion of popularization. Two trends were shaped and promoted by this triangular relationship. The first might be called the "diffusion of pleasure," as courtesan entertainment went from being enjoyed by elite men to being enjoyed by a broad urban populace. Second, in the process, the personal nature of courtesan entertainment was transformed into the abstract intimacy of the star with an audience that read the entertainment papers. The democratization of entertainment is tied in with its public marketing.

This study considers gender in the specific contexts of particular social and cultural transformations and not as an abstract, dehistoricized, analytical, and value-laden category. A gender approach would preset the issue as one between men and women, with the central issue being that of power and domination in the process of social and cultural transformation. While it is possible to approach the study of Shanghai courtesan entertainment by this route, it is too imperious and imposing as an analytical framework. A hermeneutic approach seemed more fruitful. This approach allowed the sources to reveal what turned out to be the two most important issues: entertainment's rise to become an important segment in an emerging modern cultural and public sphere and its relationship to the market.

Likewise, this study focused on the actual power dynamics of Shanghai rather than conceptualizing the city in colonial or semicolonial terms and then reading the sources in this framework. These concepts have been reified to the point that they silence the sources with their own present-day agenda and cannot help us to understand the actions or motives of the players or even their actual historical environment. The concepts of imperialism and colonialism, or the helpless hybrid semicolonialism, offer only flat frameworks for a city as complex in its legal status, inner dynamics, and overall impact as Shanghai. The city was a paradox; it consisted of many different layers. It was run by foreigners but hosted a multiethnic population, the largest part of which would class themselves as "Chinese" as opposed to "foreigners." It was created as a trading port for foreigners and quickly became one for all nationalities. The Shanghai Foreign Settlements were not a colony. The Qing government continued to hold sovereignty over the city but had ever less to say in its day-to-day management; it was not an independent Hanse-type city either, since foreign governments, most of all the French in their Settlement, retained important powers.[3] The impact of different groups and nationalities was manifold as well. Operating within the civic regulations governing the Settlements, Chinese merchants were instrumental in making the city into a cosmopolitan commercial hub, and they managed to amass such fortunes that before the end of the century, most prime real estate was in Chinese hands. To conceptualize Shanghai in terms of colonialism misses the actual power dynamics of the city and shortchanges its cultural identity. Another view claims that the very fact that Shanghai or China itself was not a colony actually shows the power of "cultural imperialism" in its purest form. Such an approach obscures the true dynamism of the city and is self-defeating in its radicalism.[4] As is typical for a multiethnic immigrant community, there was much mixing and fusing among different cultural traditions.

This study has shown a substantial Western input into Shanghai entertainment culture. There remains, however, a surprising lacuna with regard to the Japan connection, although in other fields such as painting, this impact was already visible during the 1870s and 1880s.[5] Japanese geisha and prostitutes had come to Shanghai at a very early stage in the development of the Foreign Settlements. Yet there is no strong evidence of their impact. Only by the early twentieth century was their influence on the rise. The business structures of Japanese geisha and Shanghai courtesan entertainment were utterly different. Well into the Meiji period, Japanese geisha entertainment was largely confined to enclosed quarters in or outside of the city, with the Yoshiwara district in Edo the prime example. Compared to these conditions, Shanghai courtesan establishments enjoyed much more freedom of movement within the Settlements. The same is true for their financial stature.

Foreign administration had the effect of offering, in a largely inadvertent manner, more freedom to women in terms of access to public life, even if it might have wished for this access to come through increased education for women. The vitality of economic and cultural activity in the Foreign Settlements was the result of a lack of political hegemony combined with a strictly enforced set of urban manners. Instead of imposing the heavily unifying and value-laden agenda of "colonialism," the condition of Shanghai at the turn of the twentieth century is better defined in terms of Homi Bhabha's notion of hybridity.

Bhabha describes modern hybrid communities that cannot be well defined within fixed parameters of nationality and culture. "What is theoretically innovative, and politically crucial, is the need to think beyond narratives of originary and initial subjectivities and to focus on those moments or processes that are produced in the articulation of cultural differences." The location of culture is in the structure of interrelatedness. "It is in the emergence of the interstices—the overlap and displacement of domains of difference—that the intersubjective and collective experiences of nationness, community interest, or cultural value are negotiated."[6] Shanghai and Shanghai entertainment culture are well described as the early product of a haphazard negotiation between the overlapping and displacement of different intersubjectivities and collective experiences. Whatever might have been the original intention of the various forces in opening up Shanghai, whatever the principle behind its administration, and whatever the motives of the different groups of people for moving there, the result was a unique and strong identity for the city as a whole based on the mixture of different regional and national cultural values, business practices, and civic consciousness. Politically, it became the most open and tolerant city on Chinese soil. The blossoming of Shanghai civic culture was precisely the result of this fusion and the absence of a hegemonic power structure.

Notes

Introduction

1. "Jingzhuang zhaoyan," (Rich attire dazzles the eye), *Youxi bao,* May 4, 1899, 2.

2. Corbin, *L'Avènement des loisirs.* For a study of Paris and the rise of leisure, see Csergo, "Extension et mutation de loisir citadin," 121–68.

3. Skinner, *City in Late Imperial China.*

4. For Shanghai as the engine of change, see Murphey, *Shanghai;* as the bridgehead of imperialism, see Murphey, *The Outsiders;* as the city of the workers' movement, see Roux, *Le Shanghai ouvrier des années trente;* and as the birthplace of Chinese capitalism, see S. A. Smith, *Like Cattle and Horses.*

5. For Shanghai in relation to administration, trade, and commerce, see Cochran, *Inventing Nanjing Road.* As an immigrant society, see Wakeman and Yeh, *Shanghai Sojourners;* Honig, *Creating Chinese Ethnicity;* and Goodman, *Native Place, City, and Nation.* As a thriving marketing center, see Johnson, *Shanghai.*

6. Lu Hanchao, *Beyond the Neon Lights.*

7. Henriot's book was based on his 1993 thesis "La Prostitution à Shanghai aux 19e–20e siècles (1849–1958)."

8. Corbin, *Women for Hire.*

9. In contrast, Henriot's seminal article "Chinese Courtesans in Late Qing and Early Republican Shanghai" contributes greatly to our understanding of entertainment culture by emphasizing the cultural context of the courtesan as an entertainer.

10. Hershatter, *Dangerous Pleasures,* 7.

11. Ibid., 8.

12. David Der-wei Wang, *Fin-de-Siècle Splendor,* 7.

13. Ibid., 59.

14. Ibid., 89.

15. Ibid., 72.

16. The term "model settlement" had been used to describe Shanghai since the early 1860s, in the *North China Herald,* city guides, and books on Shanghai.

17. Wright and Cartwright, *Twentieth Century Impressions,* 368.

18. Liu and Ruan lost their way while searching for medicinal plants. Half starved, they found some magical peaches and then encountered two beautiful ladies who had most sumptuous quarters all nicely prepared for them. By the time they overcame the lures of these ladies and made it back, ten generations had passed. For the entire story, see Liu Yiqing, *Youming lu,* quoted in Li Fang et al., *Taiping yulan,* ch. 41, 313–14.

The commentary to the poem reads: "When the steamship sails into Wusong Harbor, one can already see the electric lights [*dihuo*; means either gas or electric] densely covering the [city]; in an instant the boat reaches the shore and one can see Western buildings all over the place. This surely cannot be the world of the mortals." This commentary belongs to an earlier text, *Flowers from the Spring River* (Chunjiang huashi), written by Zou Tao under the pen name Xiaoxiangguan Shizhe. The poem itself was the first of one hundred poems written by Chen Qiao in praise of the Shanghai Foreign Settlements; Chen Qiao, *Shenjiang baiyong*, 79.

19. Eileen Scully argues that as a consequence of the attempted ban on prostitution and opium, crime rose steeply in Shanghai; see Scully, "Wandering Whores."

20. See Wagner, "The *Shenbao* in Crisis," 109–20. On the efforts to make Shanghai a "free city," see Pott, *Short History*, 64–66.

21. This did not exclude collective action by Chinese residents. Time and again, guilds, *landsmannschaften*, or individuals would intervene with city administrators to air their grievances and demands. In some cases, Chinese merchants took independent action to add pressure to their demands. One example is the agitation to abolish a bridge toll that was to be paid only by Chinese (see *Shenbao* reports of October 1872). For Queen Victoria's birthday celebrations in 1893, the Chinese communities joined in but incorporated their own agenda; Goodman, "Improvisations on a Semicolonial Theme," 889–926.

22. See Bhabha, *Location of Culture*.

23. The term "legal protection" here implies the protection given to business in general as practiced in the Shanghai Foreign Settlements; there was no law specifically designed to protect courtesan entertainment or prostitution. Courtesan establishments and prostitutes had been subject to licensing and taxation within the French Settlement since 1877 and in the International Settlement since 1898, which meant that the women had certain legal rights. They went to court to argue their cases on a whole range of issues, which shows the legitimate status of their business. For Qing laws on prostitution, see Ma Jianshi, *Da Qing lülie tongkao jiaozhu*, 961–62; for an English translation of these Qing laws, see *The Great Qing Code*, 352–53. On local conditions for courtesan entertainment in Nanjing during the late Ming, see Levy, "The Gay Quarters at Nanking," 1–32; for the courtesan quarters in nineteenth-century Hankow, see Rowe, *Hankow*, 194–95. For studies on regulation of courtesan establishments and prostitution for this period, see Henriot, *Prostitution and Sexuality in Shanghai*, 273–83.

24. Zhang Zhongli, *Jindai Shanghai chengshi yanjiu*, 219–36.

25. Ibid., 53–58.

26. The Qing dynasty had a most elaborate dress code. Courtesans and prostitutes were in the same category as slaves and servants and were forbidden to wear anything other than undyed coarse raw silk, coarse wool, coarse yellow cloth (a kind of native cloth), and the fur and leather made of raccoon, dog, and sheep skin. See *Qinding libu zeli*, *juan* 34: 4. For the Qing dynasty dress code, see Zhao Er, *Qingshi gao*, vol. 11, *juan* 77, 3013–98.

27. Lao Shanghai, *Hu Baoyu*, 79–80.

28. Wagner, "Role of the Foreign Community."

29. *Yangchang caizi* translates literally as "talented scholars from the foreign trading post." The term was patterned on their original name, *Jiangnan caizi* (talented scholars from the Jiangnan region south of the Yangzi River). "Yangchang" is the Chinese term for what Westerners at the time called "Foreign Settlements."

30. See Chang, *The Late-Ming Poet Ch'en Tzu-lung*; Ropp, "Ambiguous Images of Courtesan Culture"; and Wei-Yee Li, "Late Ming Courtesan."

31. Henriot, *Prostitution and Sexuality in Shanghai*, 75; Hershatter, *Dangerous Pleasures*, 70.

Chapter 1. Modeling the Modern

1. Yan Ming, *Zhongguo mingji yishu shi*; Zheng Zhiming, *Xishuo Tangji*; and Liao Meiyun, *Tang ji yanjiu.*

2. See Wang Shunu, *Zhongguo changji shi*, 264.

3. For an overview of the destruction of courtesan establishments in historically rich towns south of the Yangzi River such as Nanjing, Suzhou, and Yangzhou during the eighteenth and nineteenth centuries, see Miao Quansun, *Qinhuai guangji*, preface, 1–2; and Li Dou, *Yangzhou huafang lu*, 189. For the country as a whole, see Wang Shunu, *Zhongguo changji shi*, 201–98.

4. During the 1860s and 1870s, Shanghai newspapers reported on the new regulations issued by Qing authorities to close down courtesan houses in the walled city as well as in the Settlements. See "Chinese Theaters," *North China Herald*, Jan. 5, 1867, 2–3; and "Lun jinchang xinfa" (New law banning prostitution), *Shenbao*, Dec. 31, 1875, 1. In diaries of visitors to the city, the banning of courtesan entertainment and prostitution is also mentioned. For such a personal account, see, for example, Wuming Shi, "Jiangyunguan riji," 309.

5. Zou Tao, *Haishang dengshi lu*, 1:17–18; Chen Qiao, *Shenjiang baiyong*, 86.

6. On the conditions of streets in the walled city, see Zhang Zhongli, *Jindai Shanghai chengshi yanjiu*, 221, 233. There are also fictional depictions of the ban on carriages entering the walled city; see, for example, Sun Yusheng, *Haishang fanhua meng* (1988), 274.

7. Comments on the brightness of gas lamps and electric lights are a common feature in the narrative of the Shanghai Foreign Settlements during these decades. See, for example, Dianshizhai, *Shenjiang shengjing tu*, 2:17.

8. Timothy J. Clark, *Painting of Modern Life*, 79.

9. On courtesans in Beijing, Suzhou, and Nanjing, see, for example, *Dianshizhai huabao*, *yuan* 11, no. 86, 1897; for later examples, see *Tuhua ribao*, with serialized depictions of courtesan entertainment in Shanghai (nos. 229–304, 1910), Beijing (nos. 306–80, 1910), Nanjing (nos. 319–26, 1910), and Suzhou (nos. 327–40, 1910). On Shanghai residences, see, for example, *Dianshizhai huabao*, *wu* 4, no. 28 (1885).

10. Wang Tao, *Haizou yeyou lu*, 5649.

11. Wang Tao, *Haizou yeyou fulu*, 5694.

12. Ge Yuanxu, *Hu you zaji*, 28.

13. Many late Qing novels contain descriptions of courtesans and patrons going to shop at Hengdali. See, for example, Han Bangqing, *Haishang hua liezhuan*, 43–45; and Sun Yusheng, *Haishang fanhua meng* (1988), 78.

14. Shangwu Yinshuguan, *Shanghai zhinan* (1909), 1:7.

15. Ge Yuanxu, *Hu you zaji* (1989), 28; Yuan Zuzhi, *Chongxiu Hu you zaji*, 2:9; Han Bangqing, *Haishang hua liezhuan*, 43–45.

16. Yuan Zuzhi, *Chongxiu Hu you zaji*, 2:9; and reiterated by Sun Yusheng, *Haishang fanhua meng*, 254.

17. Sun Yusheng, *Haishang fanhua meng*, 244.

18. See "Fu yao lun" (On dressing like a demon), *Shenbao*, March 9, 1888, 1; "Lun Shanghai shimian zhi hai zaiyu she" (On extravagance as the disease of the Shanghai market), *Shenbao*, Jan. 21, 1888, 1; and Wuming Shi, "Jiangyunguan riji," 309.

19. Langyouzi, *Haishang yanhua suoji*, *juan* 4: 5–6.

20. These fans were the latest fashion and came not from the West but from Beijing. They were extremely expensive and became popular because of the courtesans; see Ge Yuanxu, *Hu you zaji*, 1989, 37–38. The fans are also mentioned in Langyouzi, *Haishang yanhua suoji*, *juan* 4: 5.

21. Langyouzi, *Haishang yanhua suoji*, *juan* 4: 6.

22. The divisions among these three top-ranking courtesan types are not completely clear

cut. However, the *shuyu* and the *changsan* are considered to have been primarily performers trained in the various arts of entertainment. In order to gain their sexual favors, patrons had to hold many lavish banquets at the courtesan house, the courtesans' main source of revenue, before such a transition could even be considered. Even then, these top-ranking courtesans normally took one main patron as a lover at one time. The client who wished to meet such a courtesan and enter her house had to be brought by a patron who was well acquainted with her. The rules of these houses were elaborate and numerous. Many guides to the courtesan houses were written between the 1860s and the 1920s. The new rules and rituals in courtesan houses in the Settlements as well as the ranking among the courtesans were noted as early as 1877. See Langyouzi, *Haishang yanhua suoji*; Zou Tao, *Haishang dengshi lu*; and Wang Tao, *Songbin suohua* (1937), 75–92. For an explanation and discussion of the courtesan guides and brush notes mentioned here, see chapter 2. For modern studies, see Ping Jinya, "Jiu Shanghai de changji"; Hershatter, "Hierarchy of Shanghai Prostitution," 463–98; Henriot, "From a Throne of Glory," 132–63; and Henriot, *Prostitution and Sexuality in Shanghai*, 22–33.

23. Huayu Xiaozhu Zhuren, *Haishang qinglou tuji*, *juan* 6: 3.

24. Chi Zhicheng, *Hu you mengying*, 163.

25. For a history of changes in the location of courtesan establishments, see Wang Liaoweng, "Shanghai jiyuan didian zhi yange," 2.

26. Hushang Youxizhu, *Haishang youxi tushuo*, 1–4.

27. "Gengzheng diaotou" (Correcting moving announcements), *Youxi bao*, Aug. 26, 1897, 2.

28. Ibid.

29. Langyouzi, *Haishang yanhua suoji*, *juan* 4: 9.

30. There is a long description of fashion, furniture, and public manners in Wang Tao, *Haizou yeyou fulu*, 5694. See also Han Bangqing, *Haishang hua liezhuan*, 150.

31. Xiaolantian Chanqing Shizhe, *Haishang qunfang pu*, *juan* 4: 19.

32. Han Bangqing, *Haishang hua liezhuan*, 301–2.

33. Huang Shiquan, *Songnan mengying lu*, 107.

34. Xiaolantian Chanqing Shizhe, *Haishang qunfang pu*, *juan* 4: 19; Han Bangqing, *Haishang hua liezhuan*, 149.

35. *Tuhua ribao*, no. 54, 1909, 7.

36. Sun Yusheng, *Haishang fanhua meng*, 254.

37. For photographs of Shanghai merchant houses and furniture, see Wright and Cartwright, *Twentieth Century Impressions*, 525–72.

38. Langyouzi, *Haishang yanhua suoji*, *juan* 3: 16.

39. Yu Xingmin, *Shanghai, 1862 nian*, 424.

40. See Zhang Mi, *Zhuanglou ji*, *juan* 3: 11.

41. Wang Tao, *Haizou yeyou lu*, 5649.

42. Xiaolantian Chanqing Shizhe, *Haishang qunfang pu*, *juan* 4: 18.

43. Jiang Ruizao, *Xiaoshuo kaozheng*. The work was first published by Shehui Xiaoshuo Chubanshe in Shanghai between 1908 and 1910. An illustrated version was published in 1918 by Shanghai Jiaotong Tushuguan. Furthermore, in *Haishang hua liezhuan*, the character Tu Mingzhu seems to be based on Hu Baoyu. See Han Bangqing, *Haishang hua liezhuan*, 149; and David Der-wei Wang, *Fin-de-Siècle Splendor*, 59–61.

44. This full-length biography, in print in 1897, is Lao Shanghai, *Hu Baoyu*. For other biographies of Hu Baoyu, see Zou Tao, *Chunjiang huashi*, *juan* 1: 13–14; and Xu Ke, *Qingbai leichao*, vol. 10, *Changji lei* (On the category of prostitution), 123–26.

45. Lao Shanghai, *Hu Baoyu*, 131.

46. Ibid., 127.

47. Ibid., 127–28. For the link between Canton courtesans and foreigners, see Zou Tao, *Chunjiang huashi*, *juan* 1: 13. Most modern scholars follow the argument that only Cantonese

prostitutes received foreign clients. My own research shows that cross-over was not uncommon; the story of Hu Baoyu is just one example. In *Youxi bao*, there are not infrequent reports of Japanese clients visiting *changsan* courtesan establishments; for example, "Dong Xiyang can" (Mixing the Japanese with the Western clients), *Youxi bao*, March 11, 1899, 2.

48. According to Zou Tao, Hu Baoyu had a Western client who treated her very generously and made her wealthy; see Zou Tao, *Chunjiang huashi, juan* 1: 13.

49. Ma Xiangbo, "Shanghai Huifeng Yinhang kaibanshi de da gudong," 1155.

50. See Han Bangqing, *Haishang hua liezhuan*, 149.

51. Xiaolantian Chanqing Shizhe, *Haishang qunfang pu, juan* 4: 19.

52. For example, a young man who goes to Shanghai with the explicit aim of visiting the courtesan house does so with the support of his wife, whose only condition is that he write down what he sees so that she, too, will be able to to experience it. See Pingjiang Yinnian, *Haishang pinghua baojian*, 1:11.

53. For an illustration of a female going to a courtesan house dressed as a man, see "Xiaqie tongpiao" (Visiting the courtesan house with one's concubine); and "Qie qie xunfang" (Bring one's concubine to visit the courtesans).

54. Courtesans or prostitutes who served female customers sexually are referred to as, among other terms, *renyao* (human monster), a term often used for transvestites. See Lao Shanghai, *Hu Baoyu*, 108–9; and also Hershatter, *Dangerous Pleasures*, 118.

55. "You qinglou jinü dai cheng huan" (Visiting the courtesan house and being entertained by a courtesan), *Youxi bao*, Sept. 19, 1887, 2.

56. Sun Yusheng, *Haishang fanhua meng*, 263.

57. Wang Liaoweng, *Shanghai liushi nian huajie shi*, 149.

58. During the 1890s, entertainment newspapers and novels such as *Haishang hua liezhuan* and *Haishang chentian ying* treated such courtesan marriages as rather normal and requiring no further explanation. Likewise, biographies of courtesans frequently mention that they had once been married but were again on their own. Judging from reports published in entertainment papers like *Youxi bao* in the late 1890s, the numbers of courtesans returning to Shanghai after their marriages had collapsed seems not negligible. Important data on ages come from four courtesan guides: *Haishang qunfang pu* (1884), *Jingying xiaosheng erji* (1889), *Haishang qinglou tuji* (1892), and *Haishang hua yinglu* (1915). The ages of the courtesans represented in these data are of particular interest. In Christian Henriot's Wang Tao data, the largest group of courtesans between 1850 and 1870 is fifteen years of age (twenty-four out of fifty-eight). In the data about the Foreign Settlements, the dominant group is substantially older, with twenty-four out of thirty-seven women whose ages are listed for 1884 being eighteen to twenty years of age, and only five being sixteen and younger. Most of the courtesans listed in these guides have also won places in the various flower competitions of the 1880s. Yet these figures are not stable. In the 1889 data, ages sixteen and seventeen are dominant. In 1892, there are peaks for ages sixteen through eighteen and for age twenty. The average age of a courtesan in the 1890s was clearly higher than suggested by Henriot's numbers for the 1860s (*Prostitution and Sexuality in Shanghai*, 28). One might assume that the rise in the reported age of courtesans had much to do with returnees who were abandoning married life. The data in fact still do not show the real picture. Two issues are of importance. First, courtesans who are already famous, such as Lin Daiyu and the three other courtesan stars, appear in earlier guides but not in later ones although they continue in business. This artificially lowers the average age of those listed. Second, it was very common for courtesans to change their names, so that what appears as a constantly renewed group of top courtesans consists in part of the same persons under different names. Being older, more experienced, and famous, these women had greater influence on the public and more control over their business. That they were able to continue in their profession also shows the increasing power they had over their own lives.

59. *Jingying xiaosheng chuji.*

60. See Alfieri, *Il gioco dell'amore*; Hibbett, *Floating World in Japanese Fiction*; and Briais, *Grandes Courtisanes du Second Empire.*

61. For a history of Yoshiwara, see Longstreet and Longstreet, *Yoshiwara*; for a contemporary study on Japanese geisha entertainment culture, see Dalby, *Geisha*; and for a history of prostitution in Japan, see Nishiyama, *Yūjo.*

62. I am grateful to Ted Huters and Craig Clunas for their questions during a talk on this subject, which helped me develop this aspect of an emerging urban "gaze culture."

63. "Lun jinjin nannü fushi zhi yi" (On the strange clothing worn by today's men and women), *Zhinan bao*, June 17, 1897, 1.

64. Langyouzi, *Haishang yanhua suoji, juan* 4: 6; Zou Tao, *Haishang dengshi lu*, 1:24.

65. Langyouzi, *Haishang yanhua suoji, juan* 4: 6.

66. Shanghaitong She, *Shanghai zhanggu congshu*, 1:6. The seventeenth-century manuscript on Shanghai life and customs, by Ye Mengzhu, was first published in 1935.

67. Ibid.

68. "Lin Daiyu yishang chuse" (Lin Daiyu in stunning dress), *Youxi bao*, Oct. 11, 1897, 2.

69. Chen Wuwo, *Lao Shanghai sanshi nian jianwen lu*, 152. For an example of this type of pearl-sewn dress, see Shanghaishi Xiqu Xuexiao Zhongguo Fuzhuangshi Yanjiuzu, *Zhongguo lidai fushi*, 310.

70. "Da Jin'gang zeqi daimao" (The [Four] Great Golden Diamond Cutters choose a date to put on their hats), *Youxi bao*, Oct. 18, 1897, 2.

71. "Yufu xuanqi" (Coachman's uniform makes for a sensation), *Youxi bao*, Nov. 2, 1897, 2.

72. Xu Ke, *Qingbai leichao*, vol. 12, *Yishi lei* (Clothes and ornaments), 53–54. This clothing fad is also mentioned in *Shijie fanhua bao*: "At present, the most fashionable courtesans wear [tops] with waists no wider than five and a half inches; the sleeves are one foot seven inches long; and the cuffs are about four inches. Even when you look at the person's whole body, [the shirt] altogether is no more than two feet seven inches long. Compared to the past, the word for fashion is 'short.'" See "Beili zhuangshi zhi" (Record of fashion among the courtesans), *Shijie fanhua bao*, Dec. 26, 1901, 4.

73. "Huayang yixin" (Each flower is unique), *Dianshizhai huabao*, *yin* 3 (1888), illustration 23.

74. "Nüban nanzhuang" (A woman dressed in men's clothes), *Youxi bao*, Sept. 20, 1897, 2.

75. *Tuhua ribao*, no. 133, 1909, 7. For a study on shoes for women with bound feet, see Dorothy Ko, *Every Step a Lotus.*

76. "Lun Haishang funü yifu" (On Shanghai women's clothing), *Youxi bao*, Nov. 7, 1897, 1.

77. Ibid. In an essay on changes in Chinese costume, written in the 1930s, Zhang Ailing attributes the tighter cut of the clothing to the political upheaval and social change of the times. She compares this clothing style to that of the Italian Renaissance, when garments were so tight that they required small slits on the side to allow for larger movements; see "Gengyi ji" (Changing clothes), in Zhang Ailing, *Zhang Ailing quanji*, 3:70–71.

78. Meihua'an Zhu, *Shenjiang shixia shengjing tushuo*, 2:5.

79. Wang Tao, *Haizou yeyou lu*, 5649. These shops are listed in Shanghai city guides; see, for example, Shangwu Yinshuguan, *Shanghai zhinan* 1 (1909): 7.

80. Wang Tao, *Haizou yeyou lu*, 5649. For details, see also Han Bangqing, *Haishang hua liezhuan*, 469; although a novel, its assertion is supported by abundant evidence of courtesans being in arrears with their tailors.

81. The impact of Shanghai fashion on the whole country was noted in, for example, Moule, *New China and Old*, 101; Xu Ke, *Qingbai leichao*, vol. 12, *Yishi lei* (Clothes and ornaments), 53–54; and city guides such as Zhonghua Tushujicheng Gongsi, *Shanghai youlan zhinan*, 1919, 3.

82. Secker, *Schen*, 64 (my translation).

83. For an example from a regular newspaper, see "Fu yao lun" (On dressing like a demon), *Shenbao*, March 9, 1888, 1; and from an entertainment newspaper, see "Lun Hushang funü fushi zhi qi" (On the exotic in Shanghai women's way of dressing), *Youxi bao*, Jan. 1, 1899, 1.

84. "Lun Hushang funü fushi zhi qi" (On the exotic in Shanghai women's way of dressing), 2.

85. "Lun jinjin nannü fushi zhi yi" (On the strange clothing worn by men and women nowadays), *Zhinan bao*, June 17, 1897, 1.

86. "Paokuai mache zhi chu fengtou" (Showing off by coach racing), *Tuhua ribao* 25:7 (1909).

87. "Lun jinjin nannü fushi zhi yi" (On the strange clothing worn by men and women nowadays), *Zhinan bao*, June 17, 1897, 1.

88. Chen Boxi, *Lao Shanghai*, 101–2.

89. Wei Yong, *Yuerong bian*, 1:69, 73.

90. J. D. Clark, *Sketches in and around Shanghai*, 49.

91. Secker, *Schen*, 21.

92. For example, see Ge Yuanxu, *Hu you zaji* (1989), 17, 52; and Huang Shiquan, *Songnan mengying lu*, 98.

93. Chi Zhicheng, *Hu you mengying*, 160.

94. This can be seen in many bamboo twig ballads published in *Shenbao* during the later years in which visitors to the city wrote down their impressions. Some of these poems are collected in Gu Bingquan, *Shanghai Yangchang zhuzhi ci*. For a list of vehicles available during the 1880s, see Chi Zhicheng, *Hu you mengying*, 160; for the 1890s, see Meihua'an Zhu, "Hu you jilüe" (Essentials for a visit to Shanghai), in *Shenjiang shixia shengjing tushuo*, 1:3.

95. Wang Tao, *Haizou yeyou fulu*, 5694.

96. "Xia ji wang qin" (Taking out a courtesan and disregarding one's family), *Dianshizhai huabao, yi*, 9 (1884).

97. Meihua'an Zhu, *Shenjiang shixia shengjing tushuo*, 1:14.

98. Reports on the courtesans' public parading are related mostly to some kind of incident, such as when a courtesan's carriage was taken in by the police for speeding, or when a passing client got off his carriage and offered it to the courtesan; see "Enke xiache" (Loving patron gets off his carriage), *Youxi bao*, Feb. 20, 1899, 2. In *Shijie fanhua bao*, such reports received regular mention in the column "Haishang kan hua riji" (Daily notes on flower viewing in Shanghai), which tracked the movements of top courtesans; see, for example "Chen Yu shouxin" (Chen Yu is in retreat), *Shijie fanhua bao*, Dec. 18, 1901, 2; and "He Ruyu douquanzi" (He Ruyu goes around in circles), *Shijie fanhua bao*, Dec. 23, 1901, 2.

99. *Jiaoshu* is an honorific for a high-ranking Shanghai courtesan. Originally meaning "book editor" or "proofreader," the term might have evolved from the tradition of singing a written text out loud for proofreading purposes. As courtesans are also singers, this might account for their title of *jiaoshu*. See Xue Liyong, "Ming Qing shiqi de Shanghai changji," 151.

100. "Ge zhang yanchi" (Relaunching their business), *Youxi bao*, Oct. 10, 1898, 2.

101. The whereabouts of Shanghai courtesans are amply documented in the city's rich literature on entertainment. See, for example, city guides such as Ge Yuanxu, *Hu you zaji*; *Shenjiang mingsheng tushuo*; Meihua'an Zhu, *Shenjiang shixia shengjing tushuo*; and the entertainment newspapers of the 1890s, such as *Youxi bao* and *Shijie fanhua bao*.

102. "Zhongguo nanyu bianfa" (It is hard to carry out political reform in China), *Youxi bao*, Feb. 18, 1899, 1–2.

103. Xiaolantian Chanqing Shizhe, *Chongding "Haishang qunfang pu,"* 1:2–3.

104. The route is described in detail in a source contained in "Zhouche lei," in Xu Ke, *Qingbai leichao*, 52.

105. Early in the twentieth century, the eastern section of Fuzhou Road developed into the "cultural street," and many of the main Shanghai publishers and bookstores set up business there. See Hu Genxi, *Si Malu*, 197–204.

106. For a detailed description of Fuzhou Road in the 1890s, see J. D. Clark, *Sketches in and around Shanghai*, 49–63.

107. Ge Yuanxu, *Hu you zaji* (1989), 53.

108. Dianshizhai, *Shenjiang shengjing tu*, 2:56.

109. For details on Zhang Garden, see Shanghaitong She, *"Shanghai yanjiu zilao" xuji*, 569–74.

110. On Zhang Garden as part of the public sphere, see Xiong Yuezhi, "Zhangyuan."

111. Zeng Pu, *Niehai hua*, 10; the translation follows Crespigny and Liu, "Flower in a Sinful Sea."

112. For studies on Nanjing Road and the commercial culture in Shanghai, see Cochran, *Inventing Nanjing Road.*

113. Xu Ke, *Qingbai leichao*, vol. 12, *Zhouche lei* (Boats and carts), 52.

114. For details, see Coates, *China Races*, 3–138.

115. Lao Shanghai, *Hu Baoyu*, 60. See also Jiang Ruizao, *Xiaoshuo kaozheng*, 169–70.

116. This practice was often reported in late Qing entertainment newspapers and courtesan novels. See, for example, "Saima shuo" (On the horse race), *Youxi bao*, May 1, 1899, 1–2; "Jingzhuang zhaoyan" (Rich attire dazzles the eye), *Youxi bao*, May 4, 1899, 2; and Jiang Ruizao, *Xiaoshuo kaozheng*, 413.

117. For a report on such an accident, see "Paokuai mache zhi chu fengtou" (Showing off by coach racing), *Tuhua ribao*, no. 25, 7 (1910).

118. "Lun zuo yemache zhi sheng" (On the fashion of nighttime carriage rides), *Youxi bao*, July 9, 1899, 1.

119. Beijingshi Yishu Yanjiusuo and Shanghai Yishu Yanjiusuo, *Zhongguo jingju shi*, 185–87.

120. On women going to the theater in Beijing, see ibid. A visitor to Beijing from Shanghai in 1911 found the separation of men and women in theaters strange, and he also reported that different days were allocated to male and female visitors at parks; see Lu Feida, "Jing, Jin liang yue ji." I thank Denise Gimpel for bringing this article to my attention.

121. "Funü kanxi zhuzhi ci."

122. *Shenbao* printed many articles on banned operas, and also came out with lists. See, for example, "Diyi fansi jinyan yinxi gaoshi" (Public announcement by the office of the Prefecture on banning obscene operas), *Shenbao*, April 27, 1890; and "Hudi yu jin nüling" (The official order banning female singers in Shanghai), *Shenbao*, Jan. 7, 1890. On the Shanghai Municipal Council's 1909 prohibition of minors under fifteen years of age in brothels, theaters, and taverns, see Henriot, *Prostitution and Sexuality in Shanghai*, 275.

123. For example, see "Guan ju xiaoji" (A reportage on the theater), *Shenbao*, March 18, 1889, 3.

124. "Huayuan yanju" (Performing in the park), *Shenbao*, Nov. 20, 1886, 3; "Huayuan yanju xishu" (A detailed report on the performance in the park), *Shenbao*, Nov. 21, 1886, 3.

125. See, for example, "Xibao ji nüyou yanju zhuzhen shi" (Charity performance by female performer reported in Western newspaper), *Shenbao*, Sept. 24, 1906, 17.

126. Huang Shiquan, *Songnan mengying lu*, 116.

127. "San xiguan zhi jizha" (The crowded chaos after the theater performance), *Tuhua ribao*, no. 29, 7 (1909).

128. Considering that one banquet cost ¥12 in the 1890s, the sum of ¥80 appears to be quite substantial. By comparison, the monthly salary of a journalist at *Shenbao* ranged between ¥10 and ¥40 at the time. See Lei Fu, "Shenbaoguan zhi guoqu zhuangkuang."

129. "Qingke fei yi" (It is not an easy matter to play host), *Youxi bao*, Jan. 7, 1899, 3.

130. On *huachuan*, see Li Dou, *Yangzhou huafang lu*, 240–42; Zeng Pu, *Niehai hua*, 58–59; and Hanshang Mengren, *Fengyue meng*, 33–34.

131. During the 1860s and 1870s, Shanghai newspapers reported on the new regulations issued by the Qing authorities to close down courtesan houses in the walled city as well as in the Settlements. See "Chinese Theaters," *North China Herald*, Jan. 5, 1867, 2–3; and "Lun jinchang xinfa" (New law banning prostitution), *Shenbao*, Dec. 31, 1875, 1.

132. Zou Tao, *Haishang dengshi lu*, 1:18b. Wang Tao, *Haizou yeyou lu*, 5675, 5680. On the ban on prostitution during the Qing dynasty, see Miao Quansun, *Qinhuai guangji*, preface, 1–2. For studies on the ban on prostitution during the Qing, see Henriot, *Prostitution and Sexuality in Shanghai*, 271–333; Xue Liyong, "Ming Qing shiqi de Shanghai changji," 152; and *Shanghai jinü shi*, 347, 356.

133. See Lao Shanghai, *Hu Baoyu*, 131–32.

134. Lu Feida, "Jing, Jin liang yue ji" (Record of a two-month visit to Beijing and Tianjin), *Xiaoshuo yuebao*, 2.9 (1911): 1; Zhongyuan Langzi, *Jinghua yanshi* (Amorous adventures in Beijing), *Xinxin xiaoshuo* (1908), 7.

135. Although a lead article in *Shenbao* around the time of the love affair between Hu Baoyu and the Peking opera singer Shisan Dan did not name Hu directly, it was strongly critical of such liaisons; see Shiwan Jinling Guanzhu, "Minghua shipin" (A famous courtesan compromises her character), *Shenbao*, Feb. 8, 1873, 2. Langyouzi, *Haishang yanhua suoji*, 3:8.

136. Lao Shanghai, *Hu Baoyu*, 128.

137. Xiaolantian Chanqing Shizhe, *Chongding Haishang qunfang pu*, 4:11.

138. Wang Tao, *Haizou yeyou fulu*, 5750; Xiaolantian Chanqing Shizhe, *Chongding Haishang qunfang pu*, 4:18; Zou Tao, *Chunjiang huashi*, 1:13.

139. "Pofu qiangwu" (A virago robber), *Shenbao*, Nov. 11, 1878, 2.

140. The stones on officials' hats indicated their ranks: "blue top" indicates *sanpin* (third rank) and "crystal top" indicates *wupin* (fifth rank). For details, see Shanghaishi Xiqu Xuexiao Zhongguo Fuzhuangshi Yanjiuzu, *Zhongguo lidai fushi*, 208.

141. "Zhengtang gongwu" (Magistrate on duty), *Youxi bao*, Oct. 15, 1897, 1.

142. See "Chinese Theaters," 3.

143. Henriot, *Prostitution and Sexuality in Shanghai*, 284–85.

144. For the year 1876, the land tax was 20,168.92 taels and the General Municipal Rate was 27,266.92 (foreign) and 48,885.35 (native), for a total of 96,321.19 taels; the combined revenue of the International Settlement was 251,166.01 taels. See Municipal Council of Shanghai, *Report for the Year Ended 31st December 1876*, 201.

145. Wang Tao, *Haizou yeyou fulu*, 5694.

146. On the difficulty of assessing the income of courtesans during this period, see Henriot, *Prostitution and Sexuality in Shanghai*, 257–58.

147. Zou Tao, *Chunjiang huashi, juan* 1: 13.

148. Wang Liaoweng, *Shanghai liushi nian huajie shi*, 35.

149. Hushang Youxizhu, *Haishang youxi tushuo*, 1:1–14.

150. Some courtesans are known to have written letters for others. See "Kelian mingshu" (The pitiable famous courtesan), *Youxi bao*, April 17, 1899, 2.

151. Hushang Youxizhu, *Haishang youxi tushuo*, 1:4.

152. Lin Daiyu traveled to Tianjin during the Boxer Uprising and the Allied invasion. She hid among refugees in the countryside, and when bandits attacked the refugees, she escaped death by offering her jewelry to the bandits. Lin Daiyu, *Beinan shimo ji*, 1065–84.

153. Wang Shunu, *Zhongguo changji shi*, 288.

154. There are many illustrations of and reports on courtesans and photography. The earliest is in Ge Yuanxu, *Hu you zaji*, 57. In his early account of Shanghai courtesans, Wang Tao mentions a fashion among them to have their photographs taken; see his *Haizou yeyou fulu*, 5720. For a study on early photography in China, see Thiriez, "Photography and Portraiture."

155. Langyouzi, *Haishang yanhua suoji, juan* 3: 11.
156. Catherine Yeh, "Creating the Urban Beauty," 419–20.
157. "Wen Jin Xiaobao qiaoqian shi yi he zhi" (A congratulatory poem on the occasion of Jin Xiaobao moving), *Youxi bao*, Sept. 21, 1897, 2.
158. Timothy J. Clark, *Painting of Modern Life*, 79–146.
159. For example, *Youxi bao*, Sept. 13, 1898, 1.
160. "Lun nüzi zhaoxiang zhi bian" (On making it easier for women to have their photographs taken), *Shijie fanhua bao*, March 8, 1905, 2.
161. Shanghai Sheyingjia Xiehui and Shanghai Daxue Wenxueyuan, *Shanghai sheying shi*, 7.
162. "Yaohua zhaoxiang shuo" (On photography in Yaohua), *Youxi bao*, Oct. 4, 1898, 2.
163. Shanghai Sheyingjia Xiehui and Shanghai Daxue Wenxueyuan, *Shanghai sheying shi*, 7.
164. "Dong xi Yaohua, guanren banjia" (In the eastern and western branches of the Yaohua studio, courtesans pay half price [for their photograph]), *Shijie fanhua bao*, March 8, 1905, 2.
165. See Tang Zhenchang, *Jindai Shanghai fanhua lu*, 253.
166. For a discussion of the demise of courtesan entertainment, see Henriot, *Prostitution and Sexuality in Shanghai*, 44–45.
167. Liu Huiwu, *Shanghai jindai shi*, 406–12.
168. Lao Shanghai, *Hu Baoyu*, 122.
169. Zhan Kai, preface to *Huashi*. For a study of Zhan Kai and his works, see Ellen Widmer, "Inflecting Gender."

Chapter 2. Shanghai Love

Some of the material in this chapter was previously published in Cathy Yeh, "Reinventing Ritual: Late Qing Handbooks for Proper Customer Behaviour in Shanghai Courtesan Houses," *Late Imperial China* 19, no. 2 (Dec. 1998): 1–63. The author thanks the editors of *Late Imperial China* for permission to republish the material here.

1. Hershatter, *Dangerous Pleasures*, 70.
2. For details on Wang Tao, see Cohen, *Between Tradition and Modernity*; Catherine Yeh, "Life-Style of Four *Wenren*," 419–70.
3. See Henriot, *Prostitution and Sexuality in Shanghai*, 76–77.
4. Wang Tao, *Haizou yeyou lu*, 5647–48.
5. Ibid., 5678. A late Qing novel describes a similar incident of local hooligans punishing a courtesan in Yangzhou for her "incivility" but in reality trying to extort money from her; see Hanshang Mengren, *Fengyue meng*, chapter 8.
6. Wang Tao, *Haizou yeyou lu*, 5678.
7. Ibid., 5671, 5675.
8. Mao Xianglin, *Moyu lu*, 2887.
9. The manuscript *Yuefu Poems on Traveling in the Bitter Sea* is held by the Suzhou University Library. It has never been printed and has largely escaped the attention of most scholars, although Yuan Jin and Alexander Des Forges have used it as a source in their work. I thank Professor Yuan Jin at Shanghai University for having a hand-copied version of the manuscript made for me.
10. Wang Tao mentions the work in his *Record of Visits to Courtesan Houses in a Distant Corner by the Sea* and quotes at length from its foreword, written by his close friend Jiang Jianren; see Wang Tao, *Haizou yeyou lu*, 5669–70. For studies on Jiang Jianren and Wang Tao, who were among the early group of sojourners who lived and worked in the Shanghai Settlements, primarily with foreigners, see Xiong Yuezhi, *Xixue dongjian yu wan Qing shehui*; and Catherine Yeh, "Life-Style of Four *Wenren*," 428–34.

11. *Bamboo Twig Ballads on the Barbarians' Market in Shanghai* (Shenjiang yichang zhuzhi ci) gives a detailed account of the new types and rankings of courtesans in the Settlements as well as their behavior and ritual practices (14).

12. Zou Tao, *Haishang dengshi lu, juan* 2: 17–18.

13. Discussed in detail in chapter 5.

14. Wang Tao, *"Haizou yeyou" fulu*, 5689, 5696. There is no evidence that any of these new categories—including the *shuyu*—and rankings were carried over from the walled city, as some scholars have claimed. Although there were high-ranking courtesan singer-entertainers in the walled city, Wang Tao gave simply their names and places and characterized them by their performance specialties. See Wang Tao, *Haizou yeyou lu*, 5671, 5675; and Mao Xianglin, *Moyu lu*, 2887. For a detailed study of the antecedents and emergence of the *shuyu* in the Foreign Settlements, see Xue Liyong, *Shanghai jinü shi*, 165–73. In his *"Haizou yeyou" fulu*, Wang Tao also quoted bamboo twig ballads by a certain Shaoxi Zuimosheng (also known as Shaoxi Mozhuang Zhuren) and claims that the ballads were a complete account of the new courtesan ritual practices in the Settlements. The two ballads, titled "Hubei zhuzhi ci," signed by Shaoxi Mozhuang Zhuren, and "Qinglou zhuzhi ci," signed by Shaoxi Zuimosheng, were first published in *Shenbao*, February 14, 1877, and March 11, 1877, respectively. For studies on the development of courtesan hierarchies before and after the establishment of the Foreign Settlements, see Xue Liyong, *Shanghai jinü shi*, 105–70; and Henriot, *Prostitution and Sexuality in Shanghai*, 22–25.

15. Yuan Zuzhi, "Hubei zhuzhi ci," 10.

16. Gu Bingquan, *Shanghai Yangchang zhuzhi ci*, 10.

17. Xue Liyong, *Shanghai jinü shi*, 155.

18. Chen Qiao, *Shenjiang baiyong, juan* 2: 7. In late Qing newspapers such as *Shenbao* and, later, *Youxi bao*, the *changsan* are always politely referred to as *shuyu* or *jiaoshu*.

19. Yuan Zuzhi, "Xu Hubei zhuzhi ci," 12–14.

20. Chi Zhicheng, *Hu you mengying*, 157. By the end of the Qing, performances by courtesan stars in such storytelling halls created a big splash in Shanghai. See, for example, the advertisements in *Shijie fanhua bao* during February 1902; and Xue Liyong, *Shanghai jinü shi*, 168–71.

21. Wang Tao, in his *Haizou yeyou lu*, mentions that rich merchants—who perhaps were residing in the walled city—sometimes called on courtesans to accompany them to open theatrical performances at Xi Garden (later known as Yu Garden). This routine was known as *xiju*, and, according to Wang, officials tried to ban it many times. His description makes it clear that *xiju* was rather unusual; see *Haizou yeyou lu*, 5680. Other practices were *chuju*, calling a courtesan to entertain, and *chawei*, calling at a courtesan house in the afternoon. Both are mentioned in a book on Ningbo courtesans by Ershi Sheng, *Shizhou chunyu*, 4:4255. The author was well known in Shanghai during the 1850s as a patron of the Shanghai courtesans. Wang Tao tells the story of a passionate love affair between Ershi Sheng and a Shanghai courtesan; see *Haizou yeyou lu*, 5672–73. The *chuju* and *chawei* rituals might thus have been brought in from Jiangnan.

22. Since the Tang dynasty, when courtesans became a major literary topic, they appeared mainly in the genres of short fiction, poetry, drama, and city guides or descriptions of capitals past and present; see, for example, Meng Yuanlao, *Dongjing menghua lu*. Guides to courtesan houses were published beginning in the Ming dynasty, but they were few in number and did not contain introductions to the rules and rituals of these houses; for example, Zhu and Zhang, *Qinglou yunyu*.

23. An example is *Muling shu jiyao* (Essentials from handbooks for local officials; 1870?), which itemizes their duties and provides examples of model behavior taken from earlier sources. I am grateful to Pierre-Etienne Will, whose talk on the structure of these handbooks in Heidelberg in July 2003 alerted me to this option.

24. It is interesting to compare these guides with Japanese guides for courtesan entertainment in Yoshiwara, the eighteenth-century Edo courtesan quarters. *Yoshiwara shusse kan* (1754) consists of a list of courtesans, from the top-rank *tayō* (a single courtesan named Hana Murasaki) to the more numerous second-rank *kōshi*, followed by a section with "judgments" (*hyōban*) giving specific comments on each courtesan. The second part of this guide is a house-by-house introduction to Yoshiwara's courtesan establishments, with illustrations and maps. Another such guide, *Yoshiwara shichifu kami* (A courtesan guide to Yoshiwara), by Ishikawa Haruyoroshi (1713), starts with three *tayō* (with Hana Murasaki in first place) and eight *kōshi*. It provides extensive introductions to these top courtesans and shorter biographies and stories for the more common ranks of courtesans; the illustrations focus mainly on the interiors of the houses. Jōjaku Koji's *Edo hanjō ki* (1832) was banned by the government between 1832 and 1836 for its depiction of licentious living and the corruption of scholars, samurai, and monks in the courtesan quarters; it offers a personal account of Edo and its entertainments. *Tai Edo bijin taku tsuki-yuki-hana jō hyōban* is a record of the competition among courtesans of the period. *Yoshiwara saiken* (1803), perhaps the most famous courtesan guide for the period, with many different editions, combines comments on individual courtesans with close observations on different aspects of life in Yoshiwara. The narrative is supplemented with rough maps of Yoshiwara showing each courtesan establishment and reproductions of their business signs plus a list of establishments and the names of the courtesans; some editions carry illustrations of different Yoshiwara scenes. These guides are written in a personal and subjective tone, and their primary aim was to offer practical knowledge of Yoshiwara. A common feature of the Japanese guides is their focus on individual courtesans and their establishments. This contrasts with the Shanghai guides, which focus on the rules and rituals governing courtesan entertainment as a whole. The Shanghai guides also differ from the eighteenth-century Japanese *sharebon*, a type of semifictional guidebook to life in the so-called floating world. *Sharebon* stories are set in courtesan houses and, together with comments by the narrator, assist the reader in understanding the inner workings of this special world. See Schamoni, *Die "Sharebon" Santō Kyōdens und ihre literaturgeschichtliche Stellung*; and Scott Miller, "Hybrid Narrative of Kyōden's *Sharebon*."

25. This work has two different author names: one appears with the author's preface, which is signed "Zhiyin Mituren," and the other is at the beginning of the text, which is signed "Langyouzi."

26. Huayu Xiaozhu Zhuren, *Haishang qinglou tuji, juan* 1: 1–2 (1892).

27. Wang Tao, *"Haizou yeyou" fulu*, 5695; Qu Yuan, *Fupu xiantan*, 17:3b.

28. Hershatter also discusses some of these rituals but does not explore the Shanghai courtesan hierarchy and services as largely products of interaction with conditions in the Foreign Settlements; see *Dangerous Pleasures*, 88–99.

29. Zou Tao, *Haishang dengshi lu, juan* 2: 17.

30. Meng Yuanlao, *Dongjing menghua lu*, 5; Wang Shunu, *Zhongguo changji shi*, 75–76.

31. Han Bangqing, *Haishang hua liezhuan*, 38–41.

32. For the multilayered economic structure of the courtesan house, see Henriot, *Prostitution and Sexuality in Shanghai*, 248–69.

33. See Dalby, *Geisha*, 173–175.

34. There has been much narrative and scholarship on courtship between client and courtesan. See, for example, Zhang Chunfan, "Haishang qinglou yange ji"; and Hershatter, *Dangerous Pleasures*, 103–16.

35. While courtesan guides of the late Qing provide no specific advice, later guides written in the 1920s suggest that guests in courtesan houses should not burden themselves with this kind of responsibility. See Wang Houzhe, *Shanghai baojian*, 3.

36. The term *zhuanju* appears in Yao Xie's narrative, but it is used to describe a courtesan following her client to several dinner parties.

37. Hershatter, *Dangerous Pleasures*, chapter 2; Catherine Yeh, "Urban Love Goes Private."

38. On the central position of *Dream of the Red Chamber* in the life and business of the Shanghai courtesans, see chapter 5.

39. During the late 1890s, courtesans advertised on the first page of entertainment papers such as *Youxi bao*, announcing that they had set up their own establishments.

40. For details about financial arrangements in Shanghai courtesan houses during the late Qing, see Henriot, *Prostitution and Sexuality in Shanghai*, chapter 10; and Hershatter, *Dangerous Pleasures*, 73–76.

41. Henriot, *Prostitution and Sexuality in Shanghai*, 233–34.

42. The complexity of the relationship between madams and courtesans, even in simple brothels, is well documented for the modern period in Wolfe, *Daily Life of a Chinese Courtesan*.

43. For details, see Sun Yusheng, *Jinü de shenghuo*, 18–19.

44. See "Lun Hu ji jixi tai shen" (The Shanghai courtesans are overdoing it), *Youxi bao*, July 20, 1899, 1; "Lun jinjin nannü fushi zhi yi" (On the strange clothing worn by today's men and women), *Zhinan bao*, June 17, 1897, 1; "Lun zuo yemache zhi sheng" (On the fashion of nighttime carriage rides), *Youxi bao*, July 9, 1899, 1; "Lun Hubin shuyu yingchou dangyi Lu Lanfen wei diyi" (Lu Lanfen should be considered as Shanghai's number one in the art of entertaining guests), *Youxi bao*, Sept. 18, 1897, 1.

45. In these advertisements, the term for a courtesan buying her freedom is *zishusheng*. The advertisements came under the general heading "Diaotou gaobai" (Announcements of changes of address); for examples, see *Youxi bao*, October 10, 1898, 1.

46. Wang Tao, *Haizou yeyou lu*, 5633–84.

47. Huang Shiquan remarks that the Spanish prostitutes are most beautiful; see *Songnan mengying lu*, 124.

48. *Shenjiang mingsheng tushuo*, 1:16.

49. Xiaolantian Chanqing Shizhe, *Haishang qunfang pu*, 4:12–13.

50. *Shenjiang mingsheng tushuo*, 1:16.

51. Zou Tao, *Haishang dengshi lu*, 2:29–30; Liangxi Chilian Jushi, *Hujiang yanpu*, 22. In Shanghai, many different coins were in use, and exchange rates were unstable. For reference, see Eduard Kann, *The Currencies of China*. Shanghai: Kelly and Walsh, 1926.

52. Liangxi Chilian Jushi, *Hujiang yanpu*, 39.

53. Huang Shiquan, *Songnan mengying lu*, 128.

54. *Shenjiang mingsheng tushuo*, 1:17–18.

55. Xiaolantian Chanqing Shizhe, *Haishang qunfang pu*, 4:20–22.

56. Zou Tao, *Haishang dengshi lu*, 2:30.

57. Ibid.

58. Huang Shiquan described a Japanese courtesan named Sansan (or Shanshan) who was very eager to learn about Tang poetry from Chinese literati; see *Songnan mengying lu*, 128.

59. Xiaolantian Chanqing Shizhe, *Haishang qunfang pu*, 4:21. According to Eileen Scully, during the early years of the Shanghai Settlements, Western prostitutes were mostly Americans who were known as the "American girls" and were quite successful in their business; see "Taking the Low Road" and "Wandering Whores."

60. Xiaolantian Chanqing Shizhe, *Haishang qunfang pu*, 4:21–22.

61. Ibid., 21–24.

62. Cao Xueqin, *Honglou meng*, chapter 12.

63. For recent studies on these novels, see David Der-wei Wang, *Fin-de-Siècle Splendor*, 53–116; Keith McMahon, "Fleecing the Male Customer"; and Des Forges, *Street Talk and Alley Stories*, 116–93.

64. See, for example, "Yeyou dang zhi zedi shuo" (On choosing the right location when visiting courtesans), *Shenbao*, March 21, 1879, 1.

65. See Xue Liyong, *Shanghai jinü shi*, 155.

66. Shanghai city guides with introductions to courtesan entertainment used as sources include Ge Yuanxu, *Hu you zaji*; Shangwu Yinshuguan, *Shanghai zhinan* (1909, 1912, 1922); Huang Renjing, *Huren baojian*; Zhonghua Tushujicheng Gongsi, *Shanghai youlan zhinan* (1919, 1923); Wang Houzhe, *Shanghai baojian*; Shen and Chen, *Shanghaishi zhinan*; and *Da Shanghai zhinan* (1933, 1947).

67. *The Illustrated Daily* was founded in Shanghai on July 1, 1909, and published for more than a year. It was among the earliest illustrated newspapers for a broader readership. The paper emphasized social reportage and serialized articles on different aspects of life in the city of Shanghai. The series referred to here is titled "Events in Shanghai Courtesan Establishments" (Shanghai quyuan zhi xianxiang); it appeared daily and ran for seventy-five installments in 1910. The series also includes depictions of Shanghai courtesans titled "Events in Shanghai Society" (Shanghai shehui zhi xianxiang). Although Shanghai courtesans and their establishments were frequently illustrated subjects, the *Illustrated Daily*'s series is unique in its systematic and detailed account of the ritual aspect of courtesan entertainment. By being at the same time historical in its reporting, the paper offers a perspective on changes and developments in these rituals during the early twentieth century.

68. For the history and modern development of the art of Japanese geisha and their training, see Dalby, *Geisha*, 97–117.

69. Xue Liyong, *Shanghai jinü shi*, 339–44.

70. See "Haishang minghua chidu," 5.

71. "Shanghai Lin Daiyu meishi dong Hangzhou Luqin nüshi" (Shanghai's *meishi* courtesan Li Daiyu [and] East Hangzhou's nüshi Luqin), in Hushang Youxizhu, *Haishang youxi tushuo*, 1:1.

72. See Wang Liaoweng, *Shanghai liushi nian huajie shi*, section "Zhuanlüe," 51; Chen Wuwo, *Lao Shanghai sanshi nian jianwen lu*, 149; Chen Boxi, *Shanghai yishi daguan*, 416; and Hershatter, *Dangerous Pleasures*, 145–52.

73. "Wang Shanbao ji Zhou Yueqing shu" (Wang Shanbao's letter to Zhou Yueqing).

74. "Chen Yuqing fu Li Peilan" (Chen Yuqing's reply to Li Peilan), 8–9.

75. "Zhu Wenqing ji He Lifu" (Zhu Wenqing's letter to He Lifu).

76. "Li Qiaoxian ji Sun Shaojiang shu" (Li Qiaoxian's reply to Sun Shaojiang).

77. "Ji Wu Chunyi" (To Wu Chunyi).

78. "Yu Zhou Wenxiang" (To Zhou Wenxiang).

79. "Shanghai Zhu Moqing ji Gusu Ma Xiaonian shu" (Letter from Zhu Moqing in Shanghai to Ma Xiaonian in Suzhou).

80. "Shanghai Lu Xiaohong ji Qian Yunsheng shu" (Letter from Lu Xiaohong in Shanghai to Qian Yunsheng).

81. Detailed discussion and translations of courtesan letters on this topic are in chapter 5.

82. Ge Yuanxu, *Hu you zaji*, 7.

83. On Yi Temple, see Huang Shiquan, *Songnan mengying lu*, 141.

84. The *juan* in the term *xuanjuan* probably referred to "precious scrolls" (*baojuan*). For an introduction to these texts, see Daniel L. Overmyer, *Precious Volumes: An Introduction to Chinese Sectarian Scriptures from the Sixteenth and Seventeenth Centuries* (Cambridge: Harvard University Press, 1999).

85. *Shenjiang yichang zhuzhi ci*, 2.

86. This trend was later summarized by Huating Wen Yehe, in "Gailun."

87. See Henriot, *Prostitution and Sexuality in Shanghai*, 22–25.

88. Ibid., chapters 9 and 10.

89. Meihua'an Zhu, "Xisu zazhi" (Random notes on Western customs), in *Shenjiang shixia shengjing tushuo*, 2:appendix, 1b.

90. Natascha Vittinghoff makes this point for the journalists as a new class bound by professional rather than regional ties; see *Freier Fluss*, chapter 3.

91. In his "Away from Nanking Road," Lu Hanchao argues that life in the Shanghai *linong* had nothing of the exotic or glamorous about it, although the great commercial streets such as Nanjing Road have assumed these qualities in historical imagination. While it is certainly true that the immigrants brought their old lifestyles with them and that these had a continuous impact, the article overlooks the behavioral forms the city imposed on its inhabitants. For example, when the Foreign Settlements were founded, they adopted the Western watch, the bell tower, and the calendar with a seven-day week, which structured time differently from the rest of China. This new arrangement in itself changed all aspects of life in Shanghai. For the gradual process in which many local time schedules brought by provincial immigrants merged in nineteenth-century Paris, see Csergo, "Extension et mutation de loisir citadin," 127.

92. For Ming courtesan guidebooks, see, for example, Zhu and Zhang, *Qinglou yunyu;* and Li Yunxiang, *Jinling baimei.*

93. For the Qing period, most records of courtesans and courtesan entertainment are modeled on Yu Huai's *Random Notes.* Such works include Penghua Sheng, *Qinhuai huafang lu;* Xixi Shanren, *Wumen huafang lu;* Xu Yu, *Baimen xinliu ji;* Fenlita Xingzhe, *Zhuxi huashi xiao lu;* Yu Jiao, *Chaojia fengyue ji;* and Shuxi Qiaoye, *Yantai huashi lu.*

Chapter 3. Playground Shanghai

1. Baoyu Sheng, *Huajian yingtie,* chapters 1 and 2.
2. Wang Tao, *"Haizou yeyou" fulu,* 5709–85. On Hu Baoyu, see ibid., 5750.
3. Wang Tao, *"Haizou yeyou lu" yulu,* 5787–5810.
4. Xiaolantian Chanqing Shizhe, *Haishang qunfang pu,* 1:1–4 (table of contents).
5. Huayu Xiaozhu Zhuren, *Haishang qinglou tuji,* 1–5.
6. Wang Tao, *Haizou yeyou lu.*
7. For nineteenth-century Beijing, see Shuxi Qiaoye, *Yantai huashi lu.* For Canton, see Yu Jiao, *Chaojia fengyue ji;* and Zhi Jisheng, *Zhujiang minghua xiao zhuan.* For Nanjing, see Miao Quansun, *Qinhuai guangji.* For Suzhou, see Xixi Shanren, *Wumen huafang lu;* and Gezhong Shengshou, *Wumen huafang xulu.* For Yangzhou, see Fenlita Xingzhe, *Zhuxi huashi xiao lu.* For Ningbo, see Ershisheng, *Shizhou chunyu.*
8. Nishiyama Matsunosuke, *Yōjo,* 164–65.
9. Wang Tao, *"Haizou yeyou" fulu,* 5758.
10. Zou Tao, *Haishang dengshi lu,* 2:28.
11. For studies on *Honglou meng* sequels, see Widmer, "*Honglou Meng Ying*" and "*Honglou Meng* Sequels." On the Settlements' print market, see Wagner, "Ernest Major's Shenbaoguan." For the development of the Shanghai print market after the Taiping Rebellion, see Wagner, "Making of Shanghai."
12. Zou Tao, *Haishang chentian ying,* 432–55.
13. See Shimizu Kenichirō's study on reading preferences among Chinese middle-school students in the 1920s, "What Books Young People Loved Best."
14. On the popularity of *Dream* among women, see Giles, *Chinese Sketches,* 14; and Widmer, "*Honglou Meng* Sequels."
15. Bamboo twig ballads provide good evidence on the city's reputation and the courtesans' role in motivating people to visit Shanghai. See, for example, the pieces selected from Liu Mengyin's *Jiang Hu zayong,* published in 1889. In his introduction to this group of poems on Shanghai, he asserts that, because of "the reputation of Shanghai as the most prosperous and stunning place under Heaven, I made a visit to my uncle and stayed for three months" (455–56).
16. See McMahon, "Fleecing the Male Customer."
17. See Shaoxi Mozhuang Zhuren, "Hubei zhuzhi ci."

18. Ibid.

19. On Hu Baoyu traveling to Hankow in men's clothes, see Wang Liaoweng, *Shanghai liushi nian huajie shi,* 35.

20. Qin, "Huile Li" (Huile Alley), in *Xinmin wanbao,* March 3, 1996, 8.

21. Wang Tao, *Haizou yeyou fulu,* 5758–59.

22. Ibid., 5753–58; "Benguan chongkai huabang qi" (Notice of our paper reopening the competition among the flowers), *Youxi bao,* July 16, 1898, 1; "Jin Cishi hu tou zijian shu" (Jin Cishi [courtesan] suddenly put in a vote for herself), *Youxi bao,* Nov. 6, 1897, 2; and Huang Shiquan, *Songnan mengying lu,* 138. For records of courtesan competitions, see Chen Wuwo, *Lao Shanghai sanshi nian jianwen lu,* 139–229.

23. Chen Dingshan, *Chunshen jiuwen,* 105.

24. Wang Tao, *"Haizou yeyou" fulu,* 5720. On newspaper reports regarding Huang Yushang, Li Qiaolin, and the Daguan Yuan theater, see "Pofu qiangwu" (A virago robber), *Shenbao,* Nov. 11, 1878, 2.

25. Huang Shiquan, *Songnan mengying lu,* 133–34.

26. "Li Qiaoxian ji Sun Shaojiang."

27. Zou Tao, *Haishang chentian ying,* 439–42.

28. Hanshang Mengren, *Fengyue meng,* 32.

29. On dramas and novels based on *Dream of the Red Chamber,* see A Ying, *"Honglou meng" shulu,* 320–403.

30. "Lun jinjin nannü fushi zhi yi" (On the strange clothing worn by men and women nowadays), *Zhinan bao,* June 17, 1897, 1; "Funü jingchuan majia yaoyan" (Women competing to dazzle the eye by wearing *majia*), *Tuhua ribao,* no. 93, 7 (1909). Both articles point out that courtesans were responsible for the fashion of wearing opera costumes. See also *Huaying jixuan.*

31. "Funü dongling yi chuan xiezi zhi jiaojian" (The vigorous stride of women wearing boots this winter), *Tuhua ribao,* no. 133, 7 (1909). This fashion was an imitation of an earlier courtesan style. On courtesans of the late Qing wearing men's boots, see *Huaying jixuan.*

32. For articles on Shanghai courtesans appearing in public in men's clothing, see "Yuanxiao xiongfei" and "Nü ban nanzhuang" (Woman disguised in men's clothing), *Youxi bao,* Sept. 20, 1897, 2. For the posture of courtesans in male dress, see *Huaying jixuan.* Also see Catherine Yeh, "A Taste of the Exotic West."

33. Huang Shiquan, *Songnan mengying lu,* 105.

34. A law of July 14, 1578, banned courtesans in Venice from dressing up in men's clothes, a practice that was reportedly popular with the most famous of Venetian courtesans. See Poli, "La Cortigiane e la Moda," 100.

35. Li Boyuan, "Benguan qianju Si Malu shuo" (On moving our office to Fourth Avenue), *Youxi bao,* Oct. 2, 1897, 1.

36. Literary and pictorial works often illustrate the interior decoration of courtesan quarters. See, for example, *Jingying xiaosheng chuji,* 3, 7, 27, 34, 47; Wu Youru, *Haishang baiyan tu,* set 3a: 4, 8, 14, 15, and set 3b: 14, 17, 20, 22; Wu Youru, "Fengsu zhi tushuo," set 10b: 9; and Huayu Xiaozhu Zhuren, *Haishang qinglou tuji,* 3:2.

37. "Lin Daiyu chong lian yu yingwu" (Lin Daiyu talks to her parrot with the blinds down), *Youxi bao,* June 23, 1899, 2.

38. Photographs taken in studios are dictated to a certain degree by the props available on location. Nonetheless, the photos show almost no duplication of settings, and one may assume that the courtesans had a say in the selection of props.

39. Cao Xueqin, *Honglou meng,* chapter 12. Not surprisingly, none of the courtesans took the name of this woman, Wang Xifeng.

40. Ibid., 572–73.

41. For descriptions and illustrations of mirrors in courtesan houses, see Langyouzi,

Haishang yanhua suoji, juan 4: 7; Huayu Xiaozhu Zhuren, *Haishang qinglou tuji*, 3:21, 5:8; *Jingying xiaosheng chuji*, 27; and Meihua'an Zhu, *Shenjiang shixia shengjing tushuo*, 2:12.

42. Xiaolantian Chanqing Shizhe, *Haishang qunfang pu*, 4:19.

43. For a study of illustrations of *Dream of the Red Chamber*, see A Ying, *"Honglou meng" banhua ji*.

44. For a study of these illustrations, see Catherine Yeh, "Creating the Urban Beauty."

45. See Haishang Baoyu Sheng, *Huajian yingtie*; and Hanshang Mengren, *Fengyue meng*, 77–85.

46. Hanshang Mengren, *Fengyue meng*, 49.

47. For details, see, for example, "Zhaolu laigao" (Publication of contributions to the paper), *Youxi bao*, Feb. 10, 1903, 2; and Huang Shiquan, *Songnan mengying lu*, 146. On these anthologies, see "Haishang minghua chidu," 2–3; and "Li Pingxiang chu shiji" (Li Pingxiang is coming out with a poetry anthology), *Shijie fanhua bao*, May 5, 1901, 1.

48. See Huang Shiquan, *Songnan mengying lu*, 146.

49. Ibid., 146–47.

50. Huang Shiquan, *Songnan mengying lu*, 108.

51. Liangxi Banchisheng, *Hushang pinghua xulu*, 5.

52. Dong Lang was a Tang poet known for his writings about the inevitable, tragic separation of the courtesan and her lover.

53. Hushang Youxizhu, *Haishang youxi tushuo*, 1:2b.

54. Qixia and Danru, *Haishanghua yinglu, erji*, after the entry "Qin Yu."

55. Bamboo twig ballads on Shanghai often are signed with pen names that pun on the name Jia Baoyu. For example, in *Shanghai News* (Shanghai xinbao), March 31, 1870, a long *zhuzhi ci* signed with the name of Baoyu compares scenes in Shanghai to scenes in *Dream of the Red Chamber*.

56. Zou Tao, *Machi lu*, 1.

57. Huang Shiquan, *Songnan mengying lu*, 133–134.

58. Zou Tao, *Machi lu*, 1.

59. The reference, *Xie nü*, is unclear but probably means a literate woman from the Xie family who had become a courtesan, such as Xie Daoyun; quoted by Xu Wei in Morohashi Tetsuji, *Dai-Kanwa Jiten* (Great Chinese-Japanese dictionary) (Tokyo: Taishūkan, 1955–60), 13 vols., 35827.172.

60. Zhan Kai, "Su Yunlan, Xie Sanbao hezhuan."

61. Huang Shiquan, *Songnan mengying lu*, 133–34.

62. Zou Tao, *Machi lu*, 3.

63. Yunshui Sanren, "Xie Tianxiang xiaozhuan."

64. For the concept of cultural capital, see Bourdieu, *Field of Cultural Production*, 29–144.

65. Many late Qing novels on courtesans have scenes with such games. See, for example, Zou Tao's *Haishang chentian ying*, in which poetry is written in the style of *Dream* (407), and card games from *Dream* are played (547). There are also fireworks based on the *Dream* motif (430).

66. Zou Tao, *Haishang chentian ying*, 433–40.

67. See *Honglou yexi pu*, 5641; Zou Tao, *Haishang chentian ying*, 548–62; and Wang Tao, *"Haizou yeyou" fulu*, 5753, 5756.

68. Wang Shucun, *Minjian zhenpin tushuo "Honglou meng,"* 102–3.

69. Ibid.

70. *"Honglou meng" gongshi*, 16b.

71. See *Chishuo si zhong*.

72. For the concept of "entering the realm of dreams" as a metaphor for entering Shanghai, see "Xu" (Introduction), in *Shenjiang mingsheng tushuo*. For Shanghai as the world's playground, see untitled introduction in Hushang Youxizhu, *Haishang youxi tushuo*.

73. Walter Benjamin, "Paris, Capital of the Nineteenth Century," 146–47.

74. Zou Tao, *Haishang chentian ying*, 707. For studies on early images of balloons and other scientific inventions in late Qing novels, see David Der-wei Wang, "Chongdu *Dankou zhi*," 430–34.

75. Ge Yuanxu, *Hu you zaji*; Dianshizhai, *Shenjiang shengjing tu*; Meihua'an Zhu, *Shenjiang shixia shengjing tushuo.*

76. For example, *Record of Dream Images of Shanghai* (Songnan mengying lu), by Huang Shiquan; *Dream Images of Visits to Shanghai* (Hu you mengying), by Chi Zhicheng; and *Dreams of Shanghai's Glamour* (Haishang fanhua meng), by Sun Yusheng.

77. Zou Tao, *Haishang chentian ying*, 361–401.

78. Zou Tao, *Haishang chentian ying*, 340.

79. See Widmer, "*Honglou Meng* Sequels."

80. Yu Da, *Qinglou meng*, 263.

81. Wang Shucun, *Minjian zhenpin tushuo "Honglou meng,"* 36–37, 40–41.

82. Han Bangqing, "Lieyan" (Introduction), *Haishang hua liezhuan*, 3.

83. Wu Jianren, *Xin Shitou ji*. The work was first serialized in *Nanfang bao* in 1905 and published in book form in 1908. For studies on Wu Jianren and this novel, see David Der-wei Wang, *Fin-de-Siècle Splendor*, 271–74.

84. See Wagner, "Life as a Quote," 463–76, and "Die Biographie als Lebensprogramm," 133–42.

85. On *Dianshizhai Illustrated Magazine* as a source for social history, see Wang Ermin, "*Dianshizhai huabao* suo zhanxian zhi jindai lishi mailuo" and "Zhongguo jindai zhishi pujihua chuanbo zhi tushuo xingshi"; Li Xiaoti, "Jindai Shanghai chengshi wenhua zhong de chuantong yu xiandai"; Chen and Xia, *Dianshizhai*; and Ye Xiaoqing, *Dianshizhai Pictorial.*

Chapter 4. Image Makers

Some of the material in this chapter was previously published in Cathy Yeh, "The Life-Style of Four *wenren* in Late Qing Shanghai," *Harvard Journal of Asiatic Studies* 57, no. 2 (Dec. 1997), 419–70. The author thanks the editors of *Harvard Journal of Asiatic Studies* for permission to republish the material here.

1. The Foreign Ratepayers' Association and its Municipal Council established the rules for the International Settlement, and the French Municipal Council governed the French Settlement.

2. Wagner, "Role of the Foreign Community."

3. Xiong Yuezhi, *Xixue dongjian yu wan Qing shehui*, 350–91.

4. A Shanghai visitor to Beijing was shocked by the absence of any notion of "being on time" in that city; see Lu Feida, "Jing, Jin liang yue ji."

5. Zhuchuan Jushi, *Xu banqiao zaji*, 4919; Levy, "Feast of Mist and Flowers," 9–18.

6. For scholarship on nostalgia for late Ming courtesans, see Wei-Yee Li, "The Late Ming Courtesan"; Catherine Yeh, "Wenhua jiyi de fudan."

7. Yu Huai's book was published in 1654, after the Ming dynasty had collapsed. For studies and translation, see Levy, "Feast of Mist and Flowers"; Catherine Yeh, "Creating a Shanghai Identity," 106–10; Ropp, "Ambiguous Images of Courtesan Culture," 27–28; and Wei-Yee Li, "Late Ming Courtesan," 47–73.

8. On Yangzhou, see Penghua Sheng, *Huafang yutan*, and Fenlita Xingzhe, *Zhuxi huashi xiaolu*. On Suzhou, see Xixi Shanren, *Wumen huafang lu*. On Nanjing after the Taiping Rebellion, see Xu Yu, *Baimen xinliu ji*. On Chaozhou, see Yu Jiao, *Chaojia fengyue ji*.

9. Catherine Yeh, "Wenhua jiyi de fudan."

10. Tourist numbers are scarce, but guidebooks stating the frequency of inland and over-

seas transportation to Shanghai demonstrate that Shanghai had established itself as an attraction by the 1880s. For example, Ge Yuanxu wrote that, by 1873, "Shanghai has surpassed Canton and Hankow in attracting visitors. There are visitors from the eighteen Chinese provinces and from the twenty-four countries abroad" (*Hu you zaji*, 7). Ge gives timetables for travel by steamship to and from Shanghai: travel by steamship to Tianjin and Yantai, twice a week; to Niuzhuang, once a month; to Guangdong province, Hong Kong, Fuzhou, and Xiamen, at least twice a week, with ships of foreign companies going even more frequently; to Ningpo, daily, except Sunday; to Osaka, Nagasaki, and Kobe, every Wednesday; to Hankow and (towns on the) Yangtze River, daily. Judging from the destinations, many of the travelers might have belonged to the business community. Judging from the inland cities on the Yangtze to and from which shipping companies offered transportation, such as Zhenjiang, Nanjing, Wuhu, Datong, Qingan, Jiuzhou, and Wuxue, with the final destination at Hankow, it is likely that these routes also would bring considerable numbers of tourists to the city. Ge provides a separate list of shipping timetables for shipping companies owned by the British, Chinese, and French governments (76–77). The 1888 edition of the same guide, by Yuan Zuzhi, indicates that shipping companies were offering transport to even more locations. These now include Tongzhou, Jiangyin, Yizheng, Anqing, Huangshi Gang, Huangzhou, Wuzhou, Xiamen, and Shantou, and the number of ships given has increased; see Yuan Zuzhi, *Chongxiu Hu you zaji*, 4:7–10. Construction on the first railroad from Shanghai to other cities began in 1898, and travel from the north was faster. By the turn of the twentieth century, according to the Shangwu Yinshuguan guide of 1909, travelers to Shanghai numbered from ten thousand to twenty thousand per day, and the guide's list of available transportation is lengthy (6:1–14). As for overseas visitors, the Reverend C. E. Darwent wrote in 1903: "The need of a guide to Shanghai has been felt for a long time. Numerous inquiries have been made for one both by new residents and tourists, who since the Boxer outbreak in 1900, have visited Shanghai in increasing numbers. The days for passing direct from Hongkong to Japan are gone by, and the growing popularity of the Siberian Railway, the service of which is but temporarily suspended, is likely to make Shanghai the starting-place for a large number of residents in the Far East, selecting that route for their return to Europe" (*Shanghai*, 1). With the Siberian Railway, the Japanese Mail Steamship Company, which began to operate between Yokohama and Shanghai in 1909, and European oceanliners to the Far East, the number of visitors to the city must have been considerable. Other sources for understanding tourism are diaries and brush notes, which record the activities of visitors to the city. On immigration, see Zou Yiren, *Jiu Shanghai renkou bianqian de yanjiu*.

11. Huang Shiquan, *Songnan mengying lu*, 126.

12. Henriot explores Wang Tao's extensive writings on Shanghai prostitution in "Chinese Courtesans," 36–49, and *Prostitution and Sexuality in Shanghai*, 21–82. See also Catherine Yeh, "Life-style of Four *Wenren*," 428–34.

13. Cohen, *Between Tradition and Modernity*, 22–23; Xin Ping, *Wang Tao pingzhuan*, 30.

14. McAleavy, *Wang Tao*, 5.

15. Ibid.

16. Li Shanlan (1810–1882), the famous mathematician who worked closely with missionaries of the London Missionary Society Press translating books of Western science, and Guan Sifu (?–1860), translator of Western medical writings, were among Wang Tao's friends at this time. For details, see Xiong, *Xixue dongjian yu wan Qing shehui*, 266–70.

17. Yu Xingmin, *Shanghai, 1862 nian*, 409, 416–19.

18. Wang Tao, *Yingruan zazhi*, 3.

19. Wang Tao, *Haizou yeyou lu*, 5637–40. For biographical data on Wang Tao, see "Wang Tao shiji kaolüe" (A study of the historical record on Wang Tao), in Shanghaitong she, *Shanghai yanjiu ziliao*, 679–89.

20. For a study on the early period of courtesan life in the walled city and afterward in the Settlements, see Henriot, "Chinese Courtesans."

21. For a detailed analysis, see Catherine Yeh, "Creating a Shanghai Identity."

22. Wang Tao, *Haizou yeyou lu*, 5633–84, *Haizou yeyou fulu*, 5685–5785, and *Haizou yeyou lu yulu*, 5787–5810.

23. Wang Tao, *Haizou yeyou lu*, 5639.

24. For a study of Wang Tao and his writings on courtesan entertainment in the walled city, see Henriot, *Prostitution and Sexuality in Shanghai*, 21–61.

25. Wang Tao, "Fu Liao Baoer xiaoji," 5667.

26. See Wang Tao, *Yingruan zazhi*, 97.

27. Wang Tao, "Mei Xiu er jiaoshu hezhuan," 15.

28. Ibid., 16.

29. Ibid.

30. Little has been published about Zou Tao's life and work. Much of his writing I have found only in the late Professor Wu Xiaoling's private collection, which he was generous enough to share with me. Zou's privately printed autobiography, *Jottings of an Old Horse* (Machi lu), a copy of which is in the Shanghai Municipal Library, provides precious new information about him. For accounts by his contemporaries, see Wang Tao's "*Haishang chentian ying* xu," his preface to Zou Tao's *Haishang chentian ying*. A short biography of Zou Tao is in Tan Wuren, *Wuxi xianzhi*, 1036–37.

31. The title *Illustrated Commentary on One Hundred Flowers of Shanghai* (Shanghai pinyan baihua tu) appears in a list of books about Shanghai courtesans and entertainment; see Shanghaitong She, *Shanghai yanjiu ziliao*, 583. The classification of courtesans in this book and the sequence in which their names are introduced match those of another work by Zou Tao, *Illustrated One Hundred Beauties of Suzhou* (Wumen baiyan tu). Although the pen names appearing in the 1880 edition of this work, Huaxia Jieren and Sixiang Jiuwei, are pseudonyms identified with Zou Tao, the foreword, which Zou Tao signed with his well-known pen name Sanjielu Zhuren, refers to the author of the work as a talented man from Suzhou who based the book on his experiences. According to Chen Ruheng, Yu Da is the real author of *Illustrated One Hundred Beauties of Suzhou* and also the author of the novel *Dream of the Green Tower* (Qinglou meng); see Chen Ruheng, *Xueyuan zhenwen*, 89. I have not been able to locate *You Hu biji* (Random notes on visiting Shanghai), a title listed on page 591 of *Shanghai yanjiu ziliao*. Most of Zou Tao's writings on courtesans appeared under the pen names Liangxi Xiaoxiangguan Shizhe, Shouhe or Shouhe Ciren, Huaxia Jieren, Sixiang Jiuwei, and Sanjielu Zhuren. Zou Tao's prefaces are in Liangxi Chilian Jushi, *Hushang pinghua lu* and *Hujiang yanpu*. Also among his publications are *Jottings from the Sanjie Hut* (Sanjielu bitan) and *Anthology of Drowning One's Sorrows [Illustrated]* ([Huitu] Jiaochou ji). He wrote one novel, *The Shadows of Heaven and Earth in Shanghai* (Haishang chentian ying). He also authored political treatises, *A Study of Contemporary International Politics* (Wanguo jinzheng kaolüe) and *Brazen Words in Favor of Learning from the West* (Yangwu zuiyan); see his *Machi lu*, 3, and *Haishang chentian ying*, 3.

32. Zou Tao, *Chunjiang huashi*, 1.

33. For a short history of *News of Benefit* (1879–99), see Ma Guangren, *Shanghai xinwen shi*, 54–55.

34. Tan Wuren, *Wuxi xianzhi*, 1037.

35. It is very difficult to verify A Ying's assertions since all writers who contributed to *The Universe* used pseudonyms. For A Ying, see his *Wan Qing wenyi baokan shulüe*, 7; for a study on *The Universe*, see Wagner, "Ernest Major," 34–37.

36. For Huang Shiquan's connection to *News of Benefit*, see Ma Guangren, *Shanghai xinwen shi*, 56. For a study on Huang Shiquan, see Janku, *Nur leere Reden*, 33–43.

37. Zou Tao, "Dushu zhi nan" (The difficulty of getting an education), in *Sanjielu bitan*, 11:2 (6031).

38. Zou Tao, *Machi lu*, 1.

39. Wang Tao, "*Haishang chentian ying* xu," 1–3. For an independent account from another friend, see Zhan Kai, "Su Yunlan, Xie Sanbao hezhuan."

40. Wang Tao, *"Haizou yeyou" yulu,* 5807–8.

41. Huang Shiquan, *Songnan mengying lu,* 136.

42. Ibid., 126, 133–34, 136, 147.

43. I have not been able to locate *Anecdotes on Courtesan Rituals.*

44. Zou Tao, *Chunjiang huashi,* 1:3–4. Zou Tao's poems dedicated to the Shanghai courtesan are found in many sources. For example, *Shanghai's Prosperity Illustrated* (Haishang fanhua tu) recorded his poem dedicated to the famous courtesan Li Sansan (Li Sansan: 2), and his *Jottings from the Sanjie Hut* is composed almost entirely of such poems.

45. Zou Tao, *Chunjiang huashi,* 1: 14–15.

46. During the early years of the Republican era, Zou Tao continued to be active in the literary realm. His "Shouhe suibi" was published in 1918 and, under the pen name Li Tian Lou, he published "Litianlou cuotan," in *The Literary Monthly* (Xiaoshuo yuebao); see Chen Yutang, *Zhongguo jinxiandai renwu minghao da cidian,* 394.

47. For a general introduction to bamboo twig ballads, see Lei Mengshui, *Zhonghua zhuzhi ci,* 1–5.

48. Yang Jingting, "Preface to 'Zayong.'"

49. For a study of Shanghai identity and bamboo twig ballads, see Mittler, *A Newspaper for China?* 322–30.

50. *Shenbao* began publishing poetry in its second issue (April 30, 1872) and ended this tradition because of lack of space in March 21, 1890. For details on this paper's role in promoting literature, see Wagner, "China's First Literary Journals"; and Chen and Yuan, *Shanghai jindai wenxue shi,* 118–20.

51. For example, "Ten Views of the Foreign Settlements of Shanghai," *The Shanghai Evening Courier,* August 31, 1874.

52. The term "Yangchang" was widely used to refer to the Shanghai Foreign Settlements from the 1870s onward; see, for example, Ge Yuanxu, *Hu you zaji,* 7. A very rich collection of such ballads is Gu Bingquan, *Shanghai Yangchang zhuzhi ci,* with nearly four thousand poems.

53. Yunjian Yishi, "Yangchang zhuzhi ci."

54. "Hushang qinglou zhuzhi ci," 431–32.

55. Huang Shiquan, *Songnan mengying lu,* 131.

56. There are two conflicting statements on this issue. Xue Liyong claims that Yuan remained in the Settlements after the Small Sword Uprising; see *Shanghai jinü shi,* 139–40. According to Xu Gongshi, however, Yuan lived in the walled city until he built his house on Fuzhou Road in 1881; see "Xu," 5.

57. Later in his life, between 1893 and 1896, Yuan became an editor for another paper, *The News* (Xinwen bao), which at the time was owned by the American Calvin Ferguson (1866–1945). By then, Yuan was in his seventies and was compiling his own literary anthology, *The Complete Works of Suiyuan* (Suiyuan quanji). Because of his busy schedule, he made many mistakes in his lead articles, which the paper later had to retract. Sun Yusheng, who was to become one of Shanghai's best-known newspaper and fiction writers, recalled that he had to rewrite many of Yuan's articles; see his "Cangshan jiuzhu yishi."

58. Zou Tao, *Sanjielu bitan,* 1:10. According to Sun Yusheng, the name came from a beautiful willow tree on the grounds where the house was built; see *Tuixinglu biji,* 30–31.

59. Chen Wuwo, "Yangliu loutai."

60. Chen Wuwo, *Lao Shanghai sanshi nian jianwen lu,* 162.

61. Yuan published most of his bamboo twig ballads and a collection of rhymed couplets in the 1888 *Chongxiu hu you zaji.*

62. During the same period, a Japanese geisha named Sansan or Shanshan lived in

Shanghai, and Yuan Zuzhi also dedicated poems to her; see Huang Shiquan, *Songnan mengying lu*, 128.

63. Zou Tao, *Chunjiang huashi*, 6.

64. Xiaolantian Chanqing Shizhe, *Haishang qunfang pu*, 1:6–9.

65. Huang Shiquan, *Songnan mengying lu*, 128; Xiaolantian Chanqing Shizhe, *Chongding Haishang qunfang pu*, 1:7; Zou Tao, *Chunjiang huashi*, 1:6.

66. Liangxi Chilian Jushi, *Hujiang yanpu*, appendix, 1; Xue Liyong, *Shanghai jinü shi*, 139. According to Wang Liaoweng, a young and rather uneducated merchant's son became enamored of Li Sansan and paid a huge sum for his first night with her. She eventually taught him literary arts. After the jealous son of another merchant shot her lover with a handgun, she refused to eat and then hanged herself. See Wang Liaoweng, *Shanghai liushi nian huajie shi*, 35–39.

67. Yuan Zuzhi, untitled *zhuzhi ci*, in Xiaolantian Chanqing Shizhe, *Chongding Haishang qunfang pu*, 1:7–8.

68. Huang Shiquan, *Songnan mengying lu*, 126.

69. Chen Wuwo, *Lao Shanghai sanshi nian jianwen lu*, 204–6.

70. Yuan Zuzhi, *Shanghai ganshi shi*; here, Yuan Zuzhi acknowledges his authorship for the first time by signing with his studio name.

71. For studies on *yuefu* poetry, see Kiyohide Masuda, *Gakufu no rekishiteki kenkyū*.

72. Gu Bingquan, *Shanghai Yangchang zhuzhi ci*, 461.

73. See Catherine Yeh, "Creating the Urban Beauty."

74. Wagner, "Role of the Foreign Community"; Kim, "New Wine in Old Bottles."

75. For a short history of the development of the Chinese illustrated magazine, see A Ying, "Zhongguo huabao fazhan zhi jingguo"; for studies on *Dianshizhai Illustrated Magazine* and Wu Youru and the immense influence the journal had on the development of Chinese illustrated magazines, see Yu Yueting, "Woguo huabao de shizu"; Wagner, "Jinru quanqiu xiangxiang tujing: Shanghai de Dianshizhai huabao"; and for a study of social life reflected in *Dianshizhai Illustrated Magazine*, see Ye Xiaoqing, *Dianshizhai Pictorial*.

76. Wagner, "Jinru quanqiu xiangxiang tujing."

77. For example, *Shenbao* reported in detail on a public fight between the courtesan stars Hu Baoyu and Li Qiaolin; see "Pofu qiangwu." Entries on courtesans ranged from enthused poems to sentimental biographies and to sympathetic reports on their fate but also included reports of their haughty arrogance, lack of feeling, and faithlessness.

78. *Entertainment* was published from 1897 to around 1910, and *World Vanity Fair* from 1901 to 1910. For studies on Li Boyuan and the *xiaobao*, see A Ying, *Wan Qing wenyi baokan shulüe*, 55–61; Wei Shaochang, *Li Boyuan yanjiu ziliao*, 450–59; and Zhu Junzhou, "Shanghai xiaobao de lishi yange."

79. *A Pair of Phoenixes Takes Off* (Feng shuang fei), by Cheng Huiying, was written between the late eighteenth and early nineteenth centuries. It remained in manuscript form until it was published in *Entertainment* as a single sheet that was included free of charge with the paper; see Li Boyuan, "Benbao fusong *Feng shuang fei* changben yuanqi."

80. Other novels of this type include *The Bureaucrats: A Revelation* (Guanchang xianxing ji), published in 1903, and *A Ballad on the National Crisis of 1900* (Gengzi guobian tanci), published in 1901. Li Boyuan also published novels by his colleagues, such as Wu Jianren's *Confused World* (Hutu shijie), in 1906.

81. *The Guide* was founded on June 6, 1896, and closed in the fall of 1897. For details, see Zhu Junzhou, "Shanghai xiaobao de lishi yange," 42 (1988): 163–67 and "Li Boyuan yu *Zhinan bao*."

82. Li Boyuan, "Chuangkan ci" (Opening words), *Zhinan bao*, June 6, 1896.

83. Li Boyuan, "Lun *Youxi bao* zhi benyi" (On the basic purpose of *Entertainment*), *Youxi bao*, August 25, 1897.

84. Li Boyuan, "Ji benbao kaichuang yilai qingxing" (On the situation of our newspaper since the time of its creation). Some papers reported on Li Boyuan's socializing with Western and Japanese friends. See, for example, "Lun Hubin shuyu yingchou dangyi Lu Lanfen wei diyi" (Lu Lanfen should be considered Shanghai's number one in the art of entertaining guests), *Youxi bao*, Sept. 18, 1897; and "Mianzhi shoujiu" (Holding on to old customs), *Youxi bao*, June 22, 1899, 2.

85. For examples, see "Zheng ming" (Correction [in regard to] reputation), *Youxi bao*, Sept. 21, 1898, 3; and "Gengzheng fangming" (Correction [regarding the writing of a] name), *Youxi bao*, Oct. 11, 1898, 3. The first case involved misinformation about a Shanghai courtesan who was happily married, and the second was a misspelling of the courtesan's name.

86. This address of Li Boyuan's home is based on information from Li Xiqi, who had been there; see *Nanting huiyi lu*, 1.59. Zhang Yilu and Wei Shaochang, however, place the office at Da Malu; see Wei Shaochang, *Li Boyuan yanjiu ziliao*, 15.

87. Li Xiqi, *Nanting huiyi lu*, 64; Cheng Bi, "Xiaoshuojia Li Boyuan," 41.

88. Cheng Bi, "Xiaoshuojia Li Boyuan," 41.

89. Li Boyuan advertised for a journalist to join him and work in the English section of town; see Li Boyuan, "Zhaoxun fangshi ren."

90. See the announcement for the literary society and its newspaper in *Youxi bao*, Nov. 10 and 11, 1; also see Zhang Yilu, "Li Boyuan yishi," 14–15.

91. From 1903 to 1906, Li Boyuan was also editor of the literary journal *The Illustrated Novel* (Xiuxiang xiaoshuo), published by the Commercial Press, in which he serialized several of his political novels.

92. Li Boyuan, "Youxi zhuren gaobai"(Announcement from the Master of Entertainment), *Youxi bao*, March 19, 1899, 1.

93. Zheng Yimei, "Nanting tingzhang."

94. Wei Shaochang, *Li Boyuan yanjiu ziliao*, 7–8.

95. See ibid., 490–91.

96. Ibid., 91.

97. Wei Shaochang first questioned the assumption that Li Boyuan was the author of *Traces of the Past*. For recent scholarship on the subject, see Zhu Junzhou, "Li Boyuan zhongyao yiwen."

98. See Wei Shaochang, 491–92.

99. See Li Boyuan, "Benguan qianju Si Malu shuo" (On moving our office to Fourth Avenue), *Youxi bao*, Oct. 2, 1897, 1; and "Bugao fang you" (An announcement to a journalist friend), *Youxi bao*, Oct. 31, 1897, 1.

100. Pang Shubo, *Hongzhi shi xiaolu*, 522. Some of Li Pingxiang's poems were also published after she returned to Shanghai; see, for example, *Shijie fanhua bao*, Sept. 5, 1906.

101. "Benguan te kai huacong Jingji teke gaobai" (An announcement of our paper holding a Special Competition with Focus on Management of State Affairs among the flowers), *Shijie fanhua bao*, June 30, 1901, 1. The results were published three months later, "Te kai huacong Jingji teke bang" (A "Special Competition with Focus on Management of State Affairs" among the flowers), *Shijie fanhua bao*, Sept. 27, 1901, 2.

102. See Wei Shaochang, *Li Boyuan yanjiu ziliao*, 522. On stories regarding Li Pingxiang, see Chen Boxi, *Lao Shanghai*, 109–10; and Qixia and Danru, *Haishang hua yinglu*, vol. 2. See also Hershatter, *Dangerous Pleasures*, 153–57.

103. Hershatter quotes from a 1920s edition of this volume, but according to the advertisement published in *World Vanity Fair*, the collection was first published in 1906. For a translation of some of the poems, see *Dangerous Pleasures*, 154–55.

104. "Lun Li Pingxiang bei ju shi" (On Li Pingxiang being detained by the court), *Shijie fanhua bao*, Dec. 7, 1901, 1.

105. Li Pingxiang bei ju ji guotang xiangzhi" (A detailed report on the arrest and trial of

Li Pingxiang), *Shijie fanhua bao,* Dec. 7, 1901, 2–3; "Li Pingxiang an jie" (The conclusion of the case against Li Pingxiang), ibid., Dec. 8, 1901, 1.

106. "Song Li Pingxiang gui Jiahe xu" (Introduction to Farewell to Li Pingxiang upon her return to Jiahe), *Shijie fanhua bao,* Dec. 9, 1901.

107. Catherine Yeh, "A Public Love Affair," 32–36.

108. "Li Pingxiang an jie" (The conclusion of the case against Li Pingxiang), *Shijie fanhua bao,* Dec. 8, 1901, 1.

109. "Li Pingxiang A Pan jieyuan" (Li Pingxiang's entanglement with A Pan), ibid., Dec. 10, 1901, 2.

110. There have been many versions of Li Pingxiang's life; for a recent study, see Hershatter, *Dangerous Pleasures,* 153–57.

111. Lu Xun, *Zhongguo xiaoshuo shilüe,* 236–68; David Der-wei Wang, *Fin-de-Siècle Splendor,* chapter 2; Alexander Des Forges, *Street Talk and Alley Stories.*

112. See Bernheimer, *Figures of Ill Repute.*

113. *Dreams of Shanghai's Glamour* was published under the pen name Sun was using at the time, Gu Hu Jingmeng Chixian. Later, he was mostly known under the pen name Haishang Shushi Sheng. His actual name was Sun Jiazhen.

114. Sun Yusheng's "Baohai qianchen lu" provides much information on the history of early Chinese newspapers.

115. Sun Yusheng, "Li Boyuan."

116. Wang Tao's *Miscellaneous Records of a Shanghai Recluse* was serialized in *Dianshizhai Illustrated Magazine,* issues 6–122 (late June 1884–mid-October 1887). See Wagner, "Joining the Global Imaginaire."

117. The novel was first serialized in *Caifeng bao* from July 27, 1898, and continued in *Xiaolin bao* from 1901 to 1902. The first book edition was published by Xiaolin Bao Guan in 1903, under the pseudonym Gu Hu Jingmeng Chixian. Sun Yusheng went on to write the sequel *Dreams of Shanghai's Glamour, Sequel* (Haishang fanhua xu meng), which was serialized in *Tuhua ribao* from 1909 to 1910.

118. Patrick Hanan has identified the original English-language version of the novel; see "The First Novel Translated into Chinese," 85–86.

119. See Catherine Yeh, "Zeng Pu's *Niehai hua,*" 195–99; Bernal, *Chinese Socialism to 1907,* 24; Nakamura, "Shinmatsu tantei shōsetsu shikō," 4:390. Serialized publication of nonfiction texts was also common in newspapers and periodicals beginning in the early 1870s.

120. David Der-wei Wang describes this group of novels as the harbingers of modernity; *Fin-de-Siècle Splendor,* 23–27.

121. Fu Xiangyuan, *"Da shijie" shihua,* 4.

122. For an initial study on *The Great World Daily News,* see Catherine Yeh, "Deciphering the Entertainment Press 1896–1920."

123. On this development, see Wagner, "The Making of Shanghai." It should be added that Shanghai was also the greenhouse and laboratory where most innovations in education were tried out and adapted; this created more important employment opportunities for men of letters.

Chapter 5. The Public Flower of the City

1. According to A Ying, about thirty-two titles can strictly be considered *xiaobao,* but according to Li Boyuan, there were about sixty; see A Ying, *Wan Qing wenyi baokan shulüe,* 51–52. Zhu Junzhou estimates the number at about forty; see "Shanghai xiaobao de lishi yange," 42 (1988): 164.

2. Examples of *xiaobao* include *Mirth* (Xiaobao), 1897; *Leisure* (Xiaoxian bao), 1897; *Fashions of the Day* (Caifeng bao), 1898; *The Entertainer* (Qubao), 1898; *Shanghai Courtesan Entertainment*

Daily (Chunjiang huayue bao), 1901–4; *Be Happy Now* (Jishi xingle bao), 1901; *Joke Forest* (Xiaolin bao), 1901; *Flower Heaven Daily* (Huatian ribao), 1902; and *The World of Flowers* (Hua shijie), 1903. Most of these *xiaobao* were published by major dailies; for example, *Joke Forest* belonged to *Shanghai East and West* (Zhongxi hubao) and *Leisure* to *Shanghai Chinese Paper* (Zilin hubao). Many were short-lived efforts, and only a few managed to be successful for a longer stretch of time. These successful papers, among which Li Boyuan's two papers stand out, are also the best preserved, while little more than the titles of the others survives.

3. On circulation numbers for *Youxi bao*, see *Youxi bao*, Oct. 4, 1897, 1.

4. Two articles on the increase in sales, both titled "Tianshe jingshou bao chu" (On establishing more sales locations for the paper), appeared in *Entertainment* in November 10 and 11, 1897.

5. See Li Boyuan, "Benguan qianju Si Malu shuo" (On moving our office to Fourth Avenue), *Youxi bao*, Oct. 2, 1897, 1; and "Lu *Tiannan xin bao* lun Shanghai Si Da Jin'gang" (Reprint from *Tiannan xinbao* [paper published in Singapore] on the Four Great Golden Diamond Cutters of Shanghai"), *Youxi bao*, May 28, 1899, 1.

6. *Kyoto Flower* (Miyako no hana) was first published in Meiji 30 (1898); it was the supplement to *Kyoto News* (Miyako shinbun). *Kyoto Flower* focused on the world of entertainment, with the courtesans and actors as central figures, and contained news, gossip, and writing on fashion.

7. There are many accounts of the lives of Hu Baoyu and Li Sansan in late Qing Shanghai courtesan guides. On Hu Baoyu, see, for example Wang Tao, *"Haizou yeyou" fulu*, 5750. On Li Sansan, see Huang Shiquan, *Songnan mengying lu*, 128. Both were fictionalized in numerous late Qing novels such as Lao Shanghai, *Hu Baoyu* and Jiang Ruizao, *Xiaoshuo kaozheng*. Li Sansan was one of the characters in Chousi Zhuren, *Haishang mingji Si Da Jin'gang zhuan qishu*.

8. "You Zhang Yuan 'Si Da Jin'gang'" (The "Four Great Golden Diamond Cutters" visit the Zhang Garden), *Youxi bao*, Oct. 12, 1897, 2.

9. In later historical stories on the Four Great Golden Diamond Cutters, Jin Xiaobao's appurtenance was in dispute. She was said to have been too young to have belonged to this august group, but judging from *Entertainment*, there is no doubt that she was the fourth Golden Diamond Cutter. There are numerous biographies, anecdotes, legends, and newspaper articles on the four courtesan stars from the late Qing onward. See, for example, Wang Liaoweng, *Shanghai liushi nian huajie shi*, 56–57; Chen Wuwo, *Lao Shanghai sanshi nian jianwen lu*, 28; and Sun Yusheng, *Tuixinglu biji*, 148–49. For studies on the Si Da Jin'gang, see Shanghaishi Wenshiguan, *Jiu Shanghai de yan du chang*, 167–68; Hershatter, *Dangerous Pleasures*, 169–71.

10. "Xuange dai bu" (An open position awaits refilling), *Youxi bao*, June 18, 1899, 2. The holdings of the Shanghai Municipal Library are missing copies of the first days of the paper, including the date when the first article mentioned in this extract appeared.

11. "Niju Shanghai piaoke Si Da Jin'gang shuo" (On the proposal of recommending the Four Great Golden Diamond Cutters among the Shanghai clients of courtesans), *Youxi bao*, July 15, 1899, 1.

12. Ibid.

13. See Janku, *Nur leere Reden*, 147–203.

14. The opera, titled *The Four Great Golden Diamond Cutters* (Si Da Jin'gang), was being rehearsed at the Mantingfang theater in the Shanghai International Settlement in 1898, but the performance was banned by Chinese officials in Shanghai County; see "Haishang fanhua" (Shanghai prosperity), *Youxi bao*, Sept. 21, 1898, 2. The novel is *The Four Great Golden Diamond Cutters from Shanghai* (Haishang mingji Si Da Jin'gang zhuan qishu), by Chousi Zhuren.

15. "Saima shuo" (On the horse race), *Youxi bao*, May 1, 1899, 1.

16. "Jingzhuang zhaoyan" (Rich attire dazzles the eye), *Youxi bao*, May 4, 1899, 2.

17. "Xili yiqian babai jiushijiu nian Shanghai chunsai disan zhi" (Third report on Shanghai's spring races of 1899), *Youxi bao*, May 5, 1899, 2.

18. "Sai xianghao" (Competition in patrons), *Youxi bao*, May 5, 1899, 2.

19. There is evidence of the relationship between Li Boyuan and Ouyang Juyuan and the four courtesan stars. For example, they all attended the meeting to create the Flower Cemetery; see Chen Wuwo, *Lao Shanghai sanshi nian jianwen lu*, 106–8. Li Boyuan also offered Lin Daiyu advice against going to Tianjin in 1900; see Lin Daiyu, *Beinan shimo ji*, 1b–2a. Li Boyuan's admiration for Jin Xiaobao is evident in the articles published in *Entertainment* during the creation of the Flower Cemetery between late 1898 and early 1899. Last, but not least, it was said that Ouyang had an affair with Lin Daiyu; see Wuli Kanhua Ke, *Zhenzheng lao Lin Daiyu*, quoted in Wei Shaochang, *Li Boyuan yanjiu ziliao*, 519.

20. See, for example, "Youyuan zaji" (Miscellanea on visiting the gardens), *Shijie fanhua bao*, Oct. 17, 1901, 2.

21. Chousi Zhuren, *Haishang mingji Si Da Jin'gang zhuan qishu*, *juan* 4: 3, 17–18. The term *mingji* is an old term for famous courtesans; its use in this context, however, changes its meaning. Their fame had previously been restricted to a small circle but had spread to the broader newspaper-reading public. The term *mingxing*, with its "star" metaphor, came two decades later with the Hollywood concept of the film star. In order to denote this public recognition, the novel's title uses the term *shixia* (fashionable).

22. "Lao bianxiang" (Transformation at old age), *Youxi bao*, March 7, 1899, 3.

23. The term *jin men* (entering the household) has an interesting range of meaning. The same term is used for marrying into a household and for a courtesan joining a courtesan establishment.

24. *Zhujia* refers to exclusive high-class courtesan establishments, which normally do not have business signs at their doors; see Langyouzi, *Haishang yanhua suoji*, *juan* 1: 1.

25. "Haishang kanhua riji" (Daily notes on flower viewing in Shanghai), *Shijie fanhua bao*, Oct. 1, 1901, 2.

26. Zhu Ruchun remained active in courtesan entertainment; after the founding of the Republic, she joined with other courtesan stars, including Lin Daiyu, and set up the Qinglou Jinhua Tuan as a school to educate young courtesans. See Wang Liaoweng, *Shanghai liushi nian huajie shi*, 156–57.

27. Li Boyuan, "Youxi Zhuren ni juxing 'Linfang hui' yi" (Comments on the "Beauty Selection Conference" planned by the Master of Entertainment), *Youxi bao*, Oct. 4, 1897, 1.

28. In the 1910s, Shanghai courtesan competitions employed Republican political terms such as "president" and "prime minister" for competition categories. See Chen Boxi, *Lao Shanghai*, 410; and Hershatter, *Dangerous Pleasures*, 171–74.

29. Li Boyuan, "Youxi Zhuren ni juxing 'Linfang hui' yi" (Comments on the "Beauty Selection Conference" planned by the Master of Entertainment), *Youxi bao*, Oct. 4, 1897, 1.

30. Early in the Qing, in 1656, a Suzhou scholar who dared to hold a flower competition in the style of the imperial examinations and gave the winners titles such as *zhuangyuan* or *bangyan* was publicly lashed to death; see Wang Shunu, *Zhongguo changji shi*, 311.

31. For an example of a "competition among flowers" during the Ming period, see Li Yunxiang, *Jinling baimei*; for a short description of flower competitions during the Qing period, see Wang Shunu, *Zhongguo changji shi*, 311–12.

32. See, for example, Liangxi Chilian Jushi, *Hushang pinghua lu*.

33. See, for example, Zou Tao, *Wumen baiyan tu*.

34. Some accounts in recent scholarship are based on incorrect or unverifiable assertions. For example, Ping Jinya, in "Jiu Shanghai de changji," states that the winners of the 1897 *Entertainment* courtesan competition were the four top-ranking courtesans Lin, Lu, Zhang, and Jin (166), yet *Entertainment*'s actual reports give the winners as Zhang Sibao, Jin Xiaobao, and Zhu Ruchun. Xue Liyong's study on the Shanghai flower competition quotes Ping Jinya's inaccurate statements and also adds some of his own, such as referring to the winner of the 1877 competition, Li Peilan, as Zhu Peilan; see *Shanghai jinü shi*, 150–58, 133–36, 149. Gail Hershatter erroneously equates the 1897 event with previous flower com-

petitions although the 1897 competition was unique in that voting took place; see *Dangerous Pleasures*, 165.

35. Wang Tao, *Songbin suohua*, 87, and *Haizou yeyou fulu*, 5753–63; also see Hua'elouzhu, "Huadi cangsang lu," in *Xinsheng* 2 (1921):1.

36. Wang Tao, *"Haizou yeyou" fulu*, 5719–20. See also Wang Liaoweng, *Shanghai liushi nian huajie shi*, 77–79; and Henriot, *Prostitution and Sexuality in Shanghai*, 65.

37. Wang Tao, *"Haizou yeyou" fulu*, 5753–58.

38. Ibid., 5753. For more details on Li Peilan, see Huang Shiquan, *Songnan mengying lu*, 107–8.

39. Examples from earlier competitions are books such as *Meeting of the Immortals on the Lotus Platform in Nanjing* (Jinling lianhuatai xianhui), Wanli 19 (i.e., 1591). See Wang Shunu, *Zhongguo changji shi*, 199; Li Yunxiang, *Jinling baimei*; and *Wu ji baimei*. For the use of the term *huachao* for a courtesan competition, see Wang Shunu, *Zhongguo changji shi*, 199.

40. Wang Tao gives a short biography of Gong Zhifang in *"Haizou yeyou" fulu*, 5753–54.

41. Xue Liyong points out that *zhu xia* is also the name of Zhuxia Xiangu, the daughter of the Daoist divinity Taishan Dijun. In this context, the image of the white crane appearing in the clouds denotes her character, her looks and style, and her skill as a storyteller or musician; see Xue Liyong, *Shanghai jinü shi*, 135.

42. Wang Tao, *"Haizou yeyou" fulu*, 5754–55.

43. See Wang Shunu's discussion on the changing aesthetic preferences in evaluations of the courtesan, *Zhongguo changji shi*, 241–52.

44. For details, see Wang Tao, *"Haizou yeyou" fulu*, 5753, 5756–57.

45. For 1880–82 competitions, see "Gengchen chunji Shenjiang huabang jianglian" (Winner list of the Shanghai flower competition, spring 1880); "Xinyi chunji Hubin huabang" (Shanghai flower competition, spring 1881); "Xinyi qiuji Hubin huabang"(Shanghai flower competition, fall 1881); "Renwu Hubin huachao yanbang" (Shanghai flower competition of 1882); "Renwu xiaji huabang" (Flower competition, summer 1882). For the winter 1883 competition held by Chiqing Zuiyan Sheng, see Xiaolantian Chanqing Shizhe, *Haishang qunfang pu*, 2:5. For the 1888 and 1889 competitions, see Huayu Xiaozhu Zhuren, *Haishang qinglou tuji*, 1:11, 2:4, 27 (which contains mention of a Wang Jinfeng from Yangzhou who won "first in the top tier" for 1888 and winter 1889).

46. See, for example, Chousi Zhuren, *The Sensational Biographies of the Four Great Golden Diamond Cutters* (Haishang mingji Si Da Jin'gang zhuan); Zhang Chunfang, *The Nine-Tailed Turtle* (Jiuwei gui); and Menghuaguanzhu Jiang Yinxiang, *The Nine-Tailed Fox* (Jiuwei hu).

47. For a short comparison, see Xue Liyong, *Shanghai jinü shi*, 137–41.

48. "Xinyi chunji Hubin huabang," 1.

49. See Qixia and Danru, *Haishang hua yinglu*, under the entries for Jin Xiaobao and Lin Daiyu.

50. Other examples are Xiaolantian Chanqing Shizhe, *A Register of Shanghai Flowers* (Haishang qunfang pu), 1884; and Huayu Xiaozhu Zhuren, *Illustrated Record of Shanghai Courtesan Entertainment* (Haishang qinglou tuji), 1892.

51. Shanghaitong She, *Shanghai yanjiu ziliao*, 584–85. This text is possibly the same as *Wumen baiyan tu* by the same author.

52. *Mirror Reflections and Flute Sounds* became the main source for late Qing courtesan illustrated guides such as the well-known *Illustrated Record of Shanghai Courtesan Entertainment*, by Huayu Xiaozhu Zhuren. It borrowed its illustrations from Wu Youru's *The One Hundred Beauties of Shanghai* (Haishang baiyan tu), published between 1890 and 1893 under slightly varying titles; see Catherine Yeh, "Creating the Urban Beauty," 419–20.

53. Wang Tao, *"Haizou yeyou" fulu*, 5709.

54. Typically this sentiment is articulated in forewords to courtesan connoisseur books or guides such as Huayu Xiaozhu Zhuren, *Haishang qinglou tuji*.

55. Newspapers such as *Shenbao* and *Entertainment* constantly carried advertisements for new publications on Shanghai courtesans.

56. Youxi Zhuren, "Fanli liutiao," 205.

57. Chen Wuwo, *Lao Shanghai sanshi nian jianwen lu*, 206.

58. Chen Boxi, "Xiaobao zhilüe" (1919), 137.

59. Due to missing sections in the Shanghai Municipal Library holdings, the record on *Entertainment's* competitions is incomplete. In this study, I compared various sources, and for dates when the newspaper's records are missing, I relied mainly on Chen Wuwo's *Lao Shanghai sanshi nian jianwen lu*, which contains reprints of many of the original articles. Unfortunately, the sequence of articles in this source is often wrong, and Chen Wuwo tends to replace the original titles with his own. Li Boyuan held three flower competitions, in 1897, 1898, and 1900; see Wei Shaochang, *Li Boyuan yanjiu ziliao*, 518–19. In addition to flower competitions, he held "elections of flowers" (*huaxuan*) in 1898, 1899, and 1900, and results were also published in book form; see Youxi Zhuren, *Gengzi huaxuan lu* (Record of the election of flowers of 1900).

60. Li Boyuan, "Youxi Zhuren gaobai" (Announcement from the Master of Entertainment), *Youxi bao*, March 19, 1899.

61. For example, see "Jin cishi hu tou zijianshu" (*Cishi* [courtesan] Jin suddenly put in a vote for herself), *Youxi bao*, Nov. 26, 1897, 2; "Jin Baoxian buyuan dengbang," 202–3.

62. See Yuan Zuzhi, "Cangshan jiuzhu zhuan Chunjiang dingyou nian xiaji huabang xu," 204–5. Due to lacunae in the holdings of the paper, dates for the competitions are not precise.

63. "Meiren Yatuo zhi Youxi Zhuren shu" (Letter by Yatuo, an American, to the Master of Entertainment), 203.

64. Li Boyuan, "Youxi zhu dake lun kai huabang zhi buyi" (The Master of Entertainment answers visitors' comments on the difficulty of holding the flower competition), 194–95.

65. Yuan Zuzhi, "Cangshan jiuzhu zhuan Chunjiang dingyou nian xiaji huabang xu" (Preface by the Old Master of Cang Mountain to the flower competition in Shanghai, summer 1898), 204–5.

66. Ibid.

67. Ibid.

68. Chen Wuwo, "Huabang jiexiao eyan" (On the errors in the announcement of the winner in the flower competition).

69. Chen Wuwo, "Zhuangyuan wu bao" (The mistake in the announcement of the winner), 43.

70. *Entertainment* claimed that out of the first ten winners of the flower competition of 1897, seven courtesans were married by 1898; see "Nan chu yizhang" (Difficulties eliminated from courtesan world), *Youxi bao*, Oct. 8, 1898, 2. There was also news of winners finding marriage partners; see, for example, "Minghua you zhu, cishi congliang" (The famous flower has a master and is getting married), *Youxi bao*, Sept. 19, 1897, 2; and "Haoyue changyuan" ([We wish] the good moon is always full), *Youxi bao*, Sept. 21, 1897, 2.

71. See Li Boyuan, "Youxi zhuren ni juxing 'Linfang hui' yi," *Youxi bao*, Oct. 4, 1897, 1.

72. When the special issue for the 1898 competition, with glued-in photographs of the top three winners, came out, *Entertainment* reported that the street outside its office was clogged. The ten thousand copies printed for that day were sold out before noon, and over the next few days the paper and the Yaohua photography studio had to reprint thousands more copies to meet popular demand; see *Youxi bao*, Oct. 1, 1898, 1.

73. Ibid.

74. Li Boyuan, "Fanli liutiao," Chen Wuwo, *Lao Shanghai sanshi nian jianwen lu*, 218–21; *Shijie fanhua bao*, June 24, 1901.

75. Li Boyuan, "Dingyou xiaji Chunjiang wubang bianyan."

76. For example, see "Ting Xiao Ruyi tan pipa yin kao erlun" (On thoughts inspired by

listening to Xiao Ruyi play the *pipa*), *Youxi bao*, Oct. 10, 1897, 1; and "Guqu xiantan" (Idle talk on *qu* [song] performance), *Youxi bao*, Oct. 14, 1897, 2. On Li Boyuan's efforts to discover new singing talents, see "Lun Shanghai jiaoshu gechang" (On the singing by Shanghai courtesans), *Youxi bao*, Oct. 8, 1897, 2; and "Dangyan guqu Lin Baozhu qingcai shicheng" (Performing *qu* at a banquet, Lin Baozhu tries to please the one who has influence [on her future]), *Youxi bao*, Oct. 24, 1897, 2.

77. "Ben guan tekai huacong Jingji teke gaobai" (An announcement on our paper holding a "Special Competition with Focus on Management of State Affairs" among the flowers), *Shijie fanhua bao*, June 30, 1901, 1. The results of this competition were published three months later in "Tekai huacong Jingji teke bang" (A "Special Competition with Focus on Management of State Affairs" among the flowers), *Shijie fanhua bao*, Sept. 27, 1901, 2.

78. *Entertainment* carried quite a few reports on literary talent among Shanghai courtesans, but, as the paper admitted with regret, this was not what clients were seeking; Shanghai had other preferences. See, for example, "Kelian mingshu" (The pitiable famous courtesan), *Youxi bao*, April 17, 1899, 2. There have been many discussions on the question of literacy among Shanghai courtesans; see Henriot, "Chinese Courtesans," 47. Judging from contemporaneous newspaper reports, literacy among the top-ranking Shanghai courtesans was higher than Henriot seems willing to consider; *Prostitution and Sexuality in Shanghai*, 29–32. This assessment is based on study of four courtesan guides: *A Register of Shanghai Flowers* (Haishang qunfang pu), by Xiaolantian Chanqing Shizhe, 1884; *Mirror Reflections and Flute Sounds* (Jingying xiaosheng), 1887; *Illustrated Record of Shanghai Courtesan Entertainment* (Haishang qinglou tuji), by Huayu Xiaozhu Zhuren, 1892; and *A Photographic Record of Shanghai Flowers* (Haishang hua yinglu), by Qixia and Danru, 1915. The data suggest that the large majority of courtesans either came directly from Suzhou or the Suzhou area or had Suzhou as their birthplace, as stated in Wang Tao's report (Henriot, *Prostitution and Sexuality in Shanghai*, 27). In general, courtesans who received their training in Suzhou and came to Shanghai appear to have been independent professionals and had a relatively high literacy rate. Courtesans also came from Changshu (Qinchuan). Although Cantonese courtesan entertainment formed an important part of entertainment businesses in Shanghai, this group is clearly underrepresented in the data. The same is true for Japanese and Western prostitutes in Shanghai. Out of ninety-eight women in *Register*, twelve were said to be highly literate. Biographies for five of the one hundred women in *Illustrated Record* state that their subjects were highly literate; "highly literate" here means that they were said to be able to compose poetry. It is probable that this number of women whose excellent literacy is especially praised signals a much greater number of other courtesans with more modest albeit substantial literacy levels. With 13 percent and 5 percent respectively of highly literate women, it might safely be said that functional literacy, which would include reading novels and newspapers, must have been several times higher and also markedly higher than among Jiangnan women in general. Henriot, based on Wang Tao, arrives at similar proportions but considers this a "low" level of literacy. I believe he misinterprets Wang Tao's information. Wang Tao mentions women with excellent literary skills that enhanced their entertainment and does not reproduce a sociological questionnaire in which "literacy" is crossed on wherever the answer is "yes." Still, as Henriot has pointed out, most of the girls who entered the trade came from poorer families, which would signal low literacy levels. The authors of the courtesan guides might simply have followed in the steps of late Ming stories about grand and very well educated courtesans. At that time, courtesan establishments were managed by officials, which might account for better courtesan education. In Shanghai, however, the business had clearly changed substantially from cultural entertainment between courtesans and literati (or candidates for the Imperial Examinations) to more down-to-earth merrymaking with musical performances and dinner companions. In addition, the leisure in which formal literary games could be enjoyed had been consumed by the urban frenzy of Shanghai. This is vividly reflected

in the *zhaoju* and *zhuanju* system, unique to Shanghai, by which courtesans were constantly on call and were expected to go from one client to another in one evening. In Shanghai, the nature of courtesan entertainment was transformed as other literacy requirements arose, such as the ability to read newspapers and novels and even do some accounting.

79. "Sutai zouma gongpan Huabang" (Sampling the flowers in Suzhou, all await the result of the competition), *Youxi bao*, May 14, 1899, 2.

80. Participants indicated their names and their origins at the beginning of their letters or provided this information in self-introductions.

81. Yunshui Xiyanren, "Zhi Youxi Zhuren lun Lin Daiyu shu" (A letter on [the courtesan] Lin Daiyu to the Master of Entertainment), *Youxi bao*, Nov. 22, 1987.

82. According to Chen Boxi, clients paid for the Shanghai flower competitions. While it is true that voters had to purchase tickets for the competition held by the New World amusement park in 1917, there is no hard evidence on buying votes in the case of the *Entertainment* competitions; see Chen Boxi, *Lao Shanghai*, 1:137–38.

83. For examples of reports on courtesan stars posing for photographs, see "Beili huarong" (The flower image of the courtesan), *Youxi bao*, May 29, 1899, 2.

84. For flower competitions held later by other entertainment papers, see Henriot, *Prostitution and Sexuality in Shanghai*, 65–66.

85. *Entertainment* carried many reports of court cases against opera singers who had love affairs with concubines; one of the most extensive reports of this kind was on the Gao Caiyun case, from March to July 1899.

86. "Zanghua chuyi" (Initial discussions on [establishing] a flower cemetery), *Youxi bao*, Oct. 5, 1898, 2.

87. Ibid.

88. Chen Wuwo, "Qunfang yizhong shimo."

89. Li Boyuan, "Nijian huazhong mujuan xiaoqi" (A notice on fund-raising for the planned establishment of a courtesan cemetery), *Youxi bao*, Oct. 8, 1898, 1. He also had argued this point in an earlier article; see Li Boyuan, "Mujuan gouzhi huazhong yi" (Discussion on fundraising for the purchase and establishment of a courtesan cemetery), *Youxi bao*, Oct. 6, 1898, 1–2.

90. "Dai jiaoshu Lin Daiyu deng ni mujuan guozhi huazhong xiaoqi" (Announcement of a draft fund-raising proposal for establishing a public cemetery for courtesans written on behalf of the *jiaoshu* Lin Daiyu and others), *Youxi bao*, Oct. 9, 1898, 1.

91. Ibid.

92. "Dai Lin Daiyu jiaoshu zhi Lu Lanfen, Jin Xiaobao, Zhang Shuyu zhu Jiaoshu quanjuan huazhong jian" (Letter written in the name of *jiaoshu* Lin Daiyu to Lu Lanfen, Jin Xiaobao, and Zhang Shuyu urging them to participate in fund-raising for the establishment of a courtesan cemetery), *Youxi bao*, around Oct. 7, 1898. See Chen Wuwo, *Lao Shanghai sanshi nian jianwen lu*, 100–9.

93. "Juanjian yizhong congtan" (Comments on the various [news regarding] the fund-raising for the courtesan cemetery), *Youxi bao*, Nov. 14, 1898, 2; Yihuashi Zhuren, "Ji Jin Xiaobao jiaoshu lun huazhong juan shi" (Report on Jin Xiaobao's comments regarding fund-raising for the courtesan cemetery), *Youxi bao*, Jan. 30, 1899, 1–2.

94. "Ren yuan li" (To each according to their abilities), *Youxi bao*, Oct. 9, 1898, 2.

95. As the number of courtesans in the 1890s was around two thousand to three thousand, handing out sixteen hundred account books for that number seems reasonable, since not all would be willing to participate.

96. Chen Wuwo, "Qunfang yizhong shimo," 106 7.

97. "Ren yuan li" (To each according to their abilities), *Youxi bao*, Oct. 9, 1898, 2; "Juanjian yizhong congtan" (Comments on the various [news regarding] fund-raising for the courtesan cemetery), *Youxi bao*, Nov. 14, 1898, 2.

98. "Juanjian yizhong congtan" (Comments on the various [news regarding] fund-raising for the courtesan cemetery), *Youxi bao*, Nov. 14, 1898, 2.

99. Ibid.

100. See "Lu *Tiannan xin bao* lun Shanghai Si Da Jin'gang" (Reprint of *Tiannan xinbao* [paper published in Singapore] on the Four Great Golden Diamond Cutters of Shanghai), *Youxi bao*, May 28, 1899, 1.

101. For example, "Fude Si Da Jin'gang chuangjian huazhong" (Poems on the Four Great Golden Diamond Cutters establishing the courtesan cemetery), *Youxi bao*, Jan. 1, 1899, 3; for a collection of poems for the occasion see *Yugou ji*.

102. "Xinshi youjian" (New poems appearing again), *Youxi bao*, Jan. 1, 1899, 2.

103. "Zhong beiwen leici huilu" (Record of epitaphs written for the cemetery).

104. Yihuashi Zhuren, "Ji Jin Xiaobao jiaoshu lun huazhong juan shi" (Report on Jin Xiaobao's comments regarding fund-raising for the courtesan cemetery), *Youxi bao*, Jan. 30, 1899.

105. Ibid.

106. "Choujuan ruji" (Embezzlement of charity funds), *Youxi bao*, (date unclear, sometime in Jan. 1899); the article was quoted by Lin Daiyu in her "Lin Daiyu zishu kuzhong han" (A letter in which Lin Daiyu tells her side of the story).

107. Lin Daiyu, "Lin Daiyu zishu kuzhong han."

108. Lin Daiyu's debt problem habitually led to marriage, with the prospective husband paying all her debts. These marriages led to quick divorces, and the routine became known as *xizao* (taking a bath). See Chen Boxi, "Lin Daiyu xiaoshi."

109. "Xue Baochai, Lin Daiyu xiangshuai maoming" (Xue Baochai and Lin Daiyu follow each other in using pseudonyms), *Youxi bao*, March 19, 1899, 2.

110. Ibid.

111. Chen Wuwo, "Qunfang yizhong shimo," 107.

112. "Jin Xiaobao cishi huazhongdi goucheng mujuan kuochong jizhi jianxiu ciyu qi" (*Cishi* [courtesan] Jin Xiaobao announces the success of purchasing the land for the courtesan cemetery and the need to raise more funds for laying the foundation and building the memorial hall), *Youxi bao*, March 13, 1899, 1–2.

113. "Lu *Tiannan xin bao* lun Shanghai Si Da Jin'gang," 1.

114. Chen Wuwo, "Qunfang yizhong shimo."

115. "Xin baihua zhong" (The new Hundred Flowers Cemetery), *Tuhua xunbao* 12 (1909): 6. There is a misprint here; number 13 was printed instead of number 12.

116. Binghong Shanren and Xiqiusheng, "Yugou hen chuanqi," 119–20.

117. On courtesan charity activities in the late Qing, see Huang Shiquan, *Songnan mengying lu*, 107–8; Zhan Kai, "Lanqiao Bieshu zhuan," 2; and "Li Jingui zhuan," 3.

118. Lin Daiyu, "Lin Daiyu zishu kuzhong han."

119. Yihuashi Zhuren, "Ji Jin Xiaobao jiaoshu lun huazhong juan shi," 2.

120. Christian Henriot concludes from the courtesans' entertainment-newspaper advertisements warning clients who had failed to pay their bills that their names would be publicized that the paper must have reached only a very small circle of courtesan patrons (*Prostitution and Sexuality in Shanghai*, 68); this argument does not take into account the eight thousand copies of the paper sold each day, which indicates that the circle of those who were very interested in this world was much larger.

121. "Diaotou gaobai" (Advertising changes of address), *Youxi bao*, Oct. 9, 1898, 1.

122. *Shijie fanhua bao*, June 24, 1901, 1.

123. The *Entertainment* issue in which Xiao Ruyi's advertisement was published is missing. Li Boyuan referred to it in his article "Shu Xiao Ruyi deng benbao zhuitao piaozhang gaobai hou" (After Xiao Ruyi's going public announcing the unpaid debts [of her client]), *Youxi bao*, Sept. 28, 1897, 1.

124. "Ting Xiao Ruyi tan pipa yin kao er lun" (On thoughts inspired by listening to Xiao Ruyi play the *pipa*), *Youxi bao*, Oct. 10, 1897, 1.

125. "Shu Yufeng Yuyin Jin Hanxiang liang deng benbao gaobai hou" (Comments after Yufeng Yuyin and Jin Hanxiang put their advertisements in our paper), *Youxi bao*, Oct. 4, 1897, 1. The papers for the dates on which these advertisements were published are missing.

126. "Shuguan feisheng" (Spreading [their] fame through [performing in] the storytelling hall), *Youxi bao*, Aug. 27, 1899, 3.

127. "Haishang yiqing" (Change of heart in Shanghai), *Youxi bao*, Aug. 28, 1899, 2.

128. For the history of state-run prostitution in Qi, see Wang Shunu, *Zhongguo changji shi*, 31; and Henriot, *Prostitution and Sexuality in Shanghai*, chapters 1 and 2.

129. "Shuchang xuzhi" (Follow-up report on the storytelling hall), *Youxi bao*, Aug. 30, 1899, 2.

130. See Xue Liyong, *Shanghai jinü shi*, 348.

131. Dianshizhai ed., *Shenjiang shengjing tu*, vol. 2, 30.

132. Chi Zhicheng, *Hu you mengying*, 157.

133. Lao Shanghai, *Hu Baoyu*, 94.

134. In *Entertainment* and other entertainment newspapers, reports on the theater were a common feature.

135. On the reason for her failure and her later return to Shanghai, see "Lin Daiyu," *Shijie fanhua bao*, May 20, 1904, 2. According to another story, she was expelled from Hankow by the military commander of the city, who was afraid of scandal; "Xiaoxiangguan zhu zhi jinxi tan" (Things old and new about the Master of Xiaoxiang studio [Lin Daiyu]), *Xinsheng* 9 (1922):12.

136. There are advertisements for Lin Daiyu's performances in other newspapers as late as 1909; see, for example, the advertisement for the Qunxian Chayuan theater in *Minli bao*, no. 91 (1911), 2.

137. I thank Joshua Fogel for giving me this piece of historical information; for details, see Fogel, "Japanese Travelogues of China," 31.

138. For courtesan involvement in charity fund-raising, see Huang Shiquan, *Songnan mengying lu*, 107–8; Zhan Kai, "Lanqiao Bieshu zhuan," 2; "Li Jingui zhuan," 3.

Chapter 6. The Image of the Shanghai Courtesan

1. Charles Bernheimer argues in *Figures of Ill Repute*, his excellent study on nineteenth-century Paris prostitution, that "the prostitute is ubiquitous in the novels and the paintings of this period not only because of her prominence as a social phenomenon but, more important, because of her function in stimulating artistic strategies to control and dispel her fantasmatic threat to male mastery" (2). I believe, however, that cities such as Paris and Shanghai, by fostering the development of this very particular type of prostitution, are very much part of the picture. In order to understand the "threat" posed to masculinity by the nineteenth-century prostitute or courtesan of Paris and Shanghai, the city itself has to be considered as a major player.

2. For the Su Xiaoxiao legend, see Guwu Molangzi, "Xileng yunji," 79–106; on the theme of the idealized courtesan, see Idema, "Shih Chün-pao's and Chu Yu-tun's *Ch'ü-chiang-ch'ih*," 217–65.

3. Jiang Fang, *Huo Xiaoyu zhuan*, 64–76.

4. Feng Menglong, "Du Shiniang nu chen baibaoxiang," 485–500. For a study of Feng Menglong and late Ming vernacular stories, see Hanan, *The Chinese Vernacular Story*.

5. See Feng Menglong, "Du Shiniang nu chen baibaoxiang," 499.

6. In *Water Margin*, see the character Yan Xipo; Shi Nai'an, *Shuihu zhuan*, 381–99. In *The Plum in the Golden Vase*, see the character Li Guijie; Xiaoxiao Sheng, *Jin ping mei cihua*, 486–92.

7. For an analysis of the novel, see Hanan, "Fengyue Meng and the Courtesan Novel."

8. In his study on the Shanghai courtesan novel *Biographies of Shanghai Flowers*, David Der-wei Wang points to the important role of the city of Shanghai; see *Fin-de-Siècle Splendor*, 89.

9. For examples, see Han Bangqing, *Haishang hua liezhuan*; Zou Tao, *Haishang chentian ying*; Erchun Jushi, *Haitian hongxue ji*; Chousi Zhuren, *Haishang mingji Si Da Jin'gang zhuan*; Menghuaguanzhu Jiang Yinxiang, *Jiuwei hu*; Zhang Chunfan, *Jiuwei gui*; and Pingjiang Yinnian, *Haishang pinghua baojian*.

10. Lu Xun, *Zhongguo xiaoshuo shilüe*, 263–64. Lu Xun gave the following examples of courtesan-client novels belonging to the *Dream of the Red Chamber* legacy: Chen Sen, *Pinhua baojian*; Wei Zi'an, *Huayue hen*; and Yu Da, *Qinglou meng*. These works preceded the Shanghai courtesan novels.

11. David Der-wei Wang, *Fin-de-Siècle Splendor*, 58.

12. Ibid., 72.

13. For studies on Western urban novels, see Wirth-Nesher, *City Codes*.

14. Lu Xun begins his discussion of the late Qing courtesan novels with works on courtesan life and biographies from the past but does not explicitly make the link; see Lu Xun, *Zhongguo xiaoshuo shilüe*, 256.

15. For the Tang capital Chang'an, *Record of the Court Entertainment Bureau* (Jiaofang ji), by Cui Lingqin, and *Record of the Northern Sectors or the Gay Quarters of Chang'an* (Beili zhi), by Sun Qi; and for the Ming capital Nanjing, *One Hundred Nanjing Beauties* (Jinling baimei), by Li Yunxiang. The Qing period literature on the courtesan was related largely to rich merchant towns, for example, *The Record of Painted Boats in Nanjing* (Qinhuai huafang lu), by Penghua Sheng; *Record of the Painted Boats of Suzhou* (Wumen huafang lu), by Xixi Shanren; and *A Small Record of Courtesan Life in Yangzhou* (Zhuxi huashi xiaolu), by Fenlita Xingzhe.

16. Li Yunxiang, *Jinling baimei*; Yu Huai, *Banqiao zaji*.

17. Wang Tao's *biji* narrative *Record of Visits to Courtesan Houses in a Distant Corner by the Sea* (Haizou yeyou lu), with a preface dating to 1860, provides the earliest description of Shanghai after it opened for international trade. Throughout the 1870s and 1880s, Wang Tao continued to devote himself to describing the Shanghai courtesan scene. In his *biji* stories and biographies of courtesans, he emphasized the notion of Shanghai as a center of entertainment brimming with wealth and glamour.

18. Huang Shiquan, *Songnan mengying lu*, 107, 146, 148.

19. Ibid., 107.

20. For sixteenth-century Venice and its courtesans and courtesan literature, see Alfieri, *Il gioco dell'amore*; for eighteenth-century Edo, see Hibbett, *Floating World in Japanese Fiction*; and for nineteenth-century Paris, see Bernheimer, *Figures of Ill Repute*.

21. A Ying, *Wan Qing xiqu xiaoshuo mu*, 89; David Der-wei Wang, *Fin-de Siècle Splendor*, 89.

22. Sun Yusheng, *Haishang fanhua meng*, 1.

23. Ibid., 1.

24. Yi Hong, *Renjian diyu*, 5.

25. Lu Xun, *Zhongguo xiaoshuo shilüe*, 264.

26. Menghuaguanzhu Jiang Yinxiang, *Jiuwei hu*, 176.

27. Pingjiang Yinnian, *Haishang pinghua baojian*, 22–23.

28. I am grateful to Laura Wu for alerting me to this. As far as I know, the two section were written with little time elapsing between them.

29. Chousi Zhuren, *Haishang mingji Si Da Jin'gang zhuan qishu*, *juan* 3: 1.

30. The novel mentions this specific incident that shows the newspapers' power in raising the status of the Shanghai courtesan; see ibid., *juan* 2: 13.

31. McMahon, "Fleecing the Male Customer."

32. Menghuaguanzhu Jiang Yinxiang, *Jiuwei hu*, 28–29.

33. Lao Shanghai, *Hu Baoyu*, 72–73.

34. Menghuaguanzhu Jiang Yinxiang, *Jiuwei hu*, 54.

35. In *Biographies of Shanghai Flowers*, a courtesan is invited by her patron's wife to Shanghai's most famous Western-style restaurant, Yipinxiang; see Han Bangqing, *Haishang hua liezhuan*, ch. 57.

36. Menghuaguanzhu Jiang Yinxiang, *Jiuwei hu*, 169–70.

37. Pott, *A Short History of Shanghai*, 18.

38. Menghuaguanzhu Jiang Yinxiang, *Jiuwei hu*, 170.

39. Sun Yusheng, *Haishang fanhua meng*, 218.

40. Ibid., 54.

41. Erchun Jushi, *Haitian hongxue ji*, 3–7.

42. On the subject of the "honest courtesan," see Rosenthal, *The Honest Courtesan*.

43. With regard to Han Qiuhe, the hero of *The Nine-Tailed Turtle*, Wang Tao, who knew the author Zhang Chunfan, stated that the novel was based on the author's love affair with a Shanghai courtesan. With regard to Zhang Qiugu, in *The Shadows of Heaven and Earth in Shanghai*, there is no direct proof, but one could reasonably assume that the character is the alter ego of Zou Tao himself; see David Der-wei Wang, *Fin-de-Siècle Splendor*, 81.

44. Works of the 1870s and 1880s generally present Shanghai as the wonderland of wealth and comfort with the courtesan as the crowning glory; examples include Wang Tao's *Appendix to "Record of Visits to Courtesan Houses in a Distant Corner by the Sea"* (*Haizou yeyou lu* yulu), with its depiction of the International Settlement, Zou Tao's *Shanghai City Lights*, and the numerous illustrated works about Shanghai from the 1880s. Works of later decades took a different view; examples include Dianshizhai's *Illustrated Grand Sites of Shanghai, Famous Shanghai Sites, with Illustrations and Explanations* (Shenjiang mingsheng tushuo), and works appearing in the 1880s such as Meihua'an Zhu's *The Latest of Famous Sites in Shanghai, with Illustrations and Explanations* (Shenjiang shixia shengjing tushuo) and Hushang Youxizhu's *An Illustrated Introduction to Shanghai Entertainment* (Haishang youxi tushuo).

45. For example, the story of Hu Baoyu going to the theater to watch the *dan* actor Shisan Dan perform was first reported in *Shenbao*; see note 135 in ch. 1.

46. For example, Feng Menglong, "Maiyoulang qiaozhan huakui," 32–73, and "Du Shiniang nu chen baibaoxiang," 485–500.

47. For studies on literary illustrations, see A Ying, *Qingmo shiyin jingtu xiaoshuo xiqu mu*, 126–41; and Hegel, *Reading Illustrated Fiction*, 164–289.

48. For an introduction to Wu Youru and *Dianshizhai Illustrated Magazine*, see Wagner, "Joining the Global Imaginaire"; and Kim, "New Wine in Old Bottles."

49. Feng Menglong, "Jiang Xingge chonghui zhenzhu shan," 5.

50. The first illustrated editions in book form I have seen of *The Nine-Tailed Fox* and *The Nine-Tailed Turtle* were published in 1917 by Shanghai Shuju.

51. In a study based on a comparison between *Flower in the Sea of Retribution* and *Amorous Adventures in Beijing*, Yingjin Zhang argues that the "close resemblance between them [the two novels] leads to this hypothesis: at the turn of the century, there was no striking difference between the configurations of Beijing and Shanghai in Chinese fiction. This situation gradually changed in subsequent decades" (*The City in Modern Chinese Literature and Film*, 120). This conclusion, I believe, is not supported by the actual text of the two novels. From its opening statement, it is clear that *Amorous Adventures in Beijing* belongs to the genre of the political novel, with a clear ideological framework as its guiding principle and the advocacy of a political reform agenda as its purpose. The fact that it focuses on the Beijing courtesan does not, in the end, make it a novel that is similar in any way to *Flower in the Sea of Retribution*. *Amorous Adventures in Beijing* comes to an end after three chapters. From the wedge chapter and the three chapters, it is difficult to discern with certainty how the work was to develop, and the meager material does not support Zhang's assertion that Beijing and Shanghai were represented as without major difference in literary works.

Chapter 7. Guides to Paradise

I am indebted to Dr. Nancy Norton Tomasko, New York, and Dr. Lothar Wagner, Heidelberg, for making their private collections of Western guides available to me. A European Association of Chinese Studies Library Visit Grant from the Chiang Ching-kuo Foundation, which allowed me to visit libraries in London and Leiden to see further materials, is also gratefully acknowledged.

1. This study on Shanghai city guides belongs to a longer study that also includes Western- and Japanese-language Shanghai city guides.

2. Charles E. Darwent, *Shanghai*, 156.

3. A more literal translation of the title is *Miscellanea by/for (Someone) Taking a Trip to Shanghai*. There are earlier records on Shanghai, and many contain valuable historical information, but this study focuses on works that have the formal features of city guides and does not include the *biji* narratives or diary and travel notes. Western-language materials were likewise restricted.

4. Ge Yuanxu, *Hu you zaji*, 1876.

5. The Japanese title renders *Hu you zaji* as *Shanghai hanji ki* (The record of prosperous Shanghai). See Zheng Zu'an, "Tiji," 5.

6. Ge Yuanxu, *Hu you zaji*, 1989, 7.

7. Ge Yuanxu, *Hu you zaji*, 8.

8. The first edition of *A Record of Essential Aspects of the Capital City* was published in 1864. I am grateful to Susan Naquin for sharing her research notes on this guide with me. The city guide as a literary genre has a long history in China. There are guides devoted to the "dead capital," the glorious cities of the past, such as Yang Xuanzhi's *Record of the Monasteries of Luoyang* (Luoyang qielan ji), written in the mid-sixth century; and Meng Yuanlao's *The Eastern Capital: A Dream of Splendors Past* (Dongjing menghua lu), written in 1147, on Kaifeng.

9. Ge Yuanxu, *Hu you zaji*, 52.

10. See Zou Yiren, *Jiu Shanghai renkou bianqian de yanjiu*, 90, 141.

11. In his foreword to *Miscellaneous Notes*, Ge Yuanxu refers to Confucius's editing of the "Book of Songs," which left many love poems in place, to justify his own inclusion of courtesan entertainment in his guide. He argues that the courtesan business had become "such an important feature in the Shanghai Concessions, that without it the guide would seem incomplete" (8). Although Ge covers the courtesan establishments in great detail, he does so mostly indirectly by inserting many poems and bamboo twig ballads on the topic.

12. See eighteenth- and nineteenth-century etchings and lithographs with such themes, which appeared either as separate prints, such as those published by the U.S. firm Currier and Ives and lithograph print shops in Épinal, France, or as illustrated papers with themes such as the Crimean War. For examples of the latter, see Bouvet, *Le Grand Livre des images d'Épinal*.

13. Dianshizhai, *Shenjiang shengjing tu*, 1.

14. Dianshizhai Zhuren, "Shiyin *Shenjiang shengjing tu* chushou."

15. Dianshizhai, *Shenjiang shengjing tu*, 1.

16. Wagner, "Ernest Major," 45.

17. See Wagner, "The *Shenbao* in Crisis," 127.

18. For Major and his publishing enterprises, see Wagner, "The Making of Shanghai."

19. One of the notable earlier guides is his *The Treaty Ports of China and Japan: A complete guide to the Open Ports of Those Countries, Together With Beijing, Edo, Hong Kong, and Macao: Guide Book and Vade Mecum; For Travellers, Merchants, and Residents in General*, published in 1867 in London and Hong Kong.

20. Most representative of the "sphere of influence" standpoint among Shanghai Western-language guides are *Twentieth Century Impressions of Hong Kong, Shanghai, and Other Treaty Ports of China: Their History, People, Commerce, Industries, and Resources* and Japan, *An official guide to eastern Asia; trans-continental connections between Europe and Asia*, published by the Imperial Japanese Government Railways, 1913–17.

21. Examples of these guides are Hotel Metropole, *Guide to Shanghai (complimentary)* (1903); Palace Hotel, *Guide to Shanghai* (1907); *Shang-hai: and the Valley of the Blue River, Madrolle's Handbooks* (1912); and Carl Crow, *Handbook for China* (1913).

22. Darwent, *Shanghai* (1903), 1.

23. See Catherine Yeh, "Representing the City."

24. Darwent, *Shanghai* (1920), 1.

25. In order to highlight the victory of public over commercial interest, and to reinforce the understanding of the conditions under which such a city was made possible, Darwent addressed the question of property rights in his 1920 edition: "Who are the owners or who is the owner of the fore-shore right? The public, rather, the Municipal Council holding it for the public" (ibid., 1).

26. Ibid., 5–6.

27. Ibid., 15, 16.

28. Ibid., 113–14.

29. See Zou Yiren, *Jiu Shanghai renkou bianqian*, 141.

30. Darwent, *Shanghai* (1903), 19.

31. Ibid., 155–56.

32. See Hughes, *Barcelona*.

33. J. D. Clark, *Sketches in and around Shanghai, etc.*, 49.

34. In the 1920 edition, Darwent openly referred to the street as a place that fosters evil; by this, he meant the opium dens. "Why is it that evil has so often more interest than goodness?" (*Shanghai*, 22).

35. Darwent, *Shanghai* (1903), 149.

36. To gain a picture of the size of the business community in Shanghai well before Darwent wrote his guide, see *The China Directory*.

37. Darwent, 203.

38. See Yeh, "Representing the City."

39. Japanese capital acquired shares in the Commercial Press in 1903 (this investment was ended in 1914). As part of the deal, Japanese advisers were sent to the publishing house, and this might have had an impact on the format and perspective of *Shanghai City Guide*. On the issue, see Gao Hanqing, "Benguan chuangyeshi." On the relationship between Japan and the Commercial Press, see Tarumoto, *Shoki Shōmu inshokan kenkyū*, 79–300.

40. Shangwu Yinshuguan, *Shanghai zhinan* (1909), 1.

41. Ibid., *juan* 9: 7.

42. Shangwu Yinshuguan, *Shanghai zhinan* (1912), 1.

43. Huating Wen Yehe, "Gailun."

44. The author who used the pseudonym Huang Renjing (Mirror of the Yellow Man) also signed in English as Wong Tsao-ling (Huang Zaoling). Huang Renjing, *Huren baojian*.

45. Ibid., unpaginated English preface and Chinese preface, 1.

46. Ibid., 124–25.

47. Ibid., 105–6.

48. Shangwu Yinshuguan, *Shanghai zhinan* (1922), 1.

49. Zhonghua Tushujicheng Gongsi, *Shanghai youlan zhinan* (1923), photographs in the opening pages.

50. Ibid., 1.

51. Ibid., 1–2.

52. Huating Wen Yehe, "Gailun," 1.

53. G. E. Miller, *Shanghai—The Paradise of Adventurers* (Chinese translation, Mile, *Shanghai, maoxianjia de leyuan*).

Chapter 8. Conclusion

1. L. S. Mercier, *Nouveau Paris*, 1799, 3:56, quoted in Csergo, "Extension et mutation du loisir citadin," 123.

2. The same was true for prostitution, although, especially in Paris, the authorities imposed health checks, which were later performed in the French Settlement as well. Christian Henriot has made use of the records of the sanitary police in the French Settlement; see Henriot, "La Prostitution à Shanghai" and "Prostitution et 'police des moeurs' à Shanghai."

3. In 1862, a discussion developed in Shanghai about changing the city's status along the lines of medieval Hanse cities with their strong political and commercial independence. The foreign consuls put an end to this.

4. Rey Chow, *Writing Diaspora*, 8.

5. Lai Yu-chih, "Fuliu qianjie."

6. Homi Bhabha, *The Location of Culture*, 1, 2.

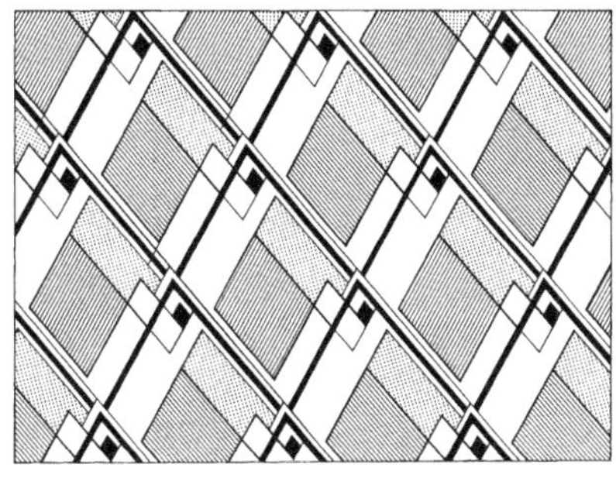

Glossary

A Bao 阿寶
Ankaidi 安塏第
anmu 案目

bai taimian 擺臺面
bailingtai 百靈臺
bakai yang 八開洋
bangyan 榜眼
Baohe 寶和
Baoshanjie 寶善街
bayin qin 八音琴
Beihailu 北海路
Beishi 北市
biaoxin liyi 標新立異
biji 筆記
Binghong Shanren 病紅山人
bowuyuan 博物院
buye zhi fangcheng 不夜之芳城

caizi 才子
caizi jiaren 才子佳人
Changfa zhan xingzong xiaozhu; Jixian li guyou xiangfeng 長發棧行蹤小住; 集賢里故友相逢
changsan 長三
chao xiaohuo 抄小貨
chawei 茶圍
chayuan mingban jiaose 茶園名班脚色
Chen Wenxian 陳文仙
Cheng Daixiang 程黛香
Cheng Jinglan 程靜蘭
Cheng Taixiang 程黛香
Chenghuang miao 城隍廟
Chengshi bianqian shi 城市變遷史
chi dacai 吃大菜
chi shuangtai 吃雙臺
chimeng 痴夢
chou 丑
chuang men tou 闖門頭
chuanqi 傳奇
chuxi 除夕
cirentang 慈仁堂
cong yi er zhong 從一而終

da chawei 打茶圍
da leyuan 大樂園
Da Malu 大馬路
Da shijie 大世界
da ziming zhong 大自鳴鐘
dacaiguan 大菜館
Daguan Yuan 大觀園
daidang 帶擋
daishu 代贖
daleyuan 大樂園
dan 淡
dan 旦
Dangui Xiyuan 丹桂戲園
daopang shumu 道旁樹木
daqiao 大橋
Daxing Lane 大興里
dayangfang 大洋房
Dayu 大玉
delüfeng 德律風
diao fangjian 調房間
diaotou 調頭
diaotou taimian 調頭臺面
dielaixin tuiboer 疊來新退勃而
difang xingzheng 地方行政
dihuo 地火
diling tuiboer 狄玲退勃而
diyu 地獄
Dong Shangren 東尚仁
Dongyang Chalou 東洋茶樓
Dongyang che 東洋車
Dongyang xifa 東洋戲法
Du Shiniang 杜十娘

duanwu 端午
duanzheng 端正
duoqing 多情
duoqing caizi 多情才子

enke 恩客
Er'ai Xianren 二愛仙人

fan taimian 翻臺面
fang shenggui 放生龜
fanhua 繁華
fanhua jingxiang ri sheng yi ri 繁華景象日盛一日
fanhua rumeng 繁華如夢
fannu 番奴
feng 鳳
Fengchang zuoxi, yi shengchuan yu goulan zhong 逢場作戲亦盛傳于勾欄中
fengsu 風俗
fu 福
Fu Jie 符節
fuben 副本
Fugui Lou 富貴樓
Fuzhou Lu 福州路

gan shimao 趕時髦
Gao Xianglan 高香蘭
gaopin 高品
Gengshang Yiceng Lou 更上一層樓
Gezhi Gongxue 格致公學
Gezhi Shuyuan 格致書院
gezhong youxi 各種游戲
Gongbu Ju 工部局
gongjia huayuan 公家花園
gongshangye 工商業
gongyi tuanti 公益團體
Gu Lansun 顧蘭蓀
Gu Yu 顧寓
gua paizi 挂牌子
guai 怪
guanbai 官白
Guang Fangyan Guan 廣方言館
Guangdong Lu 廣東路
guanshang 官商
guiju 規矩
guili 規禮
Guixian 桂仙
guji 古蹟
Gujin Tushu Jicheng Ju 古今圖書集成局

"Haishang kanhua riji" 海上看花日記
Haishang qishu 海上奇書
Haishang Si Da Jin'gang 海上四大金剛
Haishang Wenshe 海上文社
Haishang yin 海上吟
Haishang Yipin Lou Shuguan 海上一品樓書館
Han Qiuhe 韓秋鶴
hao meng 豪夢
He Airong 賀愛蓉
He Guisheng 何桂聲
heimu 黑幕
Hengdali 亨達利
Hengsimei 亨斯美
Hongkou Dianyingyuan 虹口電影院
Honglou fu meng 紅樓復夢
Hongmiao 虹廟
Hu Baoyu 胡寶玉
Hu Gongshou 胡公壽
hu hua 護花
hu hua shizhe 護花侍者
Hu Sujuan 胡素娟
Hu Xueyan 胡雪巖
Hu you xiao ji 滬游小記
Hu Yue'e 胡月娥
Hua Cuiqin 花翠琴
Hua Rongqing 花蓉卿
Hua Tianyu 花田玉
Hua Yuanyuan 花媛媛
Huang Yushan 黃玉山
Huabang zhuangyuan 花榜狀元
huabang 花榜
huachuan 花船
huadeng chuan 花燈船
huanchang 歡場
Huang Chujiu 黃楚九
Huang Cuifeng 黃翠鳳
Huang Yueshan 黃月山
huashu situihente 華庶司退痕特
huatoulubo 華頭魯勃
Huaxian 花仙
Huazhang 華彰
huazhong 花塚
Huazhonghui 華眾會
Hubeilu 湖北路
Huifan Gongtang 會審公堂
huiyan 慧眼
Huo Xiaoyu 霍小玉
huoji 夥計
Hushang 滬上

jia 假
Jia Baoyu 賈寶玉
jian 賤
Jiang Jianren 蔣劍人
"Jiang Xingge chonghui zhenzhu shan" 蔣興哥重會珍珠衫

Jiangnan caizi 江南才子
jiaofang si 教坊司
jiaoji hua 交際花
jiaoju 叫局
jiaoshu 校書
jiaotache 腳踏車
jiapin 佳品
jiaren 佳人
jie 節
jie caishen 借財神
jieju 借局
Jiemeng Lou 借夢樓
jin 金
Jin Chanxiang 金蟾香
Jin ping mei 金瓶梅
Jin Xiaobao 金小寶
Jing'ansi Lu 靜安寺路
Jinghuo Pu 京貨鋪
"Jingji teke bang" 經濟特科榜
jinmen 進門
jinrong jiguan 金融機關
jiuguan 酒館
jiuju 酒局
ju 局
juhua shan 菊花山

kaihen xitieqian'ai 開痕西鐵欠挨
ke 客
keshi 客師
kezhan 客棧
kongju 空局
kongmeng 空夢
Kuanjiabin Yipinxiang kaiyan; zou xin sheng Qizhandeng yanxi 款嘉賓一品香開筵; 奏新聲七盞燈演劇
Kuiyuan shishe 窺園詩社
Kunqu 崑曲

lajiche 垃圾車
Lang Yuan 閬苑
lanhua hui 蘭花會
Lanxian 蘭仙
Lao Shanghai 老上海
Li Di 李杕
Li Huanyao 李煥堯
Li Jinhua 李金花
Li Pingxiang 李萍香
Li Qiaoling 李巧鈴
Li Sansan 李三三
Li Shanlan 李善蘭
Li Xiangjun 李香君
Li Yuxian 李芋仙
liang 良
Lianhuan huabao 連環畫報
lianju 聯句
Liao Baoer 廖寶兒
lilong 里弄
Lin Baozhu 林寶珠
Lin Daiyu 林黛玉
Lin Fengbao 林鳳寶
lipin 麗品
liugen gelasi 六根掰拉司
liuren xunmeng zhi xiang 留人尋夢之鄉
Liyuan Gonghui 梨園公會
Lu Lanfen 陸蘭芬
Lu Saiying 陸賽英
Lüqin Nüshi 綠琴女史
lushui fuqi 露水夫妻
lutou pusa 路頭菩薩

mache 馬車
magua 馬褂
mai wen wei sheng 賣文為生
mai xiao wei sheng 賣笑為生
maiban 買辦
Maijiaquan 麥家圈
malu 馬路
maoer xi 貌兒戲
mei shi 眉史
"Mei, Xiu er Jiaoshu hezhuan" 眉繡二校書合傳
Meifeier 美斐兒
meipin 美品
meiqi deng 煤氣燈
meiren 美人
Meixianglou Zhuren 媚香樓主人
meng zhong jing 夢中境
meng zhong ren 夢中人
menghuan 夢幻
mengjian 萌奸
mengjing 夢境
mengyou 夢游
minghua 名花
mingji 名妓
mingsheng 名勝
"Mingshi sanchang fengsu gaibian" 名士散場風俗改變
mingxing 名星
Minming She 民鳴社
Mohai Shuguan 墨海書館
muzhan 拇戰

Nanjing Lu 南京路
nanshi 南市
nianhua 年畫

Niudou Ju 牛痘局
nong 濃
nü changshu chang 女唱書場
nü shuchang 女書場
nüshi 女史

pa gezi 爬格子
paiju 牌局
pan xianghao 攀相好
Pang Shubai 龐樹柏
peitang 陪堂
piaozhang 漂賬
pinghua 平話
pingtan 評彈

qi 奇
qi nüzi 奇女子
qianai 欠愛
qiangu nüxia 千古女俠
qifen 奇芬
qimeng 綺夢
Qimin Xinju Yanjiuhui 啓民新劇研究會
Qiming Nüshu 啓明女塾
qing 卿
qing 情
qing chi 情痴
qing lutou 清路頭
qinggao 清高
qinglou 青樓
qinglou ershiliu ze 青樓二十六則
qingnian eshao 輕年惡少
qingshi 情史
Qingwen 晴雯
Qingyu 清娛
Qipan Jie 棋盤街
Quanheng 全亨
"Qunfang yizhong" 群芳義塚

Riben Jiguan 日本妓館
rumeng 入夢
rumeng zhi di 入夢之地

Sai Jinhua 賽金花
sai mafu 賽馬夫
sai paoma 賽跑馬
sai xianghao 賽相好
San Malu 三馬路
sanjie 三節
sanke 三科
Sansan 三三
Sanshenglou 三盛樓
sao fangjian 掃房間
seji 色妓
shafa 沙發
Shandong Lu 山東路
Shanghai ren 上海人
Shanghai xiaojie 上海小姐
Shanghai yiyu 上海一隅
shanghao gaobai 商號告白
shanghua nongyue 賞花弄月
shangju 上局
Shanshan 姍姍
shao lutou 燒路頭
shechi 奢侈
Shen Xiaohong 沈小紅
Shenbaoguan 申報館
shengyi lang (shang) ren 生意郎(上)人
shi 實
Shi Dezhi 施德之
Shi Lu 石路
Shibata Yoshiku 柴田義桂
shier jinchai 十二金釵
shijie youxichang 世界游戲場
Shijie youxi zhuren 世界游戲主人
shimao 時髦
shimao guanren 時髦官人
Shisan Dan 十三旦
shishizhuang 時世裝
shiwai taoyuan 世外桃源
shixia ji 時下妓
shixia mingji 時下名妓
shiyi wenren 失意文人
shuangju 雙局
Shuangxiu 雙秀
shuchang 書場
Shuhua She 書畫社
Shuihu zhuan 水滸傳
shuoshu nü xiansheng 說書女先生
shushen 贖身
shuyu 書寓
Si Da Jin'gang 四大金剛
Si Malu 四馬路
si xiao jin'gang 四小金剛
sidi 私第
Sihai Shengping Lou 四海升平樓
sikaiyang 四開洋
Sima Xiangru 司馬相如
Siming Gongsuo 四明公所
sipoling paotuomoshafa 四潑玲跑托姆沙發
Situmiao 司徒廟
Su Xiaoxiao 蘇小小
Su Yunlan 蘇韻蘭
suli 俗例
Sun Juxian 孫菊仙

taitan 台毯
tanchang 彈唱
tanci 彈詞
tanci nüzi 彈詞女子
tangchang 堂唱
tanhua 探花
Taoyuan Qushuguan 桃源趣書館
teke yi deng yi ming 特科一等一名
ti ji cha 體己茶
tiaocao 跳槽
tipa'ai 梯怕哀
"Tiren nianghuo" 提人釀禍
touju 偷局
tuanyuan 團圓
tuoji 脱籍
Tushanwan 土山灣

waichang 外場
waiguo caiguan 外國菜館
waiguo jiudian 外國酒店
waiguo maxi 外國馬戲
waiguo xishu 外國戲朮
waiguo xiyuan 外國戲園
waiguo yingxi 外國影戲
Wang Yiqing 王逸卿
Wangping Jie 望平街
wei Zhongxia yi da duhui 為中夏一在都會
Wen Xiuying 文秀英
Wen Yuanyuan 文媛媛
Wen Yuyun 文玉雲
Weng Meiqian 翁梅倩
wenmo 文墨
wenren 文人
wubang 武榜
wulu caishen 五路財神
Wuxu Laoren Hui 無須老人會

xi 喜
Xi Huifang 西薈芳
Xi Huifang Li 西薈芳里
xian 仙
xiang lutou 香路頭
xiangbang 相幫
xiangqi 相契
xiansheng dao 先生到
xiangshui 香水
xianshui mei 咸水妹
xiangxia guanren 鄉下倌人
xianzhi 縣志
xiao jiating 小家庭
Xiao Jiuan 小久安
Xiao Ruyi 小如意
xiaobao 小報
Xiaoxiang Guan Shizhe 瀟湘館侍者
xie taimian 卸臺面
Xie Tianxiang 謝添香
Xie Xiang'e 謝湘娥
xiguan 戲館
Xiguo Qinglou 西國青樓
xiju 戲局
xili 西歷
Xin Baihua Zhong 新百花塜
Xinminshe 新民社
xinyou 心游
Xiqiusheng 惜秋生
Xishangren 西尚仁
Xiyang Lou 西洋樓
xiyuan 戲園
Xizi 西子
xu 虛
Xujiahui 徐家匯
"Xunpu fang" 巡捕房

yan 艷
yanbang 豔榜
Yang Guang Huopu 洋廣貨鋪
Yang Shuilong 洋水龍
Yang Si 揚四
Yangchang 洋場
"Yangchang caizi" 洋場才子
yangfu 洋蚨
Yangguan 陽關
Yangliu Loutai 楊柳樓台
yanpin 艷品
Yao Qianqing 姚倩卿
yaoer 么二
Yaohua 燿華
yapin 雅品
yaqu 雅趣
yebang 葉榜
yeji 野雞
Yeshi Yuan 也是園
yi jia yi ming 一甲一名
yi meng 囈夢
yibang 藝榜
Yibaoguan 益報館
yicha 移茶
Yichang 夷場
yiji 藝妓
ying 影
Yingchun Li 迎春里
yinghuan 影幻
yin'gou 陰溝
yiniang 姨娘
yinjing 陰井
yipin 逸品

Yipinxiang 一品香
Yiwen Lü Guan 益聞綠館
Yiwen She 藝文社
Yiyuan 怡園
you 游
you fuben 又副本
youlan shisu 游覽食宿
youtiao 油條
youxi 游戲
youxichang 游戲場
Youyuan zaji 游園雜記
yu 欲
yu 玉
yu you Haishang shiwu nian yi 余游海上十五年矣
Yu Yuan 愚園
Yu Yuan 豫園
Yue Qing 月卿
yuehu 樂户
Yuesheng 悦生
"Yugou hen chuanqi" 玉鉤痕傳奇
Yun Lin 雲林
yunpin 韻品

Zhang Baozhen 張寶珍
Zhang Fuli Gongsi 張福利公司
Zhang Huizhen 張慧貞
Zhang Qiugu 張秋谷
Zhang Shuyu 張書玉
Zhang Sibao 張四寶
Zhang Xunbo 張勛伯
Zhang Yuan 張園
Zhang Yuelan 張月蘭
Zhao Erbao 趙二寶
Zhao Puzhai 趙樸齋
zhaoxiang lou 照像樓
zhen 真
zhengben 正本
zhengtang gongwu 正堂公務
zhenqing 真情
zhiyin 知音
Zhiyin Mituren 指引迷途人
zhizao fengqi 製造風氣
Zhongguo jueda youxichang 中國絕大游戲場
Zhongnicheng Qiao 中泥城橋
zhongqiu 中秋
zhongzhi beiwen 塚誌碑文
Zhou Muqiao 周慕橋
Zhou Shuangbao 周雙寶
Zhou Shuangyu 周雙玉
Zhou Wenqing 周文卿
Zhou Xiaocui 周小翠
Zhou Yaqin 周雅琴
zhu 主
Zhu Ruchun 祝如椿
Zhu Ruxian 朱儒賢
Zhu Sulan 朱素蘭
zhuang ganshi 裝干濕
zhuangyuan 狀元
zhuanju 轉局
zhuchi shidao zhe 主持世道者
zhujia 住家
zhuo futou 斫斧頭
Zhuo Wenjun 卓文君
zhuzhi ci 竹枝詞
zilai fengshan 自來風扇
zilai shui 自來水
zilai yue 自來月
zishu 自贖
zui meng 醉夢
zujie 租界
zujie lijin 租界例禁
zuo changmian 作場面
zuo mache 坐馬車
zuo shengyi 做生意

Bibliography

A Ying 阿英. *"Honglou meng" banhua ji* 紅樓夢版畫集 (Anthology of illustrations on *Dream of the red chamber*). Shanghai: Shanghai Chuban Gongsi, 1955.

———. *"Honglou meng" shulu* 紅樓夢書錄 (A bibliography on *Dream of the red chamber*). Shanghai: Shanghai Guji Chubanshe, 1981.

———. "Qingmo shiyin jingtu xiaoshuo xiqu mu" 清末石印精圖小說戲曲目 (Index to late Qing novels and plays with lithograph illustrations). In *Xiaoshuo xiantan si zhong* 小說閒談四種. Shanghai: Shanghai Guji Chubanshe, 1985, pt. 4, 126–41.

———. *Wan Qing wenyi baokan shulüe* 晚清文藝報刊述略 (Introduction to late Qing journals of literature and the arts). Beijing: Zhonghua Shuju, 1959.

———. *Wan Qing xiqu xiaoshuo mu* 晚清戲曲小說目 (Bibliography of late Qing drama and fiction). Shanghai: Shanghai Wenyi Lianhe Chubanshe, 1954.

———. "Zhongguo huabao fazhan zhi jingguo—Wei *Liangyou* yibaiwushi qi jinianhao zuo" 中國畫報發展之經過—為 <良友> 一百五十期紀念號作 (The process by which the Chinese illustrated magazine developed, written for the celebration of the 150th issue of *Liangyou*). In *A Ying meishu lunwen ji* 阿英美術論文集 (A Ying's collected essays on art), 75–83. Beijing: Renmin Meishu Chubanshe, 1982.

———, ed. *Gengzi shibian wenxue ji* 庚子事變文學集 (Collection of literary works on the events of 1900). Beijing: Zhonghua Shuju, 1959.

Alfieri, Bruno, ed. *Il gioco dell'amore: Le cortigiane de Venezia dal Trecento al Settecento* (The game of love: Venetian courtesans from the fourteenth to the eighteenth century). Milan: Berenice, 1990.

All About Shanghai: A Standard Guidebook. Shanghai: University Press, 1934. Reprint, Hong Kong: Oxford University Press, 1983.

Appendix to Record of Visits to Courtesan Houses in a Distant Corner by the Sea. See Wang Tao, *Haizou yeyou lu yulu*.

Bakhtin, Mikhail Mikhailovich. *The Dialogic Imagination: Four Essays by M. M. Bakhtin*. Edited by Michael Holquist, translated by Caryl Emerson and Michael Holquist. Austin: University of Texas Press, 1985.

Bamboo Twig Ballads on the Foreign Settlements in Shanghai. See Gu Bingquan, *Shanghai Yangchang zhuzhi ci*.

Bao Tianxiao 包天笑. *Chuanyinglou huiyi lu* 釧影樓回憶錄 (Memoirs from the Chuanying tower). 3 vols. Hong Kong: Dahua Chubanshe, 1971. See also Tianxiao.

Baoyu Sheng 抱玉生, ed. *Huajian yingtie* 花間楹帖 (Poetry in couplets found among the flowers). Woodblock print. Shanghai: Jiboyu, 1861.

Bastid-Bruguière, Marianne, ed. *European Thought in Chinese Literati Culture*. In press.

Beijingshi Yishu Yanjiusuo 北京市藝術研究所 and Shanghai Yishu Yanjiusuo 上海藝術研

究所, eds. *Zhongguo jingju shi* 中國京劇史 (The history of Chinese opera). Beijing: Zhongguo Xiju Chubanshe, 1990.

"Beili huarong" 北里花容 (The flower image of the courtesan). *Youxi bao,* May 29, 1899, 2.

"Beili zhuangshi zhi" 北里妝飾誌 (Record of fashion among the courtesans). *Shijie fanhua bao,* December 26, 1901, 4.

"Benbao gaobai" 本報告白 (An announcement by our paper). *Xinxin xiaoshuo* 3 (1904): inside front cover.

"Benguan chongkai huabang qi" 本館重開花榜啓 (Notice of our paper reopening the competition among the flowers). *Youxi bao,* July 16, 1898, 1.

"Benguan te kai huacong Jingji teke gaobai" 本館特開花叢經濟科告白 (An announcement of our paper holding the Special Competition with Focus on Management of State Affairs among the flowers). *Shijie fanhua bao,* June 30, 1901, 1.

Benjamin, Walter. "Paris, Capital of the Nineteenth Century." In Demetz, *Walter Benjamin,* 146–62.

Bernal, Martin. *Chinese Socialism to 1907.* Ithaca, N.Y.: Cornell University Press, 1976.

Bernheimer, Charles. *Figures of Ill Repute: Representing Prostitution in Nineteenth-Century France.* Cambridge, Mass.: Harvard University Press, 1989.

Bhabha, Homi K. *The Location of Culture.* London and New York: Routledge, 1994.

Bian Yuqing 卞玉清, ed. *Shanghai lishi mingxinpian* 上海歷史明信片 (Souvenir from Shanghai). Shanghai: Tongji Daxue Chubanshe, 1993.

Bickers, Robert A., and Christian Henriot, eds. *New Frontiers: Imperialism's New Communities in East Asia, 1842–1953.* Manchester, U.K.: Manchester University Press, 2000.

Bickers, Robert A., and Jeffrey Wasserstrom. "Shanghai's 'Dogs and Chinese Not Admitted' Sign: Legend, History, and Contemporary Symbol." *The China Quarterly* 142 (June 1995): 444–66.

Bierwisch, W., ed. *Die Rolle der Arbeit in verschiedenen Epochen und Kulturen* (The role of labor in different epochs and cultures). Berlin: Akademie Verlag, 2003.

Biji xiaoshuo daguan 筆記小說大觀 (A parade of brush note fiction). Taipei: Xinxin Shuju, 1988.

Binghong Shanren 病紅山人 (Pang Shubai 龐樹柏) and Xiqiusheng 惜秋生 (Ouyang Juyuan). "Yugou hen chuanqi" 玉鉤痕傳奇 (The jade-hook mark opera). In Chen Wuwo, *Lao Shanghai sanshi nian jianwen lu,* 119–20.

Biographies of Shanghai Flowers. See Han Bangqing, *Haishang hua liezhuan.*

Bourdieu, Pierre. *The Field of Cultural Production: Essays on Art and Literature.* New York: Columbia University Press, 1993.

Bouvet, Mireille-Bénédicte. *Le Grand Livre des images d'Épinal* (The grand book of images from Épinal). Paris: Solar, 1996.

Briais, Bernard. *Grandes Courtisanes du Second Empire* (Grand courtesans of the Second Empire). Paris: Librairie Jules Tallandier, 1981.

"Bugao fang you" 布告訪友 (An announcement to a journalist friend). *Youxi bao,* October 31, 1897, 1.

Cahill, James. "The Emperor's Erotica (Ching Yüan Chai so-shih II)." *Kaikodo* (1999): 24–43.

———. "The Shanghai School in Later Chinese Painting." In Mayching Kao, ed. *Twentieth-Century Chinese Painting,* 54–77. New York: Oxford University Press, 1988.

———. "Three Zhangs." *Orientations,* October 1996, 59–68.

Caifeng bao 采風報 (Fashions of the day). May 1898–1910(?). Editor, Sun Yusheng.

"Cao Menglan beipi guanmen" 曹孟蘭被逼關門 (Cao Menglan is forced to close [her business]). *Youxi bao,* October 5, 1897, 2.

"Cao Menglan chongduo fengchen" 曹孟蘭重墮風塵 (Cao Menglan falls back into being a courtesan). *Youxi bao,* November 12, 1897, 2.

Cao Xueqin 曹雪芹. *Honglou meng* 紅樓夢 (Dream of the red chamber). Beijing: Renmin Wenxue Chubanshe, 1982.

Cao Yu 曹禺. *Richu* 日出 (Sunrise). Chengdu: Sichuan Renmin Chubanshe, 1985.

Chang, Kang-i Sun. *The Late-Ming Poet Ch'en Tzu-lung: Crises of Love and Loyalism.* New Haven, Conn.: Yale University Press, 1991.

Chartier, Roger. *The Cultural Origins of the French Revolution.* Translated by Lydia G. Cochrane. Durham, N.C.: Duke University Press, 1991.

Chen Bohai 陳伯海 and Yuan Jin 袁進. *Shanghai jindai wenxue shi* 上海近代文學史 (History of modern Shanghai literature). Shanghai: Shanghai Renmin Chubanshe, 1993.

Chen Boxi 陳伯熙. *Lao Shanghai* 老上海 (Old Shanghai). 2 vols. Shanghai: Shanghai Taidong Tushuju, 1919. Reprinted as *Shanghai yishi daguan.* Shanghai: Shanghai Shudian, 2000.

———. "Lin Daiyu xiaoshi" 林黛玉小史 (A short history of Lin Daiyu). In *Lao Shanghai,* 102.

———. "Xiaobao zhilüe" 小報志略 (A sketch of the tabloid newspapers). In *Lao Shanghai,* 137–38.

Chen Chaonan 陳超南 and Feng Yiyou 馮懿有. *Lao guanggao* 老廣告 (Old posters). Shanghai: Shanghai Renmin Chubanshe, 1998.

Chen Congzhou 陳從周 and Zhang Ming 章明, eds. *Shanghai jindai jianzhu shigao* 上海近代建筑史稿 (A draft history of modern Shanghai architecture). Shanghai: Shanghai Sanlian Shudian, 1990.

Chen Dingshan 陳定山. *Chunshen jiuwen xuji* 春申舊聞續集 (Old anecdotes about Shanghai). Taipei: Chenguang Yunkan Chubanshe, 1955.

Chen Pingyuan 陳平原. *Ershi shiji zhongguo xiaoshuo shi* 二十世紀中國小說史 (History of twentieth-century Chinese literature). Beijing: Beijing Daxue Chubanshe, 1989.

Chen Pingyuan and Xia Xiaohong 夏曉虹. *Dianshizhai: Tuxiang Wanqing* 點石齋圖像晚清 (Dianshizhai: The late Qing in illustration). Tianjin: Baihua Wenyi Chubanshe, 2001.

Chen Pingyuan, Wang Dewei 王德威, and Shang Wei 商偉, eds. *Wan Ming yu wan Qing: Lishi chuancheng yu wenhua chuangxin* 晚明與晚清:歷史傳承與文化創新 (The late Ming and the late Qing: Historical dynamics and cultural innovations). Wuhan: Hubei Jiaoyu Chubanshe, 2002.

Chen Qiao 辰橋. *Shenjiang baiyong* 申江百詠 (One hundred ballads on Shanghai). Alternative title *Shenjiang zhuzhi ci* 申江竹枝詞 (Shanghai bamboo twig ballads). Woodblock print. Shanghai, 1887. Reprinted in Gu Bingquan, *Shanghai Yangchang zhuzhi ci,* 79–92.

Chen Ruheng 陳汝衡. *Xueyuan zhenwen* 學苑珍聞 (Miscellany from the scholar's garden). Shanghai: Shanghai Guji Chubanshe, 1982.

Chen Sen 陳森. *Pinhua baojian* 品花寶鑑 (A precious mirror for judging flowers). 1849. Reprinted in Lin Jianyu, *Wan Qing xiaoshuo daxi.*

Chen Wuwo 陳無我. "Huabang jiexiao eyan" 花榜揭曉訛言 (On the errors in the announcement of the winner in the flower competition). In *Lao Shanghai sanshi nian jianwen lu,* 203.

———. *Lao Shanghai sanshi nian jianwen lu* 老上海三十年見聞錄 (A record of things seen and heard by an old Shanghai hand in the last thirty years). 1928. Reprint, Shanghai: Shanghai Shudian, 1997.

———. "Qunfang yizhong shimo" 群芳義塚始末 (Ins and outs of the collective flower charity cemetery). In *Lao Shanghai sanshi nian jianwen lu,* 106–7.

———. "Yangliu loutai" 楊柳樓臺 (Willow towers). In *Lao Shanghai sanshi nian jianwen lu,* 3.

———. "Zhongzhi beiwen leici huilu" 塚誌碑文誄詞彙錄 (Record of epitaphs written for the cemetery). In *Lao Shanghai sanshi nian jianwen lu,* 124–28.

———. "Zhuangyuan wu bao" 狀元誤報 (The mistake in the announcement of the winner). In *Lao Shanghai sanshi nian jianwen lu,* 43.

"Chen Yu shouxin" 陳玉收心 (Chen Yu is in retreat). *Shijie fanhua bao,* December 18, 1901, 2.

"Chen Yuqing fu Li Peilan" 陳玉卿覆李佩蘭 (Chen Yuqing's reply to Li Peilan). In Hushang Youxizhu, *Haishang youxi tushuo,* 1:8–9.

Chen Yutang 陳玉堂, ed. *Zhongguo jinxiandai renwu minghao da cidian* 中國近現代人物名

號大辭典 (A dictionary of the names and pen names of personalities in modern China). Hangzhou: Zhejiang Guji Chubanshe, 1992.

Chenbao 晨報.

Cheng Bi 澄碧. "Xiaoshuojia Li Boyuan" 小說家李伯元 (The novelist Li Boyuan). In Wei Shaochang, *Li Boyuan yanjiu ziliao*, 41.

Cheng bing ben xinyuan quanbu xiuxiang "Honglou meng" (Completely illustrated *Dream of the red chamber* of the Zheng and Bing manuscripts, newly compiled). In *"Honglou meng" congshu* (Collection of *Dream of the red chamber* editions). Taipei: Guangwen Shuju, 1977.

Cheng Huiying 程蕙英. *Feng shuang fei* 鳳雙飛 (A pair of phoenixes takes off). Manuscript, Qing Jiaqing period, serialized in *Youxi bao* starting November 12, 1897.

Chi Zhicheng 池志澂 (pseud. Haitian Yanzhang Man Hen Sheng 海天煙瘴曼恨生). *Hu you mengying* 滬游夢影 (Dream images of a visit to Shanghai). Original manuscript ca. 1893. Shanghai: Shanghai Guji Chubanshe, 1989.

The China Directory, for the year 1875. Hong Kong: China Mail, 1875.

"Chinese Theaters." *North China Herald*, January 5, 1867, 2–3.

Chishuo si zhong 癡說四種 (Mad talk: Four kinds). Shanghai: Shenbaoguan, 1877.

Chongding Haishang qunfang pu. See Xiaolantian Chanqing Shizhe, *Haishang qunfang pu*.

Chongtianzi 蟲天子. See Zhang Tinghua.

"Choujuan ruji" 籌捐入己 (Embezzlement of charity funds). *Youxi bao* (date unclear, sometime in January 1899). Reprinted in Chen Wuwo, *Lao Shanghai sanshi nian jianwen lu*, 128.

Chousi Zhuren 抽絲主人 (Wu Jianren 吳趼人). *Haishang mingji Si Da Jin'gang zhuan qishu* 海上名妓四大金剛傳奇書 (The sensational biographies of the Four Great Golden Diamond Cutters from Shanghai). Woodblock print. 100 *hui*, 4 vols. Shanghai, 1898. Reprinted in *Shinmatsu shōsetsu kenkyū* 15 (1992): 97–160; 17 (1994): 96–129; 18 (1995): 122–31; 19 (1996): 102–32.

Chow, Rey. *Writing Diaspora: Tactics of Intervention in Contemporary Cultural Studies*. Bloomington: Indiana University Press, 1993.

Chunjiang huayue bao 春江花月報 (Shanghai courtesan entertainment daily). 1901–4.

Clark, J. D. (John D.), ed. *Sketches in and around Shanghai, etc.* Shanghai: Shanghai Mercury and Celestial Empire, 1894.

Clark, Timothy J. *The Painting of Modern Life: Paris in the Art of Manet and His Followers*. Princeton, N.J.: Princeton University Press, 1984.

Claypool, Lisa. *The Social Body: "Beautiful Women" Imagery in Late Imperial China*. Master's thesis, Department of Art History, University of Oregon, 1994.

Coates, Austin. *China Races*. Hong Kong: Oxford University Press, 1984.

Cochran, Sherman, ed. *Inventing Nanjing Road: Commercial Culture in Shanghai, 1900–1945*. Ithaca, N.Y.: East Asia Program, Cornell University, 1999.

Cohen, Paul. *Between Tradition and Modernity: Wang T'ao and Reform in Late Ch'ing China*. Cambridge, Mass.: Council on East Asian Studies, Harvard University, 1987.

Cohn, Don J., comp. and trans. *Vignettes from the Chinese: Lithographs from Shanghai in the Late Nineteenth Century*. Hong Kong: The Chinese University of Hong Kong Press, 1990.

Corbin, Alain. *Women for Hire: Prostitution and Sexuality in France after 1850*. Cambridge, Mass.: Harvard University Press, 1990.

———, ed. *L'Avènement des loisirs, 1850–1960* (The coming of leisure). Paris: Aubier, 1995.

Crespigny, Rafe de, and Liu Ts'un-yuan. "A Flower in a Sinful Sea." *Renditions* 17 and 18 (Autumn 1982): 137–92.

Crow, Carl. *Handbook for China*. Shanghai: Hwa-mei Book Concern, 1913. Reprint, Taipei: Chengwen Chuban Gongsi, 1973.

Csergo, Julia. "Extension et mutation du loisir citadin, Paris 19e siècle–début 20e siècle" (The expansion and shifts in urban leisure of Paris during the nineteenth century). In Corbin, *L'Avènement des loisirs, 1850–1960*, 121–68.

Cui Lingqin 崔令欽. *Jiaofang ji jianding* 教坊記箋訂 (Record of the court entertainment bureau). Taipei: Hongye Shuju, 1973.

"Da Jin'gang zeqi daimao" 大金剛擇期戴帽 (The [Four] Great Golden Diamond Cutters choose a date for putting on their hats). *Youxi bao*, October 18, 1897, 2.

Da Shanghai zhinan 大上海指南 (Guide to greater Shanghai). Shanghai: Guangming Shuju, 1933, 1947.

Da shijie 大世界 (The great world)*: The Great World Daily News*. 1917–31.

"Dai jiaoshu Lin Daiyu deng ni mujuan gouzhi huazhong xiaoqi" 代校書林黛玉等擬募捐購置花塚小啓 (Announcement of a draft fund-raising proposal for establishing a public cemetery for courtesans written on behalf of the *jiaoshu* Lin Daiyu and others). *Youxi bao*, October 9, 1898, 1.

"Dai Lin Daiyu jiaoshu zhi Lu Lanfen, Jin Xiaobao, Zhang Shuyu zhu jiaoshu quanjuan huazhong jian" 代林黛玉校書致陸蘭芬金小寶張書玉諸校書勸捐花塚箋 (Letter written in the name of *jiaoshu* Lin Daiyu to Lu Lanfen, Jin Xiaobao, Zhang Shuyu urging them to participate in fund-raising for the establishment of a courtesan cemetery). *Youxi bao*, around October 7, 1898. Reprinted in Chen Wuwo, *Lao Shanghai sanshi nian jianwen lu*, 108–9.

"Dai mou jiaoshu zhi pitiao keren shu" 代某校書致皮條客人書 (Letter written in the name of a *jiaoshu* addressed to a client who failed to pay his debts). *Youxi bao*, April 27, 1899, 1–2.

Dalby, Liza. *Geisha*. Reprint, New York: Vintage Books, 1985.

"Dangyan guqu Lin Baozhu qingcai shicheng" 當筵顧曲林寶珠青睞時承 (Performing *qu* at a banquet, Lin Baozhu tries to please the one who has influence [on her future]). *Youxi bao*, October 24, 1897, 2.

Darwent, Charles Ewart. *Shanghai: A Handbook for Travellers and Residents to the Chief Objects of Interest in and around the Foreign Settlements and Native City*. Shanghai: Kelly and Walsh, 1903.

———. *Shanghai: A Handbook for Travellers and Residents to the Chief Objects of Interest in and around the Foreign Settlements and Native City*. Revised edition, Shanghai: Kelly and Walsh, 1920. Reprint, Taipei: Ch'eng Wen Publishing, 1973.

Demetz, Peter, ed. *Walter Benjamin: Reflections, Essays, Aphorisms, Autobiographical Writing*. New York: Schocken Books, 1978.

Deng Zhimo 鄧志謨. *Sensen pian* 洒洒 編. Late Ming edition in the Naikaku Bunko.

Des Forges, Alexander Townsend. "Street Talk and Alley Stories: Tangled Narratives of Shanghai from 'Lives of Shanghai Flowers' (1892) to 'Midnights' (1933)." Ph.D. diss., Princeton University, 1998.

Dian Gong 顛公. *Shanghai pianshu shijie* 上海騙術世界 (The world of trickery in Shanghai). Lithograph. Shanghai: Saoye Shanfang, 1914.

Dianshizhai 點石齋, ed. *Shanghai xian chengxiang zujie quantu* 上海縣城廂租界全圖 (Complete map of Shanghai district town, its immediate surroundings, and the settlements). Shanghai: Dianshizhai, 1884.

———. *Shenjiang shengjing tu* 申江勝景圖 (Illustrated grand sites of Shanghai). Lithograph. 2 vols. Shanghai: Dianshizhai, 1884.

Dianshizhai huabao 點石齋畫報 (Dianshizhai illustrated magazine). Shanghai, 1884–98.

Dianshizhai Zhuren 點石齋主人. "Shiyin *Shenjiang shengjing tu* chushou" 石印申江勝景圖出售 (Lithograph edition of *Illustrated grand sites of Shanghai* on sale). *Shenbao*, December 12, 1884, 1.

"Diaotou gaobai" 調頭告白 (Advertising changes of address). *Youxi bao*, October 9, 1898, 1.

"Diyi fansi jinyan yinxi gaoshi" 第一藩司禁演淫戲告示 (Public announcement by the office of the prefecture on banning obscene operas). *Shenbao*, April 27, 1890, 3.

Dolezelova-Velingerova, Milena, ed. *The Chinese Novel at the Turn of the Century*. Toronto: University of Toronto Press, 1980.

"Dong xi Yaohua, guanren banjia" 東西耀華, 倌人半價 (In the eastern and western branches of the Yaohua studio, courtesans pay half price [for their photographs]). *Shijie fanhua bao*, March 8, 1905, 2.

"Dong Xiyang can" 東西洋摻 (Mixing the Japanese with the Western clients). *Youxi bao*, March 11, 1899, 2.

Dream Images of a Visit to Shanghai. See Chi Zhicheng, *Hu you mengying*.

Dream of the Red Chamber. See Cao Xueqin, *Honglou meng*.

Dreams of Shanghai's Glamour. See Sun Yusheng, *Haishang fanhua meng*.

Duhui modeng: Yuefenpai 1910–1930 都會摩登: 月份牌 1910–1930 (Urban chic: Cigarette advertisement calendars, 1910–30). Hong Kong: Sanlian Chubanshe, 1994.

"Dumen zayong." See under Yang Jingting.

Dyce, Charles M. *The Model Settlement: Personal Reminiscences of Thirty Years' Residence in the Model Settlement Shanghai 1870–1900*. London: Chapman and Hall, 1906.

Edgren, Søren. "The *Ching-ying hsiao-sheng* and Traditional Illustrated Biographies of Women." *The Gest Library Journal* 5 (November 2, 1992): 161–73.

Elvin, Mark. "The Administration of Shanghai, 1905–1914." In Mark Elvin and G. William Skinner, *The Chinese City between Two Worlds*, 131–59.

Elvin, Mark, and G. William Skinner, eds. *The Chinese City between Two Worlds*. Stanford, Calif.: Stanford University Press, 1963.

"Enke xiache" 恩客下車 (Loving patron gets off his carriage). *Youxi bao*, February 20, 1899, 2.

Erchun jushi 二春居士 (Ouyang Juyuan 歐陽鉅源? 1883–1907). *Haitian hongxue ji* 海天鴻雪記 (Traces of the past in the world of Shanghai). Shanghai: Shijie Fanhua Baoguan, 1904.

Ershi shiji da wutai 二十世紀大舞台 (The grand stage of the twentieth century). 1904.

Ershisheng 二石生. *Shizhou chunyu* 十洲春雨 (Spring rain on Ten Island [Ningbo]). Reprinted in Zhang Tinghua, *Xiangyan congshu*, series 15, 4:4199–4278.

European Settlements in the Far East: China, Japan, Corea, Indo-China, Straits Settlements, Malay States, Siam, Netherlands, India, Borneo, The Philippines, Etc. New York: Charles Scribner's Sons, 1900.

Famous Shanghai Sites, with Illustrations and Explanations. See *Shenjiang mingsheng tushuo*.

Fang Xing 方行 and Tang Zhijun 湯志鈞, eds. *Wang Tao riji* 王韜日記 (The diary of Wang Tao). Beijing: Zhonghua Shuju, 1987.

Faure, David, ed. *Town and Country in China: Identity and Perception*. Oxford: Palgrave in association with St. Antony's College, 2002.

Fei Chengkang 費成康. *Zhongguo zujie shi* 中國租界史 (A history of the Foreign Settlements in China). Shanghai: Shanghai Shehuikexueyuan Chubanshe, 1991.

Feiyingge huabao 飛影閣畫報 (Flying Shadows Studio illustrated). October 1890–April 1893. Changed name to *Feiyingge jishi huabao* 飛影閣記士畫報. April 1993–May 1894. Changed name to *Feiyingge jishi huace* 飛影閣記士畫冊. June 1894–October 1895. Editor, Wu Youru 吳友如.

Feng Menglong 馮夢龍. "Du Shiniang nu chen baibaoxiang" 杜十娘怒沉百寶箱 (In her wrath, Du Shiniang drowns the treasure box). In *Jingshi tongyan*, 485–500.

———. "Jiang Xingge chonghui zhenzhu shan" 蔣興哥重會珍珠衫 (Jiang Xingge meets the pearl shirt a second time). In *Gujin xiaoshuo*.

———. *Jingshi tongyan* 警世通言 (Common words to warn the world). Beijing: Zuojia Chubanshe, 1956.

———. "Maiyoulang qiaozhan huakui" 賣油郎巧占花魁 (The oil seller ingeniously wins the flower queen). In *Xingshi hengyan*, 32–73.

———. *Stories Old and New: A Ming Dynasty Collection*. Translated by Shuhui Yang and Yunqin Yang. Seattle: University of Washington Press, 2000.

———. *Stories to Caution the World: A Ming Dynasty Collection, Volume 2.* Translated by Shuhui Yang and Yunqin Yang. Seattle: University of Washington Press, 2005.

———. *Xingshi hengyan* 醒世恆言 (Lasting words to awaken the world). Beijing: Zuojia Chubanshe, 1956.

———, ed. *Gujin xiaoshuo* 古今小說 (Stories old and new). Wanli era (1573–1619). Reprint, Fuzhou: Fujian Renmin Chubanshe, 1980.

"Fengsu zhi" 風俗志 (Notes on customs). *Shijie fanhua bao,* October 25, 1902.

Fenlita Xingzhe 芬利它行者. *Zhuxi huashi xiaolu* 竹西花事小錄 (A small record of courtesan life in Yangzhou). N.d. (1869). Reprinted in Zhang Tinghua, *Xiangyan congshu,* series 12, 3:3343–64.

Fischer-Lichte, Erika. *The Semiotics of Theater.* Translated by Geremie Gaines and Doris L. Jones. Bloomington: University of Indiana Press, 1992.

Flowers from the Spring River. See Zou Tao, *Chunjiang huashi.*

Fogel, Joshua A., ed. "Japanese Travelogues of China in the 1920s: The Accounts of Akutagawa Ryūnosuke and Tanizaki Jun'ichirō." *Chinese Studies in History* 30.4 (summer 1997): 3–103.

Fu Xiangyuan 傅湘源. *"Da shijie" shihua* 大世界史話 (A chronicle of *The great world*). Shanghai: Shanghai Daxue Chubanshe, 1999.

"Fu yao lun" 服妖論 (On dressing like a demon). *Shenbao,* March 9, 1888, 1.

"Fude Si Da Jin'gang chuangjian huazhong" 賦得四大金剛創建花塚 (Poems on the Four Great Golden Diamond Cutters establishing the courtesan cemetery). *Youxi bao,* January 1, 1899, 3.

"Funü dongling yi chuan xuezi zhi jiaojian" 婦女冬令亦穿靴子之矯健 (The vigorous stride of women wearing boots this winter). *Tuhua ribao,* no. 133 (1909), 7.

"Funü jingchuan majia yaoyan" 婦女競穿馬甲耀眼 (Women competing to dazzle the eye by wearing *majia*). *Tuhua ribao,* no. 93 (1909), 7.

"Funü kanxi zhuzhi ci" 婦女看戲竹枝詞 (Bamboo twig ballad on women going to the theater). In *Xu kan Shanghai zhuzhi ci,* 21–26.

Funü shibao 婦女時報 (The ladies' times). 1911–17.

Funü zazhi 婦女雜誌 (Ladies' journal). 1915–31.

Gai Qi 改琦. *"Honglou meng" tuyong* 紅樓夢圖詠 (Illustrated eulogies of *Dream of the red chamber*). Woodblock print. Shanghai, 1879. Reprint, Taipei: Yewen Yinshuguan, 1974.

Gao Hanqing 高翰卿. "Benguan chuangyeshi" 本館創業史 (The history of the founding period of our publishing house). In Shangwu Yinshuguan, *1897–1992 Shangwu yinshuguan jiushiwu nian,* 8–9.

Ge Yuanxu 葛元煦. *Hu you zaji* 滬游雜記 (Miscellaneous notes on visiting Shanghai). Shanghai, 1876. Reprint, Shanghai: Shanghai Guji Chubanshe, 1989.

"Ge zhang yanchi" 各張艷幟 (Relaunching their business). *Youxi bao,* October 10, 1898, 2.

Geertz, Clifford. *The Interpretation of Cultures: Selected Essays.* New York: Basic Books, 1973.

"Gengchen chunji Shenjiang huabang jianglian" 庚辰春季申江花榜獎聯 (Winners list of the Shanghai flower competition, spring 1880). In *Xu kan Shanghai zhuzhi ci.*

"Gengzheng diaotou" 更正調頭 (Correcting moving announcements). *Youxi bao,* August 26, 1897, 2.

Gezhong Shengshou 箇中生手. *Wumen huafang xulu* 吳門畫舫續錄. In Zhang Tinghua, *Xiangyan congshu,* series 17, 5:4823–46.

Giles, Herbert A. *Chinese Sketches.* London: Trübner & Co., Ludgate Hill; Shanghai: Kelly & Co., 1876.

Ginzburg, Carlo. *The Cheese and the Worms: The Cosmos of a Sixteenth-Century Miller.* Translated by John and Anne Tedeschi. Middlesex, U.K.: Penguin Books, 1980.

Gongyi Shushe 公益書社, ed. *Hujiang seyi zhinan* 滬江色藝指南 (A guide to the courtesans of Shanghai). Shanghai: Gongyi Shushe, 1908.

Goodman, Bryna. "Improvisations on a Semicolonial Theme, or, How to Read a Celebration of Transnational Urban Community." *The Journal of Asian Studies* 59.4 (November 2000): 889–926.

———. *Native Place, City, and Nation: Regional Networks and Identities in Shanghai, 1853–1937.* Berkeley: University of California Press, 1995.

The Great Qing Code. Translated by William C. Jones, with the assistance of Tianquan Cheng and Yongling Zhang. Oxford, U.K.: Clarendon Press, 1994.

Green, Owen Mortimer. "Introduction." In *Shanghai of To-day,* 1.

———, ed. *Shanghai of To-day: A Souvenir Album of Fifty Vandyck Prints of "The Model Settlement."* Shanghai: Kelly and Walsh, 1927.

Gronewold, Sue. *Beautiful Merchandise: Prostitution in China 1860–1936.* New York: Harrington Park Press, 1985.

Gu Bingquan 顧炳權, ed. *Shanghai Yangchang zhuzhi ci* 上海洋場竹枝詞 (Bamboo twig ballads on the Foreign Settlements in Shanghai). Shanghai: Shanghai Shudian Chubanshe, 1996.

"Guan ju xiaoji" 觀劇小記 (A reportage on the theater). *Shenbao,* March 18, 1889, 3.

Guanyuan Naideweng 管園耐德翁. *Ducheng jisheng* 都城紀勝 (A record of the splendors of the capital city). 1235. Reprint, Beijing: Zhongguo Shangwu Chubanshe, 1982.

Guichuzi 歸鋤子. *"Honglou meng" bu* 紅樓夢補 (A sequel to *Dream of the red chamber*). Shanghai: Shenbaoguan, 1879.

A Guide for Residents of Shanghai: What the Chinese in Shanghai Ought to Know. See Huang Renjing, *Huren baojian.*

Guide to Greater Shanghai. See *Da Shanghai zhinan.*

The Guide to Shanghai. Shanghai: Oriental Advertising Co., 1914.

Gujin xiaoshuo. See under Feng Menglong.

Guoli Beijing daxue Zhongguo minsu xuehui minsu congshu 國立北京大學中國民俗學會民俗叢書 (Folklore and folk literature series of National Peking University and Chinese Association for Folklore). Reprint, Taipei, 1973.

"Guqu xiantan" 顧曲閒談 (Idle talk on *qu* [song] performance). *Youxi bao,* October 14, 1897, 2.

Guwu Molangzi 古吳墨浪子. *Xihu jiahua* 西湖佳話 (Legends of West Lake). Seventeenth century. Reprint, Shanghai: Shanghai Guji, 1980.

———. "Xileng yunji" 西冷韻跡 (Poetic tidbits from West Lake). In *Xihu jiahua,* 79–106.

Haan, J. H. *Thalia and Terpsichore on the Yangtze: Foreign Theatre and Music in Shanghai 1859–1865. A Survey and a Calendar of Performances.* Vol. 1 of *The Sino-Western Miscellany, being Historical Notes about Foreign Life in China.* Amsterdam, private printing, 1988.

Haishang dengshi lu. See under Zou Tao.

"Haishang fanhua" 海上繁華 (Shanghai prosperity). *Youxi bao,* September 21, 1898, 2.

Haishang fanhua meng. See under Sun Yusheng.

Haishang fanhua tu 海上繁華圖 (Shanghai's prosperity illustrated). Woodblock print. Shanghai, 1885.

Haishang hua liezhuan. See under Han Bangqing.

Haishang hua yinglu. See under Qixia and Danru.

Haishang jing hong ying 海上驚鴻影 (Photographs of five hundred Shanghai beauties). Shanghai: Youzheng Shuju, 1913. Unpaginated.

Haishang Juewu Sheng. See Sun Yusheng.

"Haishang kanhua riji" 海上看花日記 (Daily notes on flower viewing in Shanghai). *Shijie fanhua bao,* October 1, 1901, 2.

"Haishang minghua chidu" 海上名花尺牘 (Letters by famous Shanghai courtesans). In Hushang Youxizhu, *Haishang youxi tushuo,* 1–14.

Haishang qinglou lejing tu 海上青樓樂景圖 (Illustrations of happy scenes from Shanghai courtesan houses). Lithograph. Shanghai, 1892.

Haishang qinglou tuji. See under Huayu Xiaozhu Zhuren.

Haishang qishu 海上奇書 (Sensational books about Shanghai). 1892. Periodical founded by Han Bangqing 韓邦慶.

Haishang qunfang pu. See under Xiaolantian Chanqing Shizhe.

Haishang yanhua suoji. See under Langyouzi.

Haishang yeyou beilan. See under Zhimisheng.

"Haishang yiqing" 海上移情 (Change of heart in Shanghai). *Youxi bao*, August 28, 1899, 2.

Haishang youxi tushuo. See under Hushang Youxizhu.

Han Bangqing 韓邦慶 (Han Ziyun 韓子雲, pseud. Huaye Liannong 花也憐儂). *Haishang hua liezhuan* 海上花列傳 (Biographies of Shanghai flowers). Shanghai, 1892–94. Reprint of original illustrated lithograph edition, Taipei: Huangguan Zazhishe, 1987. Unpaginated. Reprint without illustrations, Beijing: Renmin Wenxue Chubanshe, 1985.

Hanan, Patrick. *The Chinese Vernacular Story*. Cambridge, Mass.: Harvard University Press, 1981.

———. "Fengyue Meng and the Courtesan Novel." *Harvard Journal of Asiatic Studies* 58.2 (December 1998): 345–72.

———. "The First Novel Translated into Chinese." In *Chinese Fiction of the Nineteenth and Early Twentieth Centuries*, 85–109. New York: Columbia University Press, 2004.

Hanshang Mengren 邗上蒙人. *Fengyue meng* 風月夢 (Dreams of the wind and the moon). Preface 1848. First edition, Shanghai: Shenbaoguan, 1883. Reprint, Jinan: Qi Lu Shushe, 1991.

Hanshang Yugong 漢上寓公. *Xin Hankou* 新漢口 (New Hankow). N.p.: Liuyi Shuju, 1909.

"Haoyue changyuan" 好月常圓 ([We wish] the good moon is always full). *Youxi bao*, September 21, 1897, 2.

"He Ruyu douquanzi" 何如玉兜圈子 (He Ruyu goes around in circles). *Shijie fanhua bao*, December 23, 1901, 2.

Hegel, Robert E. *Reading Illustrated Fiction in Late Imperial China*. Stanford, Calif.: Stanford University Press, 1998.

Henriot, Christian. *Belles de Shanghai: Prostitution et sexualité en Chine aux 19e–20e siècle* (Shanghai beauties: Prostitution and sexuality in China during the nineteenth and twentieth centuries). Paris: CNRS-éditions, 1997.

———. "Chinese Courtesans in Late Qing and Early Republican Shanghai (1849–1925)." *East Asian History* 8 (1994): 33–52.

———. "Courtship, Sex, and Money: The Economics of Courtesan Houses in Nineteenth- and Twentieth-Century Shanghai." Paper presented at the Association for Asian Studies Annual Conference, Honolulu, April 1996.

———. "'From a Throne of Glory to a Seat of Ignominy,' Shanghai Prostitution Revisited (1849–1949)." *Modern China* 22 (1996): 132–63.

———. "La Prostitution à Shanghai aux 19e et 20e siècles (1849–1958)" (Prostitution in Shanghai during the nineteenth and twentieth centuries [1849–1958]). 3 vols. Doctorat d'état, Paris, 1992.

———. *Prostitution and Sexuality in Shanghai: A Social History, 1849–1949*. Cambridge: Cambridge University Press, 2001.

———. "Prostitution et 'police des moeurs' à Shanghai aux 19e–20e siècle" (Prostitution and the "vice squad" in Shanghai during the nineteenth and twentieth centuries). In *La Femme en Asie Orientale*. Lyon: Université de Lyon, 1988, 64–93.

Hershatter, Gail. *Dangerous Pleasures: Prostitution and Modernity in Twentieth-Century Shanghai*. Berkeley: University of California Press, 1997.

———. "The Hierarchy of Shanghai Prostitution 1870–1949." *Modern China* 10 (1989): 463–98.

Hibbett, Howard. *The Floating World in Japanese Fiction*. Tokyo: Charles E. Tuttle, 1996.

Holoch, Donald. "A Novel of Setting: *The Bureaucrats.*" In Dolezelova-Velingerova, *The Chinese Novel at the Turn of the Century*, 76–115.

Honglou fu meng 紅樓復夢 (Another dream of the red chamber). Shanghai: Shenbaoguan, 1876.

"Honglou meng" gongshi 紅樓夢觥史 (A history of *Dream of the red chamber* drinking games). In *Chishuo si zhong.*

"Honglou" yexi pu 紅樓葉戲譜 (Guide to the *Dream of the red chamber* card game). Late Qing period. Reprinted in Zhang Tinghua, *Xiangyan congshu*, series 5, ch. 20.

Honig, Emily. *Creating Chinese Ethnicity: Subei People in Shanghai 1850–1980*. New Haven, Conn.: Yale University Press, 1992.

Hotel Metropole. *Guide to Shanghai (complimentary)*. Shanghai: Hotel Metropole, 1903.

Hu Genxi 胡根喜. *Si Malu* 四馬路 (Fuzhou road). Shanghai: Xuelin Chubanshe, 2001.

Hu Shi 胡適. "*Haishang hua liezhuan* xu" 海上花列傳序 (Preface to *Biographies of Shanghai flowers*)." In *Hu Shi wencun, ji* 2, 3:1–3.

———. *Hu Shi wencun* 胡適文存 (Collected writings of Hu Shi). 1928. Reprint, Taipei: Yuandong Tushu Gongsi, 1953.

———. "Shiqi nian de huigu" 十七年的回顧 (Looking back to these seventeen years). In *Hu Shi wencun, ji* 2, 3:1–3.

Hu you zaji. See under Ge Yuanxu. See also Yuan Zuzhi, *Chongxiu Hu you zaji.*

Hua shijie 花世界 (The flower universe). 1903–?.

Hua'elouzhu 花萼樓主. "Huadi cangsang lu" 花底滄桑錄 (Record of changes in the world of flowers). *Xinsheng* 1, 2, 4, 5, 8, 9 (1921). Unpaginated.

Huang Renjing 黄人鏡 (also signed in English as Wong Tsao-ling [Huang Zaoling]). *Huren baojian* 滬人寶鑑 (A guide for residents of Shanghai): *What the Chinese in Shanghai Ought to Know*. Shanghai: Methodist Publishing House, 1913.

Huang Shiquan 黄式權. *Songnan mengying lu* 淞南夢影錄 (Record of dream images of Shanghai). Shanghai, 1883. Reprint, Shanghai: Shanghai Guji Chubanshe, 1989.

Huashi Zhuren 話石主人. *"Honglou meng" jingyi* 紅樓夢精義 (The essence of *Dream of the red chamber*). In *Chishuo si zhong.*

Huatian ribao 花天日報 (Flower heaven daily). 1902–?.

Huating Wen Yehe 華亭聞野鶴. "Gailun" 概論 (Introduction). In Zhonghua Tushujicheng Gongsi, *Shanghai youlan zhinan* (1919), 1.

Huaye Liannong. See Han Bangqing.

Huaying jixuan 花影集選 (Anthology of courtesan photographs). Shanghai, 1928. Unpaginated.

Huayu Xiaozhu Zhuren 花雨小築主人, comp. *Haishang qinglou tuji* 海上青樓圖記 (Illustrated record of Shanghai courtesan entertainment). 4 vols. Lithograph. Shanghai, 1892. Another edition with two added volumes by the same author appeared in 1895.

"Huayuan yanju" 花園演劇 (Performing in the park). *Shenbao*, November 20, 1886, 3.

"Huayuan yanju xishu" 花園演劇細述 (A detailed report on the performance in the park). *Shenbao*, November 21, 1886, 3.

"Hudi yu jin nüling" 滬地諭禁女伶 (The official order banning female singers in Shanghai). *Shenbao*, January 7, 1890, 3.

Huebner, Jon W. "Architecture and History in Shanghai Central District." *Journal of Oriental Studies* 26.2 (1988): 209–69.

———. "Architecture on the Shanghai Bund." *Papers on Far Eastern History* 39 (1989): 127–65.

Hughes, Robert. *Barcelona*. New York: Vintage, 1993.

Hujiang yanpu 滬江艷譜. See under Liangxi Chilian Jushi.

Hujiang seyi zhinan 滬江色藝指南. See under Gongyi Shushe.

Hujiang yue 滬江月 (The river and the moon in Shanghai).

Hundred Beauties of Nanjing. See Li Yunxiang, *Jinling baimei.*

"Hushang qinglou zhuzhi ci" 滬上青樓竹枝詞 (Bamboo twig ballads on Shanghai courtesan entertainment). In Gu Bingquan, *Shanghai Yangchang zhuzhi ci*, 431–32.

Hushang Youxizhu, 滬上游戲主 (Li Boyuan?), ed. *Haishang youxi tushuo* 海上游戲圖説 (An illustrated introduction to Shanghai entertainment). Lithograph. 4 vols. Shanghai, 1898.

Idema, Wilt. "Shih Chün-pao's and Chu Yu-tun's *Ch'ü-chiang-ch'ih*: The Variety of Mode within Form." *T'oung Pao* 66.4–5 (1980): 217–65.

Idle Talk on Shanghai. See Wang Tao, *Songbin suohua*.

Illustrated Grand Sites of Shanghai. See Dianshizhai, *Shenjiang shengjing tu*.

An Illustrated Introduction to Shanghai Entertainment. See Hushang Youxizhu, *Haishang youxi tushuo*.

Illustrated Record of Shanghai Courtesan Entertainment. See Huayu Xiaozhu Zhuren, *Haishang qinglou tuji*.

Illustrations of Happy Scenes from Shanghai Courtesan Houses. See *Haishang qinglou lejing tu*.

Ishikawa Haruyoroshi 石川流宜. *Yoshiwara Shichifu kami* 吉原七福神 (A courtesan guide to Yoshiwara). Tokyo, 1713.

Jameson, David, Andrew J. Nathan, and Evelyn S. Rawski, eds. *Popular Culture in Late Imperial China*. Berkeley: University of California Press, 1985.

Janku, Andrea. *Nur leere Reden: Politischer Diskurs und die Shanghaier Presse im China des späten 19. Jahrhunderts*. (Just empty talk: Political discourse and the Shanghai press during the late nineteenth century). Wiesbaden, Germany: Harrassowitz, 2003.

Japan. Tetsudōin. *An official guide to eastern Asia; trans-continental connections between Europe and Asia*. 5 vols. Tokyo: Imperial Japanese Government Railways, 1913–17.

"A Japanese Guide-book for Eastern Asia." *The Times*, March 3, 1914, 3.

"Ji Jin Xiaobao jiaoshu lun huazhong juan shi" 紀金小寶校書論花塚捐事 (Report on Jin Xiaobao's comments regarding fund-raising for the courtesan cemetery). *Youxi bao*, January 13, 1899, 1–2.

Ji Wu Chunyi 寄吳春意 (To Wu Chunyi). In Hushang Youxizhu, *Haishang youxi tushuo*, 1:12.

Jiang Fang 蔣防. *Huo Xiaoyu zhuan* 霍小玉傳 (Biography of Huo Xiaoyu). In Lu Xun, ed. *Tang Song chuanqi ji*, 64–76.

Jiang Ruizao 蔣瑞藻. *Xiaoshuo kaozheng* 小説考證 (Investigations about the novel). Shanghai: Shanghai Guji Chubanshe, 1984.

Jiangsu Guji Chubanshe, ed. *Suzhou Taohuawu muban nianhua* 蘇州桃花塢木板年畫 (Taohuawu woodblock new year prints, Suzhou). Nanjing: Jiangsu Guji Chubanshe, 1991.

"Jin Baoxian buyuan dengbang" 金寶仙不願登榜 (Jin Baoxian does not want to be on the ballot). In Chen Wuwo, *Lao Shanghai sanshi nian jianwen lu*, 202–3.

"Jin cishi hu tou zijian shu" 金詞史忽投自薦書 (*Cishi* [courtesan] Jin suddenly put in a vote for herself). *Youxi bao*, November 6, 1897, 2.

"Jin Xiaobao cishi huazhongdi goucheng mujuan kuochong jizhi jianxiu ciyu qi" 金小寶詞史花塚地購成募捐擴充基址建修祠宇啓 (*Cishi* [courtesan] Jin Xiaobao anounces the success of purchasing the land for the courtesan cemetery and the need to raise more funds for laying the foundation and building the memorial hall). *Youxi bao*, March 13, 1899, 1–2.

"Jin Xiaobao Zhu Ruchun xiangma" 金小寶祝如椿相罵 (Jin Xiaobao and Zhu Ruchun hurled insults at each other). *Shijie fanhua bao*, October 1, 1901, 3.

Jinling baimei. See under Li Yunxiang.

Jingying xiaosheng chuji 鏡影簫聲初集 (Mirror reflections and flute sounds, first collection). Copperplate engraving. Tokyo, 1887.

Jingying xiaosheng erji 鏡影簫聲貳集 (Mirror reflections and flute sounds, second collection). Unpublished manuscript, dated 1889, held in Shanghai Municipal Library.

"Jingzhuang zhaoyan" 靚裝照眼 (Rich attire dazzles the eye). *Youxi bao*, May 4, 1899, 2.

Johnson, Linda Cooke. *Shanghai: From Market Town to Treaty Port, 1074–1858*. Stanford, Calif.: Stanford University Press, 1995.

Johnston, William Crane. *The Shanghai Problem*. Westport, Conn.: Hyperion Press, 1937.

Jōjaku Koji 靜軒居士. *Edo hanjō ki* 江戸繁昌記 (A chronicle of Edo's prosperity). Tokyo: Kokki Juku, 1832.

"Juanjian yizhong congtan" 捐建義塚叢談 (Comments on the various [news regarding] fund-raising for the courtesan cemetery). *Youxi bao*, November 14, 1898, 2.

Juyuan 菊園. "Qiminshe shimo ji" 啓民社始末記 (The History of the Association for the Enlightenment of the People). In Zhou Jianyun, *Jubu congkan*, under "Getai xinshi" 歌台新史 (New history of the stage). Shanghai, 1918. Reprinted in *Minguo congshu*, 2nd series, *juan* 1, 69:25–37. Shanghai, 1990.

"Kai Guopan" 開果盤 (Serving the fruit plate). *Tuhua ribao*, no. 177 (1909), 7.

"Kelian mingshu" 可憐名姝 (The pitiable famous courtesan). *Youxi bao*, April 17, 1899, 2.

Kim, Nanny. "New Wine in Old Bottles? Making and Reading an Illustrated Magazine from Late Nineteenth Century Shanghai." In Wagner, *Joining the Global Public*.

Ko, Dorothy. *Every Step a Lotus: Shoes for Bound Feet*. Berkeley: University of California Press, 2001.

Kong Shangren 孔尚任. *Taohua shan* 桃花扇 (The peach blossom fan). Beijing: Renmin Chubanshe, 1956.

Lai Yu-chih 賴毓芝. "Fuliu qianjie: Riben wangluo yu Ren Bonian zuopin zhong de Riben yangfen" 伏流潛借:1870年代上海的日本網絡與任伯年作品中的日本養分 (Subliminal borrowing: The Japanese network in 1870 Shanghai and the Japanese nutrients in Ren Bonian's works). *Meishushi yanjiu jikan* 14 (2003): 159–242.

Laing, Ellen Johnston. "Erotic Themes and Romantic Heroines Depicted by Ch'iu Ying." *Archives of Asian Art* 49 (1996): 68–91.

Langyouzi 浪游子 (signed as Zhiyin Mituren 指引迷途人 in author's preface), comp. *Haishang yanhua suoji* 海上煙花瑣記 (Miscellaneous notes on Shanghai flowers). Woodblock print. 4 vols. Shanghai, 1877. See also Zhimisheng, *Haishang yeyou beilan*.

"Lao bianxiang" 老變相 (Transformation at old age). *Youxi bao*, March 7, 1899, 3.

Lao Shanghai 老上海 (Wu Jianren 吳趼人?). *Hu Baoyu* 胡寶玉 (Hu Baoyu). 1907. Reprinted in *Shinmatsu shōsetsu kenkyū* 14 (1991): 91–156.

The Latest of Famous Sites in Shanghai, with Illustrations and Explanations. See Meihua'an Zhu, *Shenjiang shixia shengjing tushuo*.

Lee, Leo Ou-fan. *Shanghai Modern: The Flowering of a New Urban Culture in China 1930–1945*. Cambridge, Mass.: Harvard University Press, 1999.

Lei Fu 雷夫. "Shenbaoguan zhi guoqu zhuangkuang" 申報館之過去狀況 (Past condition of Shenbaoguan). In Shenbaoguan, *Zuijin zhi wushi nian*, 28b.

Lei Mengshui 雷夢水 et al., eds. *Zhonghua zhuzhi ci* 中華竹枝詞 (Bamboo twig ballads of China). Beijing: Beijing Guji Chubanshe, 1997.

Lengxue. See Chen Jinghan, under *Xinxin xiaoshuo*.

Levy, Howard S. "A Feast of Mist and Flowers: The Gay Quarters of Nanking at the End of the Ming." Typescript. Tokyo, 1966.

———. "The Gay Quarters at Nanking." In "A Feast of Mist and Flowers," 1–32.

———. "The Gay quarters of Ch'ang-an." *Orient/West* 7.10 (1962): 121–28; 8.6 (1963): 115–22; 11.1 (1964): 103–10.

Li Boyuan 李伯元. "Benbao fusong *Feng shuang fei* changben yuanqi" 本報附送鳳雙飛唱本緣起 (The origin of the complimentary gift to our readers of the libretto to *A pair of phoenixes takes off*). *Youxi bao*, November 12, 1897, 1.

———. "Benguan qianju Si Malu shuo" 本館遷居四馬路說 (On moving our office to Fourth Avenue). *Youxi bao*, October 2, 1897, 1.

———. "Bugao fang you" 佈告訪友 (An announcement to a journalist friend). *Youxi bao*, October 31, 1897.

———. "Chuangkan ci" 創刊詞 (Opening words). *Zhinan bao*, June 6, 1896, 1.

———. "Dingyou xiaji Chunjiang wubang bianyan" 丁酉夏季春江武榜弁言 (Foreword to the 1897 summer Shanghai competition of performing artists). In Chen Wuwo. *Lao Shanghai sanshi nian jianwen lu,* 218.

——— (Youxi Zhuren 遊戲主人). "Fanli liutiao" 凡例六條 (Six rules [for the flower competition]). *Youxi bao.* Reprinted in Chen Wuwo, *Lao Shanghai sanshi nian jianwen lu,* 205.

———. *Gengzi guobian tanci* 庚子國變彈詞 (A ballad on the national crisis of 1900). Serialized in *Shijie fanhua bao,* October 1901–October 1902.

——— (Youxi Zhuren 遊戲主人). *Gengzi huaxuan lu* 庚子花選錄 (Record of the election of flowers of 1900). Reprinted in *Shinmatsu shōsetsu kenkyū* 5 (1981): 95–104.

———. "Guan Meiguo yingxi ji" 觀美國影戲記 (On viewing an American shadow play). *Youxi bao,* September 5, 1897, 1.

———. *Guanchang xianxingji* 官場現形記 (The bureaucrats: A revelation). Serialized in *Shijie fanhua bao,* April 1902–June 1905.

———. "Ji benbao kaichuang yilai qingxing" 記本報開創以來情形 (On the situation of our newspaper since the time of its creation). *Youxi bao,* January 16, 1898, 1. Reprinted in Wei Shaochang, *Li Boyuan yanjiu ziliao,* 455–56.

———. "Lun *Youxi bao* zhi benyi" 論游戲報之本意 (On the basic purpose of *Entertainment*). *Youxi bao,* August 25, 1897, 1. Reprinted in Wei Shaochang, *Li Boyuan yanjiu ziliao,* 453–54.

———. "Mujuan gouzhi huazhong yi" 募捐購置花塚議 (Discussion on fund-raising for the purchase and establishment of a courtesan cemetery). *Youxi bao,* October 6, 1898, 1–2.

———. "Nijian huazhong mujuan xiaoqi" 擬建花塚募捐小啓 (A notice on fund-raising for the planned establishment of a courtesan cemetery). *Youxi bao,* October 8, 1898, 1.

——— (Youxi Zhuren 遊戲主人). "Shu Xiao Ruyi deng benbao zhuitao piaozhang gaobai hou" 書小如意登本報追討漂帳告白後 (After Xiao Ruyi's going public announcing the unpaid debts [of her client]). *Youxi bao,* September 28, 1897, 1.

———. *Wenming xiaoshi* 文明小史 (A brief history of modern times). Taipei: Guangyu Chuban Youxian Gongsi, 1984.

———. "Youxi zhu dake lun kai huabang zhi buyi" 游戲主答客論開花榜之不易 (The Master of Entertainment answers visitors' comments on the difficulty of holding the flower competition). In Chen Wuwo, *Lao Shanghai sanshi nian jianwen lu,* 194–95.

———. "Youxi Zhuren gaobai" 游戲主人告白 (Announcement from the Master of Entertainment). *Youxi bao,* March 19, 1899, 1. Reprinted in Chen Wuwo, *Lao Shanghai sanshi nian jianwen lu,* 193.

———. "Youxi Zhuren ni juxing 'Linfang hui' yi" 游戲主人儗舉行遴芳會議 (Comments on the "Beauty Selection Conference" planned by the Master of Entertainment). *Youxi bao,* October 4, 1897, 1. Reprinted in Chen Wuwo, *Lao Shanghai sanshi nian jianwen lu,* 214.

———. "Zhaoxun fangshi ren" 招尋訪事人 (Looking for a reporter). *Youxi bao,* October 6, 1897, 1.

Li Dou 李斗. *Yangzhou huafang lu* 揚州畫舫錄 (A record of the painted boats in Yangzhou). Reprint, Jiangsu: Jiangsu Guangling Guji Keyinshe, 1984.

Li Fang 李昉 et al., eds. *Taiping yulan* 太平御覽 (Imperial digest of the Taiping reign). Taipei: Xinxing Shuju, 1959.

Li Gefei 李格非. *Luoyang mingyuan ji* 洛陽名園記 (A record of famous gardens in Luoyang). In *Congshu jicheng,* first collection.

Li Jingshan 李靜山. *Zayong* 雜詠 (Assorted songs). In Yang Jingting, *Zengbu Dumen jilüe,* 1879, 6:2.

"Li Pingxiang A Pan jieyuan" 李蘋香阿潘結怨 (Li Pingxiang's entanglement with A Pan). *Shijie fanhua bao,* December 10, 1901, 2.

"Li Pingxiang an jie" 李蘋香案結 (The conclusion of the case against Li Pingxiang). *Shijie fanhua bao,* December 8, 1901, 1.

"Li Pingxiang bei ju ji guotang xiangzhi" 李蘋香被拘及過堂詳誌 (A detailed report on the arrest and trial of Li Pingxiang). *Shijie fanhua bao*, December 7, 1901, 2–3.

"Li Pingxiang chu shiji" 李蘋香出詩集 (Li Pingxiang is coming out with a poetry anthology). *Shijie fanhua bao*, May 5, 1901, 1.

"Li Qiaoxian fu Sun Shaojiang" 李巧仙覆孫少江 (Li Qiaoxian's reply to Sun Shaojiang). In Hushang Youxizhu, *Haishang youxi tushuo*, 1:7.

Li Ruzhen 李汝珍. *Huitu Jinghua yuan* 繪圖鏡花緣 (Flowers in the mirror, illustrated). Shanghai: Dianshizhai, 1888.

Li, Wei-Yee. "The Late Ming Courtesan: Invention of a Cultural Ideal." In Widmer and Chang, *Writing Women in Late Imperial China*, 47–73.

Li Xiaoti 李孝悌. "Jindai Shanghai chengshi wenhua zhong de chuantong yu xiandai, 1880–1930" 近代上海城市文化中的傳統與現代, 1880–1930 (Tradition and modernity in Shanghai's modern urban culture, 1880–1930). In Liu and Shi, *Di san jie guoji Hanxue huiyi lunwen ji*.

Li Xiqi 李錫奇. *Nanting huiyi lu* 南亭回憶錄 (A memoir about Nanting [Li Boyuan]). 2 vols. Mimeographed manuscript.

Li Yunxiang 李雲翔. *Jinling baimei* 金陵百媚 (Hundred beauties of Nanjing). Preface 1618. Held by the Naikaku Bunko.

Liangxi Banchisheng 梁谿半痴生 (pseud. of Zou Tao?). *"Hushang pinghua lu" xulu* 滬上評花續錄 (A sequel to *A record of comments on Shanghai flowers*). Woodblock print. Shanghai, 1881.

Liangxi Chilian Jushi 梁溪池蓮居士 (pseud. of Zou Tao). *Hujiang yanpu* 滬江艷譜 (Collection of poetry on Shanghai beauties). Woodblock print. Shanghai, 1883.

———. *Hushang pinghua lu* (A record of comments on Shanghai flowers). Woodblock print. Shanghai, 1881.

Liangxi Xiaoxiangguan Shizhe. See Zou Tao.

Liangyou huabao 良友畫報 (Young companion). 1926–41.

Liao Meiyun 廖美雲. *Tang ji yanjiu* 唐妓研究 (A study on Tang courtesans). Taipei: Xuesheng Shuju, 1995.

"Liaocun gongping" 聊存公評 (There are still unbiased comments). *Youxi bao*, February 10, 1903, 2.

Libailiu 禮拜六 (Saturday). 1914–23. Reprint, Yangzhou: Jiangxi Guangling Guji Keyinshe, 1987.

Lin Daiyu 林黛玉. *Beinan shimo ji* 被難始末記 (The complete record of meeting with calamity). Preface by Ouyang Juyuan. Shanghai (?), 1901. Reprinted in A Ying, *Gengzi shibian wenxue ji*, 1065–84.

———. "Lin Daiyu zishu kuzhong han" 林黛玉自述苦衷函 (A letter in which Lin Daiyu tells her side of the story). In Chen Wuwo, *Lao Shanghai sanshi nian jianwen lu*, 128.

———. "Shanghai Lin Daiyu meishi dong Hangzhou Lüqin nüshi" 上海林黛玉眉史東杭州綠琴女史 (Shanghai's *meishi* courtesan Lin Daiyu [and] East Hangzhou's *nüshi* Lüqin). In Hushang Youxizhu, *Haishang youxi tushuo* 1:1.

"Lin Daiyu." *Shijie fanhua bao*, May 20, 1904, 2.

"Lin Daiyu chong lian yu yingwu" 林黛玉重簾語鸚鵡 (Lin Daiyu talks to her parrot with the blinds down). *Youxi bao*, June 23, 1899, 2.

"Lin Daiyu yishang chuse" 林黛玉衣裳出色 (Lin Daiyu in stunning dress). *Youxi bao*, October 11, 1897, 2.

Lin Jianyu 林健毓, ed. *Wan Qing xiaoshuo daxi* 晚清小說大系. Taipei: Guangya, 1984.

Liu Cuirong 劉翠溶 and Shi Shouqian 石守謙, eds. *Di san jie guoji Hanxue huiyi lunwen ji: Jingji shi, dushi wenhua yu wuzhi shenghuo* 第三屆國際漢學會議論文集: 經濟史, 都市文化與物質生活 (Third International Sinological Conference: Economic history, urban culture, and material life). Taipei: Zhongyang Yanjiuyuan Lishi Yuyan Yanjiusuo, 2002.

Liu Huiwu 劉惠吾. *Shanghai jindai shi* 上海近代史 (History of modern Shanghai). Shanghai: Huadong Shifan Daxue Chubanshe, 1985.

Liu Mengyin 劉夢音. *Jiang Hu zayong* 江滬雜詠 (Sundry songs on Shanghai). 1889. Reprinted as *Shanghai zhuzhi ci* 上海竹枝詞 (Bamboo twig ballads on Shanghai), in Gu Bingquan, *Shanghai Yangchang zhuzhi ci*, 417–18.

Liu, Tao Tao, and David Faure, eds. *Unity and Diversity: Local Cultures and Identities in China.* Hong Kong: Hong Kong University Press, 1996.

Liu Yiqing 劉義慶. *Youming lu* 幽明錄 (Record of the netherworld). Quoted in *Taiping yulan*, ch. 41, 313–14.

Liyuan gongbao 梨園公報 (The actor's bulletin). 1928–31.

Longstreet, Stephen, and Ethel Longstreet. *Yoshiwara, the Pleasure Quarters of Old Tōkyō*. Tokyo: Yehbooks, 1988.

Lu Feida 陸費達. "Jing, Jin liang yue ji" 京津兩月記 (Record of a two-month visit to Peking and Tianjin). *Xiaoshuo yuebao* 2.9 (1911): 1.

Lu Hanchao. "Away from Nanking Road: Small Stores and Neighborhood Life in Modern Shanghai." *Journal of Asian Studies* 54.1 (1995): 93–123.

———. *Beyond the Neon Lights: Everyday Shanghai in the Early Twentieth Century*. Berkeley: University of California Press, 1999.

"Lu *Tiannan xin bao* lun Shanghai Si Da Jin'gang" 錄天南新報論上海四大金剛 (Reprint of *Tiannan xinbao* [paper published in Singapore] on the Four Great Golden Diamond Cutters of Shanghai). *Youxi bao*, May 28, 1899, 1.

Lu Xun 魯迅, ed. *Tang Song chuanqi ji* 唐宋傳奇集 (A collection of Tang Song *chuanqi* stories). Shanghai: Beixin Shuju, 1929.

———. "Xiaxie xiaoshuo" 狹邪小說 (Fiction about prostitution). In *Zhongguo xiaoshuo shilüe*, 256–68.

———. *Zhongguo xiaoshuo shilüe* 中國小說史略 (A brief history of the Chinese novel). Beijing: Renmin Wenxue Chubanshe, 1989.

"Lun Cao Menglan beibi guanmen" 論曹孟蘭被逼關門 (On Cao Menglan being forced to close [her business]). *Youxi bao*, October 7, 1897, 1.

"Lun Haishang funü yifu" 論海上婦女衣服 (On Shanghai women's clothing). *Youxi bao*, November 7, 1897, 1.

"Lun Hu ji jixi tai shen" 論滬妓積習太甚 (The Shanghai courtesans are overdoing it). *Youxi bao*, July 20, 1899, 1.

"Lun Hubin shuyu yingchou dangyi Lu Lanfen wei diyi" 論滬濱書寓應酬當以陸蘭芬為第一 (Lu Lanfen should be considered as Shanghai's number one in the art of entertaining guests). *Youxi bao*, September 18, 1897, 1.

"Lun Hushang funü fushi zhi qi" 論滬上婦女服飾之奇 (On the exotic in Shanghai women's way of dressing). *Youxi bao*, January 1, 1899, 1–2.

"Lun jinchang xinfa" 論禁娼新法 (New law banning prostitution). *Shenbao*, December 31, 1875, 1.

"Lun jinjin nannü fushi zhi yi" 論近今男女服飾之異 (On the strange clothing worn by men and women nowadays). *Zhinan bao*, June 17, 1897, 1–2.

"Lun jiyuan yu shangwu xiang weixi" 論妓院與商務相維繫 (Mutual support between commerce and courtesan houses). *Caifeng bao*, November 18, 1898, 1.

"Lun Li Pingxiang bei ju shi" 論李蘋香被拘 (On Li Pingxiang being detained by the court). *Shijie fanhua bao*, December 7, 1901, 1.

"Lun nüzi zhaoxiang zhi bian" 論女子照像之便 (On making it easier for women to have their photographs taken). *Shijie fanhua bao*, March 8, 1905, 2.

"Lun Shanghai jiaoshu gechang" 論上海校書歌唱 (On the singing by Shanghai courtesans). *Youxi bao*, October 8, 1897, 2.

"Lun Shanghai shimian zhi hai zaiyu she" 論上海市面之害在于奢 (On extravagance as the disease of the Shanghai market). *Shenbao,* January 21, 1888, 1.

"Lun zuo yemache zhi sheng" 論坐夜馬車之盛 (On the fashion of nighttime carriage rides). *Youxi bao,* July 9, 1899, 1.

Luo Suwen 羅蘇文. "Jindai Shanghai jiaoyu, kexue, wenhua shiye de tuozhan yu tuijin" 近代上海教育，科學，文化事業的拓展與推進 (On the realization and promotion of Shanghai's educational, science, and cultural institutions at the turn of the century). *Shilin* 3 (1992): 55–62.

———. *Shikumen: Xunchangren jia* 石庫門：尋常人家 (Shiku housing: In search of the housing of common folk). Shanghai: Shanghai Renmin Chubanshe, 1991.

Ma Guangren 馬光仁. *Shanghai xinwen shi (1850–1949)* 上海新聞史 (1850–1949) (History of Shanghai journalism, 1850–1949). Shanghai: Fudan Daxue Chubanshe, 1996.

Ma Jianshi 馬建石, ed. *Da Qing lülie tongkao jiaozhu* 大清律列通考校注 (The Qing code with annotations). Beijing: Zhongguo Zhengfa Daxue Chubanshe, 1991.

Ma Junliang 馬俊良, ed. *Longwei mishu* 龍威秘書. Reprinted in Yan Yiping, *Baibu congshu jicheng.*

Ma Liangchun 馬良春 and Li Futian 李富田, eds. *Zhongguo wenxue da cidian* 中國文學大詞典 (Grand dictionary of Chinese literature). Tianjin: Tianjin Renmin Chubanshe, 1991.

Ma Xiangbo 馬相伯. "Shanghai Huifeng Yinhang kaiban shi de da gudong" 上海匯豐銀行開辦時的大股東 (Major shareholders at the time when the Hong Kong Shanghai Bank was first founded). In *Yiri yitan.* Reprinted in Zhu Weizheng, *Ma Xiangbo ji,* 1155.

———. *Yiri yitan* 一日一談 (Daily talk). Reprinted in Zhu Weizheng, *Ma Xiangbo ji.*

———. See also under Zhu Weizheng.

Mao Xianglin 毛祥麟. *Moyu lu* 墨餘錄 (Record of leftover ink). In *Biji xiaoshuo daguan,* 3:2843–2910.

Masuda, Kiyohide 曾田清秀. *Gakufu no rekishi teki kenkyū* 樂府の歷史的研究 (Studies in the history of *yuefu* poetry). Tokyo, 1969.

McAleavy, Henry. *Wang Tao: The Life and Writings of a Displaced Person.* London: The China Society, 1953.

McMahon, Robert Keith. *Causality and Containment in Seventeenth-Century Chinese Fiction.* Leiden, Netherlands: Brill, 1988.

———. "Fleecing the male customer in Shanghai brothels of the 1890s." *Late Imperial China* 23.2 (2002): 1–28.

Mei Yusheng 梅禹生. *Qingni lianhua ji* 青泥蓮花記 (Record of a lotus that remained pure in the mud). Reprint, Taipei: Guangwen Shuju, 1980.

Meihua'an Zhu 梅花盦主, ed. *Shenjiang shixia shengjing tushuo* 申江時下勝景圖說 (The latest of famous sites in Shanghai, with illustrations and explanations). 2 vols. Shanghai, 1894. Reprinted in *Guoli Beijing daxue Zhongguo minsu xuehui minsu congshu.*

"Meiren Yatuo zhi Youxi Zhuren shu" 美人雅脫致游戲主人書 (Letter by Yatuo, an American, to the Master of Entertainment). In Chen Wuwo, *Lao Shanghai sanshi nian jianwen lu,* 203.

"Meng xian huan gongzi shoujing" 夢顯宦公子受驚 (The young man from the good family is startled by the vision of an official appearing in [his] dream). *Youxi bao,* October 6, 1897, 2.

Meng Yuanlao 孟元老. *Dongjing menghua lu* 東京夢華錄 (The Eastern Capital: A dream of splendors past). Reprint, Beijing: Zhongguo Shangye Chubanshe, 1982.

Menghuaguanzhu Jiang Yinxiang 夢花館主江陰香. *Jiuwei hu* 九尾狐 (The nine-tailed fox). Shanghai: Shehui Xiaoshuo Chubanshe, 1908–10. Illustrated version, 6 vols. Shanghai: Shanghai Jiaotong Tushuguan, 1918. Reprinted in 1 vol. in *Zhongguo jindai xiaoshuo daxi.*

"Mianzhi shoujiu" 勉知守舊 (Holding on to old customs). *Youxi bao,* June 22, 1899, 2.

Miao Quansun 繆荃孫. *Qinhuai guangji* 秦淮廣紀 (Encyclopedia of Nanjing [courtesan entertainment]). Shanghai: Shangwu Yinshuguan, 1914.

Mile 密勒. *Shanghai, maoxianjia de leyuan* 上海冒險家的樂園 (Shanghai, the paradise of adventurers). Translated by Axue. 1937. Reprint, Shanghai: Shanghai Wenhua Press, 1956.

Miller, G. E. *Shanghai—The Paradise of Adventurers.* New York: Orsay Publishers, 1937. Chinese translation under Mile.

Miller, Scott. "The Hybrid Narrative of Kyōden's *Sharebon.*" *Monumenta Nipponica* 43.2 (summer 1988): 133–52.

"Ming hua you zhu, cishi congliang" 名花有主，詞史從良 (The famous flower has a master and is getting married). *Youxi bao,* September 19, 1897, 2.

"Ming jiaoshu conghui juelun" 名校書聰慧絕倫 (The famous courtesan stars were quite intelligent). *Youxi bao,* December 7, 1897, 2.

Minhu ribao 民呼日報 (Citizen voice). Shanghai, May–August 1909.

Minli bao 民立報 (Establishing the people). 1910–12.

Mirror Reflections and Flute Sounds, First Collection. See *Jingying xiaosheng chuji.*

Mirror Reflections and Flute Sounds, Second Collection. See *Jingying xiaosheng erji.*

Miscellaneous Notes on Shanghai Flowers. See Langyouzi, *Haishang yanhua suoji.*

Miscellaneous Notes on Visiting Shanghai. See Ge Yuanxu, *Hu you zaji.*

Miscellaneous Records of a Shanghai Recluse. See Wang Tao, *Songyin manlu.*

Mittler, Barbara. *A Newspaper for China? Power, Identity and China in China's News Media.* Cambridge, Mass.: Harvard Asia Council, 2004.

Montalto de Jesus, Carlos A. *Historic Shanghai.* Shanghai: The Shanghai Mercury, 1909.

Moule, Ven. Arthur E., B.D. *New China and Old, Personal Recollections and Observations of Thirty Years.* London, 1902. Reprint, Taipei: Ch'eng Wen Publishing, 1972.

Municipal Council of Shanghai. *Report for the Year Ended 31st December 1876.* Shanghai: Carvalho & Co., 1877.

———. *Report for the Year Ended 31st December 1892.* Shanghai: Kelly and Walsh, 1893.

Murphey, Rhoads. *The Outsiders: The Western Experience in India and China.* Ann Arbor: Michigan University Press, 1977.

———. *Shanghai: Key to Modern China.* Cambridge, Mass.: Harvard University Press, 1953.

Muzhen Shanren. See Yu Da.

Nagasawa, Kikuya 長澤規矩也. *Mindai sōzuhon zuroku* 明代插圖本圖錄 (Illustrated anthology of Ming dynasty book illustrations). Tokyo: Yamamoto Shoten, 1962.

Nakamura, Tadayuki 中村忠行. "Shinmatsu tantei shōsetsu shikō—hanitsu wo chūshin to shite" 清末探偵小説史稿—翻譯を中心として (Draft history of the late Qing detective novel—with a focus on the translations). *Shinmatsu shōsetsu kenkyū* 2 (1978): 121–54; 3 (1979): 236–86; 4 (1980): 372–428.

"Nan chu yizhang" 難除綺障 (Difficulties eliminated from courtesan world). *Youxi bao,* October 8, 1898, 2.

Nathan, Andrew, and Leo Lee. "The Beginning of Mass Culture." In Jameson, Nathan, and Rawski, *Popular Culture in Late Imperial China,* 360–98.

Nienhauser, William H., ed. *The Indiana Companion to Traditional Chinese Literature.* Revised edition. Bloomington: Indiana University Press, 1986.

"Niju Shanghai piaoke Si Da Jin'gang shuo" 擬舉上海嫖客四大金剛説 (On the proposal of recommending the Four Great Golden Diamond Cutters among the Shanghai clients of courtesans). *Youxi bao,* July 15, 1899, 1.

The Nine-Tailed Fox. See Jiang Yinxiang, *Jiuwei hu.*

Nishiyama, Matsunosuke 西山松之助. *Yūjo* 遊女 (Ladies of pleasure). Tokyo: Tōkyōdo, 1980.

North China Herald. 1850–1941.

"Nü ban nanzhuang" 女扮男裝 (A woman dressed in men's clothes). *Youxi bao,* September 20, 1897, 2.

An Official Guide to Eastern Asia; Trans-continental Connections Between Europe and Asia. Vol. 4, *China.* Tokyo: The Imperial Japanese Government Railways, 1913.

Oriental Advertising Company Limited. *The Guide to Shanghai*. Shanghai: The Oriental Press, 1914.

Ouyang Juyuan 歐陽鉅源. See Qu Yuan, Erchun Jushi, and Xiqiusheng (under Binghong Shanren).

Owen, Stephen. *The Great Age of Chinese Poetry: The High T'ang*. New Haven, Conn.: Yale University Press, 1981.

———. *Remembrances: The Experience of the Past in Classical Chinese Literature*. Cambridge, Mass.: Harvard University Press, 1986.

Palace Hotel. *Guide to Shanghai*. Shanghai: Palace Hotel, 1907.

Pang Shubo 龐樹柏 (Duxiao 獨笑). *Hongzhi shi xiaolu* 紅脂識小錄 (Jottings of a boudoir companion). Shanghai: Guoxue Shushi, 1925. Reprinted in Wei Shaochang, *Li Boyuan yanjiu ziliao*, 522.

Penghua Sheng 捧花生. *Huafang yutan* 畫舫餘譚 (Leftover talk of the painted boats). 1818. Reprinted in Zhang Tinghua, *Xiangyan congshu*, series 13, 4:4943–80.

———. *Qinhuai huafang lu* 秦淮畫舫錄 (A record of painted boats in Nanjing). 1817. Reprinted in Zhang Tinghua, *Xiangyan congshu*, series 14, 3901–70.

Ping Jinya 平襟亞. "Jiu Shanghai de changji" 舊上海的娼妓 (Prostitution in old Shanghai). In Shanghaishi Wenshiguan, *Jiu Shanghai de yan du chang*, 159–71.

Pinghu Huangjintai He Lou 平湖黃金臺鶴樓. *"Honglou meng" zayong* 紅樓夢雜詠 (Assorted songs on *Dream of the red chamber*). In *Chishuo si zhong*.

Pingjiang Yinnian 平江引年. *Haishang pinghua baojian* 海上評花寶鑑 (Precious mirror for judging Shanghai's flowers). 2 vols. Shanghai: Zuijingtong Shuzhuang, 1911.

Plaks, Andrew. *Four Masterworks of the Ming Novel: Ssu ta ch'i-shu*. Princeton, N.J.: Princeton University Press, 1987.

"Pofu qiangwu" 潑婦搶物 (A virago robber). *Shenbao*, November 11, 1878, 2.

Poli, Doretta Davanzo. "La Cortigiane e la Moda" (The courtesan and fashion). In Alfieri, *Il gioco dell'amore*, 99–103.

Pott, Hawks. *A Short History of Shanghai*. Shanghai: Kelly and Walsh, 1928.

Precious Mirror for Judging Shanghai's Flowers. See Pingjiang Yinnian, *Haishang pinghua baojian*.

Qian Xinbo. See Wuli Kanhua Ke.

"Qie qie xunfang" 挈妾尋芳 (Bring one's concubine to visit the courtesans). *Dianshizhai huabao*, 1880s. Reprinted in Henriot, *Chinese Courtesans*, 43.

Qin Lüzhi 秦綠枝. "Huile Li" 會樂里 (Huile Lane). *Xinmin wanbao* 新民晚報, March 3, 1996, 8.

Qinding libu zeli 欽定禮部則例 (Imperially approved collection of precedents from the Department of Rites). Reprint, Taipei: Chengwen Chubanshe, 1966.

Qing qing dianying 青青電影 (Young Cinema), 1934.

"Qingke fei yi" 請客匪易 (It is not an easy matter to play host). *Youxi bao*, January 7, 1899, 3.

Qixia 棲霞 and Danru 澹如, eds. *Haishang hua yinglu* 海上花影錄 (A photographic record of Shanghai flowers). 2 vols. Shanghai: Commercial Press (by commission), 1915. Unpaginated.

Qu Yuan 蘧園 (Ouyang Juyuan 歐陽鉅源). *Fupu xiantan* 負曝閒談 (Idle talk in scorching heat). Serialized in *Xiuxiang xiaoshuo* 6–10, 12–41 (1903–5).

Qubao 趣報 (The Entertainer). 1898.

A Register of Shanghai Flowers. See Xiaolantian Chanqing Shizhe, *Haishang qunfang pu*.

"Ren yuan li" 人願力 (To each according to their abilities). *Youxi bao*, October 9, 1898, 2.

"Renwu Hubin huachao yanbang" 壬午滬濱花朝艷榜 (Shanghai flower competition of 1882). In Liangxi Chilian Jushi, *Hujiang yanpu*, 1–2.

"Renwu xiaji huabang" 壬午夏季花榜 (Flower competition of summer 1882). In Liangxi Chilian Jushi, *Hujiang yanpu*, 2–3.

Ropp, Paul S. "Ambiguous Images of Courtesan Culture in Late Imperial China." In Widmer and Chang, *Writing Women in Late Imperial China*, 27–28.

Rosenthal, Margaret F. *The Honest Courtesan: Veronica Franco, Citizen and Writer in Sixteenth-Century Venice*. Chicago: University of Chicago Press, 1992.

Roux, Alain. *Le Shanghai ouvrier des années trente: Coolies, gangsters et syndicalistes*. Paris: L'Harmattan, 1993.

Rowe, William. *Hankow: Conflict and Community in a Chinese City, 1796–1895*. Stanford, Calif.: Stanford University Press, 1989.

"Sai xianghao" 賽相好 (Competition in patrons). *Youxi bao*, May 5, 1899, 2.

"Saima shuo" 賽馬說 (On the horse race). *Youxi bao*, May 1, 1899, 1–2.

"San xiguan zhi jizha" 散戲館之擠軋 (The crowded chaos after the theater performance). *Tuhua ribao*, no. 29 (1909), 7.

Schafer, Edward H. *The Golden Peaches of Samarkand: A Study of T'ang Exotics*. Berkeley: University of California Press, 1963.

Schamoni, Wolfgang. *Die "Sharebon" Santō Kyōden und ihre literaturgeschichtliche Stellung* (The *Sharebon* by Santō Kyōden and their position in the history of literature). Ph.D. diss., Bonn University, 1970.

Schorske, Carl E. *Fin-de-Siècle Vienna: Politics and Culture*. New York: Vintage Books, 1981.

Scully, Eileen P. "Taking the Low Road to Sino-American Relations: 'Open Door' Expansionists and the Two China Markets." *Journal of American History* 82.1 (June 1995): 62–83.

———. "Wandering Whores: American Prostitutes on the Pacific Frontier." Paper presented at the conference "Foreign Communities in East Asia (19th–20th Centuries)," MRASH, Lyon, France, Institut d'Asie Orientale, March 20–21, 1997.

Secker, Fritz. *Schen: Studien aus einer Chinesischen Weltstadt* (Shanghai: Studies from a Chinese metropolis). Tsingtau: Adolf Haupt, 1913.

The Sensational Biographies of the Four Great Golden Diamond Cutters from Shanghai. See Chousi Zhuren, *Haishang mingji Si Da Jin'gang zhuan qishu*.

Shang-hai: and the Valley of the Blue River, Madrolle's Handbooks. Paris and London: Hachette and Company, 1912.

Shanghai City Lights. See Zou Tao, *Haishang dengshi lu*.

The Shanghai Evening Courier. 1874–?.

Shanghai Laojianghu 上海老江湖. *Sanjiao jiuliu mimi zhenxiang* 三教九流秘密真相 (The true picture of [Shanghai's] secret underworld). Shanghai: Nanyang Tushu Gongsi, 1923.

"Shanghai Lu Xiaohong ji Qian Yunsheng shu" 上海陸小紅寄錢韻生書 (Letter from Lu Xiaohong in Shanghai to Qian Yunsheng). In Hushang Youxizhu, *Haishang youxi tushuo*, 1:3–4.

Shanghai Mercury, ed. *Shanghai by Night and Day*. Shanghai: Shanghai Mercury, ca. 1900.

———. *1843 Shanghai 1893. The Model Settlement. Its Birth, its Youth, its Jubilee*. Shanghai: Shanghai Mercury Office, 1893.

Shanghai of to-day: A Souvenir Album of Fifty Vandyck Prints of "The Model Settlement." Shanghai: Kelly and Walsh, 1927.

Miscellaneous Notes on Visiting Shanghai, Revised Edition. See Yuan Zuzhi, *Chongxiu Hu you zaji*.

Shanghai's Prosperity Illustrated. See *Haishang fanhua tu*.

"Shanghai quyuan zhi xianxiang" 上海曲院之現象 (Sights of Shanghai courtesan houses). *Tuhua ribao*, nos. 229–304 (1909–10).

Shanghai Sheyingjia Xiehui 上海攝影家協會 and Shanghai Daxue Wenxueyuan 上海大學文學院, eds. *Shanghai sheying shi* 上海攝影史 (History of Shanghai photography). Shanghai: Shanghai Renmin Meishu Chubanshe, 1992.

Shanghai Shi Ziliao Congkan 上海史資料叢刊, ed. *Qingdai riji congchao* 清代日記叢抄 (A collection of diaries from the Qing period). Shanghai: Shanghai Renmin Chubanshe, 1982.

Shanghai xinbao 上海新報 (Shanghai news). 1862–72.

Shanghai zhanggu congshu. See Shanghaitong She.

"Shanghai Zhu Moqing ji Gusu Ma Xiaonian shu" 上海朱墨卿寄姑蘇馬笑拈書 (Letter from Zhu Moqing in Shanghai to Ma Xiaonian in Suzhou). In Hushang Youxizhu, *Haishang youxi tushuo*, 1:8.

Shanghaishi Wenshiguan 上海市文史館, ed. *Jiu Shanghai de yan du chang* 舊上海的煙賭娼 (Opium, gambling, and prostitution in old Shanghai). Shanghai: Baijia Chubanshe, 1988.

Shanghaishi Xiqu Xuexiao Zhongguo Fuzhuangshi Yanjiuzu 上海市戲曲學校中國服裝史研究組, ed. *Zhongguo lidai fushi* 中國歷代服飾 (Chinese clothing and adornment in various dynasties). Shanghai: Xuelin Chubanshe, 1994.

Shanghaitong She 上海通社, ed. *Shanghai yanjiu ziliao* 上海研究資料 (Shanghai research materials). 1935. Reprint, Shanghai: Shanghai Shudian, 1985.

———. *"Shanghai yanjiu ziliao" xuji* 上海研究資料續集 (Supplement to *Shanghai research materials*). 1937. Reprint, Shanghai: Shanghai Shudian, 1984.

———. *Shanghai zhanggu congshu* 上海掌故叢書 (Collection of anecdotes on Shanghai). Shanghai: Shanghaitong She, 1935.

Shangshi huabao 尚時畫報 (Contemporary fashion illustrated). 1911.

Shangwu Yinshuguan 商務印書館. *Shanghai zhinan* 上海指南 (Guide to Shanghai). Shanghai: Shangwu Yinshuguan, 1909, 1912, 1922.

———. *1897–1992 Shangwu yinshuguan jiushiwu nian—Wo yu Shangwu yinshuguan 1897–1992* 商務印書館九十五年—我與商務印書館 (From 1897 to 1992, The ninety-fifth-year anniversary of the Commercial Press in Shanghai—The Commercial Press and me). Beijing: Shangwu Yinshuguan, 1992.

Shaoxi Mozhuang Zhuren 苕溪墨庄主人 (Shaoxi Zuimo Sheng 苕溪醉墨生). "Hubei zhuzhi ci" 滬北竹枝詞 (Bamboo twig ballads on the northern city of Shanghai [Foreign Settlements]). *Shenbao*, February 14, 1877, 3.

Shaoxi Zuimo Sheng 苕溪醉墨生 (Shaoxi Mozhuang Zhuren 苕溪墨庄主人). "Qinglou zhuzhi ci" 青樓竹枝詞 (Bamboo twig ballads on courtesan houses). *Shenbao*, March 11, 1877, 3.

Shen Bojing 沈伯經 and Chen Huaipu 陳懷圃, eds. *Shanghaishi zhinan* 上海市指南 (Shanghai city guide). Shanghai: Zhonghua Shuju, 1933.

Shen Yunlong 沈雲龍, ed. *Jindai Zhongguo shiliao congkan* 近代中國史料叢 (A collection of historical materials on modern China). 100 sets. Taipei: Wenhai Chubanshe, 1966–.

Shenbao 申報. 1872–1949.

Shenbaoguan 申報館, comp. *Xishi leibian* 西事類編 (Assorted information on the West). Shanghai: Shenbaoguan, 1885.

———, ed. *Zuijin zhi wushi nian* 最近之五十年 (The last fifty years). Shanghai: Shenbaoguan, 1922. Reprint, Shanghai: Shanghai Shudian, 1987.

Shenbaoguan shumu 申報館書目 (Bibliography of Shenbaoguan publications). Shanghai: Shenbaoguan 1877.

[Shenbaoguan] xu shumu 申報館續書目 (Supplement to the bibliography of Shenbaoguan publications). Shanghai: Shenbaoguan 1879.

Shenjiang mingsheng tushuo 申江名勝圖說 (Famous Shanghai sites, with illustrations and explanations). Woodblock print. 2 vols. Shanghai: Guankeshouzhai, 1884.

Shenjiang shengjing tu. See under Dianshizhai.

Shenjiang shixia shengjing tushuo. See under Meihua'an Zhu.

Shenjiang yichang zhuzhi ci 申江夷場竹枝詞 (Bamboo twig ballads on the barbarians' market in Shanghai). Manuscript of an 1860s text in the Zhongguo Kexueyuan Tushuguan in Beijing.

Shenjiang zhuzhi ci 申江竹枝詞 (Shanghai bamboo twig ballads). 1860s. Hand-copied manuscript. In *Shenjiang yichang zhuzhi ci*.

Shi Meiding 史梅定, ed. *Zhuiyi—Jindai Shanghai tushi* 追憶—近代上海圖史 (Remembrance—An illustrated history of modern Shanghai). Shanghai: Shanghai Guji Chubanshe, 1996.

Shi Nai'an 施耐菴. *Shuihu zhuan* 水滸傳 (Water margin). Beijing: Renmin Wenxue Chubanshe, 1981.

Shijie fanhua bao 世界繁華報 (World vanity fair). May 7, 1901–April 22, 1910.

Shilin 史林.

Shimizu, Kenichirō 清水賢一郎. "What Books Young People Loved Best in 1920s Beijing: Space and Structure of the Readership of *Jingbao Fukan*." Paper presented at the conference "From the Late Ch'ing Era to the 1940s: Cultural Field and Educational Vista," held at Taiwan National University, October 2002.

Shinmatsu shōsetsu kara 清末小説から (The late Qing fiction newsletter).

Shinmatsu shōsetsu kenkyū 清末小説研究 (Studies in late Qing fiction).

Shishi huabao 時事畫報 (News illustrated). 1907.

Shiwan Jinling Guanzhu 十萬金鈴館主. "Minghua shipin" 名花失品 (A famous courtesan compromises her character). *Shenbao*, February 8, 1873, 2.

"Shu Lu Lanfen Jin Xiaobao zhengou shi" 書陸蘭芬金小寶爭毆事 (Letter regarding the use of force between Lu Lanfen and Jin Xiaobao). *Youxi bao*, May 17, 1899, 1.

"Shu Yufeng Yuyin Jin Hanxiang liang deng benbao gaobai hou" 書玉峰漁隱金含香兩登本報告白後 (Comments after Yufeng Yuyin and Jin Hanxiang put their advertisements in our paper). *Youxi bao*, October 4, 1897, 1.

"Shuchang xuzhi" 書場續誌 (Follow-up report on the storytelling hall). *Youxi bao*, August 30, 1899, 2.

"Shuguan feisheng" 書館蜚聲 (Spreading [their] fame through [performing in] the storytelling hall). *Youxi bao*, August 27, 1899, 3.

Shuxi Qiaoye 蜀西樵也. *Yantai huashi lu* 燕台花事錄 (Record of events among the flowers in Beijing). Nineteenth century. Reprinted in Zhang Tinghua, *Xiangyan congshu*, series 12, 3:3365–94.

Skinner, William G., ed. *The City in Late Imperial China*. Stanford, Calif.: Stanford University Press, 1977.

Smith, D. Warres. *European Settlements in the Far East: China, Japan, Corea, Indo-China, Straits Settlements, Malay States, Siam, Netherlands, India, Borneo, The Philippines, Etc.* New York: Charles Scribner's Sons, 1900.

Smith, S. A. *Like Cattle and Horses: Nationalism and Labor in Shanghai, 1895–1927*. Durham, N.C.: Duke University Press, 2002.

"'Song Li Pingxiang gui Jiahe' xu" 送李蘋香歸嘉禾序 (Introduction to "Farewell to Li Pingxiang upon her return to Jiahe"). *Shijie fanhua bao*, December 9, 1901.

Summer, Matthew H. *Sex, Law, and Society in Late Imperial China*. Stanford, Calif.: Stanford University Press, 2000.

Sun Guoqun 孫國群. *Jiu Shanghai changji mishi* 舊上海娼妓秘史 (A secret history of prostitution in old Shanghai). Henan: Henan Renmin Chubanshe, 1988.

Sun Jiazhen. See Sun Yusheng.

Sun Qi 孫棨. *Beili zhi* 北里志 (Record of the northern sectors or the gay quarters of Chang'an). In Yang Jialuo, *Zhongguo xueshu mingzhu*, 155:25–42.

Sun Yusheng 孫玉聲. *Baohai qianchen lu* 報海前塵錄 (Anecdotes on things still remembered from the newspaper world of former times). Serialized in *Shenbao*, 1931–32.

———. "Cangshan jiuzhu yishi" 倉山舊主軼事 (Anecdotes on the old master of Cangshan). In *Baohai qianchen lu*.

——— (Sun Jiazhen 孫家振, pseud. Haishang Shushi Sheng 海上漱石生). *Haishang fanhua meng* 海上繁華夢 (Dreams of Shanghai's glamour). First serialized in *Caifeng bao* from July 27, 1898, and continued in *Xiaolin bao* from 1901 to 1902. First book edition, Shanghai: Xiaolin Bao Guan, 1903 (under pseud. Gu Hu Jingmeng Chixian 古滬警夢癡仙). Reprint, Shanghai: Shangwu Yinshuguan, 1923. Reprint, Nanchang: Jiangsu Renmin Chubanshe, 1988. Page references are to the 1988 edition.

———. "Haishang hua liezhuan" 海上花列傳 (On *Haishang hua liezhuan*). In *Tuixinglu biji.* 113–14.

———. *Heimu zhong zhi heimu* 黑幕中之黑幕 (Dark shadows behind the scene). In *Dashijie*, July 1, 1917–19(?).

——— (pseud. Haishang Juewu Sheng 海上覺悟生). *Jinü de shenghuo* 妓女的生活 (The life of prostitutes). Shanghai: Shanghai Chunming Shudian, 1939.

———. "Li Boyuan" 李伯元 (Li Boyuan). In *Tuixinglu biji*, 109.

———. *Tuixinglu biji* 退醒廬筆記 (Brush jottings from the hut of sober retreat). Shanghai, 1925. Reprint, Taiyuan: Shanxi Guji Chubanshe, 1995.

"Sutai zouma gongpan Huabang" 蘇臺走馬共盼花榜 (Sampling the flowers in Suzhou: All await the result of the competition). *Youxi bao*, May 14, 1899, 2.

Tai Edo bijin taku tsuki-yuki-hana jō hyōban 大江户美人諾月雪花娘評判 (Ranking of the beautiful women in Great Edo). Tokyo: Kyōan Dō, 1859.

Tan Wuren 談汚人, ed. *Wuxi xianzhi* 蕪錫縣誌 (Wuxi gazetteer). Shanghai: Shanghai Shehui Kexueyuan Chubanshe, 1994.

Tang Xianzu 湯顯祖 (1550–1617). *Mudan ting* 牡丹亭 (Peony pavilion). In *Tang Xianzu ji* 湯顯祖集. Beijing: Zhonghua Shuju, 1962. 4 vols.

Tang Zhenchang 唐振常, ed. *Jindai Shanghai fanhua lu* 近代上海繁華錄 (A record of Shanghai's modern splendor). Shanghai: Shangwu Yinshu Guan, 1994.

———. *Shanghai shi* 上海史 (History of Shanghai). Shanghai: Shanghai Renmin Chubanshe, 1989.

Tao Muning 陶慕寧. *Qinglou wenxue yu Zhongguo wenhua* 青樓文學與中國文化 (Courtesan literature and Chinese culture). Beijing: Dongfang Chubanshe, 1993.

Tarumoto, Teruo 樽本照雄. *Shinpen zōho Shinmatsu Minsho shōsetsu mokoroku* 新編增補清末民初小說目錄 (Newly compiled updated catalog of late Qing and early Republican fiction). Jinan: Qi Lu Shushe, 2002.

———. *Shoki Shōmu inshokan kenkyū.* 初期商務印書館研究 (Study on the early period of Shangwu publishing house). Osaka: Shinmatsu Shōsetsu Kenkyūsha, 2000.

"Te kai huacong Jingji teke bang" 特開花叢經濟特科榜 (A "Special competition with focus on management of state affairs" among the flowers). *Shijie fanhua bao*, September 27, 1901, 2.

"Ten Views of the Foreign Settlements of Shanghai." *The Shanghai Evening Courier*, August 31, 1874.

Thiriez, Regine. "Photography and Portraiture in Nineteenth-Century China." *East Asian History* 17/18 (June/December 1999): 77–102.

Tian Chunhang. See Xiaolantian Chanqing Shizhe.

"Tianshe jingshou bao chu" 添設經售報處 (On establishing more sales locations for the paper). *Youxi bao*, November 10, 1897, 1.

Tianxiao 天笑 (Bao Tianxiao 包天笑). *Suzhou fanhua meng* 蘇州繁華夢 (Dreams of Suzhou's splendor). Shanghai: Gailiang Xiaoshuo She, 1911.

———. *Xin Suzhou chubian* 新蘇州初編 (The new Suzhou, first series). Shanghai: Shanghai Gailiang Xiaoshuo She, 1910.

"Ting Xiao Ruyi tan pipa yin kao erlun" 聽小如意彈琵琶因考而論 (On thoughts inspired by listening to Xiao Ruyi play the *pipa*). *Youxi bao*, October 10, 1897, 1.

Traces of the Past in the World of Shanghai. See Erchun Jushi, *Haitian hongxue ji.*

The Treaty Ports of China and Japan: A complete guide to the Open Ports of Those Countries, Together With Peking, Yedo [Tokyo] Hong Kong and Macao. London and Hong Kong: Mayers, Dennys and Kind, 1867.

Tuhua ribao 圖畫日報 (The illustrated daily). August 16, 1909–August 1910.

Tuhua xunbao 圖畫旬報 (Weekly illustrated). 1909.

Twentieth Century Impressions of Hong Kong, Shanghai, and Other Treaty Ports of China: Their

History, People, Commerce, Industries, and Resources. London: Lloyd's Greater Britain Publishing Company, 1908.

Vittinghoff, Natascha. *Freier Fluss: Die Anfänge des Journalismus in China (1860–1911)* (Free flow: The beginnings of journalism in China, 1860–1911). Wiesbaden, Germany: Harassowitz, Opera Sinologica 9, 2002.

———. "Readers, Publishers and Officials in the Contest for a Public Voice and the Rise of a Modern Press in Late Qing China (1860–1880)." *T'oung Pao* 37 (1999): 393–455.

———. "Useful Knowledge and Appropriate Communication: The Field of Journalistic Production in Late Nineteenth Century China." In Wagner, *Joining the Global Public.*

Wagner, Rudolf G. "China's First Literary Journals." Paper presented at conference on early Chinese periodicals, Prague, 1998.

———. "The Concept of Work/Labor/Arbeit in the Chinese World: First Explorations." In Bierwisch, *Die Rolle der Arbeit,* 103–36.

———. "Die Biographie als Lebensprogramm: Zur didaktischen Funktion der chinesischen Biographik" (Biography as a life-program: The didactic functions of Chinese biographical writing). In Walter Berschin and Wolfgang Schamoni, eds., *Biographie: "So der Westen wie der Osten?" Zwölf Studien* (Biography: "The same in the West as in the East?"), 133–42. Heidelberg, Germany: Mattes Verlag 2003.

———. "Ernest Major: A Life." In *The Making of the Chinese Media Capital.*

———. "Ernest Major's Shenbaoguan and the Formation of Late Qing Print Culture." Paper prepared for the conference "The Formation of a Multiethnic Urban Culture: The Shanghai Concessions 1850–1910," Heidelberg, Germany, 1998.

———. "Jinru quanqiu xiangxiang tujing: Shanghai de *Dianshizhai huabao*" 進入全球想象圖景：上海的點石齋畫報 (Joining the global imaginaire: The Shanghai illustrated newspaper *Dianshizhai huabao*). *Zhongguo xueshu* 8 (April 2001): 1–96.

———. "Joining the Global Imaginaire: The Shanghai Illustrated Newspaper *Dianshizhai huabao.*" In Wagner, *Joining the Global Public.*

———. "Life as a Quote from a Foreign Book: Love, Pavel, and Rita." In H. Schmidt-Glintzer, ed., *Das andere China: Festschrift für Wolfgang Bauer zum 65. Geburtstag* (The other China: Festschrift for Wolfgang Bauer on the occasion of his sixty-fifth birthday), 463–76. Wolfenbütteler Forschungen, vol. 62. Wiesbaden, Germany: Harrassowitz, 1995.

———. "The Making of Shanghai into the Chinese Media Capital: The Role of the Shenbaoguan Publishing House 1872–1895." Paper presented at the Conference on Shanghai Urban History, Shanghai Academy of Social Sciences, 1997.

———. *The Making of the Chinese Media Capital: Ernest Major and Shanghai.* In preparation.

———. "The Role of the Foreign Community in the Chinese Public Sphere." *China Quarterly* 152.6 (1995): 423–43.

———. "The *Shenbao* in Crisis: The International Environment and the Conflict between Guo Songtao and the *Shenbao.*" *Late Imperial China* 20.1 (1999): 107–38.

———. "Shenbaoguan zaoqi de shuji chuban (1872–1875)" 申報館早期的書籍出版 (1872–1875) (The early publishing activities of the Shenbaoguan [1872–1875]). In Chen, Wang, and Shang, *Wan Ming yu wan Qing,* 169–78.

———, ed. *Joining the Global Public: Word, Image, and City in the Early Chinese Newspapers, 1870–1910.* In press.

Wakeman, Frederic E., Jr., and Wen-hsin Yeh, eds. *Shanghai Sojourners.* Berkeley, Calif.: Institute of East Asian Studies, 1992.

Wan Qing xiaoshuo daxi. See under Lin Jianyu.

Wang, David Der-wei. "Chongdu *Dankou zhi*" 重讀蕩寇志 (A rereading of *Record of suppressing the bandits*). In Chen, Wang, and Shang, *Wan Ming yu wan Qing,* 423–40.

———. *Fin-de-Siècle Splendor: Repressed Modernities of Late Qing Fiction, 1848–1911.* Stanford, Calif.: Stanford University Press, 1997.

———. *Xiaoshuo Zhongguo: Wan Qing dao dangdai de Zhongwen xiaoshuo* 小說中國：晚清到當代的中文小説 (Narrating China: Chinese fiction from the late Qing to the contemporary era). Taipei: Maitian Chuban Gongsi, 1993.

Wang Dewei 王德威. See David Der-wei Wang.

Wang Dingjiu 王定九. *Shanghai menjing* 上海門徑 (Key to Shanghai). Shanghai: Shanghai Zhongyang Shudian, 1932.

Wang Ermin 王爾民. "*Dianshizhai huabao* suo zhanxian zhi jindai lishi mailuo" 點石齋畫報所展現之近代歷史脈絡 (The thread of ideas running through modern history evoked in *Dianshizhai illustrated magazine*). In *Jindai wenhua shengtai jiqi bianqian.*

———. *Jindai wenhua shengtai jiqi bianqian* 近代文化生態及其變遷 (Modern cultural ecology and its changes). Nanchang: Baihua Chubanshe, 2002.

———. "Zhongguo jindai zhishi pujihua chuanbo zhi tushuo xingshi—yi Dianshizhai huabao wei li" 中國近代知識普及化傳播之圖説形式—以點石齋畫報為例 (The illustration with explanation of the form in which modern knowledge was popularly disseminated in China). *Zhongyang yanjiuyuan jindai jianjiusuo jikan*, no. 19, 1990.

Wang Houzhe 王後哲, ed. *Shanghai baojian* 上海寶鑑 (Precious mirror of Shanghai). Shanghai: Shanghai Shijie Shuju, 1925.

Wang Liaoweng 汪了翁. "Shanghai jiyuan didian zhi yange" 上海妓院地點之沿革 (On the changes in location of Shanghai courtesan houses). In *Shanghai liushi nian huajie shi*, 1–2.

———. *Shanghai liushi nian huajie shi* 上海六十年花界史 (Sixty years of the Shanghai flower world). Shanghai: Shixin Shuju, 1922.

"Wang Shanbao ji Zhou Yueqing shu" 汪珊寶寄周月卿書 (Wang Shanbao's letter to Zhou Yueqing). In Hushang Youxizhu, *Haishang youxi tushuo*, 1:1–2.

Wang Shucun 王樹村, ed. *Minjian zhenpin tushuo "Honglou meng"* 民間珍品圖說紅樓夢 (A precious work from the popular tradition: The illustrated *Dream of the red chamber*). Taipei: Dongda Tushu, 1996.

Wang Shunu 王書奴. *Zhongguo changji shi* 中國娼妓史 (The history of prostitution in China). 1933. Reprint, Shanghai: Sanlian Shudian, 1988.

Wang Tao 王韜. "Fu Liao Baoer xiaoji" 附廖寶兒小記 (Appendix: A memoir on Liao Baoer). In *Haizou yeyou lu*, 5663–68.

———. "*Haishang chentian ying* xu" 海上塵天影敘 (Preface to *The shadows of heaven and earth in Shanghai*). In Zou Tao, *Haishang chentian ying*, 1–3.

———. *"Haizou yeyou" fulu* 海陬冶游附錄 (A supplement to *Record of visits to courtesan houses in a distant corner by the sea*). Preface 1873. Hong Kong, 1883. Reprinted in Zhang Tinghua, *Xiangyan congshu*, series 20, 5:5685–5786.

———. *Haizou yeyou lu* 海陬冶游錄 (Record of visits to courtesan houses in a distant corner by the sea). Preface 1860. Reprinted in Zhang Tinghua, *Xiangyan congshu*, series 20, 5:5633–84.

———. *"Haizou yeyou lu" yulu* 海陬冶游錄余錄 (Appendix to *Record of visits to courtesan houses in a distant corner by the sea*). Preface 1878. Hong Kong, 1883. Reprinted in Zhang Tinghua, *Xiangyan congshu*, series 20, 5:5787–5810.

———. *Manyou suilu* 漫遊隨錄 (Idle travel notes). In Wang Xiqi, *Xiaofanghuzhai yudi congchao.*

———. "Mei Xiu er jiaoshu hezhuan" 眉繡二校書合傳 (The combined biographies of the *jiaoshu* Mei and Xiu). In *Songying manlu*. In *Dianshizhai huabao, yi*, no. 23, October 1884, 15, 16.

———. *Songbin suohua* 淞濱瑣話 (Idle talk on Shanghai). 1887. Reprinted in Xu Fuchu, *Xiangyan quyu*, 75–92.

———. *Songyin manlu* 淞隱漫錄 (Miscellaneous records of a Shanghai recluse). Serialized in *Dianshizhai huabao*, issue no. 6 (甲 6, June 1884) to issue no. 122 (子 2, October 1887).

———. *Tan yan* 談艷 (Talk on beauties). In *Songbin suohua*. Reprinted in Xu Fuchu, *Xiangyan quyu*, 75–92.

———. *Taoyuan chidu* 弢園尺牘 (Letters by Taoyuan [Wang Tao]). 1876. Reprinted in *Jindai Zhongguo shiliao congkan xuji* 近代中國史料叢刊續輯, vol. 100, ch. 4. Taipei: Wenhai Chubanshe, 1983.

———. *Taoyuan wenlu wai bian* 弢園文錄外編 (Appendix to the essays of Taoyuan [Wang Tao]). 1883. Reprint, Shanghai: Zhonghua Shuju, 1958.

———. *Yingruan zazhi* 瀛壖雜誌 (Miscellaneous notes from the seaside). 1870. Reprint, Shanghai: Guji Chubanshe, 1989.

Wang Xiqi 王錫祺, comp. *Xiaofanghuzhai yudi congchao* 小方壺齋輿地叢鈔 (Xiaofanghu studio collection). Reprint, Hangzhou: Hangzhou Guji Shudian, 1985.

Wanguo gongbao 萬國公報 (Review of the times). 1874–1907.

Wei Shaochang 魏紹昌, ed. *Li Boyuan yanjiu ziliao* 李伯元研究資料 (Research materials on Li Boyuan). Shanghai: Shanghai Guji Chubanshe, 1980.

———. *Wan Qing si da xiaoshuojia* 晚清四大小說家 (The four great novelists of the late Qing). Taipei: Taiwan Shangwu Yinshuguan, 1993.

———. *Wu Jianren yanjiu ziliao* 吳趼人研究資料 (Research materials on Wu Jianren). Shanghai: Shanghai Guji Chubanshe, 1980.

Wei Yong 衛泳. *Yuerong bian* 悅容編 (The arts of a beauty). Seventeenth century. 4 vols. Reprinted in Zhang Tinghua, *Xiangyan congshu*, series 1, ch. 2, 67–78.

Wei Zi'an 魏子安 (Wei Xiuren 魏秀仁). *Huayue hen* 花月痕 (Traces of the flower and the moon). 1859. Reprint, Taipei: Guangya Chubanshe, 1984.

"Wen Jin Xiaobao qiaoqian shi yi he zhi" 聞金小寶僑遷詩以賀之 (A congratulatory poem on the occasion of Jin Xiaobao moving). *Youxi bao*, September 21, 1897, 2.

Widmer, Ellen. "*Honglou Meng* Sequels and the Female Reading Public." Unpublished paper.

———. "*Honglou Meng Ying* and Its Publisher, Juzhen Tang of Beijing." *Late Imperial China* 23, no. 2 (December 2002): 33–52.

———. "Inflecting Gender: Zhan Kai/Siqi Zhai's 'New Novels' and Courtesan Sketches." *Nannü* 6.1:136–68.

Widmer, Ellen, and Kang-i Sun Chang, eds. *Writing Women in Late Imperial China*. Stanford, Calif.: Stanford University Press, 1997.

Wirth-Nesher, Hana. *City Codes: Reading the Modern Urban Novel*. Cambridge: Cambridge University Press, 1996.

Wolfe, Barnard. *The Daily Life of a Chinese Courtesan. Climbing up a Tricky Ladder: With a Chinese Courtesan's Dictionary*. Hong Kong: Learner's Bookstore, 1980.

Wright, Arnold, and H. A. Cartwright, eds. *Twentieth Century Impressions of HongKong, Shanghai, and Other Treaty Ports of China: Their History, People, Commerce, Industries, and Resources*. London: Lloyds Greater Britain Publishing Company, 1908.

Wu ji baimei 吳姬百媚 (Hundred beauties of Suzhou). 1617 edition in Hōsa Bunko, Nagoya, Japan.

Wu Jianren 吳趼人. "Hushang baiduo tan" 滬上百多談 (Talk on the one hundred "most" in Shanghai). 1914. Reprinted in Wei Shaochang, *Wan Qing si da xiaoshuojia*, 107–8.

———. *Hutu shijie* 糊塗世界 (Confused world). Serialized in *Shijie fanhua bao*, 1906. Reprinted in Lin Jianyu, *Wan Qing xiaoshuo daxi*.

———. *Xin "Shitou ji"* 新石頭記 (The new *Story of the stone*). Serialized in *Nanfang bao*, 1905. Published in book form by Shanghai Gailiang Xiaoshuo She, 1908. Reprint, Nanchang: Jiangxi Renmin Chubanshe, 1988.

Wu Youru 吳友如. "Fengsu zhi tushuo" 風俗志圖說 (An illustrated record of customs, with commentary). In *Wu Youru huabao*, vol. 3, sets 10a and 10b, 11a and 11b.

———. *Haishang baiyan tu* 海上百艷圖 (The one hundred beauties of Shanghai). In *Wu Youru huabao*, vol. 1, sets 3a and 3b.

———. *Wu Youru huabao* 吳友如畫寶 (Master works by Wu Youru). Lithograph print. Shanghai, 1908. 13 sets. Reprint in 3 vols., Shanghai: Shanghai Shudian, 1983.

Wu Zhen 吳圳. *Qingmo Shanghai zujie shehui* 清末上海租界社會 (Society in the Shanghai Foreign Settlements during the late Qing). Taipei: Wenshizhe Chubanshe, 1978.

Wuli Kanhua Ke 霧裏看花客 (Qian Xinbo 錢昕伯). *Zhenzheng lao Lin Daiyu* 真正老林黛玉 (The real old Lin Daiyu). Shanghai: Shanghai Minguo Tushuguan, 1919. Reprinted in Wei Shaochang, *Li Boyuan yanjiu ziliao*, 519–20.

Wuming shi 無名氏. "Jiangyunguan riji" 絳雲館日記 (The diary of Jiangyun Hall). Reprinted in Shanghai Shi Ziliao Congkan, *Qingdai riji congchao*.

Xia Xiaohong 夏曉虹. *Wanqing wenren funü guan* 晚清文人婦女觀 (Late Qing literati views on women). Beijing: Zuojia Chubanshe, 1996.

"Xiangchao weiding" 香巢未定 (Location of new home undecided). *Youxi bao*, October 15, 1897, 2.

"Xiao Gu Lansun" 小顧蘭蓀. In Huayu Xiaozhu Zhuren, *Haishang qinglou tuji*, 2:18.

Xiaobao 笑報 (Mirth). 1897.

Xiaolantian Chanqing Shizhe (Tian Chunhang) 小藍田懺情侍者 (田春杭). *Canghai yizhu lu* 滄海遺珠錄 (Pearls forgotten in the vast sea). Woodblock print. Shanghai, 1886.

———. *Chongding "Haishang qunfang pu"* 重訂海上群芳譜 (New edition of *A register of Shanghai flowers*). Lithograph print. 4 vols. Shanghai, 1886.

———. *Haishang qunfang pu* 海上群芳譜 (A register of Shanghai flowers). Lithograph print. 4 vols. Shanghai: Shenbaoguan, 1884.

Xiaolin bao 笑林報 (Joke forest). 1901–10?. Editor, Sun Yusheng.

Xiaoshuo huabao 小說畫報 (Fiction illustrated). 1917–20.

Xiaoshuo lin 小說林 (Novel grove). 1907–8. Editor, Zeng Pu.

Xiaoshuo shibao 小說時報 (Fiction times). 1909–17.

Xiaoshuo yuebao 小說月報 (The literary monthly). 1910–31.

Xiaoxian bao 消閒報 (Leisure). 1897–past 1903.

"Xiaoxiangguan zhu zhi jinxi tan" 瀟湘館主之今昔談 (Things old and new about the Master of Xiaoxiang studio [Lin Daiyu]). *Xinsheng* 9 (1922): 12.

Xiaoxiao Sheng 笑笑生. *Jin ping mei cihua* 金瓶梅詞話 (The plum in the golden vase). Photo reprint of Ming Wanli edition, Tokyo: Daian, 1963.

"Xiaqie tongpiao" 挾妾同嫖 (Visiting the courtesan house with one's concubine). In *Dianshizhai huabao*. Reprinted in Cohn, *Vignettes from the Chinese*, 101.

"Xibao ji nüyou yanju zhuzhen shi" 西報紀女優演劇助賑事 (Charity performance by female performer reported in Western newspaper). *Shenbao*, September 24, 1906, 17.

"Xie Yanyan cishi xiaozhuan" 謝燕燕詞史小傳 (Biography of the courtesan Xie Yanyan). *Tuhua bao*, no. 47, August 1, 1910.

"Xili yiqian babai jiushijiu nian Shanghai chunsai disan zhi" 西曆一千八百九十九年上海春賽第三誌 (Third report on Shanghai's spring races of 1899). *Youxi bao*, May 5, 1899, 2.

"Xin baihua zhong" 新百花塚 (The new Hundred Flowers Cemetery). *Tuhua xunbao* 12 (1909): 6.

Xin Ping 忻平. *Wang Tao pingzhuan* 王韜評傳 (A biography of Wang Tao). Shanghai: Huadong Shifandaxue Chubanshe, 1990.

Xin shijie baoshe 新世界報社, ed. *Huaguo baimei tu* 花國百美圖 (One hundred beauties from the kingdom of flowers). Shanghai: Shengsheng Meishu Gongsi, 1918.

Xin xiaoshuo 新小說 (New novel). 1902–6. Founded by Liang Qichao.

Xinsheng 新聲 (New voices). 1921–22.

"Xinshi youjian" 新詩又見 (New poems appearing again). *Youxi bao*, January 1, 1899, 2.

Xinwen bao 新聞報 (The news). 1893–1949.

Xinwen daxue 新聞大學 (Journalism university).

Xinwen yanjiu ziliao 新聞研究資料 (Research materials on journalism).

Xinxin xiaoshuo 新新小說 (The latest novels). 1904–7. Editor, probably Chen Jinghan 陳景韓.

"Xinyi chunji Hubin huabang" 辛巳春季滬濱花榜 (Shanghai flower competition, spring 1881). In Liangxi Chilian Jushi, *Hushang pinghua lu*, 1–2.

"Xinyi qiuji Hubin huabang" 辛巳秋季滬濱花榜 (Shanghai flower competition, fall 1881). In Liangxi Chilian Jushi, *Hushang pinghua lu*, 2–3.

Xiong Yuezhi 熊月之, ed. *Shanghai tongshi* 上海通史 (A comprehensive history of Shanghai). 15 vols. Shanghai: Shanghai Renmin Chubanshe, 1999.

———. *Xixue dongjian yu wan Qing shehui* 西學東漸與晚清社會 (The penetration of Western learning into China and late Qing society). Shanghai: Shanghai Renmin Chubanshe, 1994.

———. "Zhangyuan: Wan Qing Shanghai yige gonggongkongjian yianjiu" 張園晚清上海一個公共空間研究 (Zhang Garden: A study on a public sphere in late Qing Shanghai). In Zhang Zhongli, *Zhongguo jindai chengshi qiye, shehui, kongjian*, 334–59.

Xiqi Guguai 稀奇古怪. *Lao Shanghai jianwen lu* 老上海見聞錄 (Things seen and heard by an old Shanghai hand). Shanghai: Shanghai Guoguang Shudian, 1936.

Xiuxiang xiaoshuo 繡像小說 (The illustrated novel). 1903–6. Editor, Li Boyuan.

Xixi Shanren 西溪山人. *Wumen huafang lu* 吳門畫舫錄 (Record of the painted boats of Suzhou). 1806. Reprinted in Zheng Tinghua, *Xiangyan congshu*, series 17, 5:4763–4809.

Xixiang ji 西廂記 (The romance of the western chamber). Attributed to Wang Shifu 王實甫 (thirteenth century). Edited and annotated by Wu Xiaoling. Beijing, 1954.

Xu Fuchu 徐復初, ed. *Xiangyan quyu* 香艷趣語 (Amusing stories of courtesan entertainment). Shanghai: Shanghai Fanggu Shudian, 1937.

Xu Gongshi 徐恭時. "Xu" 序 (Foreword). In Gu Bingquan, *Shanghai Yangchang zhuzhi ci*, 1–8.

Xu kan "Shanghai zhuzhi ci" 續刊上海竹枝詞 (Sequel to *Shanghai bamboo twig ballads*). Woodblock print. Shanghai, 1880.

Xu Ke 徐珂. *Qingbai leichao* 清稗類鈔 (Qing historical anecdotes arranged by categories). 12 vols. Taipei: Taiwan Shangwu Yinshuguan, 1983.

Xu Min 許敏. "Shi, chang, you—wan Qing Shanghai shehui yipie" 士, 娼, 优— 晚清上海社會一瞥 (The intellectual, the prostitute, and the opera singer—A side-line view of late Qing Shanghai society). *Shanghai yanjiu* 9 (1993): 37–48.

Xu Qingzhi 徐慶治. *"Honglou meng" pailü* 紅樓夢排律 (Regulated verse on *Dream of the red chamber*). In *Chishuo si zhong*.

Xu Yu 許豫. *Baimen xinliu ji* 白門新柳記 (Notes on the new willows of Nanjing). Woodblock print. Preface, "Nanjing after the Taiping War," 1872. Shanghai, 1875.

Xu Zaiping 徐載平 and Xu Ruifang 徐瑞芳. *Qingmo sishi nian "Shenbao" shiliao* 清末四十年申報史料 (Historical materials on *Shenbao* from the last forty years of the Qing). Beijing: Xinhua Chubanshe, 1988.

"Xuange dai bu" 懸額待補 (An open position awaits refilling). *Youxi bao*, June 18, 1899, 2.

"Xue Baochai, Lin Daiyu xiangshuai maoming" 薛寶釵林黛玉相率冒名 (Xue Baochai and Lin Daiyu follow each other in using pseudonyms). *Youxi bao*, March 19, 1899, 2.

Xue Liyong 薛理勇. "Ming Qing shiqi de Shanghai changji" 明清時期的上海娼妓 (Shanghai prostitution during the Ming and Qing period). In Shanghaishi wenshiguan, *Jiu Shanghai de yan tu chang*, 150–58.

———. *Shanghai jinü shi* 上海妓女史 (History of Shanghai prostitution). Hong Kong: Haifeng Chubanshe, 1996.

Xueren 學人 (The scholar).

Yan Ming 嚴明. *Zhongguo mingji yishu shi* 中國名妓藝術史 (History of the artistic skills of China's famous courtesans). Taipei: Wenjin Chubanshe, 1992.

Yan Yiping 嚴一萍, ed. *Baibu congshu jicheng* 百部叢書集成. Taipei: Yiwen Yinshuguan, 1967.

Yang Jialuo 楊家駱, ed. *Zhongguo xueshu mingzhu* 中國學術名著. Taipei: Shijie Shuju, 1956–61.

Yang Jingting 楊靜亭. "Dumen zayong" 都門雜詠 (Ballads on the capital). In Yang Jingting, *Zengbu dumen jilüe*, vol. 6.

———. Preface to "Zayong" 雜詠 (Miscellaneous songs). In *Zengbu Dumen jilüe*, 1879, 6:1.

———, ed. Amplified by Xu Yongnian 徐永年. *Dumen jilüe—Xu Yongnian zengji* 都門紀略—徐永年增輯 (A record of the essential aspects of the capital city, supplemented by Xu Yongnian). Beijing: Ronglu Tang, 1864. Reprinted in Shen Yunlong, *Jindai Zhongguo shiliao congkan*, set 72, vol. 716, based on a reprinted 1907 edition.

———, ed. Amplified by Li Jingshan. *Zengbu "Dumen jilüe"* 增補都門紀略 (Amplified edition of *A record of essential aspects of the capital city*). 8 vols. Beijing: Jingdu Tang, 1879. Copy in East Asian Library, Columbia University, New York.

Yang Xuanzhi 楊衒之. *Luoyang qielan ji* 洛陽伽藍記 (Record of the monasteries of Luoyang). Reprint Zhou Zumo ed. *Luoyang qielan ji jiaoshi*.

Yangzhou meng 揚州夢 (Yangzhou dreams). Shanghai: Shanghai Guoxue Weichishe, 1915.

Yao Xie 姚燮. "Kuhai hang yuefu" 苦海航樂府 (*Yuefu* poems on traveling in the bitter sea). 1850s. Manuscript held in rare book section of Suzhou University Library.

"Yaohua zhaoxiang shuo" 耀華照像説 (On photography in Yaohua). *Youxi bao*, October 4, 1898, 2.

Ye Mengzhu 葉夢珠. *Yueshi bian* 閱世編 (Reading our times). Manuscript, seventeenth century. First published in Shanghaitong She, *Shanghai zhanggu congshu*, set 1, vol. 11.

Ye Xiaoqing. *The Dianshizhai Pictorial: Shanghai Urban Life, 1884–1898*. Ann Arbor: University of Michigan Press, 2003.

Yeh, Catherine V. "Cong shijiu shiji Shanghai ditu kan dui chengshi weilai dingyi de zhengduozhan" 從十九世紀上海地圖看對城市未來定義的爭奪戰 (The struggle for the definition of the future of Shanghai seen from nineteenth-century Shanghai city maps). *Zhongguo xueshu* 1.3 (2000): 88–121.

———. "Creating a Shanghai Identity—Late Qing Courtesan Handbooks and the Formation of the New Citizen." In Liu and Faure, *Unity and Diversity*, 107–23.

———. "Creating the Urban Beauty: The Shanghai Courtesan in Late Qing Illustrations." In Zeitlin and Liu, *Writing and Materiality in China*, 397–447.

———. "Deciphering the Entertainment Press 1896–1920: The *Youxi bao*, the *Shijie fanhua bao* and their Descendants." In Wagner, *Joining the Global Public*.

———. "The Intellectual as the Courtesan: A Trope in Twentieth Century Chinese Literature." Conference paper presented at Harvard University, 1990.

———. "Li Boyuan and His Shanghai Entertainment Newspaper *Youxi bao*." In Wagner, *Joining the Global Public*.

———. "The Life-style of Four *Wenren* in Late Qing Shanghai." *Harvard Journal of Asiatic Studies* 57.2 (December 1997): 419–70.

———. "A Public Love Affair or a Nasty Game? The Chinese Tabloid Newspaper and the Rise of the Opera Singer as Star." *European Journal of Asian Studies* 3 (2003): 13–51.

———. "Qing mo Shanghai jinü fushi, jiaju yu xiyang wuzhi wenming de yinjin" 清末上海妓女服飾, 傢具與西洋物質文明的引進 (Fashion and furniture in late Qing Shanghai courtesan houses and the introduction of Western material culture). *Xueren* 9 (1996): 381–438.

———. "Reinventing Ritual: Late Qing Handbooks for Proper Customer Behavior in Shanghai Courtesan Houses." *Late Imperial China* 19.2 (December 1998): 1–63.

———. "Representing the City: Shanghai and Its Maps." In Faure, *Town and Country in China*, 166–202.

———. "Shanghai as Entertainment: The Cultural Construction and Marketing of Leisure, 1850–1910." Paper presented at conference The Formation of a Multiethnic Urban Culture: The Shanghai Concessions 1850–1910, Heidelberg, Germany, 1998.

———. "Shanghai: 'Shijie youxichang'—wan Qing jinü shengyi jing" 上海:'世界游戲場'—晚清妓女生意經 (Shanghai, the "world's playground"—Late Qing courtesan business strategies). In Zhang Zhongli, *Zhongguo jindai chengshi qiye, shehui, kongjian*, 308–35.

———. "A Taste of the Exotic West: Fashion and Furniture in Shanghai Courtesan Houses at the Turn of the Century." In Bastid-Bruguière, *European Thought in Chinese Literati Culture.*

———. "Playing with the Public: Late Qing Courtesans and Their Opera Singer Lovers." In Bryna Goodman and Wendy Larson, eds., *Gender in Motion: Divisions of Labor and Cultural Change in Late Imperial and Modern China.* Lanham, MD: Rowman and Littlefield, 145–68.

———. "Wenhua jiyi de fudan—Wan Qing Shanghai wenren dui wan Ming lixiang de jian'gou" 文化記憶的負擔—晚清上海文人對晚明理想的建構 (The burden of cultural memory: The construction of the late Ming ideal by late Qing Shanghai *wenren*). In Chen, Wang, and Shang, *Wan Ming yu wan Qing,* 53–63.

———. "Zeng Pu's *Niehai hua* as a Political Novel: A World Genre in a Chinese Form." Ph.D. diss., Harvard University, 1990.

Yeh, Catherine V., and Christian Henriot, eds. *Chinese Urban Studies Workshop: A Reader (1850–1990).* Compiled for a workshop on Chinese urban studies, Lyon, France, 1996.

Yeh, Catherine V., and Rudolf G. Wagner, eds. *The Formation of a Multiethnic Urban Culture: The Shanghai Concessions, 1850–1910.* In press.

Yeh, Wen-Hsin. "Corporate Space, Communal Time: Everyday Life in Shanghai's Bank of China." *The American Historical Review* 100, no. 1 (February 1995): 97–122.

"Yeyou dangzhi zedi shuo" 冶游當知擇地說 (On choosing the right location when visiting courtesans). *Shenbao,* March 21, 1879, 1.

Yi Hong 倚虹. *Renjian diyu* 人間地獄 (Living hell). 1923. Reprint, Shanghai: Shanghai Guji Chubanshe, 1991.

Yihuashi Zhuren 意花室主人. "Ji Jin Xiaobao jiaoshu lun huazhong juan shi" 紀金小寶校書論花塚捐事 (Report on Jin Xiaobao's comments regarding fund-raising for the courtesan cemetery). *Youxi bao,* January 30, 1899, 1–2.

Yinghuan suoji 瀛環瑣記 (The universe). 1872–75.

Yiwen lu 益聞錄 (News of benefit). 1879–99.

Yongling 庸伶. "*Liyuan gongbao* chuban ganyan" 梨園公報出版感言 (Reflection on the publication of *Actor's bulletin*). *Liyuan gongbao,* September 5, 1928, 1.

Yoshiwara saiken 吉原細見 (A detailed guide to Yoshiwara). Tokyo, 1803.

Yoshiwara shusse kan 吉原出世鑒 (A guide to the eminent [courtesans of] Yoshiwara). Tokyo, 1754.

"You Zhang Yuan 'Si Da Jin'gang'" (The 'Four Great Golden Diamond Cutters' visit the Zhang Garden). *Youxi bao,* October 12, 1897, 2.

Youxi bao 游戲報 (Entertainment). 1897–1910(?). Editor, Li Boyuan.

Youxi Zhuren 遊戲主人. See Li Boyuan.

"Youyuan zaji" 遊園雜記 (Miscellanea on visiting the gardens). *Shijie fanhua bao,* Oct. 17, 1901, p. 2.

Yu Da 俞達 (Muzhen Shanren 慕真山人). *Qinglou meng* 青樓夢 (Dream of the green tower). Shanghai: Shenbaoguan, 1878. Reprint, Changsha: Yuelu Shushe, 1988.

Yu Danxin 余淡心, Zhuquan Jushi 珠泉居士 et al. *Qinhuai xiangyan congshu* 秦淮香艷叢書 (A collection of works on courtesan entertainment in Qinhuai). Reprint, Taipei: Guangwen Shuju, 1991.

Yu Huai 余懷. *Banqiao zaji* 板橋雜記 (Random notes on [the pleasure quarters by] the wooden bridge). 1654. Reprinted in Zhang Tinghua, *Xiangyan congshu,* series 13, 4:3637–72.

Yu Jiao 余蛟. *Chaojia fengyue ji* 潮嘉風月記 (Notes on courtesan life in Chaojia [Guangdong]). 1875. Reprinted in Zhang Tinghua, *Xiangyan congshu,* series 1, 1:241–74.

Yu Xingmin 于醒民. *Shanghai, 1862 nian* 上海, 1862 年 (Shanghai in 1862). Shanghai: Shanghai Renmin Chubanshe, 1991.

Yu Yueting 余月亭. "Woguo huabao de shizu—*Dianshizhai huabao* chutan" 我國畫報的始祖— 點石齋畫報的初探 (A preliminary analysis of the ancestor of the Chinese illustrated journals, *Dianshizhai huabao*). In *Xinwen yanjiu ziliao*, 1981.5, 149–81.

"Yu Zhou Wenxiang" 與周文香 (To Zhou Wenxiang). In Hushang Youxizhu, *Haishang youxi tushuo*, 1:12.

Yuan Zuzhi 袁祖志 (studio name Cangshan jiuzhu 倉山舊主). "Cangshan jiuzhu shu Shenjiang louxi" 倉山舊主書申江陋習 (The bad Shanghai customs described by the Old Master of Cang Mountain). In Hushang Youxizhu, *Haishang youxi tushuo*, 2:12b–14a.

———. "Cangshan jiuzhu zhuan Chunjiang dingyou nian xiaji huabang xu" 倉山舊主撰春江丁酉年夏季花榜序 (Preface by the Old Master of Cang Mountain to the flower competition in Shanghai, summer 1898). In Chen Wuwo, *Lao Shanghai sanshi nian jianwen lu*, 204–5.

———. *Chongxiu Hu you zaji* 重修滬游雜記 (Miscellaneous notes on visiting Shanghai, revised edition). 4 vols. Shanghai: Shenbaoguan, 1888.

———. "Hubei zhuzhi ci" 滬北竹枝詞 (Bamboo twig ballads on the northern city of Shanghai). *Shenbao*, September 9, 1872. Reprinted in Gu Bingquan, *Shanghai Yangchang Zhuzhi ci*, 10.

——— (pseud. Haichang Taihan Sheng 海昌太憨生). *Hushang zhuzhi ci* 滬上竹枝詞 (Shanghai bamboo twig ballads). In *Chongxiu Hu you zaji, juan* 3: 20a–22a.

———. *Shanghai ganshi shi* 上海感事詩 (Poems on Shanghai things that disturb). In *Chongxiu Hu you zaji, juan* 3: 7a. First published under the pen name Chanqing Sheng, in Ge Yuanxu, *Hu you zaji*, 49–50.

——— (pseud. Chanqing Sheng 懺情生). "Xu 'Hubei zhuzhi ci'" 續滬北竹枝詞 (Sequel to "Bamboo twig ballads on the northern city of Shanghai"). *Shenbao*, May 18, 1872. Reprinted in Gu Bingquan, *Shanghai Yangchang zhuzhi ci*, 12–14.

"Yuanxiao xiongfei" 願效雄飛 (The desire to imitate male valor). *Dianshizhai huabao, le* 樂, 1894, 95.

"Yue bao zai Xie Guixiang di yuanshu yize yinshu qihou" 閱報載謝桂香遞冤書一則因書其後 (Writing on the development of [the case of] Xie Guixiang after reading her letter defending herself against [being wronged] in [your] paper). *Youxi bao*, June 29, 1898, 1.

"Yue benbao suo ji bizhai wutai yi ze yougan er shu" 閱本報所紀避債無臺一則有感而書 (My reaction to your paper's report on "No recourse to pay back the debt"). *Youxi bao*, October 24, 1897, 1.

Yueyue xiaoshuo 月月小說 (The novel monthly). 1906–8. Editor, Wu Jianren.

"Yufu xuanqi" 輿服炫奇 (Coachman's uniform makes for a sensation). *Youxi bao*, November 2, 1897, 2.

"*Yugou ji* tici" 玉鉤集題辭 (Introduction to *The jade-hook collection*). Reprinted in Chen Wuwo, *Lao Shanghai sanshi nian jianwen lu*, 113–17.

Yūjo hyōban ki 遊女評判記 (A record of judgments on courtesans). Tokyo, 1765.

Yunjian Yishi 雲間逸士. "Yangchang zhuzhi ci" 洋場竹枝詞 (Bamboo twig ballads on the Foreign Settlements). In Gu Bingquan, *Shanghai Yangchang zhuzhi ci*, 383–87.

Yunshui Sanren 雲水散人. "Xie Tianxiang xiaozhuan" 謝添香小傳 (A short biography of Xie Tianxiang). *Youxi bao*, October 27, 1896, 1.

Yunshui Xiyanren 雲水洗眼人. "Zhi Youxi Zhuren lun Lin Daiyu shu" 致游戲主人論林黛玉書 (A letter on [the courtesan] Lin Daiyu to the Master of Entertainment). *Youxi bao*, November 22, 1897.

"Zanghua chuyi" 葬花初議 (Initial discussions on [establishing] a flower cemetery). *Youxi bao*, October 5, 1898, 2.

Zeitlin, Judith T., and Lydia H. Liu, eds. *Writing and Materiality in China*. Cambridge, Mass.: Harvard University Asia Center, 2003.

Zeng Pu 曾樸. *Niehai hua* 孽海花 (Flower in the sea of retribution). Reprint, Shanghai: Shanghai Guji Chubanshe, 1979.

Zhan Kai 詹塏. *Huashi* 花史 (History of the flowers). Shanghai: Zhuxin She, 1906.

———. "Lanqiao Bieshu zhuan" 籃橋別墅傳 (The biography of Lanqiao Bieshu). In *Rouxiang yunshi*, 2.

———. "Li Jingui zhuan" 李金桂傳 (The biography of Li Jingui). In *Rouxiang yunshi*, 3.

———. *Rouxiang yunshi* 柔鄉韻史 (The poetic history of a cozy quarter). Shanghai: Wenyi Xiaoqian Suo, 1907.

———. "Su Yunlan, Xie Sanbao hezhuan" (A joint biography of Sun Yunlan and Xie Sanbao). In *Rouxiang yunshi*, 1:30–33.

Zhang Ailing 張愛玲. *Zhang Ailing quanji* 張愛玲全集 (The complete works of Zhang Ailing). 16 vols. Taipei: Huangguan Zazhi She, 1968.

———. *Zhang Ailing zhu yi "Haishang hua"* 張愛玲註譯海上花 (*Biographies of Shanghai flowers* annotated and translated by Zhang Ailing). Taipei: Huangguan Zazhi She, 1983.

Zhang Chunfan 張春帆 (pseud. Shuliu Shanfang 漱六山房). "Haishang qinglou yange ji" 海上青樓沿革記 (A record of the evolution of Shanghai houses of prostitution). *Wansui zazhi*, 1.2–9, August 16–December 1, 1932.

———. *Jiuwei gui* 九尾龜 (The nine-tailed turtle). 1907–10. Reprinted in *Zhongguo jindai xiaoshuo daxi*.

Zhang Gongchang 張弓長. *Zhongguo de jinü yu wenxue* 中國的妓女與文學 (The Chinese courtesan and literature). Taipei: Changchunshu Shufang, 1975.

Zhang Mi 張泌. *Zhuanglou ji* 妝樓記 (Record of the tower of powder and rouge). Tang period. Reprinted in Yan Yiping, *Baibu congshu jicheng*.

Zhang Tinghua 張廷華 (pseud. Chongtianzi 蟲天子), ed. *Xiangyan congshu* 香艷叢書 (A collection of books on fragrant beauty). 5 vols. 1908. Reprint, Beijing: Renmin Wenxue Chubanshe, 1992.

Zhang Yilu 張乙廬. "Li Boyuan yishi" 李伯元逸事 (Memories of Li Boyuan). In Wei Shaochang, *Li Boyuan yanjiu ziliao*, 14–15.

Zhang, Yingjin. *The City in Modern Chinese Literature and Film*. Stanford, Calif.: Stanford University Press, 1996.

Zhang Zhongli 張仲禮, ed. *Jindai Shanghai chengshi yanjiu* 近代上海城市研究 (Urban studies on modern Shanghai). Shanghai: Shanghai Renmin Chubanshe, 1990.

———. *Zhongguo jindai chengshi qiye, shehui, kongjian* 中國近代城市企業，社會，空間 (Industry, society, and space in the modern Chinese city). Shanghai: Shanghai Shehuikexueyuan Chubanshe, 1998.

Zhao Er 趙爾, ed. *Qingshi gao* 清史稿 (A draft history of the Qing). Beijing: Zhonghua Shuju, 1976.

"Zhaolu laigao" 照錄來稿 (Publication of contributions to the paper). *Youxi bao*, February 10, 1903, 2.

Zheng Yimei 鄭逸梅. "Nanting tingzhang" 南亭亭長 (Village cop from Nanting [Li Boyuan]). Reprinted in Wei Shaochang, *Li Boyuan yanjiu ziliao*, 22–23.

———. "Sun Yusheng zhencang Li Boyuan yiyin" 孫玉聲珍藏李伯元遺印 (Seals left behind by Li Boyuan in Sun Yusheng's collection). In *Zheng Yimei xuanji*, 2:169–70.

———. *"Zheng Yimei xiaopin" xuji* 鄭逸梅小品續集 (Sequel to *Sketches by Zheng Yimei*). 1933. Reprinted in Wei Shaochang, *Li Boyuan yanjiu ziliao*, 22–23.

———. *Zheng Yimei xuanji* 鄭逸梅選集 (Selected works by Zheng Yimei). 3 vols. Harbin: Heilongjiang Renmin Chubanshe, 1991.

Zheng Zhimin 鄭志敏. *Xishuo Tangji* 細說唐妓 (A detailed narrative of the Tang courtesans). Taipei: Wenjing Chubanshe, 1997.

Zheng Zu'an 鄭祖安. "Tiji" 題記 (Introductory comments). In Ge Yuanxu, *Hu you zaji*, 1–5.

"Zhengtang gongwu" 正堂公務 (Magistrate on duty). *Youxi bao*, October 15, 1897, 1.

Zhi Jisheng 支機生. *Zhujiang minghua xiao zhuan* 珠江名花小傳 (Biographies of famous flowers in Canton). In Zhang Tinghua, *Xiangyan congshu*, series 8, 2:2003–31.

Zhimisheng 指迷生, comp. *Haishang yeyou beilan* 海上冶游備覽 (An encyclopedia on visiting Shanghai courtesan houses). Shanghai, 1883. A copy is in the Zhongyang Yanjiuyuan, Lishi Yuyan Yanjiusuo, Taipei. A reprint of this edition appeared in Shanghai, 1891. The first edition might have been published earlier. *Haishang yanhua suoji,* compiled by Langyouzi in 1877, contains most of this work's entries plus a few more, indicating that Langyouzi's 1877 book might be an enlargement of Zhimisheng's work.

Zhinan bao 指南報 (The guide). 1896–1897. Editor, Li Boyuan.

Zhiyin Mituren. See Langyouzi.

"Zhongguo nanyu bianfa" 中國難于變法 (It is hard to carry out political reform in China). *Youxi bao,* February 18, 1899, 1–2.

Zhongguo xueshu 中國學術 (China scholarship).

Zhongguo jindai xiaoshuo daxi 中國近代小說大系 (A collection of Chinese novels from 1850 to 1911). Nanchang: Baihuazhou Wenyi Chubanshe, 1991.

Zhonghua Tushujicheng Gongsi 中華圖書集成公司. *Shanghai youlan zhinan* 上海游覽指南 (Shanghai tourist guide). Shanghai: Zhonghua Tushujicheng Gongsi, 1919, 1923.

Zhonghua wenxue shiliao 中華文學史料 (Historical materials on Chinese literature).

Zhongxi Hubao 中西滬報 (Shanghai East and West).

Zhongyuan Langzi 中原浪子. *Jinghua yanshi* 京華艷史 (Amorous adventures in Beijing). Serialized in *Xinxin xiaoshuo,* vols. 5–7 (1908).

"Zhongzhi beiwen leici huilu" 塚志碑文誄詞匯錄 (Record of epitaphs written for the cemetery). Reprinted in Chen Wuwo, *Lao Shanghai sanshi nian jianwen lu,* 124–28.

Zhou Jianyun 周劍雲, ed. *Jubu congkan* 菊部叢刊 (The theater collection). Shanghai: Jiaotong Tushuguan, 1918. Reprinted in *Minguo congshu,* 2nd series, vol. 69. Shanghai, 1990.

Zhou Mi 周密. *Wulin jiushi* 武林舊事 (Anecdotes from Hangzhou). 1280. Reprint, Beijing: Zhongguo Shangwu Chubanshe, 1982.

Zhou Yuan 周蕪, ed. *Zhongguo banhua shi tulu* 中國版畫史圖錄 (An illustrated history of Chinese prints). Shanghai: Shanghai Renmin Meishu Chubanshe, 1988.

Zhou Zumo 周祖謨, ed. *Luoyang qielan ji jiaoshi* 洛陽伽藍記校釋 (Record of the monasteries of Luoyang, critical and annotated edition). Beijing: Zhonghua Shuju, 1963.

Zhu Junzhou 祝均宙. "Li Boyuan yu *Zhinan bao*" 李伯元與指南報 (Li Boyuan and *The guide*). *Xinwen daxue* 新聞大學 (Winter 1990): 48–50.

———. "Li Boyuan zhongyao yiwen: Zhengshi *Haitian hongxue ji* fei Li zhi zuo" 李伯元重要逸文— 證實 <海天鴻雪記> 非李之作 (An important document left behind by Li Boyuan—Proof that Li Boyuan is not the author of *Traces of the past in the world of Shanghai*). *Zhonghua wenxue shiliao* 1 (June 1990): 59–65.

———. "Shanghai xiaobao de lishi yange" 上海小報的歷史延革 (The historical development of Shanghai tabloids). *Xinwen yanjiu ziliao* 42 (1988): 163–79; 43 (1988): 137–53; 44 (1988): 211–20.

Zhu Weizheng 朱維錚, ed. *Ma Xiangbo ji* 馬相伯集 (A collection of Ma Xiangbo's works). Shanghai: Fudan Daxue Chubanshe, 1996.

"Zhu Wenqing ji He Lifu" 朱文卿寄何笠夫 (Zhu Wenqing's letter to He Lifu). In Hushang Youxizhu, *Haishang youxi tushuo,* 1:4–5.

Zhu Yuanliang 朱元亮 and Zhang Mengzheng 張夢徵 eds. *Qinglou yunyu* 青樓韻語 (Verses from the courtesan houses). Woodblock prints from 1616. Illustrated by Zhang Mengzheng; carved by Huang Yibin 黃一彬, Huang Duanfu 黃端甫, and Huang Guifang 黃桂芳. Held in Zhongguo Guojia Tushuguan. Reprinted in *Zhongguo gudai banhua congkan erbian* 中國古代板畫叢刊二編, vol. 4. Shanghai: Shanghai Guji Chubanshe, 1994.

Zhuchuan Jushi 珠泉居士. *Xu "Banqiao zaji"* 續板橋雜記 (Supplement to *Random notes on [the pleasure quarters by] the wooden bridge*). 1785. Reprinted in Zhang Tinghua, *Xiangyan congshu,* series 18, 5:4909–42.

Zilin Hubao 字林滬報 (Shanghai Chinese Paper). 1882–99.

Zou Tao 鄒弢 (studio name [Liangxi] Xiaoxiangguan Shizhe [梁溪] 瀟湘館侍者). *Chunjiang huashi* 春江花史 (Flowers from the Spring River). Woodblock print. 2 vols. Shanghai, 1884.

———. *Haishang chentian ying* 海上塵天影 (The shadows of heaven and earth in Shanghai). Shanghai, 1896. Reprint, Nanchang: Jiangsu Renmin Chubanshe, 1988.

———. *Haishang dengshi lu* 海上燈市錄 (Shanghai city lights). Woodblock print. 2 vols. Shanghai, 1884. Also known as *Chunjiang dengshi lu.*

———. *[Huitu] Jiaochou ji* [繪圖] 澆愁集 (Anthology of drowning one's sorrow [illustrated]). Preface, 1877. Shanghai: Dasheng Tushu Ju, 1914.

———. *Machi lu* 馬齒錄 (Jottings of an old horse). Privately printed. Shanghai, 1908.

———. *Sanjielu bitan* 三借廬筆談 (Jottings from the Sanjie hut). In *Biji xiaoshuo daguan*, vol. 28.

———. *Shanghai pinyan baihua tu* 上海品艷百花圖 (Illustrated commentary on one hundred flowers of Shanghai). Shanghai, 1880.

———. "Shouhe suibi" 瘦鶴隨筆 (Casual notes by Shouhe). In *Hujiang yue* 2, no. 5 (1918).

———. (pseud. Huaxia Jieren 花下解人), ed. *Wumen baiyan tu* 吳門百艷圖 (Illustrated one hundred beauties of Suzhou). Foreword by Sixiang Jiuwei 司香舊尉 (pseud. of Zou Tao). Woodblock print. N.p., 1880.

———. See also Liangxi Banchisheng and Liangxi Chilian Jushi.

Zou Yiren 鄒依仁. *Jiu Shanghai renkou bianqian de yanjiu* 舊上海人口變遷的研究 (Research on demographic changes in old Shanghai). Shanghai: Shanghai Renmin Chubanshe, 1980.

Index

Page numbers in italics refer to illustrations.

CPSIA information can be obtained
at www.ICGtesting.com
Printed in the USA
BVHW080026030320
573899BV00005B/14